The Book of Democracy

JAMES DAVID BARBER

PRENTICE HALL, Englewood Cliffs, New Jersey 07632

Library of Congress Cataloging-in-Publication Data

BARBER, JAMES DAVID.
   The book of democracy/James David Barber.
     p. cm.
   Includes bibliographical references and index.
   ISBN 0-13-340068-9
   1. Democracy. 2. Democracy—Case studies. 3. Political
participation. I. Title.
JC421.B27 1995
321.8—dc20   94-36188
                            CIP

Editorial Director: Charlyce Jones Owen
Acquisitions Editor: Michael Bickerstaff
Copy Editor: Carole Freddo
Cover Designer: Wendy Alling Judy
Buyer: Bob Anderson
Editorial Assistant: Nicole Signoretti
Editorial/Production Supervision
   and Interior Design: Rob DeGeorge

For Luke and Silas

©1995 by Prentice-Hall, Inc.
A Simon & Schuster Company
Englewood Cliffs, New Jersey 07632

Printed in the United States of America

10 9 8 7 6 5 4 3 2 1

ISBN 0-13-340068-9

PRENTICE-HALL INTERNATIONAL (UK) LIMITED, *London*
PRENTICE-HALL OF AUSTRALIA PTY. LIMITED, *Sydney*
PRENTICE-HALL CANADA INC., *Toronto*
PRENTICE-HALL HISPANOAMERICANA, S.A., *Mexico*
PRENTICE-HALL OF INDIA PRIVATE LIMITED, *New Delhi*
PRENTICE-HALL OF JAPAN, INC., *Tokyo*
SIMON & SCHUSTER ASIA PTE. LTD., *Singapore*
EDITORA PRENTICE-HALL DO BRASIL, LTDA., *Rio de Janeiro*

Contents

Preface

"Democracy" is government elected by the people. That is the fundamental definition. Once a nation creates a democracy, that democracy may last forever—or it may die. A democracy born of decent action can be killed by indecent action. To maintain democracy, citizens have to guard essential political principles.

How can we do that? Decent, strong, and consistent cooperation with citizens and leaders requires knowledge. The purpose of this book is to explore major political experiments in history to learn what has raised democracy up and what has cut it down. If we know what kinds of actions advanced democracy in other times and places and what kinds of actions stifled it, we will be better equipped to take the right actions for democracy in our own time and place. I have concentrated on the major events in history, from the ancient world to the present day, that I see as genuinely illuminating for this purpose.

The Book of Democracy is based on extensive research. For many years, I have been working on the histories of democracies and teaching courses titled Political Biography and Essential Global Democracy. My book *The Presidential Character*, rewritten and published four times in 20 years, is also based on the idea that focusing on historical reality helps us to make more effective political decisions now. In my work for human rights, civil rights, and international rights, for the rescue of children and grown-ups damaged and demoralized by political horrors, I have met many people who share my commitment to democracy and want to know what will work well to create and preserve democratic government.

The Book of Democracy has been improved by many experts. The historian Harold T. Parker commented on several chapters I wrote, helping me to improve them. The historian John Hope Franklin shared his essential writings about slavery. My wife, Amanda Smith, an expert writer and columnist, made extensive improvements. Each of the following professors, journalists, lawyers, and others concentrated on a draft chapter: Alex

Roland, Timothy Lomperis, William E. Scott, Susan Thorne, David Day, Dick May, Claudia Koonz, Thomas McCullough, Avinash Maheshwary, Paul H. Haagen, Peter Fish, John F. Oates, Richard Fox, Thomas D. Rowe, Jr., R. Taylor Cole, Mary T. Boatwright, William Holley, Ole Holsti, Margaret McKean, William Reddy, and David Rottmayer. Early on in this work, the following people helped me with sources: Joseph J. Kruzel, Charles R. Young, Charles W. Bergguist, Bruce Lawrence, David Canon, Marty Miller, Robert Allyn Brand, and Terry Filicko. The following experts came to my classes on Essential Global Democracy, where the students had read drafts of this book, and discussed specific aspects of democracy: Carl Gershman, James O'Dea, Holly Burkharter, Charles Patrick, Paul Haggen, Iqbal Singh, Peter Guild, Steve Crowtey, Albert Nelius, Arline Violet, and Maya Ajmera.

My excellent secretary, Lillian Fennell, repeatedly checked drafts and printed them out carefully. A fine job has been done by Carole Freddo, the copy editor, and Rob DeGeorge, the production editor at Prentice Hall. My editor, Jane Fish, was a remarkable helper who worked through each word and sentence, paragraph and chapter, of the book and contributed thousands of improvements. Roberta Bogaert was a fine reader who performed the same service for one chapter. Finally, I wish to thank the following reviewers for their helpful suggestions: William E. Kelly, Auburn University; J.A. Myers, Marist College; and Morton Schoolman, SUNY–Albany.

I am extremely thankful to every one of those who enhanced *The Book of Democracy.* And I would be glad to get information and thoughts from readers.

James David Barber
James B. Duke Professor of
Political Science and Public Policy
Duke University
Box 90204
Durham, NC 27708

About the Author

James David Barber devotes much of his energy to helping people. In addition to his human rights activities, he accomplishes this important goal through his distinguished academic career, in which he focuses on democracy, human rights, leadership, and journalism. His efforts to shed light on these topics have enabled many of his readers to empower themselves politically and, consequently, to gain control of their destiny. In addition to his extensive research and authorship, Barber has lectured widely in the United States and throughout the world.

Raised in West Virginia, Barber enrolled at the University of Chicago at age sixteen, where he received his bachelor's and master's degrees in political science. After a teaching stint at Stetson University in Florida, he enrolled at Yale University in 1957 and earned a Ph.D. In addition to later teaching at Yale, Barber was president of Yale's Political Science Association and director of the political science graduate students. In 1972, Barber became chairman of the Political Science Department at Duke Universiy. At Duke, he has taught classes in Essential Global Democracy, Political Biography, and Senior Honors for Political Science. His contributions at Duke and Yale Universities have been extensive.

Barber has written and edited many books, including two published by Prentice Hall. His book *The Presidential Character* has undergone four editions and has been profoundly influential for over twenty years. The text is used in two hundred college classes each year. Barber also coedited *Women Leaders in American Politics*.

Barber's human rights efforts earned him a position as chairman of the Board of Directors at Amnesty International USA. He has also been on the board of the Council of American Political Science, in addition to having served on many other boards. He is currently on the boards of the Association to Unite the Democracies, The Center of Public Integrity, The Poynter Institute, as well as other prominent organizations. He is also working diligently to help children who have escaped from Liberia.

Barber's wife, Amanda Smith, is also an author. His children are Silas, Luke, Jane, and Sara.

CHAPTER
1
Humans Need Democracy

Can we take action to rescue humans? That goal is great—if we *know* what to do.

Like birds flying together, human beings have related among themselves since the start of human existence. Connection is natural—people cooperate in families, sex, work, sports, education, war—and politics.

But connection creates trouble. Too often, individuals feel crowded, and react by turning away from one another, physically and psychologically. Too often, people focus on their own troubles or pleasures, ignoring the troubles and pleasures of others. And too often, people reach out beyond themselves to dominate and harm others. A dictator forces the people to do exactly as he orders, and punishes them for any differences.

Ironically, when people focus on harsh human troubles, they can make strong political progress. But to do this, they need a knowledge and understanding of real political events—in other words, political science. True political science is objective analysis of what actually happened in major events in history rather than logical theories rooted in suppositions and imaginings. Too many times in the past, political decisions have been based on fantasy rather than on accurate information, with tragic results.

In order to take the best possible action to rescue humans, we need to make a study of the past that concentrates on what went wrong and what went right in the political development of societies—what kind of politics degraded the individual and community and what kind of politics raised them up. The reason for the study of the first is obvious: we need to know what went wrong before we can know how to set things right. Unless we comprehend the horrible mistakes of the past, we are liable to repeat them, in one form or another, in the future. But it is not enough to know what went wrong. We must also understand what kinds of actions have repaired and improved the human condition. Just as a doctor needs to know what will work to heal the patient's body, we need to know what will restore the body politic.

Thus within each of the four main parts of this book, the first chapter focuses on what cut democracy down at a certain time and place in history, and the third chapter focuses on what raised democracy up in another time and place.

The outstanding achievement in the history of politics is the reality of *democracy*. Democracy is not perfect, but it is the only form of government that respects the dignity of the individual and protects the individual's human rights. This book makes the case that democracy has worked far better than alternative forms of government, such as modern fascism and communism or the old monarchies and aristocracies. Democracies have been the safest and most progressive societies in history. The most hopeful political movement in the world at this moment is the move toward democracy. We have seen three generations of democracy in Germany since the horrors of Nazi totalitarianism. This is a remarkable achievement. Japan, too has succeeded in maintaining the democracy born in the ruins of defeat in World War II. In South Africa, Russia, Latin America, and elsewhere, people are overthrowing decades—even centuries—of tyranny and taking up democracy. But the *birth* of democracy does not guarantee the *life* of democracy. We need to know how nations can not only create democracy, but sustain democracy.

THE DEMOCRACY OF THE UNITED STATES OF AMERICA

The world's first true democracy was the United States, and it has lasted through two centuries, despite the evil of slavery and the tragedy of the Civil War fought to end it. But even after two centuries, is it certain that the United States will remain a democracy? Considering the country's problems, perhaps not.

Reflect on the titles of some relatively recent significant books:

The Disuniting of America: Reflections on a Multicultural Society, by Arthur M. Schlesinger, Jr.

The Closing of the American Mind, by Allan Bloom

The New American Political (Dis)order, by Robert A. Dahl

The Party's Over: The Failure of Politics in America, by David S. Broder

Who Will Tell the People: The Betrayal of American Democracy, by William Greider

Dirty Politics: Deception, Distraction, and Democracy, by Kathleen Hall Jamieson

Why Americans Hate Politics, by E. J. Dionne, Jr.

Hollywood vs. America: Popular Culture and the War on Traditional Values, by Michael Medved

Out of Order, by Thomas E. Patterson

Democracy and Its Discontents: Reflections on Everyday America, by Daniel J. Boorstin

Hell of a Ride: Backstage at the White House Follies, 1989–1993, by John Podhoretz
Years of Discord: American Politics and Society, 1961–1974, by John Morton Blum

America is in a destructive mode of fragmentation. Killing, hurting, sickness, ignorance, divorce, abandonment, homelessness, and isolation on the scale we see today signify a breakdown of community, a breakdown of reality.

Americans recognize and publicly discuss these troubles; we know what is wrong, so the first fundamental for fixing our democracy is in place. Now we must find out what actions will work to make real improvements. For that, we need to know the three essentials of democracy and the four major requirements for democracy.

THE THREE ESSENTIALS OF DEMOCRACY

The three essentials of democracy are simple and well known:

1. Democracy is a *national government elected by the people.* The chief executive and the legislature make the rules of the nation, but the citizens decide, through elections, who will be the chief executive and who will serve in the legislature. Those elections must be clear-cut, regular, and honest. When people vote for different candidates, the candidates who get the most votes must win the positions. The citizens need to know how to predict how the different candidates will operate once in office, so knowledge of candidates' political positions is essential. Thus democracy depends on citizens freely and knowledgeably selecting political governors who recognize that their power derives from popular election and may be removed in the next popular election.

2. Democracy requires a *constitution.* The legislature makes laws, but the constitution is the law above all laws. Established at the birth of democracy, it sets forth procedures: how elections will be conducted and how the government must act. The constitution must be known to the public and truly implemented—not just asserted. The constitution can be changed, but only by a difficult procedure requiring far more discussion and votes than ordinary laws.

3. Democracy requires *human rights.* The main constitution establishes rules of procedure, but a bill of rights gives the fundamental rights of the people, typically including freedom of religion, speech, and the press; the right of assembly; and equality of all citizens under the law. For example, the bill of rights should protect individuals from arrest and imprisonment because of their political beliefs. These rights are original and should be subject to change only by the same difficult procedure for changing the constitution.

Those three basic fundamentals are known to be the basics, after they are established. But performing them, they typically get manipulated by fragmentation and impressionism. To keep making them work, these elements need to be kept simple and equally fair for all citizens, and understood by all voters.

THE FOUR MAJOR REQUIREMENTS FOR DEMOCRACY

The most significant requirements for making and keeping a democracy are addressed in the four parts of this book. Each of these requirements is treated as a challenge that has historically been both failed—in the example related in the first chapter of the part—and successfully met—in the example related in the third chapter of the part. Because democracy depends so much on choosing the right leaders, I include biographical details about major leaders and what they did wrong or right in these historical examples. The middle chapter in each part is an analysis of the requirement that suggests what can be done to make democracy live.

What are those four requirements?

Part 1: Democracy must control violence. Violence is natural to humans. For thousands of years, it has been a major instrument of control—by individuals over other individuals, by rulers over citizens, by nations over other nations. Force, torture, and killing are still widely used for political control. Democracy requires decent relationships among humans: the use of discourse and agreed upon procedures for decision-making rather than force. Force cannot be totally abandoned, however, for the government itself must sometimes use force to control violence. For domestic defense, there must be police. For national defense, there must be a military. But a democracy must control its police and military. The citizens of a democracy cannot simply assume that the military and the police will act responsibly and obey the constraints of law. They must make sure that democratic government really controls these organizations.

Many democratic governments have failed to control their police and military. Chapter 2 in Part 1 focuses on the story of Russia in 1917. Democracy was born in the spring, a hero developed it, and then in the fall it failed because the new Russian democratic government did not get control of the military. The result was a nightmare called "communism," a dictatorship of major violence that killed many millions of people inside and outside Russia.

Chapter 3, the middle chapter of Part I, discusses examples of democracies that need to manage and control their police and military in the midst of violence. We concentrate mainly on the experience of the United States, the first democracy. We briefly note violent experiences in Nicaragua, the Philippines, Panama, Argentina, Russia in the 1990s, Nigeria, Guatemala, and India.

Chapter 4 describes the great achievement of Australia in controlling force. Australia's first settlers were thousands of British prisoners, and for long years, Australia's growing democracy did not control their own military; Britain controlled it. We shall examine how the Australians achieved control, first, over their police and then, years later, over their military.

Part 2: Democracy must provide freedom and equality. Some governments see "government" as governing everything in people's lives. But a major aspect of democracy is freedom: the representatives of the people are to create and sustain liberty, rather than dictatorship. The government must therefore limit its governing. The bill of rights is to define freedoms that will be protected, not infringed, by government. Democracy is not a religion or totalitarian ideology instituted to command complete virtue. Freedom does not mean virtue. Freedom permits the existence of bigots who hate truth and damn their enemies. But it also permits the existence of decent folks. At the moment a new democracy is created, it is essential to establish freedom, not forcing "culture."

Freedom includes equality. Rather than making political distinctions between blacks and whites, men and women, or other groups of citizens, democracy demands equal liberties for all citizens.

Chapter 5 tells of the defeat of freedom in the French Revolution of 1789 (though France later did become an essential democracy). Before the Revolution, France was a monarchy: the king and his ministers and allies, insulated from the rest of France, ruled the country autocratically from Paris. After a bloody people's revolt, the leaders of the Revolution tried to enforce political purity and virtue. The result was the Reign of Terror, in which thousands of French people were murdered by their own government.

Chapter 6 relates some ancient and modern examples of totalitarianism: ancient Egypt, the Aztec Empire, Turkey, Christian tyranny in Europe, Communism in the Soviet Union and China. It then shows that the best example of freedom is the U. S. Bill of Rights and this nation's system of federalism.

Chapter 7 examines India's success. The Indians' revolution for democracy was at least as complicated as the French movement of 1789. India had a variety of religions and masses of very poor people, and was dominated by Britain. But thanks mainly to Nehru, India was established as a democracy with freedom.

Part 3: Democracy requires real law. Law is meant to provide justice: rules that are constant, steady, well known, impartial, and objective. Law existed long before democracy was invented, but law's operation is essential to democracy. If we are to behave decently, we need to know in advance what we can do and what we cannot do, rather than having our conduct condemned retrospectively by the unpredictable decisions of political leaders. Ancient governments lacked law. Then, early on, laws were instituted by religion based on moral principles required by God. Still, the king could change laws at whim for his own benefit, simply by claiming he had had a sudden new revelation from heaven. So it was significant progress when the creation of law was shifted from the king to the parliament, where law is made openly by rational discourse.

Law can deteriorate in a democracy, however. The most typical abuse is complexification by the rich, who too often quietly manipulate law in order to gain more wealth for themselves. Law is then determined by cash rather than equality. In a democracy, law must be written by the representatives of equal citizens for equal citizens.

In Chapter 8, our negative example is England in the nineteenth century, when law was harshly manipulated as the economic system changed and labor shifted from homes to factories. Those new factories were harmful for workers, including women and young children—in fact, the executives turned them into semi-slaves. The workers, led by Feargus O'Connor, organized a national movement to rescue themselves, but the new movement was manipulated and destroyed by clever politicians in the employ of the wealthy industrialists. Law was used to enforce inequality.

Chapter 9 pursues the history of law back to the times before history was written. Law seems to have originated in primitive marriage customs and ancient penalties for the taking of life and property, and to have developed more elaborately once money was invented. We trace trouble and progress in law through ancient Jerusalem, Rome, and the early United States, and show how law can be improved in today's democracies.

Chapter 10 shows how democratic law arose in seventeenth-century England: law made by parliament rather than by the king. Thanks largely to Sir Edward Coke, parliament asserted its right to create political rules.

Part 4: Democracy needs reason. Knowledge is a necessary ingredient for a good life, but it is crucial for democracy. Because we have to *know* what's wrong and what works, and democracy requires a knowledgeable citizenry participating in frequent public political discourse. But too often in democracies, education, journalism, and congressional debates display contempt for facts and logic, and far too often, people prefer fantasy to reality. When they do, democracy withers.

Chapter 11 concentrates on a tragic defeat of reason: the rise of the Nazi government in Germany. Germany became a democracy in the 1920s, thanks mostly to Friedrich Ebert. But then Hitler and the Nazis captured the German imagination with the slogan "We think with our blood." The result of this trashing of reason was unprecedented horror.

Chapter 12 explores the turn to antireason in storied Troy, ancient Greece and Rome, medieval Europe, and the United States just before the Civil War. It also discusses political ignorance and political knowledge in the modern world.

Chapter 13 discusses the use of reason in creating the world's first true democracy, the United States of America. Even as far back as the early 1600s, America had an intrepid champion of reason in Anne Hutchinson. Freedom of speech and of the press was advanced early in the next century by John Peter Zenger. Then Thomas Jefferson, George Washington, Benjamin Franklin, James Madison, and other American leaders brought their knowledge of history, experience of life and government, and tremendous reasoning powers to bear on the increasingly intolerable situation of the colonies under British rule. The decision by those late-eighteenth-century Americans to establish the United States of America as a democracy was born of a courageous confrontation with reality.

PART ONE

A Democracy Must Control Force

In ancient times, wars were fought by rather small numbers of individuals hitting one another. Modern war became "world" war, with thousands, or millions, being killed or wounded by bombs or lethal gas directed at them from a distance. Modern war often spreads quickly into the civilian population, so that ordinary citizens are suddenly astonished to find bombs raining down on them from the sky. Modern war is a tragedy.

But war has always been a tragedy. For thousands of years, governments were organized mainly for fighting wars. The ancient and medieval castles whose elegant architectures we admire were built to protect people from attack. The security they offered came at the cost of living crowded inside a rock structure without land or even enough water.

Throughout the ages, peace has been a blessing, however short it lasted. But even during times of peace, people have feared crime, which often includes violence. In our own nation—almost unique among the democracies—it is easy for citizens to obtain guns and bullets. With this easy access to guns, killing has spread from criminals to ordinary people shooting their family members and neighbors in moments of anger.

Peace and justice require control of all violence by a democratic government. Government in a democracy exercises authority over the military by retaining the war-making power for itself. The nation's armed forces are firmly under the command of the representatives of the people. Democratic governments are also responsible for preventing brutality and savagery internally, among citizens. Police must also be governed by the representatives of the people.

2

The Story
of the
Russian Revolution

Democracy Cut Down

The days of democracy for Russia! For four centuries, its citizens had been starved, enslaved, and suppressed by their high and mighty rulers. Then, in only nine days, that old system fell to the ground and broke apart. A great hope for liberty, equality, and community—for real democracy—leapt forth and thrilled the nation. A leader emerged to create democracy: Aleksandr Kerensky.

KERENSKY'S STRONG EFFORT FOR DEMOCRACY

On a Monday morning at 8:00, Kerensky's wife woke him up to take a telephone call. The message "came to me with a jolt," he said. The news was that the government had collapsed and crowds of armed soldiers were pouring out of their barracks.

It was February 27, 1917, an unusually sunny day in the long Russian winter.* The 35-year-old Kerensky—tall, muscular, called "Swifty" in the government's secret police files—jumped out of bed and pulled on his usual garb: worker-type shirt, pants, and black jacket. Neglecting hat and overcoat, he rushed

---

* In the early twentieth century, Russia still used the old Julian calendar, so all dates were 13 days earlier than dates in the Gregorian calendar used in Western Europe and the United States. Unfortunately, books on the Russian Revolution vary in which dating system they use. For consistency, this book uses the Russian dates, translating dates in those sources using Western dating into the corresponding Russian dates.

Aleksandr Kerensky.

straight to the palace in the city of Petrograd.* There the Duma (the Russian parliament) was in chaos. Soldiers were on their way to the palace, though they would not make it through the streets of Petrograd for some four hours. Kerensky stepped forth and rang the Duma bell to call the parliament together for a meeting.

On the previous Thursday evening, 100,000 striking men and starving women had crowded out into the streets; by Friday, there were 200,000, marching and cheering; by Saturday, the mood had shifted to anger: "Down with Autocracy!" they shouted. Shots went off. Police and women were beaten up. On Sunday, a day with blue sky and light snow, many workers showed up in their formal Sunday outfits. The officials ordered them to go away, but they would not

---

* The names of this same city were changed from St. Petersburg to Petrograd, then to Leningrad, then back to St. Petersburg.

leave. So the government troops shot at them, killing 50 and wounding another 48. Soldiers who had deserted and mutinied grabbed government ministers and officials and dragged them toward the palace where the Duma was gathering. Revolution was happening.

The parliament gathered. Kerensky spoke:

> What is happening confirms that we cannot hesitate. I am continuously receiving information that the troops are on edge. They will take to the streets. I am going to the regiments now. I must know what I can tell them. May I say that the State Duma is with them, that it takes responsibility upon itself, that it puts itself at the head of the movement?[1]

Later Kerensky recalled being "face to face with the most infuriated mob."

> During the first days of the revolution the Duma was full of the most hated high officials of the monarchy, numbers of the highest police officials, hundreds of gendarme officers and secret police agents. All these men, despised and detested by the whole country, had been arbitrarily arrested in various parts of the town by the revolutionaries, and brought to the Duma to be placed in my keeping. Day and night the revolutionary tempest raged round the arrested men. The huge halls and endless corridors of the Duma were flooded with armed soldiers, workmen and students....If I had moved a finger, if I had simply closed my eyes and washed my hands of it, the entire Duma, all of St. Petersburg, the whole of Russia might have been drenched in torrents of human blood....[2]

The crowd of soldiers reached the palace at 1:00 that Monday afternoon, ready to lynch the officials they had grabbed on the way. Kerensky ran out through the main entrance and saw the scene. Eyes burning in his pale face, he raised his arms to get their attention. The soldiers recognized him and parted so he could walk out. Quickly Kerensky announced that he himself was "arresting" the captive officials. Pointing to one of them, he said, "No one dare touch this man!"[3] He said to another, "Your life is in safety." To the crowd, he said, "Know this: the State Duma does not shed blood."[4]

The crowd poured into the palace and began to settle down. Kerensky, knowing "the crowd is an orchestra in the hands of its leader,"[5] could have led it to attack the officials and fill the palace with their blood. Instead, he rescued them.

Kerensky had become "the leader of the Revolution." He chose to fight with words:

> Because circumstances had put me at the apex of power during the Revolution and because my name had become a kind of symbol to the people of the new life of freedom, it fell chiefly to me to wage this verbal battle among the masses of the population. [6]

Having calmed the crowd, Kerensky spent the next days and nights in the palace, dealing with the frightened—and angered—representatives as the ragged workers and soldiers bunched into that unfamiliar building. He hardly slept, ate and drank only when someone handed him chicken or brandy or a cup of black coffee. He remembered later, "We forgot everything that was merely personal." He said "all that was merely a matter of class or caste, and became for the moment simply men conscious of our common humanity. It was a moment when every man came into touch with what is universal and eternally human."[7] More flocks of soldiers arrived—and lifted him onto their shoulders, from where he saw "a sea of heads, of gleaming, enthusiastic faces," cheering him as the champion of democracy. Later, when gunshots were heard outside the palace, the people inside flung themselves down on the floor. But Kerensky leapt up on a windowsill and yelled, "All to your posts!...Defend the State Duma....Listen: this is Kerensky speaking, Kerensky is speaking to you....Defend your freedom, the revolution, defend the State Duma! All to your posts!..."[8]

Thanks significantly to Kerensky's persuasion, the Duma rejected proposals to set up a dictatorship and instead declared a "Provisional Government" of its members. It appointed ministers—Kerensky was made minister of justice—to pave the way to a national election, scheduled for September 4. The Duma also affirmed freedom of assembly, citizen equality before the law, the right to strike, and pardon for all political crimes except treason.[9] Thus did the fractured Duma of the old regime put itself back together as a hopeful congress of the new democracy. It legislated freedoms for Russians that were stronger than those then possessed by the English and the French.

But a major complication arose: the new Provisional Government was nearly completely composed of middle-class democrats; it included virtually no soldiers or peasants. As February turned into March, another organization took form, the Petrograd Soviet of the Workers' and Soldiers' Deputies. The Soviet had a very large (and fluctuating) membership ranging from 2,000 to 3,000 workers and soldiers, and an Executive Committee of nearly 100. The Soviet's relationship to the Provisional Government was, roughly, to let the latter outfit do the governing, provided the Soviet generally agreed with its policies. Instead of grappling with urgent decisions, members of the Soviet went in for "endless, usually bombastic, oratory."[10] Kerensky was deputy chairman of the Petrograd Soviet. Significantly, he was the only Soviet member who was also in the Provisional Government.

On the morning of March 2, Kerensky finally went home and slept. But that afternoon he got up again and went before the Soviet in a huge hall, formerly occupied by perfume-smelling aristocrats, but now jammed full of masses of sweating people. Instead of marching up to the podium, he jumped onto the top of the chairman's desk and shouted his speech:

> Comrades, in my hands are the representatives of the old regime, and I have resolved to keep them in my hands. [Loud applause. Shouts of "Right"]...Once I became minister I ordered the release of all political prisoners.... [Loud applause turning into an ovation]...Since I became minister of justice...I hereby resign as deputy chairman of the Soviet of the Workers' Deputies. But comrades, I cannot live without the people, and I am ready to resume the post [of deputy chairman]

if you think you need me. [Shouts: "We ask you to."] Comrades, though I am in the Provisional Government, I remain what I have always been, a republican. In my office I need the people's support….Can I trust you as I trust myself? [Loud applause, shouts of "Comrade believe in us."] It is unthinkable for me to live without the people's support, and when you no longer trust me, kill me." [11]

He went on, calling himself a "representative of democracy," and was rewarded with roars of "Long Live Kerensky!" from the huge crowd. [12] He was lifted on their shoulders and carried off to the Provisional Government building. [13]

Kerensky was thrilled. Later he recalled:

What happened I can only describe as a miracle. Amidst the chaos and darkness of the collapse of Czarism, there rose the bright sun of liberty to shine on a country broken with suffering. And somehow the feeling of hatred and vengeance melted, and disappeared from the human heart! Turning back now to those terrifying first weeks of the revolution, I am surprised, *not* that innocent blood was shed, but that there was so little of it; that is what strikes me most now. [14]

Kerensky's popularity spread through the enormous land of Russia. He not only advocated democracy and unity, he tried hard to live them. As one admirer put it:

He was the only man who gave himself up to the wave of the popular movement with enthusiasm and complete confidence, feeling much more and much wider than the others. He perceived the whole historical grandeur of the revolution which had been accomplished from the very first day. Only he spoke to the soldiers as "we" believing that he was speaking the truth…. And he believed that the mass wanted exactly what was historically necessary for the moment. [15]

After hundreds of years the tyranny, all varieties of Russians were being brought together by the grand hope for democracy. Kerensky thrust it forward.

NEWS OF THE HOPE
FOR RUSSIAN DEMOCRACY READ IN AMERICA

Far off in the United States, *The New York Times* quoted Russia's Foreign Minister Milukoff on "the marvelous enthusiasm which today animates the whole nation." [16] A Russian in New York called it "the greatest news that ever came out of Russia." Reporters described "the suddenness and complete success of the Revolutionary movement in Russia," and wrote that "Petrograd has been the scene of one of the most remarkable risings in history…." [17] The judgment was that "Unless an improbable event occurs, Russia has today become a republic." [18]

It was the middle of World War I, and Russia was at war with Germany. America, suffering German attacks on its shipping ("THREE AMERICAN SHIPS SUNK" read *The New York Times* headline on Monday, March 19th), was on the verge of declaring war against Germany, so Americans were comforted to learn from the Russian foreign minister that his country would "fight by their side against the common enemy until the end, without cessation and without faltering." [19] The American journalist George Kennan judged that if it did not bring about civil war, the revolution would "result in tremendously increased vigor of prosecution of Russia's share of the war with Germany." [20]

The Duma, orchestrated by Kerensky, declared democracy in a list of specific rights for Russians that were familiar to Americans: "Liberty of speech and of the press; freedom for alliances, unions, and strikes…. Abolition of all social, religious, and national restrictions…universal suffrage…. [21] Foreign Minister Milukoff explained the roots of those rights:

> One of the things about us which foreigners seldom appreciate is the fact that the Russian people is deeply democratic. I do not mean that we are yet fully conscious of the democratic instinct in our political life. But we are democratic by nature, we are democratic in our daily life…. Russia is a democratic country and not an aggressive country. [22]

The New York Times editorial of March 16 expressed Americans' great hope for "The New Birth of Russia": "The Russian people, through trusted leaders in the Duma and men of loyalty and enlightenment outside the Duma, have assumed the direction of affairs in the Empire…. Moreover, the coming together of millions of men from all over the Empire, the communing one with another of those men drawn from the ranks of the people, is of deep meaning for the future of Russia."

THE FACTS OF LIFE IN RUSSIA

Though the hope for Russian democracy leapt forward when the czar "abdicated" and his son and brother—who were his potential successors—renounced their claims, the Russian reality was grim. More than two-thirds of Russians were poor peasants, unable to grow enough food to adequately feed themselves. Half of all Russian farms had never even been dug with a plow. About a third of the agricultural land was left idle each year. This vast country produced annually only about one-fifth of the amount of grain little England grew in a year. Industrialism had indeed started in Russia for millions of workers, but the conditions of labor in the factories and the coal mines were so harsh that millions of workers went out on strike time and again. In cities, and out in the countryside, violence, including murder, was widespread. The nation was fragmented: there were some 149 different ethnic groups speaking 182 different languages. The peasants were poorly educated and often downright illiterate. Drinking vodka to the point of drunkenness was common. [23]

How had Russia been ruled prior to Kerensky? And how had the relationship between the Russian people and their rulers given birth to the great possibility of democracy?

THE TYRANT IN CHARGE OF RUSSIA: CZAR NICHOLAS II

In the early twentieth century, the ruler of Russia, Czar Nicholas II, was enthroned as if he were ruling in the Middle Ages. The czar's authority had been defined in the nineteenth century in a Fundamental Law: "To the Emperor of all the Russias belongs the supreme autocratic power. To obey his commands not merely from fear but according to the dictates of one's conscience is ordained by God himself." [24] So all power was his, but he bore no responsibility to the people he ruled.

Nicholas II detested even the word "constitution," as well as any suggestion that he should adhere to law. He saw the Duma as his servants, not as an elected legislature with independent authority. In 1906, he greeted the Duma as the "best persons, whom I instructed my beloved subjects to elect from amongst themselves." [25] Ten years later, visiting the Duma (the first czar ever to do so), Nicholas II pronounced, "Let the love of the country help you and serve as the guiding star in the discharge of your duties toward the Fatherland and Myself." The Duma president responded that the great czar's visit "has strengthened the bond of union between Yourself and Your loyal people.... Long live the Great Sovereign of All Russia." [26] And this "Great Sovereign" blessed the Duma, more than a century after George Washington took the plain, honorable title of "President" and recognized the authority of the Congress of the United States. Nicholas's wife kept urging him: "Be a Czar, as the Czars of old; tell them you are still a Czar." [27]

The system of inherited monarchy and the assumption that any good king would beget another good king had always been absurd. Nicholas II had been so dominated by his father, Czar Alexander III, that he grew up to be a lonely, worried man, totally unsuited, according to scholar Adam B. Ulam, "by temperament and upbringing...to be a constitutional monarch." [28] He spent most of his time away from the duties of government, playing dominoes, boating, swimming, walking, reading dreamy novels, and saying his prayers. [29] In the spring of 1917, Kerensky finally ushered him off his throne. While acting to protect him from assassination, Kerensky "tried to fathom the former Czar's character."

> I found that he did not care for anything or anyone except, perhaps, his daughters. This indifference to all external things was almost unnatural. As I studied his face, I seemed to see behind his smile and his charming eyes a stiff, frozen mask of utter loneliness and desolation. He did not wish to fight for power, and it simply fell from his hands.... It was a new experience for him to find himself a plain citizen without the burdens of state. His retirement into private life brought him nothing but relief. Old Madame Naryshkina [the Czar's house mother] told me that he had said to her: "How glad I am that I need no longer attend to those tiresome audiences and sign those everlasting documents! I shall read, walk, and spend my time with the children." And, she added, this was no pose on his part. [30]

Nicholas II was married to a royal German lady, Alexandra, who had been raised in Windsor Castle, being the granddaughter of England's Queen Victoria. As czarina, her early occupation was producing daughter after daughter. Finally, she produced the much-desired son—only a male could inherit the throne—and motherhood of a future czar transformed her into a fervent agitator

Czar Nicholas II, his wife Alexandra, and their children.

for czarist power. She worked inside the isolated court to confirm and enhance the monarchy her son would inherit. Like the queen of Louis XIV in France or the first lady of Ronald Reagan in the United States, Alexandra is historically viewed as a behind-the-scenes czarina influencing heavily the policies of the nation via her husband's power. Kerensky saw that her "influence over the Czar was overwhelming."[31] Once, as the Duma was about to meet, she wrote her advice to the czar:

> Oh, my darling, when will you finally bang your fist on the table and shout at [Minister of the Interior] Djunkovsky and others, who are acting so wrongly? No one is afraid of you and they *should* be, they must tremble before you, otherwise they will make trouble for us.... Oh, my boy, make them tremble before you; it is not enough for you to be loved. They must be afraid to make you angry or not to do what you desire.... Be more severe, this cannot continue.[32]

As the czar's troubles grew, she prodded him to autocracy repeatedly:

> I cannot find words to express what my heart feels. You have, finally, shown yourself master, a real autocrat without whom Russia cannot exist.... The only salva-

tion is to be firm. I realize how hard this is for you, and I suffer with you.... I know your exceptionally mild disposition, and now you have overcome it and won, alone against all of them.... God anointed you at your coronation, destined you for your place, and now you have *fulfilled* your obligation. Be assured that He does not forget His anointed.... It is necessary to be severe and to put an end to all that business [presumably the Duma and all other infringements on Nicholas's power]. Dear, I am here, and don't you laugh at your silly old wifey, but I can wear trousers and can make the old man [Prime Minister Goremykin] act vigorously.... [W]e are struggling against evil. [33]

Alexandra gave Nicholas II his marching orders for dealing with questionable government officials: "Crush them all." And he—he saw what his royal marriage was, signing a letter to her as her "poor little weak willed hubby." No wonder, then, he commanded a general to crush the uprising in Petrograd in February 1917: he beat down the revolution at the wish of his wife.

Nicholas depended utterly on Alexandra, and Alexandra depended utterly on a drunken, illiterate, lying, erotic, perverse, and blasphemous monk— whom she perceived as God on earth. His name was Rasputin. He seduced her to absolute loyalty by (as she saw it) saving her son. Through Alexandra, that "afflicted, unbalanced, passionately hysterical woman," as Kerensky described her, Rasputin, in effect, became the ruler of Russia. [34]

The little son suffered from hemophilia, with uncontrolled bleeding. Alexandra was terrified her son would die. She sought a healer, and believed she found him in Rasputin. This "holy man" alone seemed able to stop the bleeding. (It may have been that he repeatedly timed his arrival at the bedside just when the boy's bleeding was about to stop anyway.) [35] To Alexandra, he was a savior. She worshipped him and called the medical monk "Our Friend." He called her "Mama" and the czar "Papa" and bragged that "The tsar thinks I'm Christ incarnate. The tsar and tsarina bow down to me, kneel to me, kiss my hands." [36]

Rasputin was actually a rugged peasant from Siberia who tramped around the royal palace wearing a sleeveless farm coat, a ragged beard that hung down over his girdled shirt, and greased-over boots. [37] To the isolated czar and czarina, he seemed to be "the people," so they took his opinions to be those of the nation's citizenry as well as those of God. Though ignorant and unpolitical, Rasputin had a special talent for inspiring women. He pursued high religion and low sex in frequent orgies with different women. Once he insisted that a woman wash his sexual organs in front of a number of other women. [38] Alexandra refused to believe these stories, arguing that "He is accused of licentiousness but did not the Apostles kiss everyone in greeting?" Indeed, she thought, "he was sent to us from God" and "he is persecuted, just as Christ was persecuted by the scribes and the pharisees." Alexandra urged Nicholas II to "take less notice of the advice of other people, then everything will be all right." She supposed that "but for him [Rasputin], it would have been all up with us long ago." [39]

Alexandra, Kerensky noted, thought that Rasputin should direct "the life of the whole country, appointing ministers, commanding the army and

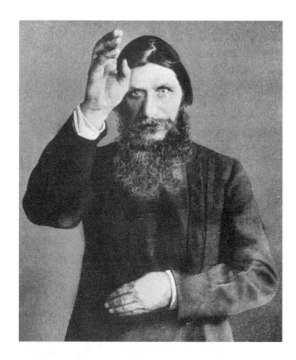

Rasputin.

choosing the time and place of the offensives [as in World War I], as he was capable of miraculously checking [the boy's] hemorrhage."[40] Rasputin cooperated by telling her what should be done. People trying to explain the madness of the results came to the obvious explanation: "Russia was being ruled by the German-born empress and the unsavory Siberian peasant who had conquered her mind."[41] In December 1916, after ten years of domination, Rasputin was poisoned with doctored wine and pastry by a group of high-level officers: a grand duke, a prince, and a Duma deputy. But he would not die, so they shot him with their revolvers. Still he would not die, so they threw him into the freezing river, and he drowned.[42] Rasputin turned out to be right in a prophecy he had given to Alexandra: "Six months after my death you will lose your throne."[43]

Rasputin's murder was hardly an exceptional experience in czarist Russia. Killings were often massive.

THE NEW MOVEMENT FOR REFORM BY THE WORKERS

Modern manufacturing was under way in St. Petersburg by 1905, but the factory workers in that city were treated as poorly as if they were rural serfs. A young and impressive Russian Orthodox priest who had worked as a prison chaplain, Father George Gapon, slowly organized a Union of Russian Factory Workers for better wages and working conditions, and also for the worker's self-improvement through the elimination of drunkenness and gambling and the encouragement of religion and patriotism. The bosses of the oldest and biggest industry, the locomotive works, reacted vigorously, firing workers who were helping Gapon organize the union. As a result, all the rest of the workers walked out of the factory and asked that their troubles be taken to their most obvious protector—the czar. Gapon developed an appeal to Nicholas II, a highly respectful request that the czar let them march to the Winter Palace and humbly "lay their needs before Thee." Gapon added that he did "guarantee the inviolability of Thy person."

That Sunday, January 9, 1906, more than 200,000 men, women, and children—completely unarmed—paraded peacefully toward the palace, many carrying ikons and portraits of the czar and singing, over and over again, "God Save the Czar." At the front marched Father Gapon, holding up a cross and bearing a scroll with the appeal to Nicholas, beginning: "Sire—We workingmen and inhabitants of Saint Petersburg... our wives and our children and our helpless old parents come to Thee, Sire, to seek for truth and protection. We have become beggars; we have been oppressed: we are breathless...." They asked for an eight-hour day, a daily wage of one ruble, an end to overtime, and the development of an elected Constituent Assembly. Their request was that Nicholas "Order and take an oath to comply with these requests and Thou wilt make Russia happy and famous and Thou wilt impress Thy name in our hearts and the hearts of our posterity forever. If Thou wilt not order and wilt not answer our prayer, we shall die here in the Square before Thy Palace." [44]

But the Czar had left town with his wife and daughters when he learned of the march. The thousands of families advancing quietly through the snow suddenly heard bugles blowing—the signal for a cavalry charge. Armed soldiers rode toward them, shot into the air, and then, pointing their rifles at the children and fathers and grandmothers, shot bullets into their bodies. In just a few minutes, hundreds fell and many died, their blood reddening the snow. [45] News of "Bloody Sunday" spread across the nation.

About 500,000 Russian workers went on strike, dangerous as that was in those days. [46] Father Gapon fled to Geneva, Switzerland, and sent a very different message to Nicholas II:

> The innocent blood of workers, their wives and children, lies forever between thee, oh soul destroyer, and the Russian people. Moral connection between thee and them may never be.... Let all the blood which has to be shed, hangman, fall upon thee and thy kindred! [47]

This gentle, czar-respecting priest had been transformed into a revolutionary by Bloody Sunday. He wrote to revolutionary parties, urging them

> to begin the business of armed uprising against tsarism.... Bombs and dynamite, terror by individuals and by masses—everything which may contribute to the national uprising. The first aim is to overthrow the autocracy. [48]

Father Gapon learned how to ride and shoot, and collected extensive funds for purchasing guns. He met with a man named Lenin, who also advocated revolution, and who found his ideas exciting. A meeting of revolutionary parties took place, but broke apart because several organizations opposed Gapon's demand for violent reprisal. So Gapon took up gun-running himself. He tried to smuggle arms from England to anti-czarist Russians, but the ship (the *John Grafton*) ran aground and blew up near Finland. Gapon made it safely back into Russia, where he unsuccessfully tried to recruit other Bloody Sunday marchers to his cause. But then, in April 1906, the priest was murdered—hanged from the rafters of a cottage.[49]

Such brutal tyranny was typical of the passive Czar Nicholas II. In 1903, he allowed his minister of the interior to encourage anti-Semitic riots, and then let his officers watch while hundreds of Jews were killed, raped, beaten, and robbed.[50] That horror had so disgusted Kerensky that he had considered assassinating the czar himself.[51] When Nicholas II appointed a famous bully as prime minister, an underground revolutionary group blew up the new official's house, killing 32 people and injuring two of his children. In retaliation, the czar authorized "field courts-martial"—quick, unappealable trials—which resulted in 489 executions in four months.[52] In Latvia, after revolutionaries attacked and killed soldiers by burning their barracks, the czar's general shot 45 men and women in reprisal. Reading the general's report, Czar Nicholas wrote in the margin, "He should have destroyed the town."[53]

Thus life degenerated in Russia. Through 1906, 768 officials were assassinated and 820 wounded.[54] The range of brutality widened. On April 4, 1912, thousands of mine workers went on strike, finally roused to action by their life of slavery underground: they were forced to work 11 to 12 hours a day, often standing in ice-cold water up to their knees.[55] When they protested, the mine managers would not even talk to them. When they marched with their wives toward the main company office, government police came out and fired at them, hitting 373 and killing 176. As Kerensky's biographer, Richard Abraham, notes, "The brutality and insensitivity of the government shook Russia's working classes out of their apathy. In April 1912 alone, half a million went on sympathy strikes, five times more than the entire number striking in the previous year."[56] Signifying the level of hopelessness in Russia, an epidemic of suicide broke out across the country.[57]

In 1915 conditions were so bad that Czar Nicholas decided to take supreme command of the army himself, a move that simply put more power to inflict brutality on the people into the hands of the czarina. On February 26, 1917, a bright sunny Sunday, many workers dressed up and marched in memory of Bloody Sunday in 1906—and were shot in the square in Petrograd by the czar's troops: 50 dead and 48 wounded.[58]

The czar, who saw himself as a kind and gentle fellow, let horror after horror happen, year in and year out. Finally, he "abdicated" and raced to get out of Russia. The tyranny of Czar Nicholas II and Alexandra and Rasputin was over. They were cast aside in favor of Kerensky and his allies. The democracy Kerensky helped bring into existence was not a sudden novelty. It had been germinating in Russia for decades.

KERENSKY'S LIFE BEFORE THE REVOLUTION

The moment was late February 1917. While not perfect, Kerensky had the spine, brain, and heart to lead a chaotic nation into the transition to liberty and justice for all. His life experience had developed those qualities in him.

Aleksandr Fyodorovich Kerensky, nicknamed Sasha, was born on April 22, 1881. His last name was derived from that of the river Kerenka, and pronounced with emphasis on the first syllable; his first name was that of a great reforming czar. His father was an educator who directed a grammar school for boys and a secondary school for girls, a man whose own father had been an impoverished parish priest in a place called the Kerensky District. Through much struggle, Aleksandr's father had acquired a university education and become a respected teacher. Aleksandr's mother had been one of his father's students; she was the grandchild of a serf who had managed to buy his freedom and get rich as a merchant, leaving quite an inheritance to his granddaughter, and thus to Aleksandr's family.

The Kerenskys' first two children—girls—were tended by a French governess, but Aleksandr and his younger brother, Fedya, were cared for by a kind, illiterate Russian *nyanya*, who had been a serf. She lived and slept with the children, prayed for them, and let them watch her kneel before her ikons. Aleksandr's mother came into the nursery at bedtime and gestured over them the sign of the cross before she kissed them good night. In those early years, his father was distant, except after a disobedient child was told "Father will teach you a lesson, just you see." But these lessons were never physical; as a teacher, Aleksandr's father believed in talking, explaining. Kerensky remembered the small town they lived in as idyllic, with flowered hills rolling down to a river stirred by steamboats when the ice melted in the spring. He recalled his childhood as "the happiest of carefree young lives." [59]

Kerensky was brought up as a Christian, seriously and pleasantly. His mother read the children stories of Jesus—as well as fairy and folk tales, poems and Russian epics. In addition to much prayer, their *nyanya* invoked Jesus to stop them from fighting. She took them walking every day. Once the boys were terrified to see convicts, chained together and their heads half-shaven, being shuffled down the street from jail to a ship at the wharf, on their way to exile in Siberia. The boys started to run away, but she stopped them, saying, "What's the matter with you? Do you really think they're going to hurt you? These poor wretches, you'd better take pity on them. Who are you to judge and condemn them? Let's be kind to them in the name of Christ." She had the boys give bread to the prisoners.

Season by season, Christianity gave them their values. On Annunciation Day, they watched caged birds set free "in recognition of the spiritual brotherhood of all creation." [60] After a loud carnival throughout the town came Lent, with 40 days of solemn silence. When the boys reached the age of seven, they got to go to the most celebratory mass of all, midnight at Easter; Aleksandr was so affected that he once saw an image of Christ he thought was alive. On Sundays, an old priest would come by and leave them pamphlets that described the major Christian holy days. Aleksandr dreamed of becoming a church bell-ringer: "to stand on a high steeple, above everybody, near the clouds, and thence to call men to the service of God with the heavy peals of a huge bell." [61]

Many years later, Kerensky looked back on that part of his life as highly significant to his worldview. "It is with a deep feeling of satisfaction that I think back to my childhood in a Russia where everyday life had its roots in religious feelings nurtured by a thousand years of Christianity," he wrote. "Religion was part of our everyday activities and entered our lives intimately and forever. These early impressions, and the image of the marvelous Man who had given His life for others and had taught but one thing—love —were the source of the youthful faith I later acquired in the idea of personal sacrifice for the people. This was the source of my revolutionary fervor and of that of many young men and women of my time." [62]

Kerensky's youth was not wholly serene. At age six, two traumas occurred. He knew an older student named Vladimir Ulyanov who went to their church and was taught by Aleksandr's father. Ulyanov's older brother called national attention to the town when he attempted to kill the czar. His arrest, conviction, and hanging shocked the community, including young Aleksandr. [63] And then Aleksandr caught tuberculosis in his hip. He had to wear a long iron boot and stay in bed for six months. While healing, he read a lot, including a book that brought tears to his eyes: *Uncle Tom's Cabin*. When he got well and went out again into the countryside, the name "Russia" flashed before him as a sign of life. "In the very depth of my heart," he remembered,

> everything that surrounded me and everything that happened was intimately linked with Russia: the beauty of the Volga, the chimes of evening bells, the bishop sitting solemnly in a carriage drawn by four horses, the convicts with heavy chains, the pretty girls with whom I went to dancing lessons, the ragged, barefoot village boys with whom I played in the summer, my parents, the nursery and *nyanya*, the Russian epic heroes, and Peter the Great. I began to ponder, to ask questions, and to try to understand some of the things I had always taken for granted. [64]

So Aleksandr was a happy and energetic child who could handle suffering and who strongly identified with the incarnation and resurrection of Christ and with the land he lived in.

When he was eight, the family moved to a larger city in a territory where his father had been appointed chief inspector of schools. [65] Aleksandr the reader became a talker. As he grew older, he saw his father as "an essential part of my life." Now that he was an educational supervisor, his father spent most of his time in an office at home, where he received consultants and visitors. He read over Aleksandr's homework and talked with him about history and literature. The boy often listened to his father's conversations with high officials about Russian life and politics. He recalled that "They always spoke in terms of the state or the country as a whole. To them the state was a living body and they placed the satisfaction of its needs above all other considerations." [66] Once Aleksandr hid behind the curtain while his father was reading aloud to his mother a shocking pamphlet by Tolstoy blasting the government and yet advocating "not resisting evil by violence."[67] Aleksandr began to speak out himself. His father taught him his motto: *Non multa sed multum*, which meant "Fewer words, more thoughts." But Aleksandr had a remarkably attractive voice and he dreamed of acting on-stage as Czar Alexander.[68] He also thought of becoming a professional actor or musician. As he approached adolescence, he sought out conversation and came to like it.

When he was 13, Czar Alexander III died. Young Kerensky wept, read all the obituary accounts, attended all the requiems, and collected money in his school class to buy a wreath.[69] He turned to the study of history, philology, and jurisprudence, determined to take up an occupation in which he could contribute to the welfare of his country.

At 18 he went off to the University of St. Petersburg, where he decided to live in the dormitory rather than in a boardinghouse because the dormitory had more "lively discussions on a variety of subjects."[70] The university offered students freedom bordering on anarchy. Aleksandr found it fun to join in student strikes, to boycott or jeer down professors brought in to replace professors fired for being too sympathetic to students. He met a charming 17-year-old named Olga, the daughter of a soldier.[71] The two of them had many discussions about current politics and literature, and read poetry to each other. Later they married.

Though he was not strongly engaged in organizations, Aleksandr was elected to a student committee[72] and to a fraternity council. He got involved in a student movement meant to "fight against the lawlessness and arbitrary conduct" of university inspectors. His voice had turned into a rich baritone and he came across as a witty, good-humored, enthusiastic fellow.[73] Near the end of his second year in college, he gave his first political speech, sudden and unprepared, to students rallied around the staircase. He urged them "to help the nation in the liberation struggle," and they cheered him loudly. Exhilarated, Aleksandr was proud when the university rector suspended him for destructive speaking and sent him home. There his thrill collapsed when he faced his angry father, who berated him, asserting that trashing his education was no way to help Russia. Aleksandr got the message—learn first, then act—and went back to the university with that purpose.

A respected philosophy professor, Nicholas Lossky, taught him that "quarreling parties, being one-sided, were partly right and partly wrong."[74] Aleksandr and his friends, as one of them remembered,

> lived entirely among ideas and ideals; they dreamed about a new world, but they wanted freedom most of all. They were unquestionably humanitarian and utterly Russian in every respect. A smoky room, a table loaded with samovar and plates of sandwiches, and groups of twelve or fifteen men and women of various ages were typical of an evening assemblage of the intelligentsia of Saint Petersburg.[75]

Kerensky transferred to law school, at first planning to be a teacher of law, but then deciding to become a practicing lawyer for political causes.

He sought out political defendants in serious need. Such clients could pay him virtually nothing, so his father regularly sent him an allowance and his pregnant wife earned some salary. Bright as he was, Kerensky could have used his training to become wealthy; instead, he focused on the causes he believed in. "My childhood dream of becoming an actor or musician," he said, "gave way to a decision to serve my people, Russia and the state, as my father had done all his life." Through his work, he got to know many poor and working-class people. [76]

The young lawyer Kerensky took up case after case to support organizations he believed in. He opposed czarist autocracy, but he also opposed the collapse of politics. For instance, he thought that the years of Russia's war with Japan

> were a cruel spiritual torture, because the…attitude towards it brought strife into the most friendly relations and divided nearly every family into two hostile camps.… [T]he memories of those long sleepless nights, spent in frenzied arguments about the war, poisoned with anger and hatred towards each other, are still painful to me, to this day. [77]

And then came Bloody Sunday. Kerensky was there, next to the crowd, and fortunate not to be shot. He wrote protesting letters and became engaged in the reaction by which "the entire country became 'unionized'" [78] as labor organizations federated in a Union of Unions. The Liberation Movement pressed the czar with explicit appeals for freedom, for civil liberties, and for a constitution. After seeing families shot down by the czar's troops, Kerensky once again decided to take upon himself "the mortal sin of killing the incumbent of supreme power who was ruining the country" [79]—an offer rejected by the anti-czarist conspiracy. [80] When another demonstration, this one in Moscow, was also crushed by troops and followed by police arrests, Kerensky wrote an angry article for a newspaper. As he and Olga and their new son were decorating their Christmas tree the evening of December 23, 1905, the doorbell rang and a police inspector came in and arrested him.

Kerensky found jail to be just the experience he needed. "Strangely enough," he recalled, "I almost enjoyed this solitary confinement, which gave me leisure to think, to look back at my life, and to read to my heart's content." He also liked tapping code messages on his cell wall and getting responses from his neighbor. But then, when he was supposed to be informed of the charge against him, nothing happened. So he went on a hunger strike—no food, no drink. "The smell of the food which was left by the side of my bed each day was almost unbearable," he wrote, and he broke down and sipped water. But then, after four days, he recalled, the hunger turned him numb and he became "almost blissful." [81] A week went by and he had to be carried into the warden's office to hear the charge against him: complicity in armed rebellion. He fainted, recovered, and not long thereafter was released. As he intended, his allies had learned of his hunger strike. He left jail determined to "devote all my efforts to the cause of unifying all democratic parties in Russia." [82] More important, he had a new reputation in revolutionary circles: through imprisonment "my revolutionary spurs were earned...I was now 'one of them' in the radical and socialist circles."[83]

Contemptuous as Czar Nicholas II was of democracy and any sort of constitution, he had allowed a consultative Duma—an elected body—to be formed. But he (or his circle) found the Duma's liberating recommendations "totally unacceptable" and therefore dissolved it on July 8, 1906.

Kerensky resumed his political legal practice, but he was depressed by the czar's action. "How could someone as anxious as I was to help people be denied the opportunity of doing so?" he wrote.[84] Still young—he was 25 in 1906—he took every opportunity to argue a case or make a speech. He stood forth for organizations like the Teachers' Union, the Peasants' Brotherhood, and the Armenian Dashnaktsutyun Party, and became known as an effective public speaker. Little wonder, then, that after the czar allowed the Duma to come back into existence, Kerensky was nominated and elected to that body. Thus he found a place to work at moving his beloved Russia toward democracy.

Year after year, Kerensky advocated laws guaranteeing justice, political discourse, freedom, and humanitarian values. His first speech as a member of the Duma in December 1912 was enraged and enraging. The subject before the parliament was the citizens' right to vote, now being tightly restricted. He said:

> In a country ruled by violence, where the masses in their millions are excluded from legislatures, are not allowed [sic] in it, where at any moment any police inspector—to say nothing of the governors—can throw any citizen into jail or arrest him, there can be no strong people, there can be no national security.

Five days later, he spoke again:

> The country says: it can't go on like this, we can't live like this.... A question cannot be decided by naked force, but should be decided by a decision of the whole popular mass, [by]...the summoning of popular representation on the basis of a universal, direct and equal franchise and the secret ballot.... There is no way out for Russia apart from democracy, there is no salvation for Russia apart from democracy.[85]

Thus his cause was government by citizens. But Kerensky was not advocating violence to advance that cause. When a well-meaning person gave his son a sword, Kerensky picked it up and broke it in half over his knee.[86] Even as he struggled in the Duma with political enemies, he believed that "Hatred and malice, hatred to the end towards political opponents is incomprehensible to us." And he thought that "we will never allow ourselves in connection with you to depart from those basic principles of righteousness, truth and love."[87]

Kerensky saw himself—and Russia—as devoted to love:

> I remain a decided adversary of every form of terror. I shall never renounce this "weakness," this humaneness of our March Revolution. The real soul of the Russian people is one of mercy without hatred. This is the heritage of our Russian culture, which is deeply humane and tested by long suffering.... It was with faith

in the justice of our cause that we launched the Revolution and sought to create a new Russian commonwealth founded upon human love and tolerance....The strength of our Russian Revolution lay precisely in the fact that it did triumph over its enemies, not by terror and bloodshed, but by mercy, love and justice, even if only for one day, for one hour. [88]

Kerensky also saw his speaking—his best talent—primarily as a way to inspire popular unity. He believed it was "necessary, by constant use of the spoken word, to counter the forces of destruction and to instill in people a sense of their individual responsibility to the nation as a whole." [89] What thrilled him most was the time when "An amazing unanimity was expressed in the enthusiastic way the conference greeted the demand for a republic voiced by speaker after speaker—from workers to capitalists, from generals to ordinary soldiers." [90]

This is the man who emerged as a leading democratic figure in Russia. A dedicated, effective public servant, Kerensky had great-faith in the humane and merciful soul of the Russian people. But the inherited Russian political culture was something far different.

WHAT RUSSIANS HAD INHERITED FROM THEIR "HEROES"

The real heritage—the heroism and the myths widely admired in that diverse nation—was one of incredible brutality.

Sir Robert Bruce Lockhart, England's consul-general in Moscow in 1917–18, observed that "There is no kinder, gentler, more superstitiously religious people than the Russian people; no people readier in their strength to sacrifice their lives for an ideal. There is also no more savage and brutally cruel people, no people readier in their weakness to betray their nearest and dearest for their own safety."[91] The English ambassador to Russia far back in 1588–90 had the same views: "The state and form of government is plain tyrannical.... It may be doubted whither is greater—the cruelty or the intemperancy that is used in the country."[92]

From the earliest days, life in Russia was war. Force was normal, peace unusual. The beautiful flat Russian steppes were continually invaded by the fiercest of Asians. The Scythians, in 700 B.C., swept in on horseback with bows and swords, cutting off the skulls of their enemies and making drinking cups of them. Eventually the dreadful Huns invaded. Then came the Avars, who when they needed their wagons pulled, did not bother to capture animals but yoked up four or five women for each wagon and forced them to drag it. [93]

Tale after tale in the national mythology celebrated human butchery, including butchery in the name of God. Nearly all of Russia's national heroes were bragged of as awesome killers. The first great Russian heroine, Olga, learned in 945 A.D. that her husband, Prince Igor, had been killed by the Drevlianians, who then sent emissaries to get her to marry their ruler. This is the story:

And Olga said to the Drevlianians: "Tomorrow I shall send for you, and you must say: 'We shall not go on horses, nor on foot, but carry us in our boat.'" And on the next day Olga sent for her guests. They sat in their boat with proud bearing and the servants brought them to Olga's palace. And they threw them, together with their boat, into a pit. And bending down toward the pit, Olga asked them: "Are you greatly honored?" They answered: "This is worse for us than Igor's death." And she ordered that they be buried alive....

Then Olga sent word to the Drevlianians: "If truly you ask that I marry your Prince, then send me your leading men, so that with great honor I may become the wife of your Prince." When the Drevlianians came, Olga ordered a bath to be prepared, saying, "After you have washed yourselves, then come before me." The guests went in, the bathhouse door was locked, Olga ordered the building set on fire, and they were burned to death. [94]

In the year 980, the famous Vladimir the Great killed his two brothers and their troops in war and took his father's throne as Grand Prince of Kiev. After converting to Christianity, he forced everyone else—by sword, if necessary—to be baptized. When he abided by Christ's words, "Resist not him that is evil," bandits began to invade the territory. Certain churchmen persuaded him that he had been "appointed by God to chastise malefactors," so Vladimir had the thieves killed. In Russia, "Christianity" was to be a continuing political contradiction: on the one hand, it justified killing others, and on the other hand, it made Russians welcome their own violent death. When a Prince named Boris found himself being murdered, he cried to heaven, "Thou knowest, my Lord, that I do not resist, do not object." [95]

After Vladimir died, his twelve sons (born of different mothers), fought over the grand princeship for 21 years. Son Yaroslav finally won. He initiated some democracy: law, a council of advisers he called the "Duma," and regular town meetings in villages.

Violence recurred steadily over the next centuries. Time and again, Asian killers invaded the land. In 1547, a 17-year-old named Ivan was crowned. He became Ivan the Terrible, one of Russia's stunning historical "heroes." Constantly invoking the name of God, Emperor Ivan ordered thousands of people tortured to death. He enjoyed deciding on the kind of torture that would be inflicted and then watching the screaming victims die. [96] As a child, he had enjoyed carrying small animals to the top of the high Kremlin tower and throwing them out the window. He learned to ride, and would whip and trot his horse through the streets, slashing people's faces. If he happened to detest the look of someone, he commanded his guards to cut off the person's head and cast it in front of him. [97]

Perhaps in memory of Olga, Ivan once dealt with a delegation of petitioners by pouring hot boiling wine on them, burning off their beards, and making them strip and lie on the floor. Then he stuck them with a metal-pointed staff and burned them with red-hot stove pans. He created a ruling gang, the *oprich-niks*, who slaughtered vast numbers of Russians for eight years. In one six-week orgy, they mutilated and burnt to death many citizens; others were thrown into the river and pushed under the ice to drown. When Ivan felt religious, he would call up his drunk torturers and rapers from the basement to hear him preach, or

Ivan the Terrible.

he would conduct a ritual of cutting ribs out of men' chests with white hot pincers. He once punished a "traitor" by sticking a shaft up through his behind and on out through his throat. The victim lived for 15 hours. His mother, a duchess, was dragged in to watch and then given to 100 gunners, who raped her to death and fed her body to the hungry hounds. In 1584, after days of howling madly through his palace, Ivan the Terrible died. He was 54. Having killed his most promising son, he was succeeded instead by his retarded deaf son, Fedor, who ruled in violence and chaos for another 14 years and set up a reign of terror for years after that. [98]

Yet another Russian "hero" was Stenka Razin, a pirate who was notorious during the 1670s. One of the most popular modern Russian folk songs tells the story of how Razin captured a lovely Persian girl and spent the night with her. When he heard rumors that she had turned him soft, he said, "In a fellowship of free men, never shall a quarrel rise. Volga, Mother Volga, take the beauty as your prize"—and he drowned the girl in the Volga River. Razin led a rebellion toward Moscow, but was defeated and captured. The czar had his assistants break Razin's bones one at a time and, before Razin died, had him quartered. [99]

Perhaps the last classic Russian "hero" was Peter the Great, who became czar toward the end of the seventeenth century. Nearly seven feet tall, with strong hands, a twitching face, and a hard drinking habit, he was known as "a furious man." He had peculiar tastes. Once when watching a dead human body being inspected, he ordered the inspectors to chew on the dead man's nerves. Peter "the Great" thought nothing of ruthlessly impressing thousands of men into his service, and watching with detachment while they died of cold, disease, exhaustion and the knout.... To build his city he dragooned into his service countless thousands of Russians,...paid them nothing, shrugged at their misery and death, and drove them onward." Under him, Russia endured much miserable war and year after year of domestic inquisition. Peter the Great, when irritated, would knock a critic unconscious with his fist or fasten iron pincers on his nose and tear out his nostrils. The extent of his torture and butchery is too great to be measured. [100]

By the time Czar Peter died, in 1725, the Russian heroic figure had been fixed in myth and memory. The heritage of violence continued through the eighteenth century, with revolutions and counterrevolutions. Those in power were guilty of terror and torture, commonly and at random. Soldiers were routinely lashed with whips, even for minor faults; sometimes they were whipped to death. At one point, nine soldiers got 6,000 lashes. [101]

Peter the Great.

On through the nineteenth century, not only did the government flog and execute citizens, but opponents of the government perpetuated violence as well. Historian Adam Ulam explains that occasional violence by civilians may have been "the only way of shaking the government out of its complacency and of making it responsive to society's aspirations." Some Russians became so tolerant of this type of violence, he says, that "they half-excused actions which clearly crossed the line separating political fanaticism from wanton criminality...." Some even tolerated the frequent murdering of czars and their children. A famous saying was "Russia is an autocracy tempered by assassination." One Russian admirer of the United States advocated finding a George Washington and adopting a U.S.-style constitution—after recruiting some assassins to get the tyrants out of the way. But, Ulam concludes, "In fact terror helped to prolong the anachronism of autocracy." [102]

The Russian habit of extreme violence gained support from a version of Christianity that exhorted people to look upward, via ritual, to God in heaven rather than to His children on earth. The Russian Orthodox Church was closely controlled by the state, which found it convenient to focus people's attention away from the harshness of the Russian reality. [103] As for the serfs—more than a third of the people in the early nineteenth century—violence was completely normal.

Added to all these factors was vodka. Throughout Russia, especially during the long winters, vodka was a popular form of entertainment and escapism. [104] When young Czar Nicholas II succeeded his father in 1894, he continued the tradition of fostering heavy tyranny. Only five years after he took the throne, the harvest of 1901 was a disaster. When starving peasants attempted to get grain for their families from the farming estates of the wealthy, Czar Nicholas's administration sent floggers into the provinces to whip them. [105]

The misrule of Nicholas II would stimulate the 1917 Revolution. The heritage of those long centuries of brutality—in heroes and myths and everyday experience—was deeply engrained in the twentieth-century Russian psyche. To create a democratic, peaceful society would be a substantial challenge.

RUSSIA'S TWENTIETH-CENTURY INHERITANCE

Germany's declaration of war against Russia in 1914 united the vast and diverse nation. Czar Nicholas II repeated the pledge Alexander I had made when Napoleon invaded Russia in 1812: "I solemnly promise not to conclude peace until the last enemy soldier leaves the soil of Russia." In St. Petersburg, crowds poured into the square in front of the Winter Palace, where the Czar viewed them from his balcony. They kneeled on the ground and sang "God Save the Tsar" and "Have Mercy, O Lord, on Thy people." [106] The Marxist supposition that the breakout of the war would trigger working-class revolutions around the world, turned out to be erroneous. Instead, the poorest of workers in Germany followed their flag, as did the poorest in Russia. As has often happened, war was met by popular enthusiasm. Russians who had suffered for years under their government volunteered to suffer and die for their country.

And many did die for their country in World War I. In contrast to the average German soldier, the typical Russian soldier was an illiterate peasant ill equipped to fight a modern war. At the start of the war, 14 million Russians were drafted—but their equipment consisted of no heavy field guns, only 4,100 machine guns, and a few light artillery with just 1,000 shells per piece (the German's artillery had 3,000 shells per piece). In the first five months of war, the Russians lost 300,000 men and 650 light cannon. In 1915, 2 million soldiers were killed and wounded and another 1.3 million were taken prisoner. [107] That August, Czar Nicholas II made himself supreme commander of the entire army, a post at which he proved even more incompetent than at his regular duties. [108] As late as January 1916, a fourth of the Russian soldiers facing the Germans on the western front had no shoes to wear. [109] Many units lacked machine guns or modern artillery. In some places, nine out of ten soldiers crouching in the trenches did not even have a rifle to fire. [110] They were told to go forward and attack anyway, watching to grab a gun from the dead. [111] With these conditions, it was no wonder that in 1916 another 2 million Russian troops were killed or wounded and 350,000 more were captured. In 1917, the Army of Russia was the largest in the world, consisting of more than 10 million soldiers. A million deserters roamed around at the rear, often spreading violence among civilians. [112] By the end of the war, more than 5 million Russians had been killed or wounded. [113]

By the fall of 1916, the mood of the country had lapsed into fear that the war would never end [114] and horror at the wild disorder at home. Far from the front lines—especially in big cities—soldiers recruited mainly from rural areas were jammed into vastly overcrowded barracks. Sailors, mainly working-class men, had been driven back into their crowded bases by the German navy. [115] Strikes in the armed forces began, and spread widely. Especially in St. Petersburg, the capital city, hordes of boxed-in soldiers and sailors kept exploding out onto the streets, searching for leadership to rescue them from virtual imprisonment.

But oddly enough, as Adam Ulam reports, "Among the bulk of the frontline troops, morale stood quite high." At the front, the rate of desertions was remarkably low, even though it was relatively easy for a soldier to escape. [116] In spite of their incredible military inferiority, the Russian troops were standing tall. At the time of the 1917 Revolution, then, Russians' experience of the war was altogether different at the front than in the country's capital.

Kerensky had recently taken command of the Revolution when Lenin arrived in St. Petersburg from Switzerland—via Germany—after more than nine years of exile from Russia. He and his fellow Bolsheviks had let the German leaders know that they wanted safe passage to Russia. The Germans saw a great opportunity: they would get this Marxist agitator away from the German front and back into Russia, where he would be sure to stir up working-class soldiers to rebel against the rulers of their own nation. So the Germans supplied Lenin not only with a sealed, nonstop train but also with money to press forward the revolution in Russia.

Early in 1917, Kerensky had been moving the country toward democracy. But when Lenin arrived in Petrograd in April 1917, he became a major factor in the fate of the nation—a profound demonstration of how the emergence of a particular leader at a particular time can shape history. Why Lenin was what he was and did what he did made a difference to the cause of democracy for Russia. He arrived in Petrograd bearing his own Russian life experiences. How would he act?

THE NATURE OF LENIN: MOVING TOWARD LEADERSHIP

Once when Lenin was listening to music by Beethoven, he said, "Nowadays we can't pat heads. We've got to hit heads, hit them without mercy."[117]

Eventually he titled himself "Lenin," but when he was born on April 10, 1870, he was named Vladimir—"Lord of the World," the name of Russia's first Christian ruler. His nickname was Volodya. His family's name was Ulyanov. He spent the first third of his life in a quiet city called Simbirsk that was home to about 30,000 people—including the Kerensky family. The structure of Simbirsk neatly illustrated the class structure of Russia. It was built on a narrow ridge overlooking windswept plains and a fork where the big Volga River was joined by a smaller tributary. It had been called "Hill of the Winds." The hill at the top of the city was known as "The Crown." Like a European castle, it had been a secure fortress for aristocrats; two peasant revolutions had failed to shake it. The Crown contained government buildings surrounded by the country mansions of the aristocrats. On the side overlooking the river lived merchants—the bourgeois. Down below, where the slopes were sometimes flooded, stood the shanties of workers. Both the Ulyanovs and the Kerenskys lived near, but not at, the Crown. They shared the stunningly beautiful view of the river but not with the Simbirskian aristocracy.[118]

Young Volodya loved where he lived and loved his family. They were strongly educated. His mother had taught herself English, French, German, and Russian, and became a schoolteacher. She taught little Volodya to play the piano and to sing as she accompanied him. And she got her children to put out a handwritten weekly magazine for the family called *The Sabbath*. She was Lutheran, but did not go to church, which made her a bit strange to the local religious community.

Volodya's father, Ilya, was a hardworking, well-educated man who became an excellent teacher of science and mathematics. The family moved to Simbirsk the year before Volodya was born, when Ilya earned an appointment as school inspector for the province (the post meant training teachers to teach well). He became chief inspector for the province and was awarded official nobility—his title was now "Actual State Councillor." The honor was defined as hereditary, and thus could be passed on to his children. He was an Orthodox Christian and attended church regularly. As a conservative liberal in politics, he was sympathetic to the people but devoted to the czar and the other powers-that-be. In fact, he named his first son Alexander, after the czar. Thanks to his hard work for 25 years, at the end of his career 434 small primary schools and several first-rate gymnasiums had been created.

Lenin.

Volodya had good times with his brothers and sisters. His sister Anna remembered him as "jovial, humorous, mischievous, self-confident, aggressive...noisy and boisterous," a boy who "loved to exhibit the growing powers of his mind."[119] He played games but "he broke his toys oftener than he played with them."[120] He and his brother Sasha often said to their cousins, "Oblige us by your absence."[121] Volodya was late in learning to walk (age three), but early in learning to read (age five). He was sent to a Russian school at age nine and a half, and, like Sasha, he got high grades and honors—not because his father was the school inspector, but because he had high intelligence, skill, and energy. Sasha taught him, and Volodya taught his little brother, Dmitri, who later recalled that he was a very strict teacher.[122]

No doubt one of the reasons Ilya had named his first son Alexander was that Czar Alexander II had sponsored a major movement of reform, including strong improvement of the people's education. But when in 1881 (Volodya's eleventh year) Czar Alexander II was killed by a terrorist bomb, a heavy reaction set in against popular education: "liberal" professors were dismissed and education was forbidden for "the children of cooks" (the lower classes). The new czar, Alexander III, not only set out to beat down the revolutionaries who had murdered his father, but also damned the reforms as "criminal error" and turned over the network of elementary schools Ilya had created to the Russian Orthodox Holy Synod.[123] In effect, Ilya's public education system was destroyed. He was forced to retire four years early on a restricted income, an ardent loyalist humiliated by the new regime. The family finances became uncertain. Then Ilya had a stroke, and on December 30, 1885, when Volodya was approaching age 16, his father died.

Brother Sasha was depressed. He came home from school and he and Volodya read hour after hour, including a book called *Capital* by Karl Marx. [124] When he returned to college, Sasha joined the revolutionary People's Freedom Party and even volunteered to kill Czar Alexander III with other members of the Terrorist Section of that party. He and his sister Anna were arrested. When a letter brought the news to the shocked family in Simbirsk, Volodya's mother ordered him to take charge of the family and hurried off to try to rescue Sasha. But Sasha refused to seek forgiveness from the administration. He sought death: "I want to die for my country." After a trial, he was sentenced to death and hanged.[125] Volodya never forgot his brother's execution. When he himself was arrested as a university student, he said, "My path has been blazed by my older brother."[126]

Volodya was deeply embittered when his Simbirsk neighbors turned their backs on his family. There was one exception: Feodor Kerensky, Volodya's father's fellow school director, whose son was Aleksandr Kerensky. Ignoring the risk of associating with the brother of a would-be assassin of the czar, Feodor awarded Volodya a gold medal for excellence in school (the decision brought Feodor reprimands from his superiors). After conferring with Volodya's mother, he also wrote a strongly positive recommendation for Volodya, who was seeking entrance to a university: "Very gifted, always neat and industrious, Ulyanov [Volodya] was first in all subjects...." He did note, in his honest style, a short-coming: "Looking more closely at Ulyanov's character and private life, I have had occasion to note a somewhat excessive tendency toward isolation and reserve, a tendency to avoid contact with acquaintances, and even with the best of his schoolfellows outside of school hours." Volodya's sister Anna agreed: in his youth, Volodya "never brought a friend home with him," she wrote.[127] But that fall, after Sasha's death in the spring, 17-year-old Volodya was admitted to the University of Kazan, where he took up the study of law.

That December, students assembled to raise demands against the university administration. Volodya—who had nothing to do with initiating the meeting and did not speak at it—sat in the front row. The university officials ordered the meeting closed, and when there was delay, they required the apparent "ringleaders" to show them their ID cards. They noted Volodya's. That night he was arrested and put in jail for several days.[128] Accused by the university rector of behaving "with deceit, dereliction, and even discourtesy,"[129] he was expelled and exiled from the city of Kazan. He and his sister Anna were allowed to move to the town of Kukushkino, where they had to live under police control. Their mother and the younger children joined them.

Volodya began studying by himself, gathering boxes of books to be read nearly all day, with a short break for meals and a swim or hike. Five months later he applied for readmission to the Kazan university. He was rejected, clearly because of his dead brother's conviction. Two months later, his mother petitioned for his readmission. Again, he was rejected. So Volodya applied for permission to go abroad for the sake of his health. But again, his request was rejected. The next fall, 1888, he was allowed to return to the city of Kazan, but not to the university. He joined a chess club and studied in the library.

His mother went to St. Petersburg and searched out officials who had been friends of her husband, begging one after another to help her boy. In a petition, she wrote that "It is a veritable torment to regard my son and see how the best years of his life slip unfruitfully away...such an existence must almost inevitably drive him to the idea of suicide." She sold the house in Simbirsk and used her pension to buy a farm in an impoverished village for Volodya to work at during the summers. "My mother wanted me to engage in farming," Volodya reportedly said. "I tried it, but I saw that it would not work: my relations with the muzhiks [peasants] got to be abnormal."[130] (Translation: He did not get along with the peasants.) His mother continued to work hard to secure his future, and at age 22 he was licensed as a lawyer.[131]

Studying all those years, Volodya learned of Marx, reading more of his other works. As a young lawyer, he began to write; eventually he would produce about 10 million words.[132] While he was living in St. Petersburg, he married a Marxist woman and repeatedly took on difficult defense cases against the government. After two years in the capital, he got permission to leave Russia. In the spring of 1895, he traveled to Berlin, Paris, and Geneva. When he returned to St. Petersburg, he published controversial articles and conspired energetically with underground workers' organizations, teaching them Marxism.

In December 1895, as a challenger of the rulers, he was arrested and put in prison. Strangely, the year he spent in jail: he slept nine hours a day and read and wrote constantly in the protected privacy of prison. He also played chess by knock code through the cell wall with his neighbor. When he was released, he was exiled to Siberia, where he settled into years of correspondence, hunting, and the resumption of his married life.

At the turn of the century, Volodya got permission to travel to Europe, where he undertook years of activity, writing and attending and speaking at meetings such as those of the Russian Social Democratic Labor Party. He became ardently devoted to a Marxist leader named George Plekhanov, an older and effective teacher in the movement. Volodya thought him worthy of "respect...reverence...infatuation."[133] Nearing 30, Volodya postured himself as the youth leader, Plekhanov as the elder. But when Volodya moved to create a journal for the emigré movement, Plekhanov harshly criticized his writing— "This is not literary work. This does not look like anything ..."[134]—splitting the organization. It was during this controversy that Volodya took the name Lenin.[135]

In 1902–03, Lenin lived in London, where he spent much time in the British Museum. He published a work that was widely translated and read, entitled *What Is to Be Done?* (the title was borrowed from a novel by his brother Sasha's favorite writer).[136] When various political disputes upset him and disrupted his sleep, his wife took him off to swim or hike.

In 1905, Lenin was advocating democratic rights, demanding "freedom of assembly" and "freedom of the press." Back in Russia, the czar was doing the same in his "Freedom Manifesto," but what he declared, he did not make happen.[137] After more than five years out of the country, Lenin returned in 1905 to St. Petersburg, where he took part in agitation against the government. Two years later, he left for Europe again—and did not return to Russia for nine and a half years, not until his famous arrival in St. Petersburg in April 1917.[138]

Lenin's most crucial life experiences were at the hands of the czarist authorities. He had lived through a brother's execution, expulsion from college, jail, exile, and harsh criticism. Through those heavy troubles, he had read many political works that he described as "calculated to evoke in the reader hatred, aversion, and contempt...calculated not to convince but to break up the ranks of the opponent, not to correct the mistakes of the opponent but to destroy him, to wipe his organization off the face of the earth."[139] He saw democracy not as fundamental, but as an expedient means of grabbing power. He believed "the congress must be simple—like a war council—and small in numbers—like a war council."[140] Lenin's ideal was the "abolition of all restrictive laws"[141] in order to create a "dictatorship of the proletariat" that "is not limited by any laws, takes no notice of any rules whatsoever and relies directly on violence."[142] He wrote in 1917 that "The seizure of power is the point of the uprising."[143]

So Lenin saw politics as violence, not as discourse. Having long been separated from school, church, and Russia, he had virtually no direct relationships with ordinary people, not even the working class he claimed to champion. Instead, he related to ideology and abstraction. His main object was destruction: to smash the powers-that-be. During World War I, he declared, "Our slogan must be a civil war," and he hoped the war would "speed up the collapse of capitalism." Later he wrote that Communists should support bourgeois or reform parties "the way a noose supports a hanging man." [144] Lenin wanted the working class to make "a violent revolution" and "shatter, break up, blow up...the whole state machinery."[145] He thought it was "a great deal better to 'discuss with rifles' than with the theses of the opposition." As for workers "found guilty of idling," he advocated "shooting on the spot one out of every ten."[146] Trying to recruit followers, he concluded that "without squabble, scandal, torture, filth, and scum this cannot be accomplished."[147] He said he wanted to "Overthrow the capitalists, crush the resistance of these exploiters with the iron hand of the armed workers, break the bureaucrat machine of the contemporary state."[148]

But what he would actually do could not be predicted by what he said, because he believed that "Promises are like pie-crust—made to be broken."[149] He lived by a totally unreal Marxist prophecy: that the state would completely fade away and the police and the regularly army would "be completely abolished and replaced by the army of the whole people; a universal militaria."[150] He advocated that "we can and *must* think of democracy without parliamentarianism,"[151] for "In parliaments, they merely chatter for the special purpose of fooling the 'common people.'"[152]

Lenin saw force as the essence of government, not the disease to be cured by a democratic government. He detested political discourse and he damned democracy.

Finally, as Aleksandr Kerensky observed, "Lenin...had absolutely no moral or spiritual objection to promoting the defeat of his own country."[153]

THE 1917 REVOLUTION FOR DEMOCRACY

The essential challenge for democracy in Russia was whether or not the representatives of the people would take control of the military.

Through March 1917, Kerensky worked with all the energy he could muster to create a democratic alternative to the czarist state. Soldiers rebelled against the czar in Petrograd, in Moscow, and throughout Russia. The Provisional Government formed on March 2nd with Prince Georgi E. Lvov as prime minister named itself "Provisional" because it saw that the creation of democracy would require a genuine national election of a Constituent Assembly to establish government by consent of the governed. Meanwhile, the Provisional Government officially declared freedom for Russia: free assembly, free speech, the right to strike, and the liberation of political prisoners. Progress toward democracy was meant to be prompt despite the war in the field and the chaos at home. The Provisional Government assured Russians that "it had no intention of using military circumstances for any sort of slowing down in the realization of...reforms...."[154] But Kerensky thought they would have to delay "all serious political changes until the end of the war." He was convinced that

> so long as Russia remains under the threat of invasion a Constituent Assembly could not deliberate with the requisite freedom. Moreover, the actual holding of the elections involves preliminary work requiring at least nine months. If women are also to have the vote, the electoral mechanism would be all the more complicated.[155]

On March 2, Czar Nicholas abdicated and the Provisional Government declared itself in charge of the country.[156] Its operations were far from serene. As minister of justice, and later minister of war, Kerensky moved constantly from crisis to crisis, trying to create political unity. He also held the office of vice chairman of the Petrograd Soviet, the enormous collection of largely impoverished and poorly educated peasants and workers gathered to represent the people of Russia. Kerensky made his position clear to the public:

> I am a socialist and a democrat, a member of the Socialist Revolutionary Party, and believe me, that when I decided to enter the Provisional Government I remained your hostage there too, the hostage of the soldiers, workers, peasants, officers and republicans, of all the citizens who want to create a free republican Russia. [Stormy applause] Believe me and know that as long as I am minister of justice, no-one will come to threaten you and no-one will dare to arise against the new regime and against free Russia.[157]

The question was how the Soviet would relate to the Provisional Government. Some factions, especially the more modern industrial workers, were in favor of Marxist rule by the working class, but Kerensky's movement for "a free republican Russia" had growing support. While he was in Moscow, a Soviet Contact Commission was formed and began to meet regularly with the government's ministers. Kerensky promised a soldiers' organization that "I will work to the limits of my powers so long as I am trusted and people are frank with me." Their chairman responded that "the army trusts you as the leader of Russian Democracy."[158]

But that part of the army in combat with Germany experienced what Kerensky described as "a terrifying moment" because "the traditional relations between the officers and men broke down immediately upon the receipt of news of the revolution and the fall of the monarchy. Civilian discipline and military discipline disappeared throughout the land. No one was prepared to obey any longer; those who were used to command no longer knew how, or did not dare."[159] Therefore "the chief object of my policy" was to prevent "the transformation of the revolution into civil war."[160]

Release of political prisoners and permission for exiles (one of whom was Stalin) to return from Siberia brought to the scene numerous aggressive advocates who burst forth with criticisms. As early as March 6, Lenin telegraphed Bolsheviks who were returning to Russia that they should have "no trust in and no support of the new government: Kerensky is especially suspect; arming of the proletariat is the only guarantee." Lenin said Kerensky's "*verbal* republicanism simply cannot be taken seriously," and his rhetoric is "political chicanery."[161] Lenin's messages were received, but they were hardly accepted. The popular atmosphere was pro-unity, pro-democracy, pro-Kerensky. According to scholar Olivia Coolidge, neither the relatively moderate Mensheviks nor the radical Bolsheviks in St. Petersburg "were entirely happy about Lenin's return. They had been getting along well enough together without him."[162] In contrast to Lenin, Kerensky had a democratic attitude toward power: "If the people don't wish to believe and follow me, I shall leave power. I shall never use force to make my opinion triumph."[163]

But Kerensky was clearly committed to using force against the Germans, for he believed Russia must win the war. Despite all the tragedy the war had brought, the military still supported it. That was clear in the spring, when soldiers jammed together in Petrograd called for land to the peasants, an eight-hour working day, and a democratic republic while carrying posters proclaiming, "We shall defeat the enemy or die," "Down with German imperialism," and "War until full victory." The right-wing Cossack cavalry put it in more traditional Russian fashion: "We shall wash our horses in German blood." Representatives of 31 frontline regiments called for strong support from Petrograd and no breakdown of the leadership: "We firmly support the Provisional Government and pledge to protect you against any threat or attack no matter from what quarter it may come." Soldiers declared that "in unity lies strength, 'dual power' leads to catastrophe."[164]

Near midnight on April 3, Lenin's train steamed into Petrograd. The Bolshevik leadership greeted him with a guard of honor, a bouquet, a band, and a march to the czar's old waiting room. The president of the Executive Committee of the Soviet met him there and addressed him—but Lenin stared at the ceiling and played with his flowers, neglecting what the officer had to say. When he answered, he spoke right past the president to the workers and soldiers.

That night, Lenin took off in an armored car illuminated with a searchlight. Outside in the dark, crowds yelled for his appearance. At corner after corner, he stopped to make a short speech, until he got to the Bolshevik headquarters—a Russian dancer's house. There he was addressed with speech after speech. But when he was finally allowed to respond to their welcome, he harshly accused them of being traitors who had played into the hands of the capitalists by failing to overthrow the Provisional Government. He went on furiously for two hours. One listener recalled, "I felt as though I had been beaten about the head that night with flails...."[165] Out on the balcony, Lenin repeated his attack deep into the night. The soldiers in the street yelled threats at him, demanding he come down into the street so they could lift him up on their bayonets.

Sailors, who had greeted Lenin as an honor guard, published a letter after they found out how he had gotten back into the country: "Having learned that Mister Lenin came to Russia by permission of His Majesty, the German Emperor and King of Prussia, we express our deep regret that we participated in his solemn welcome to Petrograd.... Down with you, go back to the country through which you come to us."[166]

Lenin firmly opposed "a parliamentary republic." He sought the "abolition of the police, the army, and the bureaucracy," and advocated "All power to the Soviets." Some Bolsheviks wanted to follow a plan of Marxist subversion: work hard to establish a capitalist-bourgeois government, and then incite the workers to revolt against that government. Lenin brushed that idea aside and demanded an immediate workers' revolution. He spoke frequently, especially to groups of soldiers, and he interrupted bourgeois meetings, heckling from the floor and taking over the platform, demanding that the war be stopped and the new government destroyed.[167] Some soldiers and workers applauded Lenin. And day by day, the political scene in Petrograd grew more chaotic.

The new commanding officer of the Petrograd Military District, General Lavr Kornilov, proposed that the Provisional Government stop the demonstrations in the streets by force. Kerensky saw Lenin's agitation as a serious threat, but he would not support military suppression of the confused soldiers and workers. "Our strength lies in moral influence," he said, "and to apply armed force would be to adopt the old road of compulsion, which I consider impossible."[168] On April 21, workers with rifles marched into the city center and started shooting, killing some people. The shocked Executive Committee of the Soviet issued a statement urging all citizens to "maintain peace, order and discipline."[169] General Kornilov found the experience frustrating: "My position is intolerable.... I was happy at the front, in command of a fine Army Corps!... and here I am in Petrograd, a hotbed of anarchy, with a mere shadow of authority."[170]

Kerensky worked hard to link the Soviets to the Provisional Government and to counter Lenin's calls for violence. On April 24, Lenin managed to get the All-Russian Party Conference of the Bolsheviks to endorse some of his main proposals: peasants should seize land, soldiers should fraternize with German soldiers, and the Soviets should destroy the Provisional Government.[171] On April 26, a worried Provisional Government issued a formal statement. The new state, it said,

> believes that the power of the state should be based not on violence and coercion, but on the consent of free citizens to submit to the power which they themselves created.... Not a single drop of blood has been shed through its fault, nor have restrictive measures been established against any trend of public opinion.[172]

It warned against the course, "well known to history, leading from freedom, through civil war and anarchy to reaction and the return of despotism." Citizens should "unite around the government which you created."[173]

There was a broad consensus in Russia that the military forces should be democratized, with soldiers electing their officers and claiming their rights. Kerensky set out to confirm the support of an enormous, diverse, and widely dispersed armed force. But he was exhausted and depressed at this point. On April 29, when he marched into the meeting of the first congress of soldiers from the front, they cheered him all the way to the stage. At first, he inspired them, saying "we can play a colossal part in world history," but "If, like worthless slaves, we are not organized in a strong state, then a dark and bloody period of internecine strife will ensue." He told them, "I regret that I did not die …two months ago: I would have died with the great dream that a new life had been kindled in Russia once and for all, that we could respect one another in the absence of whips and sticks and could administer our own state not as the former despots ruled it."

Then he addressed the soldiers in personal terms:

> Comrades, you could be patient and silent for ten years. You were able to carry out the obligations imposed on you by the old hated government. You were even able to shoot the people when that was asked of you. Why do you have no patience now? Surely the free Russian state is not a state of rebellious slaves?[174]

At the words "rebellious slaves," the audience went silent, then booed him, and that sound spread throughout the army, raising doubts about Kerensky as a friend of the soldiers.

The Provisional Government recognized increasingly that the conduct of the military was emerging as the highest-priority issue. Kerensky had not dealt with the soldiers and sailors perfectly, but at least he had gone out among them. Back in Petrograd, he plunged into major negotiations to establish a council of ministers for the government. On May 5, the ministers were named, forming the Coalition. Kerensky was appointed minister of war and navy after insisting that the complete military—both army and navy—had to be under the control of the same office.[175] He promptly sought to link the officers to the enlisted men.

On May 9, Kerensky issued a declaration of the rights of soldiers and sailors: they could not elect their officers, but, except when they were in combat, they would be free to engage in politics, discuss military policies and their relations with their officers, and join whichever party they wanted.[176] Kerensky took the train to the front, where he spoke again and again to great masses of soldiers who cheered for the idea of ending the war—and for fighting the war. Inspiring them by urging them "Forward to the battle for freedom!", he also acknowledged their pain: "After three years of the cruelest suffering, the millions of soldiers, exhausted to the last degree by the tortures of war, found themselves confronted suddenly with the questions: 'What are we dying for? Must we die?'" He won a lot of noisy respect and admiration from military units, including the radical Petrograd regiments. An English nurse at the front remembered how the soldiers responded to him: "When he left, they carried him on their shoulders to his car. They kissed him, his uniform, his car, the ground on which he walked. Many of them were on their knees praying; others were weeping. Some of them [were] cheering; others singing patriotic songs."[177]

In Moscow, he spoke to a very large audience in the Bolshoi Theater, where both the poor and wealthy jammed together. British Consul-General Lockhart was there. He wrote of the event:

> Kerensky's theme was on human suffering and human courage. All that was worth having in the world, from the physical pain of childbirth to the spiritual sorrow of the loss of a loved one, came through suffering, which alone tested character. He had been to the front. He had seen the soldiers who had nothing, but whose spirit was far better than that of the rear. All the grumbling and apathy came from the citizens of Petrograd and Moscow. They said that they were tired. What had they done to be tired? Could they not watch a little longer? Was he to go back to tell the men in the trenches that "the heart of Russia" was exhausted?
>
> He looked dead tired himself as he sank back into a chair. He was then suffering from serious kidney trouble, but he had stirred the audience to a frenzy of emotion. A rich woman threw her pearl necklace on the stage. Others did the same, and strong men wept like children.[178]

Kerensky was gaining popularity in the month of May: Lenin was not succeeding in getting the military to revolt against the democrats.

Then, on June 3, Kerensky faced Lenin in person when the First All-Russian Congress of Soviets brought them together, along with 777 socialists, of whom only 105 were Bolsheviks. Kerensky, the nation's most popular leader, entered and got a "wild ovation."

A Soviet leader spoke, mentioning that "there is not a political party in Russia which would say: hand over power to us, resign and we will take your place. Such a party does not exist in Russia." Suddenly from the floor came a shout: "It does exist!" The shouter was Lenin. He meant, as he explained the next day, that his party, the Bolsheviks, was "ready to take over full power at any moment." For starters, he recommended that they "make the profits of the capitalists public" and "arrest fifty or a hundred of the biggest millionaires." He scoffed at Kerensky, calling him "windbag."[179]

Kerensky rose to reply to Lenin's outburst. He warned the Congress against taking the track toward dictatorship:

> Comrades, I am not a Social Democrat. I am not a Marxist, but I have the highest respect for Marx, his teaching and his followers. But Marxism has never taught such childlike and primitive methods. I suspect that Citizen Lenin has forgotten what Marxism is. He cannot call himself a socialist, because socialism nowhere recommends the settling of questions of economic war...by arresting people as done by Asiatic despots....You Bolsheviks recommend childish prescriptions—"arrest, kill, destroy." What are you: socialists or jailers of the old regime?[180]

Kerensky's words were effective. A large majority of the Soviet Congress registered approval for his position. Lenin had quietly left the room.

The proposal was made that the Bolshevik and anarchist soldiers hold an "armed demonstration" to take power over the country. But the Soviet Congress forced the Bolshevik Central Committee to scrap the plan. The Bolshevik soldiers were angered at being rejected,[181] but a strong detachment of pro-government sailors was brought into Petrograd from Kronstadt,[182] and these representatives of the people—in rough form—exercised an act of control over the military. Thus Lenin's attempt to split power by force and take it for his own purposes failed.

The Congress adjourned and Minister of War Kerensky and his council planned a major strategic attack against the Germans. Kerensky left for the front, which "helped to take my mind off the troubled situation in the capital." Ironically, he found:

> A visit to the front was almost like coming home. Complications and formalities were unknown there. People were concerned with the elementary and essential business of survival, of death and life, and they felt much closer to each other in the face of the common danger.[183]

On June 24, he wrote a confidential report that the offensive against the Germans was "developing significantly less successfully than one might have hoped in view of the strength of the preliminary bombardment and the numbers of soldiers concentrated." He recommended a purge of certain senior military officers. The next day, however, came the greatest military success of the year, led by General Kornilov, who advanced some 20 miles against the Germans.[184]

That success apparently obscured the growing instability of Russia's military forces for Kerensky. For example, the general of the Tenth Army had, with much effort, induced the troops to move forward into combat—but 48 of the battalions refused to attack. Afterward, the general recalled, "I was present when the Pota regiment was handed a red banner and its soldiers swore on it to fight until death. One hour before the attack the regiment fled to the rear, stopping only after fifteen kilometers."[185]

Back in Petrograd, the Provisional Government endured its most hectic meeting yet, on July 2. The Kadets, the main right-wing party, walked out in protest over a new arrangement for the Ukrainians. Kerensky, back from the front, railed at the Kadets mercilessly: "The blood be on your heads! There on the front our armies are carrying out an attack, tens of thousands of men are giving up their lives for the motherland.... And at this moment you here desert your posts and smash the government!"[186] He stormed out of town to the front.

Then, on July 4, Bolshevik soldiers rioted in Petrograd, shooting randomly at windows from trucks and robbing liquor stores.[187] They carried a banner that said, "The first bullet is for Kerensky."[188] Lenin's colleague Leon Trotsky stopped them from killing a government minister, but several hundred people died in the chaos.[189] The next morning, Lenin slipped out of his apartment and found a hiding place. On July 7, a warrant was issued for his arrest, but he stayed hidden until August 8.

Prince Lvov, the Provisional Government's prime minister, telegraphed news of the riots to Kerensky and asked that he return. Kerensky sent back a strong demand:

> I insist on the determined prevention of treasonable demonstrations, the disarming of mutinous detachments and the handing over to the courts of all instigators and mutineers. I demand the stopping of all further demonstrations and mutinies by armed force.... The Government must immediately publish an official communiqué on the complete liquidation of the mutiny and [stating] that the guilty will suffer ruthless punishment.[190]

He stormed back to Petrograd, where he found Lvov "in terrible depression," only "waiting for my arrival to quit the government."[191] Kerensky saw that for Lvov's "gentle manner of governing the times had become too difficult. More brusqueness was required in dealing with people, more external pressure in the style of government." Lvov said he agreed: "To save the situation it was necessary to dissolve the Soviets and fire at the people. I could not do that. But Kerensky can."[192] This was the dark, risky moment when Kerensky took over as "minister-president" of Russia.

Responding to the escalations of violence, the Provisional Government cabinet decreed on July 6 that any person advocating murder, assault, robbery, "the use of force against any part of the population," or even disobedience to government orders would be sentenced to three years in prison. And any member of the armed forces found guilty of sedition would be treated as a traitor. On July 7, Kornilov was promoted to commander-in-chief, and he demanded that mutineers be punished. Kerensky agreed that all shaky units at the front must be purged. Kornilov went another step: "In view of the gravity of the moment we are going through," he wrote, no meetings whatsoever should be permitted by units at the front. The death penalty was restored, press freedom was restricted, and the order went out to disarm the Bolsheviks' Red Guard.[193]

This all happened very quickly. Then, suddenly, word came that the Germans had broken through the front of the 11th Army and the Russian troops were retreating in disorder. Kerensky again went to the front. And there, once again, he discovered a kind of relief, even joy:

> It was getting dark, the artillery preparation had started, and shells were flying overhead. All this combined to create an atmosphere of great camaraderie. The officers, the soldiers, and I all seemed to be imbued with a common sense of purpose, a common desire to fulfill our duty.
> The men of the Second Caucasian Grenadier Division told me with pride that they had rid themselves of all traitors in their midst and now wanted to be the first to go over the top, which, indeed, they were. Never in the whole course of my experience at the front had I felt so strong an urge to spend the whole night in the trenches with the soldiers and to go into action with them the next day. Never before had I been so ashamed at not doing myself what I was asking others to do.[194]

A profoundly affected Kerensky returned to Petrograd and there became a stronger, more authoritarian leader, determined to guide Russia to democracy.

At a conference with the military leaders on July 16, General Denikin, commander-in-chief of the Western Front, bitterly attacked Kerensky and the Provisional Government. The Bolsheviks, he said, were "worms in the festering wounds of the army," but it was the government that had "destroyed" the army: "Authority was abolished, the officers were humiliated. Officers up to and including the Commander-in-Chief were expelled like servants." Kerensky responded by defending the government, but as to the Declaration of the Rights of the Soldier, originally issued in millions of copies with his picture at the top—he said, "I am not defending the Declaration.... I am compelled to liquidate many things which I received as a legacy." His assistant minister of war, Savinkov, urged him to straighten out the army by appointing Kornilov as supreme commander. Kerensky hesitated, remembering how in April, after being accompanied to the War Ministry by a cheering crowd, Kornilov had asked that the crowd be shot at. But there was no other leading general, so on July 18, Kerensky nominated Kornilov, who accepted the office of Commander-in-Chief on the condition that he be responsible only to his own conscience and the nation, not to the government. He also demanded that a general recently appointed by Kerensky be discharged.

For a time, Kerensky later claimed, Petrograd saw "a steady diminution of revolutionary chaos," if not, as he also claimed, "the development of political strength and wisdom." But in the army itself, Bolshevik soldiers continued to murder their officers with bayonets or smash them to death with rifle butts. The rebellion was put down when they were bombed by their own artillery and arrested. Officers were infuriated when those arrested were not executed.[195]

On July 21, Kerensky resigned. He declared:

> In view of my inability, despite all my efforts in this direction, to broaden the membership of the Provisional Government in such a way that it would answer the demands of the exceptional historical moment which the country is passing through, I can no longer bear the responsibility before the state [while] remaining true to my conscience and understanding.[196]

But—as perhaps he knew would happen—a meeting of the ministers, the Executive Committee of the Soviet, and the Duma Committee voted overwhelmingly to draft him back into power. One man summed up their view, stating that he could not conceive how a new government could be formed

> unless A. F. Kerensky would agree to withdraw his resignation. For A. F. Kerensky is the only man whom the country still trusts and whom the country will follow. If it is impossible to form a strong government at whose centre stands A. F. Kerensky, the country will be ruined.[197]

In voting Kerensky back into power, this wide range of parties put all responsibility on him. He was to form a new government with himself authorized as dictator—or at least the one designated to take the blame for whatever went wrong.

The processes of democracy would be postponed, Kerensky pronounced, for "The national work of the salvation of the country...must proceed under conditions and in forms dictated by the severe necessity of continuing the war, supporting the fighting capacity of the army and restoring the economic power of the nation."[198] On July 28, the ministers of war and interior were given the authority to shut down all assemblies seen as endangering the state or the military.[199]

Kerensky and his new wife, Lilya, moved into the Winter Palace. He slept in the bed of Czar Alexander III, was photographed at the czar's desk, and traveled in one of the czar's trains. Like Napoleon, he wore elegant clothes, including a leather glove over the hand held at his chest.[200]

Near the end of July, 270 members of the Bolshevik party gathered in Petrograd for a meeting that lasted eight days. Despite the chaos in Russia, party membership had tripled in the last three months—some 240,000 people were now Bolsheviks. In their Petrograd meeting, the party cast aside Lenin's previous slogan, "All power to the Soviets," and called for an armed revolution against the government to gain power for an undefined revolutionary proletariat.[201]

On the last day of July, Aleksandr Kerensky visited Czar Nicholas and his family to check on their security.[202] He was 36 at this time, and clearly in charge, but troubled by the postponement of democracy and the need to use force to hold the country together. He continued to argue in favor of democracy and against "a return to autocracy or monarchy."[203] He hoped that "With the support of the masses and army, the government will save Russia and forge unity." But he worried that "If the appeal to reason, honor and conscience will not suffice, it will have to be done through blood and iron.... But the question is, would it work?"[204]

To make it work, he took resolute action. On August 2, the ministers of war and interior were authorized to exile from Russia anyone threatening state defense, internal security, or "the freedom conquered by the Revolution." On August 8, Kerensky's deputy minister of war gave him a list of 50 rightists and 50 leftists to be exiled; Kerensky approved exiling all the rightists and half of the leftists. Soon the deputy minister's own right-wing pressure infuriated him and he shouted, "You are a Lenin, but on the other side! You're a terrorist! Well then, come and kill me." To Kerensky, any military dictatorship was not only undesirable but "absolutely impossible." Yet he could not step aside:

> They accuse me of inefficiency, they think I am ambitious for power. Fools! If I could only resign, get away from all this and retire to some quiet village, I would be the happiest man in the world. But to whom could I resign my office? Where is the man? "[205]

Although the Bolsheviks were demanding that land be redistributed to the peasants, Kerensky specifically forbade changes in the ownership of land because he feared such a move might cause soldiers to desert from the war and go home to protect their farms. (In fact, many rural areas were already in chaos.) His major task now was to restore discipline in the Russian army.[206]

The key to this was General Kornilov, the short, bearded, peasant-born supreme commander who stationed Asian guards with machine guns outside whatever residence he occupied. A fellow general described Kornilov as "a man with the heart of a lion and the brains of a lamb."[207] Kornilov detested the Bolsheviks, who were increasingly hounding Kerensky. As July rolled on, he came to think that Russia could be saved only if the factories and the railways were occupied by the military, which meant canceling the Soviets and eliminating the Bolsheviks.[208] Meanwhile, the national election for a Constituent Assembly, which had been scheduled for September 4, was postponed until October 31.

THE CRISIS AT LAST

The tide of war rolled back against Russia, and Petrograd was at risk of being conquered and occupied.

Kerensky called a State Conference in Moscow for August 12–15. Some 2,400 delegates came. The Bolsheviks, banned because of their irresponsible behavior, had failed in their call for a boycott.[209] Kerensky spoke on the opening day of the conference, spelling out what had happened and what must happen:

> May everyone know, and may those know who have once already attempted to raise their armed hand against the people's government, that these attempts will be stopped with iron and blood. [Tempestuous, prolonged applause]… The situation is very grave. Our State experiences an hour of deadly danger.…
>
> For, if there was a period in the Russian revolution which was for the most part destructive, which destroyed the old foundations and created the new bases of the right to self-government for the entire people—now the time has arrived for organization, consolidation, and defense of the achieved rights of the Russian State as such.…
>
> With the support of the democratic armed forces, of the revolutionary will and free expression of our people, we came into this world with our head raised high and we remained there, equal among equals, in the great battle and at the death feast of the peoples of Europe. But we came there with our own words and our own will. Beware lest these blows at the army, these blows at the will and authority of the sovereign authority of the Russian people make a breach in the very ideas for which we fight and open the gate to the enemies of the idea of freedom which you thought we defended poorly. We desire and we will see to it that no one dare relegate the Russian empire to second place in the chorus of world nations. [Tempestuous applause] … You may rest assured that we will protect you against demoralizing influences which creep into the army from the bottom and destroy at the bottom—it is the most terrifying thing—the shame which enables people who fear death to say they do not want to fight for an idea. [Tempestuous, prolonged applause. Cries: "Bravo."] We fight them with all our strength. This anarchy from the left, this bolshevism, or whatever it is called, will find its enemy in our country, in the Russian democracy, which is imbued with the spirit of love for the State and the idea of freedom. [Applause] But I say once more: every attempt of bolshevism…any attempt to profit by the weakening of discipline, will be put to an end by me. [Tempestuous, prolonged applause.][210]

Kerensky thus declared, with clarity and enthusiasm, what needed to be; but just how this was to happen remained obscure. Many speeches followed, Kerensky's bringing out reports that, for example, in the prior year the war had cost between 40 and 50 percent of the entire Russian income. The left and the right traded off applause for different speakers of different perspectives.

Then the supreme commander walked up front, cheered by the right and booed by the left. The night before, Kerensky had tried to persuade him to limit his talk to a report on front-line action.[211] Instead, shocking everyone, Kornilov declared "with deep sorrow" that "I do not have confidence that the Russian army will staunchly perform its duty to the country." The "destructive propaganda for disorganizing the army" was continuing, and "during this short period of time since the beginning of August, the men have become like animals and, losing all semblance of soldiers, have killed the following commanders: [whom he named specifically]. All these murders were committed by soldiers in a nightmarish atmosphere of irrational, hideous club law, of interminable ignorance and abominable hooliganism." At this point, Chairman Kerensky interrupted, asking for an end of "disrespectful interruptions" from the audience.

Kornilov continued with his diagnosis and prescription:

> Thus, the army is conducting a ruthless struggle against anarchy, and anarchy will be crushed. But the danger of new debacles still hangs over the country. There still hangs the threat of new losses of territory and towns and the direct danger to the capital itself. The situation on the front is such that, as a consequence of the collapse of our army, we have lost all of Galicia, we have lost all Bukhovina and all of the fruits of our victories of the past and present years....
>
> Only an army welded by iron discipline, only an army that is led by the single, inflexible will of its leaders, only such an army is capable of achieving victory and is worthy of victory. Only such an army can endure all the trials of battle. Discipline must be affirmed in the daily, routine work of the army by vesting the superiors, the officers, and the noncommissioned officers with corresponding authority.... The prestige of the officers must be enhanced....
>
> I do not oppose committees.... But I demand that their activities be confined to the sphere of economic and internal life of the army within limitations which must be clearly specified by law, without any interference in military operations, in questions of combat, or in the selection of superiors.... The measures that are adopted at the front must also be adopted in the rear. And the principal idea governing these measures must be that they should conform to the goal of saving the native land....
>
> But I declare that there is no time to lose, that not a single minute must be lost. Resolution is necessary and the firm, steadfast execution of the measures outlined. [Applause][212]

After other long speeches, Kerensky concluded the meeting, declaring that the "enormous significance" of the occasion was that so many different views had been expressed, providing "a snapshot of the political moods of the country." Yet there had been no consensus; it would be up to the Provisional Government to reconcile the views expressed. He perceived a shortage of mutual trust:

> The Provisional Government came here with the words "The State requires order, sacrifices, and labor." And you who had to answer, each for himself, said: "We will sacrifice, we will give our labor, and we want order." Unfortunately, this was often accompanied by a qualification: "We will do this if our neighbors will do the same."[213]

Kerensky wanted the thousands before him to realize what a difficult undertaking a reconciliation of views would be for the Provisional Government:

> Is it not clear to you, citizens, from what you have heard here, that it is so difficult, sometimes almost impossible, to reconcile the various points of view, the various interests, and to establish a common understanding of things?... It is precisely this that constitutes the unbearable difficulty for the Government, which honestly strives only for this common will and these common aims.... Such a Government will always encounter many critics in its course, but few supporters, because each one feels, every class and every party feels, that his desires have not been gratified to the fullest extent, and each one thinks that this is because the shadowy power, occupying a place that does not [rightfully] belong to it, does not dare to gratify all his desires.... We are told: how quickly the Provisional Government is leading the country to ruin. There is no end to the number of crimes and sins attributed to us! But these people forget that the Provisional Government has existed for a mere six months, while the empire existed for 300 years.

The ignorance of Russian society regarding statesmanship, he said, cramped the capacity of the government to take the right actions. But even worse than ignorance was reliance on violence. "On my own behalf," he said,

> I feel that not everyone understands the necessity of a policy that does not have as its aim the use of physical force, which is demanded today. I feel that this experiment will be adopted by one side or another, but then only will you see that the power which appeared impotent was the only possible power under the present conditions. As soon as the Provisional Government or anyone else adopts the most iron-fisted, the most drastic measures in order to carry out some one task to the very end or to gratify somebody's particular interests and destroys what now exists, he will usher in a civil war and a great calamity in which all of us, perhaps, will perish. ["True!"] That is why we must defend to the last hour that one and only policy which the Government can now pursue—that of reconciling everything that can be reconciled, or leading everyone toward one objective, sweeping aside and, if need be, chopping off only those [elements] which do not want to subordinate their desires to the common will, but, on the contrary, want to subordinate the common will, by force, to their own desires. [Applause]

He said again that the situation in the army was even more extreme and more vital:

> When the army is, really, the people in arms, when the army is open from all sides to all kinds of political influence, every careless word, every statement that is too sharp, is bound to react painfully on the nerves of all those who are at the front, and I am already receiving comments regarding these discussions and the statements that have been made here.... [B]oth the Supreme Commander and I have to take urgent and drastic steps. Even here the individuals who are responsible for the army both at the front and in the rear must be allowed to do what is necessary without attracting or arousing the unhealthy curiosity which surrounds the army and those attempts at repression which are harmful to both our native land and the army. [Applause from the left]

After 1:00 in the morning, Kerensky made his final plea: that the representatives present should discourse with, and truly represent, the people, for "the power of government resides only in public opinion and in the will of the whole people," since "there is no more valuable a good and no greater a value than our native land and the people." And at the very end, he expressed the hope that "never will our native land perish; no one will ever deprive her of the freedom which was won by all the people."[214]

Thus the Conference ended with no real decisions made. The main news was Kornilov's speech demanding that military discipline be imposed on the Russian army from top to bottom, from front to rear.

Five days later the Bolsheviks won a third of the votes cast in Petrograd for the city council.[215] They then rolled into the Petrograd Soviet and demanded election to its Executive Committee. Lenin's partner Trotsky became Soviet president; he would authorize 5,000 rifles to equip Bolshevik sympathizers.[216] A big building, previously a school for daughters of the nobility with its own ballroom, was chosen by the Bolsheviks for the next Congress of All-Russian Soviets. The Bolsheviks set the scene:

> placing long tables with pamphlets at the head of every stair, crowding the gloomy, vaulted corridors with soldiers and workmen, feeding them cheaply in a vast canteen with immense caldrons of cabbage soup and hunks of black bread, commandeering the rabbit warren of rooms for offices, and dominating the lofty ballroom lighted by great chandeliers and with an empty gold frame behind the dais which nine months ago had contained the portrait of the Tsar.[217]

Meanwhile, at the front, the German army, shifting troops from the south and west, took Riga, a port city near the Baltic Sea that was closer to Petrograd than Moscow. Petrograd was in sudden danger. Masses of Russian army refugees and deserters flooded into the city. Kerensky saw the necessity for the Provisional Government to declare martial law and to move the nation's capital to Moscow. As for governing the army, he tried to work in the middle: between the radical right, which wanted the government taken over by the top military officials, and the radical left, which wanted the army to ignore the German attack and enter into internal politics. Kerensky sent his deputy minister of war to General Kornilov to order him to send a military force from the front to Petrograd to secure and implement martial law under the control of the Provisional Government. He specified that a "Savage Division" and one particular general were not to be included in that force because he distrusted them.

Kornilov supposedly agreed to Kerensky's terms on August 24, but on the following day, he sent a force from the front to Petrograd that included *both* the "Savage Division" and the general Kerensky had banned. Moreover, a prince arrived from military headquarters and pronounced to Kerensky what he declared were the orders of the supreme commander: as of that evening, the Provisional Government was to give up all authority to General Kornilov, who intended to set up a new government. If Kerensky and his deputy went to the general's headquarters and agreed to the coup, Kornilov would appoint them as ministers. Otherwise he would not guarantee their lives.

Kerensky called an emergency meeting of his cabinet. To empower Kerensky, they, in effect, canceled the Provisional Government, passing a resolution to "transfer all power to the Prime Minister in order to put a speedy end to the antigovernment movement launched by General Kornilov, the Supreme Commander."[218] They telegraphed a demand to Kornilov that he surrender his post at once. Kornilov responded: "I, General Kornilov, declare that under the pressure of the Bolshevik majority of the Soviets, the Provisional Government is acting in complete harmony with the plans of the German general staff, and simultaneously with the forthcoming landing of the enemy forces on the Riga shores; it is killing the army and undermining the very foundation of the country."[219] He then broadcast a radio message of impending defeat of Russia by the Germans: "Russian people, our great land is dying! The hour of death is near!"[220]

The war situation was truly desperate, and Kerensky realized a rudderless army meant the downfall of the country. Kornilov, as the military commander, should answer to Kerensky, but Kornilov refused to resume command, saying he had "neither the strength nor the ability" for it and thought the reappointment would be "extremely dangerous at a moment when our country is threatened by the enemy, and when the unity and freedom of our country demand speedy action to restore discipline and security in the army."[221] When Kerensky offered another general the post, the general wired back that the move would mean "systematic destruction of the army, consequently of the whole country"—and that he was "unable to follow along this path." Kerensky notified yet another general, Alekseyev, of his appointment as supreme commander, but this general asked for time to think it over.

Meanwhile, a representative of the Ministry of Foreign Affairs declared:

> A sound assessment of the situation leads to the conclusion that the entire commanding staff, the overwhelming majority of officers, and the best army units will follow Kornilov.... Apart from the factor of sheer physical force, it is necessary to take into account the superiority of their military organization to that of the weak civil authorities, the sympathy of their cause to all nonsocialist sections of the population, the growing dissatisfaction of the lower classes with the existing order, and the indifference of the majority of the rural and urban masses, who now react only to the whip.... This consideration seems to be decisive for General Kornilov, who has come to realize that only firmness can prevent Russia from hurtling into the abyss at the edge of which she now stands.[222]

General Alekseyev, the foreign minister, and the ambassadors of Great Britain, France, and Italy brought Kerensky the "friendly offer" to mediate between him and Kornilov, on the supposition that there had been some "misunderstanding." But Kerensky stood hard against any compromise with a traitor. The opposition began to crumble. Alekseyev finally whispered to Kerensky, in their exhausted conversation, that "I am at your disposal. I accept the post of chief of staff under your command." But then Alekseyev decided that "with an army so disorganized and morally broken, it is impossible to think of extensive operations." The next week he resigned as chief of staff.[223]

So Kerensky himself became the nation's military commander. As he saw it, "All officers were now under suspicion." On September 1, he issued a new order:

> (1) that all political struggle in the army cease and all efforts be devoted to building up our military power, on which the salvation of the country depends;
> (2) that all military organizations and commissars keep their work free of political prejudice and suspicion, confining themselves to activities which do not involve interference in the performance by commanding officers of their military duties....[224]

He ordered two conservative newspapers closed, as well as the Bolshevik *Pravda* and several other controversial publications.[225] The public crisis quieted down, but the crisis among leaders intensified. Kornilov's demands were neglected. But "the conspirators and their champions did not give up," according to Kerensky. "They continued to push Russia toward the abyss, stubbornly opposing what they termed a 'weak' government, in the hope of setting up a 'strong national government' under a military dictator."[226]

In Petrograd, people were called to action by the Soviet to defend themselves against a "counter-revolutionary plot." Kerensky ordered arms issued to the Bolshevik Red Guards to protect Petrograd from Kornilov's troops.[227] Bolshevik leaders were released from jail.[228] Approaching Petrograd, the "Savage Division" fell apart, as Bolsheviks urged the soldiers to ignore orders from their superiors. The general in command committed suicide and Kornilov and a few other officers were arrested.

The impact of this event was ominous: Kerensky succeeded in thwarting Kornilov's takeover, but in the process Kerensky's own reputation in the crisis-filled country was destroyed. Right-wing militants turned against him, and left-wing militants seized the initiative. As news of the whole affair spread throughout the army and navy, what little discipline existed began to collapse. Author Bruce Lockhart explains:

> Worst of all was the effect of the coup on the morale of the armed forces of the country. Regarded by soldiers as a counter-revolutionary plot, the attempt created an irreparable gulf between the lower ranks and their officers. From now on no senior officer was trusted by the men, and in many parts of the country officers of all grades were murdered in the most brutal manner, the worst fate and the greatest savagery being reserved for the officers of the Russian Navy. The March Revolution which had overthrown Tsarism had been almost bloodless. From now on murder, rape and loot were to have a free course.[229]

Kerensky was losing allies fast. One recalled seeing him "sitting alone in a corner of the Military Staff Headquarters, bowed with chagrin and disappointment. He looked like nothing but a deserted child, helpless and homeless.

Yesterday a ruler, today a forsaken idol, he sat face to face with ruin and despair.[230] On August 30, Kerensky added to his titles commander-in-chief. But throughout Russia, some 240 committees against counterrevolution had formed.[231] On August 31, the Bolsheviks achieved a majority in the Petrograd Soviet, and on September 6, they reached a majority in Moscow.

Lenin, hiding in Finland, wrote that he welcomed this "most unexpected, really incredibly drastic turn of events." He got a message to the Bolsheviks that the present situation had "put armed insurrection on the agenda."[232] As Kerensky struggled to reorganize a coalition for democracy, Lenin did all he could to undercut that possibility by demanding an immediate violent coup. Political discourse to persuade a majority was, to Lenin, a dangerous idea. "It would be naive to wait until the Bolsheviks achieve a 'formal' majority," he said, "no revolution has ever waited for that."[233]

Kerensky and others who shared his hope of salvaging a Russian democracy called another national meeting, the Democratic Conference, on September 14. Over the heckling of Bolsheviks and others, Kerensky implored the delegates "to strain every nerve and muster all the force of reason" to maintain the state. He warned the Bolsheviks: "Anyone who dares to plunge a knife into the back of the Russian army, will discover the might of the revolutionary Provisional Government, which governs with the faith and confidence of the whole country."[234] He won applause from the many Mensheviks and socialists, who had long shared his hope. The Conference, held in a grand theater, produced six days of inspiring rhetoric—but no agreed-upon course of action. Lenin cheered the outcome: "The so-called Democratic Conference is over. Thank God, one more farce is behind us and still we are advancing."[235] Kerensky, privately, was thinking the same. He wrote, "The conferences had ended in a total fiasco."[236]

Meeting after meeting followed. On September 25, the Provisional Government formed the Third Coalition Government, with Kerensky as minister-president. It issued an extensive, extremely candid declaration, which began:

> Profound discord has come once more into the life of our country....Waves of anarchy are sweeping over the land, pressure from the foreign foe is increasing, counterrevolution is raising its head, hoping that the prolonged governmental crisis coupled with the weariness that has seized the entire nation, will enable it to crush the freedom of the Russian people.[237]

October 7 saw the meeting of the Provisional Council of the Russian Republic, addressed by Kerensky:

> Never will the destructive autocracy be resurrected, nor will anyone—be it a person or a group, dare to attack the sovereign will of the Russian people, which will speak its decisive word at the forthcoming Constituent Assembly.[238]

After he left the hall, Trotsky rose to speak, angrily and powerfully. Then the Bolsheviks stalked out as the others shouted "Scoundrels" and "Go to your German friends."[239]

That night, Lenin arrived in Petrograd secretly, his beard shaved off and his bald head covered with a wig.[240] He damned Kerensky "and his Kornilovite generals" for planning to surrender Petrograd to the Germans,[241] insisting the armed uprising had to be "Now, now, or it would be too late!"[242] Lenin and the Bolshevik Central Committee conferred on October 10, expressing (among other things) their detestation for democracy: "It is senseless to wait for the Constituent Assembly that will obviously not be on our side, for this will only make our task more involved."[243]

Kerensky engaged in some secret manipulation himself. He got a secret British agent—an author by the name of Somerset Maugham—to come to the palace on October 1 and gave him a message, to be memorized but not written down, for Lloyd George, Great Britain's prime minister. The message said the British should offer the Germans a "peace without annexations or compensations," which the Germans "will refuse," allowing Britain to demonstrate to the Russian people that Germany must be dominated rather than conciliated.

Kerensky saw this deception as a necessity:

> If something of the sort is not done, then, when the cold weather comes I don't think I shall be able to keep the army in the trenches. I don't see how we can go on. Of course, I don't say that to the people. I always say that we shall continue whatever happens, but unless I have something to tell my army it's impossible.[244]

Then he met with his generals, arguing with them so heatedly that he suffered a nervous collapse lasting two days.

Meanwhile, the German army rolled on. By October 6, German troops were only 250 miles from Petrograd. Kornilov, under questioning by a sympathetic commission, declared that Kerensky had agreed with him on establishing a military dictatorship. At this point, Kerensky realized that "the poison of doubt was penetrating ever deeper into the very masses of the people,"[245] but remembering the defeat of the Bolsheviks in July, he thought that if they attempted a coup, they would be repulsed: "I only wish that they would come out [in the open], and I will then put them down."[246]

On October 24, Lenin was ready to oblige him: he wanted the Bolsheviks to rise in armed revolution rather than wait for some new confusing Congress to assemble. That very day the Provisional Council of the Russian Republic met again. Kerensky blasted the Bolsheviks, urging the authorities to act carefully, but to move resolutely against them when the time came. He demanded a vote expressing unconditional support of his authority. The Council members cheered him, but then spent hours discussing the possibility of declaring peace, peasant takeover of the land, and other issues. When they refused the vote Kerensky sought, he stalked out of the meeting, "declaring haughtily that this was the time for deeds rather than declarations."[247] Throughout the rest of the night, the Council tried desperately to recruit some armed units to come and defend them.

THE CRUNCH CAME

On October 25, Lenin's armed men occupied Petrograd's post office, telephone exchange, arsenal, and railroad stations. That morning, the Provisional Council of the Russian Republic met to continue their discussion of the night before. Men with rifles arrived and demanded that the meeting disband. Some members wanted to stay in session, but the motion was defeated. The majority then voted an angry protest and adjourned.[248]

The Petrograd City Council met throughout the day to protest the violence. Perhaps it was a sign of their irrelevance that no troops showed up to disperse them. When they decided to go to the Palace Square and join the general protest, sailors stopped them, and they were forced to return to their speech-making.[249]

That afternoon at 3:00, the Petrograd Soviet met to hear Trotsky declare that "the Provisional Government of Kerensky was dead and awaited only the broom of history to sweep it away." Lenin marched onto the stage, got a standing ovation, declared the new revolution complete, and repeated his formula advocating peace, land, and bread.

That night at 11:00, the national Congress of Soviets met, including a large minority of Mensheviks and Socialist-Revolutionaries. They turned on the Bolsheviks, expressing their fury at the outrageous armed rebellion, and threatened to walk out if the fighting did not stop and negotiation begin. Trotsky took the stand: "You are pitiful isolated individuals, you are bankrupt, your role is played out. Go where you belong from now on—the rubbish heap of history." They left.

That night Kerensky dashed out of town in a car, in search of troops to attack the Bolsheviks. One officer refused, then another. He finally found a cavalry corps he thought he could lead into battle—but it turned out to be a unit sent by Kornilov to occupy Petrograd!

Back in Petrograd, the Bolsheviks were battering the Winter Palace with rifles and artillery. They arrested the Provisional Government ministers and dragged them through jeering crowds to a fortress, where they were locked into cells the czar had used to jail revolutionaries.[250]

A nearly exhausted Lenin said to Trotsky, "You know…from persecution and a life underground to come so suddenly into power …"—and he gave a little gesture with his hand (some said it was the sign of the cross) and said, "It makes one dizzy."[251]

The evening of October 26, the Second Congress of Soviets, with Lenin as chairman and 15 Bolsheviks making up the Executive Committee, took power. Trotsky was put in charge of foreign policy and Joseph Stalin in charge of nationalities. Kerensky's friend Sukhanov surveyed the new legislature of Russia and judged them "gray and non-descript people who have crawled out of the trenches and slums. Their [alleged] devotion to the Revolution reflected but anger and despair, their 'socialism' was the product of hunger and of eagerness for peace."[252] It was not Lenin's style to introduce legislation; rather, he made decrees. He announced a "Decree on Peace," calling for an end to the war, and a

"Decree on Land," calling for all land to be owned by peasants. The Congress adjourned. As Adam Ulam has noted, "the talking period of the revolution was over."[253]

The next evening, Kerensky phoned his family and friends, promising to be in Petrograd with troops in the morning. Indeed, he did lead a small unit of Cossacks against a group of pro-Bolshevik soldiers, but he did not want them to shoot each other. Instead, he ordered his car driven between the troops and jumped up to make a speech, which motivated the soldiers to fraternize with one another—a military fiasco.[254] They left. Kerensky kept trying, again and again, to rescue his country from Bolshevism, until he became so exhausted he pondered suicide. He issued a direct appeal to the Russian people:

> Come to your senses! Don't you see that your simplicity has been abused and that they have shamelessly deceived you?… Only now, when the violence and horror of Leninist coercion, his dictatorship with Trotsky, reign, only now has it become clear even to the blind that in the period when I was in power, there was real freedom and genuine democracy.… Come to your senses![255]

He further pledged that he would attend the Constituent Assembly, whose election took place, amid the political chaos, in the second half of November.

Kerensky was elected from five different districts. The Bolsheviks—known throughout the land to have taken over the government—won only 225,000 of the nearly million votes cast. A study of the votes for the Bolsheviks has confirmed that they were cast primarily by soldiers—either those from rear garrisons or those coming back from the front. These soldiers agitated fiercely on behalf of Bolshevism though they were from districts with little or no industry. They were tired of the war, and the Bolsheviks were going to end it. One soldier sighed, "Nothing matters except to end this damned war and get home."[256] It was not, as Trotsky told the socialist journalist John Reed, that "The Army is with us." It was simply that the army was against the war.[257]

On January 5–6, 1918, the elected Constituent Assembly met. Bolshevik soldiers, who had already killed numerous young military academy students opposing them, shot demonstrators on the street. The galleries above the meeting were filled with drunken sailors casually pointing their rifles down at the Assembly members. Finally, at 3:00 A.M., guards shut down the Constituent Assembly meeting because, they said, they were tired. When the representatives showed up the next morning, the gates were locked and machine guns were set up behind them. The Constituent Assembly was over.[258]

Kerensky managed to escape Russia and eventually went to California, in the United States, where he studied and wrote books for years. His brother Fyodor was killed by the Bolsheviks that January. The Bolsheviks also located the czar and his wife and children in a basement, and shot all of them dead.[259] On December 7, Lenin's government set up Cheka, the secret police. Within one year, Cheka killed 6,300 people without trials. In contrast, in the entire nineteenth century, only 200 people had been executed in Russia for political crimes.[260]

THE RESULTS OF THE RUSSIAN REVOLUTION

Lenin had called for peace. Instead, there was a Russian civil war that lasted for nearly three years, killing hundreds of thousands of citizens, followed by systematic government terrorism on an enormous scale for decades afterward.

Lenin had called for the right of peasants to seize land from their landlords. Instead, the state grabbed the land and forced peasants into gruesome agricultural collectives.

Lenin had called for bread. For years, the farmers producing bread had it ripped away from them by armed raiders, and then, for many more years, there was a lot of bread for the powerful and much less bread for the poor.

Lenin and his allies had appeared time and again as champions of democracy with the slogan "All power to the Soviets!" In fact, for nearly half a century after Lenin's triumph, Russia stood as a prime example of modern tyranny. The dictators were not interested in equal justice under the law, the rights of life, liberty, and the pursuit of happiness, and government by consent of the governed. These new aristocrats saw to it that their own children inherited the power.

Getting rid of a tyrant does not establish democracy. Dethroning the czar opened up the possibility of government by the people, but it did not ensure it. The great effort to guide Russia in that direction failed. If 1917 was the year of hope, 1918 was the year of the death of democracy. For some 80 years, Kerensky's failure has been a stark example of how democratic hope can be crushed.

The new "Communist" government quickly banned all parties except Dictator Lenin's Bolshevists. The new secret police authorized local revolutionaries to "arrest and shoot immediately" members of "counterrevolutionary organizations." When a woman named Fanny Kaplan tried to kill Lenin by shooting him in the neck, the secret police reacted by killing 500 of her party comrades in one night. In power, Lenin was forthright: "We have never renounced and cannot renounce terror."[261] For his party, terror became the habitual mode of operation.[262]

The civil war that broke out when Lenin took power lasted for years. The czarist "Whites" and the Communist "Reds" practiced terror against each other. For example, one day the Whites filled up three railroad freight cars with the frozen bodies of Red Guards "placed in obscene positions." They sent the freight to their starving enemies, labeled "fresh meat, destination Petrograd,"[263] When the civil war finally ended, the government did not "wither away," but the Communists' wartime unity did. As author Alfred Meyer has noted, there arose "heated debates, in the course of which Lenin was outvoted more than once in the Central Committee"—a development that "prompted him to curb dissent and discussion within the party... by such devices as control over recruitment, assignment...[and] steps to silence dissenting members."[264] In 1921, Lenin pronounced policy debate in the Party Congress an "excessive luxury" and outlawed organized factions.[265]

Lenin tried to "remove" his successor, Joseph Stalin, who subsequently succeeded in sentencing to death some 50 old Bolsheviks in the 1930s.[266] The other famous member of the triumvirate, Trotsky, was axed to death in Mexico by Russian agents in 1940.

According to Boris I. Nicolaevsky, formerly of the Marx-Engels Institute in Moscow, "In the collectivization, industrialization and famines of 1929–33, it is estimated that 5 to 10 million Russians died and another 10 million were sent to forced labor under Stalin's slogan of 'the liquidation of the kulaks as a class.'"[267]

Professor Alfred G. Meyer summarizes how, in the next phase of Soviet rule, Stalin handled disagreement:

> … between 1935 and 1938 the U.S.S.R. became the stage for a veritable orgy of po-
> lice activity, in which the party, the government apparatus, the economy, the
> armed forces, the schools and universities, and all the professions were deci-
> mated, especially in their higher ranks, from which vast members of personnel
> disappeared into the labor camps or execution dungeons of the secret police. In
> the Communist Party, nearly everyone who had ever disagreed with the dictator
> was physically eliminated; and the same fate befell countless officials within the
> party and outside of it who were denounced for, or suspected of, harboring dis-
> sent. As a result, the administrative body of Soviet society was decapitated; an en-
> tire generation of leaders fell victims to the purge and an entire generation of
> younger ones moved up to fill their places.[268]

And the tragedy went on. In a study published in 1960, scholars Raymond A. Bauer, Alex Inkeles, and Clyde Kluckhohn described how a state so hated by its own people as the U.S.S.R. prevailed so long:

> More than any other modern state, the Soviet Union uses political terror and
> forced labor as an integral part of its political and economic system, and does so
> on a vast scale. Political arrests have been a marked feature of the regime since the
> time of the Revolution.[269]

And what were the material results of this ruthless recasting of a society? As late as the end of the 1980s, ordinary Russians lived like modern serfs—40 per-cent overall, and 79 percent of the elderly, existed in deep poverty. A third occu-pied housing without running water, and another third had no hot water.[270]

The death of democracy in one of the world's largest countries was an enormous and lasting tragedy. It not only resulted in unspeakable horrors for generations of Russians, it also set an example of how to seize power by force in many other countries. For, as Zbigniew Brzezinski has noted, "No communist regime ever took power as a result of the freely expressed will of the people."[271] The crux of the Russian failure was the failure of Kerensky's government to con-trol the force of the nation: the military was not commanded by the democracy.

THE POLITICAL LESSON OF THE REVOLUTION

The political sunrise of the 1990s once again raised the hope for democracy in Russia. The ideals of freedom and equal justice for all citizens, and government by elected representatives, were pronounced once more. Debate arose as to how to make democracy succeed in a nation where autocracy had continually prevailed. And in this modern age of world communication, the lust for democracy spread quickly to many countries, sparking democratic revolution in nation after nation, not simply as some mythical ideal, but as a genuine possibility.

In 1917, Russian democracy had been a possibility. Remarkably, the February Revolution unified diverse and distinctive societies against the czar. There was no significant public resistance to the Revolution. The people knew the failures of the past. Russia had experienced the liberation of the serfs—and then their virtual reenslavement. Russia had constructed a parliament—and then seen it trivialized by autocrats. Russia had produced educational and economic reforms—and then seen opportunities for ordinary citizens choked off. The czar had summoned the nation to march forth against the Germans in the Great War—and millions of pathetically armed Russians were slaughtered by a superbly equipped foe.

These tragic experiences fueled the widespread demand for major reforms. And then, in the repetitive pattern of Russian history, the monarchy went mad. The wisdom of hatred for monarchy, in Russia and elsewhere, did not arise from comparisons with the democratic alternative, but rather from long, hard, remembered experience that monarchy, given enough time, would eventually destroy human life, health, happiness, and hope.

The immediate cause of the 1917 Revolution was leadership. Kerensky was, at the outset, the strongest and best, though not the only, leader. He had one central idea: to bring about real democracy in Russia. He pursued it with high vigor. Absent Kerensky's agitation and direction, the czar might well have been replaced by another czar well before the spring of 1917.

Kerensky and his growing team and national followers made democracy a real possibility for modern Russia. The ideology, the primary institutions, the national election, the commitment to rights—all these baseline factors genuinely existed. Trouble was rampant, but so it had been in every other revolution for democracy, including those that eventually succeeded. The movement was neither a farce nor a fraud. There was a true potential for democracy in Russia, and had it been realized, the political history of the twentieth century would have been very different.

Instead, democracy lasted less than a year. Why? Nations now seeking to build and secure democracy ought to study the Russian failure in earnest to make sure the same whirlwind does not carry away the democracy they construct.

What killed Russia's democracy was violence. The Russian case points up democracy's most ancient and basic challenge: how should a democratic government deal with violence? The Russian case teaches what *not* to do.

In Russia, a long tradition of violence contended with the dream of its demise. Far more than most people, Russians grew up with stories of heroic iron and blood. The stories were real. The rulers of Russia, time and time again, had whipped, cut, tortured, and murdered, not only their enemies in the field of battle, but also helpless prisoners, old people, children and mothers. In Russia, these figures of history were held up as glorious heroes to be imitated. Ivan the Terrible was portrayed as masterful, Peter the Great as truly great, even though, in fact, they were merciless butchers.

And in ordinary Russian life, violence was a typical experience for centuries. Brutal invasions, cutthroat mobs of traveling thieves, the slaughtering of serfs—such human cruelties were not ancient or distant terrors, but regular, observable occurrences on into the twentieth century.

So Kerensky and Lenin were not expected to be St. Francis of Assisi—such a figure probably would not have gained respect. Neither the rightest Kadets nor the leftist Bolsheviks nor any of the other political organizations advocated nonviolence. The Russian culture was one of reaching out and beating up your opponent rather than speaking out and converting him by persuasion.

Russian religion also fostered violence, in two ways: through justification and benign neglect. The practice of killing in the name of God was inherited from defensive wars, when troops fell on their knees and prayed for the courage necessary to face death in defense of their homeland. Out of this experience of continually defending "Holy Russia" the idea grew that aggressive killing could be justified as a preventive measure. Thus invasions and other surprise attacks were blessed in the name of security and the guilt of murder was absolved ahead of time.

A subtler religious support for violence was the temptation to turn away from this world, to guide one's spirit into the life of heaven, way up above, recommended in a sermon by the palace priest, Rasputin. Instead of a guide to daily life, religion could be relegated to Sunday, when Russian Orthodox worshipers stood for hours in an awesome building that looked, smelled, sounded, and felt far different from their weekday homes and fields. And the hard-to-understand poetic scriptures and liturgies tended to foster passivity in the peasants, an acceptance of their lot in this world at the hands of bullying masters, floggers, and shooters. It also made the educated classes curiously passive. Rather than engage in vigorous and messy politics, they usually preferred to turn away from the ugliness of Russian life.

To be sure, there were alternative versions of Christianity, such as Kerensky's. But more often the perversions that supported ruinous alternatives of violence and passivity prevailed.

Violence took further nourishment from vodka, heavily consumed throughout Russia. The analogy with Russian religion is obvious: drinkers blasted out in rage, and then dropped off into oblivious sleep.

The violence that was so ordinary in Russia rose to extraordinary heights in the Great War of 1914. In place of teams of Cossacks galloping forth to fight for an afternoon, masses of soldiers slogged it out in deadly trench warfare that dragged on for weeks. Russians had endured this massive murder for three long years when the democratic revolution began. During 1917, Petrograd was jammed with military men; near the end, they were armed. And near the end, the Germans were next door. Violence destroys democracy repeatedly by the exigencies of "emergency." The threat seems too near, too harsh, to allow for parliamentary deliberation or the conduct of an election. World War I, in effect, destroyed the Victorian hope for a progressively more civilized society. The massive slaughter undercut Russian confidence in the Western idea of progress and confirmed the old belief that aggression is the rule of life.

Kerensky continually demanded that there be no violence in the capital, but vigorous fighting at the front. He had great hopes for Russia, an optimism and idealism that came from a harmonious childhood. His father's example and his *nyanya's* religious instruction molded him as a person of action and a responsible reformer, a man who would not only worship Christ but seek to follow his prescriptions for justice and peace. As an activist by temperament, he might well have sought a military career, but instead, first in college and then in his law work, Kerensky took his fighting spirit into politics. In that arena, he could fulfill both his childhood dream of being an actor and his responsibility to be a reformer. He witnessed violence, but he would not commit it. His jail time toughened him, but even as minister of war and navy, Kerensky hated terrorism. His hope was to persuade others by speaking to them, not by pushing them around. He held on to that ideal for years, even as it was ridiculed and killed again and again. To the very end, he argued that the solution for Russia was not force, but faith—faith in the care and tolerance of others, in the expression of truth.

Kerensky began his political career neither as a peasant nor a count, but as a middle-class reformer. Thus he was not prone to submission or to a dreamy and ineffectual idealism. Fending off extremists to his left and to his right, he tried to meld the parties of the center into an effective coalition. It's true that he was far better at rhetoric than at creating and sustaining an organization, but he had on his side the great advantage of strong and widespread popular desire for reform. Had the battle for democracy in Russia been a battle of discussion and persuasion, Kerensky might well have won.

But the battle, from the very start, was headed toward serious violence. Kerensky failed to control the military and the radicals. His own reflective observation was correct: the revolution for democracy was defeated by Kornilov when he sent armed men to rebel against the Provisional Government. Kornilov failed to win control, but he showed others how to do it. Though the Provisional Government kept shouting the principle of government by the people, it failed to establish itself as a coherent team of popular representatives who could take definitive control of violence in Russia to protect the people.

Violence had a dangerously effective advocate in Lenin. Even when absent from the scene, he was a powerful leader. Russia stank in Lenin's nostrils. Raised in the same place as Kerensky, his early experience of life was very different. After the tragedies of his teenage years, he became obsessed with power. He would never again trust liberals or anyone else—not even his closest comrades like Plekhanov, Trotsky, and Stalin. Lenin became an ardent advocate of violence, though, ironically, one of his greatest appeals to the Russian people was his advocacy of peace. He was not only in favor of ending the war, but of ending the state. He offered the people a dream of a society of love rather than oppression.

Lenin's Marxism helped to liberate him from honesty; therefore, he could say anything that he thought would enhance his power, however bizarre. Marx had made historical dishonesty a thrill for certain intellectuals because it endued them with manipulative power; like aristocrats, they could dazzle susceptible people with complexification and speculation, when what was needed to set things right was simplicity and observation. Marx's philosophical fantasies were introduced early on to imaginative Russians, who took the concepts he derived from advanced industrial economies and attempted to apply them to the primitive rural economy in which they found themselves. But none of their theories made much of a mark on the Russian masses, who were not intellectual. Not even Lenin, who regularly raided the Marxist cafeteria for stirring phrases, stuck strong with any Marxist principles.

Though Lenin did, from time to time, speak in favor of democracy, his purpose from the start was to destroy even the possibility of democracy by preventing deliberation. To Lenin, words were bombs and meetings were occasions for blasting his enemies and building his authority. He knew how to use language as a weapon, as propaganda to defeat his opponents. He and his momentary comrades were furious champions of violence who were smart enough to soften up the opposition with propaganda. They broke the essence of democracy: control over violence by the people's government.

Failure to control violence in the streets and in the armed forces has undone democracy many times in history. Democracy is never established simply by overthrowing a tyrant. Kerensky confronted a tremendous challenge. A parliament of sorts did exist—the Duma—but for years before 1917, it had only been permitted to discuss, not to decide. The Duma debated at the czar's sufferance, but it could not shape or regulate the government's activities. In a democracy, parliamentary discourse has an end: governing. In Russia, governing was done by the czar and his team, virtually completely independently of the chatter of the Duma. This mode of parliamentary discussion passed over into the new government. Kerensky inherited an assembly of representatives who went in for endless meetings and theatrical political speeches, but hadn't a clue as to how to produce the major, radical, and immediate reform Russia demanded. The challenge of actual governance seemed beyond them.

Across town there rose another complex political challenge: the Soviet. Despite this body's various pronouncements that it would be ruled by the Provisional Government, in fact it was not. Composed of an enormous crowd of workers and soldiers unused to sitting together for hours of discussion, the Soviet swung back and forth between shunning power and demanding all power. This second representative body of the people had no clearly defined operative authority or role in deciding Russia's future. Who was in charge—not only of the military, but of anything else the government would do?

Once freed from the czar's control, then, the military was, in effect, independent. Replacing the commanders in the spring of 1917, in the middle of a hard-fought war, would have been a risk. But their control over their own men was breaking down as millions were pressed to the front to face virtual suicide and millions more at the rear were threatened by robbery and murder as domestic order fell apart. In Petrograd, the Soviets and the Provisional Government tried to introduce a new kind of internal military governance, including the crazy idea that an infantry regiment marching into battle could be governed by its own troops. Kerensky managed to stave off that challenge from the left fairly easily. Much more serious was Kornilov's challenge from the right. Kornilov was in favor of the military's total control—over troops, civilians, and the government. He believed the war demanded that the government submit to him, not he to the government. Kerensky did defeat Kornilov's coup, but in doing so, he lost Russia's only viable commander-in-chief and had to take on the role himself—a role he was not equipped to play in the middle of a war.

Even if the Provisional Government had managed to rouse itself from conversation to action and exert control over the Soviet and the military commanders, the question of democracy would still have been unsettled. For in a democracy, violence must be controlled by a body of genuine representatives of the people, and that requires a national election. That crucial event was, unfortunately, postponed, and then ruled out by Dictator Lenin. Retrospective estimates are always uncertain, but a prompt, national election might have worked. It is clear that the delay of the election did not work.

Violence never disappears. But the historic advancement of democracy shows clearly that it is necessary for the legitimate government to control all violence by means of the military, the police, the prison guards, and all other officials held responsible for the repression of violence. The Russian revolution failed because, in spite of Kerensky's leadership and the Provisional Government's parliamentary attempts to establish democracy, they failed to control and counter the aggressions.

Kerensky did what he could. But the Bolsheviks got the guns.

BIBLIOGRAPHY

ABRAHAM, RICHARD. *Alexander Kerensky: The First Love of the Revolution.* New York: Columbia University Press, 1987.

ARENDT, HANNAH. *Crises of the Republic.* New York: Harcourt Brace Jovanovich, 1972.

BARGHOORN, FREDERIC C. *Politics in the USSR.* Boston: Little, Brown, 1966.

BAUER, RAYMOND A., ALEX INKELES, AND CLYDE KLUCKHOHN. *How the Soviet System Works: Cultural, Psychological, and Social Themes.* New York: Vintage Books, 1960.

BONNELL, VICTORIA E. *Roots of Rebellion: Workers, Politics and Organizations in St. Petersburg and Moscow, 1900–1914.* Berkeley, Cal: University of California Press, 1983.

BRINTON, CRANE. *The Anatomy of Revolution.* New York: Vintage Books, 1952.

BROWDER, ROBERT PAUL, AND ALEXANDER F. KERENSKY (EDS.). *The Russian Provisional Government, 1917: Documents.* Vol. I and III. Stanford, Cal: Stanford University Press, 1961.

BRZEZINSKI, ZBIGNIEW. *The Grand Failure: The Birth and Death of Communism in the Twentieth Century.* New York: Scribner's, 1989.

CARR, EDWARD HALLETT. *The Russian Revolution: From Lenin to Stalin, 1917–1929.* London: Macmillan, 1979.

COOLIDGE, OLIVIA. *Makers of the Red Revolution.* Eau Claire, Wis.: E.M. Hale, 1963.

DE JONGE, ALEX. *The Life and Times of Grigorii Rasputin.* New York: Dorset, 1987.

FEDOTOV, G. P. *The Russian Religious Mind*. Vol. II: *The Middle Ages: The Thirteenth to the Fifteenth Centuries*. Cambridge, Mass: Harvard University Press, 1966.

FERRO, MARC. *October 1917: A Social History of the Russian Revolution*. London: Routledge & Kegan Paul, 1980.

FISCHER, LOUIS. *The Life of Lenin*. New York: Harper & Row, 1964.

FRIEDRICH, OTTO. "Headed for the Dustheap." *Time*, February 19, 1990.

GOLDBERG, PAUL. *The Final Act: The Dramatic, Revealing Story of the Moscow Helsinki Watch Group*. New York: Morrow, 1988.

HOSKING, GEOFFREY A. *The Russian Constitutional Experiment: Government and Duma, 1907–1914*. London: Cambridge University Press, 1973.

HOUGH, JERRY F. *Opening Up the Soviet Economy*. Washington, D.C.: The Brookings Institution, 1988.

HOUGH, JERRY F. *Russia and the West: Gorbachev and the Politics of Reform* (2nd ed.). New York: Simon & Schuster, 1990.

JELAGIN, JURI. *Taming of the Arts*. New York: Dutton, 1951.

KERENSKY, ALEXANDER F. *The Prelude to Bolshevism: The Kornilov Rising*. New York: Dodd, Mead, 1919.

KERENSKY, ALEXANDER F. *The Catastrophe: Kerensky's Own Story of the Russian Revolution*. New York: D. Appleton, 1927.

KERENSKY, ALEXANDER F. *The Crucifixion of Liberty*. New York: John Day, 1934.

KERENSKY, ALEXANDER F. *Russia and History's Turning Point*. New York: Duell, Sloan and Pearce, 1965.

KHRUSHCHEV, NIKITA S. *The Crimes of the Stalin Era: Special Report to the 20th Congress of the Communist Party of the Soviet Union*. New York: The New Leader, 1962.

KILLINGRAY, DAVID. *The Russian Revolution*. St. Paul, Minn.: Greenhaven, 1980.

KIRCHNER, WALTER. *A History of Russia* (3rd ed.). New York: Barnes and Noble, 1963.

KLUCKHOHN, FRANK L. *The Naked Rise of Communism: A Penetrating Study of Communism—Its Origins and Doctrines, Its Strengths and Weaknesses*. Derby, Conn.: Monarch Books, 1962.

LENIN, V. I. *Selected Works*. Vol. XI. New York: International Publishers, 1943.

LOCKHART, R. H. BRUCE. *The Two Revolutions: An Eye-Witness Study of Russia 1917*. London: The Bodley Head, 1967.

MEYER, ALFRED G. *Communism*. New York: Random House, 1960.

NAHAYLO, BOHDAN, AND VICTOR SWOBODA. *Soviet Disunion: A History of the Nationalities Problem in the USSR*. New York: The Free Press, 1990.

NEUMANN, SIGMUND. *Permanent Revolution: Totalitarianism in the Age of International Civil War* (2nd ed.). New York: Frederick A. Praeger, 1965.

The New York Times: March 1917; and February 25, 1990, review of *Red Victory*.

PAGE, STANLEY W. (ED.). *Lenin: Dedicated Marxist or Revolutionary Pragmatist?* Lexington, Mass.: D. C. Heath, 1970.

PARKER, HAROLD T., AND MARVIN L. BROWN, JR. *Major Themes in Modern European History: An Invitation to Inquiry and Reflection*. Vol. II and III. Durham, N.C.: Moore, 1974.

PIPES, RICHARD. *The Russian Revolution*. New York: Alfred A. Knopf, 1990.

RIGBY, T. H. *Stalin*. Englewood Cliffs, N.J.: Prentice Hall, 1966.

SHULGIN, V.V. *Days of the Russian Revolution: Memoirs from the Right, 1905–1917*. Ed. Bruce F. Adams. Gulf Breeze, Fla: Academic International Press, 1990.

SOCIALIST UNION. *Twentieth Century Socialism: The Economy of Tomorrow*. Baltimore: Penguin Books, 1956.

STALIN, JOSEPH. *Leninism*. New York: International Publishers, 1928.

SWEARER, HOWARD R. *The Politics of Succession in the U.S.S.R.: Materials on Khrushchev's Rise to Leadership.* Boston: Little, Brown, 1964.

TOMASIC, DINKO. *The Impact of Russian Culture on Soviet Communism.* Glencoe, Ill.: The Free Press, 1953.

ULAM, ADAM B. *Russia's Failed Revolutions: From the Decembrists to the Dissidents.* New York: Basic Books, 1981.

ULAM, ADAM B. *The Bolsheviks: The Intellectual and Political History of the Triumph of Communism in Russia.* New York: Collier Books, 1965.

WALLACE, ROBERT, AND THE EDITORS OF TIME-LIFE BOOKS. *Rise of Russia.* New York: Time-Life Books, 1967.

WILSON, EDMUND. *To the Finland Station: A Study in the Writing and Acting of History.* Garden City, N.Y.: Doubleday, 1953.

WOLFE, BERTRAM D. *Three Who Made a Revolution: A Biographical Essay.* Boston: Beacon Press, 1955.

WOLFENSTEIN, E. VICTOR. *The Revolutionary Personality: Lenin, Trotsky, Gandhi.* Princeton, N.J.: Princeton University Press, 1967.

CHAPTER
3

The Challenge of Force

Government should clearly, straightly, and strongly govern force. Ironically, it may be that government was originally invented by war. That is not certain, because governments were born long before history was born, so we lack solid information as to how governments began. But there are certain hints from pre-historic times.

DID WAR GIVE BIRTH TO ORIGINAL GOVERNMENTS?

In certain old caves where humans lived long ago, there are drawings of men attacking animals. Perhaps the sketches were a magical practice meant to help the people succeed in hunting animals for food. Hunting back then, was a vital necessity that gradually took on two of the essential functions of government: planning and cooperation. Hunters had to decide where to go and who would do what. Individuals could hunt alone, of course, but early on, people discovered that they could bring home more meat working together as a team, some attacking the animals from one direction and others from a different direction. In other words, hunters took collaborate action. At first, they may have simply spontaneously joined together at the crucial moment to attack the animals. But eventually they practiced in advance, developing a system of fighting together.[1]

Then—it is supposed—hunting became competitive. A team of hunters charging against animals would see other hunters charging against those same animals and turn their weapons at the rival hunters. In the severest battles, the winners lived and the losers died. Yes, some animals were dangerous, but hunters fighting other hunters were a far greater threat. Organized leadership must have become more important as the fighting graduated from accidental skirmishes to small planned raids and then, to larger-scale warfare. War may have been the beginning of the identification of leaders, men who gathered and trained groups to fight together and who were painted or clothed to stand out in battle to signal their troops to obey them. As war expanded, going into battle without formal organization became a sure-fire prelude to disaster: troops had to be governed or they would be killed.[2]

It's likely that this early form of government was in no way democratic. Especially as weapons improved and bands of warriors increased in size, war required men to go against one of their deepest, most natural instincts: the instinct to run away from danger. At the prospect of death, the most powerful human impulse is to try to save one's own life by fleeing. It is highly doubtful that a troop referendum conducted at the front would result in a decision to go forward rather than backward, or that officers elected by their troops would order them to death. So the governance of the military emerged as an autocracy: power at the top forcing performance by those at the bottom. Those who disobeyed were killed by the commanders, as a lesson to their teammates, or hurt severely enough to persuade them to change their behavior. War was not typically carried out by the consent of the governed but by the force of the governors.

Throughout history, war has been normal: "from the year 1496 B.C. to 1861 A.D., in 3,357 years, there were 227 years of peace and 3,130 years of war, or thirteen years of war to every year of peace."[3] In the Middle Ages, European rulers ordered their lives around the goal of winning battles; this goal dictated their friends, their marriages, and the situation of their castles. Just as aggression required governance, so did defense. For example, in the centuries during which the Vikings struck out of their lands on ships ruled by a dictator-captain* to attack parts of Western Europe, again and again, the victims of these attacks were stimulated to create military governments for defense.[4]

The warrior experience created the belief that the normal system of government was autocracy: one man at the top, all others obeying. This system, which proved so successful on the battlefield, was gradually imposed at home until autocracy came to seem natural, permanent, universal, and even sacred in societies. Power, backed by force, existed only at the top; commands issuing down were to be obeyed without question.

If the rough history just sketched is essentially true, it helps to explain why wars have always proved a fundamental stumbling block to democracy. To move a society from autocracy to democracy is a major undertaking. But war remains a real challenge, so democracy cannot eliminate all wars.

Democracy is a grown-up government, the hard-won achievement of humanity as it graduated from bloody madness into humane rationality. It is essentially pragmatic, the result of wisdom based on thinking about the reality of human experience. Every democracy's survival depends on working out an

---

* It is interesting that "government" in ancient days meant "navigation."

effective and legitimate system to control force, which in all societies is primarily in the hands of the military and the domestic police. Time and again, democracies have collapsed shortly after being born because the representative government failed to take control of the military. Time and again, democracies have experienced tragedies because their governments have failed to control the force of society for the good of society.

When a government goes to war, it must fight for its survival—and for the survival of its citizens. War demands activism, technology, organization, secrecy and intelligence, planning, assignments, mutual trust, and radical inspiration. War may, at times, be necessary. The task is to see that democracy is not destroyed by it.

RECENT STRUGGLES TO CONTROL MILITARIES

Despite the hard lessons taught by ancient experience, governments around the world are being undermined by violence at the end of the twentieth century.

—In Nicaragua, Communist fighters overthrew a fascist dictatorship and established their own dictatorship. Then new revolutionaries, supported and trained by the United States, harassed the Communist regime for years, but failed to defeat it. Subsequently, the Communists permitted a national election, which, to their surprise, they lost. The newly elected president came on strong for democracy, but surprisingly, she maintained as chief of the army and the domestic police the brother of the dictator she had defeated in the election. Throughout the nation, the military which the people had rebelled against by voting—remained in control of the armed forces. Land was distributed to that Communist army—before the rebel army got their land. So for a long time after the new president officially took over the government of Nicaragua, she was still busy "negotiating" with the chief of the military, as though they had equal authority. The military was not controlled by the president or the elected representatives of the people.[5]

—In the Philippines, long after the United States had established a democracy there, a corrupt and tyrannical chieftain took over and held power for years, until a revolution for democracy threw him out. A democratic election empowered a new, highly respected president. But she, too, failed to thoroughly establish control of the military by the elected representatives. Year after year, she dealt with military leaders as though they were partners of the elected government, not public servants, tolerating their continual abuses of human rights.

—In Panama, the United States fostered a dictatorship and aided and advanced it for 19 years. Panama was ruled by a "narco-mafia" of international criminals who took over the military, which had been heavily equipped by massive U.S. aid. At last, their dictator, Noriega, was rejected by a popular election, the country was invaded by the United States military, and Noriega was arrested and taken for trial to the United States. But the new government did not take con-

Ferdinand Marcos with his wife, Imelda, after taking the oath of office as President of the Philippines. Just hours later, Marcos resigned and prepared to accept an American offer to fly him out of the Philippines for asylum.

President Corazon Aquino at a rally in the northern Philippines.

trol of the military, and the violence of the Noriega years continued.[6] Near the end of 1990, the U.S. Military Support Group was still hacking away, as U.S. Col. Jack Pryor put it, to get the government of Panama "to clean out the police some more, reward the loyalists, address some grievances and go after the civilian side of the mafia Noriega built, which has not been touched in the last year."[7] Once again, destruction of a dictatorship did not result in democratic control of the military.

—In Argentina, the military dictatorship fell apart after its defeat in a brief war with Great Britain. Still, the military was not brought under the power of a democratic regime. On the contrary, "The military still considered itself independent of the government, and even, in some quarters, above the constitution of the law."[8] The Argentine military exists as a separate nation:

> Military officers marry the daughters of other military officers. These children go to school with those of other military families. Their neighbors are military. They travel in military buses; they study in military libraries; they attend military church services; and they are buried in military cemeteries....They do not vote; they cannot openly speak their minds; and—in Argentina—they remain subject to military discipline even after they have retired.[9]

Civilian officials were given formal authority over the military, but "after three years of civilian rule, and a halving of the military budget, almost all of Argentina's old military units are still in existence; many of them are headed by commanders who express sentiments of humiliation and anger because their units are shrunken and in a poor state of operational readiness."[10]

—In the Soviet Union, President Mikhail Gorbachev repeatedly advocated democracy for the nation in the 1980s. But by the 1990s, the Soviet Army was "Coming Apart at the Seams," as headlined in *The Washington Post*. Weak control from the top fostered the rebirth of ethnic, generational, and geographic conflicts. An ominous breeze from 1917 chilled the nation. A Western diplomat asked, "If the party is no longer the leading force in the country, who is the army supposed to answer to now? ... To some extent, the Soviet military is going around looking for someone to be loyal to."[11] A meeting of 5,000 military officers in 1992 raised the tough question: Whom does this army serve? Some believed they should serve their local governments, while others felt that they owed their loyalty to the "Soviet Union"—though by this time, the Soviet Union no longer existed.[12]

—In Nigeria, some 250 different tribes were brought together by the British, taught English as the common language, trained in parliamentary government, and granted independence in 1960. For six years, democracy flourished. But then corruption and anger overcame it, and five young military officers killed the prime minister and took over the government. Soon they, too, were violently overthrown by members of another tribe, who took command of the military. In 1979, democracy was briefly reattempted, but widespread stealing and bullying instigated popular demand for a revival of military rule. A Nigerian attorney expressed the general sentiment when he said that the country needed a "strong," "ruthless," and "resolute" leader who would see that "People must be executed!...

They should pay with their lives. And the ill-gotten gains should be taken from their children." A character in a Nigerian novel summed up the country's plight this way: "When the Europeans ruled us, few people died. Now we rule ourselves, we butcher each other like meat-sellers slaughtering cows." In Nigeria, a democratic government in control of the military failed to make peace happen. [13]

—In Guatemala, a nation whose history is full of horrors, democracy seemed to triumph when genuine elections were held. In fact, the military continued to act independently of the people's chosen government. The government failed to stop soldiers from behaving in contempt of the law—the most outrageous acts went unpunished.

—In India, the Third World's prime democracy, domestic disorder in the 1990s bred local military takeovers justified by "emergencies." "We're almost sitting on a volcano today, " said one senior security force officer. Federal troops, ordinarily assigned to protect India against foreign attacks, were increasingly ordered by the government to go up against Indian citizens. "The politicians put us in this mess," said a senior police officer. Ethnic, caste, and religious tensions exploded, and instead of negotiating internal political peace, the politicians authorized military action. The results, documented by the human rights organization Amnesty International, were hundreds of deaths and abuses. The "emergency" situation triggered "a breakdown in the historic relationship between India's civilian, democratic institutions and the police and paramilitary forces," according to *Washington Post* reporter Steve Coll. An observer in New Delhi thought the military had "ensconced themselves in the belief that there will be no accountability." Sent out to quell demonstrations that turned violent, soldiers saw themselves as forced to fire their rifles without obtaining official permission. This violence, meant to stop violence, stimulated further violence. An elected government let it happen. [14]

Thus, all around the world, democracies are in danger of self-destruction because they have not succeeded in taking decisive control of the society's physical force. To understand the difficulties democracies have in controlling violence, both in wars and in domestic disorders, let us concentrate on the world's strongest democracy: the United States of America.

HOW THE UNITED STATES OF AMERICA BROKE APART

The major instance in U.S. history of the loss of national control over the military is, of course, the Civil War, a great tragedy that resulted in 620,000 deaths. Wider conditions set the stage for the breakup of the nation and the breakdown of peace, but it was the federal government's failure to maintain military order that directly led to the war.

Even on into the middle of the nineteenth century, the United States inherited its permanent constitution from the eighteenth century. At the original Constitutional Convention, one delegate came forth with a proposal "for vesting the power in the president" to make war. But no other delegate backed him up, and leading figures took the floor to oppose him. James Madison said that "executive powers...do not include the rights of war and peace." George Mason opposed "giv-

ing power of war to the executive because [he is] not to be trusted with it."
James Wilson said of the Constitution, "This system will not hurry us into
war; it is calculated to guard us against it. It will not be in the power of a single man, or a single body of men, to involve us in such distress." In 1788,
Patrick Henry forcefully stated the crux of the problem:

> Your president could easily become king.... If your American chief be a man
> of ambition and abilities, how easy is it for him to render himself absolute!
> The army is in his hands, and if he be a man of address, it will be attached
> to him.... Away with your president! We shall have a king: The army will
> salute him monarch... and what have you to oppose this force? What will
> then become of you and your rights? Will no absolute despotism ensue? [15]

The U.S. Constitution designated the president as commander-
in-chief of the military but gave Congress the power to declare war.
Despite the clarity of the Constitution regarding the national government's control of force, that control broke down. The North and South
had been fiercely contending over the issue of slavery.

To the shock and fear of the South, Illinois's Abraham Lincoln, a
determined opponent of the extension of slavery into the western territories, was elected president in November 1860, thanks to a split in his opposition. As inaugurations were scheduled then, he would not be sworn
into office until March 1861. Through those murky months of transition,
presidential power remained in the hands of James Buchanan, one of the
weakest presidents ever to occupy the White House. In December,
seething at the idea of Lincoln on the way to power, the state of South
Carolina arrogantly declared "that the Union now subsisting between
South Carolina and other states under the name of 'The United States of
America' is hereby dissolved." [16]

President Buchanan declared that South Carolina did not have
the right to secede—but he also declared that he (the president) had no
right to use force to prevent the secession, because the Union was based
on consent rather than force. On January 8, 1861, in the last speech he
gave as president, Buchanan proclaimed that "The Union must and shall
be preserved by all constitutional means" and that "The present is no
time for palliations. Action, prompt action, is required " He signaled that
by "prompt action" he did not mean military action.

The national government held Fort Sumter in the harbor of
Charleston, South Carolina. Buchanan did think of sending military rein-
forcements to the fort, but his advisers persuaded him to send instead
just one *merchant* ship with some soldiers inside. When the ship arrived
outside the harbor, it was shot at by South Carolinians. As the fort's commander prepared to shoot back to rescue the ship, it turned and sailed off.

Buchanan thus sent a message of timidity to the South. The secession movement sped up, with Mississippi, Florida, Alabama, Georgia,
Louisiana, and Texas soon following South Carolina out of the Union.

Abraham Lincoln.

These seven states (later joined by four more) formed a rebellious government called the "Confederate States of America," which proceeded to seize other United States forts, arsenals, and headquarters throughout the South. Despite Buchanan's expressed intention, his passive behavior allowed the disunion of the United States of America.

Lincoln was inaugurated on the 4th of March, 1861. Avery Craven, author of *The Coming of the Civil War*, speculated on what might have been in Lincoln's mind: "Lincoln could refuse to accept the fact of secession, hold the forts, collect the revenues, and enforce the law."[17] Whatever he was thinking, Lincoln—new president, still uncertain of the magnitude and shape of the challenges confronting him—came across as ambivalent, particularly regarding control of the military. In secret, he moved to hold forts and ships in the South, sometimes supplying the navy with ships flying the British flag.[18] And in public, he told the South:

> In your hands and not in mine, is the momentous issue of the civil war. The Government will not assail you. [But] I hold that, in contemplation of universal law and the Constitution, the Union of these States is perpetual.... No State, upon its own mere action, can lawfully get out of the Union.... I shall take care, as the Constitution itself expressly enjoins upon me, that the laws of the Union be faithfully executed in all the States.... The power confided to me will be used to hold, occupy, and possess the property and places belonging to the Government, and to collect the duties and imposts.[19]

By the time Lincoln took office, all but two forts in the South had been taken over by the Confederacy. The secretary of state, appointed by Lincoln, was William H. Seward, who had been Lincoln's major competitor for the presidential nomination; a statesman who thought of Lincoln as a country boy in need of expert guidance. Seward advised the president to seek a conflict with France and Spain, and maybe also with England and Russia, in order to reunite the North and South. When Seward thus volunteered to become Lincoln's prime minister, Lincoln said no, and on April 6, 1861, ordered a relief mission to Fort Sumter. Somehow Seward sneaked the president's signature onto an order for the mission not to go to Fort Sumter, but rather to the only other southern fort under U.S. control! Fort Sumter's commanding officer, pressed by the Confederates to surrender, said he would do so if they would wait for two days. They refused and opened fire on the fort at 4:30 A.M. on the 12th of April. [20]

Thus began the Civil War, the major failure of American democracy. Military control by the elected national government collapsed, and the result was the greatest disaster the United States has ever known. To reestablish democracy, Americans had to win a war against themselves and then, at great cost, reconstruct the political structure the Constitution had intended. The failure of the national government to control the military might well have resulted in the permanent death of the United States rather than its resurrection.

CONSTITUTIONAL CONTROL OVER THE MILITARY IS NOT ENOUGH

A bedrock condition for the survival of democracy is for the elected government to take and hold basic control over the military. That control is initially established in the unquestionable constitutional principle that the people's representatives are to guide any use of force. But for the principle to become a reality, the democratic government must rise to the challenge of actual, regular, systematic control over time, in war and in peace.

In wartime, military commanders tend to take more power. Even the United States and Great Britain; longtime democracies that have held genuine elections in the midst of wars, have acknowledged their practical dependence on military leadership in wartime. Sometimes this dependence has triggered massive disaster. In World War I, called "The Great War," in a battle in France, Britain's chief military commander, Sir Douglas Haig, ordered 110,000 of his troops to load their rifles and climb up out of their trenches and charge toward the Germans. The Germans fired machine guns at them from fortified positions. In just one day, 60,000 British troops were killed or wounded—a modern world record. Although the British people were shocked, the military did not alter its tragic practice. Months later, British troops were again ordered to attack German machine-gun positions: this time it took them five days to advance 7,000 yards, and 160,000 more of them were killed or wounded. [21] Though aware of the strategic crisis, the British Parliament did not demand or gain control over the fateful blunders of the nation's armed forces.

In the United States, military tragedies have happened when Congress decided to look the other way as presidents exercised excessive power. President Franklin D. Roosevelt allowed extensive bombing of Europe in World War II, killing many civilians. In 1945, President Harry Truman ordered atomic bombs dropped on Hiroshima and Nagasaki, destroying thousands of Japanese civilians. Later Truman started the Korean War without congressional approval, claiming it was merely a "police action." Result: 54,000 Americans were killed.[22] When John F. Kennedy took over the presidency from Dwight David Eisenhower, he inherited a secret scheme for the invasion of Cuba. He allowed the enterprise to go forward, and it turned into one of the country's most foolish and deadly failures. The next president, Lyndon Baines Johnson, tricked Congress into compliance with his plan to escalate the Vietnam War with a tale of U.S. ships being attacked in the Pacific's Tonkin Gulf. His successor, President Richard Nixon, dragged this disastrous war on for years until, with thousands of Americans dead and no liberation of Vietnam in sight, the United States finally withdrew. President Ford backed a military adventure to rescue a captured ship, at the cost of considerable casualties; and President Jimmy Carter sent a military team to rescue hostages held in Iran, a project that blew up in the desert, to the great embarrassment of the country. President Reagan went in for military surprises such as an attack on the tiny island of Grenada. He also secretly sanctioned the United States sending weapons to tyrants in such countries as Iran and Nicaragua.

Then President George Bush felt inspired to invade Panama and, later, to pour hundreds of thousands of American troops into the deserts of Saudi Arabia to fight against Iraq—a nation that owed much of its military strength to U.S. aid arranged by Bush. Bush operated initially in secret, and then through propaganda. He sent 500,000 American soldiers next to Iraq. First, after much manipulation, he got the United Nations to approve his war. Quite a bit later, he got around to requesting permission to declare war from Congress. At this point, only a few days remained until the deadline Bush had set for attacking Iraq. The extreme time pressure generated rushed, ineffective, and unreasoned speeches in Congress and a congressional resolution for war "at almost the last moment." Bush claimed this resolution was merely a nicety, since "I had the *inherent power* to commit our forces to battle after the UN resolution."[23]

All these presidential wars have perverted the U.S. Constitution and created enormous human suffering. Scholar Richard J. Barnet sums up the growth of presidential war in the last half century this way:

> Since 1945 American presidents have wielded power over national security and foreign policy beyond the dreams of tyrants. One American alone has had the authority to launch nuclear war and risk the death of the nation, even of civilization itself. For almost every one of the forty-five years since the end of World War II, presidents have ordered American soldiers into battle somewhere....
> ...In pursuit of democracy, presidents support dictators. In the pursuit of peace, they plan wars of mass destruction. In the pursuit of justice, they supply arms for repression. In the pursuit of world order, they break international law.[24]

And, as Theodore Draper has noted, "The country while prides itself on being the greatest democracy in the world has become the protector of some of the most undemocratic, die-hard, caste-conscious, otiose monarchies in the world."[25]

While such presidential actions have not extinguished American democracy, they have certainly distorted it. Time and again, the United States has fallen into military disasters, not as a result of public idiocy, but as a result of private idiocy—nondemocratic military actions taken in secrecy. To be sure, the public typically rallies around a president—labeled "Commander in Chief," as if the troops are *his* troops when he orders military action. But the question remains: Would most disasters have been avoided if the people's representatives had gathered the facts, discussed the alternatives, and decided what to do or not to do? Confidence in democracy says yes.

GOVERNMENT WAR AND PRISONER POLICIES SHOULD NOT BE SECRET

The military threats to U.S. democracy cannot be attributed solely to various presidents' characters. Another factor is the hiddenness of power within a band of elected and appointed leaders. Secrecy at the top is a hallmark of political aristocracies. Aristocratic governments typically display nothing to the public but the wonderful qualities of the rulers. History's lesson is that this is not a vision of government the people can trust. Democracy's demand for openness derives from the long, sad experience of the employment of secrecy for aristocratic profit and of military secrecy adds to the risk of violence.

In the United States, secret nondemocratic operations are often delegated by presidents. Reagan's Admiral John Poindexter said that he did not even tell the president about a wide-ranging, highly controversial military move Poindexter decided to make on his own initiative: diverting funds from U.S. arms sales to Iranians to the "Contras," an anti-Communist group rebelling against the government of Nicaragua. Poindexter assumed President Reagan would have approved of his actions if he had known of them. This unelected officer assumed presidential authority:

> I made the decision. I felt that I had the authority to do it. I thought it was a good idea. I was convinced that the president would, in the end, think it was a good idea. But I did not want him associated with the decision.... On this whole issue, you know, the buck stops here with me.

On Poindexter's authority, another unelected officer, Lieutenant Colonel Oliver North, lied to Congress to obscure his secret actions, thus corrupting democracy. He took pride as a soldier in fighting with the weapon of deceit against the people's representatives, whom he perceived as the enemy.[26]

The domestic police have also used secret, corrupt practices to subvert democracy. For example, J. Edgar Hoover, in charge of the U.S. police as FBI director, set out to destroy the civil rights leadership of Martin Luther King, Jr., by leaking secret information to ruin King's reputation.[27]

Secrecy is a major asset in state violence. Torturers, for instance, typically operate secretly; they are inhibited by publicity. Amnesty International has discovered that the most effective way to prevent the torture of those arrested is to quickly spread the information of political arrests around the world and get thousands to protest them. This mass objection is strongly communicated to those holding the particular prisoner.

In any democracy, the treatment of prisoners should be continually communicated, not only to the authorities, but also to the public. The law should ensure that no prisoner—disarmed, locked up, and thus wholly dependent upon guards—suffers violence, neither killing nor torture, or the kind of neglect that can freeze or starve or madden a human being. *Secrecy* is the greatest advantage of those who would abuse human rights, but even a certain amount of *obscurity* can protect extreme violence. People in villages neighboring the Nazi concentration camps smelled death from time to time, but tried their best to disbelieve that the horror of families being burned to death was actually happening. And distance enhances obscurity: torture conducted on the other side of the world is even easier to ignore. Since democracy is government by consent of the governed, the governed are to be informed. Abuses of violence are never to be hidden.

There is no assurance that the citizens of a democracy will stand up against the war, no matter how harsh or senseless the killing. War is often viewed romantically because its horrors typically become public knowledge only after the war is over. Still, there is an advantage in insisting that decisions for or against war be taken by the people's congress, for it is ordinary citizens who will be called upon to do the fighting, and they will not want to die except for very good concrete reasons. In contrast, top leaders and their families are unlikely to have to fight in war, so they tend to make abstract military decisions.

It can be admitted that *some* military secrecy is necessary, but this necessity has been overexpanded throughout history to hide from the public what they have a right to know. Intelligence agencies are particularly prone to hide the most disgustingly violent actions. After extensive dealings with "the Secret Team (ST)—mainly the Central Intelligence Agency and the National Security Agency—Colonel L. Fletcher Prouty of the U.S. Air Force came to view it as dangerously deviant:

> [The Secret Team] has its secrets. It has its divine and unquestioned rights and obligations. It has self-righteous power over life and death. It does not believe in anything. It does not value anything. It is utterly ruthless. Its greatest motivating force and drive is entirely undefined, because it moves by pressure. It reacts. It is therefore blind, meaningless, senseless. It will do anything in the name of anti-Communism.

Given that extensive malady,

there is but one way to control this massive ST structure. It must be uncovered. It must be made known. It must be exposed to the light. And then it must be told No. [28]

Periods of peace and security foster exposure of the wayward actions of the military and intelligence organizations, but in times of war or threat of war, these organizations become sacrosanct. Military operations depend on the enemy's ignorance. So may military diplomacy. Harmful or risky publicity, therefore, has to be forbidden. The practical alternative is not complete secrecy but deciding what must be kept secret to prevent the enemy's military advantage. Chapman Pincher's study of traitors confirms that

> in a democracy the secret services should be more accountable to the legislature, as they are currently in the USA through oversight committees, mainly to ensure that they do not infringe civil liberties. Oversight is enthusiastically supported by the civil libertarians in the hope that it would diminish the scope of the secret services, but the main reason for my advocacy is my conviction that it would improve their efficiency and reduce the risk that they would be penetrated by long-term traitors. It would also lessen, if not eliminate, the outrageous extent to which Parliament and the public have been misled by official statements on security and intelligence affairs. [29]

Military policy should, in the main, be known to the public so that the risks of war, accident, and financial corruption are minimized. Even when secrecy is a necessity, the public's representatives must be included among those who know and decide what is to happen. In this nuclear age, the elected representatives must be engaged in deciding life-and-death policies that they do not reveal to the public at large. Clearly, the general thrusts of such policies must be discussed with and approved by the citizenry, but the specific particulars—time, place, weapons, fighters, leaders—cannot be publicly disclosed. Nor can such details be shared throughout the Congress, because such sharing inevitably goes public. Instead, Congress must select its most capable and trustworthy members to put on oversight committees, and then rely on these members to do the right thing.

Unfortunately, however intelligent and responsible people may be as individuals, when they work together in committee (legislative or executive group), irrationality can take over, especially during a military crisis. Then there is a tendency to unreality. As Ervin Staub puts it, "When national security becomes an ideology, nations stop testing the reality of danger." [30] President Kennedy learned that lesson from the tragic outcome of the absurd attack on Cuba he authorized shortly after he took office. He subsequently applied it by organizing a committee capable of realistic, rational deliberation during the Cuban Missile Crisis. Kennedy's lesson never really registered with the next president, Lyndon Johnson, producer of the Vietnam tragedy. [31]

Sliding into mutually supported madness is a small-group political phenomenon that, time after time, has generated decisions that produce mass death.[32] However perceptive and moral the members of the group are, as a group, they can suddenly agree unanimously to march off into an insane and evil pursuit. Therefore, group decision making has to be carefully organized and conducted to produce rational decisions. This, in turn, requires that not only the composition of the secret-thinking team be specified, but also the process the team must use to guard against the distortions of group emotions ("groupthink").

DEMOCRACY TO GOVERN FORCE BY REASON

Democracy, we have said, demands that government operate by reason and that it regulate force. Those requirements present a serious challenge in this age of "ultimate absurdity," as Herbert York calls it, when "in the United States the power to decide whether or not doomsday has arrived is in the process of passing from statesmen and politicians to lower-level officers and technicians and, eventually, to machines."[33] Nuclear and other deadly high-tech weapons capable of killing great numbers of people immediately, are quietly spreading from nation to nation. Today "defense" requires rapid response to an attack, before one's ability to defend is suddenly destroyed. In such conditions there is no time for deliberation—not even by the president or some high-level officer. No democracy can be invoked within seconds. The only available democratic alternative is genuine, advance consent of the governed to basic emergency strategies, both offensive and defensive. Obviously, the weapons need to be carefully maintained to prevent a nuclear accident capable of ending our world. And as democracies face the looming risk of "war" that can destroy our civilization in less than a single day or night, establishing international military security through organized action becomes a top priority.

Beyond the procedures for handling military secrecy, democracy's control of violence depends on the nation's attitude toward both its foreign enemies and its own citizens. A procedure is a path, a purpose is a direction. An attitude sets the pace and style of political action. And as history shows, attitudes toward violence can change from one stage of events to the next.

Typically, when war breaks out, the public rallies around the flag, suppressing any doubts about the necessity of fighting, full scale and full speed. Hesitation feels wrong. The fantasy is to march out and win immediately. When a nation goes to war, the peacetime procedures of democracy, with their normal acceptance of internal contemplation, disagreement, and debate, are scrapped; the dignity of dissent is denied. The people are expected not only to work together toward victory but also to yearn together for it—in fact, to take victory on faith and therefore march happily on the road toward the front line. The psychology of war inspires high romance and deep suppression of doubts. Rationality is reduced to quick technical calculation. The question to fight or not to fight is a question canceled.

That mood of lively happiness on the way to deadly disaster exists perpetually as a seductive alternative to the slow, and sometimes tedious, deliberations of democracy. No wonder that when democracy becomes unclear and ineffective, the clear and effective lust for war lifts the status of the military. War has gone on for countless centuries, while democracy has existed for only two. To make democracy work, the human lust for the excitements of war has to be transformed from the physical to the verbal, from the combative to the cooperative. Ideally, the seductions of war will be recognized and rejected to be replaced by confidence in the decision of the people whether war is necessary.

But until and unless peace is secured by international cooperation and consent, war remains a strong probability, so as we practice democracy, we must also be ready to perform military action, not by turning off our minds but by turning them on. Political insanity is both the love of war and its opposite—the determination to never go to war, or put up any resistance, no matter what the threat. In the early Christian centuries, many Christians looked on martyrdom as an honor and refused to put up any resistance against vicious leaders, such as Nero, who butchered thousands of them:

> A sport was made of their execution. Some, sewn in the skins of animals, were torn apart by dogs. Others were crucified or burned, and others, as darkness drew on, were used as torches. Nero devoted his gardens to the spectacle, provided a circus, and himself, in the costume of a charioteer, rode around among the crowd, until compassion began to arise for the victims, who though deserving the severest penalties, were actually suffering not for the public good but to glut the cruelty of one man.[34]

Should Nero have been resisted? Then, as now, denial of the necessity for resistance to force can result in the defeat of democracy.

ISOLATION IS NOT THE SOLUTION

Isolationism has always been the great temptation in the United States, the belief being that ignoring the rest of the world will keep it at bay. In the American Revolution, one of George Washington's major challenges was to recruit men to serve in the military and then prevent them from going back to their isolated states before the fighting was done. After winning the Revolution, Americans longed for freedom—even neglect—from the British, the French and the Spanish, who were perpetually interfering with their new life and rousing the Indians to kill settlers on the frontier.[35]

So, in 1812, only a generation after the success of the American Revolution, Americans found themselves at war with Britain again, as the British attacked the United States, burning to the ground the Capitol and White House. For decades after the revolution, Americans turned their backs on Europe to the east and fixed their eyes on the west. Henry Clay spoke for many when he counseled that America should keep its "lamp burning brightly on the Western shore, as a light to all nations, [rather] than … hazard its utter extinction, amid the ruins of fallen or falling republics in Europe."[36] It became an American habit to romantically plunge into war when provoked far enough, and then find the experience detestable enough to retreat to isolationism at war's end. The horror of the Civil War in the 1860s confirmed Americans' dread of conflict, as did the experience of the doughboys in World War I:

We drove the Boche across the Rhine,
The Kaiser from his throne,
Oh, Lafayette, we've paid our debt,
For Christ's sake, send us home. [37]

The painful German novel *All Quiet on the Western Front* was translated into English and read by millions of Americans in the 1920s; the movie made from the book was seen by millions more in 1939.[38] Bruce Bliven of *The New Republic* saw the film and expressed the common mood: "I remember when a country that did not want to go to war was tricked and bullied and persuaded into doing so ... and so I feel, as I watch the motion picture of events unreeling on the screen of time, that I have seen it all before. This is where I came in."[39] Despite the steady growth of international interdependence, Americans longed for independence.

When Hitler emerged on the other side of the sea, Americans preferred to ignore what was happening. Selig Adler captures the emotional vogue of liberals—those citizens most in favor of freedom—of that time:

> They subscribed to a creed that held that wars solve no problems, that nations invariably fight at the fiat of selfish economic forces, and that, when democracy resorts to armed conflict, it crushes civil liberties at home and delivers itself into the hands of its reactionaries. At first, the liberals tried to persuade themselves that no real moral question was involved, arguing that one side was as bad, or almost as bad, as the other.[40]

Americans were not ignorant of Europe, or even of Japan, in those days, but military experts assured them that "Any invasion of our borders in force, even by a combination of Powers, becomes virtually impossible in the foreseeable future.[41] A public opinion poll in 1937 indicated that the overwhelming majority of Americans believed that their country's participation in World War I had been an awful mistake.[42] The economic threat of the Great Depression scared citizens more than the threat of war, so the war threat was ignored.

The public attitude was not one of strong opposition to the devil dictators who were setting forth to conquer the world, but rather the assumption that neglecting them would keep the peace. In the 1930s, Europe and Asia experienced awful slaughters, but Roosevelt could not get the United States to take military action to stop this killing of human beings, even as the horrors spread wider and wider. Only after the Japanese attack on the U.S. territory of Hawaii did the United States enter the world conflict—not only the war against Japan, but also the war against Germany. In the end, the United States and its allies won both those wars, but the cost of irrational delay in the hope of remaining isolated was enormous.

The lesson of World War II was clear: when a democracy withdraws from potential war, it may encourage and strengthen aggressive tyrants. The need for a democracy to control violence is not served by the psychological denial of the fact that war is sometimes a prerequisite for life and freedom. Democracy is not defined as government that never goes to war, but as government ruled by the people's elected representatives, who alone have the authority to decide to go to war. They alone also have the authority to set the policy for reaction by officials to unexpected military attack.

Democracies need to work together for peace, and when war is inevitable, they should join together to win it as soon as possible.

CONTROLLING VIOLENCE WITHIN THE NATION

Throughout ancient history rulers have seized power by force, and then murdered their potential rivals—even if they happened to be within their own family. Suleiman the Magnificent in the sixteenth century ruled an Islamic empire that included Turkey, Hungary, Mesopotamia, virtually the whole Mediterranean world and the eastern seas. Here is the history of that kingship:

> Suleiman's father, Selim the Grim, took the throne by killing his brothers and secured Suleiman's succession by killing all his other sons and grandsons. Suleiman, at the bidding of his scheming wife, Roxelana, had his favorite son murdered. Roxelana died, and Suleiman withdrew from active rule, leaving his remaining two sons to fight over the succession. Selim, a drunken weakling, won, and murdered his brother Bayezid with all his sons. Selim took the throne....[43]

The ancient desire to exert force over others has also marred democracies. In the United States, slavery—treating humans as if they were working animals—tormented millions of slaves for generations and eventually triggered the Civil War.

Slavery, an old and widespread condition in Africa, was not an American invention, of course, but the failure to stop it at the time of the founding of the United States was a terrible mistake. Besides being brutal and unethical toward those who endured it, slavery was a form of violence uncontrolled by the new democracy. Thomas Jefferson, although he was himself a slaveholder, tried hard to stop slavery. When drafting the revolutionary Declaration of Independence, he included this accusation against Britain's King George III:

> He has waged cruel war against human nature itself, violating its most sacred rights of life and liberty in the persons of a distant people who never offended him, captivating and carrying them into slavery in another hemisphere, or to incur miserable death in their transportation thither. This piratical warfare, the opprobrium of *infidel* powers, is the warfare of the Christian king of Great Britain. Determined to keep open a market where MEN should be bought and sold, he has prostituted his negative [i.e., veto] for suppressing every legislative attempt to prohibit or to restrain this execrable commerce; and that this assemblage of horrors might want no fact of distinguished die, he is now exciting these very people to rise in arms among us, and to purchase that liberty of which he deprived them, by murdering the people upon whom *he* also obtruded them; thus paying off former crimes committed against the *liberties* of one people, with crimes which he urges them to commit against the *lives* of another.[44]

Jefferson rightly saw slavery as a form of war, an "assemblage of horrors."

There was a real chance that slavery could have been eliminated at the birth of the United States. But his fellow revolutionaries who owned slaves realized that if they accused George III of abetting the slave trade, then they themselves would have to give up slavery; so they edited Jefferson's antislavery passage out of the Declaration. Afterward Jefferson tried repeatedly to invent some politically acceptable way to end slavery—for instance, by freeing children or by halting the trading of slaves, the slaves were chained away from politics, so Jefferson had few allies in the game. At the Constitutional Convention, Benjamin Franklin considered proposing the abolition of the slave trade, but he decided not to because he feared the controversy would ruin national unity. In the end, the Constitution allowed states to count slaves to determine how many representatives a state would have in the House of Representatives—though slaves could not vote for those representatives. It did not end the slave trade, but it prohibited any slave from escaping to freedom. Throughout, it referred to slaves as "all other persons" and "such Persons as any of the States now existing shall think proper to admit" and "Person[s] held to Service or Labour."

In the early nineteenth century, thanks to a new machine, cotton production became highly profitable and plantation slave labor created many a fortune. Rules governing slavery emerged, but enforcement was left up to the masters, an error of law. As historian John Hope Franklin explains:

> Far from being a civilizing force … the plantation bred indecency in human relations; and the slave was the immediate victim of the barbarity of the system that exploited the sex of the women and the work of everyone. Finally, the psychological situation that was created by the master-slave relationship stimulated terrorism and brutality because the master felt secure in his position and because he frequently interpreted his role as calling for that type of conduct. Many masters as well as slaves got the reputation of being "bad," and this did nothing to relieve the tension that everywhere seemed to be mounting as the institution developed.[45]

Slavery became a divisive issue in the 1840s. Abolitionists, determined to rid the nation of this moral disgrace, encouraged the use of force to free slaves. Franklin notes: "By 1850 the philosophy of force was so integral a part of abolitionist doctrine that many viewed it as a movement toward anarchy."[46] In this North-South argument over slavery, the "war of words became so bitter, and the atmosphere in the South so tense, that free inquiry and free speech disappeared."[47] Political discourse degenerated into hatred, even as Lincoln and Douglas struggled to create a political compromise to end the anti-democratic relation to slaves, reasoning through deal after deal, plan after plan. Even in the U.S. Senate, one senator actually struck another senator, symbolizing the breakdown of discourse and the rush to war.

The United States today should examine that great wound called the Civil War and commit the nation to full democracy in which all persons are protected from violence—women, children, the vulnerable elderly, everyone. It should recognize that toleration of domestic violence—taking crime for granted, beating as normal, rape as sexual excitement, bullying as a necessity—is a serious political pathology. It should realize that a perverse political culture can sicken democracy. The temptation to justify physical domination of other human beings is a deadly disease badly in need of a cure, though not by force.

CONTROL OF FORCE BY DEMOCRACY

How is democratic control of force to be accomplished? Surely education, recognized by Jefferson as an essential factor of democracy, ought to teach the history of human suffering and solutions that stopped horrors in the past. Simply knowing the mistakes is not enough. Democracy needs to cure them.

Diagnosis is not prescription. We need to know what makes life wrong, but also what makes life right. Democracy is a form of government in which decisions are made by talk, not by force. Force cannot be eliminated, but it has to be a secondary power, dependent upon the power of political reasoning. When a democracy makes mistakes, the temptation to declare an "emergency" and shift power to the military is strong. Given the long history of wars, the idea that deliberation can prevent war looks impossible. Even in the United States and other established democracies, the problem of effective control of the military comes up time and again, confirming the fact that this is a permanent, fundamental challenge to the existence of democracy.

The cases of democratic success presented throughout this book illustrate how an elected government can deal with force. Other examples can be found in historical studies that focus on law, economics, and politics. I see the following as rough generalities from successful democracies.

The nation's constitution—the fundamental law of the land—has to state, in blazing clarity, the domination over the military by the elected civilians. No ambiguity should be permitted. The United States Constitution says that Congress shall decide whether to declare war, but that the president is commander-in-chief of the armed forces. This ambiguity has plagued U.S. democracy for years, giving rise to disastrous misbehavior by presidents who have started miniwars that expanded into maxiwars. Congress too often forsakes rationality in the heat of the moment and, in a mood of gung-ho patriotism, backs the war the president has started. That is one side of the problem. The other is that presidents and Congress are sometimes inclined to delay too long in going to war when it is necessary for the nation's security. To create a clear constitution at the start is a hard thing to do: a new nation has to unify its numerous diverse groups, so compromise is the natural mode. The results often tend to be ambivalent. This is why initial devotion to constitutional simplicity is so important. The likelihood of ambivalence makes it necessary to establish a clear constitutional system for deciding what the constitution means, as well as a system for changing the constitution should that become necessary. And then, given the uncertainty as to what will result from constitutional procedures in the long term, a substantive bill of rights is essential to ensure that, whatever the process, the *result* will not infringe on the fundamental rights of citizens. Alexander Hamilton failed to comprehend this necessity. He thought that the constitution needed to contain only rules of procedure for the operation of the government, and that these rules would naturally protect citizens' rights. Very fortunately, others knew better and a bill of rights enumerating and guaranteeing specific liberties of the people was added to the U.S. Constitution. Carved across the top of the Supreme Court building in Washington, D.C., is the key demand: "Equal justice under law." The bill of rights is for every member of the society. Neither coercion nor exploitation is acceptable in a real democracy.

A constitution must actually guide the real politics of the nation. Throughout history, constitutions of striking clarity and eloquence have been written—and then ignored. Those of us who read the Soviet Constitution when we were college students found it a surprisingly inspiring document in its commitment to human rights. But it was a lie: the Russian reality was violence against the Russian people. There, as elsewhere, the crucial test of a constitution comes *after* the writing and signing. Are conflicts resolved by adherence to what the constitution says? Are the nation's laws seen as beneath the constitution, shaped, guided, and dominated by the constitution? The government must commit itself to ruling by law, under the constitution, not by whim of high officials. Within the military, rules composed in consistence with the law must be respected and enforced. In this respect, government control of the military is part of the wider rule: Democracy demands force in *support* of the law, not in subversion of it.

The ability to control force depends on exercising democratic control of the government's money. Government is funded by taxation and is responsible to the people paying the taxes for how the money is spent. For example, the U.S. government spends enormous funds for military machinery—a benefit for the rich—but enlists most of its soldiers and sailors from the working class, leaving the rich free to spend their time gaining more money. Bizarre projects have been undertaken with taxpayers' money, such as "Star Wars" (or, as its advocates preferred to call it, the "Strategic Defense Initiative"), an impractical attempt to destroy missiles in the air, and the B-1 bomber, a very expensive and ineffective airplane. Such lavish projects turn out to be far easier to start than to stop. Members of Congress, constantly in need of huge sums of money to campaign for reelection, accept contributions from military production companies and their lobbyists. They also seek political benefit by creating and maintaining military bases to supply jobs in their districts. Military economics is not only technically complex, but typically kept secret. The obfuscations benefit the defense industry and mask military absurdities from the people, who cannot see what to oppose. Unless a political party or the press digs out the information and presents it to the voters, certain members of Congress will work closely and quietly with military officials and private enterprisers to create and perpetuate expensive, military projects.[48]

The national legislature makes the laws, exercising sovereignty over all the other lawmakers. The same national legislature defines and controls money. The military is to be totally dependent on the nation's parliament for its funding;

it should never be allowed to generate its own income. As a top official under Franklin Roosevelt put it, "the budget is one of the most effective, if not the strongest, implements of civilian control over the military establishment."[49] The military must be required, not only to request its money from the legislature, but also to inform the legislature about how that money is being spent and to depend on the legislature for continued (or changed) allocations. This rule of the game is essential, though it cannot be counted on as an automatic protection against military manipulation. Since modern military technology is expensive and thus potentially quite profitable for manufacturers—whose interest in fortune often overrides their interest in the effectiveness of force— the collaboration of militants, corporate enterprisers, and legislators can result in major diversions of money. The goal of producing the best weapons for war can degenerate into the goal of producing the best profits for the manufacturer. Since there is no general competitive system for pricing big technical weapons and, before war starts, no for-sure way of evaluating their performance, the money deal typically depends on inside collaboration. The key to democratic control is the insistence of legislators on knowing exactly where the money is now going and on deciding where it will go in the future.

The military should not be permitted to engage in democratic political processes such as elections (e.g., to protect local military facilities) or lobbying in the capital (e.g., to jack up their budget). The military is an authoritarian organization naturally alien to democratic processes. It is *armed to command*, while political leaders are *authorized to persuade*. No military unit should become a political unit or operate as, or even to ally itself with, a political party.

The right to vote belongs to every citizen, including every soldier and sailor, as does the right to express an opinion on policy. But the military is by nature and function an autocracy in which the bottom line is the force of the leader to order the death of the follower. So while it is necessary to guarantee the political rights of individuals in the military services, it is just as necessary to exclude military organizations from political power.

Democracy defines human beings as equal. Political equality does not mean identity—that all people are just the same in every way—but that all citizens have to be treated equally by the government. Political equality is unrelated to religion or general morals or affection or aesthetic admiration. The awful alternative to political equality is tyranny, demonstrated in our own century most horrifically by the totalitarian Nazis and Communists. Equality is not a wispy idea. The failure of equality in politics has time and again brought on the disaster of force.

A real democrat takes pride in playing fair with all citizens, in protecting all, even those in jail, from violence. As Thomas Jefferson said, statesmen are to be condemned for "permitting one half of the citizens…to trample on the rights of the other."[50]

THE RULES OF SPORTS ILLUSTRATE CONTROL OF FORCE

The history of sports illuminates how to practice fair, peaceful politics. Competitive sports probably began as training for war—men fencing with dull sticks rather than sharp sticks. The ancient Greeks, in training themselves to hit the enemy, hit a punching bag. But as athletics evolved beyond war preparation into popular entertainment, rules developed. To take part in a Greek festival of sports, an athlete had to register, pay a membership fee, and swear to compete through the contest to the end. Before the Olympia games, "the athletes, along with their fathers and brothers, and their trainers swore that they would commit no foul play and that they had trained faithfully."[51] Closer to war was a sport called *pankration*, a general fight allowing all sorts of wrestling, boxing, and even strangleholds. But it was forbidden to bite bodies or grab eyes, and a participant had the right to halt the game immediately by a simple signal.[52] What Greek politics and Greek sports had in common was rules. Sports allowed force, but only according to the rules; politics "abhorred and strictly punished violence in civic life," by rules.[53] In those days, warfare was as common as sports and domestic politics, but in politics and sports, there was a commitment to fair rules. The Romans, on the other hand, went in for disgusting gladiator games in which human beings hacked and killed one another before thousands of cheering fans. But at least that harsh entertainment seemed to distract the Romans from war and accustomed them to action restricted by *some* rules.[54]

Today sports still prepare participants for war and generate enthusiasm in audiences for a transition from the playing field to the battlefield. And on television, in computer games, and in movies, war is romanticized. Viewers and players are often seduced from the reality of war's butchery into thrilling to war as a jazzy adventure—as if men shooting at one another were merely a form of dodgeball. Soccer fans, in England and elsewhere, have emerged from games spoiling for a fight; the typical hockey game includes the excitement of watching players striking one another with their sticks. While war, in truth, is hell, war anticipated is often posed as a marvelous sport.

In real democracy, political conflict is a healthy, permanent, rule-bound game. In politics, fair play is a value beyond victory: "Win or lose, be a good sport." Politics can be an appealing adventure, a pleasure, in comparison to the dull experience of much ordinary activity. Ideally, the political game is conducted through energetic, persuasive discourse, not hatred. The atmosphere of politics is highly significant. When that atmosphere is one of good sport, including respect for opponents and readiness to accept the bottom-line decision rendered by voting, democracy brightens human possibilities.

It is essential that the game of democracy be inclusive. Neither political nor military organizations should be class, race, geographic, or ethnic gatherings. Where there are separate military and social cultures—for instance, in Argentina—these two essentially different cultures give rise to dangerous conflicts. Scholar Claude E. Welch, Jr., makes the following observation about civilian control of the military:

> The final given is the extent of latent social differentiations.... Political disputes become increasingly polarized and linked to race, as "primordial sentiments" become more salient. These sentiments can cut across the institutional boundaries of the armed forces, resulting in their politicization and embroilment in domestic disputes.... The explosion of conflict may well incite a more marked military role in politics.[55]

Both in the Vietnam War of the 1960s and 1970s and in the war against Iraq in 1991, the American military was composed largely of working-class youths, who were in the service because they couldn't get out of the draft as easily as the middle class (Vietnam) or because they had no decent employment prospects in civilian life (Iraq). Hardly any members of Congress had sons or daughters in the service, and few of society's other leaders had relatives in any arena of the military. The warriors were, in effect, plebeians sent off to die by aristocrats.

Democracy is fundamentally opposed to this—or any other—kind of segregation. A segregated army, composed of some class, ethnic and/or geographic category of persons, tends to close in on itself; its soldiers are drawn together, not only on the battlefield, but also in their peacetime life in the nation's towns. The danger is that they will see other citizens as aliens. Psychologically, it is but a short step from seeing people as aliens to seeing them as enemies. And enemies deserve destruction. In Russia in 1917, the army fought on the side of the people; the police fought to protect the power of the czar.

In a democracy, the draft should be used to ensure that the military is composed of all categories of citizens, and brought together to protect their country. That political communion can contribute to the wholism of the society. And the mutual respect it generates makes it less likely that the military will turn against the civilian population or dehumanize the opposition.

BEYOND NATIONAL CONTROL OF FORCE

The working out of democratic control of violence is bound to vary from place to place, from era to era, from wartime to peacetime. Even after the democratic government has achieved control of the military, it will be challenged to control violence and force within the country, to use its police to protect its citizens from one another without abusing power.

The crucial question is how to make peace work, despite the real threatening circumstances peace confronts. Despite the difficulties and uncertainties, a higher hope is visible: genuine international legitimate security. If the democracies in this world do join together in the future, federated in favor of human rights, justice, liberty and equality—as well as peace—then politics may invent its best: a world in which force becomes a memory rather than an expectation.

BIBLIOGRAPHY

ADLER, SELIG. *The Isolationist Impulse: Its Twentieth Century Reaction.* New York: Collier Books, 1961.

ATKINSON, RICK, AND GARY LEE. "Soviet Army Coming Apart at the Seams." *The Washington Post,* November 18, 1990, p.1.

BAINTON, ROLAND H. *Christendom: A Short History of Christianity and Its Impact on Western Civilizations.* Vol. I: *From the Birth of Christ to the Reformation.* New York: Harper Torchbooks, 1966.

BARBER, BENJAMIN, AND PATRICK WATSON. *The Struggle for Democracy.* Boston: Little, Brown, 1988.

BARBER, JAMES DAVID. *The Presidential Character: Predicting Performance in the White House.* 3rd ed. Englewood Cliffs, N.J.: Prentice Hall, 1985.

BARBER, JAMES DAVID. "Empire of the Sun." *The Washington Monthly,* October 1991.

BARNET, RICHARD J. *The Rockets' Red Glare: When American Goes to War.* New York: Simon & Schuster, 1990.

BRADLEE, BEN JR. *Guts and Glory: The Rise and Fall of Oliver North.* New York: Donald I. Fine, 1988.

BUTTMAN, ALLEN. *Sports Spectators.* New York: Columbia University Press, 1986.

CAMPBELL, JOSEPH. *The Way of the Animal Powers.* Vol.1: *Historical Atlas of World Mythology.* London: Summerfield Press, 1983.

COLL, STEVE. "India's Security Forces Assume New Power as Role in Ending Conflicts Grows." *The Washington Post,* December 2, 1990, p. A36.

COOPER, CHESTER L. *The Lost Crusade.* New York: Dodd Mead, 1970.

CRAVEN, AVERY. *The Coming of the Civil War.* Chicago: University of Chicago Press, 1974.

CUNNINGHAM, NOBLE E. JR. *In Pursuit of Reason: The Life of Thomas Jefferson.* Baton Rouge: Louisiana State University Press, 1987.

DAVID, MAURICE R. *The Evolution of War: A Study of Its Role in Early Societies.* New Haven, Conn.: Yale University Press, 1929.

DRAPER, THEODORE. "Presidential Wars." *The New York Review of Books,* September 26, 1991, pp. 66, 71

EISENMANN, ROBERTO. "The Struggle Against Noriega." *The Journal of Democracy,* Winter 1990.

FACER, SIAN (ED.). *On This Day: The History of the World in 366 Days.* New York: Crescent Books, 1992.

FRANKLIN, JOHN HOPE. *From Slavery to Freedom: A History of Negro Americans* (5th ed.). New York: Alfred A. Knopf, 1980.

FUSSELL, PAUL. *The Great War and Modern Memory.* New York: Oxford University Press, 1975.

GARROW, DAVID J. *The FBI and Martin Luther King, Jr.: From "Solo" to Memphis.* New York: Norton, 1981.

GRAHAM-CAMPBELL, JAMES. *The Viking World.* New Haven, Conn.: Ticknor & Fields, 1980.

HIGGINBOTHAM, DON. *War and Society in Revolutionary America: The Wider Dimensions of Conflict.* Columbia: University of South Carolina Press, 1988.

JANIS, IRVING. *Victims of Groupthink.* Boston: Houghton, Mifflin, 1972.

KENNEDY, ROBERT F. *Thirteen Days.* New York: Signet Books, 1969.

KOTZ, NICK. *Wild Blue Yonder: Money, Politics, and the B-1 Bomber.* New York: Pantheon Books, 1988.

LANGER, WILLIAM L., AND S. EVERETT GLEASON. The Challenge to Isolations: 1937–1940. New York: Harper and Brothers, 1952.

LATOURETTE, KENNETH SCOTT. *Christianity Through the Ages.* New York: Harper Chapel-Books, 1965.

LEMOYNE, JAMES. "Putting Democracy in Peril." Review in *The New Leader*, December 30, 1991.

MORISON, SAMUEL ELIOT, AND HENRY STEELE COMMAGER. *The Growth of the American Republic.* New York: Oxford University Press, 1942. Vol. I

NATIONAL DEMOCRATIC INSTITUTE FOR INTERNATIONAL AFFAIRS. "Civil-Military Relations: The Argentina Experience." *NDI Report*, 1989.

O'CONNELL, ROBERT L. *Of Arms and Men: A History of War, Weapons and Aggression.* New York: Oxford University Press, 1989. Chap. 3, "Genesis."

PILARTE, DORALISA. "Nicaragua Unhappy with Government." AP, *Durham Morning Herald*, November 18, 1990.

PINCHER, CHAPMAN. *Traitors: The Anatomy of Treason.* New York: St. Martin's Press, 1987.

POLIAKOFF, MICHAEL B. *Combat Sports in Ancient World: Competition, Violence, and Culture.* New Haven, Conn.: Yale University Press, 1987.

PROUTY, COLONEL L. FLETCHER. *The Secret Team: The CIA and Its Allies in Control of the United States and the World.* Englewood Cliffs, N.J.: Prentice Hall, 1973.

PRYOR, COL. JACK. *U.S. News and World Report*, December 17, 1990.

RICE, CANDOLEEZA. "The Military Under Democracy." *The Journal of Democracy 3*, April 1992.

STAUB, ERVIN. *The Roots of Evil: The Psychological and Cultural Origins of Genocide and Other Forms of Group Violence.* Cambridge, England: University Press, 1989.

STEPAN, ALFRED. *Rethinking Military Politics: Brazil and the Southern Cone.* Princeton, N.J.: Princeton University Press, 1988.

WAISMAN, CARLOS H. "The Argentine Paradox." *The Journal of Democracy*, Winter 1990.

WELCH, CLAUDE E. JR. (ED.). *Civilian Control of the Military: Theory and Cases from Developing Countries.* Albany: State University of New York Press, 1976.

WRIGHT, QUINCY. *A Study of War* (2nd ed.) Abridged by Louise Leonard Wright. Chicago: University of Chicago Press, 1964. Chap. II, "The History of War."

YORK, HERBERT. *Race to Oblivion: A Participant's View of the Arms Race.* New York: Simon and Schuster, 1970.

CHAPTER
4

The Story of Australian Development

Democracy Raised Up

The failure of the Russian Revolution shows how democracy can die by force. The making of Australia shows how a people, after confronting long, hard agonies of force, finally won the great democratic victory: control of force by the elected representatives of the people.

WHO BECAME THE PEOPLE OF AUSTRALIA ?

Australia is a continent in the Pacific almost as large as the United States, on the other side of the world from Great Britain. Long before Great Britain took control of Australia, it took control of most of the east coast of North America. In the early 1600s, American enterprisers in the British colonies of Maryland, Virginia, and Georgia needed laborers, so they purchased convicts from the British. These servants were required to work for a certain term for those who bought them—in effect, they were slaves whose slavery had a fixed limit. An English law of 1666 authorized the transportation of persons who were "lewd, disorderly and lawless."[1] Over the next 100 years, America received about 500 convicts each year. During that same century, America also received about 47,000 slaves each year—Africans sold by Africans, mainly to Britains, who transported them across the sea. American planters preferred the African slaves, who belonged to them forever, to the convicts, who would have to be freed once their term of servitude was up.[2]

In any case, the American Revolution of 1776 put an end to the transportation of British convicts to America. But there were still a great many convicts in England, who were arrested because they refused to shift from working in their homes to working in factories or coal mines for 12 or 15 hours a day. Punishments were harsh in those days. There were some 200 crimes, including pickpocketing and "impersonating an Egyptian," for which the punishment was death by hanging. To save the government the trouble and expense of building enough prisons to contain all those criminals who had not committed capital offenses, the British took to transporting them across the ocean, first to America, and then, after 1776, to Australia.

Australia, back then, was not a nation but a continent. Some 300,000 natives lived on the continent. While they shared religion, language, and family life, they had no government, not even a king, and they were virtually unknown in Europe.[3] As early as A.D. 150, Europe's astronomer Ptolemy had included in his map a "Terra Australis Incognita"—Unknown Southern Land—on the hunch that there must be a sizable body of land out there in the vast South Pacific. In 1550, a French mapmaker mapped out an "Australia"—as a land section of Antarctica. Various Europeans sailed over there and landed at the edge of the continent, but they neither settled in nor explored the land.

In 1770, Britain's famous Captain James Cook sailed his ship *Endeavor* around the Pacific Ocean. He was watching the sky, trying to trace the movement of the planet Venus, when he bumped into the east coast of Australia on the 23rd of August. He landed at, and named, Botany Bay. He then proceeded to explore and name other capes and coasts and, liking them, he declared possession of "the whole eastern coast...in right of His Majesty George the Third."[4]

Cook's declaration eventually reached London, so Australia's eastern half of the continent was officially claimed as the property of England and named New South Wales. In 1787, the British prime minister authorized transport of convicts to Botany Bay. Most of these men and women had been found guilty of relatively mild offenses. For example, a young man who stole one loaf of bread, or a woman who stole one handkerchief, could be imprisoned and sent off as prisoners in Australia for seven years.[5]

On May 13, 1787, 11 ships with 759 convicts left England.[6] Most of the convicts had never been to sea before, so as the ships rolled on the waters, their sails pushed out by the shifting wind, many got seasick. They were locked in cells beneath the deck, four persons in each cell, which was about the size of a double bed under a ceiling height of four feet five inches; the convicts could never stand up and could barely move around.[7] No doctor or nurse was on board. More than 20 convicts died during the passage; many more sickened with cholera and influenza. After sailing eight long months through rough seas, the alive convicts arrived at Botany Bay on January 20, 1788. Of the original 759, 736 had survived to land, with 294 marines and officers and the first governor of Australia, on the coast. The chained prisoners were set to work in very harsh conditions; for example, they wore chains and cleared farmland without the aid of a plow (there wasn't a single plow in the whole territory).

Over the many years until 1868, troubled England shipped thousands of convicts to Australia. Of the 160,000 who survived the passage, about 20,000 were women and a great many others were young boys, including many orphans and deserted children.[8] On the journey, convicts suspected of planning mutiny were killed or lashed; one suspect was lashed 800 times on two successive days.[9]

These, then, were the first European settlers of Australia: crime-convicted prisoners and the marines who guarded them at work. It was a community of force without the slightest democracy.

HUMAN LIFE IN AUSTRALIA

Force was harsh. Even six-year-old children were compelled to go to work. A convict could be hanged for poaching a rabbit, or even for appearing on the high road with a "sooty face."[10] The first governor of New South Wales, commissioned by King George III in 1786, said he hoped that when Britain took possession of the country, *"That there can be no slavery in a free land, and consequently no slaves."*[11] In fact, that governor proved himself a brute. The convicts—mostly city people who knew nothing of farming and sad people—got nothing to eat if they failed to work. Nourishment was minimal in any case: for a full week, a convict got only 4 pounds of flour, 2½ pounds of salt pork and 1½ pounds of rice—barely enough to stay alive.[12] A starving man who stole 20 ounces of potatoes received 300 lashes; another who stole 3 pounds of food received 1,000 lashes.[13] Any male prisoner who attempted to enter the women's tents was shot dead. The women, falsely labeled "whores," were reserved for the sexual abuse of the military. For example, at evening dancing for the soldiers,

> all the women would join in the dances of the Mermaids, each one being naked with numbers painted on their backs so as to be recognized by their admirers who would clap their hands on seeing their favorite perform some grotesque action... with the assistance of a gallon or two of Rum. Such amusements were the talk of the soldiers for days before and after the performance.[14]

Any convict who escaped into the bush—the wilderness of scrub and forest—was likely to be speared to death by tribal natives. Work was forced, but as time went on, increased numbers of convicts were in such bad shape they really could not work.

From England, the Third Fleet of ships set forth with 1,864 convicts. On the way, a tenth of the men died, and those who arrived in Australia in 1791 were, as the governor himself said, "so emaciated, so worn away" that they could not work at all.[15] He hoped the new colony would be "formed by farmers and emigrants who have been used to labour, and who reap the fruits of their own industry," but up to 1800, only 20 free settlers arrived, though increasing numbers of convicts finished their imprisonment and started seeking their own land grants.[16]

John MacArthur.

THE RULERS OF FORCE: MACARTHUR VERSUS BLIGH

In 1790, any army officer named John MacArthur arrived and went into landowning and trade in his new home. Two years later, a new governor appointed MacArthur regimental paymaster and inspector of public works, giving him control of convict labor.[17] The next year, MacArthur took on a new line of business: liquor. When an American ship called *Hope* arrived with 7,500 gallons of rum, he bought all of it, drawing on military money from England to do so. He set up a highly profitable liquor sale system: his regiment became known as the "Rum Corps." Given the depressing conditions of life, MacArthur had no trouble selling his rum to ex-convicts and the military. In 1804, he persuaded officials in England to give him 5,000 acres so he could experiment growing Spanish sheep for wool. His business profits soared.

But then, in 1806, another new governor arrived—none other than the famous Captain William Bligh, whose sailors had mutinied against him and threw him out of his ship, the *Bounty*. Bligh survived and returned to England, where he was found guilty of abuse to sailors by the British military. Nevertheless, he was subsequently sent off to Sydney, the capital of New South Wales, to rule the region. Bligh viewed the former governor as a figure of travesty, "the ridicule of the

Captain William Bligh.

community: sentences of death have been pronounced in moments of intoxication; his determination is weak, his opinion floating and infirm; his knowledge of law is insignificant and subservient to private inclination."[18] But Bligh himself soon got into trouble. Seeing widespread starvation, he decided to prohibit the practice of paying for rum with some commodity or service. He set up harsh punishments for breaking that rule.

Bligh's downfall was MacArthur. In 1807, he ordered MacArthur's copper boilers to be sent back to England. Then, when a convict tried to escape in a boat partly owned by MacArthur, Governor Bligh captured that boat. MacArthur blasted out a complaint. Bligh had him arrested. MacArthur went to court, where he damned the judge, who owed him money, then told the six military court officers that Bligh was creating great trouble for the citizens and their property. The court became confused; it adjourned, letting MacArthur go free. But next morning, Bligh had him arrested again. This time, the six military court officers asked Bligh to release MacArthur, but Bligh refused and charged them with treason. At that point, the top officer of the military declared himself "Lieutenant Governor," signed an order to release MacArthur, and sent a message to Bligh demanding that he submit to arrest. The "Lieutenant Governor" ordered a military parade celebrating the twentieth anniversary of the first English landing at New South Wales, with flags waving and a band playing "The British Grenadiers." The troops marched into Bligh's quarters, seized him, and hauled him away. "Martial law" was proclaimed. Bligh sailed to the nearby island of Van Diemen's Land, and the "Rum Corps" took over New South Wales. [19]

THE BIRTH OF DEMOCRACY?
TROUBLE BY GOVERNORS AND WORKERS

Bligh and MacArthur exemplify, respectively, governmental uncertainty and military domination in the original colony of Australia. But in this early-nineteenth-century confusion, democracy began. Force continued to be pervasive, but law began to control it.

Given the troubles of workers in England, many probably wanted to take off across the sea, but few could afford the fare. Instead, most of the citizens who arrived in Australia voluntarily were enterprising farmers and businessmen. In Australia, when convicts finished their terms as prisoners, they were free to work for themselves. Their children were born free, and they could grow up to pursue their own endeavors. As experienced farmers from England took over more land and requested convicts to work for them, more and more convicts were assigned to that relatively more liberated work. Some worked as individuals—the one assigned worker on the farm. In New South Wales, convicts working on private farms increased from 38 in 1790 to 356 in 1800 to 10,800 in 1825. [20]

A Scottish administrator named Lachlan Macquarie was appointed governor after the Bligh fiasco. Robert Hughes, author of *The Fatal Shore*, a history of Australian settlement, describes Macquarie as "the man who cleaned up this system," the one who "began the inchmeal conversion of a jail into a colony." [21] Macquarie arrived on the first day of 1810, with his wife and his own military regiment. He had been ordered to arrest the enterprising MacArthur and the "Lieutenant Governor," but they had already sailed back to England. Bligh returned from Van Diemen's Land, raging against the way he had been treated, but Macquarie ignored him, so Bligh sailed back to England, where he died in 1817. Thus Macquarie held "all reins in his hand":

> Macquarie canceled all the civilian and military appointments and revoked all the pardons, leases and land grants made in Sydney between January 26, 1808, the day of the Rum Rebellion, and his own arrival. He reinstated all dismissed officers and got rid of MacArthur's drunken stooge of a judge-advocate, Richard Atkins, replacing him with Ellis Bent (1783–1815), the first decently trained professional lawyer to hold office in Australia, who came out with him on the same ship from England. [22]

Powerful though Macquarie was, he could not eliminate the troubles, especially the growing economic complexity and the wide range of hunger for rum. He ordered that bars be shut down every Sunday and that convicts parade to church and other requirements. He did not hate convicts; in fact, he thought they probably ought to join him at his table for dinner.[23] Though he did not doubt they had deserved to be punished, he believed they could be rehabilitated by work. Macquarie established the *rights* of convicts: the right to food, shelter, and protection from a master's punishment. The Crown of England saw convicts as "legally dead under civil law from their arrival in Australia to their emancipation." They had no rights to sue or be sued, or to witness in court. But given that the white population of Australia consisted mostly of convicts and ex-convicts, that lack of rights was impractical. The convicts were legally slaves, but they believed that because they worked, they had rights. Working for masters on farms, the convicts typically ate what the masters ate. Some claimed rights to tea, sugar, and tobacco. It was rare that an individual convict could bring his or her master to court, but convicts who worked together actually did join in such efforts at times. Convicts in Sydney, under the sight of the regime, got treated more fairly than many other convicts isolated on far-off farms. Rights by law, once put into practice, became established as ordinary and appropriate.[24]

Still, convicts' rights were limited: they did not include the right to vote or freedom of speech, for example. Even in Macquarie's time, the name "Australia" continued to be "a term of abuse" in England.[25] Governor Macquarie ruled somewhat like a king:

> All political decisions ran through his hands, who got land, where and how much, who got labour, who was pardoned, freed or sent to a penal station, what religions were celebrated, other than the established rites of the Church of England, and at what hours; who filled administrative positions, what could be said in the colony's empryonic press—a thousand matters, loaded or trivial, down to the vexed question of which side of the road the chaotic, ever increasing traffic should move on....Nowhere in the British Empire did a proconsul have wider social power than in penal Australia.[26]

Still, law existed, rights were defined, punishment required trial. Subsequently, a judge of the Australian Supreme Court declared that "the rights of prisoners were as sacred in the eye of the law as those of the free men."[27]

Given all the violence in Australia, it was not surprising that even children played flogging games—thanks in part to their lack of education and their parents' ignorance, typically unable to even sign their names. More than half the children were illegitimate. But, as often happens with children born of immigrants, the young turned away from the difficult lives of their parents and sought a better future. The hope of liberty spread.[28]

The governor following Macquarie was another Scot, Sir Thomas Brisbane. He authorized a free-press newspaper, *The Australian*. As he was leaving office in 1825, Governor Brisbane let the editor, W.C. Wentworth, bring together friends for "the first public political meeting of any kind ever held in Australia."[29] Back in 1823, the British Parliament had created legislative councils for New South Wales and Van Diemen's Land, their members to be appointed by the governor. The mainland council could approve the governor's measures and give him advice, but it could not conduct public debates.[30] In 1828, the British Parliament expanded the council to 15 members, but members were still appointed, not elected. In New South Wales, the transport of convicts was finally abolished in 1840. At that time, only about 12 percent of the Australian people were convicts. Then, in 1842, the legislative council was enlarged, and 24 of the 36 members were allowed to initiate public debate. The poor were rarely represented, because a "representative" had to own at least £2,000 in property. But at least they were elected.[31]

These were the beginnings of democracy: one free-press newspaper and a partially elected legislature. There was a long way to go.

HEAVY TROUBLES PERSIST

Convict life on the island of Van Diemen's Land was even worse than in New South Wales. For years, men were flogged at length, not only for physical rebellion against their condition, but even for complaining verbally about it (verbal complaint was termed "rebelliousness" or "insolence").[32] If a convict who had been promoted in charge of other convicts behaved badly, he would be punished by being stripped and thrown back among the same convicts he had been bossing.[33] More than 2,000 boys between 9 and 18 years of age were transported from England.[34] The black natives were slaughtered for years, typically women and children first.[35] At one point, natives were imprisoned and given clothing, new names, Bibles, and schooling, and taught how to buy and sell, as well as how to elect their own police. But to them that was a strange experience. It did not work. Many of them died.[36]

Convicts sent to Norfolk Island, the "ocean hell" off the coast of New South Wales, suffered so much that they invented a desperate game: they would meet and draw straws to specify one to be killed and one to kill him. A convict killed a convict. Then the authorities captured the killer and the witnesses and sent them off to Sydney, on the continent, for trial. Sent there, those convicts had a more likely chance to escape—off into the bush.[37] Punishment on Norfolk Island was brutal. Two convicts who made mistakes planting corn got 300 lashes apiece. Each of the following "crimes" resulted in 100 lashes: "For saying 'O My God' while on the Chain for Mutiny," "Smiling while on the Chain," "Striking an overseer who pushed him," "Insolence to the Sentry," "Singing a Song," and "Neglect of work."[38] Some convicts blinded themselves in the hope of being left alone.[39]

In 1824, largely because his fellow officers in Sydney detested him, Captain Patrick Logan was sent to take charge of the convicts in Moreton Bay, to the north of Sydney. There he established a special punishment prison. After a year, suicide was frequent: prisoners murdered one another so they themselves could be hanged, they fled to the bush to be killed by natives, they drowned themselves, cut open their veins so they would bleed to death, and deliberately misbehaved so they would be killed. Captain Logan gave prizes to his floggers. New convicts arriving had to march straight from their ship down a road where

Logan, riding his black horse, whipped them if they lagged. They had to work in the most brutal heat. If they were whipped for work failure, Logan would watch the flogging, and if the flogger did not whip hard enough, Logan would cut down the victim and order the flogger to be flogged.[40]

In 1825, Van Diemen's Land became a separate colony with its own legislative council, but this was nothing but a "rubber stamp" council governed by the governor.[41] There were public meetings in 1831 and 1832 and a "constitutional association" was founded in 1835, but both were ignored by the government.[42] The governor proposed setting up a Licensing Act so he could control the press, but the British government refused to allow it, so the governor sued his critics for libel and succeeded in sending several to jail.[43]

HOPE RETURNS

Despite more brutality toward prisoners on Van Diemen's Land and elsewhere, the movement against violence grew in Australia. One pioneer in that movement was Caroline Chisholm, who arrived at Sydney Cove in 1838. There she discovered thousands of "brides," many teenagers, living destitute and homeless. More than 600 women preferred to sleep on the rocky shore of the sea, not beside the street where they were subject to rape. Chisholm charged forward in a crusade to protect the women from vice. She traveled thousands of miles to find them jobs or respectable husbands. She worked to transform a country of "rough bachelors and wayward girls" into one of families who would care for their children. Her heroic work saved lives and helped build Australian society.[44]

Alexander Maconochie, another pioneer in that movement, was a lawyer's son from Scotland who had suffered two years of misery as a prisoner of war before he became a professor of geography in a London university. At the instigation of London's Society for the Improvement of Prison Discipline, he took a 67-point questionnaire about the treatment of prisoners to Van Diemen's Land to research conditions there in 1837. When Maconochie arrived, he found the convict system "cruel, uncertain, prodigal, ineffectual; either for reform or example...."[45] Given his character, he had to take action:

> The cause has got me complete....I will go the whole hog on it....I will neither acquiesce in the moral destruction of so many of my fellow beings nor in misrepresentation made of myself, without doing *everything* that may be necessary or possible to assist both.[46]

He decided that the goal of prison should be shifted from punishment to reform: "Let us offer our prisoners, not favors, but *rights,* on fixed and unalterable conditions."[47] Further: *"The fate of every man should be placed unreserveably in his own hands....There should be no favor anywhere."*[48]

When Maconochie and his family sailed back to England, he received the assignment to return to Australia with 300 new English convicts destined for Norfolk Island, next to New South Wales. After landing as the new commander

Caroline Chisolm.

of the prison there, he called together the "Old Hands"—1,200 convicts—and told them he had not come as their torturer, but as one determined to treat them as *English* prisoners—with rights. Cheers broke forth from the convicts. They stopped crime and moved for reform.

Maconochie refused to separate the old and new prisoners, though the governor rebuked him for it. To celebrate the birthday of Queen Victoria, on May 24, 1840, he declared a holiday for everyone on the island—including the convicts, many of whom were astonished to wake up and look out and see the great gates of the walled prison wide open! He let them wander out, go swimming in the sea, lie on the beach. There was special food and drink for that day. As Maconochie wandered among the convicts, he raised a toast to the queen. They cheered her "three times three," and then toasted him even more loudly. The convicts made music—even opera—and in the afternoon they played sports. When night came, Maconochie provided fireworks, which "banged and glittered over the prison compounds." An amazing event, at which he noted "not a single irregularity, or even anything approaching an irregularity, took place.... [E]very man quietly returned to his ward, some even anticipated the hour."[49]

When the colonists in Sydney heard of that celebration, they were shocked and infuriated. Leaders took action to push away Maconochie. He requested books for the convicts, stocking their library with moral and religious texts as well as the works of Shakespeare. He thought theatrical training could help them overcome their passions. And because he saw music as healthful, he requested trumpets, fifes, horns, drums, cymbals and seraphims, and bought music paper for them. Other officials were skeptical. Criticizing Maconochie, one declared "doubt whether he will be ever able himself to work it out" because the way "he has encouraged the Prisoners to entertain must…diminish his influence over them."[50]

Maconochie tried hard to influence the convicts. "I bade them stand up like Men, whomsoever they addressed," he wrote, and he engaged them "to act as Jurors, Pleaders, Accusers, or otherwise, as the Case may be."[51] He tore down the gallows used for hanging convicts and decreed that dead convicts would be buried with headstones or painted boards above them, not merely thrown into a hole in the ground. Through several years, he got 920 twice-convicted prisoners discharged to Sydney to begin a new life, and by 1845 only 20 of them—just 2 percent—were arrested again and reconvicted.

Though the governor saw Maconochie's system as partially good, he complained to London that Maconochie had gone too far:

> Captain Maconochie fancies himself supreme….He has contended for absolute Power….[A] most radical Change is wanted here immediately. The Place bears no more Resemblance to what a Penal settlement should be than a Playhouse does to a Church. The Public works are neglected for want of mere Labour, the Roads which were made with so much Pains [sic] are falling into Decay;…the Crops are wholly insufficient to supply the Establishment. Idleness and Insubordination prevail to a shameful extent.[52]

On April 29, 1843, Maconochie was recalled and dismissed by Lord Stanley, Britain's secretary of state for the colonies, though Lord Stanley did write that "I gladly acknowledge that his efforts appear to have been rewarded by the decline of crimes of violence and outrage, and by the growth of humane and kindly feelings in the minds of the person under his care."[53] But, as Robert Hughes points out, "the moment of reform clanged shut."[54] At the same time, the flow of voluntary immigrants from England slowed down, especially to Van Diemen's Land: in 1842, 1,446 had arrived, but in 1843, only 26 came, and in 1844, only one. In the first half of 1845, about 5 percent of the population—1,628 settlers—left that territory.[55]

MONARCHICAL VIRTUE?

Maconochie's achievement was substantial, but it was not democratic. Maconochie was the type of kindly "king" who makes monarchial government look wonderful. But a kindly king can be succeeded by a very different type of king—one whose policy is to inflict terror. And, in a monarchial system, his rule would still be legitimate. That is the horror of monarchy, even when a King Maconochie rules well.

On Norfolk Island, Maconochie was replaced by John Giles Price, who went before the prisoners in 1846 and said:

> You know me, don't you? I am come here to rule, and by God I'll do so and tame or kill you. I know you are cowardly dogs, and I'll make you worry and eat one another. [56]

Price reinstituted a regime of harsh force:

> One prisoner was flogged for mislaying his shoelaces. A man named Peart got seven days in chains for saying "good morning" to the wrong person. Another was seen walking along waving a twig; a constable saw him and demanded to know what he was up to and where he was going. "Why, I might be after a parrot," the prisoner replied, and was flogged. A cart-driver came before Price on the charge of "having a tamed bird" and got 36 lashes....It had been the custom among the convicts to wash the back of a newly flogged man, to press down his mangled skin and dress it with cool banana leaves; Price had anyone seen with a banana leaf in his possession summarily punished. [57]

But at least the numbers of convicts diminished, thanks to an economic depression in England, from 1847 to 1849, some 30,000 free emigrants sailed from England to New South Wales. The Legislative Council of New South Wales became more concerned about the cruelty inflicted on convicts. And the hope for democracy rose again, thanks to a politician named Henry Parkes.

ATTEMPTS TO STOP TYRANNY

Henry Parkes, an Australian politician, drafted an antitransportation resolution, which he presented to the Legislative Council as a "deliberate and solemn protest":

> FIRSTLY—Because it is in violation of the will of the majority of the colonists, as is clearly evinced by their expressed opinions on this question at all times.
> SECONDLY—Because numbers among us have emigrated on the faith of the British Government, that transportation to this colony had ceased forever.
> THIRDLY—Because it is incompatible with our existence as a free colony, desiring self-government, to be receptable of another country's felons.
> FOURTHLY—Because it is in the highest degree unjust, to sacrifice the great social and political interests of the colony at large to the pecuniary profit of a faction of its inhabitants.
> FIFTHLY—Because...we greatly fear that the perpetration of so stupendous an act of injustice...will go far in alienating the affections of the people of this colony from the mother country. [58]

The Legislative Council approved this protest, partly because of the support of Councilman Robert Lowe, who saw it as an act of revolution for liberty: "In all times, and in all nations, so will injustice and tyranny ripen into rebellion, and rebellion into independence." [59]

The Council pressed the governor to adopt the resolution. He agreed to send it on to London, though he added that those against bringing more convicts to Australia were merely a faction linked to a mob. But the protest widened. An Anti-Transportation League was formed by three community leaders: a publisher, a landowner, and a minister.

In Great Britain, the government acknowledged the protests, as did the press, which came out strongly against the continued transportation of prisoners. As a practical matter, Britain's available prison space had increased, so that it was now more expensive to send convicts to Australia than to jail them in England. But some convicts were sent to Western Australia, far away on the other side of the continent, until 1868, despite the protest of the Australian Intercolonial Conference. When yet another ship full of convicts arrived at the city of Melbourne, down south on the east coast, citizens demanded it be barred from anchoring; it simply sailed on to Sydney and left its 295 convicts there. Two more ships came over, putting ashore a total of 593 prisoners at Sydney. But those were the final transports of convicts. After the last of the convicts left Norfolk Island, the island was inhabited by the descendants of Fletcher Christian and his shipmates—who had done the mutiny on the *Bounty* against Captain Bligh. Living there with their Tahitian women, they tore down all the prisons. [60] The vicious transport was over. Protest had turned out to be effective. The Englishman in charge of the colonies, Lord Grey, retired.

In 1851, Australian's discovered gold. (Actually, it was a California "forty-niner" who found the first big gold strike.) The nuggets were huge. The largest ever, weighing 141 pounds and worth thousands of dollars, was found in clay only a foot or so under the ground. Generally, to get at Australian gold did not require digging out tough rocks, just clay; in the streams, the water was waiting to be panned for gold. As in America, there was a frenzied gold rush. Workers left ships, farms, mines, and factories to go get gold in Australia. In one month, September 1852, 19,000 foreigners landed in Melbourne and thousands more in Sydney. Forty thousand Chinese had come by 1857. In 1851, Australia's population was only 405,000; by 1861, it was 1,146,000—nearly tripled. [61]

VIOLENCE BY BUSHRANGERS

One Australian was persuaded that the great gold discovery "must in a few years precipitate us from a colony to a nation." [62] But the different colonies did not get together fast. Violent thieves organized their own mini-nations. As early as 1824, nearly one out of seven convicts on Van Diemen's Land escaped into the bush. Soon the escapees began to team together for survival. [63] Later many "wild colonial boys" and other troubled citizens joined these teams of outlaws, called "bushrangers." [64]

The romantic view was that the bushrangers were like Robin Hood and his merry men. They lived by stealing from the rich to help the poor. Blackening their faces with charcoal, the bushrangers would accost both travelers and home folks and demand they pass over their money or gold. [65] They stole rings and watches and used them to decorate their horses' bridles. Killing happened. J.B. Hirst describes how these bushrangers operated:

> The gangs robbed from rich and poor and made no attempt to pretend otherwise. They robbed gold-diggers, foot-travellers, carriers, Chinese and storekeepers. They took money from children and turned their horses out to feed in a poor man's crop. The only limitations the bushrangers placed on themselves were not to harm and distress women and not to take silver coins: they were prepared to leave travellers enough money to continue their journey. The bushrangers were comprehensive robbers. They held up all the travellers who passed on a road, robbed all the occupants of a coach, captured a whole town. They did not want to discriminate; to rob all was to show that they were master of all. The bushrangers were not highlighting or redressing injustice and oppression; they were displaying their own skill, daring and command. Their hatred was directed at the police and to anyone else who would stop them. [66]

There were growing anti-British sentiments because of the way Britain dominated them. Australians—even lawyers—tolerated or even admired the bushrangers. For instance, one judge said that highway robbery was a "step towards refinement and at least a manly method of taking property." [67] Farmers and drivers learned to live with these violent thieves because the police were unable to catch them. One famous robber, Ned Kelly, said of the police that he was "not a bit afraid of them and know if they alone hunted me I would never be taken." Kelly and his gang once raided a police station, locked the police in their own cells, took their uniforms, and donned them themselves. [68] And the bushrangers made it clear that they would harm those who told the police where they were. [69] They regarded the police as tyrants who deserved to die if they ventured into bushranger territory. One bushranger advised his comrades to *shoot every tyrant you come across.*" [70]

First the government had used force to torment prisoners. Now it let free thieves use violence against the rest of the population.

UNIFYING THE POLICE

Australian police were typically foreigners brought in by the British government; they were unfamiliar with both the people and the bush. Moreover, there were far too few of them to give the bushrangers any serious trouble. The police tried to enlist the help of natives—some of whom helped them—but the natives were too few to make a difference. In the first five months of 1835, mounted policemen in New South Wales caught 220 bushrangers and runaways, but many more escaped to the bush.[71] The police tried scare tactics: they would bind the arms of a prisoner standing on the ground, tie him to a horse, and ride the horse so that the man had to run hard to keep up with it. But until 1862, the police were not organized across the different districts. There were no police stations, no police uniforms, no procedural rules or shared information.[72] Efforts to unify the control of the Australian police in 1850 failed because local magistrates opposed any loss of their own authority.[73]

A national official named Charles Cowper tried to unify the police of the nation, but had only minor success. So he came up with a new plan to make the laws more severe for robbers. His Felons Apprehension Act, passed by the new Legislative Council, declared bushrangers outlaws whom anyone (not just the police) could take, dead or alive. Penalties for thieving included not only jail terms but the loss of property as well as the confiscation of their horses. Many legislators disliked the severity of the Felons Apprehension Act, but since efforts to unify the police had failed, they passed it. The main result of the act was an increase in the climate of violence and an erosion of legitimate police authority. As K.S. Inglis notes, "Nearly all the bushrangers were eventually caught or shot by the police, but the reputation of the police...was as low as it had been at any time since the force was founded five years before."[74]

Finally, in 1862, the national government took control of the police. In every town and district, a paid national official was clearly in charge of combating crime and a range of other enforcements, including overseeing school attendance, the cleanliness of dairies, the storage of gunpowder, and the care of orphans and neglected children boarded with families. These officials distributed food to newly arrived immigrants, natives, and sick people, and collected local information for the government.[75] In short, the government of Australia began.

When the government took control of physical force, the wild, diverse chaos of the bushrangers era ended. With the transfer of legal and political control from the local villages to Sydney, there was national unity. But though the continent was united, *democracy* was not yet achieved. For that, a constitution requiring rule by elected representatives had to be composed, approved, made public and put into effect throughout the nation.

THE CONSTITUTION MOVEMENT STARTS UP

From the start, Australia was a military society. Its government was a military government whose authority was based on Britain's Articles of War, written in 1749. Under those articles, the government was not answerable to the citizens, but to the king.

The town of Sydney in New South Wales (NSW) was the government's headquarters, ruled by a governor appointed by the king. His authority, absolute at first, was gradually eroded through successive reforms. As early as 1825, the governor was authorized to name a Legislative Council—though it consisted of government officials, not representatives of the public, and only had the power to approve measures the governor decided to submit to it. In 1828, the British Parliament increased the size of the NSW Council and allowed it to express "opinions." In 1842, the Council was expanded to 36 members, 24 of whom were elected locally. But only citizens who owned land worth £200 or own a house worth £20 a year had the right to vote.[76] "Popular opinion" was not respected by either the governor or the relatively aristocratic councilors.[77] In 1853, the Council changed its own constitution and created an elected Legislative Assembly. The Legislative Council, whose members were now all picked by the governor, became the "upper house." Thus, over the years, the governor lost his absolute authority,[78] and the right to vote spread somewhat: a citizen could vote if he owned land worth £100 or a house worth £10 a year.[79] There was increasing pressure to balance the legislative power of the governor and his Council and to better link the legislature with the people.[80] But the reality of government by consent of the governed was yet to happen, as was the control of force by democracy.

Soon after the discovery of Australia, the population started to spread out across the continent. The land was divided into separate colonies, all ruled by Britain's Crown Colony in New South Wales. But New South Wales was very far from London, and the new colonies were far enough from New South Wales so that, in practice, there was self-government by local commanders. As early as 1851, federal relationships began to develop: the Australasian League was established in Melbourne by delegates from the colonies of Victoria and Tasmania to oppose transportation of convicts. The league members saw Britain as making "divers promises" to stop transportation while in fact sending over "enormous masses." They designed a "handsome banner," deep blue, which eventually became the flag of an independent Australia. But there was still plenty of division; and the New South Wales government typically saw newer colonies as flouting NSW power and wisdom.[81] Through most of the nineteenth century, Australia was not seriously in danger of being invaded by another country's military. If it had been, that danger might have awakened the colonies to the need for federation.[82] But near the end of the century, the threat of invasion did arise, hastening a real coalition of force within Australia.

The governing of Australia became increasingly complex and representative in the nineteenth century, yet fell far short of democracy. Violence continued, with thieving and flogging and killing. It wasn't until the twentieth century that definite, effective democracy emerged under the leadership of Alfred Deakin.

AUSTRALIA'S LEADER FOR DEMOCRACY: ALFRED DEAKIN

Alfred Deakin became prime minister of Australia three times in the early 1900s. Australian democracy, especially the elected government's strong control over force, owes much to his heroic, unceasing efforts.

Born in Australia on August 3, 1856, Alfred was the son of a coach driver who had tried to find gold but wound up serving the gold searchers instead. Not rich, he nevertheless managed to keep his family in a modest house and give his children a good education. Young Alfred loved to read. He often read aloud at home, to his mother and sister. His mother, he recalled, had a "sweetness, patience and loving kindness." In contrast, his father seemed "more impatient, irritable, excitable, impetuous, eager, imaginative, sanguine, explosive than he really was." [83] In fact, his father hardly ever hit his son, but spoke reasonably and articulately to him and urged him to read. The encouragement paid off: Alfred liked school.

Alfred Deakin went to the University of Melbourne, where he dreamed of being a poet, a playwright, or a philosopher, but decided to become a lawyer. He did some school teaching and private tutoring. During law school he became interested in politics, took part in debates, and writing. At age 20, he was six feet tall with a dark beard and mustache, glowing eyes, and a powerful speaking voice.

In March 1877, Deakin became a lawyer, but his practice brought him few clients, so he spent much of his time writing poetry and focusing on parliamentary politics. For income, he wrote for a Melbourne newspaper called *Age*, an experience that deepened his interest in politics, writing such articles as "Politics in Australia." After five years of journalism, he had a reputation as a "Liberal," concerned for suffering people. When he was only 22, the newspaper publisher persuaded Deakin to run for local office. Deakin lost in close elections several times before he finally made it into parliament, where he sought to form a coalition for reform by bringing together the moderates of both parties. He wished, he said, "to bring about an honorable union of parties." [84] A reform bill passed in June 1881, and later that year, the first bill Deakin himself introduced, "to tighten the law for the protection of cruelty to animals," also passed. [85]

He fell in love, got married, and became the father of three children—all daughters. In his 20s, Deakin was strongly drawn to religion, becoming a leader of the "Spiritualists." He wrote a 260-page book titled *A New Pilgrim's Progress* that expressed his desire for an active religion concerned with improving human lives in the material world. He read the Christian Bible, but also the bibles of the Buddhists and the Hindus, from which he gained "insights." He described his religious belief this way: "We require to take sides in life" and "To love God is to love Goodness as a power, a principle and a person.... To love man is to love the ideal, the Perfect Man...." [86] Deakin left the Church of England and joined the Australian Church, which had been founded in the 1880s. In private, he composed prayers, 400 of which he wrote down between 1884 and 1913. He hoped God would help him see what to do: "Show me my path!" he prayed, because he had his "Birthday 29 and nothing done."

Deakin's dream was to bring Australians together to create a nation: "I especially desire to devote what energies I have to the Federal Cause...." [87] He was seen as a "federal leader." [88] He joined and helped lead the new Australian Natives' Association, which started with 235 members in 1880 and expanded to 17,000 members by 1900.

Deakin worked hard for the federal cause. He spent time in the United States and England, exploring those countries' laws as models for forming practical law for Australia in such areas as irrigation and factory life. In an 1883 meeting on Colonial Governments in London, Deakin defended his homeland and spoke out against the British decision to allow France to send convicts to Australia. Thousands of miles off from Australia, he said, Britain was bound to mistake Australia's needs. Unlike some others, he did not oppose Britain as "imperial" power with "colonial" interests, but he insisted that substantial changes were necessary in his country's relationship with Britain. His main theme was the federal unification of Australia. The meeting ended with few results, but at least Deakin had strongly articulated his democratic values: "equality of opportunity," "resistance to and destruction of class privileges," "equality of political rights without reference to creed, and without consideration of wealth or quality." [89]

After Deakin returned to London in 1887 to attend an Imperial Conference, he noted:

> If disputes ever do arise between Great Britain and Australia, surely they are much more likely to be settled in a way that would meet with the approbation of the people of these colonies, when we are united in voice and in aim, if our representations went home backed up by the high authority of a federal Parliament and a federal Government....[O]ne of the greatest difficulties which arose in connexion with the Imperial Conference...was that the representatives of the colonies could not settle their differences among themselves, so as to present a united front to the Imperial Government. [90]

When controversy spread in Australia, including labor strikes and demands by marine officers, Deakin argued that "The State would not interfere one jot or one tittle with the present conflict at this stage, but at all stages it would feel bound to preserve order..." [91] Deakin became the government's chief secretary, thus responsible for the police. He sought order—not violence. Strikes were allowed, but killing and shooting were not:

> What we have done may save the city from disorder, and riot, and pillage, but it will also mean in all probability the exclusion of every one of us from political life for all time to come. We have sought to avoid the possibility of bloodshed; we have done the right thing and we will not retreat from it, but we shall pay the penalty whether we succeed or fail. [92]

Deakin did, in fact, step down from leadership, but he continued as a member of the parliament and he stayed resolute in his purpose.

In March 1891, delegates from all six Australian colonies and New Zealand met at Sydney for the National Australasian Convention, called to plan federation. The youngest delegate was Alfred Deakin, who wrote this prayer: "Grant me wisdom and courage to scorn all other considerations except that of furthering Thy Will for the benefit of my fellow countrymen." [93] As founder of the new Federation League, he led the discussions to move federation forward.

The election for a national convention to create a constitution was set for March 1897. There, too, Deakin was the major activist. He remembered that "after an all-night sitting and under conditions of great nervous exhaustion and irritability, we have practically completed the draft bill for the Constitution of the Australian Commonwealth."[94] New South Wales initially rejected the proposal by one vote, then later approved it. Deakin and his allies arrived in London on March 11, 1900, and presented the proposal for federation to the British government. For three months, Britain's prime minister and his allies worked to revise the constitution to maintain Britain's power over Australia. But the Australians were not there to compromise. They were there to explain their demands. Serious discussions began. Before they were over, a war in Africa showed Australians just how subordinate they and their government were, under the old system, to the imperial government in London.

THE NEW RELATIONSHIP WITH BRITAIN

In July 1899, Britain had gone to war in South Africa against the Boer republics. Though 16,000 Australian volunteers went off to that war, the Australian government was scarcely consulted by the British government. Deakin, then acting prime minister of the Commonwealth, was notified, late, that a peace treaty had finally been signed. The Australian government had had no say in the decisions to go to war, how to fight that war, or when to end it. The experience led Australians to ask: Should the colonies automatically support every war that the government in London decided to engage in? Deakin answered: "I say No." Not only that Australians would necessarily refuse to help Britain, but they believed that decision should be up to them. As a loyalist, Deakin wanted to support Britain, but only by federal decision making. Years earlier, he had recommended that the colony of Victoria work up its own naval defense.

Back in 1860, Britain had set up a Royal Commission to defend the colonies. At the 1887 Colonial Conference, the Australian colonies agreed to contribute large funds for naval protection forces, provided those forces could not be withdrawn from Australia to be used elsewhere without the consent of the seven colonial governments.[95] Deakin's view was that "if you ask me whether our present action is likely to be used as a precedent for committing the colonies to spontaneous support of any and every war in which the Imperial authorities may engage, I say No."[96]

The new Australian constitution, confirmed in 1901, provided a clear and worthy democratic system as to who would decide what regarding force. Up to today, that constitution has not been changed in any fundamental way.[97]

The Commonwealth of Australia Constitution Act stated clearly who would control the military:

> 5. This Act, and all laws made by the Parliament of the Commonwealth under the Constitution, shall be binding on the courts, judges, and people of every State and of every part of the Commonwealth, notwithstanding anything in the laws of any State: and the laws of the Commonwealth shall be in force on all British ships, the Queen's ships of war excepted, whose first port of clearance and whose port of destination are in the Commonwealth.

The governor-general, appointed by the British monarch, was given authority to arrange Parliament meetings and other responsibilities, to decide about "the Queen's pleasure." But at the same time, the governor-general was "subject to this Constitution."

The major new change in Australia's government was declared in "Part V.—Powers of the Parliament," which contained provisions specifying control of force, in the military and throughout the nation.

> 51. The Parliament shall, subject to this Constitution, have power to make laws for the peace, order, and good government of the Commonwealth with respect to:…

The following areas of Parliament control were included:

> (vi.) The naval and military defence of the Commonwealth and of the several States, and the control of the forces to execute and maintain the laws of the Commonwealth.…
>
> (xxiv.) The service and execution throughout the Commonwealth of the civil and criminal process and the judgments of the courts of the States; (xxv.) The recognition throughout the Commonwealth of the laws, the public Acts and records, and the judicial proceedings of the States;

The power of the people's elected Parliament was made even clearer:

> 52. The Parliament shall, subject to this Constitution, have exclusive power to make laws for the peace, order, and good government of the Commonwealth with respect to—
>
> (i.) The seat of government of the Commonwealth, and all places acquired by the Commonwealth for public purposes:
>
> (ii.) Matters relating to any department of the public service the control of which is by this Constitution transferred to the Executive Government of the Commonwealth:
>
> (iii.) Other matters declared by this Constitution to be within the exclusive power of the Parliament.

And the Constitution set forth how the federated country would relate to the States in controlling force:

> 118. Full faith and credit shall be given, throughout the Commonwealth, to the laws, the public Acts and records, and the judicial proceedings of every State.
>
> 119. The Commonwealth shall protect every State against invasion and, on the application of the Executive Government of the State, against domestic violence.
>
> 120. Every State shall make provision for the detention in its prisons of persons accused or convicted of offences against the laws of the Commonwealth, and for the punishment of persons convicted of such offences, and the Parliament of the Commonwealth may make laws to give effect to this provision.[98]

The constitution of 1901 provided the fundamental law for the modern democracy of Australia. Eventually, all adult citizens had the right to vote. And they voted in secret, so they would be protected from coercion by their employers and others. This innovative "Australian ballot" was later imitated by other democracies, including the United States.

The military which had once been composed primarily of British troops, had become Australian troops. In 1870, the last British regiments withdrew from the country. Now Australia started its own navy, as called for in the constitution. So, in 1901, the Commonwealth of Australia assumed control of all defense matters throughout the nation, though some Australians worried about "how they could defend their country adequately and at the same time avoid the evils of militarism."[99] In 1902, at a Colonial Conference in London, Australia agreed to pay each year for naval protection. They organized a small, volunteer army in Australia that would be available for service wherever and whenever the British required it.[100]

In 1905, Deakin became prime minister of Australia. Still, Deakin was concerned that Australia lacked enough naval defense—for example, against possible attack from Japan, then at war with Russia. He even looked to America, inviting the U.S. fleet to sail to Sydney, which it did, to the excitement of the public. Until 1910, he kept trying to negotiate with Britain on naval defense, though he was careful to maintain that "when we do take a part in naval defence, we shall be entitled to a share in the direction of foreign affairs."[101] Under the new constitution, he could make such proposals, but the elected parliament had to decide them. Over in England, the slogan was "Trust the Navy!"—their own navy. But the British took its military power. Deakin wanted an *Australian* navy for Australia. Formally, the British Admiralty agreed that any Australian navy would be ruled by Australia, though in an emergency, the command of Australia's navy might quickly be shifted to the British Admiral. Deakin also pressed for the birth of a national Australian army based on three years of required training. That proposal was left suspended.[102]

Deakin saw the problem of "Imperial organization" as the "towering problem of the time." To maintain the British Empire was the "greatest national issue now before mankind." He believed that Australia's defense system must be "visibly and concretely Australian in origin, but Imperial in end and value." It needed to "take a popular form in order to fulfil all its purpose." But Britain's Prime Minister insisted that "Control of naval defence and foreign affairs must always go together."[103] London was neither prepared to give Australia any real say in Europe's foreign policy nor to forge its claim on Australia's manpower in case of war.

By 1911, Deakin was encouraged by the "remarkable change in the attitude of our people generally towards defence."[104] There was some fear of a "military caste," but a newly organized National Defence League spread across the nation, its 21 branches dedicated to awakening "Australians to realize that the defence of our country is the duty of all."[105] Australia's Commonwealth Parliament passed the Defence Act for training soldiers, and the Governor-General put it into action. The defence was to be decided by the Parliament, as the Governor General declared: "If either House of Parliament passes a resolution, at any time within fourteen days after any regulation is laid before it, disallowing any such regulation, that regulation shall thereupon cease to have effect."[106]

THE SHOCK OF WORLD WAR: CHALLENGE TO AUSTRALIA'S FREEDOM

The military debate with Britain came to an abrupt stop in August 1914, when the "World War" broke out. Quickly, Australia's Commonwealth government offered 20,000 troops to be commanded by the British government. Militarily, Australians had a strong reputation, their soldiers known for leaping into battle, even individually. Minor fights in the past had shown that the Australian soldier

> is accustomed to habits of self-reliance; he expects to be treated as an individual and not as a machine....Colonial troops will be led, but won't be driven....They are composed of first-rate men, but not men accustomed to obey orders....[107]

Australians volunteered by the thousands. The first major order from London—in 1915—sent Australian soldiers quickly to Gallipoli, in Palestine. There, faced with shattering fire, the 30,000 Australian troops stormed a steep hill, dug in, and defended their position against twice as many enemies. After eight months, they were withdrawn, without having achieved a victory. Eight thousand five hundred and eighty-seven Australian men died at Gallipoli.[108] Their commander saw it as "the bloodiest tragedy in world history."[109]

Australia's, prime minister, William Morris Hughes, was infuriated at Britain's commanders: "There Australia had been in the vanguard, but was told nothing before the landing and nothing about the evacuation....[W]e had not been given an opportunity of expressing an opinion about an operation we had been warned might involve forty percent casualties." Prime Minister Hughes rushed to London and crashed into the War Office, demanding that a representative of Australia be included in the War Office. Hughes proposed a civilian, but instead the British immediately made Hughes himself an army general operating in the War Office.[110]

In 1916, Hughes declared that "If volunteers respond in sufficient numbers there will be no need for compulsion, but to the extent that voluntary recruiting fails to supply the numbers necessary, the Government will use the authority of the people, if given, to call to the colours until the supply of single men without dependents is exhausted."[111] The constitution authorized drafting men to fight within Australia, but it did *not* authorize drafting them to be sent overseas. So the hope was how citizens would vote in a referendum: "Yes" for conscription, rather than "No" for volunteers only.

The draft for overseas service did not win automatic support. For example, Sydney's newspaper, the *Worker*, protested:

> To permit a majority to vote to resolve such a question is, we say, a prostitution of the democratic system....There are matters beyond the jurisdiction of the ballot box. This is one of them. There are issues which only the individual conscience can rightly adjudicate upon. This is one of them....[A] majority verdict in favor of conscription would afford no moral justification for forcing men to fight against their will....You cannot, by counting heads, dispose of a question that belongs to the province of the soul. In this respect the personal will is supreme and sacred.[112]

Unfortunately, Australia's splendid constitution lacked one major feature: a bill of rights. The procedures of government were clear, but the right to vote was not clear. (There had been a lengthy controversy regarding specifying rights when the constitution was written.[113]) Therefore it was possible—even plausible—for the *Worker* to declare that every individual had the right to decide whether or not to go into the army in wartime.

On September 18, 1916, Prime Minister Hughes sent forth the following startling manifesto to the people of the nation:

> After more than two years of the most dreadful war the world has known, Australia is called upon to face the test of nationhood. We, boasting our freedom, are called upon to prove ourselves worthy to be free.
>
> Though Europe has been drenched with blood, innocent non-combatants foully murdered or subjected to unspeakable outrages, millions of helpless men, women, and little children driven from their homes, their beloved country ravaged by fire and sword, not the faintest breath of such horrors has touched these favoured shores. Though many of our brave soldiers have died on the battlefields, this nation in its own home has pursued its peaceful way as though war did not exist, secure and prosperous. But we, too, must now face the dread realities of war. We have made many sacrifices, but we know nothing of the agonies which France, Belgium, Russia and Serbia have endured.
>
> …Victory can only be achieved by a tremendous effort on the part of the Allies. And that effort must be made now….
>
> Our duty and our interests alike point the way we must go. I appeal to every individual citizen of Australia to sweep aside the mist of indifference, error, and misunderstanding, and face the great realities of the hour….
>
> …Our only hope of national safety, of retaining our liberties, lies in decisive victory by Britain and her Allies over the hosts of military despotism….But we are not asked to do more than our share. Up-to-date, we have sent over 220,000 men overseas, and have 44,000 on camp….Britain has put nine millions of men into this fight! And she is calling up more men! In the face of these facts, how can we say we are asked to do more than our share?
>
> We must supply the men asked for. It is the price we are asked to pay for our national existence and our liberties. We must get men; so much is certain. The question then is how shall we get them? It is, unfortunately, only too apparent that the voluntary system of recruiting our armies does not ensure them….No patriot can deny the necessity of reinforcements; no democrat can impugn the right of the nation to demand this duty from its citizens. Democracy and nationalism are one. The supreme duty which a democrat owes to his country is to fight for it. Others may fight for dynasties and despots, but Australians fight for Australia, for democracy against tyranny, liberty against oppression. Unless a nation fights for its liberties, it can never earn nor deserve them.
>
> …Not only to ourselves do we owe the duty of supreme endeavor in the present crisis of the world's affairs. We owe it to our gallant armies who daily rush into the very jaws of death, never doubting that the Australian people will stand behind them to the end. We owe it to our heroic dead, who have already offered up their lives upon the altar of their country. We owe it to Britain, to that mighty navy under whose broad wing we have been, and are, securely sheltered, and to those great and glorious armies of Britain who daily fight our battles. We owe it to the Allies, who have fought undismayed in the same cause that protects our freedom….
>
> …Australia must not fail. In the name of Australian Democracy I adjure every man and woman in the Commonwealth to vote 'Yes.'[114]

That remarkable appeal no doubt induced many Australians to vote "Yes" in the referendum on the draft.

DEMOCRACY GOES FORWARD IN THE MIDST OF CRISIS

Prime Minister Hughes' proposal was controversial: "Was it not the cursed military system that they were now trying to force on Australia?" [115] On the one hand, Hughes said that "Everybody will be allowed full freedom of speech." But on the other hand, he said that "under the cover of speaking against conscription it will not be permissible to preach sedition, to incite persons to refrain from enlisting, or to break the law of any State or the Commonwealth." He could make this threat in a nation that lacked a definite bill of rights.

Although some politicians opposed this control of speech by the government, and the Labour party made an official protest against the prime minister, [116] from the start of the war, the military cracked hard against free speech. For example, the editor of the *Australian Woman Voter*, a weekly newspaper run by the Women's Political Association, wrote that a military officer had told them they could not publish certain antiwar statements. Subsequently, the editor said, a flock of armed guards, with several police officers, "threatened to seize the printers' plant if I persisted in publishing the matter objected to...." Her protest was successful: government officials ridiculed the anti–free speech action as "hysterical." [117] Yet censorship continued, and even became more widespread. In response, strong resistance rose up, especially in the increasingly organized women's movement.

The debate on the referendum was harsh: "The opponents of conscription were denounced as cowards, traitors and scum. The conscriptionists were represented as blood-suckers, fanatics and potential murderers of their own kin." [118]

At last in the fall of 1916, Australian citizens got to vote on the question of the draft. Of all eligible voters, 82.75% came out to vote. There were 1,087,557 votes in favor of drafting, but 1,160,033 votes against it. [119] A second referendum on the issue produced a vote of 1,015,159 "Yes" and 1,181,747 "No." [120] Perhaps the "No" vote won because of the savagery of the war: nearly 60,000 Australian soldiers were dead when the World War ended on November 11, 1918. [121] Prime Minister Hughes signed the Treaty of Peace for Australia, subject to ratification by the Commonwealth Parliament. Hughes resigned as prime minister. [122]

Whether or not Australian citizens were right about the draft, the *procedure* of the referendum was clearly and significantly democratic. In a time of crisis, the people made the nation's most important decision regarding force, and they made it against the strong appeal of their top government leader and the coercion of the military. Strongly established within Australia was the principle that the citizens and their representatives, through their votes, are to control the national use of force.

Nevertheless, Australia remained a member of the British Commonwealth of Nations and continued to accept London's military leadership. After the First World War there came another World War when, on the 1st of September 1939, the German Nazis under Hitler invaded Poland. Britain, under Prime Minister Winston Churchill, declared war on Germany. Australian forces joined the cause, fighting in Africa, Greece, and Egypt. But then, in September 1940, Japan joined with Germany and Italy, increased its fight against China, and, by 1941, was reaching south into Indochina. What would happen if Japan attacked Australia? How would the military relationship with Britain operate? The answers were not clear.

Another Japanese move suddenly clarified the situation. On December 7, 1941, Japan made a surprise attack on American forces at Pearl Harbor. The United States declared war immediately and Australia's attention quickly turned toward America. Prime Minister John Curtin came out with a frank and realistic statement:

> Without any inhibitions of any kind, I make it quite clear that Australia looks to America, free of any pangs as to our traditional links of kinship with the United Kingdom. We know the problems that the United Kingdom faces. We know the constant threat of invasion. We know the dangers of dispersal of strength. But we know, too, that Australia can go and Britain still hold on. We are therefore determined that Australia shall not go, and we shall exert all our energies towards the shaping of a plan, with the United States as its keystone, which will give to our country some confidence of being able to hold out until the tide of battle swings against the enemy. [123]

As historian Clive Turnbull notes: "So ended the last legend, the belief in Australia's inviolability behind the shield of Britannia. Australia was alone." [124] Early in 1942, Churchill wanted Australian military forces to move into India, to defend the frontiers of the Empire, but instead, the Australian government ordered the troops back to Australia. [125] Churchill was "astounded"—but Australia's decision was carried out.

The memory of these events helped lead to the formal Australia Act of 1986, passed by both the parliament of Australia and the parliament of Britain, specified as "An Act to bring constitutional arrangements affecting the Commonwealth of Australia as a sovereign, independent and federal nation." [126]

AUSTRALIA'S ENDURING SUCCESS

The government of Australia, elected by the people of Australia, became a democracy in charge of all aspects of its own force, from its local prisons and police, to its national and international military power. Today Australia stands forth as a prime example of democracy. Its people achieved that democracy despite very heavy troubles: a nation founded as a prison camp and harshly threatened by wars. The achievement took many years, and happened primarily because leaders and citizens worked hard to ensure peace and safety for everyone.

Fortunately, many Australians understood how democracy had developed elsewhere, how it had been born and sustained. That knowledge proved significant. And given the hard, long battle to control force, courage was significant. Thanks to the achievement of democracy, Australians are a free people, using their energies and gifts to achieve the lives they want.

BIBLIOGRAPHY

BARNARD, MARJORIE. *A History of Australia.* Sydney: Angus & Robertson, 1963.

BARROW, SIR JOHN. *The Mutiny on the Bounty.* Boston: David R. Godine, 1980.

CAMERON, RODERICK. *Australia: History and Horizons.* New York: Columbia University Press, 1971.

CARROLL, JOHN (ED.). *Intruders in the Bush: The Australian Quest for Identity.* Melbourne: Oxford University Press, 1982.

Daedalus: Journal of the American Academy of Arts and Sciences. "Australia Terra Incognita?" Vol. 114, No. 1, Winter 1985.

DEAKIN, ALFRED. *The Federal Story: The Inner History of the Federal Cause.* Melbourne: Robertson & Mullens, 1944.

DORNBUSCH, C. E. *Australian Military Bibliography.* Cornwallville, N.Y.: Hope Farm Press, 1963.

FINNANE, MARK, (ED.). *Policing in Australia: Historical Perspectives.* Kensington: New South Wales University Press, 1987.

FOLKARD, FREDERICK C. *The Remarkable Australians.* Sydney: K.G. Murray, 1965.

GREY, JEFFREY. *A Military History of Australia.* Cambridge, England: Cambridge University Press, 1990.

GUNTHER, JOHN. *Inside Australia.* New York: Harper & Row, 1972.

HIRST, J.B. *The Strange Birth of Colonial Democracy: New South Wales, 1848–1884.* Sydney: Allen & Unwin, 1988.

HUDSON, W.J., AND M.P. SHARP. *Australian Independence: Colony to Reluctant Kingdom.* Melbourne: Melbourne University Press, 1988.

HUGHES, ROBERT. *The Fatal Shore.* New York: Alfred A. Knopf, 1987.

INGLIS, K.S. *The Australian Colonists: An Exploration of Social History, 1788–1870.* Melbourne: Melbourne University Press, 1974.

JAUNCEY, LESLIE C. *The Story of Conscription in Australia.* South Melbourne: Macmillan, 1968.

LA NAUZE, J.A. *Alfred Deakin: A Biography.* Melbourne: Melbourne University Press, 1979.

LA NAUZE, J.A. *The Making of the Australian Constitution.* Melbourne: Melbourne University Press, 1974.

LAFFIN, JOHN. *Anzacs at War: The Story of Australian and New Zealand Battles.* London: Abelard-Schuman, 1965.

MELBOURNE, A.C.V. *Early Constitutional Development in Australia.* St. Lucia: University of Queensland Press, 1963.

NORRIS. R. *The Emergent Commonwealth: Australian Federation—Expectations and Fufilment, 1889–1910.* Melbourne: Melbourne University Press, 1975.

TURNBULL, CLIVE. *A Concise History of Australia.* London: Thames and Hudson, 1966.

PART TWO

Democratic Political Action Guarantees Freedom and Equality

As we have seen, it is essential to have a popularly elected government in control of all force in human relations throughout the society. Does that mean that a democracy is to control human life totally? No. Government is to preserve the peace, but not at the cost of trampling freedom and equality, for that would be tyranny. A democracy stands for freedom and equality. It organizes liberty and prevents discrimination against, and manipulation of, all categories of citizens.

France today is a democracy. But the strong movement of the French people for democracy in the late 1700s failed: their revolution against monarchy ended in totalitarianism. To understand why that happened is important in order to avoid similar mistakes in the modern movements for democracy.

India today is a democracy. After being governed by Britain for many years, India achieved independence after World War II. The great challenge then was to establish a real democracy. Thanks to a major political hero, Indians rejected totalitarianism and created a nation based on freedom and equality. In recent years, violence between various groups has troubled the nation, but India still stands as a democracy. After nearly a half century of democratic rule—during which Indians' lives are much improved compared to conditions under the kings and dictators of prior centuries—it is unlikely that India's government will become a dictatorship.

Part II examines the historical political experiences of France and India as they moved toward democratic freedom and equality to see what actually happened in the past so we can better decide what should happen now and in the future.

CHAPTER

5

The Story of the French Revolution

Democracy Cut Down

France is now a democracy and the French know well what a democracy must be. They know these essentials because they remember France's tragic experience more than 200 years ago when the long movement for democracy produced a revolution that led to state terrorism. They also remember the hero who worked hard to rescue his country from that fate.

THE LIFE OF GILBERT LAFAYETTE

He began life with luck. Named Marie-Joseph-Paul-Yves-Roch-Gilbert du Motier, Marquis de La Fayette, baby Gilbert was born in southern France, far from Paris, to a large and rich family whose house had 20 rooms. But when he was only two years old, his father, a French army colonel, was shot to death in a battle against the English, without even having seen his little son. A year later, Gilbert's mother, age 22, went to live with her noble father and grandfather in a palace at Versailles, the home and headquarters of the king of France. So the little boy hardly knew his physical parents. He was cared for at home by his father's mother, a woman respected by all, and her two daughters. A comrade of his father, the Duc de Broglie, also watched over him, as did his teacher, Father Raynal, who began to educate Gilbert when he was seven. Though the boy regularly went to Catholic Mass and was schooled by a priest, he did not become religious; as soon as he could, Gilbert stopped going to church. But thanks to his grandmother and aunts at home and the two men who helped raise him, he became devoted to the hero they told him about: his father, a leader of soldiers.

Gilbert was eight when a large animal, a biting hyena, escaped into the woods, a terrifying threat to the local women and children. The boy ran into the woods and for several days tried to find the hyena and fight *for* it, because, he wrote, "my heart beat in sympathy with the hyena" and "The hope of meeting it urged me on."[1] That experience imprinted itself on his memory.

He was an intelligent child. When he was ten, a visiting cousin recalled, the lad was "remarkably well-informed for his age, astonishingly forward in reason and reasoning, and extraordinary for his reflections, his wisdom, his moderation, his cool head and his discernment."[2]

When he was eleven—eight years after he had last seen her—his mother sent for him to come to Paris where she treated him with charm and intelligence, as did his grandfather, great-grandfather, and uncle.[3]

Gilbert went to a preparatory school that had existed for more than four centuries. Later he recalled, "I was distracted from my studies by my wish to study without constraint." He had "A few schoolboy successes, deriving from my love of glory, but moderated by my love of liberty." Assigned to write an essay to "Describe the perfect horse," he wrote about one who, seeing that the rider was holding a whip, bucked him off his back. Years later, Gilbert Lafayette fantasized that if his schoolmaster had punished him for this impudent essay by having him flogged, he would have either stabbed the master with his dagger or plunged it into his own heart.[4] Each summer, he liked to go home again, to the South of France.

When he was just 13, his dear mother got sick and died. Only a few days later, her father died also. Gilbert inherited from this grandfather a whopping income: about 240 times as much as a master craftsman earned in those days. Now he was under the care of his aged great-grandfather and uncle, though they hardly supervised him. They did get him a commission as lieutenant—at age 13—in the elite Black Musketeers. His unit, like others, went hunting with the king. When Gilbert was 15, the Duc d'Ayen, who was close to the king, recruited him into his regiment, where Gilbert became acquainted with Ayen's five daughters. A contract marriage between him and one of them, Adrienne, was arranged in 1772. Adrienne's mother postponed the wedding because Gilbert was so young and isolated, but he and Adrienne fell in love and married on April 11, 1774—when he was 16½ and she was 15½.

Gilbert found family life a pleasure, but the court a drag: "The awkwardness of my manners, while not out of place during great events, did not enable me to stoop to the graces of the Court, nor to the airs of supper in the Capital."[5] He could not seem to acquire the fashionable talents demanded of a young man at court in those days. When he tried to dance with pretty Queen Marie Antoinette, then only 18, he stumbled around and she laughed and said, "I shall dance with you no more, you are too clumsy!"[6] He was equally awkward riding his horse. He lacked grace in talking with the elegant court ladies dressed

Marquis de Lafayette.

in skirts 20 feet around, with hairdos so tall they had to bow down to go through doorways. Still a teenager, he began drinking liquor and gambling away his money. One night he became so drunk he had to be carried out to his carriage; he asked that his brother-in-law be told "how much I've had to drink."[7] Though dearly in love with his wife, he was persuaded to take a mistress. He did, but being unattractive, he lost her to a royal competitor. He could not fight that competitor, so he challenged his friend, Segur, to a duel, imagining that he, too, was after the same mistress. In fact, Segur was not, and, fortunately, he refused Gilbert's challenge and stayed up through the night talking him back to sanity.

Gilbert was put forward to be a "lord-in-waiting" for the king's brother, a major privilege. But, he recalled, "When my new relatives found me a place at court, I didn't hesitate to incur displeasure in order to preserve my independence."[8] At a masked ball, Gilbert walked up to the prince and made a contemptuous comment about fools who were proud of memory. The prince was outraged, but Gilbert's mentors got the prince to believe that the boy had just made a mistake, not recognizing whom he was talking to in his disguise. All Gilbert had to do was to apologize to the prince. But the next day, Gilbert walked up to the prince, who was wearing a blue suit, and said that he had actually known whom he was talking to. "And who was that?" asked the prince. "The same person, sir, I see now wearing a blue suit."[9] The prince fired him as "lord-in-waiting," and Gilbert felt liberated. He dropped the "de" in his name—which signified he was a noble—and started calling himself Gilbert Lafayette.

Lafayette's luck rose when, on August 8, 1775, he was invited to dine with a visitor to France: the brother of England's King George III, who, surprisingly, damned his brother the king, and praised the American revolutionaries. Lafayette was inspired; he talked about the American Revolution for a year. When on June 11, 1776, he and a number of other young officers had their military careers canceled and their names put on an inactive list, Lafayette decided to volunteer as an American officer. Instructed by Benjamin Franklin, America's ambassador to Paris, the American envoy, Silas Dean, welcomed Lafayette to military service.

At that time, George Washington's army had shrunk to barely 3,000 men and it was about to be beaten by the British army. Money was scarce. Lafayette, only 19, told Deane, "Hitherto you have seen nothing but my zeal. It may possibly be useful. I am going to buy a ship to carry your volunteer officers. One should show one's confidence, and it is when danger threatens that I wish to share your fortune." [11] Deane accepted his offer—and promised him the rank of major general.

Because the Americans were badly defeated that August of 1776 by the British on Long Island, the French government ordered its officers not to join the fight. That same month, America's Declaration of Independence arrived in France and Lafayette made plans to travel to America secretly. On an ordinary trip to London, where he routinely called upon the king, he wrote to his father-in-law in secret:

> I have found a magnificent opportunity of learning my trade. I am an officer in the army of the United States of America. My zeal for their cause and my candour have gained me their confidence. For my part I have done what I could for them, and their interests will one day be dearer to me than my own. [12]

To his wife, Adrienne, he wrote that he was a

> Defender of that liberty which I worship, utterly free in my own person and going as a friend to offer my services to the most interesting of Republics, bringing to the service only my candor and goodwill without ambition or ulterior motive. Working for my glory will become working for their happiness. [13]

When he returned to Paris, Lafayette faked an illness so he could stay private. He even kept away from his wife and family. Then, early in the morning, he burst into the bedroom of his friend Segur, the one he had once challenged to a duel. He locked the door and woke him up.

> *La Fayette:* I'm leaving for America. Nobody knows, but I'm too fond of you to go without telling you my secret.
> *Segur:* And how are you managing it?
> *La Fayette:* I've bought a ship, which is waiting for me at Bordeaux. I have a commission as major-general in the American Army in my pocket and here is the list of my companions, picked out by the *comte* de Broglie. Ternant and Valfort are the most capable.
> *Segur:* I'm coming with you. [14]

Lafayette set out for Bordeaux, where his ship—*La Victoire*— was being prepared. But his plans were leaked to the king, who, since France was not at war with England, quickly ordered that Lafayette quit the project. Lafayette began to obey the king, but then he received another message: the aristocrats in Paris were delighted about his enterprise. So off he went. Seven weeks later, his ship arrived at Charleston, South Carolina. From there, he set forth toward Philadelphia.

Lafayette registered in his mind an America that would be an inspiration for France. He wrote to his wife "my star":

> I can only be delighted with the reception I have been given here....The simplicity of manners, the desire to help, the love of fatherland and liberty, a pleasing equality characterize all here. The richest and the poorest man are on the same level....American women are very pretty, very simple, and of the most charming cleanliness. They rule over all here...even more than in England. What enchants me is that all the citizens are brothers. You will find in America no poor people....All citizens have a sufficient income and the same rights as the most powerful landowner.
>
>   Consider how pleasant life is for me in this country, the sympathy which puts me as much at ease as if I had known everyone here for twenty years, the resemblance of their way of thinking and mine, my love for glory and liberty, and you will see that I am indeed a happy man; but I miss you, my dear heart, I miss my friends; and there can be no happiness for me away from you and them. I ask you whether you still love me, but I ask myself the same question far oftener, and my heart always answers that you do. I hope that is right.[15]

LAFAYETTE TAKES ON AMERICA

Traveling to Philadelphia was hazardous. The roads were so bad that Lafayette's carriage broke down, forcing him to ride a horse—a challenge for him. When he and his colleagues at last arrived at the headquarters of the American Congress, they were ready to take on leading responsibilities for the war. The head of the American Foreign Affairs Committee, James Lowell, came out and told them, in effect, to get lost: "French officers are a little too eager in wanting to come and serve us without being asked. Last year, it is true, we needed officers, but this year, we have many, and very experienced ones, too."[16] Lowell turned away and reentered the hall, leaving Lafayette and company standing outside, stunned. But Lafayette was not to be repulsed. He delivered the introductory letters from Deane and Franklin to the congressmen's houses and wrote a note to Lowell, asking that it be read to the Congress:

> After the sacrifices I have made for [American] independence, I consider that I have the right to ask two favours: that of serving without pay, at my own expense; and that of serving as a volunteer (that is to say, in the ranks).[17]

The Congress finally read the material, took Lafayette seriously and accepted all the French officers into service. Lafayette was taken to dinner with General George Washington and some congressmen. Washington was somewhat stiff and haughty. "We are bound to be embarrassed at showing ourselves to an officer coming straight from French troops," he said. Lafayette, who had seen Washington's troops—exhausted, clumsy men, dressed in their own old clothes, many without shoes—replied, " I am here to learn, not to teach."[18] After their meeting, Washington was still wary. He wrote to Congress, "What the designs of Congress respecting this gentleman were, and what line of conduct I am to pursue to comply with their designs and their expectations, I know not, and beg to be instructed."[19]

Congress decided to authorize Lafayette to lead troops into combat. When the troops assigned to him hesitated to advance, he jumped off his horse, French officer style, and ran to the front, yelling at them to charge and pushing at their shoulders to shove them forward. The Americans were not motivated to advance by that appeal, but at least they stood firm. As he was urging them on, Lafayette was shot in the leg. He noticed his wound, but kept moving until the bleeding forced him to stop and get bandaged.

After that show of valor and leadership, Congress, at Washington's recommendation, authorized Lafayette to command a division—3,086 troops—of the Continental Army.[20]

His actions in America began to define Lafayette's identity. Scores of experiences could have justified his quitting. Instead, Lafayette emerged as one determined to do what had to be done to make the right thing happen. The Baron de Kalb concluded that "No one deserves more than [Lafayette] the esteem which he enjoys here. He is a prodigy for his age, full of courage, spirit, judgment, good manners, feelings of generosity and zeal for the cause of liberty on this continent."[21] Of course, at times he was discouraged or mistaken, but he made comeback after comeback throughout the war and his leadership contributed much to the liberation of America. While in America, Lafayette matured from his awkward dancing to an effective commander. He discovered how to make his beliefs operate in real life. He had embraced "the American cause," he wrote, because "I not only considered it as the cause of Honor, Virtue and universal Happiness but felt myself impressed with the warmest affection for a Nation who exhibited by their resistance so fine an example of Justice and Courage to the Universe."[22] During the war, he experienced time and again that abiding political necessity: compromise. Determined to achieve victory, he learned to adapt his efforts to those of others in order to create the most effective coalition.

And he found a father. George Washington treated him like a son, even inviting Lafayette to live in his house. Washington told Lafayette he would be pleased to have his confidence "as a friend and a father."[23] Lafayette was thrilled that "That respectable man whose talents and virtues I admire more and more as I know him better and better, is willing to be my intimate friend." And:

> His tender interest for me soon won my heart to him. I am established in his house, we live like two united brothers in the midst of a mutual intimacy and confidence. That friendship makes me as happy as I can be while away in this country. When he sent me his personal surgeon, he told him to take care of me as if I were his son, because he loved me like one.[24]

His relationship with Washington had a profound effect on Lafayette. He took back to France a political model exemplified, in his mind, by certain features of his new father. During one crisis, he wrote to Washington: "I am bound to your destiny." Washington wrote him back immediately:

> I am well aware that you are quite incapable of entertaining plans whose success depends upon lies and that your spirit is too high to stoop to seek a reputation by ignoble means and by intrigue....It is well known that neither ambition nor any ulterior motive have caused me to accept the position I fill. I have done my duty according to a uniform and inflexible rule of conduct in which I shall persevere invariably while the honour of command remains mine, without regard to what malice can do or calumny say....[25]

Lafayette learned much from the emerging American democracy. For example, when a competitor named Conway tried through Congress to take over George Washington's control of the military, Lafayette wrote to Washington, describing what this crisis had taught him:

> When I was in Europe, I thought that here almost every man was a lover of liberty....You can conceive my astonishment when I saw that toryism was as openly professed as whiggism itself. However I believed at that time that all good Americans were united together, that the confidence of Congress in you was unbounded. Then I entertained the certitude that America would be independent in case we would not lose you....You shall see plainly that if you were lost for America, there is nobody here who could keep the army and the revolution for six months. There are open dissensions in Congress, parties who hate one another as much as the common enemy, stupid men who without knowing a single word about war undertake to judge you, to make ridiculous comparisons; they are infatuated with Gates without thinking of the different circumstances and believe that attacking is the only thing necessary to conquer....I have been surprised to see the establishment of this new Board of War.[26]

Lafayette admitted that Thomas Conway, an Irish-born, French-educated Revolutionary officer who was the chief Cabalist, had "engaged me by entertaining my head with ideas of glory and shining projects, and I must confess to my shame that it is a too certain way of deceiving me."[27] Washington responded, "I am satisfied that you can have no views to answer by throwing out false colours, and that you possess a mind too exalted to condescend to dirty arts and low intrigues to acquire a reputation." He reminded Lafayette that in such a stupendous cause trouble was reality. "We must not, in so great a contest, expect to meet with nothing but sunshine. I have no doubt but that everything happens so for the best; that we shall triumph over our misfortunes and shall, in the end, be ultimately happy; when, my dear Marquis, if you will give me your company in Virginia, we will laugh at our past difficulties and the follies of others."[28]

As Olivier Bernier, the insightful author of a modern biography of Lafayette, observes:

> To La Fayette, Washington communicated his own deep-seated beliefs about free government. For the first time, Gilbert began to understand what liberty really

meant, why the people should have rights, why government ought never to proceed without the consent of those it rules. He discovered the need for freedom of the press, freedom of religion, freedom of assembly: in explaining all this, Washington transformed his disciple's life and made his American journey into a life-enduring education.[29]

Like Washington, Lafayette learned to live his beliefs, not only in his personal enterprises, but also in his day-by-day dealings with other officers and officials, with his many and various troops, and with the hosts who welcomed him to their homes for food and conversation as he led his division through the country.

Free speech was one significant lesson. When a military controversy against Lafayette went public, it infuriated him. But then he remembered Washington's wisdom:

> In a free and republican government, you cannot restrain the voice of the multitude. Every man will speak as he thinks, or, more properly, without thinking, and consequently will judge the effects without attending to the causes.....Let me beseech you therefore, my good Sir, to afford a healing hand to the wound that unintentionally has been made.[30]

Lafayette realized that free speech, in all forms, was right. And he himself spoke more freely every month in America.

Lafayette returned to France on February 6, 1779, to gain military support. He received an ambivalent welcome: first he was formally arrested for violating the king's orders by going to America, then he was celebrated as a hero. In Paris, his delightful evening parties rivaled those of Ben Franklin, although in the official daytime, the French government still resisted commitment to the American war. But Queen Marie Antoinette copied out a poem for Lafayette (which began, "What does his youth matter, since his wisdom is that of maturity?"[31]), and the French monarchy decided to send 6,000 French troops and generous supplies to America—though they were to be commanded not by young Gilbert, but by Rochambeau, an experienced major general. Meanwhile, Gilbert's loving wife was with him, and on Christmas Eve 1779, she gave birth to a son. The son was promptly named George Washington Lafayette.

Upon returning to Boston, Major General Gilbert Lafayette, then 22, was greeted with fireworks and bonfires and much applause. Again, he plunged into war. The challenges he faced were both military and political, as when he fell out with Rochambeau and then had to apologize. Honors abounded, but the fighting continued, month after month, hard as ever. Soldiers were deserting. Lafayette's way of meeting that crisis was to take a heavy risk: he pronounced that any soldier who wished to withdraw from the war was free to do so—immediately. Not one left. In fact, even a sick soldier chose to be carried along on a stretcher as the others marched forward.[32]

Washington sent General Lafayette on a mission in Virginia. There Lafayette corresponded with Virginia's governor, Thomas Jefferson. Jefferson saw this young general as a person with "accommodating temper" and advised him that military rigidity would not work well with Americans:

> Mild Laws, a People not used to war and prompt obedience, a want of the Provisions of War and means of procuring them render our orders often ineffectual, oblige us to temporize and when we cannot accomplish an object in one way to attempt it in another.[33]

When British forces advanced toward Richmond, the capital of Virginia, Lafayette raced his troops in that direction, leaving behind baggage and artillery. On April 28, 1781, the British made it to the river shore across from Richmond. The next day Lafayette's troops charged into the city and took it over. There, for the first time, he met Jefferson, his comrade in revolution, who thanked him for rescuing Richmond.[34]

That fall of 1781, Britain's General Cornwallis, his troops out of food and ammunition, and a quarter of them sick, surrendered in Yorktown. Lafayette insisted that they march forth without music and with their flags folded up.[35] The British preferred to surrender to the French, but when their troops faced Lafayette, he ordered his band to play "Yankee Doodle," the popular Revolutionary song, as loud as possible. Startled, the British turned back and surrendered to the Americans, their former subordinates.[36] The war was over, America had won.

On January 19, 1782, Lafayette again arrived in Paris. He did not go to his wife immediately because Adrienne was occupied at a court celebration: the King, and the Queen, Marie Antoinette, after a dozen years of marriage, had at last produced a son. There was to be royal procession, so Lafayette stood out in front of the door of his hotel to see his Adrienne. Queen Marie Antoinette's carriage came down the street—and stopped in front of him, as she herself had planned. Out of the carriage stepped Adrienne, so surprised and pleased to see him that she fainted with joy. They were still in love, and Lafayette was thrilled. He wrote to Washington, "The reception I have met from the nation at large, from the King and from my friends will, I am sure, be pleasing to you." He was delighted that "all the young men in this Court are soliciting a permission to go to America."[37]

On September 17, 1782, Adrienne gave birth to a daughter. In memory of Lafayette's favorite place, they named her Virginie.

As he was gearing up to go back to America, Lafayette suddenly got word that a peace treaty had been signed. Still interested in America, in June 1784, he sailed across the sea anyway. As he sailed west, Jefferson was sailing east, on his way to Paris, having being appointed by the U.S. Congress to negotiate treaties of commerce with the French.[38] In October, Lafayette wrote to Jefferson, hoping that "God grant" success to the Congress of the United States, and urging Jefferson to visit Lafayette's home and allow Adrienne to care for Jefferson's daughter, whose mother had died two years before: "My family, and anything that is mine are entirely at your disposal."[39] In America, Lafayette visited George Washington at Mount Vernon, where the two had long talks. Returning to Paris on January 20, 1785, Lafayette was "proud of his title of American citizen, eager for action and burning with the ambition

Marie Antoinette.

of rendering further service to his second country."[40] Jefferson, concentrating on the trade negotiations, wrote that he "was powerfully aided by all the influence and the energies of the Marquis de La Fayette, who proved himself equally zealous for the friendship and welfare of both nations."[41]

When the famous man of action tried to settle back into the life of French nobility—which revolved around the king and his high and mighty court—he naturally became restless. He remembered the purpose of America's war, and he continued to be influenced by Americans, working for American trade and listening to Jefferson. Seeing what was going on in France, he recalled a letter he had received from George Washington in 1783, when America seemed threatened by political anarchy: "To avert these evils, to form a Constitution that will give consistency, stability and dignity to the Union; and sufficient power to the great Council of the Nation for general purposes is a duty which is incumbent upon every man who wishes well for his Country."[42] He kept an elegant sword, created for him by Benjamin Franklin, upon which had been carved Lafayette's motto, *"Cur Non"*— which meant "Why not?"—and, next to a rising moon, *"Crescam ut Prosim"*—meaning "Let me wax to benefit mankind."[43]

Still young, and growing successful, Lafayette strode into French politics in 1789 as the French government was about to fall apart.

THE MOVEMENT FOR DEMOCRACY IN FRANCE

The news of the Americans' victory in their revolution stimulated the French to work to secure their own version of "life, liberty, and the pursuit of happiness." Money was scarce in France in the 1780s. By 1786, the government was so heavily in debt that half its revenues had to be used to pay interest on loans. Another quarter of revenues went to the armed forces. The country was ruled by a king. In order to raise taxes, the king had to appeal to the people who had money, and they naturally tried to set conditions in their favor before they would agree to pay. Various groups of nobles, brought together to approve higher and broader taxes, refused any increases. The churches collected lots of money for their own purposes, but were not about to share its revenues with the government.

Meanwhile, French working people were getting poorer and poorer. Out in the country, bad weather ruined crops two years in a row, 1787 and 1788. The peasants remembered how in the 1770s famines had forced them to eat bark off the trees and even some peasants ate other peasants.[44] Desperate people, terrified of starving, rioted, broke into food stores, and hijacked wagons and boats loaded with grain. Vagabonds, without work and with nothing to eat, roamed in bands through the countryside and into the cities, stealing what they needed to stay alive. The city people also did what they had to to stay alive. Paris then had only 650,000 people; 30,000 of them were prostitutes.[45] About five out of six Parisians were desperately poor. In the spring of 1789, an ordinary laborer had to pay more than half the money he earned in a day to buy a four-pound loaf of bread. The shortage of food and other goods was aggravated by the swelling numbers of peasants crowding into the city to find help. Many troubled folks thought they were being purposely starved so the aristocrats could control them.[46]

King Louis XVI grew increasingly desperate himself. To get the money he wanted, he had to rely on government organizations that could actually demand and collect money from the nation. But the officials of these organizations neither wanted to spare the king their own money nor force further hardship on impoverished ordinary citizens. So they resisted the king's power. That trouble generated a revolution.

The king's own administrators were failing to collect taxes and were no longer able to borrow funds. Early in 1787, one royal administrator called a meeting of the Assembly of Notables, which had last met in 1626. When the 144 men who composed the Assembly gathered at Versailles,[47] the administrator's tax plans were turned down and he was thrown out of office and exiled to England. At the Parliament of Paris, the king himself was challenged: a Parliament leader claimed that one of the king's announcements was illegal. The king replied, "That makes no difference! It is legal because I wish it!"[48]

In May 1788, the Parliament, tired of being pushed around by royal officers, issued a public declaration of fundamental law stating that, from now on, Parliament would define the rules of governing rather than bowing down to the power of the king. Two days later the king's police surrounded the Parliament building and arrested two of its members. The Parliament was forced to cancel its

King Louis XVI, with his family, during the French Revolution.

declaration and to suspend itself. Hostility to royal power rose. Protests and harsh demonstrations in the streets began. The loyalty of the army became doubtful, and here and there in France, even some nobles started to arm themselves to resist the king's forces.

Faced with this defiance, on July 5, 1788, the king announced that the following May he would organize a meeting of France's Estates-General to deal with the national crisis. The Estates-General had not met for more than 150 years. What their authority would be, compared to that of the king, was uncertain, though Louis XVI described the upcoming event as "the assembly of a great family headed by a common father"—himself.[49] No one knew how such a body would proceed.* In August 1788, yet another royal officer retracted decisions the Parliament had been forced to make, declared the Estates-General meeting for May 1, 1789—and resigned.

The Parliament of Paris returned to town in September 1788, to the cheers of the people, and pronounced that the Estates-General would be organized as it had been in 1614: there would be elections, in equal numbers, three

* Unlike in England, where the monarch was forced to deal with a powerful Parliament regularly, "in France there was no 'Whig science of politics,' no familiarity with the ins and outs of ministerial turnovers, no practice with patronage systems and interest group formations." (Lynn Hunt, *Politics, Culture, and Class in the French Revolution* [Berkeley: University of California Press, 1984], p. 43.)

Estates—the clergy, the nobles, and the citizens. Leaders in Paris, including Lafayette, petitioned that the Third Estate representatives be equal in number to the nobles and clergy together; as one put it, "What is the Third Estate? Everything."[50] Arguments over planning went back and forth, but one strong principle emerged: No more power for the king. And nearly everyone anticipated a written constitution for France, a declaration of rights, and the establishment of a regular congress to decide on taxes and laws. How everything would turn out, ironically, depended much on how the king decided to deal with it.

In the past, French kings had stimulated discussions and received various pieces of advice, while retaining all decision-making power. The king typically lived in the magnificent Palace of Versailles, twelve miles from Paris. King Louis XIV had explained to his son that "Kings are absolute lords, having full authority over all people, secular and ecclesiastical." King Louis XV, in the spring of 1766, rode into town to address the Parliament of Paris, which functioned as a law-court, not a Congress. He told them, "The Law is what I say it is."[51] And further:

> It is in my person alone that sovereign power resides....It is from me alone that my courts derive their authority; and the plenitude of this authority, which they exercise only in my name, remains always in me....It is to me alone that the legislative power belongs, without any dependence and without any division....The whole public order emanates from me, and the rights and interests of the nation...are necessarily joined with me and rest only in my hands.[52]

Kings seldom made such declarations unless they were challenged, but a regular challenge to a king was criticism of his own character. In contrast to Louis XIV, Louis XVI said, "I should like to be loved."[53] He came across as a dim, well-intentioned, but disconnected ruler, dressed up to look royal but so unplugged from reality that his palace nobles laughed at him.[54] Queen Marie Antoinette, an Austrian princess who had married him when she was 15, concentrated on jewelry, sex, and pressing him to assert absolute power.[55]

Modern European monarchies were based on inheritance: a king was not chosen by votes—or by God—but by being born to a previous king. This method of transferring power was justified as removing all uncertainty about who would be the next ruler when the present one died. In ancient Egypt, for instance, civil war broke out nearly every time a pharaoh died because succession was wildly uncertain. But the modern rule that the new monarch be the child of the previous monarch itself produced the uncertainty that an inept king like Louis XVI might inherit the thrown. A "good" king who had elevated the monarchy could be succeeded by a "bad" king who abused power, creating awful results. Thus, even so, in France, the king was seen as a King, though when he misbehaved and people starved or fought, his "absolute" definition of rule came into question.

From the start, the Estates-General was mishandled by Louis XVI. On May 2, 1789, he welcomed the First and Second Estates to Versailles. The Third Estate deputies, wearing (as the king required) plain black commoner clothes in contrast to the elegant garb of the nobles and clergy, had to wait another whole day before being permitted to see the king. On May 4, all the Estates went to a scheduled High Mass—but the commoners who happened to sit in pews at the front of the church had to give up their seats to the nobles. On the 5th, King Louis XVI spoke to the entire body, but proposed no plan for reform, only demanded of them such virtues as wisdom and prudence. His director-general of finance, Jacques Necker, then talked for three hours—about raising money.

Days passed. The different Estates worked differently, according to their different statuses. The deputies of the Third Estate, on June 17, 1789, adopted the title—invented by Lafayette—of National Assembly and declared that since they represented 96 percent of the French people, they had the true authority.[56] In effect, the Assembly crowned itself king, and called on the other Estates to join with it to accomplish "the great work of effecting the regeneration of France."[57]

The king's bumbling created a hot crisis on June 20, 1789. On that rainy day, the deputies of the National Assembly arrived in front of their regular meeting room and found royal troops barring the doors. Infuriated, they went to a nearby indoor tennis court and swore (the "Tennis-Court Oath") that they would "never abandon" the National Assembly and would "go on meeting wherever circumstances might dictate, until the constitution of the kingdom and the regeneration of the state is firmly established."[58] The king insisted that they were not a "National Assembly" and were to hold no further meetings. With 4,000 soldiers surrounding the hall, King Louis XVI walked in and criticized the deputies harshly for achieving nothing and for forgetting that none of their proposals could be effected without his approval. He demanded that they split up at once and stay apart, in separate houses. He pronounced that "the King has declared null the resolutions taken by the deputies of the Third Estate on the seventeenth of this month, as well as any subsequent ones, as being illegal and unconstitutional." He dismissed them with these words: "I command you, Gentlemen, to disperse at once, and to present yourselves tomorrow morning each in the chamber allowed to your order...."[59]

When the king marched out of the meeting, the members of the Third Estate remained sitting where they were. The Comte de Mirabeau, a noble whose liberal sentiments had got him elected to the Third Estate, spoke defiantly: "Who is it that gives these orders and dictates these laws? It is your own representative, it is one who should rather receive orders from us!" When the king's master of ceremonies tried to remove them, Mirabeau said, "If you are charged to remove us, give orders for the use of force, for we shall not leave save at the point of the bayonet." The president of the Assembly declared that they were in session, and "no-one can give orders to the nation in assembly." Despite the king's commands, the deputies reaffirmed their status as a "National Assembly." King Louis XVI sent soldiers to throw them out. But the soldiers saw and heard crowds of people supporting the deputies and were ordered by certain nobles not to even enter the hall. Thus, a military attack was forestalled.

King Louis learned of that—and abruptly dropped his demands: "Oh, well, devil take it, let them stay!"[60] Two days later he ordered the nobles and clergy to meet with the members of the Third Estate. The government changed.

The king's recent royal orders were canceled by his own statement. The work of the National Assembly began.

THE PEOPLE REVOLT

Out in the streets of Paris, the angry crowds grew larger, their orators more infuriated, the soldiers more brotherly with them. In the chaos of fighting, looting, and drunk disorder, the crowds donned weird hats and costumes. On July 14, 1789, a mob of thousands broke into a building full of arms and stole 32,000 muskets and 5 cannons. They moved on to the Bastille, the old castle-like jail of Paris symbolizing the king's power, with walls 5 to 10 feet thick, 8 round towers as tall as 73 feet, and a surrounding moat 75 feet wide.[61] The crowd had guns, but needed gunpowder, and hoped to find it at the jail. The surprised governor of the Bastille tried vainly to calm the mob, but some managed to knock down the drawbridge, which enabled the others to surge into the courtyard. There the guards shot at them—killing 98 and wounding 73.[62] The mob, in return, killed 6 soldiers.[63] The governor was knocked down and his head cut off with a pocketknife.[64] The former mayor was killed. The seven prisoners were released,[65] and the people tore down the Bastille.

At Versailles the next morning, King Louis XVI was awakened by a noble and told that the Bastille had fallen. The king said, "It is a riot." The noble replied, "No, Sire, it is a revolution."

That day the frightened king of France relinquished his authority, telling the Assembly, "It is I now who entrust myself to you."[66] He assured them that his troops would be ordered out of Paris. The Assembly stood up and cheered. In private, Louis wrote his will. When the public heard the news of his response to the Assembly, they cheered him high and loud as "Louis XVI, Father of the French, King of a Free People.[67] In Paris, the old city government was abolished in favor of a "commune"—an outfit chosen by the same kinds of voters who had elected the deputies to the Third Estates General, who were now calling themselves the "Assembly." The people elected their own mayor, a man named Bailly.[68] Lafayette was declared commander of the Paris National Guard, reporting not to the king, but to the new Paris government. He drew his sword and shouted, "I swear to sacrifice my life in the preservation of that liberty with whose defence you have deigned to entrust me!"[69] It was Lafayette who combined the colors of the city, red and blue, with the color of the royal house of Bourbon, white, to make the new red-white-and-blue flag of France.[70] The king pronounced his approval of those events.[71]

King Louis XVI went to Paris to receive the keys to the city from the mayor, who declared that "the people have reconquered their king." The mayor presented Louis with a red-white-and-blue cockade, which the king put on his hat. The monarch mind was dying. When a friend of Queen Marie Antoinette was grabbed by people in the street and hanged from a lamppost, Louis did nothing. His officer Necker told the National Assembly, "The salvation of the state lies in your hands."[72] In private, Necker explained that the king was worn out: "The king is good, but cannot easily make up his mind."[73]

Throughout France, the news that the king was no longer the nation's absolute authority spread. So did chaos and fighting. Government control collapsed as rioters and armed revolters led desperate citizens in more and more parts of the country. The great new question was: How was France to be governed?

LAFAYETTE LEADS FOR DEMOCRACY

Lafayette, in that summer of 1789, emerged as a major leader in the movement to create France's future.

When he had returned to France after the victory in America in 1781, he had been greeted as a great hero, but then he lapsed into a relaxed life. He was a wealthy man and close to the king—one of a few aristocrats who greeted the king in his bedroom every morning. Though he was a Catholic, he worked to gain French Protestants an American-style freedom, but not intensely enough to bother the king. He wrote to George Washington now and then, expressing his hope for political change in France. From a letter of 1787: "The spirit of liberty is prevailing in this country at a great rate. Liberal ideas are cantering about from one end of the Kingdom to another. Our Assembly of Notables was a fine thing."[74] He had it in his mind to become the George Washington of France—but not yet and not in violent chaos. At the start of 1788, he wrote to Washington that "I am heartily wishing for a constitution and a Bill of Rights and wish it may be effected with as much tranquillity and mutual satisfaction as possible."[75] To Jefferson he wrote cheerfully that "Many abuses may be destroyed, liberal principles be adopted and a great deal of good be done."[76] But he did not see it to be done by himself. On April 1, 1788, thinking that the Estates-General might not meet until 1792, Lafayette left Paris and rejoined the army.

Just one month later, he was infuriated. The national budget had been published, showing a whopping deficit. The king could not get the Parliament of Paris to raise taxes, so he dismissed its members. He tried to form a new tax-raising court, but many refused to serve on it. Neighbors of Lafayette's property in Brittany *"declared it infamous"* to join such courts, and Lafayette agreed with them. He woke up politically. When it turned out that the Estates-General would meet in May 1789, Lafayette organized dozens of meetings of liberal nobles at which they planned to create a constitution. On July 13, 1789, he was elected vice president of the National Assembly.[77]

Far off in the new United States, where Americans had just created their own Constitution, Alexander Hamilton and other leaders saw no necessity for a bill of rights. They believed the established constitutional procedures were adequate to protect citizens' liberties. But other American leaders demanded a bill of rights to guarantee that the government, however well and democratically structured, would not turn into a tyranny. Lafayette thought France should pursue an even better idea: "a Bill of Rights may be made if wished for the people before they accept the Constitution."[78] He proceeded to draft a Declaration of Rights for his country, conferred with Jefferson about it, and began promoting it. On July 14, 1789, the National Assembly appointed a committee to prepare a constitution. That same day the Bastille crisis interrupted the project, but roused Lafayette to revolutionary leadership.

Two major developments occurred in August of 1789. On the 4th, the National Assembly declared itself the national representative body. A few liberal nobles stood up and surprised their colleagues by voluntarily surrendering some ancient privileges of nobility, such as hunting rights and the right to own fancy places and lord it over dependent persons. Then the Assembly took on the class system. Serfdom was canceled. Tithes were abolished. Tax privileges were destroyed. In sum, "feudalism was abolished."[79] Resistance naturally arose the next day from various privileged persons, but it failed. A new decree stated: "The National Assembly destroys the feudal regime *entirely*."[80] So the National Assembly, about to undertake the job of writing a constitution, saw itself as representing not priests or princes or workers, but citizens—all of them. Later the Assembly would qualify "citizens" as "active" persons who paid taxes and restrict the vote to this class. But the main thrust of this August move was to unify the Assembly and eliminate the ability of the king to divide members by manipulation.

PRESSING FORWARD THE DECLARATION OF RIGHTS

The question of the constitution, put off during the Bastille crisis, was taken up again. Lafayette charged forward as a champion of freedom with his proposed Declaration of the Rights of Man and Citizens. Mirabeau argued that they should put off this bill of rights until they had made a constitution, but the majority disagreed and concentrated on Lafayette's proposed Declaration. Jefferson, who had earlier written Lafayette recommending "A Charter of Rights, solemnly established by the King and Nation," when he thought that France would be a constitutional monarchy, not a democracy like America,[81] was now advising Lafayette on how to improve the Declaration. Lafayette also agreed to changes by the Assembly. He started out with "Nature has made men equal...," and then changed it to "Nature has created men free and equal...," and at last to "Men are born and remain free and equal in rights."[82] The final document, with 17 rights, was not perfect, but it was a major step forward.

The U.S. Bill of Rights was relatively straightforward and simple, declaring what the government must not do. In the American document, free speech was protected flat out:

> Congress shall make no law respecting an establishment of religion, or prohibiting the free exercise thereof; or abridging the freedom of speech, or of the press; or the right of the people peaceably to assemble, and to petition the Government for a redress of grievances.[83]

The French document was blurred on this question:

> X. No one shall be disquieted on account of his opinions, including his religious views, provided their manifestation does not disturb the public order established by law.
>
> XI. The free communication of ideas and opinions is one of the most precious of the rights of man. Every citizen may, accordingly, speak, write, and print with freedom, but shall be responsible for such abuses of this freedom as shall be defined by law.[84]

More controversial was the section on religion. A draft article said "religion and morality" were necessary "to the good order of society." The churchmen demanded the declaration support a state religion. Mirabeau came out for freedom of worship and conscience. The delegates decided for neither of these two positions, but left the question of religion to be dealt with later, in the constitution.[85]

The right of "property" was called a "sacred right." The rest of the document described government rights. In composing this part of the Declaration, the Assembly drew from America the wisdom of describing rights in terms of restrictions of government power, rather than as ultimate values. The government—unlike a priest—was to relate to every citizen according to the law, and thus treat everyone equally in legal terms but not in other instances. Freedom was no perfection; free people often acted reprehensibly, but the lesson was that government, holding the power, was not to step beyond the law into the realm of morality.

As author Georges Lefebvre wrote, the Declaration "had an especially great *negative* value."[86] His description of aspects of the declaration shows that the focus was on what could *not* be done:

> Sovereignty belongs to the nation—i.e., France is no longer the property of the king. No obedience is owed except to the law —i.e., the arbitrary will of the king, and of his ministers and agents, is binding on no one. No man may be arrested or detained except by law—i.e., there shall be no more arrest by administrative orders merely. The accused is innocent until pronounced guilty—i.e., no restoration of torture. Citizens are equal before the law—i.e., there is no justification for the privileges. Resistance to oppression is allowable—i.e., the insurrection of July 14 was legitimate.[87]

The Declaration defined human relations to government much better than had ever been done before in France. Such rules, if put into effect by an operative constitution, promised to make liberty a reality.

Biographer Olivier Bernier describes Lafayette's achievement:

> This time, La Fayette was right to be pleased with himself: it was no mean achievement to have given a Bill of Rights to a country that, until then, had never known any kind of freedom. Had he done no more for the rest of his life, La Fayette would be entitled to fame and gratitude for that one achievement alone.[88]

PUBLIC REVOLUTION

On the night of October 1, 1789, the king's personal bodyguards, who were highly devoted to His Majesty, met with him for dinner. They praised him with toasts and cursed the "revolutionaries of Paris," then trampled on various cockades and ribbons the Parisians had distributed. The news of that dinner reached the hungry street crowds. Infuriated, they readied to march out to Versailles and force the royal family back to Paris. The most common slogan was "To Paris or the lamppost."[89] Since the king's troops were not allowed to shoot at women, it was decided that the revolutionary wives would march to Versailles, along with men dressed up as women, in case they had to fight.

On October 5, 1789, 7,000 hungry women and disguised men marched from Paris to Versailles in the rain, pulling along several cannons. Lafayette, in charge of the National Guard of Paris, had allowed them to go. That morning, as they approached Versailles, Mirabeau, a leading Assembly member, rushed up to the Assembly chairman and whispered in his ear:

> Mirabeau: Sir, forty thousand Parisians are marching upon us.
> Chairman: I know nothing of it.
> Mirabeau: Paris, I tell you, is marching upon us. Hurry the work of the Assembly, and prorogue the meeting.
> Chairman: I never hurry the deliberations, they are only too often hurried.
> Mirabeau: Paris is advancing.
> Chairman: So much the better. Let them kill us all. The state will be the gainer.[90]

Subsequently, King Louis, called in from hunting, allowed the people to enter Versailles. A large flock of marchers got into the Assembly and sat down with the deputies on their benches. Some embraced Mirabeau. Some told the chairman of their needs and he got the Assembly to permit him to lead a delegation of the women to the king to ask for bread in Paris. The king welcomed them graciously and promised bread. The women began to leave.

Meanwhile, back in Paris, Lafayette had been persuaded to "invite" the king to come and rule in Paris rather than in Versailles. The invitation was hardly a polite request: an army of 20,000 men plus armed crowds marched out to deliver it. The queen and leaders of the Assembly urged the king to escape before these troops arrived, but Louis refused to go, saying he did not want to be "a fugitive king!"[91] Instead, he told the Assembly that, "pure and simple," he accepted their decrees.[92]

Late that night, Lafayette, leading the National Guard, arrived in Versailles and walked alone into the palace. Some of the nobles called him a traitor, supposing he had charged in with the Parisians. He told them he had come in alone and that he obviously trusted them.[93] Lafayette then "invited" Louis to Paris. The king said he would think it over that night. But before dawn, the wild crowd raised hell. Some piled into the palace, bashed the queen's guards, and cut up her bed, from which she had escaped. There were killings. The king responded by telling one of his ministers to pass out free grain on all the roads.

To calm the armed mob, Lafayette took a heavy chance: he brought the royal family out on the balcony as the crowd kept yelling "To Paris!" and announced that the king had agreed to go to Paris and to accept the Declaration of Rights. They cheered him, and when Lafayette leaned over and kissed the trembling hand of Marie Antoinette, they cheered her too. The march to Paris began. The royal troops were disarmed and surrounded by the French National Guard. Lafayette rode his horse alongside the king's carriage, and the crowd carried the heads of two royal bodyguards, mounted on tall spikes, as they yelled, "We'll no longer lack bread. We're bringing in the baker, the baker's wife, and the baker's little apprentices."[94]

Back in Paris, Louis moved into the vacant Palace of Tuileries; later, so did the Assembly. And the Paris people, from time to time, would do what they had never been allowed to do in the past: surge into the palace garden and yell patriotic cheers.

All that turmoil left two main results: the king was forced to submit to the people and the Assembly emerged as the government of France. Thanks to the improved weather in farm country, much bread was available in Paris, so not for another two years would a Parisian crowd again revolt. Despite all the killing and hatred, a democracy seemed within near reach. The king was no longer seen as a monarch, but as a prime minister representing the Assembly. The Assembly was no longer an advisory council, but a legislative body. Thanks to the Revolution of 1789, the future looked promising.

TO MAKE AN OPERATIVE DEMOCRACY? MIRABEAU STEPS FORTH

At the start of the United States, the Bill of Rights simply set limits on the national government. Only later was it interpreted to mean that the government had to actively prevent others from violating basic human rights. In short, the American Bill of Rights was a government-limiting doctrine, not a political philosophy. In France, on the other hand, Lafayette's Declaration of Rights was a fundamental philosophy, the principles upon which the purposes of the government itself were to stand. Having won the remarkable victory of establishing fundamental beliefs for the country, the next step was to create a constitution to enact those principles.

Obviously, there were distinctive, serious problems in structuring a democratic government in a country like France. For instance, France still had a king and a state church. There remained a rich aristocracy that had been strongly entrenched for generations, an extensive peasantry, and a large, impoverished city population. To make France a democracy, the Declaration of Rights was not enough. A constitution was necessary. And it could not be a perfect document composed, at a stroke, by powers at the top. France needed a constitution worked out with the support of the wide range of people and their representatives.

Lafayette marched straight into this creative fight. He and Mirabeau led the constitutional movement in 1789. They worked together, day by day. Like Lafayette, Mirabeau saw American democracy as the best model, especially because of Americans' determination to prevent the government from empowering religion.

Mirabeau grew up with trouble. Born in 1749, as a little child he accidentally poisoned himself by drinking ink. As a teenager, he was hated by his father, who saw him as "an ill-bred youngster" on his way to becoming "an incurably perverse idiot"[95] His mother, who was also hated by his father, was a heavy gambler. One of his sisters became a nun and went crazy; another took up sin. Young Mirabeau was force-educated and then sent into the military, where he fought with his colonel and therefore spent time in prison. On his first day out of prison, he fought a duel; thereafter, "he went around swearing and fighting and giving vent to such wickedness as you never saw," wrote the family servant to his father.[96]

Mirabeau was taken up by his uncle, who thought he had so "much brilliance of mind" that "If he is not worse than Nero he'll be better than Marcus Aurelius...."[97] At age 21, Mirabeau received permission from his father (who still detested him) to take the family title of Count de Mirabeau. His parents got him married, but he ran away with another woman. In Amsterdam, Mirabeau went to work writing and translating for a publisher. But his life continued to be troubled: he went through a series of money crises, mistress after mistress, and battles with

Mirabeau.

his parents. He drank heavily and even spent several more years in jail. He lived in England for a while, and visited Germany. But through it all, Mirabeau's mind remained keen.

In 1778, he thought "The English government seems to be crazy," while America was "the most worthy nation in the world!"[98] He had come to hate religion:

> I hate and fear pious people, and I prize toleration as the one thing which can give the civil authority a real and firm control over the whole ecclesiastical body, and maintain social tranquillity in spite of fanaticism, hypocrisy and superstition....As a general rule, have no sort of confidence nor even, so far as you can avoid them, social relations with anybody infected with religious zeal. One can never depend in anything upon people who sanctify perfidy, and refer all moral questions to a system which, even were it not false, absurd and pernicious, incessantly contradicts the passions, interests and general course of human life....I am deeply convinced that *true believers* are...either credulous ignoramuses or interested hypocrites or artful rogues or dangerous enthusiasts.[99]

For many years, church officials in France had been appointed by the government. They were dependent on the aristocracy and the king for their power and financial support. But very many French people had become indifferent to religion in the eighteenth century because it seemed ignorant and superstitious in the Age of Reason.

Mirabeau supported the monarchy, though he thought the king should have only limited governing power. He believed there should be some free trade, free emigration, free army enlistment. And he thought the king ought to bring the military under civil control. As for the aristocracy, he wrote, "The most absolute monarch's interests are coincident with the principles of popular government. It is not kings that the peoples fear and resent; it is their ministers, their courtiers, their nobles—in a word, aristocracy."[100] Mirabeau envisioned a new government that would be "linked to a constitutional scheme which would save us from aristocratic conspiracies, from democratic excesses and from the utter anarchy into which authority, though wishing to be absolute, has plunged itself and us."[101]

He stressed history and realism in his pamphlets and speeches and private advice. For example, he told the king that the legislators "will never forget the natural alliance of Throne and People against divers aristocracies, whose power could only be established upon the ruin of royal authority and of the common weal."[102] He saw that politics based on the abstractions of philosophers was unworkable: it produced fanciful politicians who insisted on their imaginative "truth in its impelling purity," whereas a reasonable politician "is bound to take previous events, difficulties and obstacles into account."[103] He understood that genuine discourse and compromise, though difficult, was the fundamental practical challenge in politics. He once said to an agent apropos of two government council members, "I like neither of them, and I don't suppose they care for me; but it matters little whether we like each other if we can come to an understanding. I am appealing to you to arrange a meeting with them."[104]

For months, despite their differences of personality, Lafayette and Mirabeau collaborated on moving the constitution forward in the National Assembly. As Lafayette's biographer Bernier puts it, "By mid-October [1789], only two men were popular enough to run the government effectively: Mirabeau, because of his eloquence, and Lafayette, because of his popularity. Neither man, however, could form a ministry without the other."[105] Actually, Mirabeau dominated the formation of the new ministry, meeting with Lafayette to damn most candidates and to propose a few others. Lafayette proceeded with less certainty. One night at dinner with Gouverneur Morris, the American statesman, then in Paris on business, Lafayette confided his uneasiness about the morality of some candidates for the ministry. Morris explained to him that "Men do not go into Administration as the direct Road to Heaven." Instead, they are "prompted by ambition or avarice."[106]

Mirabeau backed Lafayette as a real chief minister, hoping Lafayette would pick the members he wanted, including Mirabeau who was anxious to get some money. But Lafayette decided he would not take on that role. And he tried to get Mirabeau to let it delay, but Mirabeau pressed for it. Lafayette offered him substantial money, but Mirabeau refused the money though he wrote to Lafayette: "Whatever may come, I shall be yours to the end."[107] They continued to work together toward a constitution, yet each man found it hard to maintain confidence in the other. Mirabeau complained about Lafayette's feeble thinking: "What a man! What an outlook! I am afraid…he will pretty soon ball things up."[108]

Each met with many others in the Assembly and took on issue after issue—offices, duties, and economic policies. Both hoped to make French democracy a reality. But Lafayette had a vaster vision. In his view, the purpose of the constitution was:

> To continue to defend the National Assembly against public enemies, to insure the inviolability of the Representatives of the Nation and the freedom of their debates as well as the rights of a beloved monarch whose personal happiness is a necessity as well as an obligation for us, and to maintain with firmness the decrees of the National Assembly and particularly those that united by every tie of fraternal equality all parts and all citizens of the Empire are the principles to which our honor mutually binds us and for which we are ready to shed the last drop of blood.[109]

Mirabeau had a much more cynical vision: he saw the National Assembly as "a wild ass, which could be mounted only with a great deal of maneuvering."[110] He was impatient for results, though his mode of negotiation was often marred by harsh and insulting rhetoric, both publicly and privately. Tension between the two men became significant. Lafayette made high and wide speeches, while Mirabeau kept pushing forward proposals for change.

Then in January 1790, Mirabeau secretly sold out. He took money from the king on a continuing basis and began to subtly agitate in favor of the king, that made as little change in the king's status as possible. Thus the effort to create a democratic constitution became Lafayette's responsibility alone.

LAFAYETTE TAKES OVER THE MOVEMENT

Despite the tensions among Lafayette, Mirabeau, the king, the queen, and others, important steps were taken toward government by law in the year after the Bastille revolution. Largely owing to Lafayette's initiatives in the National Assembly, laws were passed. But it was uncertain whether these laws would be executed—laws such as the kings right to veto, to make peace and war, to abolish inherited titles, and laws regarding the relation of the state to the church. Increasingly, Mirabeau and Lafayette grew to dislike each other, and Lafayette regarded the king and queen as "just big children who will not swallow the medicines which are good for them without being frightened by tales of werewolves."[111] But those attitudes remained private. In public, Lafayette and Mirabeau were respectful of one another and willing to cooperate despite their interpersonal attitudes. Lafayette explained: "Believe me, if I care above all for liberty and the principles of our constitution, my second wish, my very ardent wish, is for the return of order, of calm, and the establishment of public vigor."[112] He joined with Mirabeau in working out how the new government would declare war. Mirabeau now thought the king should be responsible for war and he tried to persuade the Assembly accordingly. But at last the Assembly decided that "war could be declared only by a decree of the legislature voted upon the formal and necessary proposal of the king and subsequently sanctioned by His Majesty."[113] The members applauded the two who had led the discussion: Lafayette and Mirabeau. And so it went. The two stood strong, speaking neither as rabble rousers nor lecturing philosophers but as make-it-happen politicians. They took up tough, important issues. The National Assembly did reach decisions, but as July 1790 approached, the constitution was still unfinished.

On July 14, 1790, there was a great celebration in Paris in honor of the Bastille revolution one year earlier. For this festival, a huge piece of land was required. At a place called Champ-de-Mars, it took workers and volunteers—some 150,000 citizens, including ladies and gentlemen and children—eight days to clear the ground and construct a grand altar. One day Lafayette mounted his white horse, rode out, and set to work with them. He dug the earth with a pickax, shoveled the soil into a wheelbarrow, and rolled it over to the mound at the side of the field. That action impressed ordinary citizens.[114]

The more he thought about it, the more committed Lafayette became to the July 14 event. At first, he had wanted it postponed until the nation could celebrate the existence of a new and permanent constitution. But he changed his mind as the celebration day approached and he saw the excited anticipation throughout the community. Lafayette addressed the National Assembly:

> Finish your work, Gentlemen....Now carry on and put strength into authority of the state. The people owe to you the glory of a free constitution, but they ask of you, they expect, that stability at last which cannot exist without a strong and thorough organization of government.[115]

The current president of the National Assembly (a new one was elected every two weeks) shared Lafayette's ambition for lasting democracy. He saw as "the finest day of the National Assembly" the one on which it would build and stabilize for the future an operative constitution.[116] The king himself spoke out in support of Lafayette's appeal:

> Defenders of public order, friends of law and liberty, remember that your first duty is the maintenance of order and submission to law; that the benefits of a free constitution should be equal for all; that the freer one is, the more serious are the offenses he commits against freedom [and] the more criminal the acts of violence and force that are not required by law.[117]

So all the important players in the drama seemed to agree on the essential point: the nation should have a constitution. But a constitution had not yet been created.

THE PUBLIC CELEBRATION OF THE HOPE FOR DEMOCRACY

The great theatrical festival on July 14, 1790, strengthened popular support for a strong democracy. At about eight o'clock in the morning, the march to Champ-de-Mars began, with Lafayette at the front of the cavalry and some 50,000 National Guards, who had been waiting since dawn. There was also a battalion of 400 children, carrying a sign that read "The Hope of the *Patrie*,"[118] as well as a group of 100 young mothers with their babies in cradles decorated with tricolor ribbons.[119] The marchers were cheered all along the way. Whenever they paused, people fed them cakes and bread and wine—this at a time of harsh hunger. A storm burst from the sky, with pelting rain and wind, but it hardly slowed the march.

A fellow came up to Lafayette and offered him a glass, saying "General, you are warm. Have a drink." But what was the liquid? Wine? Poison? Lafayette hesitated only a moment before drinking it down and handing back the glass with thanks to the giver. The fellow had noticed the general's brief hesitation, so Lafayette poured himself another glassful and drank it down. The spectators cheered.[120]

On they rode. Lafayette ordered the artillery to fire to signal the approach of the National Assembly, who were dressed in their plain black coats. They made it to the huge field at about one o'clock, approaching the great Altar of the Fatherland, with a woman on one side representing the constitution. Some 400,000 French citizens were there.[121] From the altar came a pronouncement of three "sacred words":

> The Nation, the Law, the King
> The Nation, that is you
> The Law, that is also you
> The King, he is the guardian of the Law[122]

A large body of clergy, some 300 chaplains and priests, arrived and established themselves with their bishop, Talleyrand, who told them, "Sing and weep tears of joy, for this day France has been made anew."[123] Hundreds of musicians and drummers played for the arrivals. When Lafayette was seen riding in, the applause burst forth more loudly. The troops settled near the priests, and everyone waited for the king, whose chair—oddly in front of but below the chair of the National Assembly president—had been transformed into a throne by being draped with purple velvet embroidered with gold. As the heavy rain fell— "Heaven were washing away the sins of the nation"[124]—and the waiting continued, soldiers joined the singing and some danced around, laughing, on the muddy ground.

Signaled by a salvo of artillery, King Louis XVI, dressed in bright regalia, arrived to an enthusiastic ovation and settled into his thronely chair. The ceremony began with a mass celebrated by the priests under Bishop Talleyrand. Lafayette signaled 83 official flag bearers to approach, and they were blessed. The bands played. The cannons boomed. The spectators applauded. Then Lafayette signaled the Paris National Guard to form a lane before him, through which he rode his horse toward the king. He dismounted, marched up the stairs, saluted the king, and asked for orders. The king gave him the text of the oath to be taken by the soldiers present—more than 14,000, representing the 3 million National Guardsmen throughout France who had elected them. Lafayette saluted the king again, walked down, and drew his sword and lifted it high as he advanced toward the altar. He marched up the steps and, as trumpets sounded, placed his sword upon the altar. In the sudden silence, he turned to the soldiers and read loud and clear the new military oath:

> We swear to be forever faithful to the Nation, to the Law, and to the King; to maintain with all our power the Constitution decreed by the National Assembly and accepted by the King; to protect, in keeping with the Laws, the safety of persons and of property, the circulation of grain and of other supplies within the realm, the collection of taxes in whatever form they may have; [and] to remain united with all Frenchmen by the indissoluble bonds of brotherhood.[125]

Thousands drew their swords and held them high as they declared, "I so swear."

The cannons fired. Lafayette walked back down the steps as the band played. When he came to the National Assembly members, he signaled for the music to stop and shots to be fired. The Assembly president recited the members' oath:

> I swear to be faithful to the Nation, and to the King, and to maintain with all my might the Constitution decreed by the National Assembly and accepted by the King.

The members answered, "I so swear." The crowd cheered as the artillery fired again.

At last it was time for the king to swear his oath. Suddenly, a miracle seemed to happen: the rain stopped and the sun came out. Lafayette signaled and Louis XVI stated that

> I, King of the French, swear to employ all the power delegated to me by the constitutional law of the state, to maintain the constitution decreed by the National Assembly and accepted by me, and to attend to the execution of the laws.

Cheers broke out through the enormous crowd of citizens: "Hurray for the king!" Suddenly the queen stood and lifted her little boy up for the crowd to see, and the cheering increased. Some of the military started toward Marie Antoinette, but Lafayette rode over and ordered them back.

The ceremony was nearly over. The priests returned to the altar and chanted the *Te Deum*. The king departed. Lafayette started away, but a cheering person shouted, "Look at M. de Lafayette galloping down the centuries to come!"[126] People crowded around him, touching and kissing him and patting his horse. The day was done. A friend of Lafayette's wrote to Thomas Jefferson:

> The day of the Fourteenth went off happily, thank God, to the satisfaction of the kindly people and of its good king, to the honor of Lafayette, to whom security, public order, the safe outcome of the whole thing had been confided....Everyone is united here in saying, but each according to his inclination and system, some blessing, some cursing, that the French are copying the Americans and Lafayette their Washington.[127]

Clearly the great theme of the celebration was the need to have a constitution in place. In America, after the victorious Revolution, James Madison and his determined associates had succeeded in making a lasting constitution. The French were now determined to do the same for France. All three oaths had insisted on that. Lafayette was the hero of the day, upon whom the whole national community focused their devotion. They saw him as both the champion of the constitution and a resolute military leader who was singularly equipped to lead the nation to the basic law that would transform it from a monarchy into a democracy.

ACTION FOR DEMOCRACY DELAYED

The probability of immediate democracy lapsed. Lafayette did not wish to become king of France or a dictator like England's Cromwell, whom he had already been accused of imitating. In fact, Lafayette's direct responsibilities as a military commander loomed larger, taking up more and more of his time. Mirabeau, having secretly sold out to the king, worked to strengthen the monarchy. In the ceremony at the Champ-de-Mars, the king had sworn to support a constitution, but there was virtually no way to determine what he was really committed to—as his future actions would demonstrate. Even at the time of the July 14 celebration, King Louis and Queen Marie Antoinette were being pushed this way and that, responding day by day as they thought they had to in order to survive.

Until the day of the festival, Lafayette had led France on the basis of his belief in American democracy. His vision was not abstract, but concrete, influenced primarily by his adopted father, George Washington, and secondarily by Thomas Jefferson and Benjamin Franklin, as well as by what he knew of the work of James Madison and Alexander Hamilton. All these men were practitioners of democracy. Their thinking had indeed been affected by philosophers, but it was molded much more by their own basic values and real situations. When Lafayette, their student, took a break from political leadership, a very different approach to politics emerged in France.

FRANCE'S NEW APPROACH, BY ROUSSEAU AND ROBESPIERRE

An eloquent French philosopher named Jean-Jacques Rousseau was born in 1712 in Geneva, Switzerland. His life experience affected his thought. As a child, he was abandoned three times, first when his mother died, then when his father deserted him, and finally when he was ousted from his uncle's house.[128] When he reached 16, he ran away from all his family. Much later, in his *Confessions*, he wrote of his feelings at the time: "I was entering the wide world confidently, my value was going to fill it. By showing myself I was going to be the center of attention of the entire universe."[129]

As a boy, Rousseau learned to deal with the harshness of his life by dedicating himself to perfect and universal ideals, and by defining himself as a god. Young Jean-Jacques tried to gain admiration by his productions: engraving, toy-making, music composition, reading his writings in public, chess-playing and even by exposing his naked buttocks in elegant, populated courtyards. His peculiar mindset grew firm:

Jean Jacques Rousseau.

> I did not doubt that in the end I would become better than all of them and that was enough, in my opinion, to support me. I used to say to myself: whoever is best at something is always sure of being sought after. Let's be best, then, at no matter what; I shall be sought after, opportunities will present themselves, and my worth will do the rest.[130]

He won an academic prize for an essay, a victory that started him off on his career as a writer concentrating on philosophy. He described himself as a person who had been "good" but then "I became virtuous, or at least drunk with virtue."[131] In his behavior, Rousseau was not constrained by virtue—he had numerous adulterous affairs with women. But in writing, his perception of virtue ruled his thought.

He wrote much. As for politics, Rousseau's fundamental idea was that of the "general will." He believed the general will should dominate and even define the individual's will:

> *Each of us puts his person and all his power in common under the supreme direction of the general will, and, in our corporate capacity, we receive each member as an indivisible part of the whole.*[132]

As political scientist John H. Hallowell explains, "Rousseau argues that...each individual gave himself and his rights up completely and unreservedly to the community as a whole."[133] Rousseau was quite clear that "general will" did not mean some tentative or ambiguous agreement to live by "majority rule." It was a fixed commandment:

> Whoever refuses to obey the general will shall be compelled to do so by the whole body.
> *The general will is always right and tends to the public advantage.*
> We see at once that it can no longer be asked whose business it is to make the laws, since they are acts of the general will; nor whether the prince is above the law, since he is a member of the State; nor whether the law can be unjust, since no one is unjust to himself....
> He who dares to undertake the making of a people's institutions ought to feel himself capable, so to speak, of changing human nature, of transforming each individual, who is by himself a complete and solitary whole, into part of a greater whole from which he in a manner receives his life and being; of altering man's constitution for the purpose of strengthening it....[134]

Thus Rousseau advocated total rule of all members of society based on absolute principles of human nature.

In 1758—when Rousseau had 20 more years to live—Maximilien Marie Isidore Robespierre was born in Arras, France, four months after his mother and father were married. His father was a lawyer, as had been his father and grandfather. His mother was the daughter of a successful innkeeper and brewer. Arras, though it was the capital of a province, was a serene country village where the Robespierre family had been living for 300 years. The baby's life began happily.

But Maximilien Robespierre's happiness was short-lived. When his mother gave birth to a baby in Maximilien's sixth year, the baby died. Not long after, his mother died. Two years later, Maximilien's father left town and the children were distributed to relatives; Maximilien, age eight, went to a pair of aunts. His sister Charlotte wrote that their childhood was "filled with tears, and each of our early years was marked by the death of some cherished object. This fate influenced, more than one can imagine, Maximilien's character; it made him sad and melancholy." [135] He became a lonely boy who "rarely shared the games and pleasures of his comrades. He liked to meditate in silence and passed hours in reflection." [136] Instead of playing with friends, he stayed by himself, often making lace or taking care of pigeons.

Robespierre might have been permanently defeated early in life had it not been for the strength of his intellect. His boyhood teachers were "secular clergy" in a school formerly run by Jesuit priests (the Jesuits had been thrown out of France two years before Maximilien entered the school). He did well, so well he won a scholarship to one of the best schools in Paris, the College Louis-le-Grand. There he stayed for 12 years, winning prizes for his quiet studies of the classics. A teacher of rhetoric inspired him and trained him to speak well, especially about contemporary philosophies. At age 17, Robespierre was honored by an invitation to speak before the king and the queen, who smiled on his performance.

One of young Robespierre's teachers recalled the boy's intellectual devotion: "Everything went into his studies," and "His study was his God." [137] Student Robespierre read Rousseau. He was enthralled by Rousseau's *Confessions*. This

Maximilien Robespierre.

story of a tragic life remarkably similar to his own, yet braced by strong ideals, shaped Robespierre. Years later, he wrote a dedication addressed to Rousseau:

> Divine man, you taught me to know myself: while I was still young you made me appreciate the dignity of my nature and reflect upon the great principles of the social order....I saw you in your last days....I understood all the pains of a noble life devoted to the cult of truth. They did not frighten me. The consciousness of having wanted the good of his fellow beings is the recompense of the virtuous man....I wish to follow your venerable footsteps, even if I were to leave only a name which fails to interest the centuries to come: happy if, in the perilous career that an unprecedented revolution just opened before us, I remain constantly faithful to the inspirations I found in your texts![138]

Rousseau's texts shaped Robespierre. Like Lafayette, Robespierre found a father: he saw himself as "the spiritual son of the author of the *Confessions*."[139]

Like his actual father, Robespierre decided to be a lawyer. After being licensed in Paris in August 1781, he returned home to Arras, where he was appointed an "Episcopal Judge." Getting money was not his purpose,[140] but he had trouble even getting cases, and lost some of those few he did manage to get. Then (as now) lawyers had to concentrate on evidence as well as on the law itself, and Robespierre tended to focus solely on theoretical principles, ignoring facts. Biographer James Michael Eagan describes Robespierre's typical approach as "urging adherence to the spirit of the law rather than to its letter."[141] Concrete information about a case did not interest him. He once took on the defense of a wealthy man who had a lightning rod—Benjamin Franklin's invention—put up on the top of his house. The man's neighbors, frightened that the rod would attract lightning to the neighborhood and then divert it to their houses, had filed suit against him. Instead of gathering and presenting to the court facts about the operation of the lightning rod, Robespierre concentrated on the principles involved in the case—including what the philosophers Galileo and Descartes would have had to say about it. (In this instance, Robespierre did win his case, perhaps by dazzling the sleepy judge with his grasp of philosophical principles.)

Robespierre also was active at the local academy, where he could expound philosophy. Echoing Rousseau, he declared that virtue

> demands that all special interests, all personalities, yield to the general welfare. Each citizen, being part of the state is obliged to watch over the safety of his country whose rights are entrusted to him. He should spare no one when the safety of the republic demands his punishment.[142]

By 1788, when he was 30 years old, Robespierre's law practice had declined to nearly nothing. So that year, when the Estates-General was called into session for the first time since 1614, Robespierre welcomed the chance to be elected to the Third Estate, the commoners. He campaigned by advertising his virtue. One of his pamphlets read, "Oh, you who are citizens who burn with that sacred fire of patriotism to which is bound the hope and the safety of the nation, unite to oppose the fearful conspiracy hatched against it."[143] He got elected and borrowed money for the coach fare to Versailles. There, admiring the glorious monarchical palace and gardens,[144] he began a new career.

In his maiden speech, Robespierre recommended that the clergy be invited to join the Third Estate. That proposal was rejected, but it impressed Mirabeau, who made it his business to get to know Robespierre.[145] From then on, Robespierre spoke repeatedly. He declared his devotion to politics as the core of virtue: "The fundamental principle of democracy is virtue, the love of the country and its laws."[146] He was devoted to an abstraction he called *"le peuple,"* which he saw as "always worth more than the individuals."[147] At the same time, he proclaimed, "I am the people myself!"[148] He was devoted to "love of the Fatherland," the nation, but insisted that the government of France must be transformed.[149] He was devoted to Rousseau's pronouncement that "he who would undertake to create a people should see himself as involved, so to speak, in changing human nature."[150] In 1789, the other representatives thought him interesting, but too radical. But outside the National Assembly, he was growing very popular. He spoke frequently, and the public began to see politics as fulfilling needs. As scholar Lynn Hunt notes, for Robespierre, "Politics was not an arena for the representation of competing interests. It was rather an instrument for reshaping human nature, making citizens out of subjects, free men out of slaves, republicans out of the oppressed."[151]

Robespierre favored Lafayette's Declaration of Rights, but he did not want the king in charge of it. He proposed that the king "be called the first public functionary, the chief of the executive power, but never the representative of the nation."[152]

When, in 1789, the Bastille revolution and the march on Versailles induced the king and the Assembly to move to Paris, some 200 angry conservative members resigned. Numerous nobles were already leaving France, terrified of what was to come. But Robespierre was at home in Paris, where he had long gone to school. He lived alone, without any sex or love affairs or even close friends. He rose at 6:00 A.M., spent an hour getting properly dressed, and left for the court at 10.[153]

Later he walked over to a new club formed for secret political discussions: the Society of the Revolution, later nicknamed the Jacobin Club because the group had rented the library of an old Dominican monastery called the Convent of the Jacobins. The Jacobin Club's first president was Mirabeau, who was subsequently reelected. In February 1790, the Jacobins went public and adopted for their formal name the Society of Friends of the Constitution. There were other clubs in Paris, which Robespierre did not take part in: the Society of Friends of the Rights of Man, in which a man named Danton took part, and the club called the Friend of the People, from which a radical named Marat emerged.[154] But the Jacobin Club grew—and not only in Paris; there were about 1,000 chapters throughout France. Robespierre became its leader: he was titled "Savior of the Jacobins."[155] He urged that virtue be the first criterion for membership; those who were not "pure patriots" should be excluded from Jacobin Clubs.[156] So the clubs got into the habit of investigating, assessing, selecting and rejecting people for membership based on the purity of their "patriotism." In one chapter, five different purges cut membership from 300 to 171.[157] Women were excluded from membership.[158] Ironically, since Robespierre believed that the state—not the church—was the authority of all virtue, the Jacobin Clubs often met in churches, called together by the bell. Many of them published journals. The purpose was simple, as Robespierre defined it: "Spread the ideas and sentiments of patriotism among our citizens" and "the sacred flame which you possess will spread everywhere."[159] An oath required by one of the clubs put the Jacobin credo succinctly: "I shall never have any other temple than that of Reason, other altars than those of *la patrie*, other priests than our legislators, nor other cult than that of liberty, equality, fraternity."[160]

In the months following July 14, 1790, Lafayette, having broken with Mirabeau and having been assigned wider responsibility for commanding the military by the king, stopped attending the National Assembly regularly. Robespierre did attend regularly and became a leading figure. He spoke against limiting voting to those who paid taxes equivalent to three days' wages and against restricting the citizenship of Jews, actors, Protestants, and domestic servants.[161]

As the government grew desperate for money, it became more militant against the Catholic Church. On August 4, 1790, the church was required to abolish the tithe payments members had been required to pay to their churches. Since the French had revolted against paying taxes and the government's credit was so bad it could not borrow funds, there was nowhere to turn for money but to the Church. The state took over Church property and the funds of the clergy and required priests to swear allegiance "to the nation, the law, and the King."[162] In private, Marie Antoinette was infuriated by the government's takeover of Church funds and property, though in public she and Louis seemed to approve of the action.

In the spring of 1791, Mirabeau died. Near the time of his death, despite excruciating pain, he kept speaking to the National Assembly on many issues, especially on preserving the authority of the king.[163] By this time, the king and the queen were in such despair they decided to run away. They tried to escape to Austria in a coach on the night of June 20, 1791, the king disguised as a common valet. But they were caught, arrested, and brought back to Paris, where they were jailed in their own castle. Marie Antoinette's hair turned white.[164] Robespierre insisted that the king should be brought to trial, but the Assembly members voted to simply suspend him until he should sign their (still unfinished) constitution.

On July 17, 1791, mobs rioted again, demanding that the king be deposed. The Assembly declared martial law. Lafayette, in charge of the National Guard, had to disperse demonstrators at the Champ-de-Mars. Someone there shot at and nearly hit him. In the turmoil, Lafayette ordered the guards to fire at the crowd and they killed approximately a dozen of the rioters.[165] The riot was stopped, but public reaction was hard against Lafayette. The common people now saw their former hero as a murderer. Robespierre and the Jacobins damned him in public.

THE CONSTITUTION IS BORN

The constitution was finally completed in August 1791. Hope for democracy was renewed. In September, the king was reinstated so he could approve it. He did. A general amnesty forgiving the government's enemies was decreed. Acting on a proposal by Robespierre, the members of the National Assembly, despite their valuable experience, ruled that they would not be eligible for membership in the new legislature to be elected under the constitution. They resigned from the Assembly and departed from Paris. In October, Lafayette resigned his military command, glad to go off to live in a village (perhaps thinking of George Washington's passion for Mt. Vernon) and happy for the victory of democracy. "It is as a lover of liberty and equality," he said, "that I enjoy the change which has put all citizens on the same level and given preeminence only to the lawful authorities." [166]

A new Assembly of 745 members, restricted to one term apiece, was elected. The constitution put nearly all power in their hands. The king had virtually no power. Compared to England's George III or to President George Washington, Louis XVI was constitutionally transformed into a symbolic clerk. A rule was that he would be dethroned if he traveled more than 50 miles from Paris. Control of both the military and the top ministers of government was constitutionally in the hands of the new Assembly. The Assembly members, new at national politics and power, were much affected by two relatively experienced political parties—the Jacobins and the Girondins. The latter were militant ideologues in favor of making war and taking over of the king's army. [167] Indeed, war was approaching. Austrian forces were moving toward France. Robespierre, now out of the Assembly, became the editor of a newspaper. He advocated the defense of the constitution but, with the rest of the Jacobins, he opposed war.

As in the United States, the new constitution in France had to be put into practice after it was formally instituted. In December 1791, Lafayette, hoping to help do that, returned to Paris and spoke to the Assembly. King Louis greeted him coldly. Lafayette was vigorously concerned about the Austrian war threat. But the king, given his character, was secretly hoping that the French army would be defeated so that the nation would demand the cancellation of the new constitution and reinstate him as absolute king to defend France. In contrast, Lafayette took off to the war front to defend his country. Thanks to his American experience, he was able to weld the disorganized, confused, angered soldiers into an army.

LAFAYETTE CHECKS OUT

In January and February of 1792, the new Assembly began to confiscate private property and conduct a witch hunt against supposed traitors, as well as to suppress priests even further. It produced paper money, whose value quickly plummeted. On March 14, 1792, the king was forced to appoint new ministers of war and the interior. Lafayette grew worried: "The Assembly are wildly uninformed and too fond of popular applause, and the King slow and rather backward in his daily conduct." [168] For different reasons, both the king and the Jacobins worked to see Lafayette defeated by the Austrians.

On April 20, 1792, France declared war against Austria by action of the king and the Assembly. Angered French soldiers rioted in masses. In a clash with Austrian troops on the Belgian border, French troops deserted and murdered their own general. In Paris, the minister of war and the commander-in-chief resigned from office. [169] The king lost support and the Jacobins gained it. On June 16, 1792, General Lafayette, perhaps unaware of the king's plot for his and the army's defeat, wrote a letter to the Assembly, asking them to give His Majesty independent authority. He wanted the Jacobins stopped, believing that they had "caused all the disorders" in the Assembly: "Organized like an empire throughout the country, blindly led by a few ambitious men, this sect forms a separate body amid the French people whose power it usurps by subjugating its representatives." [170] His enemies blasted him. Danton said, "There is no doubt that Lafayette is the head of the nobles who are allied with the tyrants of Europe," and Robespierre declared, "Strike Lafayette and the nation is safe." [171]

On June 20, 1792, a Paris mob crowded into the king's palace and forced him to put on a red hat and drink red wine to toast the Revolution. When Lafayette hurried to Paris and urged the Assembly to enforce the constitution and stop the chaos, Jacobins yelled out for his head to be cut off. A majority of the Assembly approved Lafayette's demand, but did not carry it out. He returned to the army and wrote secretly to the king, proposing that his National Guard meet and protect him, arrest the Jacobins, and restore the constitution. [172] But the king did not approve the proposal. On July 14, at the second celebration of the Bastille revolution, King Louis wore a protective breast-plate under his robe to guard against assassination. [173]

Robespierre induced the government to transfer Lafayette's military command to France's Northern Army, whose soldiers were not familiar with General Lafayette. Robespierre denounced him again, saying, "Freedom will be in danger as long as Lafayette is at the head of an army." [174] On July 15, 1792, a member of the Assembly demanded that Lafayette be charged with treason. The majority voted that down, but then on July 20, Robespierre demanded his arrest: "If Lafayette is not punished, it means we have no constitution, for there can be no constitution where a man is above the law." [175] On July 29, Robespierre explained to the Jacobins that "Serious ills call for drastic remedies." [176] On August 4, a committee in the Assembly proposed to indict Lafayette for treason, but the full Assembly voted against indictment, 406 to 224. Some 500 military representatives from Marseilles, singing prowar songs, came to Paris and met with the Jacobins. All regions of Paris joined in a petition to eliminate the king and bring together a new National Convention. Parisians rioted again on August 10, and again invaded the king's palace. He and his family escaped to the Assembly, where, after violent debate, a majority declared the king suspended and sent him and his family to prison.

THE CONSTITUTION IS BROKEN

Arresting and suspending the king broke the constitution. The Assembly collapsed. An Insurrectionary Commune was formed and took command. Robespierre was elected a member on August 11, 1792, and the Commune empowered him as "the true mayor of Paris."[177] Given the state of emergency, the Commune suspended the free press, arrested monarchists, and closed down monasteries and convents.[178] Hearing the news of Paris, Lafayette tried to rally the troops in defense of the constitution. He succeeded in getting the new government commissioners arrested, but he did not succeed in getting the troops to swear an oath to "The Nation, the Law, the King," as the constitution required. Instead, they swore an oath to "Liberty, Equality, and the National Assembly."

That persuaded Lafayette to escape. He and a small squadron headed toward the Belgian coast to take a ship to the United States, but on the way, they were caught and imprisoned by the Austrian army.[179] In Paris, Robespierre insisted that Lafayette "must be declared a traitor to the country."[180] The Assembly continued to exist, but did virtually nothing. Six weeks went by until a new National Convention was elected in September 1792, with the intention of drafting a new constitution for France.

With Mirabeau dead, Lafayette gone, and the king in prison, Robespierre emerged as the national leader. A country that had a Mirabeau wheeling and dealing, a Lafayette pushing for an American-inspired practical system of democracy, and a king who was ambivalent about yielding power to a popularly elected Assembly had a certain advantage: its first constitution had been composed through compromise, taking into consideration the interests of various political perspectives. With its three most influential political leaders removed from the scene, France's future was uncertain. What kind of new constitution would be created with Robespierre and the Paris Commune in power?

In September 1792, a wave of incredible violence swept Paris. It had been prepared for by two actions. A month earlier, about 500 rioters, mostly drunks, had tramped up from Marseilles and camped in the capital. Then, for some reason, the Paris Commune had released from prison a number of people convicted of crimes of violence, including murder.[181] For six days that September, gangs tore through Paris from one prison to another, killing more than a thousand prisoners, including women and children. Those murdered were not all identified as enemies of the government. Some were nobles, but others were prostitutes and common criminals and priests. For example, 150 priests—unarmed, naturally—were grabbed from a convent. The mob set up a table in the corridor supposedly to give the priests a trial two at a time. They were condemned and shoved down the steps into a garden, where 119 of the priests were murdered by the mob in less than two hours.[182] A princess, Mme. de Lamballe, was pushed before the "trial" table. When she refused to declare that she hated the king and queen of France, she was pushed down into the mob. They killed her with a spear, cut out her beating heart and ate it. They also cut off her arms and legs and shot them through a cannon.[183] Some 1,500 people were killed in the frenzy, including 33 boys aged 12 to 14 and a number of 10-year-old girls, sliced to death by swords.[184]

Amazingly, on September 3, 1792, the Commune of Paris actually put out a proclamation in support of the vicious chaos:

> The Commune of Paris hastens to inform its brothers in the Departments that many ferocious conspirators detained in its prisons have been put to death by the people—acts of justice which seemed to be indispensable in order to terrorize the traitors concealed within its walls at a time when it was about to march on the enemy. The whole nation will without doubt hasten to adopt this measure so necessary to public safety, and all the French people will cry out as did the Parisians, "We will march on the enemy, but we will not leave brigands behind us to murder our wives and children."[185]

The National Assembly failed to stop the killing, and the Insurrectionary Commune took part in it. Minister of justice Danton commented, "I don't give a damn about the prisoners,"[186] and the minister of the interior declared the killing was "a kind of justice."[187] When Robespierre learned about the violence, he took no action against it.

Instead, the new government focused on how to handle the king. The royal prisoner was now widely seen as a traitor to France. Robespierre argued that there need be no trial for him because his fault was so clear. Nevertheless, the king was tried in December 1792. Robespierre spoke against him: "We talk of a republic, and Louis still lives! We talk of a republic, and the person of the King still stands between us and liberty!" Though Robespierre had opposed the death penalty, he now said that "because the country must live, Louis must die."[188] The Assembly voted for his guilt, but a separate vote for his death won by a majority of only one.[189] On January 21, 1793, King Louis XVI had his head cut off.

Robespierre and his Jacobin organization moved to rule France, overcoming their Girondin opponents and replacing the National Assembly with their emergency operations. The war with Austria went on, despite Robespierre's opposition to it, and on February 1, 1793, the Convention even declared war on England due to money problems.[190] In June, Robespierre became a member of the Committee of Public Safety.

That year, 1793, mob killings were rampant in much of France. In the province of Brittany, for example, a child-hater emerged as a mob leader. "They are all little whelps," he said, "and they must be butchered without mercy." So 500 boys and girls were driven out into a field, where they were shot down and beaten to death. In another instance, 200 men were tied together and killed with small iron balls.[191]

ROBESPIERRE'S NEW "DEMOCRACY" FOR VIRTUE

From Robespierre's point of view, a new France—a real republic—was now possible. With the malicious and obstructionist king gone, France could establish a real democracy, based on deliberative actions by a national legislature elected by the people. He said there should be no more executions. He defined his cause based on his Rousseauistic thinking:

> It is not enough to have overturned the throne: our concern is to erect upon its remains holy equality, and the imprescriptible rights of man. It is not an empty name, but the character of its citizens, that constitutes a republic. The soul of a republic is *vertu*—that is, love of one's country, and a high-minded devotion which sinks all private interests in those of the community as a whole....The temple of liberty must be rebuilt upon the foundations of justice and equality.[192]

In May 1793, the meetings of the National Assembly were moved into a theater. The seats faced the stage. Given that arrangement, members did not turn toward one another to debate, but rather faced toward the leading actors up front. In Paris, Catholic churches were closed and more than 400 priests were forced to resign.[193] In July, Robespierre took over the new Committee of Public Safety, which was now the true governing body of the country. Having emerged as France's supreme leader, he spoke theatrically to the Assembly. That May he declared that "Man is born for happiness and freedom" and "The object of society is the preservation of his rights, *and the perfecting of his nature*."[194]

What Robespierre believed in became highly significant for the fate of France. "The Revolution was his whole life," historian Robert Sobel points out: "He did not care for wine or food, friends or family. Robespierre's entire existence was dedicated to his ideas."[195]

Time and again, Robespierre presented proposals based on his vision of the mission of the state. The Republic, he determined, would transform ordinary, messy human life into virtuous existence; it would create a heaven on earth through politics. And he lived solely for that grand ideal. "Yes," he said,

> this charming land of ours, this pampered child of nature, was made to be the realm of liberty and happiness; its proud and sensitive people was born for glory and goodness....I am a Frenchman, thy representative....Accept the sacrifice of my whole being! Blessed is the man who lives in thy midst! Thrice blessed he who can die for thy happiness!...[196]

He explained his credo of politics this way:

> We wish to substitute morals for egotism, honesty for love of honor, principles for conventions, duties for good wishes, the rule of reason for the tyranny of fashion, the hatred of vice for the scorn of unhappiness, pride for insolence, grandeur of the soul for vanity, love of glory for love of gold, good people for "good company," the charm of happiness for the boredom of luxury, the grandeur of man for the pettiness of the great, a magnanimous, powerful, happy people for a lovable, frivolous and miserable one; that is, we must substitute all the virtues and miracles of the republic for all the devices and the ridiculousness of a monarchy.[197]

To Robespierre, virtue was not distinct from politics but essential to it. "Not only is virtue the soul of democracy," he said, "but it can exist only in such a government."[198] As biographer David P. Jordan notes, to Robespierre "the Revolution was morality in action."[199] What a politician should do, declared Robespierre, is "Think of nothing but the good of the country and the interests of humanity. Welcome every institution and doctrine that consoles and elevates the soul."[200] And "Patriotism must be a marked characteristic of everyone. Republican spirit and a very pronounced love of France are the first conditions for the employment or designation of citizens for public functions of all kinds."[201]

Robespierre did not see the ethical complexities that others did: "There exists for all men but one morality, one single conscience."[202] And virtue had a natural development: "The more a man is endowed with sensitivity and genius, the more he attaches himself to ideas that enlarge his being and elevate his heart; and the doctrine of this kind of man becomes the doctrine of the universe. Ah! How could such ideas not be true?"[203] That spring a military academy declared for a republic

> where every citizen is a soldier, each man owes his life to the defence of the fatherland and must make himself fit to serve it well.
>   Parents must be guided by the principle that children belong first to the general family, the Republic, and only secondly to individual families. Without this principle there can be no republican education.[204]

Robespierre's Articles, proposed as the law of the land in May 1794, began with these sweeping statements:

> Article I. —The French people recognizes the existence of the Supreme Being, and the immortality of the soul.
> Article II.—It recognizes that the proper worship of the Supreme Being consists in the practice of human duties.[205]

Subsequently, the legislators did not create laws by voting for them, but by remaining silent about new laws propagated by Robespierre and his Jacobin allies.[206]

Given Robespierre's determination to force a republic of complete virtue—one where every citizen was dedicated to the "glory and goodness" of the state—he had to appeal to the public for support of his new government. He did so theatrically and with great effect. But not every French citizen loved him that spring of 1794. He took a box seat at a theater to watch a play about the classic tyrant Nero. When, in the play, the actors yelled "Death to the tyrant!" a good portion of the audience on the main floor cheered loudly, jumped up, and shook their fists at Robespierre up in his box. He paled. He waved to them.[207]

Still, Robespierre was nearly unanimously elected president of the Convention. The final Article he proposed announced France's first "National festival in honour of the Supreme Being." The festival, in effect, declared God's blessing on the Republic's political perfection.[208] That astonishing celebration, designed by the great artist Jacques-Louis David under Robespierre's supervision, was performed on June 8, 1794. Robespierre was the star, as Lafayette had been at the festival of 1790. The festival presented to the world Robespierre's vision for France.

A marvelous mountain was constructed on the Champ-de-Mars, high and wide enough for the Convention to stand upon it, along with orchestras and others. Moral symbols were put up: an ancient oak tree, a 50-foot-high pillar with a statue of Hercules on it, holding "Liberty" in his hand. There were tombs, a temple with 20 columns, and candels with torches.[209] Citizens and children were trained to sing new songs "like the rumble of a troubled sea which the winds of the South raise and prolong to an echo heard in distant valleys and forests," wrote David. Robespierre had the "Hymn of the Supreme Being" recomposed to suit his moral purposes.

At five o'clock in the morning on June 8, 1794, the bugles blew to wake the people. The day was fine, the sun coming up. Robespierre, in a special suit of yellow pants and blue jacket, was dressed like the Rousseau-drenched hero of a popular novel by Goethe.[210] He stepped out onto the street and howled, "Oh nature, how sublime and delicious is your power. How tyrants will pale before the idea of this holiday!"[211] Holding flowers, he marched along the old king castle, well ahead of the deputies. The people cheered. He did hear a few ugly whispers: "There's the dictator! He wants all the people's attention fixed on him! It's not enough to be king! He wants to be God!"[212] But far more admirers roared forth in his favor.

Twenty-four hundred citizens sang as a choral group, separated into men, women, girls, boys, and small children. Great bands of girls in white lawn dresses carried baskets of fruit.[213] Robespierre arrived at his lone chair up front. He spoke to the masses of his vision for France:

> French Republicans, first people of the world. The day has arrived that the French people consecrate to the Supreme Being. Never has the world which He has created offered such a spectacle worthy of His regards. He sees a whole nation, fighting the oppressors of the human race, suspend the course of its heroic work to raise its thoughts and vows towards the Great Being who gave it the mission to undertake it and the force to express it. Was it not He who engraved on the heart of man the code of justice and equality? Did He not decree the existence of the Republic, and give liberty, faith, and justice to all peoples? It was He who created man to arrive at happiness through virtue which is the love of France....O generous ardor of the nation, naive and pure joy of young citizens....O majesty of a great people, happy in the felling of its force and glory. The day has arrived of the union of the first people of the world!....The Supreme Being created the universe to proclaim His power. He made men to help and love one another, and to be happy through virtue....All that is good is His work because it is Himself. Evil belongs to depraved men who oppress their fellows. The Author of Nature has bound all mortals by the great chain of love and felicity....French Republicans, you must purify the earth that they [tyrants] have soiled, and recall the justice that they have banished. Liberty and virtue issued forth together from the Divinity. One cannot live among men without the other....People, deliver us to Him, to the just transports of joy. Tomorrow, once more, we shall combat vices and tyrants. We shall give to the world the example of republican virtues....[214]

Robespierre then took up the torch, blazing before him and approached a great big statue made of paper, a symbol of atheism, and set it afire. The paper burned away—revealing a great statue of the Goddess of Wisdom. "It has gone back to nothingness," he declared, "this monster which the spirit of kings had vomited upon France; with it let all the crimes and misfortunes of the world disappear!"[215] The crowd wept.

Then Robespierre preached out against kings: "Crush the impious league of kings by the grandeur of our character more than through the force of arms." He appealed to the "Being of all beings, Author of Nature," praying

> we have no unworthy prayers to offer Thee. Thou knowest the creatures of Thy hands; their needs no more escape Thine eyes than their most secret thoughts. The hatred of bad faith and tyranny burns in our hearts together with the love of justice and our country. Our blood flows for the cause of humanity. Here is our prayer, here is our sacrifice, here is the worship we offer Thee.[216]

With his prayer raised to the sky, he stepped forward to lead the procession of half a million people—Robespierre twenty paces out front.[217] His followers chanted more prayers to the "Father of the Universe," and sang the new hymns of patriotism, accompanied by cavalry and trumpeters, followed by a hundred drummers and three military bands. All the deputies carried bouquets. Blind children filled a cart, singing the "Hymn to Divinity." Then came mothers bearing roses, and fathers leading their sons armed with swords. At the end of all came a great coach pulled by eight oxen, their horns painted gold.[218] On the top of the coach was a princess of Liberty, holding a club beneath another great oak tree, with a printing press and a plow beside her in the coach.[219]

The festival joined the new politics to a new faith. Poetry was read. The new hymn, "Father of the Universe," was sung, as were others to the tune of the national anthem, "Marseillaise." Cannons fired. Children threw their flowers into the air. Mothers gave thanks to the Supreme Being for their fertility and girls swore they would marry no one who failed to serve the nation. Like Moses descending from Mt. Sinai, Robespierre walked down the mountain on the Champ-de-Mars. The enormous crowd burst out with cheers for their leader.

To him, that was "Oh day forever blessed." To the "Being of Beings," he prayed, "Did the day of Creation itself—the day the world issued from thy all-powerful hands—shine with a light more agreeable in thy sight than that day on which, bursting the yoke of crime and error, this nation appeared in thy sight in an attitude worthy of thy regard and its destinies?"[220]

In this massive celebration, Robespierre damned atheism. He saw himself as son of Rousseau, but also son of God—a direct son who needed no earthly priest as intermediary. His strong determination, his faith and fervor, concentrated on reforming France, and in this work he saw religion as an absolute necessity.

In the early years of the Revolution, France had seemed done with religion. The movement for "reason" in effect, to replace the ancient Catholic faith. In 1792, when the state seized the property of the Catholic Church, some priests swore allegiance to the constitution, canceled their faith in the Word of the Lord, and got married.[221] The state even changed the calendar to eliminate Sunday, the Sabbath, and renamed the days, months, and numbers of the years, which had traditionally been counted from the birth of Christ. More extreme measures followed. For example, 2,000 soldiers broke into a community church and knocked down the statues and pictures. They took a cross from a chapel and carried it around town, inviting citizens to spit on it. When one citizen refused to spit on the cross, a soldier grabbed him and cut off part of his nose. Elsewhere, a priest, betraying his church, went through a cemetery knocking down all religious emblems and replacing them with a sign that read "Death is but an eternal sleep."[222] Others stole a bishop's robes and dressed donkeys in them and led a shocking parade through the streets. In churches, stained glass was smashed, hymnals burned. The bishop of Paris, grabbed in his bed and forced to resign, gave in and said, "There should be no other public cult than liberty and holy equality."[223] The church's Eucharistic liturgy was transformed to read: "Verily I say to you, my brothers, this is the blood of kings, the true substance of republican communion, take and drink this precious substance."[224] In Paris, the Commune ordered all churches closed. Throughout France, churches were shut or plundered or used for the worship of the new ideology.[225] In Paris's grand Cathedral of Notre Dame, a ceremony was held with a liturgy glorifying the "Temple of Reason,"[226] in which every reference to Jesus Christ was deleted. Notre Dame was stripped of all Christian symbols, and a cardboard Greek cathedral was set up in the nave, where an opera actress performed as the "Goddess of Reason." Hot dancing happened up front: wild whirling men without pants, women without shirts. The revolters blessed the worship of Virtue, and damned the worship of "that Jew slave" Jesus and his mother Mary, "the adulterous woman of Galilee." One declared that "a religious man is a depraved beast. He resembles those animals that are kept to be shorn and roasted for the benefit of merchants and butchers."[227]

Robespierre was shocked. Neither Catholic nor Protestant, he nevertheless believed that religion was a necessity in a virtuous state. So, as historian Charles Breunig says, Robespierre "set about devising an official religion which would serve the needs of the state."[228] Robespierre condemned the new corrupt ceremonies as "ridiculous farces" put on by "men without honor or religion."[229] He wrote a report "On the connection between religious and moral ideas with republican principles and national festivals."[230] In essence, he defined, "Republic" as moral citizenry: "Immorality is the basis of despotism, as virtue is the essence of the Republic."[231] "Atheism is aristocratic," he proclaimed. "I demand then that this society purge itself of this criminal horde!" Of atheists, he said, "Why does the Convention waste its time on these people? The People are sick of them."[232]

Robespierre was not, however, in favor of France's old Christianity. "What do priests have in common with God?" he asked. "Priests are to morality what charlatans are to medicine. How different the God of nature is from the God of priests! There is nothing which resembles atheism as much as the religions priests have made."[233] Since the church had failed to produce virtue on earth, the *government* must do it: the state must be the people's church.

This high ideal of salvation through the state led Robespierre to make some extreme proposals. He thought the state must make education an instrument to uplift the youth of the nation. "What thing above all should citizens learn?" Robespierre asked, and answered "the rights of humanity…the duties of each man toward his fellows…the divine principles of morality and equality." Education had a political purpose: "It is no longer a question of forming gentlemen, but rather citizens." Indeed, he thought, "The nation alone has the right to raise children," a duty not to be left "to the pride of families nor to the prejudices of individuals." Such prejudice creates "aristocracy and domestic feudalism" and eventually "destroys, equally, all the foundations of the social order." Robespierre agreed with education planner, Lepeletier, who had said, "I am convinced of the necessity for a complete regeneration and, if I can thus express myself, the creation of a new people." [234] Robespierre's own Declaration of Rights included this Article: "Society ought to encourage the progress of public intelligence, with all its might, and bring education within the reach of every citizen." [235]

France needed a uniform education system because, Robespierre said, "There exists for all men but one morality, one single conscience." [236] Therefore, "education must be common to everyone and universally beneficial." [237] In Robespierre's plan, all children would be turned over to the state from age 5 to age 12 because it was necessary "to seize children at the time when they receive the most decisive impressions, at the time when they begin to form habits." [238] Any parents who failed to turn their child over to the state's school would lose their rights as citizens and be forced to pay double taxes. After being taken from their parents and moved to a government school in a simple house, the student children would sleep on a hard bed, wear simple, uniform clothing, do all the household cleaning and service, eat simple food, and follow a strict schedule of training. The program would attempt "to strengthen the bodies of children, to develop them by gymnastic exercises, to accustom them to handwork, to harden them to all sorts of fatigue, to shape their character and spirit by useful instructions, and to give them the knowledge necessary to every citizen whatever his profession might be." [239] All were to be taught the constitution, morals, and how to work the soil. Girls would be taught civic songs and "lessons of history proper to the development of the virtues of their sex," as well as mending and sewing. [240] Boys would learn shop work. Punishment for unfinished work would be to postpone the student's next meal and then force the child to eat alone. Textbooks, to be generated and approved by the state, would teach morals, especially the "most striking tales of the history of free peoples and of the French Revolution." [241]

The strong ethical purpose of the Republic imposed many demands on adult citizens as well. Revolutionary leader Antoine-Louis Saint-Just proposed that "Every man 25 years old [be] obliged to declare in the temple who his friends are. This declaration must be renewed every year.…If a man abandons his friend, he must explain his reasons before the people, in the temples.…If he refuses, he is banished." [242] Journalists would be required to "Spread the ideas and sentiments of patriotism among our citizens"—and forbidden to do otherwise. [243]

Robespierre's purpose was total rule by government to make all human beings superior—and identical. He believed that sin had to be corrected by the state, with whatever methods proved necessary. His hope was that "We can now present to the universe a constitutional code infinitely superior to all moral and political institutions, a work…which presents the essential basis of public happiness, offering a sublime and majestic picture of French regeneration."[244] To achieve the moral France he dreamed of, he saw the necessity of unity: "The body politic, like the human body, becomes a monster if it has several heads."[245] He thought that federalism, advocated by the Girondist party, was dead wrong. He blasted the Girondists for

> the intention of turning the French Republic into a congeries of federal republics which would always be at the mercy of civil disorder of foreign attack. Let us declare that the French Republic is a single state under a single system of constitutional laws. Only the certainty of the strongest possible union between all parts of France can enable us to repulse our enemies with energy and success.[246]

Community was essential to virtue, and the community was now the nation: "Men are nothing, France is everything: it commands, you must obey."[247] At the top was needed "the organization of a revolutionary tribunal and all other measures for the punishment and suppression of rebels."[248] The French armed forces were sent to conquer rebellious villages and bring them under government control. Government authorities were to "punish traitors and royalists promptly and severely, especially the chiefs and principal agents of Girondist intrigues." They were warned: "Do not be deluded by the signs of patriotism they affect." In addition, they were told to "send throughout the Republic a small number of strong commissioners, supplied with sound instructions, and above all, with good principles, to restore public opinion to unity and republicanism." The commissioners were to go out in pairs, "one strong man with another whose patriotism is less certain."[249] An order signed by Robespierre declared that "*all* authorities become revolutionary armies."[250]

Robespierre insisted on weeding out all arrogant enemies of the Republic speedily because "This is not the time to paralyze the national energy." Judges and juries should be committed to "innocence and patriotism, but be unbending to all enemies of *la Patrie*"[251] "Enemies" included the unenthusiastic: "Patriotism must be a marked characteristic of everyone.…Keep from your lists all those men who are cold, egotistical or indifferent to the Republican revolution.…National opinion will strike them among us with political death.…The Republic, one and indivisible, can best be served, defended, and administered by those who love it with as much warmth as constancy."[252] But the worst "enemies" of France, declared Robespierre, were the aristocrat "who founds popular societies, the fanatic who attacks religion, the royalist who cheers republican victories, the noble who professes a love of equality, and the tyrant who scatters flowers on the tomb of defenders of victory."[253] He saw these enemies as most dangerous because they were subtle obstructionists:

> Ask them to act: they talk. Ask them to deliberate: they are for instant action. The country is at peace: they oppose every change. It is at war: they desire to reform everything. You propose measures against sedition: they remind you of Caesar's clemency. You propose to rescue patriots from persecution: they urge the severity of Brutus.[254]

Virtue was missing in any person "clawing his way up at court or humiliating himself at the feet of a minister or a mistress." Even someone who had done something wrong in the past—"once in his life"—lacked virtue forever.[255]

In other words, all kinds of people could potentially harm the government's achievement. Robespierre thought that "we must protect patriotism even when it goes astray."[256] He called for "the prosecution of writers who attack the principles of liberty; who arouse the people over the death of a tyrant...[and] those who wish to cause civil war by designating Paris as 'suspect' to the department." He condemned wrong writing and said of one particular publication, "I demand that the offensive issues of this journal be burned in the hall of the Society!"[257] Not only news writers but play writers were to be restricted to advocating the current Jacobin approaches.[258] Even people who wore the hats or emblems or medallions or insignias were to be corrected by the state. Robespierre insisted that foreigners and nobles, priests and bankers, be thrown out of the Jacobin Clubs.[259] Before long, anyone whose name was removed from the Jacobin membership list was likely to be sentenced to death. And Robespierre's officials would not allow the accused to speak out in their own defense, lest they confuse the people and delay the Republic's march toward virtue. One of Robespierre's Articles of public principles stated that "Any individual who usurps the sovereignty may at once be put to death by free men."[260] He wrote that "the first maxim of your policy must be to guide the people with reason and the people's enemies with terror....Terror is nothing other than justice, prompt, severe, and inflexible; it is therefore an emanation of virtue."[261] Since right-wing deputies were enemies of the state, "The only way to establish liberty is to cut off the heads of such criminals."[262]

THE RESULTS OF THE REVOLUTION FOR CITIZENS

The government execution of citizens whose minds were seen as evil spread through France. Robespierre was not alone in instigating these killings. For example, when he was away from the Committee of Public Safety for 45 days, 1,285 people were condemned to death.[263] Others arrested drunks, jokers, and cynics, whom they perceived as anti-France. The Jacobin Clubs throughout the country took it upon themselves to curb and correct immoral persons. Saint-Just was of the view that "the repression of all evil will bring forth the good" and that all should be the same: "Every party is criminal....Every faction is criminal."[264] Still, as Robespierre's biographer James Michael Eagan perceived, Robespierre's religious convictions made it "much more comforting to him to believe that men were guillotined in defense of religious principles than because they differed with him personally or politically."[265] Fifty-four "Robespierre's assassins" had their heads chopped off.[266] It was Robespierre himself who demanded that "the Jacobins and all the good citizens seize and arrest upon the spot anybody who dares to insult the National Convention." Those who denied the existence of "the Supreme Being" would be arrested; those who dared to say the "Sacred name of God" would be killed.[267]

On April 6, 1794, 14 *Jacobin* leaders, convicted for conspiracy, were guillotined.[268]

That summer, masses of prisoners were sent into Paris from the provinces, where there were probably ten times as many prisoners as Paris's 7,000 to 8,000. A new law stated that if a defendant was convicted, the sentence *must* be death. "Any kind" of evidence could be used to convict; the "standard of judgment" of evidence was "the conscience of the jurymen enlightened by patriotism." The jury did not even have to hear witnesses. The law said that no "conspirator" could have a lawyer to defend him. Executions abounded. In May, 346 people were killed; in June, 689; and in July, 936.[269]

Some 25,000 priests had already fled the country, no doubt remembering that previously more than a hundred priests had been captured, dragged out into a garden, and either hacked to death with knives and axes or shot or beaten to death.[270] Scores of young boy criminals were slaughtered together, as were some 40 prostitutes.[271] Delinquent military officers were brought out in front of their own troops and shot dead.[272] Savage riots took place; in one outbreak of violence, 1,600 houses were torn down.[273]

France's usual mode of execution was the guillotine—a long, sharp piece of metal dropped by a rope to cut off the whole head. It had been invented by a doctor as quicker, cleaner, and more kindly than having a drunken executioner wield an ax at the victim's neck. The Republic's executioner became very efficient at the guillotine: once 32 heads were chopped off in 25 minutes; a week later, a dozen heads were cut off in a mere 5 minutes. Other methods of execution were developed. In one place, 60 prisoners were tied together and shot with a cannon; those remaining alive were sliced to death. In another place, 113 people were executed in one day. Twenty peasant girls were killed. One had a baby nursing at her breast. The guard jerked away the baby.[274]

A man wrote to his brother in Paris:

> Still more heads and every day more heads fall! What pleasure you would have experienced if, the day before yesterday, you had seen national justice meted out to two hundred and nine villains. What majesty! What imposing tone!...PS, say hello to Robespierre....[275]

Actually, that time of killing concluded with 1,905 people dead.[276]

Generals oversaw the killing of civilians. Women were raped, mutilated, and killed; children were mutilated and killed. One general, to save gunpowder, had his troops do the killing with their swords. Another general forced 200 old people, mothers, and children to dig a big grave pit and kneel down in front of it so they would fall into the pit when they were shot. Thirty children and two women fell into the grave alive, suffocating to death when the dirt was shoveled over them. [277]

In Paris, as the Terror went on, Robespierre said that "a river of blood would now divide France from its enemies." [278] Everyone in Paris was in danger. [279]

Prisoners suffered great humiliation and deprivation before they were executed. In jail, they were often denied enough air or water and forced to live on a floor crowded with shit and wet with urine, where they were attacked by bugs and rats. [280] When Queen Marie Antoinette was arrested, her seven-year-old son, Louis-Charles, cried loudly for an hour. Then he was taken away from her and put alone in a room below her. She could hear him sobbing, day after day. He was sick. His mother was killed. Her boy was stuffed, like a caged animal, into a dark and filthy place, where he eventually died. [281] An old man, while waiting to have his head cut off, was forced to watch the heads of his daughter, his granddaughter, and her husband cut off. [282] Suicide spread.

In Paris, the guillotine operation became too slow, given the numbers of victims. So, instead, men and women were stripped of their clothes, which were taken by a soldier to sell. Then a man and a woman would be paired, tied together in a "republican marriage," and thrown into the river to drown. But even that became too time-consuming. So barges were filled with priests and laymen, tied up, and sunk in the swirling depths of the Loire River. [283]

The guillotines, removed for Robespierre's grand Festival in Honor of the Supreme Being, were afterward reinstalled for three days. Parisians angrily complained that the streams of blood flowing from them were stinking up their city.

Just two days after the festival, the Convention passed a new law declaring that political crimes were far worse than ordinary crimes. Henceforth citizens would be arrested and brought before the Revolutionary Tribunal—with no lawyer, no witnesses, and no alternative to acquittal but the death sentence allowed—for the following political crimes: "slandering patriotism," "seeking to inspire discouragement," "spreading false news," and "depraving morals, corrupting the public conscience and impairing the purity and energy of the revolutionary government." Robespierre had hinted that voting against the measure would be immoral. The Convention passed it. Under the new law, masses of officials were arrested and brought to Paris: 674 were acquitted, 2,156 were killed. [284]

Many people were executed for the most casual or careless speech. A tailor said that "the men who work in government offices are all wretches." He was killed. A woman said she needed a spinning wheel (*rouet*); someone thought she said she needed a king (*roi*). She was killed. A young carpenter's apprentice lost at cards and cursed. His opponent said, "Good patriots don't talk like that." He yelled back, "Fuck good patriots!" He was killed. [285]

A woman carrying hidden knives tried to approach Robespierre, but failed. He said, "I am the most miserable of men," but then "I have a stout heart, a resolute soul. I have never known how to bend under the yoke of baseness and corruption." [286]

CRISIS IN THE GOVERNMENT

Robespierre began to stay away from the Jacobins, the Convention, and the Committee of Public Safety. Some members of the Convention wondered how long it would be before they themselves were suddenly accused and executed. One day, Robespierre did come in, for the first time in three weeks. He spoke about good and bad citizens, and warned that a new conspiracy was brewing—inside the government. "People!" he called out to the members. "You should be informed that there exists within your bosom a league of scoundrels who are at war with public Virtue!"[287] Purging the government would be necessary: "We must not slander it, but we mush recall it to its first duties, simplify it, reduce the number of its agents."[288] He named some of the conspirators and hinted that there were others.

Suddenly a member shouted, "I am opposed to the printing of this speech! There are many grave accusations in it that ought to be clarified." Robespierre was stunned. A man he had accused rushed up and took the rostrum, shouting, "The mask must be torn away! I would rather my corpse should serve as the throne of an ambitious man than that by my silence I should become the accomplice of his crimes!" Another went to the rostrum and revealed a secret: "Robespierre has drawn up a list and my name is said to be on it."

"The list! The list!" went up the cry.
"Name those whom you have accused!" demanded a deputy.
"Name them! Name them!" echoed the Convention.[289]

Robespierre refused to give the names and left the hall. The Convention members were furious. Robespierre took a walk. That night he gave the same speech to the Jacobin Club—and they cheered him on.[290]

But the next day, July 27, 1794, when the Convention opened, a member damned the Jacobins: "These people are planning to murder the Convention!" he shouted. He saw a Jacobin in the gallery. "I see one of those who dared menace the Convention sitting among us now." The crowd yelled "Arrest him! Arrest him!" and at once the police seized him and took him out.

Robespierre came to the Convention. A deputy roared, "I demand the arrest of Robespierre!" Robespierre tried to speak, but got shouted down—and then laughed at. He cried out, "For the last time, will you let me be heard, President of Assassins!" They demanded a vote for his arrest because, as one shouted, "The monster has insulted the Convention!"[291]

Robespierre rushed down from the rostrum and ran over to the deputies of the Left. But they shouted "Get away from here!" So he turned to the Center, calling "Men of purity! Men of Virtue! I appeal to you. Give me the leave to speak which these assassins have refused me!" They yelled at him, so Robespierre scrambled over to the Right and fell onto a bench. But those on the Right moved away from him, one of them shouting "Monster!" He turned to the gallery—the audience—but they, too, shouted "Arrest him!" as the Jacobins hurried out of the room. Robespierre screamed, "Brigands! Hypocrites! Scoundrels!" The crowd yelled out again, "Arrest him!" An usher handed him the arrest paper, but he did not even notice it. The president of the Convention called out, "He refuses to obey the Convention's decree of arrest!" Members yelled, "Then carry him down to the bar!" So guards carried him out, as Robespierre shouted, "The brigands have triumphed!"[292]

He was taken off to the Hotel de Ville where his supporters gathered. The Convention continued into the evening and at 9 P.M., it pronounced Robespierre sentenced to death—along with four others—without trial.

At 2:00 A.M., a guard broke into Robespierre's room. Robespierre's brother, Augustin, climbed out the window and jumped down from the second floor, nearly killing himself. Another fellow pulled out two pistols, gave one to Robespierre, and shot himself dead. Robespierre also shot himself, blowing apart his lower left jaw. Despite this deep and bloody wound, he survived. The next morning he was carried on a board to the Convention, but they refused to let him into the hall because, they said, "To bring a man covered with crime into our hall would be to diminish the glory of this great day"[293] and "the body of a tyrant can bring nothing but pestilence."[294] He was put on a waiting room table, where he passed out. Much later, a noisy crowd outside woke him up with loud damnations, as well as kind words of encouragement. A doctor came, pulled out some of Robespierre's teeth, and bandaged his jaw.

Around the middle of the day, he was carried in an armchair, along with others, to a guillotine at the same place where King Louis XVI had been killed. A crowd gathered. They cheered and laughed, men flinging their hats and singing. Women danced around the wagons carrying Robespierre and the other condemned men, and one shrieked out, "Monster! I am drunk with joy to see you suffer. You are going to Hell with the curses of all wives and mothers following you!"[295]

Robespierre was only half awake. When the executioner tried to tie him onto the guillotine plank, the jaw bandage got in his way, so he ripped it off. Robespierre screamed in pain again and again until the guillotine blade flashed down and cut off his head. Robespierre was silenced.[296]

THE FUNDAMENTAL FAILURE
OF THAT FRENCH MOVEMENT FOR DEMOCRACY

Why did the French Revolution's noble promise of democracy turn into tragedy? How did high moral purpose degenerate so quickly into deep evil—the murder and torture of thousands in a few years, a reign of terror that struck fear into the hearts of millions more?

The great mistake was totalitarianism. The Revolution was taken over by men whose determination to construct a state that would reconstruct human nature damned human beings. These dictators—Robespierre chief among them—

thought that by force they could transform the minds, hearts, and lives of the French people to make them into "virtuous republicans." To achieve that ultimate end, they created a government that attempted to take total charge of people's lives, to regulate their thoughts as well as their actions. Instead of controlling violence, the government instigated it. Instead of delivering the freedom and equality that were the hope of the Revolution, Robespierre and his colleagues set themselves as gods and made the French people their terrified victims on the altar of ultimate ethics.

The case of the French Revolution is neither unique nor irrelevant to the present. The potential for government terror exists in every revolution for democracy—and even in existing democracies. The romance of revolution—its engaging efforts to overthrow tyranny, its high moral purposes, its admirable heroes—none of that justifies cheating, hurting, and slaughtering human beings. Democracy is to control violence, not use violence to control citizens.

France's great error was to try to create ultimate ethics through politics. Politics is meant to be practical, not metaphysical; to be conditional, not ultimate; to persuade, not force. The basic purpose of politics is to create a system that controls power and citizen actions in a way that makes *possible* an admirable life.

The basic aims of politics are liberty and equality. Liberty means citizens have the freedom to do and say what they want, with very few and mild limits. That does not mean that what people say or do must be characterized by virtue. The great lesson learned over thousands of years of human experience, is liberty requires toleration: individuals should be restricted only when they physically harm others. What they believe is their own business, not the government's.

Take the democratic guarantee of free speech. Free speech has been a long, hard achievement, a practical lesson learned by democracy from experience with government speech control. Liberty requires allowing people to say what they want to say, no matter how false or harsh their expression.

As for equality, consider human experience before the idea of political equality was invented. There was no such thing as universal justice. People were discriminated against when they were placed in ethnic, class, race, gender, religious, and other political categories. The right of all adult citizens to vote equally is fundamental to democracy and the regular, universal, and equal administration of justice. Equality does not mean citizens are ethically or morally equivalent. It does not ensure that they will even vote ethically. Some—probably many—people vote *un*ethically, to gain or protect wealth or privilege against others. But political equality—applied directly and consistently, without ethical evaluation—is essential for democracy.

Politics must not be total. Those in charge of the French Revolution after 1791 made extensive and arrogant judgments about the moral lives of their fellow citizens. In the name of a great ideal, they exercised extraordinary cruelty. But a democratic government is not intended to be the primary agent for moral reform of society. The state is not the church. Any society that tries to make a church of the state will find hell occupying that temple.

THE END OF DEMOCRACY'S CHAMPION

In the summer of 1794, a prisoner in Paris tried to gain release. She was Adrienne, wife of Gilbert Lafayette. Given the pace of executions, she knew she might soon be killed. Indeed, on the Fourth of July, children jailed with her were guillotined, and then she was alone. But on January 21, 1795, six months after Robespierre's death, she was set free. Under the care of friends, Adrienne recovered and set out with her two daughters, Anastasie and Virginie, on a strenuous journey over rough roads to Austria to find her husband, who was still in prison in that country.

Lafayette had meanwhile worked out a plan for his own escape. After bribing some guards, he did get out—though at the cost of a piece of his finger, bitten off by an unbribed guard who grabbed him. Galloping away on a horse, he came to a fork in the road and took the wrong turn. He was caught and sent back to his cell. Later Adrienne recalled his reaction to her appearance at his prison with their two daughters: "Just imagine how M. de La Fayette must have felt, when after eight months spent seeing only his jailers, who refused to tell him whether we were still alive, suddenly, without any preparation, he saw us walk into his cell!" [297] He looked like a ghost. He had been ill and left in a cold, dank cell day after day. His only way to communicate had been by whistling a code to a fellow outside the fortress.

The Lafayette family was allowed to stay together in the prison. The daughters were put in a separate cell, as was Adrienne. She met with her daughters for breakfast at eight o'clock in the morning and with Gilbert for lunch at noon. The family then stayed together until eight o'clock in the evening, when the daughters were locked away. Adrienne paid for the food, which they ate from soiled wooden bowls. She had brought with her three silver forks, but they were taken away, forcing them to eat with their hands.

Adrienne soon became ill herself from this regime. She wrote to the emperor of Austria, asking permission to go to a doctor, but he replied (months later) that if she left the prison, she would not be allowed to return to it. She chose to stay. The girls, living in these hellish conditions, stayed amazingly cheerful toward their father and mother. Long after the childish novelty of living in jail had passed, they maintained their love and hope.

From across the sea, a letter arrived from U.S. President George Washington to his ambassador to France, Charles Cotesworth Pinckney: "I need hardly mention how much my sensibility has been hurt by the treatment [Lafayette] has met with; or how anxious I am to see him liberated therefrom; but what course to pursue...is not quite so easy to decide on." [298] He did not want a personal concern to interfere with his presidential responsibilities in foreign affairs, but finally, on May 15, 1796, Washington wrote to the emperor of Austria:

> I take the liberty of writing this *private* letter to your Majesty....Permit me only to submit to your Majesty's consideration, whether [Lafayette's] long imprisonment and the confiscation of his Estate, and the Indigence and dispersion of his family—and the painful anxieties incident to all these circumstances, do not form an

assemblage of sufferings, which recommend him to the mediation of Humanity? Allow me, Sir! on this occasion to be its organ; and to entreat that he may be permitted to come to this country....[299]

Lafayette was not released. Meanwhile, the French government allowed Lafayette's appeal to reach the new leader, General Bonaparte. Bonaparte did demand of Austria his freedom, but time continued to pass. At last the family was released, though Lafayette would not agree to the Austrian emperor's requirement that he go to America rather than to France. In October 1797, the Lafayette family made it to Holland, where Adrienne, though she herself was sick, cared for her husband and daughters.

After overcoming many barriers, they finally arrived in France. Their young son, George Washington Lafayette came back from America where he had served in the military. He joined his family with joy. They lived in an old feudal building with a moat and towers and a stone bridge that they were kept busy fixing up. Lafayette wrote, "My political life is over. I will be full of life with my friends...."[300] And so he was. He did occasionally meet and confer with Bonaparte, whose view of government he fundamentally disagreed with. But for Lafayette, politics was finished, though his memory was not.

He was saddened by the news that father George Washington had died on December 14, 1799. But Gilbert Lafayette must have been comforted by the knowledge that Washington had received the following letter from him shortly after he was freed from prison:

> In vain would I attempt, my beloved General, to express to you the feelings of my filial heart, when, at the moment of this unexpected restoration to liberty and life, I find myself blessed with the opportunity to let you hear from me—this heart has for twenty years been known to you—words that, whatever they be, fall so short of my sentiments, could not do justice to what I feel.[301]

Years later, on December 20, 1823, Gilbert Lafayette wrote to his friend Thomas Jefferson:

> Every account I receive from the United States is a compensation for European disappointments and disgusts. There our revolutionary hopes have been fulfilled, and although I must admire the observations of such a witness as my friend Jefferson, we may enjoy the happy thought that never a nation has been so completely free, so rapidly prosperous, so generally enlighted. Look, on the contrary, to old Europe....You have been a sharer, my dear friend, in my enthusiastic French hopes; you have seen the people of France truly a great nation, when the rights of mankind, proclaimed, conquered, supported by the whole population, were set up as a new imported American doctrine, for the instruction and example of Europe, when they might have been the sole object and the glorious price of a first irresistible impulsion, which has since been spent into other purposes by the subsequent vicissitudes of government; the triple counter revolution of Jacobinism, Bonapartism, and Bourbonism, in the first of which disguised Aristocracy had also a great part, has worn out the springs of energetic patriotism. The French people are better informed, less prejudiced, more at their ease on the point of property, industry, habits of social equality in many respects, than be-

fore the Revolution. But from the day when the National Constitution, made, sworn, worshiped by themselves, was thrown down on a level with the edicts of arbitrary kings, to the present times…so many political heresies have been professed, so dismal instances of popular tyranny are remembered, so able institutions of despotism have crushed all resistance, that, if you except our young generations, egotism and apathy, not excluding general discontent are the prevailing disposition. In the meanwhile, all adversaries of mankind…are pushing their plot with as much fury but much more cunning than they had hitherto evinced.[302]

BIBLIOGRAPHY

BERNIER, OLIVIER. *Lafayette: Hero of Two Worlds.* New York: Dutton, 1983.

BLUM, CAROL. *Rousseau and the Republic of Virtue: The Language of Politics in the French Revolution.* Ithaca, N.Y.: Cornell University Press, 1986.

BOORSTIN, DANIEL J. (ED.). *An American Primer.* Chicago: University of Chicago Press, 1966.

BREUNIG, CHARLES. *The Age of Revolution and Reaction, 1789–1850.* New York: Norton, 1970.

CHINARD, GILBERT (ED.). *The Letters of Lafayette and Jefferson.* Baltimore, Md.: The Johns Hopkins Press, 1929.

CLARK, RONALD W. *Benjamin Franklin: A Biography.* New York: Random House, 1983.

COBB, RICHARD AND COLIN JONES, (EDS.). *Voices of the French Revolution.* Topsfield, Mass.: Salem House Publishers, 1988.

EAGAN, JAMES MICHAEL. *Maximilien Robespierre: Nationalist Dictator.* New York: Columbia University Press, 1938.

FUEY, MAURICE DE LA, AND EMILE BABEAU. *The Apostle of Liberty: A Life of La Fayette.* New York: Thomas Yoseloff, 1956.

GOTTSCHALK, LOUIS, AND MARGARET MODDOX. *Lafayette in the French Revolution: From the October Days Through the Federation.* Chicago: University of Chicago Press, 1973.

HALLOWELL, JOHN H. *Main Currents in Modern Political Thought.* New York: Henry Holt and Company, 1950.

HEMMINGS, F.W.J. *Culture and Society in France: 1789–1848.* Great Britain: Leicester University Press, 1987.

HUNT, LYNN. *Politics, Culture, and Class in the French Revolution.* Berkeley: University of California Press, 1984.

JORDAN, DAVID P. *The Revolutionary Career of Maximilien Robespierre.* Chicago: University of Chicago Press, 1947.

LEFEBVRE, GEORGES. *The Coming of the French Revolution.* Trans. by R.R. Palmer. Princeton, N.J.: Princeton University Press, 1947.

LOOMIS, STANLEY. *Paris in the Terror: June 1793–July 1794.* New York: Dorset, 1989.

PALMER, R.R. *A History of the Modern World.* New York: Alfred A. Knopf, 1952.

PARKER, HAROLD T. *The Cult of Antiquity and the French Revolution: A Study in the Development of the Revolutionary Spirit.* New York: Octagon Books, 1965.

SCHAMA, SIMON. *Citizens: A Chronicle of the French Revolution.* New York: Alfred A. Knopf, 1989.

SEVERY, MERLE. "The Great Revolution." *National Geographic,* 176, July 1989.

SOBEL, ROBERT. *The French Revolution: A Concise History and Interpretation.* New York: Ardmore Press, 1967.

SYDENHAM, M.J. *The French Revolution.* New York: Capricorn Books, 1965.

THOMPSON, J.M. *Robespierre and the French Revolution*. New York: Collier Books, 1967.

VAN DOREN, CARL. *Benjamin Franklin*. New York: Viking, 1938.

WELCH, OLIVER J.G. *Mirabeau: A Study of a Democratic Monarchist*. Port Washington, N.Y.: Kennikat Press, 1968.

CHAPTER

6

The Challenge
of Totalitarianism

Long ago, when the Greek city of Athens was governed partially as a democracy, Aristotle wrote that "A basic principle of the democratic constitution is liberty."[1] Throughout history, governments have often destroyed liberty by attempting to dictate citizens', ideology and faith, doctrines and tenets—to control not only their actions but their minds and hearts as well. The brilliant discovery of democracy is that the government is authorized to control some behavior, but not belief. The state is not the church.

DEMOCRACY IS NOT A RELIGION

In the Christian religion, the most fundamental rule of life, inherited from Israel and confirmed by Jesus Christ, is this:

> Thou shalt love the Lord thy God with all thy heart, and with all thy soul, and with all thy strength, and with all thy mind; and thy neighbor as thyself.[2]

Devotion to God in that faith is not satisfied by occasional reading of the Bible or Sunday morning visits to a distinctive building where the Christian takes a rest from weekday work. The devotion is total: the believer's life belongs to God. But as history shows, the worst interpretation of Christianity—or of any other religion—is for leaders to use the power of the state to force "neighbors" to adopt and obey their faith. That is when Satan plays God.

In the case of the French Revolution, we saw how a set of essentially religious principles became the foundation of state power. Intense devotion to this political religion and its transformative power led the Jacobin leadership, culminating in Robespierre, "the Incorruptible," to move from persuasion to force. Regardless of what one thinks of the Jacobins' principles, the results for human life in France were tragic: hideous, massive butchering of people the government was supposed to serve.

Such political horrors were not peculiar to the eighteenth-century French. Democracy has been travestied many times by rulers determined to mold human nature to their own ideals. Democracy is not intended to be the ultimate focus of life. Democratic government serves citizens best when it is only a secondary factor in their lives. But totalitarians cannot accept this restriction on the state. They believe the society's security depends on the absolute power of the state. This fundamental error is made most often in times of war and anarchy.

ANCIENT EGYPT'S GOVERNMENT

In ancient Egypt, society broke down into chaos time and again before 1528 B.C. The government could best be described as an extremely unstable kingship. A king would seize the throne, then often be overthrown himself. Whenever a king died or left the country, revolution broke out. Masses of people died in the fighting. At last a ruler emerged who described himself not as mere god, but as "King of the Gods."[3] When the new king was crowned, he recited this prayer:

> O Red Crown, O Inu, O Great One,
> O Magician, O Fiery Snake!
> Let there be terror of me like the terror of thee.
> Let there be fear of me like the fear of thee.
> Let there be awe of me like the awe of thee.
> Let there be love of me like the love of thee.
> Let me rule, a leader of the living.
> Let me be powerful, a leader of spirits.
> Let my blade be firm against my enemies.
>   Oh Inu, thou has come forth from me;
> And I have come forth from thee.

Then the new king received praise:

> The Great One has borne thee;
> The Exalted One has adorned thee;
> For thou art Horus who hast fought
> For the protection of thine Eye.

A prayer was spoken to empower him:

Stand (as king) over it, over this land which has come forth
from Atum,
The spittle which has come forth from the beetle.
Be (king) over it; be high over it,
That thy father may see thee,
That Re may see thee.
...
Let him grasp the Heavens
And receive the Horizon;
Let him dominate the Nine Bows
And equip (with offerings) the Ennead.
Give the Crook into his hand
So that the head of Lower and Upper Egypt
Shall be bowed.[4]

"Lower and Upper Egypt" refers to the duality of the land of Egypt: North and South, the Nile River and the desert, the sun and the moon. So the king became a god called Pharaoh, exalted above Egypt's two main unearthly gods, Seth and Horus.

For a century and a half after 1528 B.C., there was stability in Egypt. The power of the king had become virtually infinite. The Egyptian religion, fused together from many different tribal cults, lasted about 1,500 years. The pharaoh was called "Thou sole god," the one who "settest every man in his place."[5]

Given the previous history of revolution when a king died, much thinking went into the planning of monarchical succession. The king-to-be was generally the present king's eldest son—sometimes the child of the king and his sister. At times a daughter was declared to be a son and made the heir or a male child was adopted as son and heir. The young king-to-be was kept visible and given increasing responsibilities. When the king died, the long funeral included prayers for the new king, who was seen as created by the gods "in the egg"—that is, the new king had been crowned before he was born. The old king, resurrected, watched over his successor from heaven as, in exquisite ceremonies, the new king was crowned, divinized, and given royal weapons. He sailed in his boat up and down the Nile, from village to village, where he performed ceremonial washings, broke bread, and hosted elegant feasts to declare his divine promotion. Then the new king, the Pharaoh, faced his three main duties: "the interpretation of the will of the gods; the representation of his people before the gods; and the administration of the realm."[6]

Under this system of government, art and poetry were created, and a monumental architecture, but for the great mass of the approximately seven million commoners, life was slavery. They worked long days under the command of the pharaoh's officers, and slept in crude houses of mud and thatch. The work was dull: road work, farming, or dragging huge stones long distances to make tombs for the pharaohs. One pyramid tomb required 100,000 men to labor for 30 years.[7] Subjected to such suffering, ordinary Egyptians' lives were brief. On occasion, to satisfy some god of the pharaoh, every citizen was required to kill his first-born son as a sacrifice. When the king is God, ordinary humans are seen as animals.

THREE THOUSAND YEARS LATER: THE AZTECS

Totalitarian state religion was practiced for tens of centuries, independently, in many widely separated places. The Egyptian version enslaved most of the populace regularly and involved occasional commands to sacrifice all first-born sons. But much later, on the other side of the world, the Aztecs of Mexico in the fifteenth century A.D. had a version of totalitarian state religion that required mass human sacrifices on a regular basis. In these religious ceremonies, the Aztec king called all the local rulers to a feast held at a tall stone tower built to worship the holy sun. Four staircases rose on the four different sides—north, south, east, and west. The king, worshipped as a god, addressed the local rulers:

> Do you see the likeness of the Sun?
> Do you see the image of him who warns you
> With his heat and with his fire,
> Most excellent Lord of Created Things?
> You have come here to give honor to this image;
> For that purpose have I bid you come.[8]

On the day of the feast, the king and his chief adviser arrived, totally blackened with soot from head to toe to invite to their darkness the light of the sun. Crowns adorned their heads, and they were outfitted with sheaths, mantles, loincloths, and sandals decorated with gold and jewels and feathers to symbolize their status as king and priest; the jeweled plugs stuck through the holes in their noses and the flint knife each of them carried also symbolized this status.[9] The five priests of sacrifice also wore many religiously symbolic decorations. But their bodies, in stunning contrast to those of the darkened king and his chief adviser, were painted from head to foot with red ochre.

Masses of war prisoners, all naked, were lined up. The first prisoner was forced to climb all the way up the high tower and stand upon the holy stone altar. The priests then threw him over on his back, grabbed his arms and legs, and tied down his neck. The king held high his royal knife. He cut open the man's breast, grabbed his heart and yanked it out, and held it up high as an offering to the holy sun. He poured the man's blood into his hand and sprinkled it out toward the sun. He threw away the heart and the priests threw the victim—whose body was sometimes still pulsing—down the steps. The next prisoner was forced to climb up to meet the same fate. On and on it went, cutting out and lifting high as many as a thousand hearts. Later came many other ceremonies, and then a feast—at which human bodies were eaten. Later great piles of skulls were collected, tied onto poles, and paraded around.

To supply sacrifices in the desired numbers, the Aztecs went to war often, struggling hard to capture their enemies rather than kill them on the battlefield. Many human beings were murdered as sacrifices to the gods in various other ways. Some 2,000 were killed at one time to honor the god of fire in a sacrifice that started at midnight and lasted almost the whole next day. The priests were thrilled:

> Triumphant and joyful, the priests were bathed in blood, and the vessels filled with human blood were sent to smear the lintels of the doors, posts and altars of the temples, and to sprinkle the statues of the gods.[10]

The overwhelming focus of the Aztec government in those days was to use the power of the state to please their gods by ripping out human hearts and squirting forth showers of human blood. That culture's totalitarianism exceeded even the Egyptian pharaoh's enslavement of thousands to build their self-glorifying tombs.

IN THE TWENTIETH CENTURY: TYRANNY IN TURKEY

Mass killings can be motivated not only by religious enthusiasm but also by religious fear. Take the example of Turkey in the early twentieth century. For centuries before World War I, Turkey was governed by the Muslims. The Turkish government was headed by a king. Since he was not only the secular ruler, but also the spiritual leader of the Muslim faith, his power was vast. Turks of other religions were second-class citizens in this Islamic state. For instance, non-Muslims could testify in court, but Muslims' testimony was officially evaluated as automatically truer than other testimony. Any non-Muslim who murdered a Muslim would be sentenced to death, but a Muslim who killed a non-Muslim would not. A Muslim man could marry a non-Muslim woman, but a non-Muslim man could not marry a Muslim woman. Armenians, living under Turkish rule, could not own guns or ride horses, and they were required to provide housing for migratory Muslim Kurdsmen, who often beat them, raped their daughters, and stole their goods.[11]

This religious-political arrangement continued into modern times. In 1894–96, authorized Turkish troops massacred more than 200,000 Armenians, smashed their churches, robbed their houses, and raped Armenian women. In the spring of 1909, there was another Turkish attack in which some 30,000 Armenians were slaughtered. When the Armenians called attention to the awful abuses they had suffered and demanded their rights, the only result was an increase in tensions between them and the Muslims.

As scholar Ervin Staub points out, in 1911, the state of Turkey justified its actions as follows: "Sooner or later the total Islamization of all Turkish subjects must be accomplished, but it is clear that this can never be achieved by verbal persuasion, therefore the power of arms must be resorted to."[12] Note the classic totalitarian formula: since "verbal persuasion" will not work—in this case, to control citizens of another religion—resorting to "the power of arms" is justified. One of the delegates declared that Turkey's new purpose should be "wiping out of existence the Armenians who have for centuries been constituting a barrier to the Empire's progress in civilization." [13]

The new project was put into action. First the Turkish government killed the Armenian leaders. A letter to America's President Woodrow Wilson describes what followed:

> And so they drove the whole people—men, women, hoary elders, children, ex-pectant mothers and dumb sucklings—into the Arabic desert, with no other ob-ject than to let them starve to death.
>
> …They drove the people, after depriving them of their leaders and spokesmen, out of the towns at all hours of the day and night, half-naked, straight out of their beds; plundered their houses, burned the villages, destroyed the churches or turned them into mosques, carried off the cattle, seized the vehicles, snatched the bread out of the mouths of their victims, tore the clothes from off their backs, the gold from their hair. Officials—military officers, soldiers, shepherds—vied with one another in their wild orgy of blood, dragging out of the schools delicate or-phan girls to serve their bestial lusts, beat with kudgels dying women or women close on childbirth who could scarcely drag themselves along, until the women fell down on the road and died….
>
> Even before the gates of Aleppo [a city in Syria] they were not allowed to rest…the shrunken parties were ceaselessly driven barefooted, hundreds of miles under the burning sun, through stony defiles, over pathless steppes, enfeebled by fever and other maladies, through semi-tropical marshes, into the wilderness of desolation. Here they died—slain by Kurds, robbed by gendarmes, shot, hanged, poisoned, frozen, parched with thirst, starved.
>
> …I have seen maddened deportees eating as food their own clothes and shoes—women cooking the bodies of their new-born babes. [14]

So in the name of the Muslim god, thousands of human beings were tor-mented to death. What the Muslim god made of it is obscure, but the politics of it clearly failed. By executing the Armenians, who could have helped their defense in World War I, the Turks made it easier for the Russians to invade and defeat them in 1916. But their effort does exemplify yet another focus of mass murder: elimination of a category of human beings within a nation who are seen by the powers-that-be as a degraded semihuman people threatening the religious purity of the nation.

"SAINT" AUGUSTINE: A CHRISTIAN TYRANT

Despite Christ's commandment to his disciples to "love one another," Christian rulers have at times practiced incredible cruelty and justified it as their religious inheritance. Christ himself inherited from his Hebrew culture the stories that Moses ruled rightly, though absolutely, because he could hear God's instructions, that King David waged nearly constant war by God's commandment, and that King Solomon's authoritarian wisdom came from the mind of God. It is puzzling that subsequent tyrants, claiming to be Christian, somehow brushed aside the fact that Jesus Christ did not take on the rule of politics.

Well before the advent of tyrants who pledged their loyalty to Christ, Roman rulers were practicing tyranny extensively. Emperor Nero, for example, in the first century after Christ had masses tortured and killed. He even had his own mother murdered. But Nero did not profess Christianity.[15]

Centuries later, when the Roman empire was crumbling, a new Christian leader rose to power.

Augustine—later designated *Saint* Augustine by the Christian church—was born in 354 A.D. in present-day Algeria. His family was middle class and his religion was Manichee, a complex faith which, for example, allowed him at age seventeen to go away with a concubine who then produced a child.

Augustine became a professor of rhetoric, but asthma destroyed his ability to speak well, which depressed him. Perhaps that is why he converted to Christianity. A great bishop baptized him: led him down into the deep, dark pool under the cathedral of Milan and three times shoved the naked Augustine into the water. Then Augustine put on a white robe and was handed a candle. Emerging as a Christian, he saw that the Church in Milan was strongly engaged in political rule.

His speechmaking ability gone, Augustine took up writing. "The House of the Lord," he wrote, "shall be built throughout the earth."[16]

He was sure that God had established the power relations:

St. Augustine.

> It is You who make wives subject to their husbands…you set husbands over their wives; join sons to their parents by a freely-granted slavery, and set parents above their sons in a pious domination. You link brothers to each other by religious bonds tighter than blood….You teach slaves to be loyal to their masters, masters to be more inclined to persuade than to punish. You link citizen to citizen, nation to nation, you bind all men together in remembrance of their first parents, not just by social bonds but by common kinship. [17]

Thus Augustine's central political belief was: "You teach kings to rule for the benefit of their people, and warn the peoples to be subservient to their kings." [18] As scholar Paul Johnson notes, Augustine believed in "the idea of a total Christian society," a faith that "necessarily included the idea of a compulsory society." [19] Of the church and government, Augustine wrote, "The two states are bound together in this world until they are separated by the last judgement." [20] God commanded the Christian ruler to command all of human life. And if the ruler's commands were not voluntarily obeyed, they should be imposed by force so that the earthly city would become "The City of God."

Augustine became a leading bishop, with substantial power over government enforcements. At first he was hesitant to advocate cruelty to build the City of God, but state torture was already a regular practice in the empire. Secret police dragged in the victims. A "vestal virgin" who lost her virginity was flogged and then buried alive. The prisons had torture racks, whips with lead attached, and red-hot plates for burning flesh. Because the Church was taking over the government, Augustine thought the Church would have to use the same methods. Early in his career as a bishop, he advocated inhibited cruelty: heretics were to be examined "not by stretching them on the rack, not by scorching them with flames or furrowing their flesh with iron claws, but by beating them with rods." [21] Augustine's own town of Hippo had been, in his view, "brought over to the Catholic unity by fear of the imperial edicts." As he saw it, fear worked; it "made us become earnest to examine the truth…the stimulus of fear startled us from our negligence." Reading the Bible, he thought Christ himself had used "great violence" to "coerce" St. Paul into Christianity. He found his idea confirmed in a phrase in the Gospel of St. Luke (14:23): "Compel them to come in." [22]

Torture was even more appropriate for probing suspects than for punishing convicted criminals: "The necessity for harshness is greater in the investigation, than in the infliction of punishment," wrote Augustine, and "it is generally necessary to use more rigor in making inquisition, so that when the crime has been brought to light, there may be scope for displaying clemency." [23] Augustine saw public debate as encouraging heresy and therefore as a danger to Christian faith:

> Far be it from the Christian rulers of the earthly commonwealth that they should harbour any doubt on the ancient Christian faith…certain and firmly-grounded on this faith they should, rather, impose on such men as you are [heretics] fitting discipline and punishment….Those whose wounds are hidden should not for that reason be passed over in the doctor's treatment….They are to be taught; and in my opinion this can be done with the greatest ease when the teaching of truth is aided by the fear of severity. [24]

Essentially, he wrote, "when a man does not serve God, what justice can be considered to be in him?"[25]

Given his totalitarian philosophy, Augustine's behavior was predictable. He appeared, as Johnson notes, as "a clever man stooping low for the purpose of vulgar appeal, remorselessly exploiting popular prejudice, an anti-intellectual, a hater of classical culture, a mob orator, and a sex-obsessive."[26] He not only thunderously condemned the sort of adultery he had practiced for many years, he also confessed to being ashamed at the "sin" of having wet dreams.

Shortly before Augustine's death in A.D. 430, the Vandals invaded his city and the rest of North Africa. They butchered and tortured all types of people and tore down and burned Christian churches. Near the end of his life, Augustine wrote, "This life, for mortals, is the wrath of God. The world is a small-scale Hell."[27] Despite his utter failure to heed Christ's commandment to "love one another," Augustine inspired Christian rulers for centuries. His theory and practice guided generations of Christian tyranny in the name of God.[28]

CHRISTIAN TYRANNY BEYOND AUGUSTINE

Augustine's view that the king is God's representative on earth and the state is the church lived on long after him. He had proclaimed that war was a virtue, provided God commanded it. And who would know if He did? The king. War seemed especially acceptable—even admirable—if undertaken against non-Christians. Through the Dark Ages, European Christian leaders claimed to have God's approval to go to war to defend Christians. Christian warriors who took up arms against non-Christians were often made saints by the Church; at the very least, they obtained forgiveness of all their sins. Through these same centuries, there was also a Christian movement for peace, based on the commandment to love others. But the religion of fighting proved more appealing and soon grew typical. War seemed more normal than love in the Dark Ages.

In 1095, the pope set in motion the First Crusade. Its objective was to destroy the Muslims down south in the "Holy Land," on the ground that they had no right to inhabit their part of the earth, while for a Christian "the whole world is his country."[29] Jews were also killed by the Christian Crusaders. In one year, 1096, 12 Jews were killed one place, 500 in another, 1,000 at a third. Even "non-Latin" Christians were murdered in heavy numbers by the Crusaders. One account says that their babies were hung on cooking spits and roasted over fires. When the Crusaders conquered Jerusalem, they massacred Muslim and Jewish men, women and children. In this First Crusade, some 100,000 Europeans—young and old, rich and poor, male and female—converged on the Holy Land. Ten years later, almost all of them were dead. The experience was bizarre, but it did not discourage future Crusades against the East.

In 1204, Crusaders went to war against their fellow Christians in the East and Constantinople, "to the honor of God, the Pope and the empire." The soldiers, permitted to steal and rampage for three days, broke into the cathedral, ripped away the hangings, and shattered the large silver crosses. They raped nuns and set a prostitute on the Patriarch's throne to sing a dirty French song. They threw down the sacred Bibles and guzzled the holy wine at the altar.

Such "Christian" horrors continued until the end of the thirteenth century. The Crusaders built gigantic castles, well protected as long as the soldiers hunkered down in them. But whenever they marched off to find and fight the enemy, the castles were occupied by the enemy, and the returning Christian soldiers were locked out and killed.

Furthermore, as such warmongering increased, the Christian military leaders naturally took over, forcing the clergy to obey their orders. In 1209, Crusaders killed 15,000 humans, "showing mercy neither to order, nor age nor sex." Prisoners were blinded, dragged by horses, and used for target practice.[30] In 1212, great crowds of children, led by two young boys, set off with shepherds on a Crusade. As they passed through Paris, they kept shouting, "Lord God, exalt Christianity! Restore the True Cross to us!"[31]

Terror hit the Church. Sometimes they even condemned dead persons, already buried in the church cemetery. They dug them up, dragged them through the street, burned them in garbage pits, and then smashed down their houses and transformed them into sewers or dumps. The Inquisition system began. Males as young as 14 and females as young as 12 had to swear allegiance every two years to the Catholic church and pronounce their detestation of all heretics. In the early days of the Inquisition, suspects were locked away in prison. Then leading Christians, previously reasonable and sympathetic thinkers, nevertheless emerged as torturers, preaching their justification to torment any victim:

> But if, having been tortured reasonably[!], he will not confess the truth, set other sorts of torments before him, saying that he must pass through all these unless he will confess the truth. If even this fails, a second or third day may be appointed to him, either *in terrorem* or even in truth, for the continuation (not repetition) of torture; for tortures may not be repeated unless fresh evidence emerges against him; then, indeed, they may, for against continuation there is no prohibition.[32]

No woman was to be tortured while pregnant: "we must wait until she is delivered of her child."[33] Young children and old persons *could* be tortured—though less severely than the norm. As the prisons grew crowded and gave rise to diseases that spread beyond their walls, many suspects were burned to death.

Scholar Paul Johnson has written of that awful era, which dragged on for hundreds of years:

> The total Christian society of the Middle Ages was based on an intense belief in the supernatural. It tended to live on its nerves. Lacking any kind of system for determining the truth scientifically and objectively, society was often bewildered....The enthusiasm of faith so easily toppled over into hysteria, and so became violently destructive....One man's Christ was another man's Antichrist. The official Church was conventional, orderly, hierarchical, committed to defend Society as it existed, with all its disparities and grievances. But there was also, as it were, an anti-Church, rebellious, egalitarian, revolutionary, which rejected society and its values and threatened to smash it to bits.[34]

For hundreds of years after the horrors of the Crusades, Christian religion was invoked time and again as justification for empowering rulers to use force against dissident thinking. This Augustinian precept was embraced by Protestants as well as Catholics, as the careers of Martin Luther, John Calvin, and Oliver Cromwell make clear. Absolute rule justified by theology became the ideology of kings who trampled on citizens' human rights. It took centuries of tragedy to learn that human rights could not be guaranteed except by the separation of church and state. The clearest, most lasting monument to that idea is the government of the United States of America.

The Christian experience of religious totalitarianism is not unique. Around the world, other religions—in the Middle East, Africa, and India, for example—have used the power of the state to advance their religious beliefs. It seems a certain type of religious mind cannot conceive of relying on persuasion for conversion. But the principle of the separation of church and state did spread after the Americans adopted it, first throughout the British Empire and then elsewhere. In our own generation, Christian tyranny is rare, while Christian support of democracy is typical.

But there are other forms of political totalitarianism besides those based on orthodox religion, as we saw in the chapter on the French Revolution. Instead of being based on ancient texts and traditions, these newer forms use a secular political ideology to justify the absolute rule of the state and create new festivals and ceremonies to glorify that rule.

THE POLITICAL RELIGION OF COMMUNISM

In the nineteenth century, a former journalist, living in London, Karl Marx, studied the French Revolution and wrote about it. Marx thought the Reign of Terror had been a tactical mistake, but not a moral crime; he admired the Jacobins and Robespierre, and declared, "The classical period of political reason is the French Revolution." [35] He was far from forswearing killing by the state. "Certainly," he wrote, "in periods when the political state as such comes violently to birth in civil society, and when men strive to liberate themselves through political emancipation, the state can, and must, proceed to *abolish and destroy religion*; but only in the same way as it proceeds to abolish private property, by declaring a maximum, by confiscation, or by progressive taxation, or in the same way as it proceeds to abolish life, by the *guillotine*." [36] Marx advocated revolution—the new state coming "violently to birth"—and a political "religion" of his own to replace traditional religion.

Marx was right in his description of the unjust exploitation and suffering of workers in England and elsewhere—a genuine horror that the aristocrats obscured by making it complicated. As a witness, Marx put his finger on the problems that those who would struggle for democracy needed to understand. As a prophet, he failed. To suppose that to know the evil makes you also know the good is false: a doctor who is a genius at diagnosis can be a disaster at prescription. Marx presented extraordinarily extensive and complex prognostications of

Karl Marx.

the future, so complex that a Marxist could derive from them all sorts of conclusions: Marx's predictions as to the time and place of the great Communist revolution, for instance, could be wrenched out of all recognition. Various intellectuals with a fatal weakness for complexifying became attached to his multifaceted, eclectic and diverse analyses. But some of his suppositions were bizarre, such as the prediction that a successful revolution by the working class would result in the "withering away" of the state. Guessing what Marx or his chief apostle Friedrich Engels would actually advocate in a specific political situation in another time and place was nearly impossible.

Still, his influence was enormous. Marxism as an ideology spread across the world. Its appeal was essentially religious. For example, the famous Hungarian-born author Arthur Koestler became devoted to Communism because, he said, "Faith is a wondrous thing; it is not only capable of moving mountains, but also of making you believe that a herring is a race horse." [37] The equally famous French writer André Gide described his feelings about Communism this way:

> My conversion is like a faith. My whole being is bent towards one single goal, all my thoughts—even involuntary—lead me back to it. In the deplorable state of distress of the modern world, the plan of the Soviet Union seems to me to point

to salvation. Everything persuades me of this. The wretched arguments of my opponents, far from convincing me, make me indignant. And if my life were necessary to assure the success of the Soviet Union, I would gladly give it immediately. I write this with a cool and calm head, in full sincerity, through great need to leave at least this testimony, in case death should intervene before I have time to express myself better. [38]

The British poet Stephen Spender took on faith of Communism:

Your friends are allies and therefore real human beings with flesh and blood and sympathies like yourself. Your opponents are just tiresome, unreasonable, unnecessary theses, whose lives are so many false statements which you would like to strike out with a lead bullet as you would put the stroke of a lead pencil through a bungled paragraph. [39]

Author Louis Fischer noted that "Communists addressed one another as 'comrade.'…The Party expected [one] to be a model of antireligious zeal, ideological loyalty, personal morality, and political devotion. Lapses were severely punished." [40] Ignazio Silone, the Italian writer, who also converted to the new faith, later recalled:

What struck me most about the Russian Communists, even in such really exceptional personalities as Lenin and Trotsky, was their utter incapacity to be fair in discussing opinions that conflicted with their own. The adversary, simply for daring to contradict, at once became a traitor, an opportunist, a hireling. *An adversary in good faith* is inconceivable to the Russian Communists.… To find a comparable infatuation one has to go back to the Inquisition. [41]

This religious devotion to Communism that so many intellectuals of the twentieth century had in common did not mean that they agreed on tactics or strategies or even political principles. Lenin took power, not by convincing even all the Bolsheviks, let alone the Mensheviks or the rest of the Russian population, that the time was ripe for a revolution in the name of Marxist principles. He overthrew Kerensky by taking control of the military. Once in power, he quickly established a personal dictatorship. Lenin's political policies shifted up, down, and around in the less than five years he was in charge of Russia—especially in the area of economics, the heart of Marx's theory from the first. Lenin seemed against totalitarianism at times, and in favor of it other times, as when he pronounced in 1918 that there was "absolutely *no* contradiction in principle between Soviet (that is, socialist) democracy and the exercise of dictatorial powers by individuals." [42]

When Lenin died, Stalin took over and ruled the Soviet Union completely for 25 years. Totalitarianism was accomplished.

For years before either man came to power, the totalitarian potential had existed in Russia. The word for "state" in Russian is *gosudarstvo*, translatable as "lordship" and reflecting, according to Leonard Shapiro, "the exercise of power over subjects by an all-mighty ruler." [43] Russia's traditional culture strengthened the religious aura of Marxism. Maurice Latey writes, "The quasi-religious character of the ideology became even more evident when it was transplanted to Holy

Russia, the land of millennial sects, with the Orthodox seminarist Stalin as its high priest. Marx came to be treated as John the Baptist to Lenin's Messiah. Trotsky became the Devil."[44] Bertrand Russell perceived the equivalents:

> Yahweh = Dialectical Materialism
> The Messiah = Marx
> The Elect = the Proletariat
> The Church = the Communist Party
> The Second Coming = the Revolution
> Hell = the punishment of Capitalists
> The Millennium = the Communist Commonwealth [45]

In 1921, a group of Russian writers saw the "Great Russian Revolution" as a grand fulfillment of Russia's destiny: "God's way on earth."[46]

Under Stalin, the old religious language was reborn in the service of the state and many martyrs were made. Incredibly, "heretics" about to be shot to death by one of Stalin's firing squads loyally shouted "Long live Stalin!"[47] Scholar Adam Ulam sees Stalin as "a man of religious temper," a ruler who

> proceeded to people the Soviet citizen's universe with "good men" surrounding the Leader, and "renegades," "traitors," and "wreckers" constituting between them a latter-day collective Antichrist. The setting was religious, almost medieval, in which the Good were received into the bosom of Abraham while the wicked were given their just desserts.[48]

Stalin's father had actually been a priest, and Stalin himself had been educated in a local church school and then, through a scholarship, in a Russian Orthodox theological seminary. His mother wanted him to become a priest also,[49] but he refused. He exchanged his Russian Orthodox faith for the religion of Bolshevism. *Pravda* once quoted him:

> A Bolshevik is one who is devoted to the end of the cause of the proletarian revolution. There are many such among nonparty people. Either they haven't had time to enter the party's ranks or they see it as so holy that they want to prepare better to enter the party's ranks. Oftentimes such people, such comrades, such fighters stand even taller than many and many a party member. They are faithful to it to the grave.[50]

Stalin called his country "a fatherland."[51] It was one in which he himself was worshipped as the Almighty Father, as when a woman shouted out "Glory to Stalin!" and 3,000 people stood up and cheered him.[52] Once André Gide, traveling in Russia, stopped at a post office to send a telegram to Stalin. It began, "Passing through Gori on our wonderful trip I feel the impulse to send you—" The translator said he could not address Stalin as "you." Something had to be added. He proposed—actually required—"You leader of the workers" or else "You Lord of the people."[53]

Power was the fundamental belief of the Communist religion begun by Marx, advanced by Lenin, and firmly established by Stalin. Leonard Shapiro ob-

Josef Stalin.

serves that "Stalin's was, in fact, the first truly personal despotism to have existed in a modern state." [54] Shapiro writes:

> There was no longer any need to persuade by argument where fear could do the work better. But ideology remained of ever greater importance as a means of ensuring conformity. It set a norm, or pattern, in accordance with which the foundations of the national creed, or the accepted interpretation of history, or of foreign policy, or of any other question considered by Stalin to matter, had to be expressed by all. Anyone who deviated from the norm, whether prompted by originality or by intellectual dissent, was immediately exposed and could be dealt with. [55]

A prisoner put it in poetry:

> Stalin, my golden sun,
> If death should be my fate,
> I will die, a petal on the road
> Of our great country. [56]

The ideology Stalin adopted was totalitarianism. The enabling ideal was that government action would eventually transform the Soviet Union into a "classless society" in which the government would "wither away." [57] In this brand-new idealistic society achieved through the "dictatorship of the proletariat," individuals would love one another, and care nothing for their own material advancement, and work for the common good. Citizens would not need a government to tell them what they must and must not do. In order to create this future, leaders were justified in taking any action—no matter how brutal—today. Stalin gladly took on the mission. He saw his Communist Party as "not only the highest form of class association of the proletarians" but "an *instrument* in the hands of the proletariat *for* achieving the dictatorship when that has not yet been achieved and *for* consolidating and expanding the dictatorship when it has already been achieved." [58]

How should a nation achieve that goal? Stalin described the process:

> Now, what does to "maintain" and "expand" the dictatorship mean? It means imbuing the millions of proletarians with the spirit of discipline and organization; it means creating among the proletarian masses a cementing force and a bulwark against the corrosive influences of the petty-bourgeois elements and petty-bourgeois habits; it means enhancing the organizing work of the proletarians in re-educating and remolding the petty-bourgeois strata; it means helping the masses of the proletariats to educate themselves as a force capable of abolishing classes and of preparing the conditions for the organization of socialist production. But it is impossible to accomplish all this without a party which is strong by reason of its solidarity and discipline. [59]

There could be free discussion, Stalin said, but it must stop once a decision is made, so that there will be no "breaking up of the unity of will." Progress cannot happen so long as the "petty-bourgeois groups" are tolerated because they keep insisting on "the spirit of hesitancy and opportunism, the spirit of demoralization and uncertainty." [60] So those who were encouraged to have as their ultimate goal the abolishment of government must now devote their lives to total government power. Stalin said, "A strong and mighty dictatorship of the proletariat—that's what we need now to smash to pieces the last remnants of the dying classes and breakup their thieving machinations." [61]

The rule of law, Stalin thought, could also delay progress. According to his chief legal theorist, Stalin's proposition was that "there are times, moments in the life of society and in our life in particular, when laws turn out to be obsolete and have to be set aside." [62] In the finally achieved ideal society, law would be eliminated because people would no longer need to be ruled by it. But now it should be eliminated to allow the government to rule by force so progress could be made toward that ideal society. Similarly, the goal of a "classless society" had to be set aside for the moment. In army, military ranks that had been abolished were reestablished by Stalin. He also decided to "abolish wage equalization" and set up wage differences to "take into account the difference between skilled and unskilled labor." And Stalin changed one word in a famous pronouncement by Marx. Whereas Marx had proclaimed, "From each according to his abilities, to each according to his needs," Stalin proclaimed, "From each according to his abilities, to each according to his work." [63]

In Stalin's future Communist Party, all citizens would be included. But that could not happen, he said, unless many people were expelled from the present Party. Between May and December 1934, some 190,000 Communists were thrown out of the Party. Stalin's *Pravda* newspaper explained: "It must be understood that if we want to destroy all enemies in the shortest possible time, our first task is to overcome the organizational disorders in our own ranks, to put our own party house in order."[64] And though Stalin published the "most democratic constitution in the world," its guarantee of free speech was postponed.

Thus did Stalin take control of the nation's social life in order to take control of citizens' beliefs. In essence, force makes faith.[65]

THE RESULT OF COMMUNISM

Communist faith created Communist terror. The terror was not an invention by Stalin, but by Lenin. Lenin had ordered violent repression back in 1918, when revolt challenged his new government. He told his authorities to use "merciless mass terror against kulaks, priests, and White Guards," and his "Red Terror" decree stated that "the Soviet republic should be made secure against class enemies by isolating them in concentration camps."[66] Four years later he wrote to a justice official that "The court must not eliminate terror." Regarding farmers, Lenin demanded that the government "Lay it down more precisely that owners of grain who possess surplus grain and do not send it to the depots and places of grain collection will be declared *enemies of the people* and will be subject to imprisonment for a term of not less than ten years, confiscation of their property, and expulsion forever from the community."[67] Under Lenin's rule, masses of people suffered and died.

But Stalin grossly transcended Lenin's terror. He proclaimed 1929 "The Year of the Great Turn." The great turn was to collectivized farming—a complete change in the country's system of agriculture. The "kulaks," farmers who were at least somewhat better off than the poor peasants, were damned. Stalin made that clear when he said, "To take the offensive against the kulaks means to get ready for action and to deal the kulak class *such a blow* that it will no longer rise to its feet."[68] So 180,000 agents of the Soviet trade unions were dispatched into the countryside to create the new collective farms. They went after the "kulaks," who often farmed away from their neighbors. The agents took their property and jammed kulak families into boxcars of trains destined for far-off slave labor camps. Many died on the way. Their methods succeeded: early in 1930, about 14 million peasant households had been "collectivized,"[69] and by 1931, nearly 2 million people were imprisoned in labor camps.[70]

Here is the memory of one young kulak boy sent with his family to a labor camp:

> Strangers came to the house. One of them was from the G.P.U. and the chairman of our Soviet was with him too. Another man wrote in a book everything that was in the house, even the furniture and our clothes and pots and pans. Then wagons arrived and all our things were taken away and the remaining animals were driven to the *kilkhoz*.... They put us all in the old church. There were many other parents and children from our village, all with bundles and all weeping. There we spent the whole night, in the dark, praying and crying, praying and crying. In the morning about thirty families were marched down the road surrounded by mili-

tiamen. People on the road made the sign of the cross when they saw us and also started crying. At the station there were many other people like us, from other villages. It seemed like thousands. We were all crushed into a stone barn but they wouldn't let my dog, Volchok, come in though he'd followed us all the way down the road. I heard him howling when I was inside in the dark. After awhile we were let out and driven into cattle cars, long rows of them, but I didn't see Volchok anywhere and the guard kicked me when I asked. As soon as our car filled up so that there was no room for more, even standing up, it was locked from the outside. We all shrieked and prayed to the Holy Virgin. Then the train started. No one knew where we were going.[71]

Some 7 million human beings lost their homes to the dictator's agents and about half that many people were dragged off to labor camps or sent away to the freezing north or the wasteland of Siberia.[72] By the middle of 1937, 93 percent of kulak households (some 18.5 million) had been seized by the government.

Meanwhile, millions of peasants and their children were starving to death as a result of a terrible famine that had spread across the country. One major cause of the famine was that Stalin's government had seized millions of tons of grain and sold them overseas. At night, "barbers"—mainly mothers of starving children—sneaked out into the fields and clipped off grain with their scissors. Others, forced to carry off grain for the government, stuck some into their pockets or under their shirts. Hearing of this, Stalin decreed that such starving thieves should be imprisoned or executed. In just five months, 54,545 people were convicted and 2,110 were killed.[73] Peasants, in desperation, ate grass, dogs, bark, horses and—many, many times—other humans.[74] Starving beggars banged on doors and fought one another over garbage.

Stalin had read a good deal in Machiavelli's *The Prince* and he admired Ivan the Terrible, so when resistance to his rule arose, he was prepared to act fast and brutally. After one of his officials was killed, Stalin saw to it that 94 White Guardist prisoners were executed.[75] So began the second phase of Stalin's horror, the Great Purge. Thousands, especially leaders who had supported *Lenin's* dictatorship, were murdered or sent off to Siberia after losing all their possessions.[76] Stalin himself created a new law called "On Measures Against Crime Among Minors" to terrify accused parents with the threat that one of their children might also be subjected to criminal punishment if the parents did not cooperate.[77]

The purging of Leninists, police, and even the Red Army continued. Millions were arrested and killed or locked into slave-labor camps. Often their loved ones were also hurt. For instance, one woman was taken to prison and

stripped naked, and put in a cold dark cell with rubber walls. Once the cell door opened, a light shone in, someone touched her back with the tip of his boot, and she heard a man say, "Those enemies of the people sure knew how to pick their women." Another door opened, a flashlight was trained on her, she heard a man's outcry, and thought the voice was her husband's.[78]

The massive terrorism went far beyond what any other major nation in history had ever done.[79] All kinds of people could be arrested if they were denounced—

by anyone. Children were urged to denounce their parents. Being thrown into jail was no great alternative to death, since often more than 100 people were jammed into a cell built for 20 prisoners. Torture became the norm; the screams prisoners heard often terrified them into confessing to anything. Cruelty escalated: prisoners were forced to stand for hours, given no water, had their fingers crushed by doors, their faces burned by cigarettes, their genitals beaten with rubber truncheons. In 1937 and 1938, from 4.5 to 5.5 million people were arrested and from 800,000 to 900,000 were condemned to death. Of those who went to prison camps or jails—probably 3 to 4 million in those two years—few ever made it home again.[80] In the "trials," the accused were demeaned as the "scum of humanity," "a foul-smelling heap of human garbage," "the acme of monstrous hypocrisy, perfidy, jesuitry, and inhuman villainy."[81]

How was it possible for human beings to spend years maiming and murdering millions of their fellow humans? It was ideology—the totalitarian religion of Communism—that drove the killers and torturers. Scholar Adam Ulam notes that "Many Communists who were being victimized in the mid or late 1930's felt that they had approved of (or indeed ordered) so many frightful things to be done to the 'class enemy' only a few years earlier that—why quibble at the disposal of this or that member of the Party elite? This appalling 'historical' cynicism was yet another factor smoothing Stalin's path."[82] Those who had imitated Stalin in ruthlessness came to feel his ruthlessness themselves.* But so strong was the ideology that some of these victims volunteered for their own death or torment.

Totalitarianist brainwashing allowed leaders to acquiesce in the sacrifice of millions of lives to build the ideal society in the ever-receding future. The president of the Ukrainian Republic of the Soviet Union was once questioned by an American labor organizer who had come over to work in a Ukrainian factory. The American said that the workers had told him that peasants were dying all over the country and that 5 million had already died that year (1933). When the American asked the president what he should tell the workers, the president answered, "Tell them nothing! What they say is true. We know that millions are dying. That is unfortunate, but the glorious future of the Soviet Union will justify that. Tell them nothing!"[83]

In the Marxist mode of "rationality," even the definition of a human being could be distorted. In 1937, a woman who had been tortured, kept awake for seven-day periods at a time, protested to her interrogators that "This is a Soviet institution where people can't be treated like dirt." But they answered her in Stalinist fashion: "Enemies are not people. We're allowed to do what we like with them. People indeed!"[84]

---

* Robert C. Tucker relates the following anecdote about the private Stalin: Stalin frequently smoked his pipe in his room and stalked back and forth thinking. Occasionally he would spit on the floor. A small parrot in a cage imitated him. When Stalin saw the parrot spit, he reached with his pipe into the cage and struck the bird dead. (*Stalin in Power: The Revolution from Above, 1928–1941* [New York: Norton, 1990], p.147.)

COMMUNIST TOTALITARIANISM IN CHINA

When Lenin came to power in Russia, he tried to get "proletariats" around the world to revolt. He especially hoped that the "toilers of the East" would emerge as "revolutionary masses" who would ignite the "fire of the world revolution." He thought that "the way to Europe is through Asia." Later Stalin demanded that China use guerrilla warfare in the farmlands of that enormous nation.[85]

The winner in the Chinese Revolution of 1949 was Mao Tse-tung. That October 1, Mao, as if he were imitating Robespierre, stood on a great rostrum at "the Gate of Heavenly Peace in Peking" and declared the birth of "The People's Republic of China," rousing masses of devoted followers down below to cheer him.[86] Mao became a god whose pictures were considered sacred in factories, communes, and homes throughout the nation. All Chinese people were supposed to worship Mao in a ceremony each morning and evening. First came readings from his bible of quotations. Then followed the singing of three hymns: "The East Is Red," "Sailing the Seas Depends on the Helmsman," and "Father and Mother Are Dear but Mao Tse-tung Is Dearer." Finally, there was a prayer for Mao's advice for the future.[87] Year after year, that holy leader dictated the life of one of the world's most populous nations, showing the way to total dictatorship in other nations.

Mao had been elected to the Central Committee of the Communist Party of China in the 1920s and for decades thereafter, was a chief mover in revolutionary strategy and action. He was a Marxist, but one who believed that Marxism had to be adjusted to China. He said Marxism's "foreign stereotypes" must be set aside and its "dogmatism must be laid to rest," to be replaced by a "fresh, lively Chinese style and spirit."[88] Instead of urban workers, peasants were "the people" for whom the new China was being created. Mao created his own Communist faith and commandments to fit his vision for China. Dennis Bloodworth, who titled his book about Mao and China *The Messiah and the Mandarins*, paints Mao "an ambitious Puritan."[89] He worked all night, slept in the morning, smoked cigarettes one after another, and stalked around his study in black cotton shoes, often forgetting to eat.

Mao saw Communism not as the creation of a loving community but as "a hammer for destroying the enemy."[90] Though since childhood, he said he had hated Confucius, he nevertheless put the classic Chinese philosopher in the new Chinese Community pantheon along with Marx. Mao thought hard work was good for people, that physical trouble intensified their spirit and motivated them to change the government. Arguments, too, would help: "Capitalize on contradictions to win over the majority, and crush your enemies separately," he advised.[91] Mao indicated he hated Confucius's preference for moral propaganda and ideology rather than law and a constitution. And he certainly did not believe that all Chinese people were equal: "the people" meant the working poor only. Mao also believed that learning should be restricted—"We shouldn't study too many books"[92]—and that human happiness was debilitating—"failure is the mother of success."[93] When his actions were criticized, he pushed for instant

Mao Tse-tung.

Communism, not debates about programs.[94] Political thinking, he made clear, was up to him, not the Party. The military, too, had to take on Mao's "living ideology."[95] Traditional Chinese family life and moral standards were rejected as outdated.[96] Chinese Communism was to transform everything.

Like that other notable Marxist dictator, Stalin, Mao ruled absolutely, he himself deciding what was logical and what the society's values were to be. But his reasoning lacked both logic and human values because Marxism disdains reality, factual calculation, and, most important, genuine care for all citizens. Granting himself the dictator's license to fix all, Mao set out on the path to murder. He said, "A revolution is not a dinner party...to put it bluntly, it is necessary to create terror...proper limits have to be exceeded in order to right a wrong."[97] Mao Tse-tung also said, "It isn't good to kill people" and "We should arrest and execute as few as possible." But then, a writer said of Mao, "Today he uses sweet words and honeyed talk to those whom he entices, and tomorrow he puts them to death for fabricated crimes." Mao neither denied nor damned this statement. He welcomed it—and circulated that document throughout his Party.[98] He declared that the masses would be unsatisfied "if we did not kill some tyrants."[99]

And so, kill he did. In the middle of 1951, Mao advertised that his government had just exterminated 800,000 people, but the press—the official Party press—claimed the Maoists had killed "over one million armed bandits." In 1953, there was a report that 2 million had been killed; it was later hinted that twice that many died.[100] Believing that "forced labor would compel [people] to change themselves and so become new men," Mao had masses of workers and businessmen dragged off to labor camps and forced into slavery. The work included digging fake wells, uprooting growing plants, and beating other people. Many escaped by suicide.[101]

From the revolution of Mao to this day, China has been a tyranny, its government run by men who succeeded in grabbing and holding power, not to benefit "the people," but themselves.

There have been varieties of Marxist governments other than Stalinism and Maoism, but their common factor has been totalitarianism. The rulers have been dictators. Liberty and equality have been absent from the calculations, as has reality. Marxists prided themselves on their "scientific" interpretation of history, but their version of history was filled with false information and illogical interpretations—for example, the bizarre idea that government would "wither away."

In 1975, Aleksandr I. Solzhenitsyn noted that "Marxism is not only not accurate, is not only not a science," but has "failed to predict a *single event* in terms of figures, quantities, time-scales or locations." So "only the cupidity of some, the blindness of others and a craving for *faith* on the part of still others can serve to explain this grim jest of the twentieth century: how can such a discredited and bankrupt doctrine still have so many followers in the West!"[102]

DEMOCRACY DEMANDS LIBERTY AND EQUALITY

Democracy invented political liberty and equality, and those inventions have turned out to be remarkably conducive to human progress and happiness. The purpose of democracy is not to rescue human beings nor to transform them totally. Democracy is a restricted government. In contrast to totalitarianism, it concentrates on what must *not* be done rather than on what must be done.

An ancient analogy is the Ten Commandments. Moses did not march down from Mount Sinai and declare to the people what they must do and how they must be—totally. The Ten Commandments do prescribe a few actions: "Honor thy father and thy mother" and "Keep holy the Sabbath day." But primarily they proscribe actions that insult God—worship of idols and blasphemy—and harm other human beings—murder, adultery, stealing, false witnessing, and conniving to take what belongs to others.

The establishment of democracy is based on reliable knowledge of human difficulties in history rather than on an abstract philosophy. That is the kind of knowledge that has built the modern democracies of Germany and Japan. In Germany, since the defeat of Hitler's Nazi tyranny, "The authority of the President of the Federal Republic has been sharply limited; there is no provision in the Basic Law for the President's assuming wide powers for an emergency decree...." The German Supreme Court can "use these principles in declaring unconstitutional any law that blatantly violates human dignity or human rights...." And though political parties "can be freely formed," it is understood that "their internal organization must conform to democratic principles." [103]

The new Bill of Rights established in Japan after the Second World War includes 31 articles. Among these articles are: "The people shall not be prevented from enjoying any of the fundamental human rights" and "Their right to life, liberty, and the pursuit of happiness shall...be the supreme consideration in legislation and in other government affairs." The Japanese Bill of Rights contains other important statements:

> Many more specific rights are also expressly detailed—equality under the law, which has entailed the scrapping of the whole peerage, the people's "inalienable right to choose their public officials and to dismiss them," "the right to own and to hold property," "freedom of thought and conscience," "freedom of religion," "freedom of assembly," "academic freedom," freedom of the individual "to choose and change his residence and to choose his occupation," and even the equal rights of men and women in marriage, which "shall be based only on the mutual consent of both sexes," and "shall be maintained through mutual cooperation with the equal rights of husband and wife as a basis."...[I]n addition there are certain newer rights....[such as] "the right to maintain the minimum standards of wholesome and cultured living," "the right to receive an equal education," "the right and the obligation to work," and "the right of workers to organize and to bargain and act collectively." [104]

Since U.S. democracy is the pattern many other nations have followed in setting up democracies that would guarantee liberty and equality, let us consider a few of the essentials of U.S. democracy. The new German and Japanese democracies have not been operated perfectly. Neither has the older democracy of the United States. But all three of those governments have avoided resorting to dictatorship in emergencies and have very seriously and effectively applied the principles of liberty and equality in their dealings with their citizens. Like the Ten Commandments, the Bill of Rights is more proscriptive than prescriptive: it says what the government is *not* to do. The government specifically restricted its own power so that citizens can choose their own beliefs and most of the own behaviors. Thomas Jefferson put it this way: the Bill of Rights "is what the people are entitled to against every government on earth...and what no just government should refuse...." [105]

The very First Amendment of the U.S. Bill of Rights begins, "Congress shall make no law respecting an establishment of religion, or prohibiting the free exercise thereof...." Jefferson understood well how the mastering of religion by the state both destroys true religion and leads to political horrors:

> [The] presumption of legislators and rulers...have assumed dominion over the faith of others, setting up their own opinions and modes of thinking as the only true and infallible, and as such endeavoring to impose them on others, have established and maintained false religions over the greatest part of the world and through all time.... [106]

Jefferson's solution was not to eliminate religion, but rather to eliminate state religion and to guarantee citizens the right to freely practice whatever religion they chose. Even such "religions" as Marxism and Fascism are allowed to individuals—though emphatically not to the government.

The principle underlying the U.S. Declaration of Independence is that human rights are not intellectual constructs but gifts of God: human beings "are endowed by their Creator with certain unalienable rights" and "to secure these rights, Governments are instituted among Men." It concluded that the failure of a government to secure these rights justifies revolution.

Democracy does not require citizens to love one another, only to respect one another—politically. When this kind of respect breaks down, people start to think of their political enemies as less than human. During the conflict of slavery, for instance, a Kansas abolitionist writer concluded that proslavery "invaders" from Missouri were "wild beasts" who deserved to be killed:

> I always believed it was right to kill a tiger, and our invaders are nothing but tigers. Christ says, "if a *man* smites thee on the one cheek, turn to him the other also." These Missourians are not men....I made up my mind that our invaders were wild beasts, and it was my duty to aid in killing them off. When I live with men made in God's image, I will never shoot them; but these pro-slavery Missourians are demons from the bottomless pit and may be shot with impunity. [107]

With this kind of demonizing rhetoric on both sides, "Bloody Kansas" became a battleground in which some proslavery and antislavery advocates were willing to kill their unarmed political opponents.

Human beings are still human no matter what their ideas, politics, or religion. The democratic principle of equality can be traced to the Gospels, where Jesus Christ insisted that the second great commandment, "Thou shalt love thy neighbor as thyself," defined all human beings as neighbors, even alien persons with alien religions. In the United States, as in other democracies, it took years to fully establish the equality of all citizens, as in the right to vote. The Declaration of Independence says "All men are created equal"—'men' here meaning humans, not males, but it took another century and a half for women to gain the right to vote. It took even longer for African Americans to gain the *effective* right to vote.

After the principles come the procedures. Real democracies did not create noble-sounding constitutions simply for show or occasional invocation by a Robespierre, a Stalin, or a Mao. They create workable constitutions with clearly defined procedures—for election, inaugurations, parliamentary discourse, judicial process, and so forth—and they act on them.

Two procedures are most significant: federalism and free speech. Federalism is a system of sharing differentiated powers between the national government and state or local governments. It recognizes that the variety of the nation in terms of religions, regions, occupations, ethnicities, ideologies, and so forth, requires secondary governance. Federalism does not undo or deviate from the national government but adds to it in order to benefit the peculiar needs and ambitions of local communities. The states themselves typically imitate that national state. In theory, federalism recognizes the national government as the ultimate sovereign. In practice, it can crack apart this logical concept of sovereignty and create puzzles and uncertainties. But federalism also allows for adaptation when necessary.

Decisions of adaptation require political discourse and political discourse requires free speech. "Free speech" does not mean *good* speech. It does not even mean *true* speech. It means that *all* speech is to be tolerated, because the history of government control of speech is abominable. As author J. L. Talmon understands, "Freedom has no meaning without the right to oppose and the possibility to differ."[108] Governments that punish free speech in order to make speech "pure" make speech obscure. Controlled public speech often deteriorates into extraordinarily complex messages. Under Communism, Soviet citizens had to guess what some phrase in a government publication really meant: they could not simply read what it said. So the fundamental lesson is negative: government control over speech harms democracy.

The positive side of free speech has proved essential to democracy by moving conflict and decision making from the sword to the mind. The citizens must think through what is to be done, so all kinds of assertions and controversies must not only be permitted but even encouraged. Criticisms against the current government must be spoken out and respected as potentially improving. The democratic state governed by "the consent of the governed." To consent rationally, the citizens need to be informed of the relevant facts, principles, and arguments. That requires the liberation of journalism to pursue its professional objective: to make reality interesting, so that citizens will vote with their heads, not their guts. In the parliament, of course, genuine free discourse is essential if the members are really going to decide what is to be done in the nation.

What we need to remember most from the history of totalitarianism is this: the tyrants depicted themselves as saints. Their appeal was for salvation, but their governments created hellish societies. Government matters much to human life, but it is a lie that government creates and rules life. Democracy creates, better than any other kind of government, the conditions for human progress. The challenge of making democracy work without transforming it into totalitarianism is one of the most daring and admirable aims of life.

BIBLIOGRAPHY

AVINERI, SHLOMO. *The Social and Political Thought of Karl Marx*. Cambridge, England: Cambridge University Press, 1968.

BLOODWORTH, DENNIS. *The Messiah and the Mandarins: Mao Tsetung and the Ironies of Power*. New York: Atheneum, 1982.

BOARDMAN, JOHN, JASPER GRIFFIN, AND OSWYN MURRAY (EDS.). *The Roman World*. New York: Oxford University Press, 1988.

BOORSTIN, DANIEL J. (ED.). *An American Primer*. Chicago: University of Chicago Press, 1966.

CHAPMAN, BRIAN. *Police State*. New York: Praeger, 1970.

COHN, NORMAN. *The Pursuit of the Millennium* (2nd ed.). New York: Harper Torchbooks, The Academy Library, 1961.

CONANT, JAMES BRYANT. *Germany and Freedom: A Personal Appraisal*. Cambridge, Mass.: Harvard University Press, 1958.

CROSSMAN, RICHARD (ED.). *The God that Failed*. New York: Bantam Books, 1952.

DANIELS, ROBERT V. (ED.) *A Documentary History of Communism*. New York: Random House, 1960.

DURAN, FRAY DIEGO. *Book of the Gods and Rites and the Ancient Calendar*. Translated and edited by Fernando Horcasitas and Doris Heyden. Norman, OK: University of Oklahoma Press, 1971.

DURAN, FRAY DIEGO. *The Aztecs: The History of the Indies of New Spain*. Translated by Doris Heyden and Fernando Horcasitas. New York: Orion, 1964.

EARL, DONALD. *The Moral and Political Tradition of Rome*. Ithaca, N.Y.: Cornell University Press, 1967.

EDITORS OF NEWSWEEK BOOKS. *Thomas Jefferson: A Biography in His Own Words*. Vol. 1. New York: Newsweek, 1974.

FRANKFORT, HENRI. *Kingship and the Gods: A Study of Ancient Near Eastern Religion as the Integration of Society and Nature*. Chicago: The University of Chicago Press, 1978.

GARDINER, ALAN. *Egypt of the Pharaohs*. New York: Oxford University Press, 1964.

HANSEN, MOGENS HERMAN. Translated by J.A. Crook. *The Athenian Democracy in the Age of Demosthenes: Structure, Principles and Ideology*. Oxford, England: Basil Blackwell, 1991.

JOHNSON, PAUL. *A History of Christianity*. New York: Atheneum, 1985.

LATEY, MAURICE. *Tyranny: A Study in the Abuse of Power*. London: Macmillan, 1969.

LEE, STEPHEN J. *The European Dictatorships, 1918–1945*. New York: Metheun, 1987.

PERRY, LEWIS. *Radical Abolitionism: Anarchy and the Government of God in Antislavery Thought*. Ithaca, N.Y.: Cornell University Press, 1973.

REISCHAUER, EDWIN O. *The United States and Japan* (3rd ed.). Cambridge, Mass.: Harvard University Press, 1981.

RILEY-SMITH, JONATHAN. *The Crusades: A Short History*. New Haven, Conn.: Yale University Press, 1987.

SABINE, GEORGE H. *A History of Political Theory*. New York: Holt, Rinehart and Winston, 1961.

SHERWIN-WHITE, A.N. *The Roman Citizenship* (2nd ed.). Oxford, England: Oxford University Press, 1973.

SOLZHENITSYN, ALEKSANDR I. *Letter to the Soviet Leaders*. New York: Harper & Row, 1975.

STAUB, ERVIN. *The Roots of Evil: The Origins of Genocide and Other Group Violence*. New York: Cambridge University Press, 1989.

TALMON, J.L. *The Origins of Totalitarian Democracy*. London: Secker & Warburg, 1952.

TRAGER, FRANK N., AND WILLIAM HENDERSON (EDS.). *Communist China, 1949–1969: A Twenty-Year Appraisal*. New York: New York University Press, 1970.

TUCKER, ROBERT C. *Stalin in Power: The Revolution from Above, 1928–1941*. New York: Norton, 1990.

URBAN, G.R., (ED.). *Stalinism: Its Impact on Russia and the World*. New York: St. Martin's Press, 1982.

WALLBANK, T. WALTER, AND ALISTAIR M. TAYLOR. *Civilization Past and Present*. Chicago: Scott, Foresman, 1955.

CHAPTER

7

The Story of India's Nationality

India is one of the world's most important democracies. It included roughly 500 former kingdoms and accommodates some 16 languages with more than 1,500 dialects, six major religions, and many other divisions. Despite all those differences, after World War II the nation became "one nation with regular elections, an independent judiciary, a free press, and an apolitical military."[1] No democracy is perfect, but compared to the tragic alternatives we have seen all over the globe in recent decades, India stands forth as a prime example for other modern governments to imitate.

This chapter focuses on how India, despite tumultuous conditions, succeeded in establishing democracy after World War II. India might have fallen into the kind of totalitarian tragedy that gripped France after the French Revolution if it had had the ill luck to have leaders whose primary aim was to seize power and grind the citizenry into a conformity that matched their political vision. But India's leader established a government that set political conditions—by law—for common justice and equality.

INDIA'S POLITICAL PAST

Indian civilization emerged more than 4,000 years ago with the founding of large cities. The country was called "India" after its long central river, the Indus. Spanning a wide area, India includes deserts that are lower than the sea and mountains that are among the highest in the world.[2] Traditionally, the great mountains in the north were a barrier to military invasions from countries above. Down south, the intense heat made it hard to grow food; nor was there enough gold or iron for trade.

Poverty was ordinary. And so, for centuries, was warfare and slavery; slaves could be "exiled at will" or "slain at will."[3] Given the harshness of life, many Indians longed for "a deep dreamless sleep," a life in which the pain of reality could be ignored and happiness gained through the concentration of imagination. Monarchy was the typical form of government in India for thousands of years. The ancient kings were trained to fight against the "six enemies" of "lust, anger, greed, vanity, haughtiness, and exuberance,"[4] but this moral education did not stop them from claiming up to a fourth or even half of all the crops raised in the land nor from paying their bureaucrats huge salaries at the expense of ordinary people. The monarch typically saw himself as a benevolent father and the Indian people as his "children."[5]

One ancient king, named Ashoka, came forth with moral politics, including "liberality to friends, relations, brahmans, and ascetics," the rejection of "the slaughter of living creatures," the toleration of different "sects," and "compassion" and "truthfulness." In his reign, there emerged an admiration of law. King Ashoka declared:

> Both this world and the other are hard to reach, except by great love of the law, great self-examination, great obedience, great respect, great energy....[T]his is my rule: government by the law, administration according to the law, gratification of my subjects under the law, and protection through the law.[6]

Then, for several centuries, India was politically fragmented, with various kings ruling different areas. The Hindu religion spread throughout the land. Hindus believed in strict moral standards of behavior, and also in reason and discourse, including arguments. Eventually, the religion of Islam was born thereby creating Muslims. In contrast to Hindus, Muslims urged martial fervor rather than toleration. Bloody wars led to the destruction of some ten thousand Hindu temples. Time and again, a king would work to improve people's lives, and then another king would make a priority of feeding his enormous war elephants—each of whom would eat some 600 pounds of grain a day—rather than trying to feed starving Indians. Even into the sixteenth century A.D., tens of thousands of Indians were killed in wars or tormented, as when 800 Muslim sailors had their hands, ears, and noses cut off. A European described India as "very barbarous, vicious, and without inclination to virtue, no constancy of character, no frankness."[7] The nobles of India, often bullied by their emperor, in turn bullied their own dependents.

In the eighteenth century, India once again split into several realms, each with "independent kings." That division stimulated war. Some 30,000 were slaughtered. The technology of slaughtering was significant. For example, about 10,000 Indians attacked 230 Europeans, but the Europeans, equipped with cannons and muskets, overwhelmed the Indians despite being greatly outnumbered. Thus India's enormous population of citizens and soldiers did not win these wars. They often lost.

ENGLAND TAKES OVER INDIA

English businessmen traveled to India to exploit it, profiting from the "universal distress of the miserable natives." [8] British business sought to rule the nation, and in 1793 their leader put forth a "Code of Forty-Eight Regulations," supervised by their judges and enforced by their police. British taxes were imposed on Indians—including a tax on the sale of salt. Britain began to take over. As historian Stanley Wolpert notes, "By reducing all Indian princes—one at a time—to virtual impotence, British power gradually brought an almost revolutionary state of peace and tranquility to most of the subcontinent." [9] Wide ranges of Indians learned the English language through business and education. Slavery had been abolished and human rights proclaimed: "No Native of the said Territories, nor any natural-born Subject of His Majesty resident therein, shall, by reason only of his religion, place of birth, descent, colour, or any of them be disabled from holding any Place, Office, or Employment under the said Company." [10] Indian communities, wide apart, linked with one another through British-built railroads, post mail and telegraph systems, and English-language newspapers. But resentment against British rule had been building up. As Wolpert puts it, "Virtually all the bridges so painstakingly erected between the British and Indian cultures were destroyed by fear and hatred." [11] Widespread anger against the British united the Indians.

War between India and British in 1857–58 ended with British victory, so the British Parliament voted the "Government of India Act," transferring "all rights" of companies from the businessmen to the King of England. Once again, the high principle of human rights was proclaimed. Queen Victoria issued a proclamation stating

> it to be our royal will and pleasure that none be in anywise favored, none molested or disquieted, by reason of their religious faith or observances, but that all shall alike enjoy the equal and impartial protection of the law; and we do strictly charge and enjoin all those who may be in authority under us that they abstain from all interference with the religious belief or worship of any of our subjects on pain of our highest displeasure. [12]

In fact, the transfer of power to the British government led to exploitation on a greater scale than ever and brutality continued. In 1885, 73 representatives of the Indian provinces convened as the Indian National Congress. The Congress declared its loyalty to the British Crown, but complained about the governed. Its president stated the representatives' request "that the basis of the Government should be widened and that the people should have their proper and legitimate share in it." The Congress leaders saw themselves as "the true interpreters and mediators between the masses of our countrymen and our rulers." [13] The British-controlled bureaucracy, pressured to extract as much wealth as possible from

India to send to Britain, hardly responded to the needs and wants of Indians. Frustrated at getting nowhere with the British, a group of revolutionary leaders within the Congress formed the New Party, a development that divided the Congress for years.

EMERGING LEADERS: JINNAH AND GANDHI

Trouble continued. India's most popular religion, which focused not only on the afterlife but also on life on the earth, was Hinduism. Hindus kept generating a revolutionary movement to gain control of the nation. Meanwhile, a smaller religious group, consisting of about sixty million, were the Muslims, who formed their own congress called "League." The Muslims mainly lived in towns and were descended from merchants, soldiers, and officials, and thus were more aristocratic than the Hindu peasants.[14] Early on, the British gave Muslims privileged voting status: "A Muslim could become a voter if he paid tax on an income of only Rs 3,000 per year while a Hindu had to have an income of Rs lakhs (rs 300,000)."[15] Muslims, naturally, elected fellow Muslims.

Typically, the Muslims backed the British until a tragic assassination made them join the movement for Indian self-government. The emerging hero of the Muslims in India was Mohammed Ali Jinnah. Born in 1876 to a middle-class family, Jinnah was sent off to London to study law when he was 18. He did well in school and practiced law in London for a while, but then returned to India, where he was elected to the Legislative Council in 1910.

The emerging hero of the Hindus—and all India—was Mohandas Karamchand Gandhi. He was born in 1869. His father was prime minister under a king in a small state, although "Gandhi" meant "grocer" and most of his family were merchants. As a boy, Mohandas was married to a child-wife. He went to a university in India and then was sent to London to study law. There he remained a vegetarian, which was a fundamental principle of strict Hinduism, and learned much about liberal and Christian principles even as he experienced British racism. When he returned to India, Gandhi practiced law, though somewhat ineptly. Later, he recalled that once when he stood up to cross-examine a witness, "my heart sank into my boots. My head was reeling and I felt as the whole court was doing likewise....I could think of no question to ask. The judge must have laughed."[16]

Gandhi traveled to British-ruled South Africa. There he raised a family and for 20 years worked to help an Indian community of 40,000 by teaching them the English language and becoming their advocate for increased rights under the government. He also took up the study of various religious faiths, partly because of his membership in the Society of Friends, where he collaborated with a Jew, as well as with Christians, fellow Hindus, and humanitarians of all kinds. He read many books and wrote some. Later, because of his belief in nonviolence and in "holding fast to the truth," he came to be called "Mahatma," meaning "Great-Soul."[17]

Mahatma Gandhi, being taken through a crowd in a ricksha.

INDIA AND WORLD WAR I

Great Britain declared war against Germany on August 4, 1914, and automatically included India as its ally. The Indians united in support of Britain, dreaming that service in the British army and victory in the war would secure their country's freedom. All but 15,000 English troops were quickly pulled out of India to fight in Europe, and of India's own 1,200,000 new soldiers, 800,000 became combatants.[18] Soon the romance of war collapsed: in two months some 7,000 Indian troops were killed, wounded, or missing in action.

As the carnage went on, the British encountered more and more resistance in India. The Sikhs—a monotheistic religious group that had been treated as inferior to both the Hindus and the Muslims by the British—rebelled and some members were shot. The Muslims, led by Jinnah, called for "self-government similar to that enjoyed by the self-governing members of the British Empire." They demanded that a certain number of seats in the Indian National Congress be specified for Muslims, and insisted on "equality in respect of status and rights of citizenship" for members of their religion.[19] Gandhi, back in India now, advocated nonviolent resistance to the British. He appealed very effectively to the Indian masses because he dressed like a peasant and appealed to their fundamental religious beliefs.

The war gave birth to massive new industries in India, but these had little effect on the lives of the common people. Indian soldiers who had gone to Europe to fight and discovered how much better French and English "peasants" lived than Indians, joined groups demanding "complete popular control" of government when the war was over. When Muslims were put down by the British, Jinnah and his allies declared that "The fundamental principles of justice have been uprooted and the constitutional rights of the people have been violated at a time when there is no real danger to the State."

During the war, the British had actually pledged ultimate self-government for India.[20] In 1917, the House of Commons had declared that

> The policy of H.M. government, with which the Government of India are in complete accord, is that of the increasing association of Indians in every branch of the administration, and the gradual development of self-governing institutions, with a view to the progressive realization of responsible government in India as an integral part of the Empire.[21]

And in 1919, Parliament passed the Government of India Act, allowing the election of Indian ministers to share power with the appointed British governors.

But tragedies continued. Disease spread through the nation, killing some 12 million people. When approximately 10,000 unarmed Indian men, women, and children gathered to celebrate a Hindu festival, a British army unit shot 1,650 bullets at them, killing 400 and wounding 1,200 more. The British government punished the unit's commander for that harsh mistake by removing him from office, but the Indians remembered it as the worst tragedy. An Indian named Nehru—father of the great leader who later emerged—spoke to a meeting of 8,000 delegates and a crowd of about 30,000. He said that "if our lives and honour are to remain at the mercy of an irresponsible executive and military, if the ordinary rights of human beings are denied to us, then all talk of reform is a mockery."[22]

GANDHI LEADS INDIA

When he had returned to India in 1914, Mahatma Gandhi found shocking poverty, disease, and violence. Identifying with the poor, he cast aside his British clothing and began to dress like a peasant. For several years, he remained quiet, taking the advice of a friend to keep "his ears open and his mouth shut."[23] Then he was imprisoned for two years by the British for organizing a protest. When he was released, he fasted to prepare himself to assume his great mission as leader of the people of India. He looked like a peasant and talked like a saint. Gandhi was described as follows:

Soft dark eyes, a small frail man, with a thin face and rather large protruding eyes, his head covered with a white cap, his body clothed in coarse white cloth, barefooted. He lives on rice and fruit, and drinks only water. He sleeps on the floor—sleeps very little, and works incessantly. His body does not seem to count at all. There is nothing striking about him—except his whole expression of "infinite patience and infinite love."[24]

Gandhi's ethical beliefs were both deep and wide. They centered not on the specifics of Hinduism, but on a strong devotion to all humanity. He believed in truth, to be pursued with all his strength. He saw all Indians—including the segregated Untouchables, whom he called "Children of God"—as worthy human beings not at all inferior to Europeans. Naturally, his beliefs appealed to the ordinary people, for whom he was not only a personal hero but also an activist leader for progress.[25]

Indians of all kinds turned to Gandhi because he turned to them. He led the Indian National Congress and presented the first article of the Congressional Constitution, declaring that "The object of the Indian National Congress is the attainment of complete self-rule by all legitimate and peaceful means."[26] His work centered on his faith in God, whom he believed to be the God of all—Hindus, Muslims, Christians, everyone. This deep and constant faith in a universal God enabled him to reach the millions who longed to come together as a people. He saw Hindu-Muslim unity as "the breath of our life." Gandhi urged Indians to "forget fear," despite the horrors they had undergone. He even believed that India's great suffering was a blessing because

the purer the suffering, the greater is the progress. Hence did the sacrifice of Jesus suffice to free a sorrowing world....If India wishes to see the Kingdom of God established on earth, instead of that of Satan which has enveloped Europe, then I would urge her sons and daughters...to understand that we must go through the suffering.[27]

Gandhi's democratic deficit was his hope for religious governing; he wanted a universal faith to be the principle of government. He wrote that "those who say that religion has nothing to do with politics do not know what religion means."[28] This is dangerously analogous to the ideal of the French Revolution. His great democratic asset was his insistence on the full political inclusion of every human being in citizenship. He was for universal political rights from the start, in contrast to the founders of American democracy, who allowed slavery and did not even consider giving women the vote.

Gandhi's new Congress Constitution set forth the goal: "the attainment of Svaraj [self-rule] by the people of India by all legitimate and peaceful means." He said "self-rule" would mean "that we can maintain our separate existence without the presence of the English."[29] Gandhi's method was nonviolent noncooperation. He urged Indians to "refuse civilly to obey...unjust, subversive" laws,[30] to buy no British products, to take their children out of British schools and colleges, to decline to take part in British law courts and councils, and to refuse all British titles and honors.

Despite his national following, Gandhi's revolution was broken. There were riots and disturbances, and in the year 1921 alone, the British jailed some 20,000 Indians. Muslims initiated a "holy war," killing many Europeans and wealthy Hindus and forcing Hindu peasants to convert to the Muslim religion. They organized politically to demand that they be specially represented in major areas, even where they were minorities. Hindus turned against Muslims, some forcing Muslims to "wash their pollution" by throwing them into rivers. Thus the fragile political unity of Hindus and Muslims fell apart, although some Muslim-Hindu gangs did unite to attack Europeans, including Christians and Jews living in Bombay. Gandhi himself perceived that "God...has warned me...that there is not as yet in India that non-violent and truthful atmosphere which alone can justify mass disobedience, which can be at all described as civil, which means gentle, truthful, humble, knowing, willful yet loving, never criminal and hateful."[31] The British arrested him and jailed him for two years. After his release, Gandhi stayed silent until 1929.

NEHRU MOVES IN

A new, younger leader emerged, with the strong blessing of Gandhi: Jawaharlal Nehru, who later became the president of the National Congress and the prime minister of India. Nehru stressed universal political rights. On January 6, 1930, designated Independence Day, millions of people pledged that

> We believe that it is the inalienable right of the Indian people, as of any other people, to have freedom and to enjoy the fruits of their toil and have the necessities of life, so that they may have full opportunities of growth. We believe also that if any government deprives a people of these rights and oppresses them, the people have a further right to alter it or to abolish it. The British Government in India has not only deprived the Indian people of their freedom, but has based itself on the exploitation of the masses, and has ruined India economically, politically, culturally, and spiritually.[32]

Despite the assertion of these great principles, the British continued to rule the country, arresting thousands and at times even shooting at Indians. Nehru perceived that words were not enough. Political action was needed.

Meanwhile, Gandhi had reemerged into public life, receiving popular support and worldwide attention for his renewed campaign of civil disobedience. In the 1920s, the British government of India had doubled the salt tax. Since salt was such an important part of the Indian diet—to replenish salt lost through sweating in the extreme heat—Gandhi chose to center his political campaign on a protest against the salt tax. At the age of 61, he led huge numbers of Indians on a march of 240 miles to the ocean, where they illegally gathered their own salt from the beach. Gandhi was blessed by the people—one woman shouted "Hail, law breaker!" and great numbers of other women throughout the nation joined the protest.[33] But the British arrested tens of thousands of Indians who had joined his protest.

Jawaharlal Nehru at UN Headquarters with Sir Pierson Dixon, the United Kingdom's Permanent Representative to the UN.

In April 1930, Nehru was arrested, and then, in June, the entire Congress's Working Committee was arrested. At least 100 people had been killed during the campaign and some 400 had been wounded. Finally, Gandhi himself was arrested. In 1932, he began a fast to protest the government's treatment of the Untouchables, because as "a man of religion," he had "no other course left open" to him than to die for his convictions.[34] After six days, the British gave in and announced a policy more favorable to the Untouchables. In 1935, the British Parliament passed a law allowing the election of independent provincial governments in India, but this was not enough to satisfy the independence movement.

Meanwhile, the Muslims and the Sikhs were moving further away from the Indian National Congress, demanding separate electorates for their communities. Jinnah led the Muslim fight against the Hindus. He damned the Congress as having "killed every hope of Hindu-Muslim settlement in the right royal fashion of Fascism." Nehru thought Jinnah's "astonishing course" was "aggressively antinationalist and narrow-minded" and "a negative program of hatred and violence, reminiscent of Nazi methods." By 1938, India's Congress was torn apart by factional fighting.[35] Gandhi urged Nehru to lead the Congress again, but Nehru refused. The democratic movement for independence seemed broken. And then, in September 1939, World War II started.

India was called to war by the British Empire without even being consulted, let alone allowed to vote for or against it. The country's hope for liberty was smashed as Britain set aside the issue of Indian independence because of the war emergency. India's government committee rebelled and resolved that "A free democratic India will gladly associate herself with other free nations for mutual defence against aggression and for economic co-operation," but "co-operation must be between equals and by mutual consent." Since there had been no "mutual consent," the Indian Congress's high command ordered all provincial ministers to resign. Further breaking the nation's unity, Jinnah, in an address to 100,000 Muslims, declared that Britain could get support for the war from the Muslim community if it supported their demands. He made it plain that he was not for the unity of India: "the only course open to us all is to allow the major nations separate homelands by dividing India into autonomous national states." He said "one Indian nation" was a "misconception" because "The Hindus and Muslims belong to two different religious philosophies, social customs, and literatures. They neither intermarry nor interdine together and, indeed, they belong to two different civilizations."[36]

Jinnah's speech "deeply hurt" Gandhi, who denounced "the vivisection of India." Gandhi believed the "two-nation" theory was wrong and argued, according to Wolpert, that there were many Indian Muslims whose "language, dress, appearance, food, and social life made them virtually indistinguishable" from Hindus.[37] Gandhi shared with Jinnah the concern over the extent to which the Muslims and Hindus shared beliefs, personal habits, and their social emotions. But Jinnah saw "India" as an artificial construct: "India is held by the British power and that is the hand that holds and gives the impression of a United India and a unitary Government. Indian nation and central government do not exist." A government of India would require "the previous approval of Muslim India."

The fact that many Muslims were in the Indian Army strengthened Jinnah's argument. Nehru and Gandhi had appealed to Indians to resist the war effort nonviolently. Nehru was arrested, but Gandhi would not give up: "It is 'do or die,'" he said. "There is no turning back. Our case is invulnerable. There is no giving in."[38]

Geography made India vital to the war in Japan and China, so Britain badly wanted Indians' military help and was ready to go along with whatever *internal* independence India demanded. But Gandhi's last great campaign was for Britain to "Quit India" altogether, to "Leave India to God." English men, women, and children were shouted at throughout the country to "Quit India." Gandhi fasted for three weeks, but the war in 1942 was going so harshly for the British that this tactic no longer worked with them. In desperation, they arrested some 60,000 Indian Congress supporters. The violence spread, and the following year starvation was so extreme that 1 million—perhaps even 3 million—died.

Mohammed Ali Jinnah, President of the All-India Moslem League, addresses the League's Legislators' convention in 1946.

NEHRU TAKES LEADERSHIP AT THE END OF WORLD WAR II

After World War II ended, the major Indian leaders met, including Gandhi, Jinnah, and Nehru. They all sought independence from Britain, but the Muslims demanded a separate nation for themselves, to be called Pakistan, in those northern areas of British-ruled India where they formed a majority. Within the rest of India, they wanted "control in all matters vital to their culture, religion, and economic and other interests." Jinnah saw India's National Congress as nothing but a *Hindu* Congress. As the interreligious controversy continued, Nehru insisted that an independent India divided between the majority Hindus and minority Muslims would still need to have "some over-all power to intervene in grave crisis breakdown." Jinnah disagreed; he thought that what Nehru had proposed was "a complete repudiation of the basic form upon which the long-term scheme [of independence] rests and all of its fundamentals." Jinnah denounced the "bad faith" of the government and said, "We have exhausted all reason." Violence recurred among Muslims, Sikhs, and Hindus in which thousands were killed.

In one incident, on August 16, 1946—declared Direct Action Day by the Muslim League in Bengal, where they had formed a Muslim government—demonstrations turned into riots in which Muslims killed Hindus. In Calcutta, the Sikhs killed men, women, and children of the Muslim minority. Throughout India, there were thousands of funeral pyres. Huge numbers of people, trying to escape from one city to another, were turned back and killed.[39]

Nehru tried to restore peace and re-create the government. But when he attempted to form a new government of 14 elected ministers, including Muslims, Jinnah insisted that no Muslim could be elected in a general election; all would have to be selected by the Muslim League. So Nehru's effort at cooperation failed. The British, still in formal control of the country, stepped in. On August 24, 1946, India's Interim Government was announced under the leadership of Nehru.[40]

Nehru traveled to London for further negotiations. The British no longer desired to rule India, so they sent Lord Louis Mountbatten to help arrange India's independent future. Nehru returned to India and declared that "we have now altogether stopped looking towards London." Gandhi prayed publicly for unity, which convinced many Hindus, who could no longer conceive of any kind of union with the hated Muslims, that he was a traitor to his religion. Jinnah threatened the Congress that the choice was Pakistan or chaos. In 1947, Britain's House of Commons declared that "two independent Dominions" would be established, "to be known respectively as India and Pakistan." The latter nation was composed of East and West Pakistan, the two regions separated by 1,000 miles of Indian territory. Such was the result of "partition of religion."

Independent India chose Jawaharlal Nehru as its first prime minister, a position he would hold for the next 17 years. Nehru declared, "At the stroke of the midnight hour, when the world sleeps, India will wake to life and freedom,"[41] and he stepped forward as the most likely leader to establish democracy despite India's history of brutality and injustice.

NEHRU'S CHARACTER CREATED BY HIS LIFE

Nehru's past is a fascinating story worth knowing. His ancestors served as bureaucrats under Indian kings. But as early as the start of the 1800s, a British leader wrote, "We are now the complete masters of India, and nothing can shake our power, if we take proper measures to confirm it."[42] The Nehru family was able to gain a fortune under British rule because they spoke the English language. Nehru's father, Motilal, was born in 1861 and grew up, his son said, to be "one of the leaders of the rowdy element of the college," and then a man "attracted to Western dress and other Western ways at a time when it was uncommon for Indians to take to them." Motilal Nehru became a lawyer and later a national political leader. His third son, born to his second wife on November 14, 1889, was named Jawaharlal, a name the boy did not like. As years went on, Jawaharlal saw his father as a laugher, but also as a hero:

> I admired Father tremendously. He seemed to me the embodiment of strength and courage and cleverness, far above all the other men I saw, and I treasured the hope that when I grew up I would be rather like him.[43]

Jawaharlal enjoyed his father's affection—he often sat on his father's knee—but sometimes he was frightened by Motilal's temper toward others and his tendency to act like a high-handed aristocrat. Motilal was not religious, for "He was too absorbed by the daily struggle here and now to bother about the hereafter." Also, his ingrained rationalism prevented him "from being swept off his feet by the tides of Hindu revivalism, which rose high at the turn of the century." His son grew up "English by education, Muslim by culture, and Hindu by an accident," concentrating on "secularism, reason, free-thinking, science and progress," his fundamental "Five Principles."[44] The Nehrus' attitude toward religion was unusual in a land noted for the intensity of its religions. Many Hindus believed that "The basis of national unity in India is Hindu religion." They wanted India to emerge from British oppression as "a religious nation" that would begin the "golden age of Hinduism."[45] The Nehrus did not support this notion of a "Hindu nation," nor did they support the ambition of Muslims to take over parts of India to set up their own religious state. Jawaharlal's father admired the British lifestyle, which he thought the Indians should try to achieve, and allowed only English to be spoken at home.

When Jawaharlal was ten, his father bought a home named Abode of Happiness."[46] When he was 15, his father sent him to England to study. There Jawaharlal received a letter from Motilal saying, "In you we are leaving the dearest treasure we have in this world."[47] Jawaharlal's seven-year stay in England, where he was called "Joe," had a mixed effect on him. He wrote to his father that "I cannot mix properly with English boys. My tastes and inclinations are quite different," But living in a land with such a glorious history, he found, "Visions of similar deeds in India came before me, of a gallant fight for freedom."[48] Later he recalled that "in my likes and dislikes I was perhaps more an Englishman than an Indian. I looked upon the world almost from an Englishman's standpoint."[49]

Jawaharlal followed with keen interest the elections in England. He and his father wrote letters back and forth about politics. As a teenager, Joe began criticizing his father as "immoderately moderate," going along too easily with the British government in India. His angry father nearly ordered him back to India, but Joe apologized—"I am sure you will pardon me for an offence I did not intend to commit"—and his father forgave him—"My love for you knows no bounds." When he entered Cambridge University, Joe thought he "had got out of the shackles of boyhood and felt at last that I could claim to be a grown-up."[50] Through their many letters, his father kept urging him to achieve the best. His son wrote back, "You distress me greatly by confidently expecting me to get a First."[51] But his father wisely advised him that "every man will stand or fall by that which is in him and not what follows his name on paper."[52] Joe agreed with his father about a main Hindu concept that annoyed both of them: "repeated references to the spiritual mission of India," the idea of India as " 'God's chosen country' " and "the Indians as the 'chosen race.' "[53] At the same time, he resented anti-Indian discrimination, as did his father. He described himself as "always, like my father, a bit of a gambler, at first with money and then with highest stakes, with the biggest issues of life."[54]

Back to India he came. He was welcomed by his father, and when they arrived home on horseback, Jawaharlal swung off his saddle and ran to hug his mother, lifting her up above him. He went to work as a lawyer for eight years. He was not a remarkable speaker, but he became an effective newspaper writer. He wrote much about politics, once railing that "Ours have been the politics of cowards and opium-eaters long enough and it is time we thought and acted like live men and women who place the honour and interests of their country above the frowns and smiles of every Tom, Dick and Harry." [55] Leaning toward socialism, he described capitalism as "democracy manipulated by the unholy alliance of capital, property, militarism and an overgrown bureaucracy, and assisted by a capitalist press," which "has proved a delusion and a snare." At the same time, "Orthodox socialism does not give us much hope," for "an all-powerful state is no lover of individual liberty." [56] Much experience followed, including an active role in politics and imprisonment by the British for that role. Nehru came to believe that "Pure idealism divorced from realities has no place in politics," and that violence "is today in India the very reverse of revolution." [57] He saw the new national flag of India as meaning that "All those who stand today under this flag are Indians, not Hindus, not Muslims, but Indians." [58]

In 1930, his father died. Jawaharlal missed him immensely. Like his father, Jawaharlal admired Gandhi, so much so that he not only read all Gandhi's writings but also gave up smoking for five years and even experimented with vegetarianism to please the Mahatma. [59] But Nehru opposed Gandhi's "religious and sentimental approach to a political question" and thought "his frequent references to God—God has made him do this, God even indicated the date of the fast, etc.—were most irritating." [60] No doubt he recalled how his father had told Gandhi, "I leave unworldly things to you and my wife. While I'm on earth I will be earthy." [61]

Nehru's growing number of enemies said he did not understand the "soul of India." [62] But he declared that "All those people who talk in terms of Hindu rights and Muslim interests are job-hunters, pure and simple, and fight for the loaves and fishes of office. How long are you going to tolerate this nonsense, this absurdity?" [63] He anticipated their future goal: "The next step should obviously be for the Muslim League and Hindu Mahasabha, in the sacred name of religion, to join together to protect their respective vested interests against the incursion of the common people of India. This is a fascist development. Behind the veil of religion and culture, there is this attempt to consolidate vested interests and groups of privileged people." [64] In contrast, Nehru saw "my people as the Indian people as a whole." [65] Given the tough realities in India, Nehru knew that "We have got a stiff time ahead of us here." [66] In 1932, for example, his own mother, in a protest march, was struck hard by a policeman with a wooden cane, leaving her badly bleeding. That infuriated Nehru. [67]

The same year, the British prime minister declared elections separate among people, so Gandhi began a "fast unto death," which made Nehru confess he was "shaken up completely and I know not what to do." [68] When he received some positive response on unity, Gandhi stopped his fast, but the next year Gandhi fasted for 21 days, which again greatly disturbed Nehru. [69]

Nehru spent much time in jail in the 1920s and 1930s—in one period of four years, he was free for only six months. Finding it "a terrible thing when brutality becomes a method of behaviour,"[70] Nehru began to despair. He wrote that *"it is not possible in any vital matter to rely on anyone. One must journey through life alone; to rely on others is to invite heartbreak."*[71]

But through the many difficulties, Nehru led the way to independence. In 1947, with strong support by Gandhi, he was elected president by Congress and then prime minister of India.

On August 14, 1947, Nehru dedicated the new nation:

> At the stroke of the midnight hour, when the world sleeps, India will awake to life and freedom. A moment comes, which comes but rarely in history, when we step out from the old to the new, when an age ends, and when the soul of a nation, long suppressed, finds utterance....Peace has been said to be indivisible. So is freedom, so is prosperity now, and so also is disaster in this Old World that can no longer be split into isolated fragments.[72]

Every member of the new assembly pledged service to India, and throughout the nation, the people celebrated independence with parades and firework displays and massive meetings. Gandhi was honored as the "Father of the Nation" and England's Mountbatten, was honored for freeing the nation from Britain. Nehru's public honor was the prospect for his future.

THE MOVEMENT FOR UNITY

As the British left India, their prime minister, Winston Churchill, worried that "India is to be subjected not merely to partition, but to fragmentation, and to haphazard augmentation. In handing over the Government of India to these so-called political classes, we are handing over to men of straw, of whom, in a few years, no trace will remain."[73] Indeed, unity was an enormous challenge. Within India's borders were 550 states. Fighting erupted within the year. About 12 million people—Hindus, Muslims, and Sikhs—left their homes to find safer places to live, yet half a million people died in the violence.[74] Nehru's government sent the Indian Army, which had been professionally organized during World War II, to establish peace and to secure every state as part of India, under the rule of the Indian government.

In the capital city of Delhi, Nehru himself went out onto the streets. He rescued two Muslim children who were hiding for safety on a roof. Riots erupted. When the unarmed Nehru came upon some Hindus robbing Muslim shops as the police stood by and watched, he rushed into the angry crowd and called for sanity. That did not work, so he turned to the police and ordered them to shoot the Hindu robbers. Then violence stopped in Delhi.[75]

But violence continued to spread throughout India. Gandhi called for peace. In Calcutta, an enormous city, people were killing one another in large numbers. Gandhi began another fast, "to end only if and when sanity returns to Calcutta." For 24 hours, the entire Calcutta police force joined him in his fast. Within four days, there was complete peace. Gandhi prayed before the people and thousands of Hindus and Muslims came together and even embraced one another.[76]

Gandhi saw the need for "heart friendship" among the conflicting religions. He even thought the national Congress should "dissolve," given its constant controversies. Gandhi reached out to the Muslims: he fasted again, old as he was, to secure a promise from India to give Pakistan, the separate Muslim nation, £40 million. Every member of the nation's cabinet came to his bedside and confirmed the promise. Nehru urged Gandhi to stay alive, because his death would be "the loss of India's soul." But there were Indians who chanted, "Let Gandhi die!" Mahatma Gandhi stopped his fast and walked with many to a garden to pray. On the way, just before sundown, a young man approached him and bowed before him. Then that same young man shot Gandhi dead. It was January 30, 1948. Nehru announced to the nation, by broadcast, that "The light has gone out of our lives and there is darkness everywhere." But the spirit of Gandhi lived on. Ironically, by his death, as historian Stanley Wolpert perceived, he "came closer to achieving his goal of Hindu-Muslim unity [in India] than he ever did in his lifetime."[77]

Nehru confronted his toughest early challenge with Gandhi's spirit of harmony. The part of India next to the Muslims' new nation of Pakistan was Junagadh, a state of 700,00 mostly Hindu people whose ruler was a Muslim. When Pakistan tried to take over Junagadh, Nehru met with the Defence Committee of the Indian Cabinet and declared that "The Government of India does not want a war with Pakistan or anyone else and would like to avoid it at almost every cost." Though he knew that "Any war with Pakistan would undoubtedly end in defeat and ruin of Pakistan provided no other nations are dragged in," he also saw clearly that such a war "may well mean the ruin of India also for a considerable time." Therefore, he declared, "we do not accept...the accession of Junagadh to Pakistan." He stated that

> we are entirely opposed to war and wish to avoid it. We want an amicable settlement of this issue we propose therefore, that wherever there is a dispute in regard to any territory, the matter would be decided by a referendum or plebiscite of the people concerned. We shall accept the result of this referendum whatever it may be as it is our desire that a decision should be made in accordance with the wishes of the people concerned. We invite the Pakistan Government, therefore, to submit the Junagadh issue to a referendum of the people of Junagadh under impartial auspices.[78]

He was determined to solve the problem democratically, through elections, rather than by killing.

Indian troops invaded Junagadh, occupied the capital, and disarmed the state's soldiers and police—fortunately, with no resistance. In February 1948, Junagadh and neighboring states voting overwhelmingly in a referendum to join India.[79] After that, the hundreds of small states of India were consolidated into larger units and all these new states joined the uniform national structure of democracy.[80]

Both Muslim leader Jinnah and Britain's Lord Mountbatten objected to Nehru's method of using military invasion to ensure peaceful negotiations and voting. Nehru's answer was that "War is a prolonged affair, and if we resort to it, many new problems may arise. We have therefore been trying to solve this problem by negotiation, but that does not mean we are afraid of following the path of war."[81] Peace was not complete; people continued to die in the sometimes violent and always complicated arguments over whether a state should join India. But the primary result of Nehru's policy was a decisive and mostly peaceful definition of the nation. In the middle of 1948, India's government issued a White Paper and a map of the nation showing "the progress of political reorganization of States according to integration and merger schemes up to 31st May 1948." The vast land of India was mapped and the government clearly ruled every foot within the nation's boundaries. Historian H.V. Hodson sees this as "an astonishing transmutation, in order out of chaos, to have been accomplished in less than ten months."[82]

Now that the land of India was united, in what manner were Indian *citizens* to be unified? Nehru understood that "After the achievement of independence, the basic problem of India, taken as a whole, is one of integration and consolidation....India must build up for herself a unity which will do away with provincialism, communalism and the various other 'isms' which disrupt and separate."[83]

Pakistan, to the north, developed as a totalitarian state with a government dictated by religion. The preamble to its 1956 Constitution begins: "In the name of Allah, the Beneficent, the Merciful; whereas sovereignty over the entire universe belongs to Allah Almighty alone, and the authority to be exercised by the people of Pakistan within the limits prescribed by Him is a sacred trust..." And Article 25, a "Directive Principle of State Policy," states:

(1) Steps shall be taken to enable the Muslims of Pakistan individually and collectively to order their lives in accordance with the Holy Koran and Sunnah.

(2) The state shall endeavor, as respects the Muslims of Pakistan—

    (a) to provide facilities whereby they may be enabled to understand the meaning of life according to the Holy Koran and Sunnah;

    (b) to make the teaching of the Holy Koran compulsory;

    (c) to promote unity and the observance of Islamic moral standards; and

    (d) to secure the proper organization of zakat, wakfs and mosques.

Article 198(1) says that "No law shall be enacted which is repugnant to the Injunctions of Islam as laid down in the Holy Koran and Sunnah...and existing law shall be brought into conformity with such Injunctions."[84]

In contrast, largely through Nehru's efforts, the "unity" of India was not achieved at the price of imposing one common religion on all Indians. Instead, the unity was political, based primarily on common rules of what must not be done, rather than on rules of what must be done. Nehru visited the United States and returned to India with a devotion to the kind of fundamental bill of rights that had been adopted by America more than a century and a half earlier. [85]

CREATING A CONSTITUTION

India's new constitution for the Sovereign Democratic Republic and Union of States became national law on the twentieth anniversary of India's Independence Day, January 26, 1950. It established the following principles:

> to secure for all its citizens…JUSTICE social, economic, and political; LIBERTY of thought, expression, belief, faith, and worship; EQUALITY of status and opportunity; and to promote among them all FRATERNITY assuring the dignity of the individual and the unity of the Nation.

In contrast to the French Revolution, Indian independence resulted in a secular, nonreligious government—the opposite, as Nehru saw it, of the "caste and priest-ridden society" some had wanted. [86]

In March 1950, the government of East Pakistan proposed to force the Hindu professional and commercial classes out of the country. Nehru's leading ally in government, the Hindu nationalist Patel, actually welcomed that plan, for it gave him the excuse to advocate "ten eyes for an eye"—throwing ten Muslims out of India every time one Hindu was thrown out of East Pakistan. But Nehru stood up against that idea, because it would have destroyed India's secularism and damned the nation by increasing the hatred and violence between Hindus and Muslims. [87] Nehru's biographer M.J. Akbar says that "Nehru never fought a senseless fight or made the dangerous mistake of treating life as a black-and-white battle.…Of all the burdens Nehru had to carry, none was greater than preventing India from further fragmentation." [88] The radical Hindu nationalist solution was to convert all Indians to Hinduism. For example, one leader in the Congress insisted that Muslims be forced to adopt a "Hindu culture" if they were to be allowed to continue to live in India. Nehru said no.

THE CHALLENGE OF "COMMUNALISM"

The philosophy of communalism defines people completely by their religion. Such labeling exposes individuals to a religious prejudice that resembles racism, classism, genderism, nationalism, and ancestorism. Indian communalism was opposed by Nehru as antidemocratic and tending to totalitarianism. [89]

Author Bipan Chandra describes what communalism means in India:

> It is a belief that in India Hindus, Muslims, Christians and Sikhs form different and distinct communities which are independently and separately structured or consolidated; that all the followers of a religion share not only a community of religious interests but also common secular interests, that is, common economic,

> political, social and cultural interests....i.e., religion has to become the basis of their basic social identity and the determination of their basic social relationships....They never think, feel or act in any other manner or category except as members of such homogeneous communities whose interests, outlook, way of life, etc., are the same.[90]

Recognizing the strength of this belief, Chandra concluded that "divisive and disintegrative movements will break out again and again and continue to impede the processes of national integration and social transformation, even endangering the considerable though limited achievements of the last 100 years in this direction."[91]

Despite the totalitarian movements, Nehru led India to secular democracy, in which all humans are seen as equal, and the government would neither reward nor punish anyone because of religious affiliation or any other association. India's constitution included Article 25(1):

> Subject to public order, morality and health and to the other provisions of this Part, all persons are equally entitled to freedom of conscience and the right freely to profess, practice and propagate religion.[92]

And so India became a "secular state," which is defined this way by Professor Donald Eugene Smith:

> Freedom of religion means that the individual is free to consider and to discuss with others the relative claims of differing religions, and to come to his decisions without any interference from the state....The state cannot dictate religious beliefs to the individual or compel him to profess a particular religion or any religion....All religious groups have the right to organize, to manage their own affairs in religious matters, to own or acquire property, and to establish and administer educational and charitable institutions....
>
> The secular state views the individual as a citizen, and not as a member of a particular religious group. Religion becomes entirely irrelevant in defining the terms of citizenship; its rights and duties are not affected by the individual's religious beliefs....[93]

Historian Percival Spear praises Nehru for "his care for secular democracy in India,"[94] and Nehru's biographer Michael Brecher concludes that "Perhaps his most notable accomplishment is the creation of a secular state."[95]

Under Nehru's guidance, India emerged as the world's largest democracy: 173 million citizens.[96] The system was federalist: the Indian states were responsible for such matters as police, education, and agriculture. The national legislature was bicameral: the lower house, called the House of the People, represented citizens by population (like the U.S. House of Representatives), while the upper house, called the Council of State, represented the states equally (like the U.S. Senate).

Nehru had strong ideals and beliefs, but he was also an active and effective political leader. For the first major election, he traveled throughout the land, urging support for his Congress Party in up to nine speeches a day. His party won a sweeping victory in the elections for the new House of the People.

Nehru worked directly with the legislature and the Congress Party for progress, though it was often difficult. In September 1949, he confronted trouble: "As I see things happening in India, in the Constituent Assembly, in the Congress, among young men and women, which take us away step by step from those ideals, unhappiness seizes me."[97] But he was never tempted to abandon party politics and become a dictator. As M.J. Akbar, the author of a major biography of Nehru, asserts:

> The one thing…that Nehru would never contemplate was leaving the Congress. He understood better than others its strengths. He would never go so far as to do anything which would break the party; he wanted only to rescue it from those opposed to the Gandhian commitment.…As Nehru once said, the Congress was the central fact about India.[98]

Congress grew strong. The amazing first general Indian election—which took six months of voting—elected many representatives who would work with Nehru, and a poll of 176 million voters made it clear that Nehru had strong support as the nation's leader.[99]

Akbar says that "Of all the burdens Nehru had to carry, none was greater than preventing India from further fragmentation.…His greatest success, perhaps, was the fact that he kept…India united." Given India's tremendous diversity, Nehru did the only practical thing: he established English as a common language throughout the nation so all citizens could communicate in deciding politics. Nehru saw that "First things must come first, and the first thing is the security and stability of India."[100] He believed in the wisdom of simplicity. He saw that unity in democracy never meant total identity, but rather shared basic rules for the game of politics. Whatever else citizens believed, they were to believe in liberty and equality.

Trouble helped. The nation's population grew up quickly, but food production remained difficult throughout India. So the government instituted generalized economic campaigns, assisted by the U.S. Ford Foundation. While the government supported "the establishment of a socialist pattern of society" in 1954, in fact the economy was primarily free enterprise. Leftist and rightist economic arguments cut across religious arguments, focusing on welfare rather than faith.

Nehru was also the primary leader in India's foreign policy. Again, fundamentals ruled public policy, not detailed, rigid dogma. "In general," Wolpert notes, "Nehru worked to identify India's foreign policy with principles that were integral to India's history: anticolonialism and antiracism were preeminent among them, born in reaction to British rule."[101] He got India to remain within the British Commonwealth, but did not hesitate to support Third World peoples against colonial rulers—for example, condemning the Dutch for their "police action" in Indonesia. Nehru was determined not to have Pakistan divide India: "The Muslim League can have Pakistan if they want it, but on the condition that they do not take away other parts of India which do not wish to join Pakistan."[102]

A Chinese attack on India's northern border led India to align itself militarily with the United States, but even that major crisis did not degenerate into an aggressive ideological war.

Fundamental democracy focuses on relations among all people. The government is the government of every citizen; it does not govern its citizens by religious, gender, or racial categories. Nehru once explained his faith in the individual this way:

> I do believe that ultimately it is the individual that counts. I can't say that I believe in it because I have no proof, but the idea appeals to me without belief, the old Hindu idea that if there is any divine essence in the world every individual possesses a bit of it...and he can develop it. Therefore, no individual is trivial. Every individual has an importance and he should be given full opportunities to develop—material opportunities naturally, food, clothing, education, housing, health, etc. They should be common to everybody. [103]

India had 60 million Untouchables, poor people discriminated against by high-caste Hindus. The government set quotas for the Untouchables in government service work at the local, state, and national levels, and set aside seats for them in the state legislatures and the national House of the People. Those initial, unequal quotas later led to trouble, but at least they made it clear that Indian politics intended to include those who had always been excluded.

Indian women—another long-excluded category of people in political life—were brought into the democracy. Gandhi had succeeded in getting large numbers of women to enter the national movement, but many old Indian laws made women nearly slaves, and Indian women's rate of suicide was the highest in the world. Under Nehru, women gained the right to vote, as well as the right to serve in any political position, including the prime ministership. Complicated laws restricting ranges of marriage were removed, as were restrictions on divorce. Female children won the right to equal inheritance of family property. A new law let women adopt children and gave these adopted children rights equal to those of natural children. These early government policies paved the way for Indian women to emerge as full political citizens in the years to come. [104]

Education was another controversial political issue. Early on, Indian education used two languages, English and Hindi, throughout the nation. Though many Indians could not read or write, for schooling was far from universal, having but two common languages in the educational system contributed to the political integration of widely different cultures. Separatists opposed to Nehru's platform demanded that a variety of languages be used in schools. Nehru got a commission to study the matter, and when the governmental organization of federal states shifted, demand for common national language was revitalized. Yet the agitation for different provincial languages always bothered Nehru because he saw it as an attack upon the nation's federal democracy, and the issue was never really laid to rest. [105] Even so, the percentage of Indians who could read doubled from 15 percent to 30 percent. [106]

NEHRU'S ACHIEVEMENTS

Nehru lead the Indian democracy from independence in 1947 until he died, working in his office, on May 27, 1964. His achievements have survived. The essential accomplishment, without doubt, was the nation's fundamental decision to separate the government from religion, as well as from ideologies like Fascism and Communism. The government was to set laws, not beliefs, to make peace with liberty, not by cruel power, and to establish political equality, not political aristocracy.

Jawaharlal Nehru clarified his hope for democracy in his book, *The Discovery of India*, which he wrote in jail in five months. Nehru's vision remains significant:

> The modern mind, that is to say the better type of the modern mind, is practical and pragmatic, ethical and social, altruistic and humanitarian. It is governed by a practical idealism for social betterment. The ideals which move it represent the spirit of the age....It has discarded to a large extent the philosophic approach of the ancients, their search for ultimate reality, as well as the devotionism and mysticism of the medieval period. Humanity is its god and social service its religion. This conception may be incomplete, as the mind of every age has been limited by its environment, and every age has considered some partial truth as the key to all truth. Every generation and every people suffer from the illusion that their way of looking at things is the only right way, or is, at any rate, the nearest approach to it....We have therefore to function in line with the highest ideals of the age we live in, though we may add to them or seek to mold them in accordance with our national genius.... [107]

Even had he been religious, Nehru could still have seen the need for government to avoid aligning itself with religion. But perhaps his lack of religion helped him to do what needed doing. In his last will and testament, Nehru wrote:

> I do not want any religious ceremonies performed for me after my death. I do not believe in any such ceremonies....My desire to have a handful of my ashes thrown into the Ganga at Allahabad has no religious signification, so far as I am concerned. [108]

Ironically, crowds of millions, mourning his death, cried, Nehru "has become immortal." [109]

CRISIS AND HOPE

Thanks to Nehru's strong, long, and humane political career, India has stood out for decades as having the best government of justice in its region of the world. There has been trouble through the years, but so far, Indian democracy has held fast. In the 1990s, mob violence and even deaths in police custody did occur. In 1992, when hundreds of people began fighting over religious differences, the Indian government responded to the crisis and attempted to revitalize justice. The prime minister went "scrambling to restore the government's authority," arresting leaders who were fighting. [110]

How does India compare to other nations whose revolutions have led, not to imperfect democracy, but to ideological power politics?

In China, the Communist dictatorship has continued to imprison and execute citizens for their beliefs, to stifle free expression, and to use the police to enforce social conformity.

In Yugoslavia, after a revolution that overthrew a Communist government, the nation blew apart into hatred, which led to rape, murder, starvation, and torture on a massive scale.

Throughout the continent of Africa, where the end of colonial rule did not generally result in democracy but in corrupt dictatorships and suppression, violence has roared in nation after nation. Recently in Liberia, force was used to establish totalitarianism. In Rwanda, tribal hatreds have led to mass murder and perhaps the greatest refugee problem the world has known as millions fled their native land to escape the savagery.

And in Russia, whose people were so full of hope for democracy a few years ago, a new dictatorship seems to be emerging.

Such horrors of the 1990s may possibly be cured, but in comparison to India they were tragically worse.

In India, the memory of the original democracy has risen time and again to political minds to revitalize the courageous struggle to maintain real democratic government. Grandson Rajiv Gandhi, said in 1985:

> What Nehru and the founding fathers gave us has stood the test of time, the test of tremendous tensions. Democracy has reached deep into the average Indian. I don't think anybody could change the system today. In 1984…people did not know what was going to happen. But the system really held together. I think we got it right at the very beginning. [111]

India's democracy is government, not dictating humans.

BIBLIOGRAPHY

AIYAR, S.P. (ED.). *The Politics of Mass Violence in India*. Bombay: Manaktalas, 1967.

AKBAR, M.J. *Nehru: The Making of India*. London: Penguin Books, 1989.

BASHAM, A.L. *The Wonder That Was India: A Survey of the Culture of the Indian Sub-Continent Before the Coming of the Muslims*. New York: Grove Press, 1959.

BOWLES, CHESTER. *A View from New Delhi: Selected Speeches and Writings*. New Haven, Conn.: Yale University Press, 1969.

BRECHER, MICHAEL. *Nehru: A Political Biography*. Abridged edition. Boston: Beacon Press, 1962.

CHANDRA, BIPAN. *Communalism in Modern India*. New Delhi: Vikas, 1984.

DUBE, S.C. *Indian Village*. London: Routledge & Kegan Paul, 1961.

EMBREE, AINSLIE T. *Utopias in Conflict: Religion and Nationalism in Modern India*. Berkeley: University of California Press, 1990.

ENGINEER ASGHAR, ALI (ED.). *The Role of Minorities in Freedom Struggle.* Delhi: Ajanta, 1986.

ERIKSON, ERIK H. *Gandhi's Truth: The Origins of Militant Nonviolence.* New York: Norton, 1969.

GANDHI, MOHANDAS K. *An Autobiography: The Story of My Experiments With Truth.* Boston: Beacon Press, 1960.

GUPTA, N.L., AND VINOD BHATIA (EDS.). *Jawaharlal Nehru: Statesman, National Leader, and Thinker.* New Delhi: Panchsheel, 1989.

HARDGRAVE, ROBERT L., JR., AND STANLEY A. KOCHANEK. *India: Government and Politics in a Developing Nation.* 4th ed. New York: Harcourt Brace Jovanovich, 1986.

HODSON, H.V. *The Great Divide: Britain-India-Pakistan.* London: Hutchinson, 1970.

"Holy War in India." *Newsweek.* December 21, 1992.

KHAN, WALI. *Facts are Facts: The Untold Story of India's Partition.* New Delhi, Vikas, 1987.

KOHLI, ATUL (ED.). *India's Democracy: An Analysis of Changing State-Society Relations.* Princeton, N.J.: Princeton University Press, 1988.

MENON, V.P. *The Story of Integration of the Indian States.* New York: Macmillan, 1956.

MOHAN, RADHEY (ED.). *Composite Culture and Indian Society: Problems and Prospects of Integration.* New Delhi: Vichar, 1985.

NAIPUL, V.S. *India: A Wounded Civilization.* New York: Alfred A. Knopf, 1977.

NANDA, B.R. *Mahatma Gandhi: A Biography.* Woodbury, N.Y.: Barron's Educational Series, 1965.

NEHRU, JAWAHARLAL. *The Discovery of India.* Garden City, N.Y.: Anchor Books, 1960.

The New Republic. Editorial. September 7, 1987.

PANDIT, H.N. *Fragments of History: India's Freedom Movement and After.* New Delhi: Sterling, 1982.

PANDIT, VIJAYA LAKSHMI. *The Scope of Happiness: A Personal Memoir.* New York: Crown, 1979.

PANIKKAR, K.M. *The Foundations of New India.* London: Allen & Unwin, 1963.

RADHAKRISHNAN, SARVEPALLI, CHARLES A. MOORE (EDS.). *A Source Book in Indian Philosophy.* Princeton, N.J.: Princeton University Press, 1973.

SAGGI, P.D. *We Shall Unite: A Plea for National Integration.* New Delhi: Indian Publications Trading Corporation, 1968.

SMITH, DONALD EUGENE. *India as a Secular State.* Princeton, N.J.: Princeton University Press, 1963.

SPEAR, PERCIVAL. *A History of India.* Vol. II. New York: Penguin Books, 1984.

Time. Editorial. October 21, 1985.

WADE, H.W.R. *Government and Citizens' Rights: New Problems, New Institutions.* Delhi: National, 1974.

WOLPERT, STANLEY. *A New History of India.* 2nd and 3rd eds. New York: Oxford University Press, 1982 and 1989.

PART THREE

Political Action to Make Democracy Rule by Law

The third requirement for democracy is rule by law. Law in a democracy is made by representatives of the people, who are elected through fair voting procedures. It is simple and straight-forward, clearly stating what actions must happen or must not happen, and it is known by the whole society. Democratic law is also consistent and persistent, until or unless it is changed in the set legal manner. Finally, it is enforced, fairly and impartially.

Contrast this to law under monarchy and aristocracy. In an absolute monarchy, the king rules, period. Law is the king's momentary, often inscrutable, and always powerful preference. In an aristocracy, law is more complex, though just as inscrutable. An elite group of people manipulate law for their advantage and increase their wealth and power at the expense of ordinary citizens. They do this usually not by killing opponents or by taking absolute rule, but by complicating the society's thinking and by acting in ways that result in the enhancement of their own position.

Established democracies are less often threatened by military takeover or totalitarian tyranny—forms of monarchial law—than by fragmentation in which government becomes so diverse and various that the result is an appearance of liberty but a reality of political inequality.

Rule by law is meant to safeguard the people from the obscure and shifting demands of rulers. Democratic law is not perfect, but it is far better for humans to make laws under a democratic constitution than to live under laws handed down by hereditary or entrenched power holders.

8

The Story of England's Nineteenth Century

Democracy Cut Down

Did England in the 1800s have a plain, straight, definite constitution? In contrast, look how Edmund Burke, then a famous author and a member of the House of Commons, described this complicated British constitution as "far better than any sudden and temporary arrangement by actual election." He wrote that the constitution

> is a choice not of one day, or one set of people, not a tumultuary and giddy choice, it is a deliberate election of the ages and of generations; it is a constitution made by what is ten thousand times better than choice, it is made by the peculiar circumstances, occasions, tempers, dispositions, and moral, civil, and social habitudes of the people, which disclose themselves only in a long space of time.[1]

British politics in the nineteenth century provides a prime example of the third major threat to democracy: complexification. The historians Harold Parker and Marvin Brown have noted the difficulties of writing the history of England in this extremely complicated period: "The history of the nineteenth century, it has been suggested, cannot now be written. We know too much about it."[2] Indeed, the twistings and turnings of the politics of the period have been described in numerous books. But the main feature that stands out in these accounts is that too often a form of government that was supposed to be established for *the* people was actually exploited by a *few* people. This was done, not by violent tyranny, but by legal manipulation.

Even in its primitive beginnings, an important function of law was to control and advance the society's forms of material production. Economic changes too often generate legal changes. Great Britain in the late eighteenth and nineteenth centuries exemplified that process.

BRITAIN'S COMPLEX CONSTITUTION

In 1688, Parliament essentially took over the British government, shunting aside the king's power to exploit taxes and property to expand his own power and wealth. Over the next century and a half, England moved from primitive to modern economics by taking advantage of the nation's natural wealth of coal, iron, cotton, wool, and other resources. And by creating a remarkable series of mechanical inventions that utilized the power of steam, oil, and electricity, the volume of products increased considerably. Another advantage was England's location by the sea. Especially after the development of canals and railroads to transport goods to ports and steamships to transport them overseas, new British products could be sold abroad on a massive scale. This great expansion in production and trade led to the modern development of big capitalism.[3]

There was the usual linkage between changes in economics and changes in laws. The new enterprisers replacing Britain's oldtime industrialists used their wealth to persuade members of Parliament to alter the laws for their business profit. They were especially interested in opening up overseas markets. The new enterprisers therefore pressed Parliament to do away with laws taxing products coming into England in the hope that other countries would respond by eliminating their taxes on English imports. The old-style producers who had habitually relied on tariffs to prevent competition lost influence to the new free-traders, and the tariffs were repealed.

Even more important to the new capitalists were laws governing workers. Traditionally, people worked at home, at farming and family-produced manufacturing. But new technological inventions led to factory production; workers were recruited to leave their home areas and come to work in a building owned and run by the producer. The new capitalists pressed for and succeeded in changing old laws which had restricted local workers to be aided only by their own local church and to be rejected from any other community which did not want them there. The old laws regarding worker training had restricted the master of a company to taking on only one person at a time and had required the master to coach that person for seven years. But lengthy training was unnecessary to work with the new machines in factories; a factory hand could learn how to operate a machine in seven days or even seven hours. So worker training laws were changed and industrialists hired thousands. The new capitalists also managed to eliminate the possibility that workers would organize to better their working conditions by getting labor unions condemned as secret revolutions and outlawed.[4]

Why did the members of the House of Commons take on such new laws? Well, mainly because they were offered money to do so, and because they could use legislation to exploit new economic policies to increase their own fortunes.

The election of England's lawmakers to the House of Commons was complicated. Three hundred of the 513 House of Commons members were legally elected only by "proprietors" in different communities. This meant that to get elected, one had to pay money—a substantial price that was advertised in the newspapers. In other words, one needed support from the rich. Known as the "king's friends" in Parliament, they voted as he wanted them to. In those years, the king of England still had significant, if not absolute, powers. And at least most of the people who could afford to attend the theater worshiped him: those who failed to join in the customary anthem "God Save the King" before the play started had their hats smashed by nearby members of the audience.[5]

Most people in Great Britain did not have the right to vote. In Scotland, for example, only about one out of 500 people could vote, and England's new industrial towns of Manchester, Birmingham, and Leeds—each with a population of about 100,000—were not entitled to even one representative in Parliament. So the House of Commons was, in fact, occupied by uncommon representatives who represented different forms of property rather than the great numbers of ordinary citizens, and they made laws to benefit "the landed, the mercantile, the ecclesiastical, and the noble."[6] Efforts to widen representation were continually voted down in Parliament.

Nineteenth-century England, then, was hardly a democracy. But from the viewpoint of the aristocracy, the nation was making stunning progress: gaining major new wealth and inventing marvelous new technologies that increased industrial and agricultural production. It was necessary, they believed, to change the nation's laws to see that this progress continued.

CONDITIONS OF WORKERS, INCLUDING CHILDREN

A "factory" in the nineteenth century was not what it is now. Quickly constructed to house the exciting new machines, the buildings typically had low ceilings, little light, and poor ventilation. After some use, they became muddy and dirty; the air was not only filthy, but extremely unhealthy. The newly invented machines were unbearably noisy and unprotected by any safety devices, so workers were often injured. If a worker's hand was cut off by accident, it was considered the worker's own fault; workers maimed on the job got no money for medical care. Unlike farm work, which varied in kind and intensity according to the hour of the day and the season of the year, and unlike independent work done at home at the worker's own pace, factory work required people to labor for fixed hours doing fixed actions hundreds of times each day. It was hard, machine-ruled, intense, and tedious. Packed into dim, dirty, airless rooms, sweating over the hot machines, workers were prone to cholera, asthma, lung disease, rheumatism, crippled limbs and other deadly illnesses and conditions not curable in those days. And their homes were in filthy slums in crowded towns, where they lacked warm clothes and food worth eating:

The potatoes which the workers buy are usually poor, the vegetables wilted, the cheese old and of poor quality, the bacon rancid, the meat lean, tough, taken from old, often diseased cattle, or such as have died a natural death, and not even fresh then, often half decayed.[7]

In 1843 in Glasgow, typhus infected 32,000 people. A third of them died.[8]

To make workers forget such hardships, managers gave them cheap gin, beer, and whiskey. Workers were not only pressed to drink on the job but also typically received their pay at a bar.[9] In Glasgow, every Saturday night about 30,000 men got drunk.[10] Men who labored as long as 15 hours a day too often sought relief by exploiting young women workers for lust at night. "Crime, drunkenness and immorality were rife in the industrial areas," where "many of the mills…[were] little better than brothels," and "an unhealthy, stunted, short-lived race was rising."[11]

Men suffered in factory work. And so did children and women. Traditionally, children and women had worked at home, but now many working men could not afford to support their families unless their children and wives also earned factory wages.[12] In the factories where cotton was turned into cloth,

The London Match Makers: This engraving depicts women working in an East End factory in nineteenth-century England.

for example, half the workers were children.[13] During the 1830s, tens of thousands of children worked in cotton mills,[14] where they typically started at dawn and did not stop until late at night. Some of them were only four or five years old. Sir William Napier visited one factory, where he discovered "a hellish system":

> The noise of the machinery was deafening, the heat intolerable, the smells disgusting, and the haggard faces and distorted forms of the women and children employed were heart-sickening.[15]

There are many horrifying accounts of child labor in those days. In 1832, in Westminster, children of eight or nine—and sometimes as young as five—worked in factories, enduring 90-degree heat, for 16 to 18 hours a day, often including Sundays. Sometimes these exhausted children would fall into the machines; those who were crippled by factory work were "treated worse than dogs."[16] In 1840, child cotton workers in Lancashire had to crawl down a broken stepladder into a cellar "dug out of an undrained swamp," whose walls ran with dirty water. In that cellar, they worked by candlelight, which strained and weakened their eyesight.[17] In 1844, child workers "were held in bondage" in factories. In order "to perform their task-work they were compelled under cruel punishment to walk as much as twenty miles a day, [and] that their day's work lasted for from twelve to sixteen hours, were the facts or allegations which aroused the pity and the wrath of the nation."[18]

Children were frequently hired to make nails. The youngest ones blew air into the bellows, the seven- and eight-year-olds started constructing the nails, and those aged ten to twelve, working in high heat and smoke, each had to turn out a thousand nails a day.[19] Little girls in a lace-making factory in Northamptonshire spent their workday in similar tension:

> The girls had to stick ten pins a minute, or six hundred an hour; and if at the end of the day they were five pins behind, they had to work for another hour....They counted to themselves every pin they stuck, and at every fiftieth pin they called out the time, and the girls used to race each other as to who would call out first.[20]

A mistress supervisor sat there with a cane in her hand; a child "looking off" and thus "losing a stitch" was beaten with the cane.[21]

Beating child workers was not unusual. In some factories, children constantly worked many whirling wheels with both their fingers and feet, and their boss might hit them or punish them for faltering at this unnatural activity. Many children imprisoned in this kind of labor became upset, their nerves making them jump or shake or hit out. Often they were given drugs, such as opium, to calm them and they became addicted. No wonder Lord Shaftesbury described little children walking out of the factories in the evening as "sad, dejected, cadaverous creatures."[22]

This woodcut depicts child labor in nineteenth-century England. These children are carrying clay in a brick yard.

Children were employed in the coal mines because they were small enough to drag coal through small, cramped tunnels.

> The youngest children were of necessity employed in the thin seams, in roads [i.e., tunnels] which were occasionally found as low as 16 to 18 inches. In many of the small pits of the West Riding, girls had to leave the pits when they reached the age of fourteen to eighteen, being by that time too big to crawl through passages of 22 to 26 inches. Growing girls must have suffered intolerable pain and weariness in sustaining this crouched position for hours on end, with no opportunity to straighten their backs. [23]

Other children carried baskets of coal up ladders all day long. As late as 1842, girls five and six years old were working all day in darkness, opening and shutting doors. Boys, girls, and women dragged heavy loads of coal down in the pits. One investigator saw them

> Chained, belted and harnessed like dogs in a go-cart, black, saturated with wet, and more than half naked, crawling upon their hands and feet, and dragging their loads behind them—they present an appearance indescribably disgusting and unnatural. [24]

Children abandoned by their families were assigned to factories by public officials to earn their keep. They were provided with shabby, dirty beds nearby, and took turns sleeping and working on different shifts. A slave-master from the West Indies who saw the life of child workers in England said:

> I have always thought myself disgraced by being the owner of slaves, but we never in the West Indies thought it possible for any human being to be so cruel as to require a child of nine years old to work twelve and a half hours a day, and that, you acknowledge, is your regular practice.[25]

A newspaperman thought that "The children of Israel, while under Egyptian bondage, did not work nearly so many hours as the people in factories."[26]

Child workers in England's factories and mines got virtually no education, except training in how to operate particular machines faster. So they grew up extremely ignorant. After-work schooling failed; imagine a child trying to learn algebra after 12 hours of factory work. Since many children had to work until midnight Saturday, they probably learned little from Sunday School the next day.[27] One investigation discovered a 17-year-old boy who could not add two plus two, a flock of boys who had never heard of London, and more who did not know who the queen was, as well as a child who "does not know who Jesus Christ is, but had heard the name."[28]

Children who did not or could not work well in this new industrial system were often sentenced to jail. A former Royal Navy captain, Edward Pelham Brenton, who founded the Children's Friend Society, investigated conditions on one floating jail named the *Euryalus*:

> Who would have believed in the existence of such a ship, and for such a purpose, as the *Euryalus* at Chatham:—417 boys, between the ages of nine and sixteen, confined as convicts for seven years, each to cost between £/70 to £/100.—A floating Bastille;—children in iron cages, who should have been in a nursery garden;—children pining in misery, where the stench was intolerable…And while unfortunate girls were starving for want of needlework, these boys were confined in dungeons, making shirts for convicts.…I denounce this system as atrociously extravagant, cruel and vindictive, and I challenge any man to come forward and justify it.…[29]

Men, women, and children working in the new industries had thoroughly miserable lives, even when compared to the farming work they had left behind. Friedrich Engels thought that, by comparison, farm work for children had been "a comfortable and peaceful existence," because

> They were not forced to work excessive hours; they themselves fixed the length of their working day, and still earned enough for their needs.…Children grew up in the open air of the countryside, and if they were old enough to help their parents work, this was only an occasional employment, and there was no question of an 8 or 12 hour day.…[30]

The statistics and the conditions are shocking, but even more appalling are the actual stories of the workers. For example, Richard Pilling, a worker brought to trial for protesting conditions in the 1840s, told the court his story:

Gentlemen, I am somewhere about forty-three years of age. I was asked last night if I were not sixty. But if I had as good usage as others, instead of looking like a man of sixty, I should look something like a man of thirty-six.

I have gone to be a hand-loom weaver, when I was about ten years of age—in 1810. The first week I ever worked in my life, I earned sixteen shillings a-week by the hand-loom. I followed that occupation until 1840. Then I was the father of a family—a wife and three children. In 1840 I could only earn—indeed the last week I worked, and I worked hard, I could only earn six and six pence; but I should do that or become a pauper. I should go to the factory, which I detested to the bottom of my heart, and work for six and six pence a-week, or become a pauper. But although I detested the factory system, yet, sooner than become a pauper on the parish I submitted. I was not long in the factory until I saw the evil workings of the accursed system—it is a system, which above all systems, will bring this country to ruin if it is not altered....

After working in the factory seven years, a reduction began to creep in, one way or another. There were some masters always who wanted to give less wages than others. Seeing this to be an evil, and knowing it to be injurious to the master...I became an opponent to the reduction of wages of the working men, I became an opponent to the reduction of wages to the bottom of my soul....[T]he masters combined all as one man against me, and neither me nor my children could get a day's employment. In 1840, there was a great turn-out in Stockport, in which turn-out I took a conspicuous part. We were out eight weeks. We were up every morning from five to six o'clock. Upwards of 6,000 power-loom weavers were engaged in that turn-out. We had our processions....No one meddled with us—no one insulted us. We were never told, at this time, that we were doing that which is wrong....

In 1840 the master manufacturers, to the number of about forty, had a meeting, and they conspired together—if there is conspiracy on the one side there is conspiracy on the other—and they gave us notice for a reduction of one penny a cut. Some people think a penny is a small reduction, but it amounts to five weeks' wages in the course of the year. It is 2s. 6d. a week. Thus by the reduction they were robbing every operative of five weeks' wages....Myself and my two sons were then working at the mills for twelve-pence half-penny a cut....I was in very poor circumstances then, having a wife and seven children to support; and only three of us earning wages, as I told you....

My Lord, and gentlemen of the jury, it was then a hard case for me to support myself and family. My eldest son but one, who was sixteen years of age, had fallen into a consumption last Easter and left his work. We were then reduced to 9 3/4d a cut, which brought our earnings down to something like sixteen shillings a week. That is all I had to live on, with my nine in family, three shillings a week going out of that for rent, and a sick son lying helpless before me. I have gone home and seen that son—

[Here Pilling was moved to tears, and unable to proceed for some time.]

I have seen that son lying on a sick bed and dying pillow, and having nothing to eat but potatoes and salt. Now, gentlemen of the jury, just put yourselves in this situation, and ask yourselves whether seeing a sick son that had worked twelve hours a day for six years, in a factory—a good and industrious lad—I ask you, gentlemen, how you would feel if you saw your son lying on a sick bed and dying pillow, with neither medical aid, not any of the common necessaries of life?—Yea, I recollect some one going to a gentleman's house in Ashton, to ask for a bottle of wine for him; and it was said," Oh, he is a chartist, he must have none. [Great sensation in court.] Oh, such uses from the rich will never convince the chartists that they are wrong. Gentlemen, my son died before the commencement of the strike....

I have seen in the factory in which I have worked, wives and mothers working from morning till night with only one meal; and a child brought in to suck at them twice a day....Mr. Orrel, employs 600 hands, and he will not allow one *man* to work within the mill. I have seen husbands carrying their children to the mill to be suckled by their mothers, and carrying their wives' breakfasts to them....In consequence of females being employed under these circumstances, the over-lookers, managers, and other tools, take most scandalous liberties with them....I have a nervous wife—a good wife—a dear wife—a wife that I love and cherish, and I have done everything I could in the way of resisting reductions in wages, that I might keep her and my children from the workhouse, for I detest parish life.

It is wages I want. I want to be independent of every man, and that is the principle of every honest Englishman; and I hope it is the principle of every man in this court....And, now, Gentlemen of the jury, you have the case before you; the masters conspired to kill me, and I combined to keep myself alive.[31]

Pilling's talk of his distress brought tears to the eyes of the judge and the jury, and even the prosecutor was so upset that he had to leave the room for a while.[32]

Similar experiences were endured by countless numbers of citizens in Great Britain. In the new age of manufacturing, millions of people died early from overwork and extreme poverty and millions more fled Great Britain for the United States. From Ireland alone, three million people emigrated in three years.

THE LEADERS' VIEWPOINT

Britain's Prime Minister Robert Peel seemed to have hardly noticed what was happening; he claimed that the existing state of things "has secured for us during 150 years more of practical happiness and of true liberty than has been enjoyed in any country excepting the United States of America, not excepting any other country."[33] But the truth was coming forth. Given the domination of the rich,

Too harshly ruled, the poor man learns to hate
And curse the oppressive law that bids him serve the great.[34]

Before the start of the nineteenth century, though, there were leaders who thought it would be just fine for ordinary citizens to take on tough work. A divine said that work would lead to virtue, because "the lesser time for idleness any trade allowed, the better it was." Another declared that "Nothing is more favorable to morals than habits of subordination, industry, and regularity." And decades later, still another minister proclaimed that "There can be no training of the volatile minds of youth equal to that which is maintained at the factories."[35] Others thought the new work must be interesting—even fun—because of its novelty and efficiency.

Then, early in the nineteenth century, a few aristocrats moved to reform industrial practices. Their stance was one of benign lords concerned to have the workers ruled sympathetically. Sir Robert Peel was so shocked by the sicknesses of his own 1,000 apprentice workers, he proposed a bill that would limit work hours, stop night work, and force owners to have the walls of factories washed

Sir Robert Peel.

down, improve the air quality in their buildings, and provide some education, religious instruction, and dormitories for their workers. His Health and Morals of Apprentices Bill was passed in the House of Commons, but it made hardly any impression because government inspection of factories soon dropped off. In 1815, concerned about the harmfulness of the new steampower, Peel tried again. He proposed a bill that would prohibit hiring children under the age of 10, limit children under 18 to 10½ hours of labor a day, and prohibit night work. The bill also made some provision for education. Opponents succeeded in blocking Peel's bill by claiming it would encourage viciousness among England's children: "the deterioration of morals increases with the quantity of unemployed time." A modified version of his proposal eventually did pass, but it was barely enforced, because any worker who came forward as a witness of violations of the law in his factory was "flung out of employment."[36]

In the 1830s, major political conflicts began as the factories spread out across the land. Knowledge of the terrible working conditions could no longer be evaded in the House of Commons. Members moved to improve the situation—but with mild and ineffectual methods. In 1830, farm workers rioted in large numbers in the south of England because they were being repressed by Lord Melbourne, the home secretary for the Whig government. Many workers were arrested; 9 were hanged and 457 were "transported" to Australia.[37] In 1833, a Royal

Commission appointed to investigate factory conditions was told by manufacturers that if the work hours of children were cut back, the hours their parents worked would also have to be cut back, and companies would lose so much labor they would no longer be able to make a profit. Parliament went ahead and passed the Factory Act anyway, which did limit children's hours, but only in the textile factories. The coal mines, pottery industries, the tailoring trade, and other abusive enterprises were untouched. In the textile industries, the law forbade the employment of children under 9 altogether, and limited the workday of those aged 9 to 13 to 9 hours, and of those aged 13 to 18 to 12 hours. The Factory Act also said that children under 13 were to have schooling 2 hours a day. But only four inspectors were assigned to supervise these reform measures, which meant they were rarely enforced.

The House of Commons did include benevolent members, but most were not ready to take radical action to alleviate the workers' troubles.[38] Enforcement of what laws they did pass was a joke. For example, one mill owner, prosecuted for overworking children, said he would close down his mill rather than conform to the law. So he was fined—one shilling. By early 1835, 177 owners had been fined, but the Factory Act "was widely broken, education was generally ignored and it proved impossible to check ages," according to researcher J. T. Ward.[39]

In 1834, a Poor Law was passed. The law was well titled, for it was a regressive measure overturning 300 years of more decent precedent. It said that those who could not find regular work would no longer receive any "outdoor" welfare relief, but instead would be required to go into a government workhouse back in the town where they had originally come from. In these workhouses, children were separated from their parents and wives from their husbands, and even harder, heavier work was demanded than in factories. The discipline was harsh and the food sparse.[40] The Poor Law hurt the unemployed poor and frightened the workers. A fellow making shoes in those days later wrote that "the fact is undeniable"

> that the labourers of England believed that the new poor law was a law to punish poverty; and the effects of that belief were, to sap the loyalty of the working men, to make them dislike the country of their birth, to brood over their wrongs, to cherish feelings of revenge, and to hate the rich of the land.[41]

The winter after the Poor Law was enacted, the weather became severe, forcing many unemployed workers to ask for relief. When they were shuttled off to a workhouse instead, they went on demonstrations. One crowd called for "blood or bread," until it was dispersed by the police. Another crowd began to destroy a workhouse, but was stopped by troops. In some places, laborers took over the workhouse they were forced into and demanded their regular relief. The separation of men and women was seen as a plot to keep the poor from breeding; rumor said the workhouse food had in it an antifertility drug. Anglican churchmen spoke out against the Poor Law.[42]

The bad effects of the Poor Law were obvious: the poor were subjected to injustice, bullying, and downright brutality. Ironically, though, the law had one good effect, and that was the spread of concern about social conditions through the citizenry and leadership in England. One tavern keeper wrote to advise a House of Commons leader that he should "give [people] employment and they will sleep away politics."[43]

ENGLAND'S NEED FOR DEMOCRACY

That the permanent solution for suffering people is the charity of leaders is wrong. There have nearly always been charitable, kind leaders who have succeeded in helping citizens, and thus gained public loyalty for their independent power. But good leaders eventually pass on, and bad leaders take their place, leaders who pervert their authority by blessing themselves with money while citizens suffer. English workers experienced this transition from good to bad leaders. The House of Commons did not condemn workers as evil or inferior, nor did it send troops out to kill them, nor did it demand total control of the country. Instead, it was willing to pass legislation to assist the workers—but only if it would benefit the rich. Because the legislation was complicated and its action requirements uncertain, it continued, even intensified, a bad way of life for the working people of England—which was far worse than the life the leaders themselves were experiencing.

The people of England called for democracy. They began to demand, not help from the nobles, but the right to elect their representatives. Eventually the famous political philosopher John Stuart Mill told his English brothers and sisters that

> A person who is excluded from all participation in political business is not a citizen. He has not the feelings of a citizen. To take an active interest in politics is, in modern times, the first thing which elevates the mind to large interests and contemplations; the first step out of the narrow bounds of individual and family selfishness, the first opening in the contracted round of daily occupations. The person who in a free country takes no interest in politics unless from having been taught that he ought not to do so, must be too ill informed, too stupid, or too selfish, to be interested in them; and we may rely on it that he cares as little for anything else which does not directly concern himself or his personal connections. Whoever is capable of feeling any common interest in his kind, or with his country, is interested in politics; and to be interested in them and not wish for a voice in them is an impossibility. The possession and the exercise of political, and among others of electoral rights, is one of the chief instruments both of moral and intellectual training for the popular mind; and all governments must be regarded as extremely imperfect until every one who is required to obey the laws, has a voice, or the prospect of a voice, in their enactment and administration.[44]

As far back as 1777 in England, Major John Cartwright initiated a reform campaign with specific demands:

1. Universal Manhood Suffrage
2. Annual Parliaments
3. Equal Electoral Districts
4. Abolition of the Property Qualifications for Members of Parliament
5. Payment of Members
6. Vote by Ballot [45]

Pressure for the right to vote by the people, and fears in the government that England might have a violent revolution similar to those spreading through Europe, persuaded the House of Commons in 1832 to consider a voting reform bill. But in the end, the House merely fixed some of the most bizarre districts and extended the right to vote to men who owned or rented property with an annual rental value of at least £10. The aristocrats found plenty of reasons to oppose universal suffrage. A Parliament so elected would refuse to "fulfill the engagements entered into between the people and the public creditor," they claimed. "Universal suffrage would be fatal to all purposes for which government exists," and moreover, it was "utterly incompatible with the very existence of civilization," which rested "on the security of property." They believed universal suffrage would destroy England's "mixed constitution, balancing Queen, Lords, and Commons." [46]

The new voting law enfranchised about 200,000 more citizens, but at the same time, it actually disenfranchised some workers who had previously had the right to vote. Its overall effect was to distinguish the upper and middle classes as voters and the working class as nonvoters. [47] Thus, in the guise of reform, the rulers in Parliament passed an election law meant to recruit allies in the middle class and to exclude workers. Given the kind of electorate this "reform" created, nearly every member of the House of Commons who had supported universal manhood suffrage lost his seat in the next election. [48] Meanwhile, the life of factory workers, hardly ever observed by aristocrats, further deteriorated. A complex law helped harm the poor.

THE "LION OF FREEDOM": FEARGUS O'CONNOR

With the help of new leadership, the poor did not give up. The most important new leader was Feargus O'Connor, an Irish member of the House of Commons who created a remarkable organization of workers throughout Britain to agitate for the right to vote. O'Connor was a tall, husky, muscular Irishman, with big round shoulders, curly red hair, and appealing face and manners, and a strong voice. [49] At least when things were going well, he was "a genial, jovial, friendly, sympathetic person." [50] In Ireland, his father and uncle had been leaders in the failed revolution against England in the 1790s, and his uncle had suffered imprisonment. O'Connor's father, as a wealthy Protestant landowner, was not a typical Irishman, though he was sympathetic to the poor Catholic population.

Feargus O'Connor grew up knowing his father was linked with English agitators—at home, the radical newspapers had to be read.

Feargus O'Connor started out on his own political career when he left home with one of his brothers and went to live at a nearby farming community in the house of their older brother. Naturally he spent time in the society of the local gentry, but he also reached out to the peasants and made friends among them. He supported their desire to stop paying tithes and rents. In his mid-20s, O'Connor published *A State of Ireland*, dedicated "to the people of England," which openly attacked the Irish aristocracy—the landlords, clergy, grand jurors, and magistrates—and expressed concern about England's suppression of the Irish people's rights and liberties. This publication threatened to get him arrested in Ireland, so he went to London. According to his own story, he and his closest brother stole two horses from their older brother, sold them in town, and used the money for boat fare to London. O'Connor came back to Ireland after a year to take up farming and law studies, which he finished in London in his 30s. To be licensed as a lawyer, he had to take an oath of allegiance to the government. His father believed that was a wrong pledge to be made by descendants of ancient Irish kings—so he disinherited Feargus. It was probably in London in those days that O'Connor wrote a novel called *The White Boy*, as well as two tragedies, one comedy, and a farce.[51]

Back in Ireland, Feargus O'Connor stood up as a champion of Irish rights. He came on strongly for the classic political reforms—universal suffrage, annual parliaments, and ballot voting—as well as Irish independence. He was determined to organize a united mass protest against the unjust operations of the law, and he even worked to get his church to have fair orders for all the members. A fellow campaigner said, "Feargus's strongest point was his great physical energy. He was indefatigable in his agitation."[52] When he opposed the rule forcing people to pay tithes, he was arrested, because it was illegal "to excite terror and alarm." But the charge against him was dropped. Then O'Connor emerged as a major speaker—one of the best in Ireland—sounding forth with "a mystical spirit in the man that found an utterance in pouring out his feelings to an impassioned peasantry." People were "charmed with the melodious voice, the musical cadences, the astonishing volubility, the imposing self-confidence of the man, and the gallant air of bold defiance with which he assailed all oppression and tyranny."[53]

O'Connor pushed for democratic voting to choose the leaders of his county in Ireland. He solicited widespread support, and his movement won. He himself won a seat in the House of Commons, and so left for London as the representative of the largest county in Ireland.

Many Irish people lived in England, and Irish leaders in London had already aroused to organize for reforms in the government. O'Connor joined their effort. In the House, he quickly opposed an effort by the Whig Party to extend its rule in Ireland, fiercely arguing that if the Whigs succeeded in dominating Ireland, they would soon achieve the same kind of domination in England. He said it was time for the "Irish agitators and the radicals of England to unite for their common safety."[54] Workers in England were beginning to organize protests at this time, even though the police attacked them.

When the 1832 House of Commons made the manipulative proposal to expand voting rights only slightly, O'Connell said his pro-workers should postpone opposition until they became better organized. But O'Connor declared, "Our Great General will not lead the little band to fight—I WILL....[T]he battle must be fought. Of course we shall be beaten." He said he "depreciated the Moderates as 'Wait-a whiles'; we looked upon the moment as having arrived when all Ireland would cry aloud for liberty."[55] But a majority of the party went for the postponement, so O'Connor withdrew his opposing motion. O'Connell, according to author James Epstein, was "a parliamentary tactician, a pragmatic opportunist,"[56] and thus helped to complicate the law. Back home, O'Connor received more and more support. Because he was trying to change the law to mandate annual elections to Parliament, he decided that he himself would resign at the end of any year the people turned against him.[57] He disliked the Whig Party, the nominal liberal party in Parliament: "They have promised everything—they have performed nothing;—they have violated every pledge they made to the people of Ireland."[58] O'Connor not only repeatedly spoke out for the workers but also continually called for freedom of the press—for example, he opposed government charges brought against a paper for advocating tax reforms.[59]

In Ireland, O'Connor's opponents managed to knock him out of the House of Commons when they discovered that he did not own a freehold worth £600, as required of an M.P. So, despite his strong popularity, O'Connor was forced to leave Parliament in 1835. He then became a full-time leader of British working-class protest. The newly founded Radical Association wrote a Declaration of the Rights of Man that started with: "The end of society is the *public good,* and the institution of government is to secure *every individual* the enjoyment of his rights." More than 3,000 radicals attended the Association's first public meeting. O'Connor, who chaired the meeting, declared that "The people must now take matters into their own hands."[60]

In June 1836, O'Connor put together the Universal Suffrage Club, whose purposes were:

> To elevate the moral, intellectual, and political character of the Working Classes; to afford them opportunities for friendly intercourse with each other; and for forming a more substantial compact between them and such men of learning, and political and moral integrity, as are desirous of making common cause with their less affluent brethren; for placing happiness within the reach of all;—to soften, and eventually subdue, the asperity of the aristocracy and the middle classes towards the working portion of the people;—to prove to all their enemies the fitness of the working classes to manage their own affair, both locally and nationally....[61]

He did not oppose factories using machines, but he opposed the way machinery was allowed to harm workers. He wanted to organize a National Convention to meet in London as a rival of the Parliament. Sometimes he became irritated that his fellow "radicals" were being divided from other radicals.[62] But more organizations arose, thanks to his initiative and enterprise.

O'Connor advocated direct challenges to the established order: "Your moral influence can only be established by straightforward and consistent conduct, and by proper demeanor."[63] He asked, "What have the people ever got by cringing, by going with cap in one hand and petition in the other, a posture beneath the dignity of a freeman....?"[64]

O'Connor started, and wrote extensively for, a newspaper called the *Northern Star,* which became the most important medium of national communication for the workers' movement.[65] By December 1837, the *Star* was the most widely circulated provincial newspaper in Great Britain.[66] It was so free and independent that it even printed criticisms against O'Connor himself: "He let every rival speak," Epstein writes.[67] The *Star*'s profits went to support radical political prisoners and their families.[68]

But of all of Feargus O'Connor's actions and agitations, the most important was the Chartist movement that emerged in 1838.

THE DEVELOPMENT OF THE CHARTIST MOVEMENT

The Poor Law operated, as O'Connor said," to leave working men completely at the mercy of their masters."[69] It was passed by a Parliament in which ordinary working people and the poor had no voice. Thus there was strong need for real democracy in England, especially the right to vote for all citizens. In February 1838, the House of Commons had a motion before it, petitioned by more than 100,000 men and women, to repeal the Poor Law Act. The members overwhelmingly rejected that petition, and the workers concluded that they would "never petition again."

In fact, petitions were crucial for the Chartist movement. O'Connor said he had "ceased to think of any other question but universal suffrage."[70] Throughout the country, the workers' movement argued about whether to use "moral" or "physical force" for the cause of rescuing workers from their awful working conditions. Many "took on the slogan peaceably if we can, forcibly if we must."[71] Though England's attorney general "claimed that the government had been successful in putting down Chartism without bloodshed by legal and constitutional means,"[72] England was in real danger of "one of the most bloody revolutions the world ever saw."[73]

In 1838, King William IV died, and a new young queen, Victoria, was crowned. Scottish weaver and leader James Hyslop said, "If a woman can rule, surely women could and should have the vote."[74] Many thousands of women workers had joined and helped lead the new Chartist movement, and there were now more than a hundred female radical associations. Support for women's right to vote was widespread.[75]

After the crowning of the new monarch, there was a national election, which, under the restrictive voting rules, hardly increased workers' representation in Parliament.[76]

In May 1838, William Lovett founded the London Working Men's Association, which called for democracy as it had been demanded in 1777. Lovett's People's Charter called for "manhood suffrage, vote by ballot, payment of members of Parliament, annual Parliaments, equal electoral districts, and the abolition of the property qualification for M.P.'s."[77] While Lovett and his organization thought of these reforms as a step-by-step process, based on improved public education, O'Connor was for immediate sweeping reform. In the late summer and fall of 1838, there were mass demonstrations throughout England. O'Connor went from meeting to meeting, speaking to the crowds.[78] He was seen as "The only man who could be said to have a party." Almost all delegates and constituencies knew him personally.[79] The people had begun to join together and look to particular leaders to advance their cause, because they had "discovered the advantage of combination and submission to leaders." One newspaper wrote of the new phenomenon, "There has been nothing like it in the history of the people of this country."[80] People began to arm themselves.

The major step forward, in 1839, was the National Convention to ratify the People's Charter. Ironically, under English law, such a convention had to consist of delegates who were not elected by specific organizations, but rather by public meetings. This meant that the leaders of the Chartist movement had to leave London and other cities and travel throughout the nation to organize local public meetings for the election of delegates.[81] To block them, the British government sent letters to all the magistrates in the country, offering to supply guns and ammunition to any groups of "respectable" citizens who would form volunteer corps to defend "order and property" against the Chartists.[82] Even so, the Chartist elections took place—with masses of people voting in very many communities. The Convention brought together 53 elected delegates on February 4, 1839, at the British Coffee House in London.

Of the delegates, 29 were middle class and 24 were workers; the latter risked losing their jobs by going to the Convention. Some, primarily middle-class members, thought of their mission as only to present the petition of the People's Charter to the House of Commons. But that limitation on action was rejected by the majority. The middle-class delegates then resigned and were replaced by young working men.[83] The main problem was that all the delegates thought the petition would be rejected by the House of Commons and were uncertain about what to do when that happened. Lovett, secretary of the Convention, and O'Connor tried hard to hold the delegates together in mutual respect and cooperation, but options were hard to decide on. O'Connor kept pushing the delegates to reach a decision, because, he said, "You see the position into which delay has brought this country."[84]

The Convention worked for months after the start of February. In May, it moved to Birmingham. There were some riots, but ordinary meetings were more common. A crew of 70 Metropolitan Police were sent by train from London on July 4. At that evening's meeting an article was read from a Chartist journal by a man on the platform when, with no warning, the police drew out their batons and attacked the crowd—beating men, women, and children.[85] The crowd was terrified. Then the Chartists tore down wooden rails and attacked the police. This event triggered a riot in which property was destroyed and the troops were called in to make arrests. Seldom before in England had any type of law justified arresting people at peaceful meetings.

The National Petition for the People's Charter was signed by 1,283,000 people and submitted to the House of Commons. On July 12, 1839, the House took up the proposal. M. P. Thomas Attwood declared that "the people of England [were] the most miserable and discontented on the face of the earth" and that wrongly the "House disregarded the prayer of the people." Joseph Hume presented the arguments of the petitioners, who had stated that "The energies of a mighty kingdom had been wasted in building up the power of selfish and ignorant men...." Petitioners complained that "they had been bitterly and basely deceived." Hume put their questions before the House:

> Now, could any man lay his hand to his heart and say there was not much of truth in these statements? Could any man say that the House at present represented fully, fairly, and freely the sentiments of the people of England? Why, it was notorious that at present the House was chosen by less than a sixth part of the male adult population.[86]

He then proceeded to argue their case:

> [N]o man could be considered as a freeman who had not a voice in the election of those representatives who were to make the laws under which he was to live, and were to impose the taxes which he was to pay. The Chartists said, that they were slaves, as they had no voice in the election of those who had the power to make laws affecting their lives, their liberties, and their patty pittances of property; and stated, that their sufferings arose principally from the source, that the laws were passed for the benefit of the few, and not for the benefit of the many. Now, could any one deny that the laws were partial, and administered unequally among the rich and the poor?[87]

The Chartist movement for fair law, Hume said, was similar to the proposal that a member had brought before the House 30 years earlier:

> The remedy I have proposed is simple, constitutional, practicable, and safe, calculated to give satisfaction to the people, to preserve the rights of the Crown and to restore the balance of the constitution.

Currently, the Chartists advocated fair and equal representation:

> To deprive any member of the community of his right to vote, in making the laws, or electing those who are to make them, was neither more nor less than an outlawry of such individual....[88]

The fundamental demand was that law be made by representatives elected by all citizens. The Chartists were petitioning "for peaceable and legal efforts to obtain justice for the working classes," advocating "that the Commons of

England ought to be the Commons of England." They insisted England was not well governed by aristocrats: "men born in the clouds, and living in the clouds, could not understand the mere interests, and wants, and necessities of people living on the earth...." Indeed, the Chartists "thought that foxes ought not to represent geese—that wolves ought not to represent sheep—and that hawks ought not to represent pigeons."[89]

OPPOSITION TO THE CHARTIST MOVEMENT

Opponents of the Chartists rose to speak. One M.P. said it was wrong and sad that advocates of the petition "have been found going through the country, from town to town, and from place to place, exhorting the people in the most violent and revolutionary language...."[90] The "universal suffrage" attributed to the United States of America was called a mistake that England would be unwise to imitate.[91] Some members of Commons insisted that most English people did not want voting reform, "that there was an overwhelming majority in this country totally opposed to universal suffrage."[92] Others argued that the Chartists' hopes that universal suffrage would bring prosperity to the working class was "a complete delusion." Instead, they believed workers could be helped by increasing their wages and making it easier for them to buy property. One member admitted that some workers were "conscientious persons," but thought others "very designing and insidious persons" who try "to produce a degree of discord—to produce a degree of confusion—to produce a degree of misery, the consequence of which would be to create a great alarm, that would be fatal, not only to the constitution as it now exists, not only to those rights which are now said to be monopolized by a particular class, but fatal to any established government." It is a "fallacy" that "social evils would be cured by political rights."[93]

The House of Commons voted, 235 to 46, to reject the Chartist petition without even holding a hearing on it.[94]

Dismissed so overwhelmingly by the House, the Chartists began to think about calling for a "sacred month," a national strike by workers for 30 days. But while they were discussing this action, many Chartists were arrested throughout the nation.[95] The Chartist Convention, depleted by these arrests, withdrew the plan for a "sacred month" and instead recommended a National Holiday—a three-day strike in August—during which petitions would be signed requesting the queen to dismiss her ministers. The National Holiday went off as planned, and the result was the arrest of more people than had ever been arrested in English history.[96] Dragged into court, the Chartists were manipulated: urged to plead "guilty" to charges such as conspiring people to arm, "seditious conspiracy, unlawful association or other such rather vague charges." Most of those who agreed to plead guilty were sentenced to keep the peace—usually for two years—and then allowed to go home. Hundreds gave in to this deceptive compromise, and magistrates who had allowed false confessions as evidence claimed the light sentence was merciful. Still, several hundred more stubborn Chartists were tried and imprisoned. The trials took place over 12 months.[97]

William Lovett, the Chartist Convention's secretary, was one of those arrested. He had protested against the police, claiming "a wanton, flagrant and unjust outrage has been made upon the people of Birmingham by a bloodthirsty and unconstitutional force from London." Both Lovett and Birmingham's leader of workers were thrown into jail for nine days before they were released on bail. Tried for "seditious libel," Lovett was found guilty by a jury that hated Chartists and was sentenced to 12 months' imprisonment. In jail that winter with no fire to warm him, eating dreadful prison fare and enduring dangerously unsanitary conditions, he still managed to write a book: *Chartism: A New Organization of the People*. But his health was seriously hurt and he was infected by despair. Later he broke with O'Connor and the other radicals and proposed a long-run educational plan through which the common people would *earn* the right to vote.[98]

O'Connor also was arrested and, along with 58 others, charged with "seditious conspiracy." The attorney general focused his attack on O'Connor, who had encouraged the three-day strike in his *Northern Star*. He pointed to the nonviolence of the legal process and took pride in not once damning the revolutionaries. "I have, I hope," he said, "abstained from using one solitary expression of harshness." To the jury, the attorney general said:

> I desire to give no character to these offenses beyond that which the law does, and has done; I desire not to raise your feelings, from any sense of danger, that you will not do justice. I invoke you as dispassionately as it is possible under these circumstances to do, calmly and boldly, but firmly, to assist in the administration of the law.[99]

LEGAL COMPLEXIFICATION

Indeed, the trial was run politely. But it exemplified the use of incredible legal complexification so common to the rulers of the time. After much testimony, the attorney general summed up the charges to the jury, "which are not very easy for you to apprehend; indeed, not always easy for persons familiar with such subjects, fully to appreciate." The "conspiracy" was defined "as being a combination of two or more persons, either to do, or to cause others to do, an illegal act, or to bring about a legal act by illegal means." But, he said, he wished "to guard myself against laying down a rule that nothing is conspiracy but what comes within this definition." He pointed out the reason so many "counts" had been lodged against the defendants. This "variety of separate charges" was necessary, he said,

> Each count states the charge in a somewhat different manner, for fear the charge, if stated in the manner in which it might appear in the first count, might not be borne out by the evidence, and the party might be acquitted. The charge is therefore stated in a variety of ways.[100]

The Attorney General also stated to the jury, "You may be satisfied, taking the law from me, that in order to convict all, or any, of the defendants, you must convict them of one and the same conspiracy;—*one and the same.*" But, he added, "I do not mean that every one of the defendants used exactly the same influence."[101]

The result of all that gentlemanly complexification of law was sure and simple: conviction. Feargus O'Connor—former member of the House of Commons—was jailed in York Castle from May 1840 to August 1841. Being the high-class Chartist in the convicted crowd, he got the best room, which he was allowed to furnish. He supplied his own food, as well as wine, candles, coals, books, newspapers, birds to keep him company, and was permitted to receive doctors and other visitors. Only one restriction was seriously imposed: no writing of political articles for publication. Despite that rule, prisoner O'Connor was able to smuggle articles out of prison to the *Star*.[102]

Some 1,500 other Chartists, including practically all the leaders, were arrested. In Newport, thousands of Chartists marched, in the style of soldiers, across the hills in the rain and on to a hotel where the military had imprisoned another crowd of Chartists. Not attacked, but feeling at hazard, the military fired a volley of shots at the crowd, who ran away. The three Chartist leaders of the march were arrested—and sentenced to death for treason. Though the British cabinet agreed with the sentence, the three were eventually exiled for life through England's infamous "transportation" punishment.[103]

Despite O'Connor's public appeal he often had problems getting along with other leaders, which made it difficult for the Chartist organization to draw together the increasing millions of workers. Another Chartist leader, M'Douall, addressed the movement: "I implore you to unite, unite, unite! organise, organise, organise!"[104] O'Connor proposed a new Land Law to allow peasants to obtain free farmland, so there would be fewer factory workers competing for bad jobs. But the complications of current land law made reform in this area so difficult that the Land Law movement declined into insignificance.[105]

Prime Minister Peel explained why he was in favor of complex law:

> you must break up, in some way or other, that formidable confederacy which exists in that country [Ireland] against the British government and the British connection. I do not believe you can break it up by force....You can do much to break it up by acting in a spirit of kindliness, forbearance, and generosity.[106]

The Chartist movement changed as economic hard times in the 1840s made it even more difficult for workers to risk their jobs by becoming active Chartists. But the greatest obstacle to Chartism remained English law. The law made it impossible for workers to gain the right to vote in elections for the House of Commons, where they might succeed in passing humane laws to govern profit making. Still, the vast Chartist movement persistently tried to further its cause by overcoming the aristocracy's legal entanglements. For example, English laws regarding the relations among different branches or divisions of a national organization were complicated. To avoid those legalities, the National Charter Association tried its best to transform itself into one general national organization, without divisions. It advanced a petition, signed by two million people, for the release of all Chartist prisoners. [107] (The freed O'Connor refused to take payment when he became the treasurer of the NCA. [108]) Members became increasingly hesitant to protest because national troops surrounded their crowded demonstrations. Instead, they set up local operations, such as "cooperative stores, temperance societies, burial clubs, schools and democratic chapels." [109]

Feargus O'Connor, again voted into the House of Commons, strongly opposed these diverse local enterprises—which he scornfully condemned as "Church Chartism, Teetotal Chartism, Knowledge Chartism, and Household Suffrage Chartism"—because he thought they splintered the national organization and therefore weakened the drive to achieve real democracy. [110] He also opposed the Complete Suffrage movement, which appealed to some middle-class national leaders, because he thought it was a middle-class movement that was trying to dupe workers into voting for free trade. [111]

Despite the constant presence of troops, there were immense demonstrations which focused more and more on gaining the vote for all citizens. Demonstrators shouted, "All labour shall cease until the People's Charter becomes the law of the land," or

> Men of England, ye are slaves
> Though ye rule the roaring waves,
> Though ye shout from sea to sea
> "Britons everywhere are free." [112]

As historian Dorothy Thompson notes, "1842 was the year in which more energy was hurled against the authorities than in any other of the nineteenth century." [113] That year the House of Commons again took up a Chartist petition—supported by nearly 3,500,000 people. It had a "'greater number of signatures than any petition ever before presented," and it utilized "the soundest constitutional principles to advocate universal suffrage." [114] Despite the numerous arrests in the country and the increased anger by the Chartists, the House of Commons again sympathized and even approved of those who advocated the change, describing the "peaceable, respectful, and orderly demeanour of the individuals who came down with the petition yesterday…characterised by forbearance, regularity and decorum." [115] There were members of the House of Commons clearly against the demand for workers to have the right to vote. For instance, one member thought that allowing citizens without property to vote would mean "sinking into barbarism," but still, he declared, "I am far from bringing any charge against the great body of those who have signed this petition." [116] Some ventured that "the surest way to prevent revolutions was to listen to the complaints of the people." [117] And the M.P.'s against the Chartists even applauded when one member said that "he never witnessed more honest sincerity, or more real and sterling worth, than the working men of England exhibited." In general, members said they felt "compassion for their sufferings," as well as admiration for "the fortitude and forbearance with which those sufferings are endured." [118]

So Great Britain's House of Commons did not rouse itself to anger, hatred, violence, or totalitarian force. Nevertheless, the majority of M.P.'s remained against granting the Chartists' demands. They saw the petition as a mistake: "a petition which does not represent the sentiments of those who signed it—a petition that is utterly at variance with the judgment and good sense of the 3, 000,000 of petitioners...."[119] They wondered that the petitioners did not consider "that universal suffrage will be incompatible with the maintenance of the mixed monarchy under which we live." The proposal was seen as "wild, dangerous, and visionary."[120] Some gentlemanly members suggested that rather than legislate universal suffrage "suddenly," it should be implemented by "gradual extension."[121] They saw the leaders of the Chartist movement as the types of people they did not want as colleagues on the benches of the House of Commons. After much respectful discussion, the House voted 287 to 49 to deny approval of the petition.[122]

Chartism would not die, however. Historian Dorothy Thompson notes that "By 1848, Chartism had become the accepted political standpoint of the working people of Britain."[123] That year, more than five million citizens petitioned the House of Commons once again. One member of the House discovered that every 100,000 signatures on this monster petition included approximately 8,200 women."[124]

O'Connor had said that "I would rather die than give up one particle of the Charter,"[125] and the *Northern Star* declared that a new Chartist convention would be held in London to make a new petition and to plan more action. In Halifax, thousands of Chartists met and then marched out past the army barracks; the soldiers cheered them as they passed by. Would workers and soldiers ally to agitate for Chartism? No. A few days later, because of this incident, those soldiers were transferred to Dublin. About 5,000 Chartists walked with them to the railroad station, inspired by a brass band and a tricolor flag. The government sent away the Chartist soldiers, separating them from the Chartist workers.[126]

In economics, the government advocated free trade rather than tariffs restricting the entrance of foreign products into England: the traditional conservatives had been outvoted by the new middle-class members linked with the new factory movement. The workers felt they should take a stand on this question, but they were confused: which would benefit them, free trade or tariffs? Fragmentation on this question made it harder for them to stick together on the fundamental issue of democracy: universal suffrage. In contrast, middle- and upper-class leaders did stick together in determined opposition to working-class voting. The Revolutions of 1848 in Europe aroused great fear (among the ruling classes) and hope (among the workers) in England. The government used the new electric telegraph system and railroads to extend national control over the military so that troops could be moved quickly to put down riots. In contrast to this decisive action, the Chartists leaders pondered: Should they continue to petition peacefully or should they turn revolutionary? This disagreement also divided the Chartists.[127]

The great crowds of Chartists that had demonstrated so effectively were restricted when the government began enforcing a law that made it illegal for more than 20 people to bring a petition into the House of Commons or even to meet closer than a mile to the House itself. And in April 1848, the House quickly passed a "gagging bill" making "seditious speech" a felony and harshly raising the penalty for such speech to "transportation." [128] Thus was free speech effectively outlawed in England. O'Connor did what he could to get Chartists to gather together for peaceful demonstrations. One comrade urged him to do "nothing rashly," to "aim not to destroy the government, but to render a class government impossible." [129] O'Connor spoke to some 20,000 people in London one day, and then the members spread out around the city. Returning to meet again that night, feeling "angry, hungry, footsore," they were barred from the meeting place by troops and police at the city bridges. [130] Throughout the year of 1848, many more Chartists, both leaders and members, were arrested and brought to trial, and many were jailed for at least a year.

THE END OF THE EFFORT

In July 1849, the House of Commons once again took up a Chartist petition for the right to vote. It was decisively rejected, 222 to 17. [131] In ten years, the Chartists had actually *lost* ground in Parliament, for the House vote in 1839 (235 to 46) had not been quite so lopsided.

In 1851, Feargus O'Connor called yet another Chartist Conference, but nothing much was achieved at it. In 1852, he briefly visited the United States. Upon his return, he argued again in the House of Commons, where, in June, he spoke strangely. The sergeant-at-arms removed him from the House. O'Connor was declared insane and put in an asylum, where he stayed until 1854. A doctor then let him go live in his sister's house. On August 30, 1855, Feargus O'Connor died. [132] Twenty thousand people came to his funeral.

Lacking O'Connor, the Chartist movement collapsed into a minor English organization. [133] Many years later, some workers were allowed to vote, but the "one man one vote" principle was not established in England until after World War II. [134]

The demand for democracy in nineteenth-century England was a demand for human welfare. An insightful movement saw from the start the need for government to act by consent of the governed, with elected representatives chosen by the *people,* rather than by some category of aristocrats. The lesson of history is sharp: The poor cannot depend upon the charity of the rich. The power of the state must be ultimately dependent upon the expressed consent of the entire citizenry. With the clarity of a bill of rights, government by a true majority is far less likely to deteriorate into exploitive power than any other type of government. England had no bill of rights, and its complex unwritten constitution allowed aristocrats to treat vulnerable citizens virtually as slaves for many, many years.

Not only the constitution but ordinary law as well was used by the elite to disregard the common people's welfare. Citizens were controlled, not by obvious military power or totalitarian governance, but by the perversion of law from its essential meaning. Law is meant to be clear, general, lasting, and fair. England's law was distorted into highly complex, virtually unintelligible rules. England's aristocrats presented themselves as benevolent, but connived shrewdly to complicate the law so much and so long that appeal to the law by the poor became impossible. Economically, many false political alternatives arose despite the supposed basic devotion to law itself.

Two extreme philosophies of law warred in the nineteenth century. In one, the "free-market" philosophy, it was demanded that the government leave business alone. In the other, it was demanded that the government control all businesses in their every aspect. This Communist view eventually prevailed in Russia and elsewhere. Both of these extreme philosophies of law helped torment, injure, and kill millions of men, women, and children, generation after generation.

The democratic hope has always been that the people will elect a government that rules by law only. Rule by law by no means demands that everything be political, but rather that politics be restricted to the making and enforcing of universal, knowledgeable, persistent, and just rules of the game of life. Clear law is essential for life, liberty, and the pursuit of happiness.

BIBLIOGRAPHY

BRADFORD, SARAH. *Disraeli*. New York: Stein and Day, 1982.

BRADLAUGH, C. *The Real Representation of the People*. 2nd ed. London: Freethought, 188(?).

BRASHER, N.H. *Arguments in History: Britain in the Nineteenth Century*. London: Macmillan, 1968.

BRIGGS, ASA (ED.). *Chartist Studies*. London: Macmillan, 1959.

BURGESS, KEITH. *The Origins of British Industrial Relations: The Nineteenth Century Experience*. London: Croom Helm, 1975.

COLE, G.D.H. *Chartist Portraits*. London: Cassell, 1989.

COLLIER, FRANCES. *The Family Economy of the Working Classes in the Cotton Industry, 1784–1933*. Manchester, England: Chetham Society, 1965.

DICEY, A.V. *Lectures on the Relation Between Law and Public Opinion in England*. London: Macmillan, 1920.

EPSTEIN, JAMES. *The Lion of Freedom: Feargus O'Connor and the Chartist Movement, 1832–1842*. London: Croom Helm, 1982.

GASH, NORMAN. *Aristocracy and People: Britain, 1815–1865*. Cambridge, Mass.: Harvard University Press, 1979.

GASH, NORMAN. *Politics in the Age of Peel: A Study in the Technique of Parliamentary Representation, 1830–1850*. London: Longmans Green, 1966.

GROVES, REG. *But We Shall Rise Again: A Narrative History of Chartism*. London: Secker and Warburg, 1938.

Hansard's Parliamentary Debates. Third Series. 2 Victoriae 1839, Vol. XLIX, 8 July–6 August, 1839, Fifth Volume of the Session, 63515; 5 Victoriae 1842, Vol. LXIII, 3 May–16 June, 1842, Forth Volume of the Session, 63529; and 11 Victoriae 1847–1848, Vol. XCVIII, 7 April–26 May, 1848, Fourth Volume of the Session, 63564.

HARRISON, J.F.C., AND DOROTHY THOMPSON. *Bibliography of the Chartist Movement, 1837–1976*. Atlantic Highlands, N.J.: Humanities Press, 1978.

HUNT, E.M. *British Labour History, 1815–1914*. Atlantic Highlands, N.J.: Humanities Press, 1981.

JACKSON, T.A. *Trials of British Freedom*. New York: Burt Franklin, 1968.

MAITLAND, F.W. *The Constitutional History of England*. Cambridge, England: Cambridge University Press, 1963.

PARKER, HAROLD T., AND MARVIN L. BROWN, JR. *Major Themes in Modern European History: An Invitation to Inquiry and Reflection*. Vol. II *The Institution of Liberty*. Durham, N.C.: Moore, 1974.

PINCHBECK, IVY. *Women Workers and the Industrial Revolution, 1750–1850*. London: Virago Press, 1985.

PINCHBECK, IVY, AND MARGARET HEWITT. *Children in English Society*. Vol. II: *From the Eighteenth Century to the Children Act 1948*. London: Routledge & Kegan Paul, 1973.

PREST, JOHN. *Liberty and Locality: Parliament, Permissive Legislation, and Ratepayers' Democracies in the Nineteenth Century*. Oxford: Clarendon Press, 1990.

READ, DONALD. *Peel and the Victorians*. Oxford: Basil Blackwell, 1987.

SEYMOUR, CHARLES. *Electoral Reform in England and Wales: The Development and Operation of the Parliamentary Franchise, 1832–1885*. New Haven, Conn.: Yale University Press, 1915.

STEVENSON, JOHN. *Popular Disturbances in England, 1700–1870*. London: Longman, 1979.

The Trial of Feargus O'Connor, Esq., (Barrister at Law,) and Fifty-Eight Others, at Lancaster, On a Charge of Sedition, Conspiracy, Tumult, and Riot. London: John Cleave, 1843.

THOMPSON, DOROTHY. *The Chartists: Popular Politics in the Industrial Revolution*. New York: Pantheon Books, 1984.

WALLBANK, T. WALTER, AND ALASTAIR M. TAYLOR. *Civilization: Past and Present*. Chicago: Scott, Foresman, 1956.

WARD, J.T. *The Factory Movement, 1830–1855*. London: Macmillan, 1962.

WEISSER, HENRY. *British Working-Class Movements and Europe, 1815–48*. Manchester, England: Manchester University Press, 1975.

WEST, JULIUS. *A History of the Chartist Movement*. Boston: Houghton Mifflin, 1920.

CHAPTER
9
Law for Democracy

Law is one of the most significant human creations. Without law, society is brutal and anarchic, and justice is impossible. This is not to say that the rule of law guarantees justice—that is only possible in a democracy, where law is made and enforced by a government elected by the people—but that life without any rules to temper power is totally uncivilized.

Law was created and enforced long before recorded history, so the reasons for its original development are obscure. One possibility is that law arose in very ancient times to stabilize a new human practice—marriage.

MARRIAGE LAW

Apparently, in the distant past, people did not realize that babies were produced through sexual intercourse between a man and a women. Therefore, males were not required to take responsibility for their own children. Possibly the mother would rely on her brother for protection and aid in rearing her children, provided she had a brother. In any case, the need for one woman and one man to join together in a stable commitment was a great human hunger, for trouble alternatives—incest, casual sex, neglected children and youth, or the aged deprived of family caring—created disasters in relationships. After many years of such troubles, the wonder of marriage was born: one man and one woman promised faith to each other for the rest of their lives. Thanks to the known, simple, stable law of wedlock, children could rely on care from a bonded pair of adults. And adult needs were taken care of in marriage. Men gained the security of household and domestic care, while women gained protection for themselves and for their children. Both adults gained the advantage of a regular sex life and a stable place in society.[1]

Even in primitive times, simple laws became more complicated. Somehow the rule of marriage came to require that the man and woman come from *different* tribes—perhaps because tribes were quite small and marriage within them seemed incestuous, and also because marriage between members of different tribes cemented tribal alliances and prevented war. Further complications of marriage laws arose with the accumulation of power and material goods. For example, a man who emerged as powerful leader could take, not just one wife, but scores of wives.[2] Families began to demand payment for marriageable daughters. A wealthy man might have to give valuable gifts to gain a bride, putting much of his own property into her hands or the hands of her relatives. For instance, a marriage in one tribe cost the husband "360 arrows, five copper bracelets, and two knives of jet," while in another tribe, the husband had to deliver "two or three slaves, two or three necklaces, and two or three empty bottles."[3] Elsewhere, men gained great power over their wives and children sometimes over their very lives. Where this happened, a man was entitled to slaughter a wife who committed adultery. In some places, if a father died, his children had to pay back his debts or be killed.[4] In others—India and China, for example—a father had the right to sell his child in order to pay his debts.[5]

THE DEVELOPMENT OF SETTLED COMMUNITIES AND LAW PENALTIES

As economies developed, law became more dependent on power relations. In primitive societies, life depended on success in gathering food. There was as yet no idea of property, and hence no property law. People searched for edible plants in groups of 10 or 15. Eventually, they discovered that saving the roots of these plants and planting them in the soil would give them a stable food source.[6] The women became planters, while the men were often away hunting or fighting against enemies. Strong communities developed, especially after it was determined that the best places to settle were next to great rivers, where floods and silt enriched the soil for cultivation and the river waters provided fish to supplement the community's diet. The women who stayed at home and fostered agriculture, ruled the whole community, including the men whenever they returned to the home base.[7]

Then a major development came when hunters began capturing animals and taking them home to breed them for a stable source of meat and milk. Once the men stayed home to raise livestock, they became the essential rulers of the communities and lawmakers.[8] Property law began to develop. Prosperous herds, were often attacked by starving neighbors, which led the men in charge of the settled communities to organize powerful militaries. War entailed the capture of enemies who became slaves—human beings owned by and forced to labor for others. Slaves were a form of wealth; they did not legally exist as human beings, so they were not entitled to the protection of the community's law. They could be disposed of as their owner wished. It was not uncommon for slaves to be put to death when their owner died. In one tribe, when a significant leader died, about 20 of his slaves would be killed, half of the bodies buried with him and the other half eaten by the community at the funeral feast.[9]

These ancient settled communities developed laws to deal with human relationships and property rights. Penalties were established in oral tradition (written laws came much later) for certain defined offenses. Some offenses were punished by death, but many more were punished by fines. In one primitive community, the following penalties were exacted for the offenses named:

Homicide (except by accident)	
Of a man	14 cows, l bull*
Of a woman	7 cows, 1 bull
Of a child	6 cows, 1 bull
Homicide (accidental)	
Of a man	7 cows, 1 bull
Of a woman	4 cows, 1 bull
Of a child	According to sex
Injuries (intentional or not)	
Loss of a finger:	l cow, 1 bull
Loss of a toe	l bull, l goat
Loss of a leg or arm	7 cows, l bull
Loss of both legs or arms	14 cows, l bull
Loss of an ear	5 goats
Loss of an ear (accidental)	2 goats
Tearing an ear	1 goat
Loss of an eye	l cow, l bull
Loss of both eyes	14 cows, l bull
Loss of a tooth	l goat
Loss of a tooth (accidental)	Pot of tembo
Loss of nose	1 cow, 1 bull
Loss of a testicle.	4 cows, 2 bulls
Loss of both testicles	14 cows, 1 bull
Loss of penis	14 cows, 1 bull
Homicide or injury by a person of the same village or family	Half composition
Adultery	1 bull, 1 goat
If a child is born and dies before compensation for adultery is paid	2 bulls, 2 goats
If woman dies	Blood-money
Rape	1 large bull equal to 1 cow
Bride-price	3 cows, 2 bulls
Theft	
General	Restitution plus 1 bull
Honey-barrel stealing or habitual stealing	Kingole

---

* This list is taken from A.S. Diamond, *The Evolution of Law and Order* (London: Watts, 1951, p.115.) In the numerous cases where it is mentioned, one bull was paid to the tribunal of justice as a kind of court fee.

Similar sanctions were created in primitive societies for centuries. Notice how property payments sufficed for physical maimings and even murder. The biblical rule of "An eye for an eye, a tooth for a tooth" was hardly typical.

Primitive laws were simple, certain, known to all, and had real application. But over time, owing to various crises and developments, law came to consist of thousands of complicated rules people could hardly understand or remember. To solve this problem, a fundamental distinction was invented, at least as early as 2000 B.C.: the written *code* of law. The earliest codes were basic rules carved onto stone: Moses' tablets containing the Ten Commandments and King Hammurabi's law code of the second millennium B.C. were powerful landmarks. Later developments included the Hebrew Code of Law found in the early books of the Bible and, in 450 B.C., the Twelve Tables that registered the basic law of Rome. [10]

Law developed also in religious communities. For example, the rules of behavior for a Benedictine monk were written out in 73 chapters. But, as the introduction to the Benedictines' "Holy Rule" book says, "Laws and rules of life, unlike dogmas, call for changes and adjustments to suit the requirements of different times and places." [11] It seemed more natural and easy, in both secular and religious communities, to simply add new laws to the old ones than to expunge old laws when they became obsolete. Thus the body of law grew and became more complicated and difficult to know and follow. This situation was similar to the one that had led to written law in the first place, only now that the law was written down, it was even more susceptible to manipulation by the powerful. Fines for certain offenses became ever more differentiated to suit the ruling class.

Bas relief in the Louvre, Paris, depicting the Summary of Hammurabi's Code of Law, dating back to 2000 B.C.

For example, if a common serving-maid was seduced, the seducer had to pay 6 shillings, but if the seduced maid served a noble, the fine was 12 shillings, and if she served the king, it was 50 shillings.[12] And as written laws grew more elaborate, falsification by copyists became more common.[13] Moreover, there were frequent contradictions between religious and secular law. In medieval Europe, church laws increasingly contrasted with the king's law. For example, under church law, a murderer could escape the death penalty ordained by the king's law by taking refuge in a church sanctuary.[14] All of these factors made the actual operation of the legal system unjust.

MONEY AND THE LAW

A.S. Diamond, English barrister and author of *The Evolution of Law and Order*, sees economic development as the main explanation for the complexification of law:

> A rule of law is formed mainly by the impact upon economic circumstances of general human emotions or physical reactions....In a vast number of cases the origin of a rule of law or a judgment is but economic expediency, and this is no less true of modern law, with its vast bulk of rules that pertain only to the organization of the State, its departments, and its functions.[15]

One economic invention that greatly transformed law was money. For most of human existence, trade consisted of swapping goods. Then various forms of exchange were created to make trading easier. Cattle was one of the most popular forms, a fact that is reflected in language: for instance, the Latin word for money, *pecunia*, was derived from the word for cattle, *pecus*; and the modern English word *fee* was derived from the Old English word for cattle, *feoh*.[16] Money—that is, currency—gradually became the accepted medium of exchange or measure of value in all the more advanced societies. Because it was easier to steal money than cattle, laws against money theft had to be expanded.[17]

Laws governing debt were also developed. Early on, persons who failed to pay back a loan on time could be killed. As towns grew larger and trades became more specialized, special laws were needed to govern the diversity of economic relationships. Economic contracts of all kinds required laws to make them enforceable. As banking developed, that, too, required laws. And as law became more and more complicated, a new profession was created: that of the lawyer.

LAW IN ANCIENT JERUSALEM: AN EXAMPLE OF PERVERSION

Other factors besides economics complicate law and lead to the breakdown of justice. Consider one of humanity's worst legal decisions: the condemnation and execution of Jesus Christ.

Detailed information about the trial of Jesus of Nazareth 2,000 years ago comes to us from the four New Testament evangelists, Matthew, Mark, Luke, and

John, who wrote their accounts many years after the trial. It is thought that none of them was an eyewitness at this event, and the gospels are heavily colored by later theological interpretations, so they cannot be considered historically accurate in their details. [18] Yet the basic story they narrate—that Jesus was arrested and tried before a Jewish court on a charge of blasphemy, found guilty, then taken before the Roman governor, who was reluctant to pronounce the death sentence but was pressured into doing so—is probably accurate. At any rate, the story is an interesting and significant one and helps us to think about the law.

Palestine in 30 A.D.—the approximate date of this trial—was ruled by Rome. The districts of Judea and Samaria were under the direct rule of a Roman governor, or procurator, while the district of Galilee was ruled by Herod Antipas, a local tetrarch (ruler) responsible to Rome. Technically, Roman law prevailed over all local law, though to keep the peace, Rome allowed the local Jewish leaders quite a bit of latitude in applying religious law.

There were three main Jewish parties at the time and they were divided concerning the law. The wealthy, aristocratic Sadducees, based in Jerusalem, collaborated with their Roman overlords. This group dominated the Jewish Supreme Court (Sanhedrin) with its 71 judges, and furnished its chief justice (high priest). The Sadducees thought of God's law as only the "Written Law." [19] The more popular party, the Pharisees, thought God's law included both the "Oral Law" and the "Written Law." Blasphemy, the crime Jesus was accused of, was an offense in the Written Law but not in the Oral Law. [20] The third party, the Zealots, refused to obey the Roman emperor and advocated killing Romans and Roman sympathizers. A Zealot band known as the "Assassins" eventually assassinated the Sadducee high priest because of his pro-Roman stance. [21]

The most powerful Sadducee at this time was Annas, a rich and energetic judge who had served as high priest and who managed to get five of his own sons, a grandson, and a son-in-law also appointed to the high priesthood. The ordinary people detested Annas. But he had a magnificent house, thanks to his business dealings in the Temple, where money changers and sellers of animals had profitable operations. Annas was angered when Jesus, on the Monday before his arrest, threw the money changers out of the Temple because they were corrupting the holiness of the House of God. Annas and his colleagues also feared the effect his miracles might have on the public—particularly his raising Lazarus from the dead. So Annas agreed with the high priest, his son-in-law Caiaphas, that "it is expedient for us that one man should die for the people." [22] High Priest Caiaphas was a tough, ambitious fellow. Historian Frank J. Powell writes of him, "In religion he found, not a conviction, but a career." [23]

Pontius Pilate, the Roman governor of the province, had landed in Palestine in 26 A.D. In Caesarea, he had stayed in the palace of Herod Antipas, and he brought his 6,000 soldiers with him to another palace of Herod in Jerusalem. [24] Pilate despised the Jews and he tried to abolish their laws. One Hebrew law even prohibited "images," not just actions. But in honor of Caesar, Pilate brought from Caesarea many images, which generated massive protests from the people for six days. Pilate ordered his soldiers to hide their weapons in their clothes and join the

Engraving showing Christ before Pontius Pilate.

crowd, then took his place on a judgment seat in front of the protestors. When they continued to harangue him about the images carried into Jerusalem, Pilate ordered his soldiers to reveal their weapons and threaten the protesters with death. The protesters threw themselves onto the ground and bared their necks, saying they would welcome death rather than allow one of their gravest laws to be violated. Pilate was shocked. Surprisingly, he gave in and ordered the "images" to be taken away from Jerusalem.[25]

When Pilate decided Jerusalem needed a better water supply, he set about building an aqueduct into the city. But the people found out that he was dipping into the sacred Temple treasury for the project and tens of thousands of them protested. In response, Pilate again sent soldiers with weapons hidden under their clothes among the crowd. This time when they refused to disperse, he gave the order to attack and the soldiers beat and killed many protesters.[26]

Under Roman law at this time, if an accuser failed to show up in court to express his accusation, the person he accused was to be instantly discharged. But in Jerusalem, dealing with non-Roman citizens, Pilate had full discretion to decide on all legal questions. His appointment by the emperor gave him "absolute power of life and death."[27] Nevertheless, Pilate's determined preference was "to assume his full judicial responsibility."[28]—that is, to rule by law. Rome was home to a variety of religious practices and many deities were worshipped, but Roman law was strongly biased against followers of non-Roman religions:

> Prophets were to be beaten and expelled from the city; if they came back they were to be imprisoned or deported. Persons consulting with reference to the life of the Emperor were punished with death. Those who took part in the exercise of

magical and diabolical arts were to be crucified; the magicians themselves, to be burnt alive. Even to keep books on the subject was a crime; the books were to be burned and the owners severely punished....[P]ersons *introducing new kinds of worship,* unknown to custom or reason, disturbing weaker minds, were to be punished, if persons of rank, with deportation; if not of rank, with death. [29]

No doubt Pilate had this Roman law in mind during the trial of Jesus Christ.

Early in the gospel according to St. Matthew, Jesus said, "Think not that I am come to destroy the law, or the prophets: I am not come to destroy, but to fulfil. For verily I say unto you, Till heaven and earth pass, one jot or one tittle shall in no wise pass from the law, till all be fulfilled." [30] Even so, the Pharisees and the scribes accused Jesus of being a sorcerer, and anyone who declared him as the Messiah, or Christ, was expelled from the synagogues. In Jerusalem, those who acknowledged him to be the Christ were excommunicated. [31] Challengers tried repeatedly to "entangle him in his talk" with such politically loaded questions as "Is it lawful to give tribute to Caesar, or not?", [32] but without success. It was Jesus' miracle of raising Lazarus from the dead that triggered his arrest. The miracle was not denied, but rather was regarded as a dangerous piece of magic. So High Priest Caiaphas, well before Jesus came to trial, decided that Jesus should die. [33] Caiaphas would have preferred to delay the arrest until the great annual Jewish Feast of Passover was past, for at the feast there were dangerous revolutionary crowds in Jerusalem, [34] but after Jesus received a tumultuous palm-waving reception on his entrance into the city the Sunday before the feast, it was decided to arrest him as soon as possible.

So Jesus was arrested stealthily, at night, the next Thursday and taken to Annas. Annas had him bound and sent to Caiaphas. No one came forth to accuse him, so legally he should have been discharged. But instead, Caiaphas himself kept querying Jesus, even though Hebrew Law stated that "Our law condemns no one to death on his own confession." [35] Jesus called for a witness, saying, "Why askest thou me? Ask them which heard me, what I have said unto them; behold, they know what I said." An officer of the court reached out and struck him, yelling, "Answerest thou the high priest so?" Jesus said, "If I have spoken evil, *bear witness* of the evil: but if well, why smitest thou me?" [36] High Priest Caiaphas, in effect, "threw all semblance of law to the winds," demanding that Jesus "tell us whether thou be the Christ, the Son of God." [37] Jesus said yes. And the high priest convicted him: "He hath spoken blasphemy; what need have we of witnesses? What think ye?" [38] They yelled that he was guilty and should be killed, as the high priest tore his clothes and others spit at him and covered his face.

In that court of law, there was no valid investigation and no justice. Trials for blasphemy, when they lacked free speech, were to be decided on evidence of what had happened *before* the trial, not confession *at* the trial. Yet another rule of law stated, "If they found him innocent they set him free; *otherwise they leave his sentence over until the morrow."*

The Sanhedrin judges pondered what to do with Jesus. Roman law did not allow them to carry out the death penalty themselves, but how would they persuade Pilate to execute Jesus when Pilate, as a Roman, was not interested in crime of blasphemy? They decided to damn Jesus before Pilate as a criminal guilty of high treason against Caesar because he himself had claimed to be a king. And if Pilate failed to agree to kill him, they would arouse the people to threaten to denounce Pilate as a traitor to Caesar himself.[39] No one defended Jesus as one who had expressly said that his kingdom was "not of this world."[40]

When Jesus Christ was taken to Pilate, he could reasonably have expected that Pilate, an admirer of law, would behave as he would have behaved in Rome: fixing a future trial date and giving public notification of it.[41] But Pilate did no such thing. Instead, he asked the officials who brought Jesus to him, "What accusation bring ye against this man?"[42] The answer was simply that he was a "malefactor"—an accusation not based on any evidence or past behavior. Pilate tried to dismiss the whole case: "Take ye him and judge him according to your law."[43] But, wanting Jesus dead, they responded that "It is not lawful for us to put any man to death."[44] They expanded the charge: "We found this fellow perverting the nation, and forbidding to give tribute to Caesar, saying that he himself is Christ a King."[45] Pilate turned to Jesus Christ and asked him to tell about it: Jesus would not; he had said nothing about the emperor of Rome, nothing about himself being a king in this world.

Pilate then had Jesus brought inside his judgment hall, and asked him privately, "Art thou the King of the Jews?"[46] Jesus' reply can be seen as making a point of law regarding confession and accusation: "Sayest thou this thing of thyself, or did others tell it thee of me?"[47] What did Pilate mean by the word "king"? Pilate did not answer him directly, but asked, "Am I a Jew? Thine own nation and the chief priests have delivered thee unto me."[48] Then Jesus said plainly, "My kingdom is not of this world."[49] Pilate then went out to the chief priests and said, "I have no fault in him."[50] In effect, he declared Jesus "not guilty." The trial was over.[51]

Or was it? The crowd was infuriated and said so. So Pilate, although intending to be devoted to the law, suspended his verdict and passed Jesus over to Herod. Legally, Herod could not decide a case beyond his authority over Judea. This Herod, son of Herod the Great, friend of Pilate, and murderer of John the Baptist, seems to have thought that Jesus might be John the Baptist risen from the dead. Jesus had previously spoken of Herod as "that fox,"[52] so it is not surprising that Herod's cross examination of Jesus elicited no answers. Infuriated, Herod and his soldiers mocked Jesus, forced him to wear a fancy robe, and sent him back to Pilate.

Pilate said to the crowd:

> Ye have brought this man unto me, *as one that perverteth the people:* and, behold, I, having examined him before you, have found no fault in this man touching those things whereof ye accuse him: No, nor yet Herod: for I sent you to him; and, lo, nothing worthy of death is done unto him. *I will therefore chastise him, and release him.*[53]

But they demanded that Pilate kill Jesus. They refused his offer to amnesty Jesus in honor of the feast of Passover and instead demanded the release of a man who had murdered a Roman. As he sat on the judgment seat, Pilate's wife sent him a note saying she had dreamed of Jesus and wanted him saved. So Pilate was again pulled between his sense of justice and the public outcry. He resolved his problem by washing his hands in water before the people, symbolizing through the Hebrew tradition that he was innocent. Then he let his soldiers whip Jesus Christ, cut his head with a crown of thorns, dress him in a robe, and mock him as king, as they hit him time and again with their hands. Pilate again pronounced, "I find no fault in him," but the crowd said, "We have a law, and by our law he ought to die, because he made himself THE SON OF GOD." [54] They demanded that he be crucified, the most degrading method of death.

Again, Pilate spoke in private to Jesus, who had been bloodied by the soldiers. Pilate asked, "Whence art thou?" But Jesus remained silent. Pilate said, "Speakest thou not unto me? knowest thou not that I have power to crucify thee, and have power to release thee?" Then Jesus spoke out: "Thou couldest have no power at all against me, except it were given thee from above." [55]

Pilate returned to the crowd. He sought to release Jesus. But the crowd cried out to him, "If thou let this man go, thou art not Caesar's friend: whosoever maketh himself a king speaketh against Caesar." Pilate brought Jesus forth again and said, "Behold your King!" They yelled for Jesus to be crucified. Pilate asked, "Shall I crucify your King?" The chief priests said, "We have no king but Caesar." [56]

Pilate got the message: if he failed to kill Jesus, the chief priests would charge him with condoning treason against Caesar. The Roman procurator gave up. As Powell puts it, "He abandoned his high duty as Judge to do right and justice to the Accused without fear or favour, partiality, affection or ill-will; in an attempt to save himself from a charge of treason, he gave way to the clamour of the mob." [57]

Because of Pilate's final decision, Jesus Christ was killed by being nailed to a cross. As he hung dying, he said, "Father, forgive them, for they know not what they do." [58]

The lesson of the case against Jesus is this: Law can be admired, even revered—and yet perverted for cruelty. The law of Rome and the law of the Hebrews were both significant achievements in those ancient days. Both laws were designed to protect people from the perpetual danger of being harmed by another person's false accusation. There were good laws in the trial of Jesus Christ; justice failed because neither Roman nor Hebrew law was followed. The Jews could not produce the witnesses the crime of blasphemy demanded under their law, so they disregarded the law. There was no evidence of the crime of treason, as demanded by Roman law, so Pilate, under pressure, ignored the law and permitted the execution of a man he knew was not guilty. The "trial" of Jesus Christ was not a true trial because there was no intention to find out the truth of the issues under examination. It was a perversion of justice for political ends. The result was one of the world's great legal and moral disasters.

THE LAW OF ROME

Western law is primarily an invention of the Romans, who spread Roman law throughout the known world and enforced it by the power of their empires. The Romans conceived of law as universal and true for all civilizations. The Roman politician Marcus Tullius Cicero once said:

> True law is right reason consonant with nature, diffused among all men, constant, eternal; which summons to duty by its command and hinders from fraud by its prohibition, which neither commands nor forbids good men in vain nor moves bad ones to either....It needs no interpreter or expounder but itself, nor will there be one law in Rome and another in Athens, one in the present and another in time to come, but one law and that eternal and immutable shall embrace all peoples and for all time, and there shall be as it were one common master and ruler, the god of all, the author and judge and proposer of this law.[59]

The scholar John H. Hallowell saw in that statement "the conception of natural law which is to dominate Western political thought for at least eighteen hundred years." He noted that "The idea of a universal law and the idea of the state being founded upon consent together laid the foundation for the conception of individual rights—a conception which was lacking in ancient Greek political thought." The classic Digest of Roman Law demanded that "The precepts of law are these: to live uprightly, to injure no one, to render to each his right."[60]

While that idea of law lasted thousands of years, it was practiced—never perfectly, but generally—for only 200 years of Roman history, through the reign of Marcus Aurelius. Emperor Aurelius believed the essence of law was linkage. He wrote:

> Meditate often on the bond between all things in the universe, and their mutual relationship to one another. For all things are in a way woven together and all are because of this dear to one another. For one thing follows on another in order because of the stress movement and common spirit and the unity of all being.[61]

That principle of law as "the bond between all things" broke down after the death of the great Marcus Aurelius in 180 A.D.

His son, Commodus, inherited the empire. For three years, Commodus allowed Aurelius's remaining senators, administrators, and counsellors to guide him as ruler. But one day as he returned to his palace through a dark and narrow portico, a man approached him, waving a sword and shouting, *"The senate sends you this!"* Guards grabbed that attacker and Commodus soon found out who had sent him: his own sister. Her crowd of lovers had conveyed to her their "desperate fortunes and wild ambition," and she conspired with them to take power. Commodus had the conspirators all killed, including his sister. After that experience, he deeply feared and hated the Roman Senate. Senators long considered "the most distinguished of the Romans," were spied on by Commodus's paid informers, who told him every anti-Commodus remark the senators made. Senators, including the noblest, were killed one after another. Commodus turned

Marcus Aurelius.

the Senate's power over to a man named Perennis, an ambitious government minister who had murdered his predecessor. By confiscating the fortunes and estates of senators, Perennis accumulated such a treasure that he aspired to take over the empire himself. As controversy inside Rome proceeded, not by argument, but by violence, Roman law disintegrated.

Meanwhile, 1,500 soldiers from Britain marched on Rome to protest the policies of Perennis. To appease them, Commodus had Perennis killed. Disorder followed, in which soldiers and deserters took over the highways. A soldier named Maternus organized a band of robbers and freed the prisoners from the jails. He asked slaves to join them in setting off to Gaul and Spain to rob undefended cities. The provincial governors set up successful defenses, so Maternus dissolved his group with the plan of reconvening it back in Rome. Their mission was to kill Commodus.

A former slave named Cleander had gained the confidence of Commodus, who appointed him as the new chief minister, following Perennis. Cleander sold Senate seats to those who would pay enough. The law was hardly working at all: accused criminals who could pay were found innocent and released; those who lacked money were found guilty. In his three years in power,

The emperor Commodus in the guise of Hercules.

Cleander collected enormous wealth. He brought great presents to Commodus and laid them at his feet. On behalf of the emperor, Cleander built baths, porticos, and gyms for the people. But pestilence and famine struck Rome, and the poor were especially hard hit, partly because the rich had a monopoly on grain, the food staple. There was a mass revolution. Cleander ordered his soldiers to disperse the crowds, which they did by killing and trampling people with their horses. The starving people fought back, throwing stones and darts at cavalry soldiers, and the foot soldiers joined the people. Together they pushed the cavalry back and mobbed the gates of the palace. Inside the palace, Commodus "lay dissolved in luxury and alone unconscious of the civil war." His two favorite concubines— one of them his sister—rushed in crying and fell at his feet, revealing the crimes of his chief minister and telling the emperor that the enraged people were about to break in and kill him. Commodus resolved the crisis by ordering Cleander's head cut off and thrown out to the crowd. The appeased mob then dispersed.

All Emperor Commodus cared about was his personal pleasures. He was addicted to fine food. He had sex with 300 women and as many boys. If his attempt at seduction failed, he used violent force. He had no interest in law. Even as a child, Commodus had "discovered an aversion to whatever was rational or liberal, and a fond attachment to the amusements of the populace—the sports of the circus and amphitheater, the combats of gladiators, and the hunting of wild beasts."

Much earlier, Roman sports had adopted rules so that games were highly competitive, but disciplined by laws. However, Commodus had no use even for the laws of sport. He killed animals brought to him by slaves, rather than hunting in the forest. He named himself "the Roman Hercules" and put a club and a lion's skin next to his throne. He would throw darts to kill a hundred lions in one day, before a massive crowd. Much of the crowd was appalled when Commodus presented himself as a gladiator, for his gladiatoring was hardly fair sport: he fought 735 times to victory. Hatred of him spread. His favorite mistress, thoroughly frightened by his behavior, got him drunk one day and a young wrestler came in and strangled Commodus to death.

Chaos followed his death. Emperor after emperor came into and fell out of power. The Praetorian Guard—the elite imperial guard whose true allegiance was to venality—once sold the empire at public auction to a "wealthy and foolish senator." (Commodus had once advised his sons, "Make the soldiers rich and don't trouble about the rest." [62]) One man assumed the empire as his own "personal property." In the years after Commodus, "the ruined empire seemed to approach the last and fatal moment of its dissolution." [63] Law was killed for money.

Governing by law is essential to democracy. The destruction of law—even long before democracy existed—led to human tragedies even worse than the tragedies of the wilderness. The power of the government became a power against the people, a power to exploit humans or, if exploitation was impracticable, to destroy them. But eventually, law rose again after the Romans had canceled it.

THE ORIGINAL TROUBLE OF LAW IN AMERICAN DEMOCRACY

Thanks to the development of historical reality, as opposed to many ancient fictitious stories, new generations could actually learn about law, even while they suffered without it. Democracy was born long after real Roman law, in the form of a nation called "The United States of America." To that progression of human life, law was essential. The American revolution against British tyranny was inspired and guided by a great pronouncement of legal principles and objections to injustice: the Declaration of Independence in 1776. After the war, in the 1780s, the newborn national government was defined by the Constitution of the United States, the fundamental restraining authority on the power of every government official. The birth of American democracy was a blessing for Americans and a potential blessing for the world, the significance of which is explored in Chapter 13.

But during the early stages of democracy, certain laws failed, largely because of the greed of the wealthy. A prime example was the initial failure to abolish slavery, a failure which eventually resulted in that massive killing of Americans by Americans known as the Civil War.

In 1619, a Dutch ship delivered 20 African slaves to the James River in Virginia. Soon after, the English wholeheartedly took up the slave trade, a profitable commercial enterprise. Eventually some 300,000 slaves were imported into the 13 English colonies of America. In 1712, 1726, and 1768, several states taxed the costs of the imported slaves. In 1771 and 1774, the colony of Massachusetts tried to abolish slavery, but the British Crown vetoed that attempt. [64]

Thomas Jefferson grew up with about a hundred slaves on his parents' Virginia estate. Later, on his grand Virginia estate called Monticello, Jefferson himself owned slaves. But as a political leader, he proposed the abolition of slavery again and again. He found the existence of slavery obnoxious. In his *Notes on the State of Virginia*, he wrote:

> The whole commerce between master and slave is a perpetual exercise of the most boisterous passions, the most unremitting despotism on the one part, and degrading submissions on the other. Our children see this, and learn to imitate it; for man is an imitative animal.... [65]

In 1769, in the Virginia colonial legislature, Jefferson introduced a bill to allow owners to free their slaves. But it failed to pass. [66] In 1776, in the Revolutionary Continental Congress, he pressed a bill to allow "neither slavery nor involuntary servitude" to exist in any new state. As his biographer Fawn Brodie wrote, "No single legislative proposal in American history had so much promise for preventing future mischief from escalating into calamity." [67] But the southern states stood firm against the bill, so Jefferson got only six of the seven state votes he needed to win. Jefferson was saddened, as he wrote to James Madison, that "South Carolina, Maryland and !Virginia! voted against it." [68]

Thomas Jefferson drafted the 1776 Declaration of Independence, which stated the principles for which the American Revolution was fought:

> We hold these truths to be self-evident, that all men are created equal; that they are endowed by their Creator with certain unalienable Rights; that among these are Life, Liberty, and the pursuit of Happiness. That, to secure these rights, Governments are instituted among Men, deriving their just powers from the consent of the governed; that, whenever any Form of Government becomes destructive of these ends, it is the Right of the People to alter or to abolish it, and to institute new Government, laying its foundation on such principles, and organizing its powers in such form, as to them shall seem most likely to effect their Safety and Happiness. [69]

The Declaration presented a list of complaints against George III, the king of England. Jefferson's draft included the following:

> He has waged cruel war against human nature itself, violating its most sacred rights of life and liberty in the persons of a distant people who never offended him, captivating and carrying them into slavery in another hemisphere, or to incur miserable death in their transportation thither. This piratical warfare, the opprobrium of *infidel* powers, is the warfare of the Christian king of Great Britain. Determined to keep open a market of where MEN should be brought and sold,

he has prostituted his negative [veto] for suppressing every legislative attempt to prohibit or to restrain this execrable commerce; and that his assemblage of horrors might want no fact of distinguished die, he is now exciting these very people to rise in arms against us, and to purchase that liberty of which he deprived them, by murdering the people upon whom *he* also obtruded them; thus paying off former crimes committed against the *liberties* of one people, with crimes which he urges them to commit against the *lives* of another.[70]

Given the focus of the Declaration, this passage naturally focused on the king's faults rather than on those of American slavers. But Jefferson's passage damning slavery was cut from the Declaration by the Continental Congress at the insistence of representatives from South Carolina and Georgia—who, according to Jefferson, struck out the clause because they "had never attempted to restrain the importation of slaves" and "on the contrary, still wished to continue it." Further, he wrote, "Our northern brethren also, I believe, felt a little tender under those censures; for though their people had very few slaves themselves, yet they had been pretty considerable carriers of them to others."[71]

The arguments about slavery took up quite a bit of the Congress's time. Samuel Chase of Maryland contended that Jefferson's statement was completely wrong because Negroes were not to be classified as persons, but as property, like cattle. John Adams disagreed, and proceeded to argue against slavery from the economic perspective: slaves, he said, should be considered legal persons because they produced as much wealth as white laborers produced. James Wilson also disagreed with Chase because he thought Chase's idea would "permit the Southerners to reap all the economic benefits of slavery and Northerners to bear the burden of it."[72]

During the American Revolution, thousands of slaves escaped into freedom and many, where permitted, joined state armies to fight against the British. Georgia and South Carolina refused to allow former slaves to enlist in their armies because they believed the practice would encourage slaves to escape from ordinary work.[73] On the other hand, a year after the Declaration, New Jersey and Pennsylvania argued that Congress should not draft only whites, because that would deplete the numbers of free workers in the North and leave all the slaves in the South working—which would benefit rich southerners. When many slaves escaped from the deeper South and migrated to Maryland, Maryland congressmen argued that "one state shall not be burdened with the maintenance of the poor."[74] All these developments confirmed Jefferson's suspicion that financial considerations were being allowed to decide an issue of fundamental human rights: "It has sometimes been said, that slavery is necessary, because the commodities they raise would be too dear for market if cultivated by freemen; but now it is said that the labor of the slave is the dearest."[75]

In 1778, Jefferson did manage to get Virginia's legislature to pass a law forbidding any further importation of slaves.[76] And in 1787, after the war was won, the national Congress took an action that historian John Hope Franklin sees as "perhaps the high water mark of the postwar anti-slavery movement": it passed a law prohibiting slavery or involuntary servitude in the Northwest Territory.[77]

Then the principle that "all men are created equal" collapsed. To create a constitution for a United States of America, the Constitutional Convention needed to decide how many representatives each state would elect and how much taxes each state would have to pay. North and South argued. The northerners wanted slaves assessed as property for tax purposes, but not counted as persons for representation. The southerners did not want the slaves freed or allowed to vote, but they wanted them counted by the government for purposes of representation so the South would have a stronger voice in the Congress. Arguments got hotter. Rufus King of Massachusetts demanded that slavery never be recognized in the Constitution, while Charles Pinckney of South Carolina demanded that the Constitution never prohibit slave trade.

Compromises were reached. The first article of the Constitution was made to say that

> Representatives and direct taxes shall be apportioned among the several States which may be included within this Union, according to their respective Numbers, which shall be determined by adding to the whole Number of free Persons, including those bound to Service for a Term of Years, and excluding Indians not taxed, three fifths of all other persons.[78]

"Other persons" meant slaves. Thus the primary law of the nation deemed a slave to be three-fifths of a person.

The Constitution makers also could not agree on slavery migration or importation, so they compromised by postponing the decision:

> The Migration or Importation of such Persons as any of the States now existing shall think proper to admit, shall not be prohibited by the Congress prior to the Year one thousand eight hundred and eight, but a Tax or duty may be imposed on such Importation, not exceeding ten dollars for each Person.[79]

Economic compromise was continually used to shape laws concerning slavery, for the Constitution makers and their successor politicians came to agree that "government should rest upon the dominion of property,"[80] in contrast to the Declaration of Independence, which declared that "Governments are instituted among Men, deriving their just powers from the consent of the governed." The controversy over slavery continued for decades, but once slaves were categorized as countable property items rather than as human beings, the possibility of real democratic results was eliminated. To be sure, in 1807, both England and the United States passed laws prohibiting slave importation—but those laws were not enforced.[81] Thousands of slaves were freed, but many more thousands were enslaved. Breeding slaves for sale and kidnapping free blacks and selling them as slaves was profitable.[82] Despite the law against slavery in the West, Missouri joined the Union in 1820 as a slave state."[83] And the deprivation of humanity continued. Indeed, many laws were created to govern slavery, but the slaves themselves, not being citizens, had no recourse to any laws:

A slave had no standing in the courts: he could not be a party to a suit at law; he could not offer testimony, except against another slave or a free Negro; and his irresponsibility meant that his oath was not binding. Thus, he could make no contract. The ownership of property was generally forbidden him....A slave could not strike a white person, even in self-defense; but the killing of a slave, however malicious the act, was rarely regarded as murder. The rape of a female slave was regarded as a crime, but only because it involved trespassing.[84]

As he approached his death, Thomas Jefferson recalled the glorious significance of the Declaration of Independence:

All eyes were opened, or opening, to the rights of man. The general spread of the light of science has already laid open to view the palpable truth, that the mass of mankind has not been born with saddles on their backs, nor a favored few booted and spurred, ready to ride them legitimately, by the grace of God.[85]

The history of slavery in the United States must never be forgotten, for it exemplifies a temptation to pervert democracy for the advantage of some. Americans held high the banner of human rights, which all the world needed. They forced the inclusion of a Bill of Rights in their Constitution in order to make it certain that American democracy would be committed to the real substance of human protection. But they allowed the manipulation of law in favor of wealth to preserve slavery. And they paid for it in the tragedy of the Civil War. That outcome should remind Americans and thinkers throughout the world of what can happen when greed is allowed to infect the law so that it is used as an instrument of oppression.

CHALLENGES IN MODERN LAW

In our own time, law is in danger and, therefore, so is democracy itself in danger. To make the law serve democracy, citizens and leaders must be genuinely committed to and continuously active for clear and just law. Faith in political justice in the abstract, private sense is not enough. The corruption of law that led to the execution of Jesus Christ, the destruction of Rome, and American slavery can not be considered a "historical problem" that has been largely overcome, for we confront the very same kind of threats today. That human progress automatically occurs with the passage of time is a myth, and belief in this myth makes us vulnerable to lasting tragedies.

Arthur R. Hogue, a scholar of English law, makes it clear that law needs to keep alive the fundamental principles of democracy even as it develops to accommodate new social changes:

Throughout its long history the English common law has borne directly on the raw facts of daily life in English society. The rules of common law are social rules; never remote from life, they serve the needs of a society once feudal and agricultural but now industrial and urban. Gradually, as social changes have occurred, the law has been adapted by judicial interpretation to meet new conditions. It continues as always to reflect the character of the social order.[86]

In the modern world, democracy is seriously threatened by fragmentation. Communities, nations, and international alliances are splitting apart. Too often, laws are dissected into gross complex alternatives which can be exploited by rich money seekers.

Within the United States, for example, there are dangerously fragmented communities where people are divided into different camps. In Southern California in 1992, a jury made a strikingly erroneous decision. An amateur videotaped policemen beating a black driver, who had jeopardized their lives by forcing them to drive very fast to catch him and arrest him for speeding. The video evidence showed clearly that the police officers broke the law by beating a person they had arrested, so they were tried in court for this crime—and a jury found them not guilty. Fury arose in Los Angeles—and throughout the country—at this perversion of the law.

So, what was the reaction? Did the infuriated citizens firmly decide to mobilize a political movement to press the national, state and local governments to enforce the law, and to elect representatives adamantly devoted to justice? No. Instead, violent revolution broke out in Los Angeles by the citizens themselves. They beat one another. Fifty-four human beings were killed, 2,383 injured. The mobs burned and damaged some 5,200 buildings, probably costing over a billion dollars, and destroyed businesses that had employed approximately 40,000 people. The police moved slowly. The violence only ended when the state's military forces entered the city to stop it. Eventually about 17,000 people were arrested.[87]

Why did this tragedy happen? A clear cause was that Los Angeles lacked community and commitment to law. Its citizens were hostiley divided. To be sure, different ethnic populations occupied the city: roughly 40 percent were Hispanics, 37 percent white, 13 percent black, and 10 percent Asian. This variety was partly due to the fact that approximately 300,000 people were flowing into the city each year. But they were not only different but separate. As Michael Meyer wrote in *Newsweek:*

> Los Angeles has not been a triumph for the melting pot, at least not yet. Even before the riots, it sometimes resembled a city under siege. Los Angeles is a town where merchants pack guns, where inner-city neighborhoods are divided into precincts with names like "Little Beirut" or "the Kill Zone," where wealthy neighborhoods are fenced off and posted with warnings of ARMED RESPONSE. "This is a bunker mentality," says the head of one of L.A.'s 3,500 private security firms. Lacking any center, barricaded into nervous camps, Los Angeles has little common ground upon which its diverse citizenry can meet.[88]

Nowhere in the country is the gap between rich and poor so evident, nowhere are racial and ethnic relations so complex, as in Los Angeles. Economic competition among the poor, as well as money manipulations by the rich, enhanced tensions in 1992. As in much of the United States, law was expensive—

that is, those who could afford to hire lawyers and pay bonds and fines were far more likely to stay out of jail than those who could not afford such payments. Thus the 1992 Los Angeles tragedy—death, injury, destruction, poverty, and unemployment—is to be blamed on a failure of democracy: the fragmentation of community, the consequent inequality and injustice under the law, manipulated economic competition. Law is not only perverted by the greed of the rich, but can be perverted by the poor as they seek money.

Fragmentation—the breakdown of cooperative politics—is not only a crisis of democracy in certain American cities. Even the national government of the United States has been fragmented. Consider Congress. Members of Congress are supposed to represent the people by meeting to debate, discuss proposals, and determine laws by their votes. Law is supposed to be created by common parliamentary discourse participated in by the full crowd of elected representatives in the House and Senate. Instead, the Congress has divided itself into more than 300 committees and sub-committees, each specializing in some particular subject matter. This form of fragmentation typically benefits those members with chairs or vice chairs on restricted, distinctive committees. It does not benefit the American people.

On occasion, members do make speeches in the chambers of Congress, supposedly to persuade their colleagues on some issue. In fact, the speeches are typically expressed to television cameras, not to fellow members of Congress—who are largely absent. (Congress has prohibited television from showing the rows of empty seats in the chamber) Members of Congress do go to the chamber to vote, but this does not mean they have participated in any discourse on the particular law to be voted for or against. Quite often a bell rings in their offices, calling them to come in to vote, and on their way to the chamber, they turn to a staff member to get a quick signal on whether to vote yes or no. Hence the production of a huge number of laws whose content is not known by those who voted them into being. No wonder so many of our laws are difficult to understand and difficult to enforce. Such a system greatly empowers the government's administrators, who not only decide on how to enforce law, but too often also on which laws to enforce and when to enforce them. Instead of coming together as a team to discuss and agree on laws for the American people, the Congress behaves like a collection of experts who care about their own diverse issues only. The result is not *common* law.

Members of Congress spend too much time taking care of their own power and wealth. Years ago, elected members of Congress typically served for only a limited time, because they wanted to return home to their states and pursue their family fortunes. That was when congressional salaries were more modest. In 1987, members raised their annual salaries from $77,400 to $89,500. In 1989, they increased their pay again—by 51 percent. In 1991, they awarded themselves $120,900 per year, and in 1992, their pay reached $125,100 per year—a wage higher than the wages of 97 percent of American households.[89] These self-awarded raises were put through by a tricky procedure: the raise would go into effect automatically if the Congress did not vote *against* it by a certain date. Many members did vote against the raise—the day after the deadline. Thus "members could demonstrate their disdain for the raise back home while pocketing the money." A national poll showed that 85 percent of Americans opposed the 1992 pay raise, so Congress could hardly claim to be representing the people on this issue.[90]

Members of Congress have created many other privileges and benefits for themselves. For example, they are not required to obey certain laws pertaining to civil rights and employee relations. And they have a variety of communication, transportation, housing, parking, and other privileges. These aristocratic benefits further divide them from ordinary citizens.

Members of Congress spend considerable time and energy, not discussing and making laws, but planning how to win reelection, which now costs much money. They secure for themselves far more money for communication and travel than their opponents could get from the government. They also spend much time in Washington catering to business organizations trying to persuade Congress to vote for their interests. Organizations for the poor generally lack the money to be as persuasive as the rich, so Congress is typically much more influenced by rich lobbyists than by troubled people. Lobbyists find ways to give members of Congress money for campaigning. Often they use these donations not only to pay campaign costs, but also to pay for personal luxuries. Thus members of Congress are rarely defeated by an outsider trying to take their place.

Washington politicians no longer depend upon the political parties for guidance and financing but run for office on individualized platforms and raise their own funds. For example, in October and November 1988, after an extensive advertising campaign and heavy news coverage in newspapers, magazines, television, and radio, a national poll showed that roughly a third to a half of the voters did not know which candidate for president was running with which candidate for vice president. The party "platform," traditionally a one-page paper focused on the few major goals the party hoped to achieve, has been transformed into a big book of detailed statements that are not only too complicated to be understood by the average citizen but are also meaningless in relation to what the party's candidates will actually do if they win. It has become nearly impossible for people to determine which candidates to vote for in terms of getting laws they favor enacted.

Given the fragmentation of Congress and the parties, politics has become much more dependent upon journalism. Journalism has been a significant factor in democracy from the first, because the consent of the governed must be based upon genuine knowledge. But today journalism itself is fragmented, particularly television news coverage. Not long ago, national news was all that the citizen could find to watch on television in the early evening, but now the national news programs are in competition with game shows, movies, sports, and pop music. Hence the tendency to present news as entertainment: jagged, exciting, not related to history, but sudden and immediate. Because of the decline of education in the United States, many citizens find it difficult to follow news about law or politics even when it is clearly presented.

Many other aspects of American life have become fragmented. Universities are divided into highly specialized departments and subdepartments, neighborhoods and shopping malls are increasingly segregated by class, and even families are often broken up or separated geographically. Recently, a scholarly fad called "multiculturalism"—an idea that originated long ago in Paris and then passed out of fashion there—damaged the crucial value of democracy. Democracy requires shared political beliefs and rules and common political actions that bring together all citizens, regardless of their race, gender, religion, or ethnic origin. Ironically, the distraction by complexity from the left supported manipulation from the right. Rich Americans got their wealth vastly increased, thanks to concealed helps from the government.

Government by consent of the governed, by means of law, depends not only on citizens' motivation but also on their being genuinely informed and engaged in political discourse. Typically the super-rich in a formal democracy prefer political/legal obscurities they have figured out how to exploit . And they have a free hand when ordinary people do not want to know the truth about how they are being governed. As author William Greider concludes in his book on the high-handed way in which an unelected Federal Reserve Board runs the nation's economy behind the scenes, Americans seemed to want mystery: "The mystery was necessary...to sustain social faith. Knowledge was disturbing. Not knowing the secrets was reassuring. If Americans were afraid to look inside the temple, perhaps it was because they feared to see the truth about themselves. [91]

In the early 1990s, when the U.S. economy was stuck in recession, top government officials made optimistic announcements assuring Americans that they would soon benefit from a projected recovery. The secretary of the treasury said, "We're in a cyclical downturn. It'll return to a good strong level sometime in 1991." The Council of Economic Advisors proclaimed that "the economic downturn is not likely to last long and...a recovery will begin by the middle of 1991." And the president declared, "I think the economy is recovering. I think it will be more robust as we go along here. Job creation is fast." [92] There was an economic recovery—but only for the wealthiest Americans. Economic conditions for ordinary working people grew worse. In 1992, journalists Donald L. Bartlett and James B. Steele assessed that "we are in the midst of the largest transfer of wealth in the nation's history." [93] And it is the government that has made this happen:

> They have created a tax system that is firmly weighted against the middle class.
>
> They have enabled companies to trim or cancel health-care and pension benefits for employees.
>
> They have granted subsidies to businesses that create low-wage jobs that are eroding living standards.
>
> They have undermined longtime stable businesses and communities.
>
> They have rewarded companies that transfer jobs abroad and eliminate jobs in this country.
>
> They have placed home ownership out of reach of a growing number of Americans and made the financing of a college education impossible without incurring a hefty debt. [94]

The result of American fragmentation has not been equal paralysis across the range of classes. Instead, the rich have gotten richer and average citizens have sunk into more and more desperate economic trouble.

THE NEED FOR LEGAL ACTION AROUND THE WORLD

The current news raises grand hope for the future of humanity: democracy is being born and raised all over the world. Approximately a fourth of all nations are currently democracies. But the memory of the Russian Revolution of 1917 makes us realize that the birth of democracy does not ensure its survival. A lasting democracy requires continuing careful attention. And the world's democracies are more secure when they support one another.

Unfortunately, while economic and military linkages among nations are strengthening, political linkages are weakening. For example, central government banks in the United States, Japan, Britain, France, Germany, Italy, and six other industrialized countries agreed in 1988 to create a new major system to coordinate capital bank operations by 1992.[95] And the United Nations, which is composed of tyrannies as well as democracies, has been undertaking more and more military operations. But politically, nations are breaking apart. The Soviet Union is no longer a union, Eastern Europe is no longer a political bloc, and Yugoslavia and other nations are convulsed in civil war. The defeat of Communist tyranny has let loose old ethnic hatred that are smashing nations apart. Political unification—or at least a coalition—of the two halves of Europe is a grand hope: "One day this may be seen as a turning point in history, the moment when Western Europe reached out to embrace the other half of Europe, so long separated from it by artificial barriers."[96] But the countries fell adrift.

Meanwhile, military technologies, including nuclear weapons, are quietly spreading from nation to nation, increasing the potential for disastrous future wars. And economic interdependence is also quietly spreading, increasing the potential for strong nations to exploit weaker ones. Technological upheavals whose end we cannot see are another factor that is affecting democracy. As the scholar Benjamin Barber and the journalist Patrick Watson note, "If democracy survives into the future, it will have to adjust to a world of space stations, laser weapons, underwater agriculture, genetic engineering, and medical microrobots capable of dredging human arteries."[97]

History warns us that the breakdown of nations is not a plus for democracy. Over the centuries, such breakdowns have led to exploitation and war more often than not. The German historian Samuel Pufendorf saw the essential need for community back in 1672:

> It is quite clear that man is an animal extremely desirous of his own preservation, in himself exposed to want, *unable to exist without the help of his fellow-creatures*, fitted in a remarkable was to *contribute to the common good*, and yet at all times malicious, petulant and easily irritated, as well as quick and powerful to do injury. For such an animal to live and enjoy the good things that in this world attend his

condition, *it is necessary that he be sociable,* that is, *be willing to join himself with others like him,* and conduct himself towards them in such a way that, far from having any cause to do him harm, they may feel that there is reason to preserve and increase his good fortune.[98]

Our fragmented world is in horrible danger. It needs a coalition of democracies that works, not only for military security and economic benefits, but also for justice and human rights. The established democracies should carry that great action forward by reaching out to fledgling and potential democracies to help them strengthen their own internal unities under the rule of law—law that is fair, coordinated, and beneficial for all.

While working for the common good is a necessity, total unification is not desirable. Democracy is limited government at home: democratic government decides what particular common conditions it is necessary to control for human advantage. Law for democracy requires open, fair rules truly made by the peoples' representatives in the interest of the people.

BIBLIOGRAPHY

ALDEN, JOHN RICHARD. *The South in the Revolution, 1763–1789.* Baton Rouge: Louisiana State University Press, 1957.

BARBER, BENJAMIN, AND PATRICK WATSON. *The Struggle for Democracy.* Boston: Little, Brown, 1988.

BARTLETT, DONALD L., AND JAMES B. STEELE. *America: What Went Wrong.* Kansas City, Mo.: Andrews and McMeel, 1992.

BIRLEY, ANTHONY. *Marcus Aurelius: A Biography.* New Haven, Conn.: Yale University Press, 1987.

BOORSTIN, DANIEL J. (ED.). *An American Primer.* Chicago: University of Chicago Press, 1966.

BRODIE, FAWN. *Thomas Jefferson: An Intimate History.* New York: Norton, 1974.

CLARKE, JAMES FREEMAN. *Anti-Slavery Days.* New York: AMS Press, 1972.

DIAMOND, A.S. *The Evolution of Law and Order.* London: Watts, 1951.

FRANKLIN, JOHN HOPE. *From Slavery to Freedom: A History of Negro Americans.* 5th ed. New York: Alfred A. Knopf, 1980.

GIBBON, EDWARD. *The Decline and Fall of the Roman Empire.* Abridged version edited by Dero A. Saunders. London: Penguin Books, 1987.

GREIDER, WILLIAM. *The Trouble with Money.* Knoxville, TN: Whittle Direct Books, 1989.

GREIDER, WILLIAM. *Secrets of the Temple: How the Federal Reserve Runs the Country.* New York: Simon and Schuster, 1987.

GUINESS, ALMA E. (ED.). *Mysteries of the Bible: The Enduring Questions of the Scriptures.* Pleasantville, N.Y.: Reader's Digest, 1988.

HALLOWELL, JOHN H. *Main Currents in Modern Political Thought.* New York: Henry Holt, 1950.

HAWKES, NIGEL (ED.). *Tearing Down the Curtain: The People's Revolution in Eastern Europe.* London: Hodder & Stoughton, 1990.

HOGUE, ARTHUR R. *Origins of the Common Law.* Indianapolis, Ind.: Liberty Press, 1966.

KOCH, ADRIENNE, AND WILLIAM PEDEN (EDS.). *The Life and Selected Writings of Thomas Jefferson.* New York: The Modern Library, 1944.

MERRY, ROBERT W., Executive Editor of *Congressional Quarterly*. Quoted in *Durham Herald-Sun*, May 14, 1992.

Newsweek, May 18, 1992.

POWELL, FRANK J. *The Trial of Jesus Christ*. London: The Paternoster Press, 1949.

STEIN, PETER. *Legal Evolution: The Story of an Idea*. Cambridge, England: Cambridge University Press, 1980.

VERHEYEN, REV. BONIFACE (TRANS.). *The Holy Rule of Our Most Holy Father Benedict*. 8th ed. Atchison, Kan.: The Abbey Student Press, 1935.

WALLBANK, T. WALTER, AND ALASTAIR M. TAYLOR. *Civilization: Past and Present*. Chicago: Scott, Foresman, 1956.

10

The Story
of England's Law Invention

Democracy Raised Up

The reality of law is the *use* of law: law is meant to operate throughout the governing of the nation. In a democracy, the term "law" describes three of the major components of government.

The first component is the *constitution:* the fundamental procedure of political operations. The constitution embodies the basic rules of the game of government. It is created through widespread, thoughtful discussion and voting by the parliament and the people. Once established, the constitution is not meant to be changed simply by ordinary majority vote. Change requires an extensive, special type of voting. The constitution is meant to be the norm for political action.

The second component of law consists of *rights:* rules for the protection of the people. A substantial bill of rights states what actual behavior is not allowed to do. Clear definitions are even more essential here than in the constitution. Fundamental rights are liberty and equality: all citizens are regarded as human beings who cannot be pushed around, whatever their group identity or behavior, so long as that behavior is within the law. Like the constitution, the bill of rights is meant to be created through wide discussion and to be changed only by special public voting.

The third component is *regular, normal law* decided by the parliament. Normal laws are to be made by definite, open, majority votes by representatives whom the people have elected as their government agents. Unlike the constitution or the bill of rights, these laws can be changed or replaced or confirmed by ordinary voting in the parliament. Regular law governs the government itself as well as the nation. All members of government—those who have been appointed as well as those who have been elected—are obliged to see that normal laws operate well, day by day.

Those are the three essentials of law in a democracy. One more thing is required to make government work well for the people over time: devotion to law itself. History tells us that if people want good government, they must be committed to creating honest law and seeing that it is carried out. They cannot rely only on the character of their rulers. Indeed, there have been monarchs and aristocrats who have governed well and benevolently. There have also been times when the people have risen up violently and achieved advantages for themselves. But neither personal rules nor mass action can be depended on, for personal rule can easily become tyranny and mass action can degenerate into anarchy. Devotion to law is a crucial requirement for human welfare.

We saw how England's law was perverted by business in the nineteenth century as ordinary citizens were wrenched from their homes and farms and subjected to the tough new experience of factory work. But many years before, England stood forth in the world, as the champion of law. Far back in the Middle Ages, England had formed a parliament, but until the seventeenth century, as Orlando Patterson has noted, "Parliament was nothing more than a court of the king which he summoned when he pleased, usually not to obtain advice but to communicate his demand for new taxes and to ensure that these taxes were effectively collected and that the charters he had granted were being fairly applied."[1] In that century there emerged a remarkable jurist who stood up to several English Monarchs in defense of the English common law and whose writings mark an epoch in the history of law.

HERO OF LAW FOR ENGLAND: SIR EDWARD COKE

A prime leader in the 1600s was Sir Edward Coke (pronounced Cook). Even after he died, legal decisions he had authorized lived on, and law books he had written were sailed across the sea. When the English colonies in North America were on their way to becoming the United States, Coke's books greatly impressed certain Revolutionary lawyers: John Adams, Thomas Jefferson, John Quincy Adams, and James Madison. Jefferson said that Coke's writing, much of it done when Coke was 76 years old, "was the universal lawbook of students."[2] Partly because of Coke's work, law developed as an essential element of what became the world's strongest democracy: the United States of America. As author Stephen D. White declares, "for two centuries after his death, his writings exerted a profound influence on English and American law."[3] Sir David Lindsay Keir, author of *The Constitutional History of Modern Britain Since 1485*, assesses Coke as "The most learned lawyer of his day."[4] Because of Edward Coke, according to historian Ernest Barker, "What made English history in the seventeenth century was the legal profession."[5] James H. Rutherford estimates that "Coke's Dictum has been considered the single most important source of what became in American constitutional law the concept of judicial review."[6] The great historian, Sir W.S. Holdsworth saw Coke as a hero: "What Shakespeare has been to literature, what Bacon has been to philosophy, what the translators of the authorized version of the Bible have been to religion, Coke has been to the public and private law of England."[7]

Edward Coke was born February 1, 1552, the son of a lawyer. He grew up in the countryside, along with six sisters. He was educated at home, until, at age nine, his father died and Edward was sent to the Free Grammar School in the city of Norwich, where his fellow students were the sons of landowners, merchants, lawyers, priests, and others. His early experience taught him not to give up— "Fallynge down dis paire not"—and that he should teach people with care— "Teche that thou hast learned lovingly." As a youth, he joined in the religious revolution that made England Protestant. He and the fellow students knelt morning and evening, on the stone schoolroom floor to pray. He believed one should "Honor God and the Common Laws of England." In those days, history was rarely taught in school, but after school, Edward learned much of it on his own.

When violence erupted in England, with rebels yelling "Kill the gentlemen!" the young Coke noticed that men who spoke in favor of the rebels had their ears cut off. After he entered college at age 15, he saw that even young boys were hanged. Still, he thought England's Cambridge University, where Erasmus had once taught, was superb. While he was at college, his mother died. He left Cambridge after three years of courses and went off to the Inner Temple to study

Sir Edward Coke.

law for eight years. There he forcefully advocated the students' protest that they lacked the food they needed. One person noticed that he stated the students' cause well and exactly "that all the House admired him and his pleading it, so that the whole Bench took notice of him."

Coke won law positions locally, and then nationally. He became a member of the Parliament, and then its leader, or speaker. Eventually, he became Queen Elizabeth's attorney general.[8]

Upon becoming speaker of the parliament, Coke praised Queen Elizabeth and pressed for liberty. Addressing the queen in the Commons, he said, "Your Majesty's most loving subjects…have nominated me, Your Grace's poor servant and subject, to be their Speaker." His actual appointment would be up to her: "Though their nomination hath hitherto proceeded…yet…their nomination was only a nomination and not election until Your Majesty giveth allowance and approbation." Queen Elizabeth, through her Lord Keeper, approved Coke's election:

> …Her Majesty, by the influence of her virtue and wisdom, doth enlighten you, and not only alloweth and approveth you, but much thanketh the Lower House and commended their discretion in making so good a choice and electing so fit a man. Wherefore, now, Mr. Speaker, proceed in your office, and go forward to your commendation as you have begun.

So authorized, Coke gave the queen his recommendations for the liberties of the House of Commons itself:

> Now am I to make unto Your Majesty three petitions in the name of the Commons: First, that liberty of speech and freedom from arrest, according to the ancient custom of Parliament, be granted to your subjects; secondly, that we may have access to the royal person, to present those things that shall be considered among us; and lastly, that Your Majesty will give your royal assent to the things that are agreed upon.

Queen Elizabeth did not agree to Coke's petition for freedom of speech. Again through her Lord Keeper, she explained to Coke and the Commons:

> …To your three demands, the Queen answereth…privilege of speech is granted, but you must know what privilege you have; not to speak every one what he listeth, or what cometh into his brain to utter of it; but your privilege is, Aye or No….[T]o your persons, all privilege is granted, with this caveat, that under color of this privilege, no man's ill-doings or non-performing of duties, be covered and protected. The last, free access, is granted to Her Majesty's presence, so that it be upon urgent and weighty causes, and at times convenient and when Her Majesty may be at leisure from other important causes of the realm.[9]

In other words, the queen told the Commons to censor themselves to avoid offending the Crown.

Even so, there were members of the House of Commons who presented laws for reform. For example, one introduced a bill to reform the operation of ecclesiastical (i.e., church) courts. Speaker Coke studied it and found it too complex

Queen Elizabeth.

and obscure; he asked that it be clarified, and promised to keep it secret until the revisions were made. But he was called to the queen and asked, not to read the bill to her, but to tell her what was in it. He did. The next morning, Coke related to the House of Commons the Queen's response:

> ...It was not meant we should meddle with matters of state or in causes ecclesiastical; she wondered that any would be of so high commandment to attempt a thing contrary to that which she hath expressly forbidden....Her Majesty's present charge and express command is that no bill touching the matters of state or reforms in causes ecclesiastical be exhibited.[10]

In short, members of Parliament were not to get the notion they could create the law of the land. Parliament operated at the suffrance of the monarch, who usually called it into session to organize ways of acquiring money for the Crown. Coke even described Parliament's members as "the little bees" who "have but one governor whom they all serve," whose business is "seeking honey from every flower to bring to their king."[11]

In ancient Rome, Cicero had declared that "True law is right reason, harmonious with nature, diffused among all, constant, eternal; a law which calls to duty by its commands and restrains from evil by its prohibitions...."[12] A Roman jurist in the second century A.D. had seen that "by the law of nature all men were born free."[13] But the English view, even as far back as the reign of Henry III, was that "The King himself ought no to be subject to man, but subject to God and to the law, for the law makes the King."[14] In 1297, King Edward I stated that all "justices, sheriffs, mayors and other ministers, [are] under us and by us have the laws of our land to guide."[15] So Queen Elizabeth in her statement to Parliament was just asserting monarchical authority that had been asserted repeatedly for centuries.

When he became Elizabeth's attorney general, Coke was responsible for meeting with the House of Lords, advising them about law, conveying messages to the House of Commons, and prosecuting state trials.[16] For 300 years, England's kings had maintained their dominant sovereignty, even over the Pope.[17] In acknowledgment of the queen's power, Parliament members meeting with her dropped to the floor on their knees whenever she arose. As the new attorney general, Coke expressed the need for "right reason and the common law."[18] But in those days, not even a common law judge would question royal authority. England's Star Chamber, a secret court authorized by the queen, sometimes favored poor men, but it operated without any public law. Queen Elizabeth, partly because she had received several assassination threats, demanded strict laws against gentlemen who dropped into London. Persons accused of crime were typically imprisoned in the dark of London Tower and tortured at the authorization of the queen, not the Parliament.[19]

Yet the House of Commons did meet, at least when brought together to raise money for the monarch, and members clearly addressed one another. Back in 1547, the Commons had moved its meetings to a chapel. The speaker sat in front of the altar, and the members divided themselves to sit in the left and right choir stalls, directly facing toward their opposite groups. They had no desks. Occasionally, a member fell asleep and dropped onto the floor. Because they met in a church, members were never allowed to take swords or spears with them to meetings, nor were they permitted to use obscenity in their debates. There was no fireplace, so they wore their outdoor clothes and sat huddled close to one another.[20] In this way, England's elected representatives began to work as a group, to share thinking and action for government by law.

THE NEW MONARCH: KING JAMES I

In 1603, Queen Elizabeth died and Scotland's King James VI became King James I of England. He was 37 years old and had been king of Scotland from the age of six months.[21] Edward Coke stayed on as attorney general.

King James I is remembered by all English-speaking people as the monarch who authorized the great English version (1611) of the Bible still called by his name. Shakespeare's plays had stimulated excitement about the English language, but reading was still rare. Most people were illiterate. Those who did read mostly scanned Latin, not English. Books were rare. But when King James' Version of the Bible appeared, it became "the most influential book ever published in England." For at least 300 years, this Bible taught the English language to readers.[22]

The new translation stimulated English interest in law, divine and human. In the Book of Exodus, written centuries after the death of Moses, it says that after the Hebrews left Egypt and went into Sinai, "Moses sat to judge the people: and the people stood by Moses from the morning unto the evening."

Moses' father-in-law asked him, "What is this thing that you doest to the people? why sittest thou thyself alone, and all the people stand by thee from morning until even?"

Moses explained, "Because the people come unto me to enquire of God: When they have a matter, they come unto me; and I judge between one and another, and I do make them know the statutes of God, and his laws."

Moses' father-in-law found that disturbing: "The thing that thou doest is not good. Thou wilt surely wear away, both thou, and this people that is with thee: for this thing is too heavy for thee; thou art not able to perform it thyself alone." He advised Moses to "teach them ordinances and law.'

Moses took his father-in-law's advice and chose able men and made them judges over the people in all ordinary disputes: these "rulers of thousands, rulers of hundreds, rulers of fifties, and rulers of tens...judged the people at all seasons: the hard causes they brought unto Moses, but every small matter they judged themselves."

Moses "went up into God" on Mt. Sinai while the people remained below. When he came down, he gathered the people's elders before him and told them the rules God had said, which included: "...ye shall be unto me a kingdom of priests, and an holy nation. These are the words which thou shalt speak unto the children of Israel." The people bought that rule; they said, "All that the Lord hath spoken we will do." The only one allowed to do so, Moses went again to the mountain, and returned. He announced that God wanted all of them to wash their clothes, and they washed them. He returned to them with God's Ten Commandments—simple, clear rules of conduct that included "Thou shalt not kill. Thou shalt not commit adultery. Thou shalt not steal. Thou shalt not bear false witness against thy neighbor." Written much later, Exodus preserves both this original Mosaic law and the elaborations of subsequent centuries: detailed rules addressing very specific situations, list after list of hundreds of laws, put in Moses' mouth. For example: If men strive, and hurt a woman with child, so that her fruit depart from her, and yet no mischief follow: he shall be surely punished according as the woman's husband will lay upon him; and he shall pay as the judges determine." And "If a man shall steal an ox, or a sheep, and kill it, or sell it; he shall restore five oxen for an ox, and four sheep for a sheep." People did misbehave, but Moses was described as repeatedly trying and eventually succeeding in getting them to accept all these laws as the laws of God.[23]

King James I, sponsor of the English-language Bible, was inclined to act like Moses, declaring that he himself was the profound pronouncer of God's law—law created above humans, who must obey it. James believed that God had created the king, as a "little God to sit on his Throne and rule over other men." The people were to be "without resistance but by sobbes and teares to God."[24] James wished to rule England as he had ruled Scotland, by declaring laws. He intended to rule England and Scotland with a new unity: "What God hath conjoined let no man separate. I am the husband and all the whole isle is my lawful

King James I.

wife; I am the head and it is my body; I am the shepherd and it is my flock."[25] He believed that the king was the essence of government because there had been kings "before any Parliaments were holden, or laws made." English leaders devoted to James, agreed that "The King is the law speaking," "It is clear by the word of God in the Scripture that judges are but delegates under the King," and "The twelve Judges of the realm are the twelve lions under the throne."[26] James said, he thought it stupid to have some "Jack and Tom and Will and Dick…meet and at their pleasure censor me and my Council and all our proceedings."[27] So much for Parliament. He explained to an ambassador that

> The House of Commons is a body without a head. The Members give their opinions in a disorderly manner. At their meetings nothing is heard but cries, shouts, and confusion. I am surprised that my ancestors should ever have permitted such an institution to come into existence. I am a stranger, and found it here when I arrived, so that I am obliged to put up with what I cannot get rid of.[28]

To minimize the power of Parliament, James proclaimed that "General laws, made publicly in Parliament, may by the King's authority be suspended upon causes known only to him."[29]

An example of James' force: Early in his reign, a thief was arrested who confessed to having followed the king's traveling retinue and stealing from their purses. James ordered the man hanged—without any law trial or even a hearing. His method was consistent with ancient Roman law: "What pleases the prince has the force of law." But following King James' traveling disturbed a knight of England: "I heare oure new King hath hanged one man before he was tried; 'tis strangely done: now if the winde bloweth thus, why may not a man be tried before he hath offended?"[30] Despite England's principle against it, prisoners were tortured. One servant, named Little John, killed himself in prison rather than spend another day hung up by his thumbs.[31]

The rule of law had gone up and down in England, but one law was consistently adhered to: if the king needed to raise public taxes, Parliament had to agree to it. A medieval doctrine held that "The King may not rule his people by other laws than they assent unto, and therefore he may set upon them no imposition, i.e. tax, without their assent."[32] Yet the Parliament was not free to dissent from the king. As modern Prime Minister Winston Churchill explained, "No Parliament could meet without the summons of the King, or sit after he had dismissed them. Little else but financial necessity could compel the King to call a Parliament."[33] Thus a king who could manage to raise money other than through taxes could prevent a meeting of the Parliament for years. Eventually, of course, financial necessity would force him to call it into session. King James drained money from the Treasury by giving generous gifts to his favorite followers. By 1606 three years after this "stranger" came to England, he had increased the Crown's debt from £365,000, the debt left by Elizabeth, to £600,000.[34] Thus King James, was repeatedly constrained to call Parliament into session. Each time it met, the House of Commons would be born again and members would renew their determination to gain authority.

SIR EDWARD COKE VS. KING JAMES I

In the year 1606, Sir Edward Coke was appointed chief justice of Court Commons Pleas, one of several royal courts of justice. Coke stood forth for law made by Parliament. He believed that '"the law of the realm cannot be changed but in Parliament"[35] and insisted that "The King is under God and the law!" He even advised James that "The King cannot take any cause out of any of the courts and give judgment upon it himself."[36] When James condemned religious Puritans—"I shall make them conform themselves or I will harry them out of the land"—Coke spoke out in support of the Puritans: "No man ecclesiastical or temporal shall be examined upon secret thoughts of his heart or of his secret opinion."[37]

One day in 1608, as Coke was speaking, King James interrupted him to say that Coke "spoke foolishly." Coke replied, "The common law protecteth the King." Then the king of England shouted, "A traitorous speech! The King protecteth the law, and not the law the King! The King maketh judges and bishops. If the judges interpret the laws themselves and suffer none else to interpret, they may easily make, of the laws, shipmen's hose!" But then Coke humbly prayed that the king would respect "the Common Lawes of his land, &c."[38] He steadfastly maintained "that the King hath no prerogative, but that which the law and the land follows."[39]

In 1609, desperate for money, King James brought the Lords and Commons before his throne. At first he proclaimed his respect for law: "I am not ignorant, that I have been thought to be an enemy to all prohibitions, and an utter stayer of them," but "the least cause of any man" is "to dislike the common law." But then he insisted that the king ruled law:

> The state of monarchy is the supremest thing upon earth. For Kings are not only God's lieutenants upon earth and sit upon God's throne, but even by God himself they are called Gods...for that they exercise a manner or resemblance of divine power upon earth. For if you will consider the attributes of God, you shall see how they agree in the person of a King. God hath power to create or destroy, make or unmake at his pleasure, to give life or send death, to judge all and to be judged nor accountable to none. Kings make and unmake their subjects; they have power of raising and casting down; of life and death...and make of their subjects like men at the chess, a pawn to make a Bishop or a Knight, and to cry up or down any of their subjects as they do their money....[40]

So the Parliament disbanded.

Meeting that winter of 1609–10, Coke defended the authority of law. He sent the king a careful treatise:

> Actes of Parliament are to be interpreted by the judges of the laws of England and not by any canonist or ecclesiastical judge....When an Act of Parliament is against common right and reason, the common law will control it and adjudge such Act to be void.[41]

Thus he was claiming that the "common law" was a constitution, limiting even the king. Later on, Coke declared that "The King cannot change any part of the common law, nor create any offence by his proclamation, without Parliament, which was not an offence before."[42] He succeeded in having the following proclamation accepted by Parliament: "*It was resolved:* That the King by his proclamation cannot create any offence which has not an offence before, for then he may alter the law of the land by his proclamation in a high point....[T]he law of England is divided into three Parts: Common Law, Statute Law, and Custom; but the King's Proclamation is none of them."[43] King James was not pleased. He sent a message to Parliament saying, "No house save the house of Hell could have treated him as the commons had been doing."[44] In 1612, James promoted Coke to chief justice of the King's Bench, where the king thought he could better control him.

But Coke was determined that English law be real, living justice. He urged judges to make law live with courage:

> And you, honourable and reverend Judges and Justices, that do, or shall, sit in the High Tribunals or Seats of Justice, as aforesaid, feare not to do right to all, and to deliver your opinions justly according to the law; for feare is nothing but a betraying of the succours that reason shall afford....[45]

Coke was also concerned about the fundamental nature of law. He thought that "a statute should have prospective, not retrospective operation," that "no one should be twice punished for the same offence," and that "every man's house is his own castle."[46]

Trouble persisted between King James and Coke. In 1616, Coke was the chief of the 12 common law judges. King James insisted his right to dictate the judges' opinions. When he demanded a meeting with them on a specific case, Coke got the judges to decide the case in advance, defying the king's right to interfere.

In response, James summoned the 12 judges to stand before him and damned them so harshly that all 12—including Coke—fell down on their knees. Eleven of them apologized and promised to consult the king before they ruled on any future cases that interested him. Only Coke kept silent. James said to him, "Well, Sir Edward, and you, how will you behave?" Coke answered, "I shall do what it befits an honest and just judge to do." At this, the king dismissed him and appointed another judge.[47] In fact, James was so angry at Coke for trying to limit the king's power that James not only fired him, but also forced him out of London. But only one year later, Coke was back in London as a member of the Privy Council—the body of officials who advised the king. Perhaps he had been allowed to return because he had managed his daughter to marry the brother of a member who was the royal favorite.

When Coke was elected to Parliament again in 1621, the king had him arrested and imprisoned in the Tower of London and ordered his books and papers confiscated. It certainly seemed that Coke's career in government was finished, but he got himself released from prison that same year and made it back into Parliament.

King James was more determined than ever to rid himself of the Parliament. Parliament was just as determined to survive. The king wrote to the speaker of the House of Commons that "Fiery and popular spirits of the House" were debating matters that were "far above their reach and capacity." He commanded the members "not to meddle henceforth with any thing concerning our government or deep matters of state." To another person, King James wrote, "We think ourselves very free and able to punish any man's misdemeanors in Parliament." But the House of Commons stood up against him. Coke said, "There have been errors of relation." He declared that "The privileges of this House is the nurse and life of all our laws, the subject's best inheritance. If my sovereign will not allow me my inheritance, I must fly to Magna Charta and entreat explanation of his Majesty.... When the King says he cannot allow our liberties of right, this strikes at the root. We serve here for thousands and ten thousands."[48] In response, the king dismissed Parliament, but the members defied him and stayed in session until night, resolving upon the following principle:

> That the liberties, franchises, privileges, and jurisdictions of Parliaments are the ancient and undoubted birthright and inheritance of the subjects of England; and that the arduous and urgent affairs concerning the King, State, and defence of the

realm and of the Church of England, and the maintenance and making of law, and redress of mischiefs and grievances which daily happen within this realm, are proper subjects and matter of counsel and debate in Parliament; and that in the handling and proceeding of those businesses every member of the House of Parliament hath, and of right ought to have, freedom of speech to propound, treat, reason, and bring to conclusion the same.[49]

KING CHARLES AND PARLIAMENT: THE RISE OF LAW

King James died in February 1623, and his son Charles, at age 24 became King Charles I of England. Though Charles had disagreed with his father on particular policies—he had, for instance, wanted to go to war against Spain when his father had not—he agreed with James that the king was answerable only to God. "I must avow," he said, "that I owe the account of my actions to God alone."[50] But the House of Commons took even more control over law limiting the king's money-getting to be done only one year at a time. In 1626, King Charles removed Coke from the Commons by appointing him a sheriff in Buckingham, far away from London. Then, in a controversy with the Commons, the king dissolved them. They asked for two more days in session, but Charles ordered "Not a minute!"[51] Thinking he now had a free hand to raise money as he wished, he simply ordered citizens to pay taxes to him. More and more refused, even though many were thrown into jail. The situation grew so tense that King Charles, who had said that "Parliaments are of the nature of cats. They ever grow cursed with age," had to release the non-paying prisoners and call Parliament back to a meeting. The Commons had to be elected, and indeed, many who had refused to pay were reelected. That resistance created what Catherine Drinker Bowen sees as "an extraordinary Parliament, one of the two most celebrated in English history."[52] Bowen explains:

> Parliament stood up again for the importance of law, recalling Magna Carta, an ancient, famous law, proclaiming that No freeman shall be taken or imprisoned or disseised by any free tenement or of his liberties or free customs, or outlawed or exiled, or in any other way destroyed, nor will we go upon him nor send upon him, except by the lawful judgment of his peers or by the law of the land. To no one will we sell, to no one will we refuse or delay, right or justice.[53]

One leader declared that the current difficulty "is the crisis of Parliaments. We shall know by this if Parliament live or die....Men and brethren, what shall we do?"[54]

Coke, now in his mid-70s, again led the movement for rule by law. He was praised as "King of the Law." The Commons passed four strong and significant resolutions:

> no freeman to be imprisoned without cause shown, even at the King's command; habeas corpus not to be denied; a prisoner brought to court on habeas corpus must be either bailed or freed; no "tax, taillage, loan, benevolence" to be commanded or levied without consent by act of Parliament.[55]

King Charles I.

Coke believed that "The greatest inheritance that a man hath is the liberty of his person, for all others are accessory to it." He saw to the root of the dispute between the monarch and those who insisted that the people's rights and liberties be protected by law: "When the King doth a thing 'of grace,' it implies that it is not our right."[56] Responding to the Parliament's concerns, King Charles brought the Lords and Commons together and proclaimed his view that there was no need for law since his subjects could rely on his character:

> he holdeth Magna Charta and the other six statutes insisted upon to be all in force. He will maintain all his subjects in the just freedom of their person and safety of their estates. You shall find as much security in his Majesty's royal word and promise as in the strength of any law ye can make. And therefore his Majesty desires that no doubt of distrust may possess any man, but that ye will all proceed unanimously to his business.[57]

But Coke would not be put off. He presented a range of specific laws, which the Commons discussed at length. Coke then proposed, "Let us put up a Petition of Right! Not that I distrust the King, but that I cannot take his trust but in a Parliamentary way."[58]

The Petition of Right was passed by the House of Commons and sent to the House of Lords. After three days of pondering, the Lords approved it—but added the following: "We humbly present the petition to your Majesty, not only with a care of preserving our own Liberties, but with due regard to leave entire that sovereign Power, wherewith your Majesty is trusted, for the Protection, Safety, and Happiness of your People." But the Commons found the phrase "to leave entire that sovereign Power" problematic. One asked, "What is this 'sovereign power'? Let us give that to the King the law gives him, and no more." And Coke said, "To speak plainly, this will overthrow all our Petition....Let us hold our privileges according to the law."[59] Even though the members' oath to Parliament started "I (name) do utterly testify and declare in my conscience, that the King's Highness is the supreme Governor of this Realm in all causes...", the House of Commons did bring forth their new Petition of Right.

King Charles came to Parliament, announcing that he would "perform my promise" and "give you as much content as in me lies." The Petition was read aloud. It included the four other specifics, that "soldiers and sailors should not be billeted on private individuals against the will of these individuals" and "commissions for martial law should not be issued in the future."[60] The substantive laws were significant. They were based on long, hard experience of what was definitely needed for fair law and justice. But beyond that, The House of Commons was pressing for a constitutional determination that law would be made by them. For that, they sought the blessing of the King. As Coke put it, "Let right be done as is desired."[61]

The king heard it all. The members looked to him. What would he say? His Lord Keeper spoke for him:

> The King willeth that right be done according to the laws and customs of the realm and that the statutes be put in due execution, that his subjects may have no cause to complain of any wrong or oppressions, contrary to their just right and libertie: to the preservation whereof, he holds himself in conscience as well obliged, as of his prerogative.

This sounded as if King Charles agreed with Parliament. But there was a telling obscurity in the statement. Charles agreed, in general, that there should be law and justice, but he would not approve the Petition of Right. Coke was stunned. He called for the Commons to assemble again and explain their grievances to the king. But the next day, King Charles announced that the Commons would be dismissed within a week and that they were to "entertain no new matters."[62]

The members of Commons gathered in their chapel. The first speaker said sadly, "If ever my passion were wrought upon, it is now. I hear this with grief of the saddest message of the greatest loss in the world. I perceive that towards God and man there is little hope, after our humble and careful endeavors. We came hither full of wounds, and we have cured what we could. Yet what is the return of all but misery and desolation?" There was a general attitude of despair. One member proposed, "Unless we may speak of these things in Parliament, let us arise and be gone, or sit in silence." They sat in silence. Another rose to speak, but wept and sat down. Many wept, including Sir Edward Coke and the speaker. At last they decided to transform their meeting into a Committee of the Whole, in which they could talk freely, in private, about what they should do.

Coke rose: "We have dealt with that duty and moderation that never was the like, after such violation of the liberties of the subject. Let us take this to heart....Now, when there is such a downfall of the state, shall we hold our tongues?...What shall we do? Let us palliate no longer! If we do, God will not prosper us." Of the king, he said, "Let us set down the causes of all our disasters and they will all reflect on him." The speaker walked out to meet with the king, and returned to close down the Parliament until the next day, ordering "all committees to cease in the meantime." But they sent word to the king, asking him for "a clear and satisfactory answer" before the full Parliament the next day regarding the Petition of Right. Two days later, the king came to them. When asked if he approved the Petition specifically, King Charles requested that it be read aloud again. It was. The Commons cheered it. The clerk went before the king. The king said simply, "*Soit droit fait, comme il est desire*"—that is, "Let justice be done as is desired."[63]

They had won: the king had approved the Petition of Right. The Commons loudly cheered their victory and the news that there was a great hope for the people quickly spread throughout England. Parliament had at last heeded the voice of a leading knight who once cried, "O improvident ancestors! O unwise forefathers! to be so curious in providing for the quiet possession of our lands, and the liberties of Parliament, and to neglect our persons and bodies, and to let them lie in prison....If this be law, what do we talk of our liberties?"[64]

The Petition of Right "curbed the power of the King to a greater extent than any document since Magna Carta."[65] The principle of rule by law had triumphed over rule by monarchical whim. In practice, however, King Charles did not give in so easily and follow the law made by the Commons. He raised money in his own way. He dissolved Parliament—though members of the House rushed forward and grabbed the Speaker and held him in his chair while the House voted on three strong resolutions: "anyone paying tunnage and poundage, anyone advising its collection, and anyone introducing innovations in religion was 'a capital enemy to this kingdom and commonwealth.'"[66] Then they let the speaker up and they left for home.

King Charles did indeed distribute thousands of copies of the Petition of Right throughout England. But, in one last gesture of resistance, he did not sign at the end of his strong, simple assent he had given to Parliament—"Let justice be done as is desired"—but rather he put forth his previous statement *against* the Commons, the one that had made the members weep.[67]

THE INHERITANCE OF LAW FOR THE FUTURE OF ENGLAND

In later years, many troubles of the parliamentary law of liberty and justice were alleviated and law evolved. Indeed, King Charles dissolved Parliament, arrested members who opposed him, and held some of them in prison for years. He ruled without Parliament for 11 years. But in November 1640, Parliament convened again, revitalized, and remained in session for more than 12 years, even through civil war.[68] By 1660, Parliament "was in a far stronger position than it had been before the Civil Wars."[69] As historians Harold Parker and Marvin Brown observe, "Legislation was henceforth to be grounded upon clear majorities in legally elected Parliaments. Parliament's consent was now necessary to both taxation and legislation. Parliament could now freely discuss any issue involving the welfare of the kingdom."[70]

Through all the troubles of succeeding centuries, Coke's principles were kept alive. Derek Hirst sees what Coke's demand for fundamental rules against tyranny established for the future of democracy: "The most common formula for ending...oppression, and for curtailing the abuses of power, was the oldest. Power should be submitted to the rule of law."[71] Laws were to be made by a current Parliament, not simply inherited from some ancient parliament. Law was not only to be what had been established originally, but also what was needed for the present.

Coke had devoted himself not simply to ensuring that the king would follow law. He was just as concerned with the substance of law. Justice, he believed, could only be attained when law was simple and clear rather than obscure and complex. Conrad Russell, a historian of the Parliaments of the 1620s, notes the thoughts of Coke and his allies that "wretched is the slavery where law is wandering or unknown."[72] Common law, Coke believed, had to reach out to include military law, the governing of religion, government funding, and all other matters that came under government rule. And each specific dimension had to be controlled by one law, not a variety of laws. Coke knew that "two laws will never stand together in England," for "We have a national appropriate law to this kingdom. If you tell me of other laws, you are gone."[73]

Indeed, the king retained specific authority: he "could make war and peace, he could pardon offenders, he could grant letters and he could strike coin." But "The King had these prerogatives because he was granted them by law."[74] Law was no longer merely what the king wanted. Coke proclaimed of the king that "One cannot be judge in his own case."[75]

On the other hand, government by law did not transform the king and councils into mechanical executors of the law. Laws were general and specific, not precise; thus they had to be continuously interpreted. That did not mean that the king and his ministers could arbitrarily decide what the law was. England in this period moved decisively from a government in which the king was God's representative on earth to one in which the king was the executor of the law decided by the representatives of the people. The government moved toward democracy, in which law was justice for all.

In short, Sir Edward Coke's remarkable writing brought the world these lessons:

Law is to be made by parliament.

Law is to be written down.

Law is to be learned, by studying it.

Law is to be knowable, not obscure.

Law is to be open to the public.

Law is to be applied universally, to all citizens and leaders.

Law is to be interpreted by judges, not by monarchs.

Law is to be understood by cases of its application in the reality of history.

Law is to be adjusted, if necessary, by parliament's amendment.

Law is to protect citizens by ensuring their human rights.[76]

Despite England's troubles, England originated the modern principle of law, which spread throughout the world, an essence of democracy. After thousands of years of monarchy and aristocracy, hundreds of years have now existed in which government action operates by open rules, made by lawmakers the citizens choose. Politicians have a deep responsibility: to make law just.

BIBLIOGRAPHY

AIKEN, WILLIAM APPLETON, AND BASIL DUKE HENNING (EDS.). *Conflict in Stuart England*. New York: University Press, 1960.

BAGEHOT, WALTER. *The English Constitution*. London: Oxford University Press, 1949.

BOWEN, CATHERINE DRINKER. *The Lion and the Throne: The Life and Times of Sir Edward Coke (1552–1634)*. Boston: Little, Brown, 1957.

CHURCHILL, WINSTON S. *A History of the English-Speaking Peoples*. Volume II: *The New World*. New York: Dodd, Mead, 1983.

CORWIN, EDWARD S. *The "Higher Law" Background of American Constitutional Law*. Ithaca, N.Y.: Cornell University Press, 1955.

ELTON, G.R. *The Tudor Constitution: Documents and Commentary*. Cambridge, England: Cambridge University Press, 1960.

FLETCHER, ANTHONY. *The Outbreak of the English Civil War*. New York: New York University Press, 1981.

HEXTER, J. H. (ED.). *Parliament and Liberty from the Reign of Elizabeth to the English Civil War*. Stanford, Cal.: Stanford University Press, 1992.

JAMES, CHARLES WARBURTON. *Chief Justice Coke: His Family and Descendants at Holkham*. London: Country Life, 1929.

JANSSON, MAIJA. *Two Diaries of the Long Parliament*. New York: St. Martin's Press, 1984.

JENNINGS, IVOR. *Parliament*. 2nd ed. Cambridge, England: Cambridge University Press, 1969.

JONES, J.R. (ED.). *Liberty Secured?: Britain Before and After 1688*. Stanford, Cal.: Stanford University Press, 1992.

JONES, COLIN, MALYN NEWITT, AND STEPHEN ROBERTS (EDS.). *Politics and People in Revolutionary England*. Oxford, England: Basil Blackwell, 1986.

KEIR, DAVID LINDSAY. *The Constitutional History of Modern Britain Since 1485*. 9th ed. New York: Norton, 1969.

LAPRADE, WILLIAM THOMAS. *British History for American Students*. New York: Macmillan, 1928.

LYON, HASTINGS, AND HERMAN BLOCK. *Edward Coke: Oracle of the Law.* Boston: Houghton Mifflin, 1929.

MAITLAND, F.W. *The Constitutional History of England.* Cambridge, England: Cambridge University Press, 1963.

PARKER, HAROLD T., AND MARVIN L. BROWN, JR. *Major Themes in Modern European History: An Invitation to Inquiry and Reflection,* Vol. 1 and 2. Durham, N.C.: Moore, 1974.

PATTERSON, ORLANDO. *Freedom. Vol. I: Freedom in the Making of Western Culture.* New York: Basic Books, 1991.

PREST, WILFRID R. *The Rise of the Barristers: A Social History of the English Bar, 1590–1640.* Oxford: Clarendon Press, 1986.

ROBERTS, CLAYTON. *Schemes and Undertakings: A Study of English Politics in the Seventeenth Century.* Columbus: Ohio State University Press, 1985.

ROBERTS, CLAYTON, AND DAVID ROBERTS. *A History of England.* 3rd ed. Vol. I and II. Englewood Cliffs, N.J.: Prentice Hall, 1991.

RUSSELL, CONRAD. *Parliaments and English Politics, 1621–1629.* Oxford: Clarendon Press, 1979.

RUTHERFORD, JAMES H. *The Moral Foundations of United States Constitutional Democracy.* Pittsburgh: Dorrance, 1992.

STONER, JAMES R., JR. *Common Law and Liberal Theory: Coke, Hobbes, and the Origins of American Constitutionalism.* Lawrence: University Press of Kansas, 1992.

WHITE, STEPHEN D. *Sir Edward Coke and "The Grievances of the Commonwealth," 1621–1628.* Chapel Hill: University of North Carolina Press, 1979.

WILSON, DAVID HARRIS. *A History of England.* New York: Holt, Rinehart and Winston, 1967.

PART FOUR

Political Action to Make Democracy Rule by Reason

Democracy depends on reason. When reason dies, democracy dies. That is not a hypothesis. History shows that time and again political irrationality has destroyed democratic government and caused great human suffering. The hope of democracy is to bring reasoning to steady and trustable performance so that the decisions and actions of the government are reasonable. In practical terms, the requirements for rule by reason in a democracy are elections and parliamentary debate. But those requirements depend upon the workings of reason in the citizenry, which can be either developed or eroded by education, journalism, and entertainment.

Rule by reason means that law is made after carrying out research to discover what is actually happening in the society, what rules are most likely to work, how different laws are to be linked with one another, and how new laws can best be enforced. Thus rule by reason requires lawmakers to both conduct a strong search for information and do substantial logical thinking. When fantasy and illogic reign in government, rule by law is perverted and justice is impossible.

To ensure liberty and equality, democracy requires a government that recognizes clear limits, that is firm in protecting basic human rights but refuses to try to rule all aspects of life. Like rule by law, this requirement cannot be fulfilled without reason. Not only the top leaders and the parliament but also the citizens must be capable of reasoning, for democracy is, after all, "government by the people." In order to vote responsibly in elections, the citizens of a democracy need to know what has happened, what is happening, and what may happen to the best. Before citizens take action in the voting booth, they need accurate political information and the ability to think about that information logically. It is the government's obligation to see that they have both. Governments fulfill this obligation by practicing truthful disclosure and by establishing a sound system of public education.

We saw earlier that the first requirement for democracy is control of force—inside and outside the nation—by a freely elected government. But wars happen despite the best diplomacy, and when they do, governments are tempted to use secrecy and propaganda to obscure the truth of the nation's situation. It is said that the first casualty of war is truth. War typically does suspend reason. Citizens of military age are indoctrinated through months of training to charge into combat and face death—not a rational thing to do. The last thing an army wants is for its soldiers to stop and think. And on the home front, the soldiers' families, friends, and neighbors are urged to suspend reason in favor of emotional patriotism. But government by emotion, wishful thinking, and propaganda must be resisted. Defending a democratic nation by irrational, undemocratic means is dangerous for that nation's future.

Democracy is essential for decent, free, humane life. And rule by reason is essential for democracy.

11

The Story of Nazism

Democracy Cut Down

The Nazi experience of Germany is a prime example of how a democracy may be killed by fantasy. Democracy rose in that country after the Germans were defeated in World War I, and it lasted for over a decade. But then the deterioration of reason in both German leaders and the German people destroyed Germany's democratic government. The story of how that came about is a warning to all modern movements for democracy to concentrate on reality.

During World War I, in which many millions died, reason was rejected by the Allies as well as by Germany. The British government became so adroit at twisting the truth through propaganda that "The prevailing opinion in the trenches was that anything might be true, except what was printed."[1] The only communication the government allowed British soldiers to send home was a "Field Service Post Card" that was printed with choice forms of good news, one of which the soldier was supposed to mark. The card warned that *"If anything else is added the post card will be destroyed."*[2]

The truth of what was happening was horrible. Take one dreadful example. On the morning of July 1, 1916, 110,000 British soldiers along a 13-mile front climbed up out of their trenches and tramped forward with their rifles, clambering over barbed-wire fences. A week before that day, British artillery had bombarded the German trenches with a million and a half bombs. But the six German defending divisions had dug down into the ground below their trenches to make caves, where they hid safely from the bombs. So on that morning of July 1, when the British artillery shifted their bombing so their own troops could go forward, the German soldiers came up from the ground with machine guns and fired at the approaching British soldiers. Before the day was over, they had killed or wounded 60,000 British soldiers. Thousands of the wounded lay screaming on the ground, the massive fire power of the Germans preventing the British first-aid men from rescuing them.[3] This brutal trench warfare continued with unprecedented casualties on both sides. The United States entered the war on the side of the British and the French and tipped the balance for an Allied victory.

To secure the peace for future generations, President Woodrow Wilson proposed founding a League of Nations to settle international disputes. But he failed to persuade his own country to join the League and Americans elected the theatrical president Warren G. Harding, one of the worst presidents in U.S. history, to succeed the exhausted Wilson.

GERMANY'S POSTWAR DEMOCRACY LED BY FRIEDRICH EBERT

Despite the German army's stunning defeat in the war, a remarkable opportunity for democracy emerged in Germany at the end of the conflict. The leading figure in the democratic cause was Friedrich Ebert.

Born on February 4, 1871, in a small house in Heidelberg, Friedrich was the fourth child of his Catholic father, a hardworking tailor, and his Protestant mother, a farmer's daughter. There was little political conversation at home, though Friedrich's grandfather and father held a few political positions. Friedrich's father respected ordinary workers. The father and mother appreciated each other's religions. In fact, it was Friedrich's mother who decided the children would be brought up in their father's Catholic faith.

Friedrich found school boring and he was glad to leave it to go to work for a producer of horse saddles. But that also turned out to be boring, since he had to run errands and clean the workshop rather than ride horses, so he entered a vocational school. There he won a first prize, and also studied various classical authors such as Goethe. But just four weeks before his apprenticeship was to end, Friedrich got bashed on his ears by his angry master. Friedrich stalked out and quit—an act quite unusual for a teenage worker in those years. His father was shocked and told him to go back to finish his apprenticeship. Instead, Friedrich left home.

He traveled around for three years, trying several different jobs. Eventually, with the help of his uncle, he got a job in a factory. He joined the Social Democrat organization and began organizing local unions in various cities. His union activities got him fired time and again by irritated masters. In the spring of 1890, Ebert took part in the campaign for elections to the national parliament. His party did well. The next year, young Ebert settled in the city of Bremen, where he took a job as a saddle maker and was elected chairman of the union. He got to know the workers and spoke out to them about working conditions—and, once again, was fired by the boss. Ebert then became editor of the local labor newspaper, for which he wrote a widely read article on "The Situation of Workers in the Baker's Trade of Bremen," revealing the shameful working conditions of the bakers, which was news to most people. As German scholar

Friedrich Ebert.

Willi Eichler pointed out, Friedrich Ebert "learned to distinguish between facts and mere commentaries, rapidly to grasp a situation, and cleverly to participate in discussions."[4]

Later, Ebert married his 19-year-old girlfriend, Luise Rump. The couple rented a restaurant and beer hall, which she operated while he was absorbed in politics. Her mother straightened him out about one aspect of his personality: "Don't go about looking so glum. They will believe that your beer is as sour as your face and there will not be many guests."[5] He learned to speak with hope and stood forth for poor people. He and Luise had four sons and one daughter.

In 1899, Ebert was elected to the city parliament as a representative of the Social Democratic Party. For five years, he took care of the workers. When he was elected secretary of the national Social Democratic Party's Executive Committee in 1905, he and his family moved to Berlin, where he introduced typewriters and telephones into the party's national office. In Berlin Ebert became a practical mediator between the party's left and right wings. He became chair in the party's Young Workers, whom he encouraged to become more active.

Ebert craved concrete information to act upon; he was not merely interested in political abstractions. He supported a Social Democratic Party that was not "very susceptible to theoretical questions," one that pursued "a policy of facts." He thought that arguing about theories was an "unnecessary inconvenience," and "the SDP probably had better things to do than making itself the arena for a continuous theoretical struggle."[6] He was by no means a dictator, though. He declared at a party convention that the unity and purpose of the Social Democrats should be decided "after having thoroughly discussed matters."[7] A fellow politician praised him for his "outstanding skill for negotiating and his objectivity."[8]

In 1912, Ebert was elected to the national parliament, where the SDP had become the strongest party. When the SDP leader died in 1913, the 473 party convention members unanimously elected Ebert as the party's new chairman.

On July 29, 1914, Ebert heard that war was being considered and that the party leaders would probably be arrested. He departed for Switzerland, but soon returned to Berlin. When, in early August, Germany did declare war against Russia and France, Ebert supported the war decision. His party agreed, but not completely. As the war continued, however, various leftist Social Democrats increasingly protested it. They were expelled from the party. Ebert regretted the split. He said that "we shall condemn any war of conquest" and urge a peace movement.[9] But the war raged on and Germany justified its drive to conquer neighboring countries. They falsely justified their war as "defense."

Ebert went along with the war. But during the long months of battle, he complained that the improvement of Germany's government was being delayed. On June 7, 1916, he spoke to the national parliament:

> The war has now been going on for 22 months. During that long period it would certainly have been possible to smooth the path for new things to come. But scarcely any of the chains of archaic police methods have been loosened nor do we hear anything about a reform of the class-suffrage in Prussia and other Federal States. [One has not] found the courage for safeguarding food supplies and protecting the populace against usury....The press is at the mercy of censorship. All this is filling a wide circle of our population...with misgivings and bitterness....We demand that some goodwill should be shown to the people that...have done so much, that they be helped in the development of justice and freedom and betterment of their economic and social conditions. As the Government has been failing in these respects, we will draw our own conclusions and will vote against the budget.[10]

On into 1917, as leader of the Social Democratic Party, Ebert stressed that "The Party Convention demands the immediate fulfillment of the German people's longing for democracy....Nothing would be more likely to strengthen in the people the will for national defence than granting them equal civil rights in the fullest sense."[11]

After the United States entered the war on the side of the Allies, the stalemate was broken and Germany began to lose. But this fact was kept from the German people. More importantly, it was the German Supreme Army Command, led by Hindenberg and Ludendorff, that initiated negotiations for a cease-fire and a peace settlement on September 29, 1918—and this, too, was concealed from the public. The generals also proposed a genuine parliamentary system of government, one in which the people's elected representatives would take on actual power. Why did they do this?

THE END OF THE WAR: THE START OF DEMOCRACY

By the fall of 1918, the situation of the German army was hopeless. The generals knew this, but did not care to take public responsibility for losing the war. Instead, they devised a way to pass that responsibility off to a civilian government that had had no voice in conducting the war. It was the democratic parties in the national parliament—led by Ebert's Social Democrats—that were seen to be surrendering and suing for peace terms. This is the origin of the "stab in the back" accusation that later helped Hitler rise to power: It wasn't the German army that lost the war, the people were led to believe, but a craven liberal civilian government. The German people, stunned by the sudden capitulation of their country in a war they thought they were winning, were ready to believe this lie.

Another reason the German generals were now so willing to back a democratic government was, no doubt, the peace proposals of President Woodrow Wilson of the United States. President Wilson thought that no deal made with the German military could be trusted unless it was supported by the German public. He was for the destruction of "every arbitrary power anywhere that can separately, secretly, and of its single choice disturb the peace of the world."[12] The German military apparently thought that if Germany went democratic, the United States and the other Allies would simply let the army withdraw to its own borders without officially surrendering.

At the same time, the German parliament latched onto Wilson's proposal for democracy, a change which could empower Ebert and company. On October 20, 1918, they decided on this response to Wilson:

> The new government has been formed in complete accord with the wishes of the representatives of the people....The leaders of the great parties of the Reichstag [i.e., parliament] are members of this government. In the future, no government will be able to take or continue in office without possessing the confidence of the majority of the Reichstag. The responsibility of the chancellor of the empire to the representatives of the people is being legally developed and safeguarded.[13]

On October 26, Ebert and allied parties in the parliament most significantly determined that the chancellor would from now on be responsible to the parliament and the military would answer to the civilian government. Conservatives shouted against that change, which they saw as a move toward Russian Communism. But the necessary constitutional amendments were adopted and signed by the kaiser. By law, Germany was now a parliamentary state.

Democracy was far from firmly established, however. Ebert led a movement to abolish imperial rule and the kaiser left Berlin the night of October 29. But with the defeated nation in chaos and violent public demonstrations spreading, the German parliament virtually fell apart.

To be sure, there were tentative successes. On November 9, the assent of the kaiser to the elimination of the throne was announced and Ebert became chancellor of the "German Republic." Though Ebert supported the creation of this provisional republic, he insisted that such change "must be decided by a constituent assembly."[14] He proclaimed that "The new Government will be a people's government. Its main endeavor will be to bring peace to German people as speedily as possible and to reinforce the freedom it has achieved....Citizens! I am entreating you: leave the streets! Keep law and order!"[15] On December 19, the parliament voted 400 to 50 to schedule elections for a national assembly on January 19,

1919. The kaiser fled to Holland and all the German states overthrew their rulers. As historian William Halperin notes, Germans rallied for democracy "because they believed that a republic had the best chance of obtaining peace terms for the Allies." [16]

Tensions quickly developed in the provisional government. The left pushed for governance by workers and soldiers rather than by all citizens. Ebert supported that view temporarily, but he again stated that such decisions should be made by the constituent assembly, and should include freedom of assembly, association, speech, and the press, along with equal, direct, secret, and universal suffrage. Ebert hated violence: two of his sons had been killed in the war. He wanted to work out democracy step by step.

But 1918–19 was a time of terrible suffering in Germany—people starving, killing, jobless, confused, and afraid. Ebert managed to hold on to the administration and bureaucracy of the government until, in December 1918, left-wing demonstrators were shot by soldiers in Berlin. In parliament, left-wingers tried to grab authority before the coming elections. Three thousand sailors took over the government building in Berlin. Ebert sent the army, which drove off the sailors with artillery fire. In reaction, the Communist Party called for "a great mass demonstration" to bring down Ebert. [17] Even Ebert's Social Democratic Party proclaimed a general strike, because, they said, "We refuse any longer to allow ourselves to be terrorized by lunatics and criminals." [18] There were huge demonstrations and more blood-letting. Shooting in January 1919 killed more than 1,000 people and in March, about 1,200 died in the violence. In April, a crowd in the city of Munich proclaimed itself a "soviet republic," but before long, they were ruthlessly liquidated.

But that same January, on the 19th, 30,000,000 Germans went out and voted in the scheduled elections for a new national government. The Social Democrats got the most votes, almost 11,500,000. On February 6, 1919, Ebert opened the assembly. Thanks to his constant thinking and acting, democracy was becoming a reality. On February 11, after enacting a provisional constitutional law, the assembly elected Ebert president of the German Republic by 277 out of 379 votes. Ebert promised to represent all the people, not just his own party, and quickly moved to create a cabinet. He exhorted the nation to honor rule by reason and work to defeat the corrupting influence of violent political emotion. To a friend in Sweden, Ebert wrote:

> The brutal attitude towards our national independence and the continuous sadistic attacks on our national feelings must whip up national passions and help to spread nationalist demagogy among the young. They…are the greatest enemy of German democracy and the strongest impulse for turning to Communism and Nationalism. [19]

In April, 1919, the peace requirements were to be determined at Versailles, near Paris. On a special train, 180 German diplomats and experts set out, but the French operated the train at only ten miles an hour so the Germans would see the vast lands they had devastated. Arriving at Versailles, they were taken into an isolated hotel surrounded by barbed wire, sent upstairs carrying their own baggage, and confined for a week, while the Allies negotiated among themselves. Finally the Germans were brought in to receive and sign rules. It was decided that neighbor nations would take back areas the Germans had occupied, that German military forces would be minimized, and that the German government would be required to acknowledge "causing all the loss and damage to which the [Allies] have been subjected as a consequence of the war imposed on them by the aggression of Germany."[20]

The Germans were shocked at losing land, though the Allies could have invaded all of Germany. The danger of resistance was obvious: it would revitalize a war they would lose. In the midst of various party factions damning the Versailles document Ebert brought together a cabinet to sign the peace treaty. After violent debate, the parliament voted in favor of the treaty, though members asked to discuss certain terms with the Allies. The Allies refused, saying "the time of discussion is past."[21] Ebert called the treaty a "peace of violence"[22] and urged the United States to reach out beyond the treaty and support the German Republic. But in the end, Germany signed the treaty; it had no alternative. But bitterness over the terms further divided the parties and threatened the new democracy. This threat stimulated Ebert to think and act harder.

On July 31, 1919, Germany's new constitution was adopted by a vote of 262 to 75 in the parliament and Friedrich Ebert was the president of the German Republic. A professor proposed by Ebert, Hugo Preuss, was the constitution's principal composer. The new constitution gave the national government far more power than it had had in the past. But more important was the essentials of democracy. The cabinet was made responsible to the parliament. Article 41 stated that "The president of the Reich shall be elected by the whole German people."[23] The president was to serve for seven years and be eligible for reelection. If one-tenth of the voters agreed on a bill or a constitutional amendment, they could present it to the parliament for consideration. German voters now had "proportional representation" in their parliament, meaning that the number of representatives of each party would be determined by the percentage of votes they received from the electorate.

The fundamental basics of democracy were retained: government governed by a constitution, elected by the citizens, and enacting law through discourse and voting in the parliament. Substantive rights were included. Historian William L. Shirer wrote:

> The wording of the Weimar Constitution was sweet and eloquent to the ear of any democratically minded man. The people were declared sovereign: "Political power emanates from the people." Men and women were given the vote at the age of twenty. "All Germans are equal before the law....Personal liberty is inviolable....Every German has a right...to express his opinion freely....All Germans have the right to form associations or societies....All inhabitants of the Reich enjoy complete liberty of belief and conscience...." No man in the world would be more free than a German, no government more democratic and liberal than his. On paper, at least.[24]

Article 48 of the constitution dealt with public emergencies: "If public safety and order are seriously disturbed or threatened…, the president of the Reich may take such measures as are necessary to restore public safety and order. If necessary, he may intervene with the help of the armed forces." But the article stipulated that though the president was not required to get the parliament's permission in advance of taking emergency action, the parliament could cancel any such measures by the president.[25]

Article 118 of the constitution declared that "every German has the right, within the bounds of the general laws, to express his opinion freely in word, writing, print, picture, or in any other manner" and "There is no censorship…." As author Modris Eksteins notes, the constitution makers "gave their readers an unending feast of reason and decency….They believed in truth, they believed in human understanding, and they believed that truth and human understanding led to mastery."[26]

Ebert struggled to translate this paper democracy into an actual one. After the new constitution was voted in, a right-wing revolt in 1920 stimulated a left-wing general strike, which became the largest strike the world had ever seen. In the election of 1920, Ebert's party lost 51 seats and there was a general swing to the right. But Ebert did not give up. In fact, despite all the tensions and violence of these first few years after World War I, Germany retained the essential democracy Ebert had brought forth.

But nothing was certain. The army was still led primarily by the Great War commanders. Would they back Ebert's democracy? The German legal system was not yet clearly committed to the constitution's eloquent declaration of rights such as free speech. Conservative German judges sentenced liberals to long terms in prison for "treason" because they had revealed government or military secrets, or had denounced in the press or in public speech the army's violations of the Versailles Treaty. Would these judges also imprison right-wing killers revolting against the German Republic?

THE NEW CRISIS: INFLATION

In the early 1920s, wracked by the destruction and chaos brought on by the war, the German economy collapsed and the German money fell in value till it became nearly worthless. The basic German cash was the mark. Its value, in 1921, declined with 75 marks equal to one American dollar. In 1922, it took 400 marks to equal one dollar. In desperation, the German government asked permission to delay payments to the Allies required by the peace treaty. But the French said no. In early 1923, 7,000 marks equalled one dollar. Germany failed to deliver required timber obligations to France, so the French army invaded Germany's industrial Ruhr, the area where four-fifths of German coal and steel were produced. When Ruhr workers went on strike, the French arrested, deported, and even executed some of them. This exacerbated the national crisis. The mark plunged unbelievably: by January 1923, to 18,000 per dollar; by July 1, to 160,000; by August 1 to 1,000,000; by November to 4,000,000. Thereafter, German currency was utterly

During the 1920s, inflation was so high in Germany that it was cheaper to start fires with the German mark than it was to buy kindling wood with it. The woman shown here is lighting a cooking fire with the almost worthless currency.

worthless. German savers lost all their money; German workers saw their wages collapse to nothing.[27] Working people had to be paid at noon every day; they grabbed their big sacks full of money and ran off to the nearest store to buy whatever they could, before the prices leaped higher.[28]

Businesses went bankrupt, unemployment soared, food was scarce and its prices were out of reach for most of the populace. It's no wonder that in that atmosphere the German masses grew angry enough to demand a new government and a new war against the French. In the fall of 1923, Ebert's chancellor, Gustav Stresemann, announced that, by necessity, there would not be resistance to the French occupation of the Ruhr nor further delay in Germany's reparation payments. Communists and right-wing nationalists blasted the government equally. So Ebert, drawing on Article 48 of the constitution, declared an emergency and shifted absolute power to the minister of defense and the commander of the army. On September 30, 1923, troops led by an army major seized three forts to the east of Berlin, but Ebert's general forced them to surrender. Down south in Bavaria, a radical newspaper vigorously damned the German Republic and was ordered to cease publication. Its editor was Adolf Hitler.

Hitler salutes some of the hundred thousand Nazi leaders whom he addressed on the zeppelin field at Nuremberg.

THE EMERGENCE OF ADOLF HITLER

Adolf Hitler appealed to the head of the Munich military district to be allowed to hold mass meetings. He assured the general on his word of honor, that he would not attempt to take over the government or even direct any antistate action. That persuaded the general to give him permission to meet six times rather than the 12 Hitler requested. But Hitler did hold twelve meetings.[29]

On the evening of November 8, 1923, in a big beer hall in Bavaria, some 3,000 angry Germans gathered to drink and express their fury. While the "oom-pah music" blared out from the band and waitresses quickly passed around heavy mugs of beer, the air filled with cigar smoke and ale fumes.[30] Three national military leaders entered. Crowds waited outside. As a local supporter of public anger made the keynote speech, Adolf Hitler approached the beer hall and told the police they should control the area in case of trouble, which they agreed to do. Entering with several of his followers, Hitler was handed a mug of beer, but he did not drink it. An officer slipped in and whispered to him, "They have arrived!" "They" were steel-helmeted storm troopers in trucks, led by Hitler's Nazi officer Hermann Goering, who, with the permission of the police, ordered the troops to guard the beer hall doors.

As Hitler pressed through the crowd to interrupt and make a speech, a police major stepped toward him with his hand in his pocket. Hitler thought that policeman was drawing a pistol, so he drew out his own pistol and pointed it at the policeman's forehead, snapping "Take your hand out." The officer did; his hand was empty. Goering, steel helmet on and wearing a pistol, climbed onto a table, kicked the mugs of beer away, and yelled "Silence!" The chaotic crowd hardly noticed. So Hitler shot his pistol at the ceiling. Shocked, the mob shut up and looked at him. He shouted:

> The National Revolution has begun! This building is occupied by six hundred heavily armed men. No one may leave the hall. Unless there is immediate quiet I shall have a machine gun posted in the gallery. The Bavarian and Reich governments have been removed and a provisional national government formed. The barracks of the Reichswehr [army] and police are occupied. The Army and the police are marching on the city under the swastika banner.[31]

Hitler's claim that he controlled the army and the police sounded true—after all, hundreds of his storm troopers were surrounding the beer hall—but he was lying. He turned away from the crowd and had the three national military leaders herded into a private room to meet with him. The crowd grew frenzied. One man yelled, "Don't be cowards as in 1918. Shoot!" Helmet-headed Goering tried to quiet them. "There is nothing to fear," he shouted. "We have the friendliest intentions. For that matter, you've no cause to grumble, you've got your beer!"[32]

Inside the private room, Hitler melodramatically told the three men, "No one leaves this room alive without my permission." He demanded that they join his new revolutionary government and swore he would make them leaders. They stayed silent. He harangued them further. They remained silent. Finally, Hitler took out his gun and pointed it at them: "I have four shots in my pistol! Three for my collaborators, if they abandon me. The last bullet for myself!" He pointed it at his own head. "If I am not victorious by tomorrow afternoon, I shall be a dead man!"[33] One of the men responded, "Herr Hitler, you can have me shot or shoot me yourself. Whether I die or not is no matter." Another accused Hitler of breaking his sworn word that he would capture the police. Hitler admitted this, but when one of the officers started speaking to another, Hitler snapped, "Halt! No talking without my permission!" Because they would not agree with him, Hitler called in his officer to guard them with a machine gun. He then dashed out to the crowd and announced that the three generals had sworn to join him in forming a new national government.[34] Loud cheers arose from the crowd. Hitler then took a general named Ludendorff into the private room. Ludendorff was angry that Hitler, merely a former army corporal, had declared himself the dictator of Germany: Ludendorff felt that he, as a general, was better qualified. Ludendorff did not influence the other three. They went out with Hitler and the others and made short statements confirming the audience's belief that they were aligned with Hitler. The crowd sang "Deutschland über Alles."[35]

Hitler raged victory. The meeting ended and the crowd strolled out of the beer hall. Several government ministers, bankers, police chiefs, and city counselors were arrested by Hitler's Storm Troopers, to be held as hostages till the coup was completed.

The three captive leaders escaped from Hitler and quickly denied their loyalty to him. One even ordered a placard posted throughout the city of Munich, declaring this:

> The deception and perfidy of ambitious comrades have converted a demonstration in the interests of national reawakening into a scene of disgusting violence. The declarations extorted from myself, General von Lossow and Colonel Seisser at the point of the revolver are null and void. The National Socialist German Workers' Party, as well as the fighting leagues Oberland and Reichskriegflagge, are dissolved.
>
> VON KAHR, General State Commissioner [36]

Hitler's gang heard the news, via an intercepted radio message from Berlin, that the three had turned against him, and also that the government had announced its intention to arrest Hitler and his allies.[37] President Ebert proclaimed to the nation:

> Whoever supports this movement is guilty of high treason. Instead of helping our brothers in the Rhineland and in the Ruhr who are fighting for Germany, certain persons are plunging Germany into misfortune, endangering her food supply, exposing her to the risk of foreign invasion and destroying all possibility of restoring economic well-being. The latest measures taken by the German government in regard to the currency have resulted, during the last twenty-four hours, in a vast appreciation of the mark in foreign money markets. Everything will be lost if this mad attempt in Munich meets with any success. In this critical hour for the German people and the German Reich, we appeal to all friends of the Fatherland to stand forth in defense of unity, German order and German freedom. All necessary measures for the crushing of this attempt and the restoration of order have been taken, and will be enforced with ruthless energy. [38]

Early on the morning of November 9, General Ludendorff and Hitler led a massive march of some 3,000 Storm Troopers into the city of Munich. Ludendorff had told his wife that he wanted to hang President Ebert "and Co." and would be glad to watch them dangle from the gallows, but that he did not want to kill policemen and soldiers. Goering marched up front with the two leaders, and when they were stopped by the police, he told the police to let them pass or he would have the hostages—who were being dragged along at the end of the march—killed immediately. Hitler, wearing his helmet and war uniform, yelled "Surrender! Surrender!" But as they approached the city military headquarters, a police leader answered no: stop and go back. Hitler's gang refused. The first shots were fired. Suddenly Goering was shot in the leg and 16 Nazis and 3 policemen were killed. Hitler, who was knocked down when the man next to him was shot, was grabbed and shunted into a car that sped him away to a house in the country.[39] Two days later, the police found him hiding in the wardrobe closet of his hostess and arrested him.[40] He was tried for treason, convicted, and sentenced to five years in prison. Actually, he spent a little less than nine months in a privileged prison where he dictated *Mein Kampf (My Struggle)*, his autobiography.[41]

In February 1924, the Bavarian government gave evidence of a new, strong allegiance to Ebert's national government,[42] and the state of emergency, invoked under Article 48, was canceled. In effect, the crisis was over. Hitler had failed, Ebert had won. Inflation was down, the economy was recovering, and democratic procedures were being revived. For the next six years, German politics as well as economics seemed to be working.[43] Germany looked like a real democracy. It had shown itself able to deal with emergencies and violence and injustice, not by transforming itself into a dictatorship, but by keeping faith with the constitution and holding elections for representatives who grappled with the nation's problems. Ebert's leadership was essential, and so the nation's commitment to democracy seemed secure.

But Hitler, a man of remarkable violence and dishonesty, was not permanently lost to German politics. He was not over with.

HITLER'S CHARACTER

Adolf Hitler's early life shaped his personality, which later shaped Germany's personality. He was born on April 20, 1889, in Austria, near the border with Germany. For his parents, his birth was a significant event. Alois Hitler, borne illegitimately by a mother who died when he was five, worked for many years as a civil servant. He married three times: his first two wives had died, as had some of their children. His current wife, Klara, was his second cousin. They married when he was 48 and she was 25. Four months and ten days later, their first child was born, a boy who died in infancy, as did the next child, a girl.

So when Adolf survived, his parents were delighted, though both his father and his mother neglected and mistreated him from time to time. His father retired at age 56, when Adolf was 4. From then on, his father spent much of his time drunk at a tavern. After idle talk with the neighbors, he typically returned home to beat his wife and child and their dog. Adolf's mother loved him, but when he was five, she had another son, and two years later a daughter, both of whom shifted her attention away from Adolf. Over the years, his father bought and sold property, which forced the family to move from one place to another.

Adolf started school at six, and did well at first. At eight, he transferred to the Catholic Benedictine Monastery, which he liked. He sang in the choir and took singing lessons, and dreamed of becoming an abbot. But the monastery kicked him out after he was caught smoking in the garden. That same year, his little brother died. His father forced Adolf to go to another school. There the boy did poorly. He failed a class year and had to take it over, then failed again and took the same class a third time. He shifted to another school, one he hated, and again did poorly. There he got drunk for the first and last time in his life.

When Adolf was 13, his father died suddenly. Adolf convinced his mother to let him stay at home, dreaming and drawing. At age 16, he was diagnosed as having a lung ailment and spent much time in bed. He returned to school briefly, but the only subject he did well in was drawing. He fell in love with a girl named Stefanie; for four years, he gazed longingly at her as she strolled by. He wrote many love poems to her—but he never met her or even sent her any of the poems.

In 1907, at age 18, Adolf moved to Vienna. Before the next Christmas, his mother was dead of breast cancer. Hitler was alone.

Thus Adolf Hitler grew up in trouble with his parents and teachers. But what did that mean for his basic identity? How did he himself see his responses to his early life? Hitler's book, *My Struggle*, most of which he wrote in prison, is full of lies. Ralph Manheim, who translated that book into English, notes:

> [Hitler] makes the most extraordinary allegations without so much as an attempt to prove them. Often there is no visible connection between one paragraph and the next. The logic is purely psychological: Hitler is fighting his persecutors, magnifying his person, creating a dream-world in which he can be an important figure. [44]

Hitler's preferred interpretation of his early experience centered on his resistance to his father's demand. Adolf Hitler asserted:

> It was his basic opinion and intention that, like himself, his son would and must become a civil servant. It was only natural that the hardships of his youth should enhance his subsequent achievement in his eyes, particularly since it resulted exclusively from his own energy and iron diligence. It was the pride of the self-made man which made him want his son to rise to the same position in life, or, of course, even higher if possible, especially since, by his own industrious life, he thought he would be able to facilitate his child's development so greatly.
>
> It was simply inconceivable to him that I might reject what had become the content of his whole life. Consequently my father's decision was simple, definite, and clear; in his own eyes I mean, of course. Finally, a whole lifetime spent in the bitter struggle for existence had given him a domineering nature, and it would have seemed intolerable to him to leave the final decision in such matters to an inexperienced boy, having as yet no sense of responsibility....
>
> And yet things were to turn out differently.
>
> Then barely eleven years old. I was forced into opposition for the first time in my life. Hard and determined as my father might be in putting through plans and purposes once conceived, his son was just as persistent and recalcitrant in rejecting an idea which appealed to him not at all, or in any case very little.
>
> I did not want to become a civil servant.
>
> Neither persuasion nor "serious" arguments made any impression on my resistance. I did not want to be a civil servant, no, and again no. All attempts on my father's part to inspire me with love or pleasure in this profession by stories from his own life accomplished the exact opposite. I yawned and grew sick to my stomach at the thought of sitting in an office, deprived of my liberty; ceasing to be master of my own time and being compelled to force the content of a whole life into blanks that had to be filled out. [45]

According to *My Struggle*, given his stark rejection of his father's plan for his future, Adolf felt he had to decide on an alternative. That decision brought on a new conflict:

As long as my father's intention of making me a civil servant encountered only my theoretical distaste for the profession, the conflict was bearable. Thus far, I had to some extent been able to keep my private opinions to myself; I did not always have to contradict him immediately. My own firm determination never to become a civil servant sufficed to give me complete inner peace. And this decision was immutable. The problem became more difficult when I developed a plan of my own in opposition to my father's. And this occurred at the early age of twelve. How it happened, I myself do not know, but one day it became clear to me that I would become a painter, an artist. There was no doubt as to my talent for drawing; it had been one of my father's reasons for sending me to the *Realschule* [i.e., school], but never in all the world would it have occurred to him to give me professional training in this direction. On the contrary.[46]

That same significant year, Adolf's 12-year-old heart and mind turned to an imagined alternative father when he saw the first opera of his life, Wagner's *Lohengrin*.

I was captivated at once. My youthful enthusiasm for the master of Bayreuth knew no bounds. Again and again I was drawn to his works....All this, particularly after I had outgrown my adolescence (which in my case was an especially painful process), reinforced my profound distaste for the profession which my father had chosen for me. My conviction grew stronger and stronger that I would never be happy as a civil servant....I wanted to become a painter and no power in the world could make me a civil servant.[47]

So it was the confrontation with his father that confirmed to Adolf his basic identity.

When for the first time, after once again rejecting my father's favorite notion, I was asked what I myself wanted to be, and I rather abruptly blurted out the decision I had meanwhile made, my father for the moment was struck speechless.
"Painter? Artist?"
He doubted my sanity, or perhaps he thought he had heard wrong or misunderstood me. But when he was clear on the subject, and particularly after he felt the seriousness of my intention, he opposed it with all the determination of his nature. His decision was extremely simple, for any consideration of what abilities I might really have was simply out of the question.
"Artist, no, never as long as I live!" But since his son, among various other qualities, had apparently inherited his father's stubbornness, the same answer came back at him. Except, of course, that it was in the opposite sense.
And thus the situation remained on both sides. My father did not depart from his "Never!" And I intensified my "Oh, yes!"
The consequences, indeed, were none too pleasant. The old man grew embittered, and, much as I loved him, so did I. My father forbade me to nourish the slightest hope of ever being allowed to study art. I went one step further and declared that if that was the case I would stop studying altogether. As a result of such "pronouncements," of course, I drew the short end; the old man began the relentless enforcement of his authority. In the future, therefore, I was silent, but transformed my threat into reality. I thought that once my father saw how little progress I was making at the *Realschule*, he would let me devote myself to my dream, whether he liked it or not.
I do not know whether the calculation was correct. For the moment only one thing was certain: my obvious lack of success at school.[48]

Because of his psychological state during his youth, Adolf Hitler's deep, strong, essential identity decision shaped his future. Its significance is confirmed by his three years of failure at school, where he shunned nearly all objective learning, in rebellion against his father. He desired to produce artistic impressions, not to learn facts. His future association with government would never, in his mind, include either *civil* or *servant*. And his father's death—almost as if killed by his son's rebellion—confirmed to Adolf Hitler his victory of identity.

In school, only one academic course, taught by another alternative father, attracted him: history. What he absorbed was that "history" was to be exploited, not learned:

> To "learn" history means to seek and find the forces which are the causes leading to those effects which we subsequently perceive as historical events. The art of reading as of learning is this: *to retain essential, to forget the non-essential.*[49]

His beloved teacher was described by Hitler as an exploiter of history for political ideology:

> He used our budding nationalistic fanaticism as a means of educating us, frequently appealing to our sense of national honor. By this alone he was able to discipline us little ruffians more easily than would have been possible by any other means.
>
> This teacher made history my favorite subject. And indeed, though he had no such intention, it was then that I became a little revolutionary.
>
> For who could have studied German history under such a teacher without becoming an enemy of the state which, through its ruling house, exerted so disastrous an influence on the destinies of the nation?[50]

Living in Vienna from 1908 until 1913, Hitler tried again and again to get into the Academy of Art and then into the Architectural School, but both rejected him. He obtained an orphan's pension and inherited some money from his family, but he also supported himself by doing dull jobs, in which he had virtually no relationship with the other workers. He spent his free time reading many books and articles about politics. But given his decisive attitude, Hitler read into the works what he wanted, rather than having his thinking shaped by their information. Walter C. Langer, author of *The Mind of Adolf Hitler*, notes that Hitler read

> not with the idea of understanding the problem as a whole, which might have enabled him to form an intelligent opinion, but to find arguments that would support his earlier conviction. This is a trait that runs throughout his life. He never studies to learn but only to justify what he feels. In other words, his judgments are based wholly on emotional factors and are then clothed with an intellectual argument.[51]

Adolf's decisive preference for emotion and his contempt for reason distinguished him from his civil servant father. He rejected more than his father's choice of career for him; he rejected the kind of steady work grounded in the real world that his father represented. Adolf was damning thought and cheering feelings.

In 1913, Hitler went to Germany and moved into a cheap, furnished room above a tailor's shop in Munich. There he earned some income by painting pictures. As historian Otis C. Mitchell points out, "Hitler's life in Munich was little changed from his earlier life in Vienna." In fact, "The few people who knew him in Munich describe a man who lived in his own world of fantasy...."[52]

In 1913, the Austrian government sent the Munich police a message to arrest Hitler for evading military draft. He appealed that accusation, saying that he was too ill and weak to be drafted—an untrue statement. Appearing before a draft board, he managed to appear sick, persuading them that he was indeed unfit for war. So he returned to his isolated painting in Munich. Hitler then found a way to get the emotional conversation he wanted: he joined beer-drinkers at a tavern—though he himself did not drink—to chat at great length with drunks about politics.

In August 1914, when Adolf Hitler was 25, Germany declared war on France and Russia. He was thrilled: "Even to this day I am not ashamed to say that, in a transport of enthusiasm, I sank down on my knees and thanked Heaven from an overflowing heart."[53] He joined the army, where he was assigned to run messages between companies in the field and regimental headquarters—a dangerous job that required zipping through and around battle areas. In October 1916, Hitler was hit by a piece of shrapnel and sent to a hospital, and then sent back to Munich. Within two days, he sent a letter to his commanding officer, asking to return to combat. He soon did. In October 1918, he was temporarily blinded and made speechless by an attack of mustard gas. While in the hospital, the war ended with Germany's defeat. Though he had regained his sight and speech, Hitler became so depressed at that news that "Everything went black again before my eyes; I tottered and groped my way back to the ward, threw myself on my bunk, and dug my burning head into my blanket and pillow....So it had all been in vain."[54]

Hitler joined the reserve army. His peacetime assignment was to visit with soldier friends and find out which ones were Communists, then report them to the authorities so they could be executed. Hitler described that work as his "first more or less political activity."[55] At this time, he was also assigned to visit various political organizations to discern how people in them related to the military. He began to develop his speaking abilities during this tour of duty as an "education officer."[56] He strongly appealed to his listeners, though "it was often the *way* Hitler said things, rather than what he actually said" that affected people.[57] His speeches were highly emotional, alternating between violent, threatening pronouncements and soft, sentimental appeals. At one moment he would thunder, "There will be no peace in the land until a body hangs from every lamppost,"[58] and at the next he would shift gears to his gentle mode. An observer said, "Almost anything might suddenly inflame his wrath and hatred....But equally, the transition from anger to sentimentality or enthusiasm might be quite sudden." Another noted that "the slightest difficulty or obstacle could make him scream with rage or burst into tears."[59]

He joined a small political party, called the German Workers Party, and quickly recruited many more members from the thousands attracted to hear and see him speak. He changed the party's name to the National Socialist German Workers Party, which, in German, was contracted to "Nazi." On March 31, 1920, Hitler quit the army reserve in order to work full time for the party. He drew as many as 6,500 people per speech. He attributed his appeal to his capacity to go "straight to the heart of his hearers."[60] Hitler saw the public as "feminine": "The masses are like a woman.…The people, in an overwhelming majority, are so feminine in their nature and attitude that their activities and thoughts are motivated less by sober consideration than by feeling and sentiment."[61]

For all his growing popularity, the private Hitler was tormented by secret fears and a sense of isolation: "I am the loneliest man on earth."[62] He would wake up and scream at night, so terrified of being poisoned that he began to fear going to sleep at all. And he could not stand debate or opposition. If anyone in the crowds listening to his speeches contradicted or questioned him, he had his party officers strike or throw that person out of the hall. Once he decided on a course of action, no information could dissuade him. Years later he confessed, "I follow my course with the precision and security of a sleepwalker."[63]

Thus Hitler transmuted his private identity of emotion and violence into an effective public rhetoric of emotion and violence. He emerged as a leader of the Nazi Party because of his strongest political talent: oratory. He would not reason with others, nor did he ever truly collaborate. He was a loner who could move crowds. Typically he scheduled his speeches for late in the evening, after an assistant had given a short speech that generally left the audience sleepy and vulnerable. Hitler would then appear at the back of the hall, with a group of Storm Troopers. The band would strike up a military march as he strode to the speaking platform. He would begin to speak, nervously at first, but once he saw the audience reflecting the emotion he was feeding them, "suddenly he got the 'feel' and was able to go on."[64] An observer described his speaking:

> The beginning is slow and halting. Gradually he warms up when the spiritual atmosphere of the great crowd is engendered. For he responds to this metaphysical contact in such a way that each member of the multitude feels bound to him by an individual link of sympathy.[65]

Here is Hitler himself on his speaking mode:

> The psyche of the broad masses does not respond to anything weak or half-way. Like a woman, whose spiritual sensitiveness is determined less by abstract reason than by indefinable emotional longing for fulfilling power and who, for that reason, prefers to submit to the strong rather than the weakling—the mass, too, prefers the ruler to a pleader.[66]

Generally he worked himself up to such a pitch during his speeches that "When he stopped speaking his chest was still heaving with emotion."[67] He made no attempt to inform his audiences; his desire was to fill them with slogans. He said, "There is only so much room in a brain, so much wall space, as it were, and if you furnish it with your slogans, the opposition has no place to put up any pictures later on, because the apartment of the brain is already crowded with your furniture."[68]

Hitler's contempt for reason was thoroughgoing. In his view, the meaning of a book had nothing to do with what the author intended. Rather, it was up to the reader to define and exploit the author's written words for his own purposes:

> In "reading," to be sure, I mean perhaps something different than the average member of our so-called "intelligentsia." I know people who "read" enormously....True, they possess a mass of "knowledge," but their brain is unable to organize and register the material they have taken in. They lack the art of sifting what is valuable for them in a book from that which is without value....[T]here arises [in them] a confused muddle of memorized facts which not only are worthless, but also make their unfortunate possessor conceited.[69]

He saw rational education as contemptible:

> Of secondary importance is the training of mental abilities.
>   Overeducated people, stuffed with knowledge and intellect, but bare of any sound instincts.
>   These impudent rascals [intellectuals] who always know everything better than anybody else....
>   The intellect has grown autocratic, and has become a disease of life.[70]

Thus Hitler perceived education, reading, and—especially—political rhetoric and discourse as essentially emotional. In this rejection of rationality, he was imitating his despised father's drunk and violent life.

Hitler loved romantic fictions, which he saw as far more appealing than dull factual learning. From his very first experience of Wagnerian opera at the age of 12, he became an intense Wagner fan. Years later, he said that "Whoever wants to understand National Socialist Germany [i.e., the Nazi Party] must know Wagner."[71] There were reasons for Hitler's strong affinity for the composer. Wagner, of course, never proposed that Germany rule the world, but he "scorned parliaments and democracy and the materialism and mediocrity of the bourgeoisie"[72]—all of which Hitler also detested. At his 1924 trial for treason, Hitler shouted at the court, "When I stood for the first time before Richard Wagner's grave, my heart swelled with pride."[73] Later, Hitler's Nazi propagandist, Joseph Goebbels, said Hitler had seen Wagner's opera *Die Meistersinger* more than a hundred times. In his book and speeches, Hitler adopted "Wagner's stylistic faults: painful repetition, crank tangents, offensive grandiloquence, emotion to the point of hysteria."[74] He even imitated the composer's vegetarianism and repeatedly visited his grave and attended Wagner festivals. In the midst of political conversations, Hitler would suddenly hum Wagner's music to himself. He declared, "What joy each of Wagner's works has given me!"[75]

Hitler's political creed emerged:

> What luck for governments that people don't think. Thinking may be done only when an order is given or executed. If this is different, human society could not exist.[76]

THE GERMAN ROMANCE AGAINST REASON

Hitler's romantic love of the irrational was not peculiar in Germany. As Langer put it, "It was not only Hitler, the madman, who created German madness, but German madness that created Hitler."[77] Author Elmer Davis explained that "three generations of Germans have been conditioned by [Wagner's] *Ring* operas to the conviction that the German Hero can never be struck down except by a stab in the back."[78] Author Peter Viereck thought that "one hundred years of romantic literature and philosophy made Germany more susceptible to Nazi concepts than any other country in the world, already long before Versailles."[79] And author Horst Von Maltitz perceived that in Germany, "The romantic antithesis which was strangest but was quite generally accepted was culture against civilization, that is, German *Kultur* against Western civilization." Von Maltitz thought that the romance of irrationality had deeply infected the German language: "The language did, in fact, come to reflect the romantic dominance of emotions and senses over rationality, and all the lack of clarity, certainty, and definition which this implies." He saw that "An important practical result of Romanticism, in the present context, was that it created a general climate of inexact thinking, an intellectual and emotional dream world, and an emotional approach to problems of political action to which sober reasoning should have been applied."[80]

As Ebert struggled to establish a rational democracy, which required both a government and an electorate capable of reasoning, Germany's irrational popular art of fantasy undermined his work repeatedly. There was, for instance, a vast outpouring of plays with nameless generic characters, such as "The Father" or "The Son," who "worked out their violent and rather unreal destinies."[81] Both the audience and the actors shouted to release their emotions; if a play aroused this kind of immediate emotional response, its performance was repeated. A typical German drama of the 1920s, such as the popular one about "Dr. Caligari," featured a "madman who shows the sane world to be insane"; such plays dramatized the fashionable idea that "there's no distinction between the world and a madhouse nowadays."[82] There were inane plays in which an actor would stand up and read from a newspaper while an electric bell rang so loudly that the audience could not hear what he was saying. Or an artist drawing pictures along a wall would be followed by a man who erased everything the artist had drawn.[83] One play of 1925, with the cheery title *The Merry Vineyard*, got tremendous applause and rave reviews. Because it mocked the Nationalists, riots broke out 63 times at its performances—largely demonstrating that riots helped a play's popular success.[84] On the other hand, plays by Bertolt Brecht damned Ebert and the

Weimar Republic, even during the period when the government was contributing significantly to the economic recovery of Germany and the freedom of the German people.[85] What the plays of both the German left and right shared was an attraction to wild, fantastic, dreamy experiences—and the audiences loved them. These theatrical fantasies did not offer weary citizens an escape from politics. They *were* politics—the politics of romantic negation. Dadaists, who dedicated themselves to deliberate irrationality in art and literature, posted slogans claiming "Dada is political." This "diverse and argumentative group"[86] was quite influential for a time. There were "accidental poems"—composed of random words picked up from newspapers—and "simultaneous poems"—verses put together out of different languages—and "sound poems"—made up of meaningless, newly invented words.[87]

A sculptor made art by tearing up scraps of paper, throwing them down onto a board, and gluing them wherever they landed. Jazz songs included "Yes, we have no bananas" and "Tomorrow's the end of the world."[88] Opera and symphony going were no longer typically serene experiences: a German observer attended an opening night in December 1925, at which "There were fist fights…angry challenges shouted across the orchestra seats and from the boxes, deriding laughter, boos, and hostile whistles that threatened for some time to overpower the small but, at last, vigorous group of believers."[89]

Even classical dancers went wild. For example, Anita Berber, originally a serious student of ballet, danced completely naked, took many lovers of both sexes, consumed quantities of cocaine, morphine, and alcohol, and showed up with a band of thugs at prizefights and bicycle races.[90]

Movies were extremely popular in Germany. In 1913, the nation had 28 movie theaters. Despite the war, the number of theaters had grown to 245 in Germany by 1919, and after that, they spread even more rapidly throughout the country.[91] Adolf Hitler, busy as he was, got into the habit of watching two movies every night.

Films were a completely new type of art. Films came on with "deep layers of collective mentality which extend more or less beyond the dimensions of consciousness."[92] The German government was quick to see film's propaganda potential. During World War I, the Military Press Agency distributed films designed to boost popular support for the war. From their perspective, "If the film's emotional impact created an irrational hatred for the enemy and equally irrational loyalty to the fatherland, it deserved praise."[93]

Early on in Germany, films from the Soviet Union, England, and the United States (especially cowboy movies) were the most popular, but after the war, Germany created its own distinctive film style. Sex was an important feature of this style. Many movies had racy titles—*Lost Daughters, Hyenas of Lust, A Man's Girlhood, The Loves Lost Pharaoh*.[94] The sex they portrayed ranged far beyond the ordinary. Pornographic debauchery helped sell movies:

> Debaucheries are often an unconscious attempt to drown the consciousness of deep, inner frustration. This psychological mechanism seems to have forced itself

upon many Germans. It was as if they felt paralyzed in view of the freedom offered them, and instinctively withdrew into the unproblematic pleasures of the
flesh. An aura of sadness surrounded the sex films.[95]

A second feature of German film style was spectacle used to debunk the
idea of progress in history. Psychological historian Siegfried Kracauer explains
why the nihilism of these historical films so attracted people:

> [T]he majority of people lived in fear of social changes and therefore welcomed
> films which defamed not only bad rulers but also good revolutionary causes.
> These films outrightly encouraged the existing resistance to any emotional shift
> that might have enlivened the German Republic. Their basic nihilism made them
> indulge also in images of utter destruction, which…reflected forebodings of a
> final doom.[96]

Most postwar Germans had an "aversion to realism."[97] Demoralized by
defeat, divided by political extremes of left and right, wracked by dizzying inflation that destroyed people's faith in the meaning of work and savings and property, Germans "eagerly tended to withdraw from a harsh outer world."[98] The
early German expressionist films such as *The Cabinet of Dr. Caligari*, presented
strange, distorted visions of a world. "Instead of stimulating critical thought and
encouraging audiences to contemplate democratic forms of social interaction, ex-
pressionist-style films drew attention away from everyday reality, focused it on
psychological phenomena, and promoted an irrational, conservative, and sometimes even apocalyptic world view."[99]

The violent irrationality that permeated German art was reinforced by
real events. Many Germans who watched movies at night joined street demonstrations by day. In March 1920, soldiers were marching through a city when a
small boy laughed at them. Two troopers stepped over and hit the boy with their
rifle butts and kicked him with their boots. The crowd was stunned into silence,
but then someone hissed at the bullies. Soldiers aimed their machine guns toward
the whole crowd and fired several shots, which hit several people. Then the soldiers turned away and marched on—singing.[100] Elsewhere at another time, ten
Red Cross nurses were seen carrying pistols, so, wrote a youthful soldier, "We
shot those little ladies with pleasure—how they cried and pleaded with us to save
their lives. Nothing doing! Anyone with a gun is our enemy."[101]

The violent emotionalism of German film, art, poetry, theater, music, and
even architecture in the 1920s and early 1930s helped to weaken democratic reasoning. As Otto Friedrich observed, "Once inside the legislature the brown-
shirted invaders [i.e., Nazis] enjoyed parliamentary immunity, and every subsequent debate became a scene of shouted insults, loud singing, and threats of
violence."[102] Eventually, Kracauer notes, "The surrender to the Nazis was based
on emotional fixations rather than on any facing of facts."[103]

Once Hitler came to power, Nazi romanticism infested all of German culture. Hitler's grandiose fantasies relieved people of the need to think. Nazi
philosophers often advocated myth with reasoning words, as did George Sorel:

"In the *course* of this *study* one thing has always been present in my *mind*, which seemed so *evident* that I did not *think* it worth while to lay much stress on it."[104] Sorel saw myths as ideal, "a happy choice," "not descriptions of things, but expressions of a determination to act."[105] Unlike information or logic, "A myth cannot be refuted, since it is, at bottom, identical with the conviction of a group…unanalyzable into parts which could be placed on the plane of historical descriptions."[106] For Sorel, shouting and singing were preferable, a wonderful alternative to argument.

Hitler concluded that ordinary citizens could hardly think:

> The receptivity of the masses is very limited, their intelligence is small, but their power of forgetting is enormous. In consequence of these facts [sic], all effective propaganda must be limited to a few essential points.…These slogans must be repeated until every last member of the public understands what you want him to understand.[107]

THE FANTASY OF JEWS AS DEVILS

The Nazis promoted one simple vicious idea as the answer to all of Germany's troubles: hatred of Jews. False propaganda was used to damn Jews for years, especially under the growing leadership of Hitler. Eventually, millions of Jews were killed or tortured by the government, one of the most horribly unjust and inhuman actions ever done. Germany's disrespect for the reality of history helped create conditions in which such terror could be marketed as justice.

Even as a young man, Hitler had been spouting anti-Semitism, though he claimed he had never heard his father speak against Jews nor had his teachers preached hatred of Jews. In his memoir, he claims that one day, he ran into a man with "a black caftan and black side-locks" and wondered "Is this a Jew?" After reading some of the anti-Semitic literature, he found that "Wherever I went I began to see Jews, and the more I saw, the more sharply they became distinguished in my eyes from the rest of humanity.…Later I often grew sick to the stomach from the smell of these caftan wearers." Staring at one, "I recognized the Jew as the cold-hearted, shameless and calculating director of this revolting vice traffic in the scum of the big city, a cold shudder ran down my neck." So "Gradually I began to hate them.…For me this was the time of the greatest spiritual upheaval I have ever had to go through. I had ceased to be a weak-kneed cosmopolitan and become an anti-Semite."[108]

Hitler began to attribute to Jews all traits of mind he considered undesirable. For instance: "Conscience is a Jewish invention. It is a blemish like circumcision."[109] He became obsessed with Jews. Author Walter C. Langer concludes that "In Hitler's case all his undesirable characteristics were projected onto the Jew."[110]

Thus Hitler rid himself of his weak-knee and his conscience by hating Jews. This gave him great relief. It also gave relief to many Germans to focus on one imagined cause of all their troubles: the Jews. For the ordinary German, battered by an incredibly rapid series of crises, from war and inflation to depression and violence, had developed neurotic anxieties, since most of these crises could neither be predicted nor avoided. So the almost mystical anti-Semitism preached by the Nazis seemed to cure the confusion and self-doubt that had arisen among non-Jewish Germans since the war.

Propaganda against the Jews was nothing new in Germany. It had been going on for centuries. For example, the medieval-minded Martin Luther had demanded that Jews' "assets be sequestered, their homes razed, their synagogues leveled, that they be driven off the roads…assigned to the mines and quarries, compelled to fell trees…in misery and captivity as they incessantly lament and complain to God about us." [111] Nor was perverse hatred of Jews peculiar to German history. In France and Spain, in Russia and elsewhere in Europe, murderous persecution of Jews had broken out from time to time. But only in Germany, in the second third of the twentieth century, did a government turn to total war against the Jews. Only the Germans conceived the idea of annihilating every last Jew on earth. What makes this so bizarre is not only that it happened in one of the most advanced nations on earth, but also that it happened in a nation where Jews were not that numerous and where they were known as assimilated and patriotic.

Early on in the 1900s, only about 600,000 Jews lived in Germany. In World War I, 100,000 of them served in the armed forces, 80,000 of these in the front-line trenches. Proportionally, more Jews (12,000) died in combat than any other German population. Thirty-five thousand Jewish soldiers were honored for bravery. After the war, more Jews came to Germany. Many succeeded in business. In 1924 in Germany by one account, Jews controlled 57 percent of the metal trade, 22 percent of the grain trade, and 39 percent of the textile trade. In Vienna, between 50 and 90 percent of lawyers, dentists, physicians, boot and shoe industrialists, newspaper owners, bankers, wine traders, cinema owners, and other businessmen were Jews. In Berlin, 50 percent of the members of the Chamber of Commerce were Jews, as were 1,200 of the 1,474 members of the Stock Exchange. Some non-Jews detested Jewish success. One told the British ambassador that "The mass of people are discontented because they find that they themselves are poor while the Jews are rich, and they ask, 'why has the government allowed this?'" Even the government included a remarkable number of Jews. In 1924, a quarter of the Social Democrats in the Parliament were Jews. [112]

Thus many Jews were visibly successful in Germany, and many other Germans came to blame their own economic difficulties on the Jews. One embittered survivor of the era complained:

> The 1920s were governed, in science, medicine, in culture, by the Jews.…The professors of the university were Jews. If a student was a Jew, he would get the best job. If you had a Jewish lawyer, you would win a case, but if you didn't, you would lose. And any job which promised to get money out of it was in the control of the Jews. For us, for the Germans, it was very bad. [113]

It became commonplace to insist that Jews were not true Germans. A German citizen who said "A Jap is a Jap, a Jew is a Jew," was challenged by a man who asserted "A German is a German." The citizen answered, "Of course, it's a matter of blood." [114]

THE EMERGENCE OF PRESIDENT HINDENBURG

The years 1924–25 saw three fateful events in Germany.

First, in 1924, President Friedrich Ebert was falsely accused by a local court of committing treason during the war. Through the war, "He had preached reason and moderation towards the enemy and had hoped for a negotiated peace,"[115] but he had never betrayed his country. In the postwar judicial system in Germany, however, leftists were far more often convicted than rightists of treason and other crimes, and were sentenced to far longer prison terms, so Ebert's innocence was no guarantee of acquittal. In fact, his enemies did not succeed in convicting him, but they did mortify and depress him: "The pain I feel in my heart is the worst....They have murdered me politically and now they want to murder me morally. I will not survive this shame."[116] Fortunately, the national cabinet unanimously declared their loyalty to him and he did not give up: "I have to fight for my honour. No, not my honour but rather the honour of the Head of State." He kept up his courage, in spite of "This flood of dirt that is rising up all around me!"[117]

Second, in December 1924, Hitler was released from prison.

Third, on February 28, 1925, President Ebert died. Surgery had come too late to rescue him from sudden appendicitis. At his funeral thousands of workers with black armbands marched, bands played, and politicians praised him. Throughout the nation, millions mourned the loss of this democratic leader.

German democracy survived Ebert's death. A national election for a new president was held and the different parties and organizations put up candidates among them. Seven candidates got votes, but because none received a majority of votes cast, a run-off was necessary. The moderates and Socialists came together and agreed on ex-Chancellor Wilhelm Marx for their candidate, the Communists put up their leader Ernst Thalmann, and the conservatives nominated the 77-year-old war hero Marshal Paul von Hindenburg. Because the Communists split the leftist-moderate vote, the conservative won: totals were 14.6 million votes for Hindenburg, 13.7 million for Marx, and 1.9 million for Thalmann.

President Hindenburg was a tall retired general who had been responsible for some early German victories in World War I. He had publicly called Germany's defeat a "stab-in-the-back" by the liberal democratic government. Hindenburg had been born in 1847, before a "Germany" existed. In 1925, though he sometimes grew sleepy and stumbled over his speech texts, he was well respected. Some said that with his election, "We have witnessed the *birth* of the German Republic." As the constitution required, Hindenburg swore the oath of office before the parliament, and gave a speech emphasizing "the constitution's *republican* and *democratic* character."[118] Friedrich Ebert's heritage lived on through the 1920s and into the 1930s with national elections held regularly.

Marshall Paul von Hindenburg.

PROPAGANDA DESTROYS DEMOCRACY:
HITLER'S PAUL JOSEPH GOEBBELS

In 1924–25, the Nazi Party had only some 27,000 followers, and therefore was not powerful enough to win the election. After Hitler was released from jail in 1925, however, the party was revitalized through Hitler's theatrical speeches and the remarkable propaganda talents of Paul Joseph Goebbels.

Goebbels was a short man with a harshly deformed foot that made him limp. As a teenager in 1914, he had been rejected for service in the army because of his bad foot. That rejection—which he should have anticipated—broke his heart. He locked himself in his room. His mother pleaded to come in, but he refused to open the door to her. He cried loudly and refused food all that day. But then he did come out, and he survived. This was the pattern of behavior Goebbels followed much of his life. As his biographer Helmut Heiber wrote:

> His despair and disappointment were genuine; the young man had fooled himself, had believed what he wanted to believe and had been torn from the absurd illusionary world of his fantasy. There would be many other such scenes in his life, when the dreamer needed help in order to regain contact with reality. [119]

The young Goebbels wrote in his diary that "Life is shit." But in school, he was usually near the top of his class. He did especially well in religion classes, and his Catholic parents wanted him to become a priest. Like Hitler, Goebbels rejected the world; but where Hitler had turned to art, Goebbels turned to literature. He became a man of letters. After moving from one university to many others, he eventually finished a dissertation entitled "Wilhelm von Schutz as Dramatist: A Contribution to the History of the Drama of the Romantic School." He thought that "the spirit of our time and the spirit of the early Romantic period are brothers."[120] He chose to quote Dostoevski: "Reason and knowledge have always played a secondary, subordinate, auxiliary role in the lives of peoples, and this will always be the case."[121]

Like Hitler, Goebbels rebelled against his parents, separating himself from them and repudiating the Catholic Church. Goebbels wrote a novel titled *Michael* that damned ordinary religion and stated that life "has nothing to do with either knowledge or education."[122] Graduating from a university at age 24, in 1921, as a Herr Doktor—a titled intellectual doctor—Goebbels stayed at home and wrote plays, essays, articles, and even poems with such moody titles as "Deep in Dreams I Wandered the Dark Wood."[123]

Goebbels made his first foray into politics as a speaker before a bunch of Communists. When they shouted that he was nothing but a "capitalist pig," he pulled out his billfold and showed it empty of money—which got their attention. His writing was not accepted for publication, so he became managing editor of a Nazi *National Socialist Letters*, but he proved a poor manager. By contrast, Goebbels' speechmaking improved, gaining him impressive attention and applause. He even once claimed that "If I had told them to jump from the fourth-floor window, they would have done so."[124]

In 1925, he saw Hitler. For a while he disliked him: once he even shouted "I demand that the petty bourgeois Adolf Hitler be expelled from the Nazi Party!" But then he heard Hitler speak, and his attitude changed. To Hitler he wrote, "Like a rising star you appeared before our wondering eyes, you performed miracles to clear our minds and, in a world of skepticism and desperation, gave us faith."[125] Goebbels was so taken, he gushed, "Adolf Hitler, I love you, because you are both great and simple."[126] So Hitler recruited Goebbels as his propaganda chief. Goebbels had shifted from Communism to Nazism. He declared that "True National Socialism is instinct, not knowledge."[127]

Goebbels developed his own type of shock speech. Once he was speaking in a crowded hall where Nazi and Communist factions smashed at each other. Goebbels got ten wounded Nazis brought up front to bleed and groan while he railed against the "Red mob."[128] Taking advantage of his limp, Goebbels would refer to "Those of us who were shot up in the war,"[129] implying that he had been crippled by a war wound.

But Goebbels found his true calling as the Nazi's strategist and tactician for winning public support. In the election of 1924, a Nazi-type organization, called the "Freedom Movement," lost 18 of the 32 parliamentary seats it had held. Goebbels took that setback as a challenge: "The battle is fought, and now the bugle summons us to rally our strength. There's no use denying it: we lost this battle, and the enemy conquered all along the line." To win in the future, he exhorted, "is worth any sacrifice, even the sacrifice of lives and property!" To Goebbels, the defeat was actually good news—he said, "We have every reason to welcome the results of this election"[130]—because it inspired future fighting.

Goebbels seemed to be a democratic advocate, appealing for the general public to support and elect the Nazis. He didn't want people to think about details. He didn't want them to think, period. "Life is an enormous monkey show,"[131] he said. And in appealing to those German monkeys—his fellow citizens—there was no need for reasoned argument: "One doesn't prove the obvious. One states it."[132] He believed that political success depended on one thing—the ability to use propaganda: "The most modern of all political methods is propaganda….[o]nly propaganda becomes, as it works, unstoppable." Truth never entered into Goebbels' calculations, only results: "The propaganda which produces the desired results is good and all other propaganda is bad….Propaganda is always a means to an end."[133] Hitler agreed completely. He condemned the "immorality of Weimar rationalism" and exclaimed, "Propaganda, propaganda, propaganda. All that matters is propaganda."[134] Goebbels constructed for the Nazis

Paul Joseph Goebbels.

a type of propaganda that reflected what he saw as the nature of the German public: "We were simple because the people are simple. We thought in primitive terms because the people think in primitive terms. We were aggressive because the people are radical."[135]

He seized on popular media: "Radio! Radio! Radio in the house! The German with his radio will forget about his occupation and his Fatherland! Radio!"[136] He determined "to see that the press be so artfully organized that it is so to speak like a piano in the hands of the government, on which the government can play...."[137] To arouse blind loyalty in the Nazi rank and file, he decided "to hammer the party faith so completely into the heads of the members that they can parrot it back in their sleep." Then they "will put themselves on the line with a blind fanaticism and a heroic willingness to sacrifice themselves." It does not work, Goebbels said, to try "to compete with Jewish literary cosmopolitans in flashy style and intellectual pyrotechnics."[138] Goebbels' propaganda required repetition:

> If someone reads a slogan once, he will perhaps laugh. However, when it is to be met on every corner, when it can be seen a thousand times on the poster pillars, on every available space on fences, in railroad cars and streetcars, and who knows where else, then the very omnipresence of this brief sermon exerts an appeal. In the end one is tempted, if only for his own peace of mind, to believe that which at first he was unwilling to swallow.[139]

Finally, propaganda must work rapidly because "It is necessary to keep the party breathless."[140]

Goebbels, who believed that "state power begins in the street,"[141] organized mass meetings, such as National Socialist Freedom Day. At one meeting, crowds of Communists showed up "to beat the murdering brown bastards to pulp," but instead, 83 of them were beaten up. Goebbels organized a mass meeting of 5,000 Nazis to hear Hitler for the first time. He started a new newspaper, in which he "didn't give a damn for objectivity."[142] He invented a new action for Nazis: team up and physically attack any "bold, presumptuous, and arrogant" Jews. When Goebbels' own bullies were arrested, he used it as a cause to protest. In 1928, few Nazis were elected, but Goebbels was one of them. Now, when charged with crimes by the government, he could claim parliamentary immunity. When he was physically attacked by Communists pushing at his car, he scared them away by firing blanks from his gun.

Goebbels was tireless. He set up a school to train Nazi speakers. When the Prussian state government prohibited Nazis from wearing their brown shirt uniforms, Goebbels got all of them to wear white shirts. When the police grabbed Nazis and removed their brown pants, the Nazis kept marching—pantless.

Through the 1920s, despite all this action, the Nazis failed to add significantly to their numbers or to make strong gains at the polls. But after the 1929 Wall Street crash, a worldwide depression spread out from New York City. Germany was hit hard. Banks collapsed in Berlin; in one year, unemployment more than doubled; in one week, five bankrupt businessmen committed suicide.

The chancellor resigned and the German parliament fell into confusion. Responsibility fell to President Paul von Hindenburg, a sleepy old man who was prone to mental lapses. Article 48 of the Weimar Constitution authorized the president, at a time of emergency, to seize complete power. But the 83-year-old Hindenburg hesitated.

ELECTIONS TO CUT DOWN DEMOCRACY

Goebbels did not hesitate. He saw the economic tragedy as a great advantage for the Nazis: "We'll conduct a campaign, the likes of which the big-shot establishment parties in the parliament have never seen."[143] Mass meetings spread throughout the country. Posters spread out and the party's newspapers increased their circulations tenfold. When the pacifist movie *All Quiet on the Western Front*, which berated Germans for starting the war, came out and angered Goebbels, he physically attacked it: stink bombs were thrown and white mice released in the theater. The movie was banned. Goebbels mailed out 50,000 small phonograph records of propaganda. He had a speech of his own filmed, to be shown night after night in downtown Berlin. Nazi propaganda films were sent to many movie theaters. And he built up a radio program for Nazi propaganda broadcasting.[144]

Germans swung over to the Nazis by the tens of thousands. The party had had only about 17,000 members in 1926. It swelled to 120,000 in the summer of 1929, to 210,000 in March 1930, and then to about 1,000,000 in the fall of 1930.[145] In the national election of 1930, the Nazis went from 12 to 107 seats which made them the second-largest party in the parliament. Their total votes exploded from 810,000 to 6,500,000. The Social Democrats lost seats, while the Communists won 77 seats.[146]

Why the Nazis suddenly appeared so attractive to the German electorate is uncertain. Clearly the economic crisis triggered fear and confusion, but why did so many fearful and confused citizens turn to the Nazis? Erich Fromm, author of *Escape from Freedom*, thought the lower middle class was swayed by "their love of the strong, hatred of the weak, their pettiness, hostility, thriftiness with feelings as well as with money, and essentially their asceticism." Wilhelm Reich, author of *The Mass Psychology of Fascism*, thought that the trend toward Nazism happened because "In its pure form fascism is the sum total of all the *irrational* reactions of the average human character."[147] And as millions of Germans saw their world crumbling once again, they were in no mood to be rational.

The Nazis saw the 1932 elections as their great opportunity. Unemployment had continued to soar since 1930. People were hungry and bitter. Goebbels said, "I hope to make the election campaigns this year into masterworks of propaganda."[148] He persuaded Hitler to run for president against Hindenburg. Goebbels distributed a million posters, 8 million pamphlets, and 12 million extra copies of the Nazi newspaper throughout Germany. He staged 3,000 meetings a day. Films were sent out. Trucks drove around broadcasting propaganda from loudspeakers to people on the streets.[149] On July 17, 1932, Goebbels rallied

120,000 people to come to hear a speech by Hitler.[150] Yet Hindenburg decisively defeated Hitler, 18,600,000 to 11,400,000 votes. Still, Nazi gains in the parliament that July were ominous. The party had surged from 107 to 230 seats, making it almost twice as large as the next largest party of representatives in the parliament, the Social Democrats. Hitler demanded that he be made chancellor, with full power under the constitution. President Hindenburg refused to appoint him. Hitler then threatened to use the Nazi dominance of the parliament to paralyze the government. In a strange, conflictual meeting, the parliament voted 512 to 42 that they had "no confidence" in the current chancellor, who had been attempting to form a government. The Nazi leader Hermann Goering led the opposition, insisting that "I am firmly resolved to maintain…the rights of Germany's popular representatives to continue to exercise their proper constitutional functions."[151]

President Hindenburg then dissolved the parliament and called another election the same year, for November 6, 1932. This time the Nazis lost some 2 million votes, their seats dropping from 230 to 196, while Communist seats rose from 89 to 100. But the parliament again rejected Hindenburg's chancellor. The president considered appointing Hitler as chancellor, but again refused to do it. Instead, Hindenburg worked with administrators to try to split the power of the Nazis. Hitler stormed against their attempt: "If the party falls apart, I'll put an end to it all in three minutes with a pistol."[152] He wept, as did Goering and Goebbels.

The Nazis continued their agitation, in the government and in the streets, and Hindenburg finally did appoint Hitler chancellor in January 1933. Goebbels said, "All of us are dumb with emotion. Everyone clasps the Führer's hand."[153]

Hitler immediately demanded a new election. The election was set for March. Goebbels figured that the Communists might again gain votes at the Nazis' expense, so he arranged a highly secret adventure to destroy them: he sent Storm Troopers to set the parliament building on fire—which they achieved—and then publicly insisted that the Communists had done it! Hitler used this shocking catastrophe to demand that President Hindenburg sign a decree "for the Protection of the People and the State." The old man was bullied into signing this decree, which suspended the Weimar Constitution guarantees of freedom of speech, press, and assembly; privacy of letters, telegrams, and telephone conversations; protection against house searches; and confiscation of property by the state. Another decree authorized the arrest of Communists—which resulted in the jailing of some 4,000 of them—and crushed the left-wing press.[154] The day before the election, Goebbels organized a celebration throughout Germany, which he called the Day of the Awakening Nation. Legions dressed in brown marched in every city and burned "freedom fires" on nearly all the hills and mountains, so that "all Germany seemed a single, enormous, flaming banner."[155]

In the March election, Hitler won 44 percent of the vote, but the Nazis still did not have a majority in the parliament. So Hitler created a Nazi majority by banning the Communists from the parliament and arresting their leaders. He then demanded that the parliament pass an "enabling act" authorizing him to rule by decree. It did, and German democracy was over.

The flag of the Weimar Republic was replaced by the Nazi swastika flag and the republic was replaced by the Third Reich. All political parties except the Nazi Party were declared illegal.[156]

Goebbels was thrilled:

> Now it will be easy to carry on the fight, for we can call on all the resources of the State. Radio and press are at our disposal. We will stage a masterpiece of propaganda. And this time, naturally, there is no lack of money.[157]

He insisted that the Nazis were devoted to the welfare of the German people:

> This Government is, in the truest sense of the word, a People's Government. It derives from the people and it will always execute the people's will. I protest most passionately against the notion that this Government is the expression of some reactionary will and that we are reactionaries....We want to give the people what belongs to them, albeit in a different form than has been the case under parliamentary democracy.[158]

This "different form" included the permanent suspension of individual and civil liberties and the takeover of citizens' minds. The sole purpose of Goebbels' new Ministry for Popular Enlightenment and Propaganda was to "work on people until they are addicted to us."[159] Hitler himself was clear that Nazi "culture" would be forced on all Germans: "We must not forget that all the benefits of culture must be introduced more or less with an iron fist."[160]

After the March 1933 election, the parliament met in a Berlin opera house to decide on Hitler's proposed Law for Removing the Distress of People and the Reich. This "law" gave the power of the parliament—including control of the national budget, approval of foreign state treaties, and the initiation of constitutional amendments—to the cabinet for four years. Further, the bill said that laws enacted by the cabinet would be drafted by Chancellor Hitler and "might deviate from the constitution."[161] Hitler prepared a calm and moderate speech in which he promised that "The government will make use of these powers only insofar as they are essential for carrying out vitally necessary measures."[162]

Despite Hitler's reassuring words, a dozen representatives of the Social Democrats had been "detained" by the police and outside the opera house, Storm Troopers were shouting "Full powers, or else!" Even so, the Social Democratic party's leader, Otto Wells, stood forth to declare their honor:

> We German Social Democrats pledge ourselves solemnly in this historic hour to the principles of humanity and justice, of freedom and socialism. No enabling act can give you the power to destroy ideas which are eternal and indestructible.[163]

Otto Wells's courageous allegiance to democracy enraged Hitler, who jumped up and roared at him:

> You came late, but yet you come!...You are no longer needed....The star of Germany will rise and yours will sink. Your death knell has sounded....I do not want your votes. Germany will be free, but not through you![164]

The Nazis cheered. The vote was taken: 441 for Hitler's proposal and 84—all Social Democrats—against. The Nazi members of parliament jumped up and shouted and stamped their feet. The Storm Troopers crowded into the opera house and burst into song,

> Raise high the flag! Stand rank on rank together. Storm troopers march with steady, quiet tread....[165]

On July 13, 1933, Hitler announced that 61 of his opponents had been shot to death.[166] On August 1, 1934, the day before President Hindenburg died, a new law transferred the powers of the president to the Chancellor.[167]

DEMOCRACY KILLED BY FANTASY

The German Republic established by Friedrich Ebert and his allies vanished in 1933. A decade of government by consent of the governed, with liberty and equality and the rule of law, was wiped out in one spring by Hitler. Germany—supposedly the world's most intellectual nation—became the world's most shocking tyranny. How could this have happened?

First of all, democracy had not been established in Germany by popular desire but by default: the German right, the aristocrats and the military, who had started the war, pushed off on the democrats in the parliament the responsibility for ending it on what turned out to be highly humiliating terms. Then they foisted on the German people the "stab-in-the-back" lie. So democracy did not get started in Germany on the best possible footing.

Second, twice in a generation, the Germans underwent devastating economic crises. The Weimar Republic mastered the first crisis reasonably well, but it did not seem to have a clue as to how to handle the Great Depression of the early 1930s.

Third, the Nazis masterfully manipulated democracy to kill it. Hitler used elections and the Weimar Constitution to take power *legally*, and once he had it, he proceeded methodically to wipe out or cow all of his opponents so there would be no possibility of free elections again.

Most of all, though, democracy died in Germany because of the rejection of reason. There was in German culture a deep strain of romantic irrationality, exacerbated by the social-economic crises of the time and exploited repellently but brilliantly by Hitler and Goebbels. Hitler's vicious ranting against the Jews, Communists, socialists, and democrats struck a response in a good part of the populace. Recall, the Nazis did succeed in getting 44% of the vote in free elections in the spring of 1932. Hitler openly condemned reason and offered a powerful appeal to "blood" and "will" to a susceptible people, a people who were tired of reality and wanted fantasy.

Once in power, the Nazis made Germany a totalitarian state. They tortured and killed their enemies, but always they reached out for the support of the masses through relentless propaganda. They killed democracy by eliminating from the government anyone who represented reason. And to make sure it stayed dead, they set out to erase reason from the minds of all Germans and replace it with emotions they defined as desirable. The essence of Nazism is a slogan invented by the Italian Fascist Benito Mussolini's official philosopher Giovanni Gentile: "We think with our blood." [168] This slogan was very popular in the Third Reich.

An essential program to secure the Nazis' future power was the conversion of German youth. Young Germans were taught to mistrust reason and idealize feeling and faith. Here is Reich Youth Leader Baldur von Schirach on the superiority of romantic faith:

> We interpret the National Socialist Revolution as the rising of German feelings against the arrogance of cold intellect. Its victory signifies the triumph of the soul over everything that is only mechanic....Faith has overcome doubt. It rules the lesser forces that dared to deny it. The motto of our lives must be Adolf Hitler's profound saying "Woe to the one who has no faith!" [169]

True education, focused on reason, could weaken Nazism. So an essential Nazi strategy was the takeover of education. Thinkers, teachers, and books deemed antithetical to Nazism were to be eliminated. On May 10, 1933, Nazi youths stormed into libraries and hauled away vast numbers of books Goebbels had identified as hateful. They piled them up downtown and set them on fire, dancing around and shouting "Burn Karl Marx! Burn Sigmund Freud!" and the others. Goebbels was delighted: "This is a strong, great, and symbolic act." [170]

Hitler used the Nazis' success with German youth to taunt his opponents. Speaking in 1933, he said:

> When an opponent declares, "I will not come over to your side," I calmly say, "Your child belongs to us already....What are you? You will pass on. Your descendants, however, now stand in the new camp. In a short time they will know nothing else but this community." [171]

In 1937, he brazenly declared, "This new Reich will give its youth to no one, but will itself take youth and give to youth its own education and its own upbringing." [172] From his youth, when he had revolted against the education his father wanted him to achieve, he detested learning: "Today we suffer from over education. Only knowledge is prized. The know-it-alls are the enemies of action. What is needed is instinct and will." [173] His hatred of intellect was matched by his glorification of physicality: "The whole education by a national state must aim primarily not at the stuffing with mere knowledge but at building bodies which are physically healthy to the core." [174] The nation, he said, "has to direct its entire education primarily not at pumping in mere knowledge but at the breeding of absolutely healthy bodies....especially the promotion of willpower and determination....and only as the last thing scientific schooling." [175]

Pro-Nazi "educators" wholeheartedly supported Hitler in redefining "education." His Inspector of National Political Educational Institutions asked,

"What good is a boy who is endowed with great intellectual gifts but who for the rest is a weak, hopelessly irresolute, and slack fellow?"[176] A school principal declared, "We German educators must rid ourselves altogether of the notion that we are primarily transmitters of knowledge."[177] Children as young as age two to six wore Nazi clothes, learned the new greeting "Heil Hitler!", marched to train as future soldiers, and prayed grace to Hitler before taking their meals. Upon joining Hitler's Young Folk, a boy would swear this oath:

> In the presence of this blood banner, which represents our Führer, I swear to devote all my energies and my strength to the savior of our country, Adolf Hitler. I am willing and ready to give up my life for him, so help me God.[178]

The boys in these Young Folk groups were given daggers to carry and trained in martial arts; the girls were trained at farms and in city households to become proper mothers. Both underwent the strictest discipline and were exhorted to practice "blind obedience" to their leaders. Students were informed upon graduation that they should "realize and keep in the bottom of their hearts that they are now dedicated to the Order for life and death and that they must obey it without question....[T]here is no road back....He who fails or would betray the party or the leader will be destroyed by this Order."[179] At age 18, to be accepted as a member of the Hitler Youth, boys had to swear to uphold Nazi dogma, which included the following:

1. The Leader is always right
2. Never violate discipline
3. Never waste time in idle chatter, not in self-gratifying criticism, but take hold and help....[180]

Youths to be trained as elite Nazis went to Adolf Hitler Schools for a course of intense Spartan discipline. After six years of Nazi rule, the number of university students in Germany had dropped from 127,920 to 58,325.[181]

Teachers had to get used to the new "deconstruction." By law, all teachers, from kindergarten through university level, had to join the National Socialist Teachers' League, which was legally "responsible for the execution of the ideological and political co-ordination of all teachers in accordance with the National Socialist doctrine." Teachers were required to be "the executors of the will of the party-supported State" and to swear to "be loyal and obedient to Adolf Hitler." Jews were forbidden to teach at any level.[182]

In elementary school, the primary topic was race consciousness: the celebration of the Germans as superior to all other peoples. Teachers of history had to lecture students to be "full of hope and faith that the German victory, the victory of Nordic humanity over Jewish-westish plutocracy, may not be too far away."[183] As William Shirer points out, "History was so falsified in the new textbooks and by the teachers in their lectures that it became ludicrous."[184] Geography teachers had to convince students to see a much wider boundary for Germany than was on the map. Teachers of biology had to focus primarily on sex education to protect the health of German youth. Physics teachers had to teach *German* physics. And all the teachers were to declare to students, not to engage in discourse. A teacher's manual warned that "National Socialist ideology is to be a sacred foundation: it is not to be degraded by detailed explanations or discussions."[185] Teachers who failed to obey were fired: by 1936, 1,630 professors and teachers had been dismissed.[186]

Teachers who bought into Nazi ideology taught students to hate democracy, especially that of the United States of America. The following scene was not untypical:

> The teacher launched into a devastating diatribe that made short shrift of the United States, that country which had joined the last war just to make money. He worked himself into an emotional fervor.
>
> He explained that during the centuries there had been many men and women who could not get along in Europe. Most of them were criminals and crooks, reprobates and renegades...undesirables. Whenever they tangled with the law...they got on a boat and went to the United States. There they married each other. The children in turn mingled with Jews and Negroes....There are many other weaknesses as a result of this lack of racial purity....Their government is corrupt. They have a low type of government, a democracy. "What is a democracy?"
>
> Answers of the students: "A democracy is a government by rich Jews." "A democracy is a government in which people waste much time." "A democracy is a government in which there is no real leadership." "A democracy is a government that will be defeated by the Führer."[187]

In 1938, the German government manual for upper-school teaching said under "Literature": "Of course, only such selections should be chosen as point in the direction of the New Germany, help prepare the new world outlook, or give instances of its innermost will."[188] The teacher was not to help students understand the author's purpose and perspective, but to warp the author's meaning to serve Nazi purposes and perspectives. A German professor explained how Nazi educators exploited and perverted literature:

> *Hamlet* was denounced as embodying the "flabbiness of soul" that the Nazis condemned in Russian writers like Dostoevski and Tolstoi, the "soft Slavic soul" that in Tolstoi even went so far as pacifism. So in Shakespeare I could assign *A Midsummer Night's Dream*, which in normal times I should not have bothered with, just so that I could say to the students, "The music for this was written by Mendelssohn. Your parents all know the music. Mendelssohn was a Jew. We don't play his music any more."[189]

The Nazi idea of education is eerily echoed in the recent fashion for deconstruction in American universities. This theory of criticism displays the same contempt for reason and reality the Nazis did. One of the most prominent deconstructionists of the 1970s and 1980s, Professor Paul de Man, wrote much Nazi propaganda in Europe in the 1940s . Because he dismissed reason as an illusion, de Man saw only two intellectual possibilities—"fictional discourse" and "empirical event."—and thought "it is never possible to decide which one of the two possibilities is the right one." [190] As one expert on the deconstructionists notes, "There is no doctrine of human rights in the literature of deconstruction," but merely "a methodology useful for attacking entrenched power and established thinking." [191]

William Shirer described the effect of Nazi education on students: "Though their minds were deliberately poisoned, their regular schooling interrupted, their homes largely replaced so far as their rearing went, the boys and the girls, the young men and women, seemed immensely happy, filled with a zest for the life of a Hitler Youth." [192] The Nazis relieved people of the trouble of thinking and decision making and responsibility. They removed all doubt, and in return for "blind obedience" provided thrilling spectacle and song, romantic adventure, the prospect of conquest, and the assurance of belonging to the "master race."

THE RESULTS OF NAZI DISHONESTY AND FANTASY

The results of Nazism were some of the worst in all of human history. Millions of innocent people were tortured and killed. It was a line of life of injustice, violence, abuse of power, and lawlessness.

The Nazis started war. The result was the death and damage of enormous numbers of people. For nearly two years, democratic England stood nearly alone defending the world from Nazi barbarism. With Western and Central Europe conquered, Hitler blitzed England night after night with bombing raids to terrify the population. This is one woman's memory of the experience:

> My husband once was coming home on leave through London. He was days late because he kept stopping at buildings, pulling out the dead. It was awful.
>
> I had four daughters, all except one born during the war. When I went to have one of them, we didn't have ambulances. I had to go out into the blitz with all the fires raging, to try to get a phone you could still use, call my doctor. He sent two men with a little truck, with a plank across it. I lay on it. There was no light and no signs, in case the Germans came. These two men were so hopeless, I almost gave birth in the truck. We fell down a big bomb crater and I almost tipped over. But you took it all in your stride. It looked as if you were going to live this way the rest of your life.
>
> When I had my third baby, I stood in the room and said, "please, God, if you're going to kill us with these bombs, let's all die together now, at night." One didn't know how many children to take under you, like a bird, put them under your wing. I thought if I had two here, and that one was over there, she might get killed and leave me with these two. You had to sort of lay on top of them, so that you'd all be killed together. Never thought I had it in me.
>
> I never thought I could sit and read to children, say, about Cinderella, while you could hear the German planes coming. Sometimes a thousand a night came over, in waves. We had a saying, [says it staccato] I'm gonna getcha, I'm gonna getcha. That's how the planes sounded. You'd hear the bomb drop so many hundred yards that way. And you'd think, Oh, that missed us. You'd think, My God, the next one's going to be a direct hit. But you'd continue to read: "And the ugly sister said"—and you'd say, "Don't fidget, dear." And you'd think, My God, I can't stand it. But you bore up. And I wasn't the bravest of people, believe me. [193]

But this was nothing compared to what the Nazis inflicted upon their greatest "enemies," the Jews. For years before he came to power, Hitler had attacked Jews in the most violent and disgusting terms. Once in power, he deprived Jewish citizens of their livelihoods, property, and finally, their lives. From all over Germany and every land the Nazis conquered, Jews were herded into cattle cars and sent to concentration camps to be slaughtered. Some were permitted to survive as slave laborers until they became too weak to work and the Nazis decided to kill them.

The famous CBS radio reporter Edward R. Murrow accompanied Allied troops as they entered one of these killing camps, Buchenwald, in April 1945. Murrow, his hands shaking, broadcast a radio report across the sea to the United States:

> ...Permit me to tell you what you would have seen, and heard, had you been with me on Thursday. It will not be pleasant listening. If you are at lunch, or if you have no appetite to hear what Germans have done, now is a good time to switch off the radio, for I propose to tell you of Buchenwald. It is on a small hill about four miles outside Weimar, and it was one of the largest concentration camps in Germany, and it was built to last....
>
> There surged around me an evil-smelling horde. Men and boys reached out to touch me; and they were in rags and the remnants of uniform. Death had already marked many of them, but they were smiling with their eyes. I looked out over that mass of men to the green fields beyond where well-fed Germans were ploughing.
>
> A German, Fritz Kersheimer, came up and said, "May I show you around the camp, I've been here ten years."...I asked to see one of the barracks....I was told that this building had once stabled eighty horses. There were twelve hundred men in it, five to a bunk. The stink was beyond all description....I asked how many men had died in that building during the last month....They totalled 242. Two hundred and forty two out of twelve hundred in one month....
>
> As we walked out in the courtyard, a man fell dead. Two others—they must have been over sixty—were crawling toward the latrine. I saw it but will not describe it.
>
> In another part of the camp they showed me the children, hundreds of them. Some were only six. One rolled up his sleeve, showed me his number. It was tattooed on his arm. D-6030, it was. The others showed me their numbers; they will carry them till they die.
>
> An elderly man standing beside me said, "The children, enemies of the state." I could see their ribs through their thin shirts. The old man said, "I am professor Charles Richer of the Sorbonne." The children clung to my hands and stared. We crossed to the courtyard. Men kept coming up to speak to me and to touch me, professors from Poland, doctors from Vienna, men from all Europe. Men from the countries that made America.
>
> We went to the hospital; it was full. The doctor told me that two hundred had died the day before. I asked the cause of death; he shrugged and said, "Tuberculosis, starvation, fatigue, and there are many who have no desire to live. It is very difficult...."
>
> We went again into the courtyard, and as we walked we talked. The two doctors, the Frenchman and the Czech, agreed that about six thousand had died during March. Kersheimer, the German, added that back in the winter of 1939, when the Poles began to arrive without winter clothing, they died at the rate of approximately nine hundred a day. Five different men asserted that Buchenwald was the best concentration camp in Germany; they had had some experience of the others....

There were two rows of bodies stacked up like cordwood. They were thin and very white. Some of the bodies were terribly bruised, though there seemed to be little flesh to bruise. Some had been shot through the head, but they bled but little. All except two were naked. I tried to count them as best I could and arrived at the conclusion that all that was mortal of more than five hundred men and boys lay there in two neat piles....

If I've offended you by this rather mild account of Buchenwald, I'm not in the least sorry....[194]

The Germans had dozens of other concentration camps in Germany and farther east, in Poland, where millions of prisoners were systematically gassed or shot to death and burned, or buried alive.

Subsequently, Germans who worked at these camps revealed some of their "scientific" experiments on prisoners. Here is how one such German tried out a new killing gas:

Early in August, 1943, I received eighty inmates who were to be killed with the gas Hirt had given me. One night I went to the gas chamber in a small car with about fifteen women this first time. I told the women they had to go into the chamber to be disinfected. I did not tell them, however, that they were to be gassed....

With the help of a few S.S. men I stripped the women completely and shoved them into the gas chamber when they were stark naked.

When the door closed they began to scream. I introduced a certain amount of salt through a tube...and observed through a peephole what happened inside the room. The women breathed for about half a minute before they fell to the floor. After I turned on the ventilation I opened the door. I found the women lying lifeless on the floor and they were covered with excrements.[195]

Some 200 prisoners were subjected to another experiment:

I have personally seen through the observation window of the decompression chamber when a prisoner inside would stand a vacuum [sic] until his lungs ruptured....They would go mad and pull out their hair in an effort to relieve the pressure. They would tear their heads and face with their fingers and nails in an attempt to maim themselves in their madness. They would beat the walls with their hands and head and scream in an effort to relieve pressure on their eardrums. These cases usually ended in the death of the subject.[196]

This is the barbarism that the Germans sunk to under the leadership of Adolf Hitler. This is what emotional political fantasy, carried to extremes, led to. Having read these accounts of the horrors of Nazism, please remember that these events originated in Germany's contempt for rule by reason.

Near the end of the war, with Germany on the verge of being conquered, Hitler shot himself in the mouth in the underground bunker where he was hiding from Allied air attacks.[197]

After the war, Germans themselves realized how awful had been the results of political fantasy and created an honest democracy that has lasted for half a century.

BIBLIOGRAPHY

ALLEN, WILLIAM SHERIDAN. *The Nazi Seizure of Power: The Experience of a Single German Town, 1930–1935.* Chicago: Quadrangle Books, 1965.

BULL, HEDLEY (ED.). *The Challenge of the Third Reich: The Adam von Trot Memorial Lectures.* Oxford: Clarendon Press, 1986.

BURNS, EDWARD MCNALL. *Western Civilizations: Their History and Their Culture,* 4th ed. New York: W.W. Norton, 1954.

CHILDS, HARWOOD L. (TRANS.). *The Nazi Primer: Official Handbook for the Schooling of Hitler Youth.* New York: Harper & Brothers, 1938.

CLARK, R.T. *The Fall of the German Republic: A Political Study.* New York: Russell & Russell, 1964.

COHEN, CARL (ED.). *Communism, Fascism, and Democracy: The Theoretical Foundation.* New York: Random House, 1962.

COLLIER, JO LESLIE. *From Wagner to Murnau: The Transposition of Romanticism from Stage to Screen.* Ann Arbor, Mich.: UMI Research Press, 1988.

CONWAY, JOHN (TRANS.). *The Path to Dictatorship, 1918–1933.* New York: Frederic A. Praeger, 1967.

DOBKOWSKI, MICHAEL N., AND ISIDOR WALLIMANN (EDS.). *Towards the Holocaust: The Social and Economic Collapse of the Weimar Republic.* Westport, Conn.: Greenwood Press, 1983.

ENGLEMANN, SUSANNE CHAROLOTTE. *German Education and Re-Education.* New York: International Universities Press, 1945.

EKSTEINS, MODRIS, *The Limits of Reason: The German Democratic Press and the Collapse of Weimar Democracy.* London: Oxford University Press, 1975.

EYCH, ERICH. *A History of the Weimar Republic.* Cambridge, Mass.: Harvard University Press, 1962.

FRIEDRICH, CARL J., AND ZBIGNIEW K. BRZEZINSKI. *Totalitarian Dictatorship and Autocracy.* Cambridge, Mass: Harvard University Press, 1956.

FRIEDRICH, OTTO. *Before the Deluge: A Portrait of Berlin in the 1920s.* New York: Fromm International, 1986.

FROMM, ERICH. *Escape from Freedom.* New York: Rinehart, 1959.

FUSSELL, PAUL. *The Great War and Modern Memory.* New York: Oxford University Press, 1975.

GOEBBELS, JOSEPH. *My Part in Germany's Fight.* New York: Howard Fertig, 1979.

HALLOWELL, JOHN H. *Main Currents in Modern Political Thought.* New York: Henry Holt, 1950.

HALPERIN, S. WILLIAM. *Germany Tried Democracy: A Political History of the Reich from 1918 to 1933.* New York: Thomas Y. Crowell, 1946.

HARTSHORNE, EDWARD YARNALL, JR. *The German Universities and National Socialism.* Cambridge, Mass.: Harvard University Press, 1937.

HEIBER, HELMUT. *Goebbels.* New York: Hawthorn Press, 1972.

HERZSTEIN, ROBERT EDWIN. *The War That Hitler Won: Goebbels and the Nazi Media Campaign.* New York: Paragon House, 1987.

HIRSCH, DAVID H. *The Deconstruction of Literature: Criticism After Auschwitz.* Hanover, N.H.: University Press of New England, 1991.

HIRSCH, HERBERT. "Nazi Education: A Case of Political Socialization," *The Educational Forum* 53, (1), Fall 1988.

HITLER, ADOLF. *Mein Kampf.* Trans. Ralph Manheim. Boston: Houghton Mifflin, 1971.

KAEES, ANTON. *From Hitler to Heimat: The Return of History as Film.* Cambridge, Mass.: Harvard University Press, 1989.

KOLB, EBERHARD. *The Weimar Republic.* London: Unwin Hyman, 1988.

KRACAUER, SIEGFREID. *From Caligari to Hitler: A Psychological History of the German Film.* Princeton, N.J.: Princeton University Press, 1974.

LANGER, WALTER C. *The Mind of Adolf Hitler: The Secret Wartime Report.* New York: Basic Books, 1972.

LAQUEUR, WALTER. *The Terrible Secret: Suppression of the Truth About Hitler's "Final Solution."* Boston: Little, Brown, 1980.

LAQUEUR, WALTER Z. *Young Germany: A History of the German Youth Movement.* New York: Basic Books, 1962.

LEHMAN, DAVID. "Deconstructing de Man's Life." *Newsweek,* February 15, 1988.

LIFTON, ROBERT JAY. *The Nazi Doctors: Medical Killing and the Psychology of Genocide.* New York: Basic Books, 1986.

LILGE, FREDERIC. *The Abuse of Learning: The Failure of the German University.* New York: Macmillan, 1948.

MARX, KARL, AND FREDERICK ENGELS. *The German Ideology.* Part I. New York: International Publishers, 1985.

MAYER, MILTON. *They Thought They Were Free: The Germans, 1933–1945.* Chicago: University of Chicago Press, 1955.

MITCHELL, OTIS. C. *Hitler Over Germany: The Establishment of the Nazi Dictatorship (1918–1934).* Philadelphia: The Institute for the Study of Human Issues, 1983.

MORRIS, WARREN B., JR. *The Weimar Republic and Nazi Germany.* Chicago: Nelson-Hall, 1982.

MOSLEY, LEONARD. *The Reich Marshal: A Biography of Hermann Goering.* New York: Dell, 1974.

MOSSE, GEORGE L. *Nazi Culture: Intellectual, Cultural and Social Life in the Third Reich.* New York: Schocken Books, 1981.

MURRAY, BRUCE. *Film and the German Left in the Weimar Republic: From Caligari to Kuhle Wampe.* Austin: University of Texas Press, 1990.

NICHOLS, ANTHONY, AND ERICH MATTHIAS. *German Democracy and the Triumph of Hitler.* London: Allen and Unwin, 1971.

NITZSCHK, V., AND P. WEIGT. *Friedrich Ebert.* Bonn: Freidrich-Ebert-Stiftung, 1968.

PERSICO, JOSEPH E. *Edward R. Murrow: An American Original.* New York: McGraw-Hill, 1988.

PEUKERT, DETLEV K. *The Weimar Republic: The Crisis of Classical Modernity.* London: Penguin, 1991.

ROSENBERG, ALFRED. *The Myth of the Twentieth Century: An Evaluation of the Spiritual-Intellectual Confrontations of Our Age.* Torrance, Cal.: Noontide Press, 1982.

SCHUMAN, FREDERICK L. *The Nazi Dictatorship: A Study in Social Pathology and the Politics of Fascism.* New York: Alfred A. Knopf, 1936.

SHIRER, WILLIAM L. *Berlin Diary: The Journal of a Foreign Correspondent, 1934–1941.* New York: Popular Library, 1961.

SHIRER, WILLIAM L. *The Rise and Fall of the Third Reich: A History of Nazi Germany.* New York: Simon and Schuster, 1960.

SPEER, ALBERT. *Inside the Third Reich.* New York: Collier Books, 1970.

SPERBER, A.M. *Murrow: His Life and Times.* New York: Bantam Books, 1987.

STEIN, GEORGE H. (ED.). *Hitler.* Englewood Cliffs, N.J.: Prentice Hall, 1968.

STERN, FRITZ. *Dreams and Delusions: The Drama of German History.* New York: Alfred A. Knopf, 1987.

SWALLOW, ALAN (ED.). *Readings on Fascism and National Socialism.* Denver: University of Colorado, 1952.

TERKEL, STUDS. *"The Good War": An Oral History of World War Two.* New York: Ballantine Books, 1984.

VIERECK, PETER. *Metapolitics: The Roots of the Nazi Mind.* New York: Capricorn Books, 1961.

VON MALTITZ, HORST. *The Evolution of Hitler's Germany: The Ideology, the Personality, the Moment.* New York: McGraw-Hill Book Company, 1973.

WELCH, DAVID (ED.). *Nazi Propaganda. The Power and the Limitations.* Totowa, N.J.: Barnes & Noble Books, 1983.

WELCH, DAVID. *Propaganda and the German Cinema, 1933–1945.* Oxford: Clarendon Press, 1983.

CHAPTER

12

Reason

Essential for Democracy

Fantasy is not always bad. Dreams can give us insight, visions can inspire hope, fiction can tell much about life, art can stimulate the imagination in healthy ways. Without emotion, we would not be human. Indeed, the desire to help other human beings is a matter of faith. But if the people suffer a fundamental lapse in reason and become dependent on fantasy, it can be disastrous, especially in the politics of democracy. Successful democratic politicians rely on reason. Ideally, the politician's time for fantasy is after work—a movie in the evening or dreams at night. Politicians primarily must read news and history and then, some weekend, perhaps a wondrous novel or a visit to an inspiring art museum. The crux is that fantasy can be a blessing, but we have to take care of the real world necessities through reason.

Democracy is not the product of a dream but of rational conclusions drawn from thousands of years of human experience. That long history shows repeatedly that fantasy can destroy democracy. Hitler's remarkable rise to power was not based primarily on force or totalitarianism or complexification of law, but on his success in warping reason. After he took authority under the constitution, he systematically abolished reason throughout German society. Education, philosophy, journalism and other communication media, political discourse and decision making—indeed, all rational processes in Germany—were taken over and twisted to serve Nazi fantasies. That part of German civilization that had been powerfully influenced by the Age of Reason was shut down.

Elsewhere, at many times and places, in a wide variety of circumstances, reason has been abolished from human affairs with shocking consequences for society.

LACK OF INFORMATION DESTROYED ANCIENT TROY

More than a thousand years before the birth of Christ, the Greeks fought a war for more than a decade. Their military, led by Odysseus, had tried time and again to breech the fortified walls of Troy, across the sea from Athens, without success. Then one day the Trojans looked out over their walls and saw an astonishing thing: the Greeks had given up at last and were leaving! They had set their military shacks along the shore on fire and had cast away the stones anchoring their ships at the beach. All the Greek ships were seen sailing away, filled with the fighting men who had been attacking Troy for ten years.

But left behind was an amazing sight: a huge wooden statue of a standing horse. It startled and intrigued the Trojans, to whom the horse was a sacred animal. They would have liked to take the great wooden horse into their temple, but it was so large it could not possibly be dragged through the castle gate. Some Trojans thought that since the Greeks had withdrawn, it would be safe to break the gate to the city, and even part of the walls, to bring that holy horse into their city.

Troy's King Priam was amazed at his good fortune. The war was over and the Greek attackers had left a grand gift! He and his council went out and glanced at the great wooden horse. They decided to bring it into the city and take it to the temple. But crowds of Trojan citizens who had been fighting against the Greeks cried, "Burn it! Hurl it over the rocks into the sea! Cut it open!" And the priest of the temple, Laocoön, called to them, "Do not trust it, Trojans; Do not believe this horse. Whatever it may be, I fear the Greeks, even when bringing gifts." [1] Laocoön took his spear and threw it as hard as he could at the huge wooden horse; it hit and stuck in the wood—and suddenly people thought they heard the horse moan.

But then the Trojan guards dragged in a Greek prisoner, Sinon, who said that the Greeks were escaping, but they turned against him and forced him not to escape with them. King Priam demanded that Sinon tell the truth about the wooden horse. The prisoner explained that it was indeed a respectful offering to their goddess Athena, and that the Greeks had made the horse enormous so that the Trojans could not take it into their city as a symbol of their final victory in the war. He warned the Trojans that destroying the great horse would be a profanity for which they would be doomed. If they took it inside, he said, it would ensure the safety of Troy. The crowd was beginning to believe him when suddenly two giant snakes sprang from the sea and killed Laocoön.

King Priam ordered the gate and wall torn down and had rollers line the ground so the horse could be dragged into Troy. As the huge horse was being towed forward, it jammed to a stop four times, and people thought they heard the sound of metal clangs inside it. Nevertheless, they hauled it into the city and over to the great temple. The Trojan citizens cheered. In great happiness that the long war was over, they began feasting and drinking. Only the king's daughter, Cassandra, dissented and in terror cried out, "O miserable people, poor fools, you do not understand at all your evil fate."[2] The happy drunks mocked her, saying her prophecy was "windy nonsense." Seeing that they would not believe her, Cassandra seized an axe and a torch and marched out to destroy the horse herself, but the people stopped her. The celebration went on well into the night, until finally the drunk Trojans dropped off to sleep, dreaming of peace.

They awoke to a different reality. In the middle of the night, Sinon crept out to fulfill the secret mission he had been assigned by Odysseus: he went over to the horse and opened its trap door. Out spilled a troop of armed Greek soldiers—including Odysseus. Some of them were nearly blinded by their long stay in that dark confinement, others were weeping. Though their muscles were stiff, they recovered quickly and ran through the city, opening all its gates, while Sinon waved a flaming torch to signal the nearby Greek ships to return. The ships had not sailed for home, as the Trojans thought, but only out of sight of the city. The ships landed and the masses of troops charged into Troy. The Trojan men, drunk and sleepy, were slaughtered, the women raped, the houses burned, and Trojan treasures stolen. Ironically, the Trojans found that the war was indeed over: Trojan heroes and families were butchered and the city of Troy burnt.[3]

After succeeding for years in defending their city against military invasion, the Trojans were fooled by a clever trick. All they had to do to save themselves from disaster was to walk out and open the wooden horse to see what was inside of it. Empiricism—checking out the facts—was essential to human survival long before the Trojan tragedy, and is still. No government can be effective unless it gathers real information and makes decisions based on that intelligence. This is especially true of military decisions. Again and again, government leaders have preferred to act on emotion and imagination rather than reach out for genuine factual information in making decisions for war or peace. The irrationality of so many wars in the past makes it essential in a democracy that the *people* demand accurate information.

A sudden and surprising threat can confuse leaders because they are not prepared for the unusual. There is not always time to gather the desirable amount of information before acting. But even in an emergency, there is enough time to use reason. Leaders who are in the habit of reasoning are much more likely to be able to size up a situation quickly and accurately then those addicted to fantasy.

SOCRATES DISCOVERED THE DANGERS OF RHETORIC

Fantasy can not only fail defense against an emergency, but can even create an emergency. Socrates, one of the most thoughtful humans in Greece, centuries after the Trojan horse crisis described himself as "the only or almost the only Athenian living who practices the true art of politics." He said, "Nor shall I be surprised if I am put to death."[4] In the end, the thinker, Socrates was brought to death, in part because of the politics in Greece.

Socrates.

The great surge toward the eventual birth of democracy in Greece was rhetorical. Not only was there a grand theater with seats for thousands, but speeches, long before any microphones existed. Speakers spoke loud and clear to reach out to the masses of citizens. But as Socrates revealed in his dialogue "Gorgias," the rhetoric was primarily fantasy.

The famous and very active rhetoric leader Gorgias told Socrates that "persuasion is the chief end of rhetoric"[5] rather than reason. Socrates asked if he meant that "the rhetorician need not know the truth about things?" Gorgias replied, "Yes, Socrates, and is not this a great comfort?—not to have learned the other arts, but the art of rhetoric only, and yet to be in no way inferior to the professors of them?"[6] Socrates disagreed: such "rhetoric, according to my view, is the ghost or counterfeit of a part of politics....Ignoble, I should say."[7] In caring primarily for how artfully they came across as speakers rather than for bringing people knowledge, Gorgias and his fellow rhetoricians, Socrates pointed out, were corrupting Athens. They clouded people's minds so the people could not see what was truly happening in their city:

> You praise the men who feasted the citizens and satisfied their desires, and people say that they have made the city great, not seeing that the swollen and ulcerated condition of the state is to be attributed to these elder statesmen; for they have filled the city full of harbors and docks and walls and revenues and all that, and have left no room for justice and temperance.[8]

Gorgias' young student Polus entered the discussion and, under Socrates' questioning, insisted that the great achievement of the speaker was to dominate the audience, to exercise force over them, even if that meant injustice or cruelty toward his listeners. Skill at rhetoric gave a man power; the greatest rhetorician could become the greatest tyrant because of the hold he exercised on people's minds. To lead meant not to inform people but to rule them through superior powers of persuasion.

Socrates questioned a third rhetorician, Callicles, who believed that rhetoric was a theatrical performance that gave pleasure to the audience. Callicles saw philosophy—the love of wisdom and truth—as foolish: "I feel towards philosophers as I do toward those who lisp and imitate children."[9] He admitted that Socrates was "a votary of the truth," but saw no use in truth for human happiness. Callicles insisted instead "that luxury and intemperance and license, if they be provided with means, are virtue and happiness," while "all the rest is a mere bauble, agreements contrary to nature, foolish talk of men, nothing worth."[10] Socrates hardly saw this view of happiness as shallow and wrong, as his question makes clear:

> Do the rhetoricians appear to you always to aim at what is best, and do they seek to improve the citizens by their speeches, or are they too, like the rest of mankind, bent upon giving them pleasure, forgetting the public good in the thought of their own interest, playing with the people as with children, and trying to amuse them, but never considering whether they are better or worse for this?[11]

In the end, after showing rhetoricians to be highly effective evokers of emotional response, but so in love with their own artistry and the power it gave them that they had no concern for truth or reason, Socrates offers another way. He implores his audience:

> Follow me then, and I will lead you where you will be happy in life and after death, as the argument shows....When we have practiced virtue together, we will apply ourselves to politics....Let us, then, take the argument as our guide, which has revealed to us that the best way of life is to practice justice and every virtue in life and death.[12]

Thus the saint of ancient political philosophy fervently presents the case for reasoned argument as a means of arriving at justice and virtue. Through reason, Socrates could see the great harm antireason does in politics—and even see how that disease could be cured.

THE FALL OF THE ROMAN REPUBLIC

A weakness for strong rhetoric was the Greeks' downfall. For the Romans, it was an addiction to the violent spectacle.

For centuries, the Roman Republic, though not like a modern democracy, was a remarkable government dedicated to the welfare of its citizens. In this, it contrasted sharply with Roman governments both before and after it. Edward Gibbon's classic work sums up "the deep foundations of the greatness of Rome":

> The fidelity of the citizens to each other and to the state was confirmed by the habits of education and the prejudices of religion. Honour, as well as virtue, was the principle of the republic; the ambitious citizens laboured to deserve the solemn glories of a triumph; and the ardour of the Roman youth was kindled into active emulation as often as they beheld the domestic images of their ancestors. The temperate struggles of the patricians and plebeians had finally established the firm and equal balance of the constitution, which united the freedom of popular assemblies with the authority and wisdom of a senate and the executive powers of a regal magistrate. [13]

This relatively good political arrangement eventually fell apart and then destroyed by Roman emperors. When the republic was replaced "The happiness of an hundred millions depended on the personal merit of one or two men, perhaps children, whose minds were corrupted by education, luxury, and despotic power." [14]

A major factor in the downfall of the Roman Republic was the ancient games called "gladiator circuses." These games started as rituals: men would fight, even unto death, in solemn sport to honor the memory of the dead. But over the years, the gladiator games became widely popular entertainment. As early as 358 B.C. 307 prisoners of war were killed in one circus. When the population of the world was much less than it is now, often 50,000, and sometimes even 200,000, citizens would show up to watch fighting done by as many as 10,000 gladiators and 10,000 animals. Over time, the games became more theatrical and spectacular, even including ships attacking one another in a big pond.

Augustus, the first Roman emperor, arranged gladiator circuses 66 days a year to entertain his subjects. Under later emperors, the circuses took place 175 days a year, or more. Thus spectators spent nearly half their lives watching these exciting bloody shows. They were profoundly affected: "Gladiators became so ingrained in the Roman mind and soul that all manner of strange superstitions proliferated around them." [15] The playwright Seneca noted how the games affected him:

> ...nothing is so damaging to good character as the habit of lounging at the games, for then it is that vice steals subtly upon one through the avenue of pleasure. What do you think I mean? I mean that I come home more greedy, more ambitious, more voluptuous, and even more cruel and inhuman—because I have been among human beings. [16]

The circuses kept the people amused and gave them a vision of life as exciting battle. Gladiators, including women and children, were forced to kill or be killed. Those who survived became heroes in the audience's imagination, and the losers' deaths were romanticized—which led to an idealization of the contest to the death. This idea carried over into Roman politics. In becoming ruler of the circuses, the emperor strengthened his rule over the whole nation. As the scholar Keith Hopkins notes, "Gladiatorial shows were political theater." [17] Some eight emperors actually fought in gladiatorial contests—always victoriously, of course—and increasingly the spectators divided into fanatical adherents of different gladiator teams. The circuses coarsened Romans' minds by accustoming them to brute killing of opponents in games. The spectacle of the fight unto death so filled the people's imagination that they began to regard it as entirely natural for political contests to end in the murder of the losing side. The circuses also led to centuries of warfare as audiences vicariously experiencing war in the arena began to hunger for it. So war became Rome's primary human adventure.

"Games were part of the political order," [18] and the kind of irrational sensibility the games induced was incompatible with the demands of a rational constitutional republic. When the games killed reason, the Roman Republic died.

THE ROMANCE OF KILLING CHILDREN

Today, in the media, and especially in movies, violence is displayed romantically. The theatrics of Roman gladiator circuses exemplify one of the most horrible effects of fantasy on democracy—the circuses led to centuries in which war became the primary human adventure. In the early thirteenth century, wars of crusade, extending from Europe to Jerusalem, were a religious romance, resulting in widespread battles and death. One time, even children took part in fighting the political–religious adventure. Their experience was tragic. Two young boys, one of them a shepherd, led crowds of children into Paris, chanting "Lord God, exalt Christianity! Restore the True Cross to us!" [19] They were accompanied by many adults. The largest group of children traveled far down the Rhine River and over the Alps into Italy, where many dispersed, with a significant group going on to Genoa. Some made it to Marseilles, where they were deceived by men claiming to offer them assistance. Instead, the child crusaders were put into two ships bound for North Africa—where they were sold into slavery.[20]

That children would be attracted to the adventure of a Crusade is understandable. But the adults who guided them on their tragic journey from Paris must have been deranged to hold the wild supposition that hurling crowds of young children against Muslim armies would end in anything but the children's slaughter. Centuries later, enormous numbers of children joined the Nazi Youth Party. They were guided by equally deranged adults who were so devoted to Hitler's romantic propaganda that they enlisted children in a crusade of conquest by the "master race."

War, portrayed as a grand human enterprise, has lured citizens away from dull troubles at home to great adventure abroad thousands of times. In wartime, "patriotism" is likely to shift from devotion to citizens' welfare to devotion to winning the war. Democracy is often suspended, "for the duration of the war," but typically when the war ends, the wartime dictatorship lives on. The romantic propaganda that governments so often use to enliven and unify citizens during wartime has repeatedly crushed democracy. Only infrequently have nations—such as the United States in World War II—maintained democracy even while the war was on.

WITCH HUNTS

In Europe, for two and a half centuries, propaganda and myths about witchcraft led to the execution of thousands upon thousands of people. Mass fear of witchcraft—what scholar Charles Mackay described as a "cruel and absurd delusion"[21] —began in earnest at the shift from the fourteenth to the fifteenth century, an unsettling time of change. Witches were burned throughout Europe. In Germany, 600 people, on average, were killed annually for the "pretended crime" of witchery. In France, Joan of Arc was burnt as a witch in 1431 after a trial by churchmen. In Switzerland, just in the years 1515 and 1516, 500 so-called "Protestant witches" were burned to death. In Scotland, some 17,000 witches were killed in 39 years. In some places, even children could be considered witches; on one occasion, 56 children found guilty of witchcraft were sentenced to punishment that ranged from imprisonment to being forced to run a gauntlet and being whipped publicly once a week for 12 months.

Many times, the only requirement for prosecuting a witch was an accusation: anyone *accused* of being a witch was determined a witch. At other times, in the interests of "justice," it was decreed that no one would be burned who did not confess to witchery. The accused was put on the rack, a torture mechanism that stretched a person's body until his or her mouth cried out the desired confession. Other techniques used to extract confessions were beating and whipping, gagging and smothering, often followed by filling the victim with whiskey so he or she would give up resistance. Torture often made the victim accuse others.

Obviously, torture destroyed truth. The victims were "so horribly tortured, that reason fled."[22] Frequently the confessions of the tortured were so wild that they surprised even the torturers. Some victims admitted that the devil had produced their children or that they had gone to church and seen a great black goat, who spoke to them and made them kiss him. A sexually exciting idea to torturers was the popular belief that a woman witch would not confess until the "mark of Satan" was found on her body. Children who were tortured often came up with the story that the devil had forced them to become witches. Imagination was stimulated by harsh pain.

Through those witch-hunting centuries, formal trial procedures were being invented, but using reason to arrive at justice was rare. Most of the victims were too poor and ignorant to be able to argue their innocence. Witnesses in witchcraft cases, in contrast to other cases, could be little children or senseless adults. And some trial procedures strike us as insane. For instance, under King James I of England, accused witches had their thumbs tied to their opposite feet and were wrapped in big cloths and laid out on the surface of a pond or river. Those who sank were declared innocent—which did them no good, since they were drowned. Those who floated were declared guilty—and were pulled out to be burned. Another test required the accused to recite the Lord's Prayer or the Creed, and if the slightest mistake was made, the person was considered a witch. Accused children had to clearly pronounce "Lord Jesus" or "Christ"; if they did not, they were found guilty. In some courts, accused persons were condemned if they could weep no more than three tears from the left eye. Others were weighed against the local church's big Bible: if they weighed less, they were guilty; if more, they were innocent. Very little evidence was needed to convict; anything a person said might be considered proof of guilt. When one woman who was accused of talking to the devil said that she had merely been talking to herself, her accuser triumphantly declared that only witches talked to themselves and she was burned. Other accused witches were required to reach out and touch a masked girl; if the girl began to shake—and most were nervous enough to do so—the accused person was guilty.

No trials were models of rationality in those days, but witchcraft trials were much more irrational than the norm—and purposefully so. As one French leader explained:

> The trial of this offence must not be conducted like other crimes. Whoever adheres to the ordinary course of justice perverts the spirit of the law, both divine and human. He who is accused of sorcery should never be acquitted, unless the malice of the prosecutor be clearer than the sun; for it is so difficult to bring full proof of this secret crime, that out of a million of witches not one would be convicted if the usual course were followed![23]

Mackay quotes one witch hunter, who titled himself "The Grand Judge of Witches," on the necessity for very loose standards of evidence. The crime of witchcraft was so horrible, he said, that

> a mere suspicion of witchcraft justifies the immediate arrest and torture of the suspected person. If the prisoner muttered, looked on the ground, and did not shed any tears, all these were proofs positive of guilt! In all cases of witchcraft, the evidence of a child ought to be taken against its parent; and persons of notoriously bad character, although not to be believed upon their oaths on the ordinary occasions of dispute that might arise between man and man, were to be believed, if they swore that any person had bewitched them![24]

At last in the seventeenth century, a Jesuit named Frederick Spee wrote a book exposing the madness behind the witch hunts and the idiocy of the trials. By the middle of the eighteenth century, it was generally recognized in Germany, France, England, and Scotland that witchcraft trials were a vulgar mistake. To be sure, the witchcraft insanity broke out from time to time in that century, but there was a new respect for reason that henceforth made madness in Western politics and judicial proceedings rather than the norm.

The witch-killing movement, once started, was hard to stop. For more than two centuries, this horror sustained itself simply because it had become the norm—an example of the irrationality of assuming that what has been should continue to be. In a democracy, traditional practice should be evaluated on the basis of how well it continues to serve citizens. Democratic government should not obstinately maintain the policies of the past simply because they are traditional.

The opposite style of political irrationality is the assumption that whatever is past is dead. The demand to reject lessons learned in the past commonly occurs during a widespread crisis, such as an economic depression or a massive health disaster. The mistake here is to suppose that the present is so different from the past that that *nothing* done before, with whatever success, can be repeated successfully in the present. This insistence on novelty can be as detrimental to political reason as rigid adherence to past practice. Clearly one of the appeals of Fascism in the 1920s and 1930s was its novelty; this was also true of Communism in much of the world in later decades. Perhaps the greatest irrationality of all is the destruction of an established democracy in favor of some radical mode of government.

DETERIORATION OF REASON SINKS THE UNITED STATES TO CIVIL WAR

The United States was founded during the Age of Reason. In the eighteenth century, reason was revered, not only in government, but also in the nation's schools and homes. But then in the nineteenth century, American cultural values began to change. A romantic movement emerged, and by the 1840s, "all the recognized values of orderly civilization were gradually being eroded," according to scholar David Donald.[25] In that decade, politician Henry Clay privately said that he "lamented the necessity, real or imagined…of appealing to the feelings and passions of our Countrymen, rather than to their reasons and judgments." But, though he regretted the need for it, Clay did make use of fantasy to gain election.[26]

The chief exponent of the romantic idea that only individual feelings could be trusted was the New England literary leader Ralph Waldo Emerson. He exhorted Americans "To believe your own thought, to believe that what is true for you in your private heart is true for all men—is genius." He assured them that "Nothing is at last sacred but the integrity of your own mind."[27] Emerson advocated rejecting reality: "Let me admonish you, first of all, to go alone; to refuse the good models, even those which are sacred in the imagination of men....Yourself a newborn bard of the Holy Ghost, cast behind you all conformity...."[28] Author David Donald saw that Emerson's views became popular: "Every aspect of American life witnessed this desire to throw off precedent and to rebel from authority."[29]

Emerson applied his imagination to government:

> In dealing with the State we ought to remember that its institutions are not aboriginal, though they existed before we were born; that they are not superior to the citizen; that every one of them was once the act of a single man; every law and usage was a man's expedient to meet a particular case; that they are all imitable, all alterable; we may make as good, we may make better. Society is an illusion to the young citizen. It lies before him in rigid repose, with certain names, men and institutions rooted like oak-trees to the centre, round which all arrange themselves the best they can. But the old statesman knows that society is fluid; there are no such roots and centres, but any particle may suddenly become the centre of the movement and compel the system to gyrate round it....[30]

Americans responded enthusiastically to Emerson's rejection of the reasoned principles on which the world's best government had been founded and began to crave the excitements of novelty and irrationality. The American of the eighteenth century was a thinking citizen concerned with coming together with other citizens to establish rule by reason. That American's idea was that government would make certain laws to ensure "life" and "liberty" and would leave citizens largely free to "pursue happiness" as they saw fit. The post-Emerson American was concerned with feelings and was concerned with change for change's sake. Ironically, in view of Emerson's emphasis on individuality and nonconformity, nineteenth-century Americans were prone to mass movements that preyed on their emotions. As David Donald notes:

> Huddling together in their loneliness, they sought only to escape their freedom. Fads, fashions, and crazes swept the country. Religious revivalism reached a new peak in the 1850s. Hysterical fears and paranoid suspicions marked this shift of Americans to "other- directness." Never was there a field so fertile before the propagandist, the agitator, the extremist. [31]

At least by the 1850s, imagination ruled northerners' and southerners' definitions of themselves and each other, and the country was split and weakened. As scholar Avery Craven notes, even today, "The ante-bellum South is shrouded in romance and hidden by the lingering clouds of abolition propaganda. Friends and foes have conspired to distort realities." From the North, southerners looked "indolent, licentious, intemperate, and overbearing." Since "Slavery was imagined, not investigated," southerners saw northerners as "haughty nabobs, intemperate and lax in morals, dwelling in great white-pillared houses, wringing wealth from those in bondage and sorrow, and seeking to destroy the best government on the face of the earth." Throughout the nineteenth century, "From decade to decade details were added to the fiction and the pattern stereotyped." [32] Slavery became more profitable and more morally troubling, so southerners turned to romance and mythology to justify treating humans as animals. But romantic mythology was also common up North: "Where argument and appeal to reason failed, the abolitionists tried entertainment and appeal to emotion." [33]

The prime example of northern mythology about the South was *Uncle Tom's Cabin*, a remarkable novel published in 1852 by an "oppressed and broken hearted" Yankee. Harriet Beecher Stowe's imaginary account of slavery in the South sold an amazing number of copies in the United States—nearly as many as the Bible—and quite a few throughout the world. Her novel was dramatized for the stage, where "it did more to make the theater respectable in rural America than any other single influence. The fictitious Uncle Tom became the stereotype of all American Negro slaves; Simon Legree became the typical slaveholder." [34] In both North and South fiction was preferred over news, drama over history, emotional appeals over reasoned discourse. In short, for Emerson's children, feeling was superior to thinking.

An outstanding exception to this trend was a lawyer named Abraham Lincoln. Lincoln emerged as a national politician by engaging in extensive debates and giving thoughtful speeches on the subject that was ripping the country apart. Lincoln cited history, not vaguely, but carefully, factually. He showed how the founders of democracy in the United States had tried to forbid slavery in the new national territories. He urged southerners to stop their "malicious slander" and northern Republicans to "strive to keep harmony in the Republic." But most strongly, he urged both sides to rely on reason. "Though much provoked," he said, *"let us do nothing through passion and ill temper."* Though he believed southerners were wrong about slavery, he beseeched the Yankee to "calmly consider their demands and see what will satisfy them." Lincoln wanted to revitalize true discourse, which he saw as an essential duty of democracy. Therefore, he proposed:

> Neither let us be slandered from our duty by false accusations against us, nor frightened from it by menaces of destruction to the Government nor of dungeons to ourselves. LET US HAVE FAITH THAT RIGHT MAKES MIGHT, AND IN THAT FAITH, LET US, TO THE END, DARE TO DO OUR DUTY AS WE UNDERSTAND IT.[35]

Alas, the Congress of the United States failed in its duty to rely on reason for making decisions. Consider the nature of the debates in that body before Lincoln's election in 1860.

Four years earlier, in 1856, in another presidential election, democracy itself was already under attack in America. The election debates centered on whether the territory of Kansas would or would not be allowed to have slavery. Emotions were so hot that some politicians even ridiculed the idea of elections in the territory. At a convention in the North, one politician told the audience:

> You are looking to ballots, when you should be looking to bayonets; counting up voters, when you should be mustering arms and none but armed emigrants; electioneering for candidates for civil rules, when you should be inquiring for military rulers....Political action is our greatest hindrance, because it delays the only remedy for the wrongs of Kansas.[36]

In the Senate of the United States, the chief leader against slavery, and the South's greatest enemy was Charles Sumner of Massachusetts. Sumner, who was famous for his startling rhetoric, had been raised in Boston by serious, strict parents. At college, he became known as "The Chatterbox"—that is, as "a first-rate declaimer, orator and public speaker."[37] When he went to Washington to represent Massachusetts, he found the Senate "a godless place." His leading opponent, Stephen A. Douglas, he described as "a brutal vulgar man" who "looks as if he needed clean linen and should be put under a shower bath." He grew depressed at the thought that "We have before us a long season of excitement and ribald debate, in which the Truth will be mocked and reviled."[38]

Douglas harshly opposed the idea that Kansas should be admitted to the Union as a free state. In response, Sumner spent two months composing a 112-

Senator Charles Sumner.

page speech entitled "The Crime Against Kansas." When he stood to deliver it, so many people filled the Senate galleries that the doors were blocked.

Sumner's approach to the controversy was accusatory and insulting. His opponents hoped, he said, for "the rape of a virgin territory, compelling it to the hateful embrace of slavery." He blasted Douglas as a manipulator of "apologies": Douglas's "Apology *tyrannical*" was backing the proslavery Kansas legislature. His "Apology *imbecile*" was denying the power of the president of the United States to stop slavery in the territory. His "Apology *absurd*" was a "poor mummery of a secret society," the so-called free-soil Kansas Legion. And Douglas's "Apology *infamous*" was succeeding in getting a New England outfit to hold back a supply of arms to Kansas abolitionists. Sumner's damnation of apologists for slavery was rhetorically fancy. He ended his first day of the speech by proclaiming, "I am proud to believe that you may as well attempt, with puny arm, to topple down the earth-rooted, heaven-kissing granite which crowns the historic sod of Bunker Hill, as to change her fixed resolves for Freedom everywhere, and especially now for freedom in Kansas."[39]

The next day Sumner continued his speech by pronouncing a *"Remedy of Tyranny,"* a *"Remedy of Folly,"* a *"Remedy of Injustice and Civil War,"* and a *"Remedy of Justice and Peace."* He condemned the proslavery stance of Senator Butler of South Carolina, declaring Butler "has chosen a mistress to whom he has made his vows, and who, though ugly to others, is always lovely to him; though polluted in the sight of the world, is chaste in his sight…the harlot, Slavery." He called Douglas "the squire of Slavery, its very Sancho Panza, ready to do all its humiliating offices."[40]

Sumner's rhetoric surprised and insulted many senators. Douglas, the primary butt of Sumner's attacks, muttered, "That damn fool will get himself killed by some other damn fool." But Sumner went on attacking Douglas, and Butler as well, who, he said, "cannot open his mouth, but out there flies a blunder." He attacked Senator James M. Mason of Virginia as one who "represents that other Virginia, from which Washington and Jefferson now avert their faces, where human beings are bred as cattle for the shambles."[41]

When Sumner finally concluded, the dean of the Senate stood up and pronounced his speech "the most un-American and unpatriotic that ever grated on the ears of the members of this high body." Douglas condemned the speech as "personal assaults and...malignity," as well as "classic allusions, each one only distinguished for its lasciviousness and obscenity." He then asked, "Is it his object to provoke some of us to kick him as we would a dog in the street, that he may get sympathy upon the just chastisement?" Senator Mason said, "I am constrained to hear here depravity, vice in its most odious form uncoiled in this presence, exhibiting its loathsome deformities in accusation and vilification against the quarter of the country from which I come...because it is a necessity of my position, under a common Government, to recognize as an equal, politically, one whom to see elsewhere is to shun and despise."

> Sumner faced Senator Douglas, declaring that he should "remember hereafter that the bowie-knife and bludgeon are not the proper emblems of senatorial debate....I say, also to that Senator...that no person with the upright form of man can be allowed—" and he hesitated.
>
> Douglas blustered: "Say it."
>
> "I will say it," Sumner went on; "no person with the upright form of man can be allowed, without violation of all decency, to switch out from his tongue the perpetual stench of offensive personality....The noisome, squat, and nameless animal, to which I now refer, is not the proper model for an American Senator. Will the Senator from Illinois take notice?"
>
> "I will," Douglas retorted; "and therefore will not imitate you, sir."
>
> "Mr. President," Sumner replied haughtily, "again the Senator has switched his tongue, and again he fills the Senate with his offensive odor."
>
> Turning finally upon Mason, Sumner reminded him that "hard words are not argument; frowns not reasons; nor do scowls belong to the proper arsenal of parliamentary debate."
>
> Reporters understood Mason to mutter: "The Senator is certainly *non compos mentis* [not of sound mind]," and the debate closed.[42]

Sumner's speech received much attention and much criticism. Even one of his Boston friends admitted that the senator from Massachusetts was "essentially a man of emotions and sentiments," and "it is very easy for him to believe anything to be true that he wishes to....I do not think he has a truthful mind."[43] Massachusetts politician Edward Everett thought that "Language equally intemperate and bitter is sometime heard from a notorious parliamentary blackguard, but from a man of character of any party I have never seen any thing so offensive."[44]

Other reactions were phrased less genteelly. A Tennessee congressman said that "Mr. Sumner ought to be knocked down, and his face jumped into." Congressman Preston S. Brooks of South Carolina thought that Sumner had insulted his state, and decided to do something about it. He did not sue Sumner for libel. Nor, though he was a southern gentleman, did he challenge Sumner to a duel, because it was believed down South that that would have been too great an honor for Sumner. Instead, this 6-foot-tall, 170-pound, 36-year-old congressman went into the Senate, where he saw Sumner writing at his desk. Brooks asked the sergeant-at-arms to remove the ladies from the room. Then he walked with his cane over to Sumner's desk and spoke: "Mr. Sumner." Sumner looked up. Brooks said, "I have read your speech twice very carefully. It is a libel on South Carolina, and Mr. Butler, who is a relative of mine—." As Sumner started to stand up, Brooks, in the chamber of the Senate of the United States, lifted his cane and whacked the senator. He beat Sumner faster and harder, smashing him until blood filled his eyes. Sumner struggled to get up, grabbing his desk so hard he broke it off the floor. He stumbled down the aisle, but Brooks kept beating him hard. Sumner bumped across other desks and fell down. Brooks grabbed the label of Sumner's coat and beat him straight on. Smashed by about 30 blows, Sumner fell unconscious.

Kentucky Senator Crittendon ran up and, shocked by "such violence in the Senate chamber," yelled, "Don't kill him!" Brooks said, "I did not intend to kill him, but I did intend to whip him." Representative Keitt from South Carolina held up his own cane against Crittendon and yelled, "Let them alone, God damn you." A doctor hurried in and stitched Sumner's bleeding wounds. The scene was over.

When Sumner regained consciousness, he said, "I could not believe that a thing like this was possible." Brooks was arrested, but upon paying $500 bail, he was let free. The Senate decided that it could not act against him because he was a representative. Eventually, all Brooks suffered was a fine of $300 for his brutal crime. Senator Sumner was so badly hurt he stayed out of the Senate for three years.

This violent event shocked and thrilled the public. Politicians split strongly, North versus South, over the incident. A Massachusetts leader said Brooks' attack was to be condemned "not only as a cowardly assault upon a defenseless man, but as a crime against the right of free speech and the dignity of a free State."[45] Southern leaders sent Brooks a new cane inscribed "Hit him again," and the governor of South Carolina and students at the University of Virginia sent him other new canes. A Louisiana applauder wrote, "Were I in the House I should certainly propose a vote of thanks to Mr. Brooks."[46] In the House and Senate, speakers yelled threats and insults at one another, such as "You are a liar!"

So, a few years before the Civil War, reasonable discussion became impossible in the Congress of the United States. In the Senate and House of Representatives, whose members were elected by the people to come together, gather the facts, and rationally discuss and decide the policy of the nation, but emotional mythology, melodrama, and revenge prevailed. Congress continued to meet and to vote, but the serious business of the nation was no longer seriously addressed. In a sense, there was no longer a Congress of the United States. As this supposedly democratic parliament declined into irrational warring camps, it helped to excite violence throughout the nation.

Sumner's rhetorical violence led to Brooks' physical violence. The fashion of ridiculing reason and appealing to emotion led to American democracy's worst failure, the Civil War. Historians Randall and Craven concluded "that the Civil War was caused by the irresponsible emotionalism of politics far out of proportion to the real problems involved."[47]

POLITICAL IGNORANCE

Even today, some democracies are seriously failing to serve human welfare because of the decline of reason. Consider modern Mexico. That nation's turn to democracy has been a blessing to Mexicans, bringing relative peace and stability compared to other Central and Latin American nations. But Mexican politics have been thoroughly dominated for decades by one political party—though two others, a leftist and a rightist party, have begun to seriously compete in elections.

Accurate information is a basic requirement for citizens in a democracy so that they can take rational responsibility for the direction of their government. For this, a free press is essential. Officially, the Mexican government does not censor the nation's press. But in fact, political reasoning in Mexico has long been hampered by complicated relationships between the government and the media. Authors Benjamin Barber and Patrick Watson point out that when thousands of Mexicans protested against government policies before the 1968 Olympic Games, Mexican soldiers fired at them, killing up to 500 and arresting more than 5,000. But the government announced that only 50 had been killed, and this grossly false figure was printed in most Mexican "independent" papers. In 1971, police bullied students in another controversy, and the press hardly noted the incident. Journalists themselves have been killed from time to time in Mexico—perhaps 30 or 40 in the past two decades—a story sure to be headlined within a healthy democracy, but one not even reported in Mexico.

The Mexican government controls the news not by legal means but by economic means: by controlling supplies. The government has a monopoly on newsprint and ink. Further, the government supplies up to 70 percent of newspaper advertising revenues by purchasing ad space for government-composed stories—which are not differentiated from the newspaper's own stories, so that readers do not know their source. The government also supplies "bonuses" to the media—significant amounts of money—that naturally disincline editors and journalists to reveal government mistakes and government corruption. An English correspondent says, "Journalism in Mexico is prostitution." A few small, genuinely independent newspapers do exist in Mexico, but they are the exception. In general, the media do not try to inform Mexicans of the truth. Given these conditions, Mexico's extensive crime and drug business is no surprise.[48]

Even when the media are truly free, as in the United States, democracy will erode if the majority of citizens rarely bother to inform themselves about politics and history. Americans' ignorance of both is discouraging in a nation that pioneered universal education. And this ignorance preceded the blanketing of the country with television, which is often blamed for it. In June 1952, as Adlai Stevenson was moving toward the Democratic nomination for the presidency, 66 percent of the public did not know who he was or what he stood for. In 1955, only 33 percent of Americans knew who Karl Marx was and only 22 percent had ever heard of Sigmund Freud. Typically, less than half of Americans know who their representative is and only a bare majority can name even one of their senators. Far fewer know who has been elected to conduct their local government.

The ignorance extends to the institutions of government. In 1945, people were asked, "What do you know about the Bill of Rights? Do you know anything it says?" Nearly four out of five Americans could not answer. That same year, 55 percent did not know the answer to "How many Senators are there in Washington from your state?" In 1955, only 35 percent knew what the electoral college was and only 19 percent could give a correct answer to "Will you tell me what the three branches of the Federal Government are called?" [49]

Political ignorance has made Americans highly susceptible to political fiction. The president elected in 1980, Ronald Reagan saw himself as essentially an actor: "Politics is just like show business." Substance has come to matter less and less; the style of the political actor is what counts. In September and October 1988, shortly before a presidential election and after presidential and vice presidential debates, television features, and an enormous number of magazine and newspaper stories on the election, approximately one-third of the American voters did not know which Republicans were running together for the presidency and vice presidency, and roughly 50 percent did not know the pair of Democratic candidates. Shortly after that election, the new president, George Bush, was asked by a journalist how he intended to fulfill promises he had made during the campaign. Bush answered, "That's history. It doesn't mean anything anymore." In other words, Bush regarded his campaign promises, not as real commitments he would try to honor, but as fantasies he assumed would be forgotten. And in 1992, many citizens actively working for the presidential election of businessman Ross Perot did not know anything about his life or business, or even how to spell his name. To them, he was an impressive figure on TV whose major appeal was that he could "clean up the mess in Washington" because he knew nothing about politics.

Thus for a long time now, "government by the consent of the governed" has been weakening in the United States because the populace is too ignorant of even the simplest and most significant facts relevant to their political future to give their informed consent. Meanwhile, basic American education has so deteriorated that not even college graduates know much about the history of the democracy they live in. The deterioration of professional ethics among professors has contributed to the substitution of fantasy for knowledge. Certain professors teach fiction and claim it is history. In some courses, students get good grades only if they accept the professor's politics. These attitudes have helped to transform much of American political discourse from rational dialogue into theatrical assertions.

POLITICAL KNOWLEDGE

True history demonstrates that reason is fundamental to democratic politics. There will never be perfect government, but appreciation of rational government has grown in the second half of our century, along with understanding of the horrors of political fanaticism.

After Japan's defeat in World War II, a Japanese leader named Yoshida expressed the hope that his country would be successful in "adapting democracy to actual conditions."[50] He and others knew that popular education had to be reformed if Japan was to become and remain truly democratic. The Fundamental Law of Education, enacted in 1947, set as the goal of Japanese education "the full development of personality" and resolved to train people "who shall love truth and justice."[51] To keep partisan politics from corrupting the new Japanese democracy, another law was enacted, the Temporary Law to Ensure Observance of Political Neutrality in Compulsory Education Schools, which stated that "no one or no organization may instigate or incite teachers to support or oppose a political party or activity."[52]

Also in Germany after World War II, as scholars Dennis Bark and David Gress noted, "education becomes a crucial factor" in ensuring the longevity of the new democracy: "Perhaps the single most important task for the Allied occupiers in 1945 was that of restructuring the educational system at all levels, primary, secondary, and university. Without clearly defined educational policies, principles, and practices, no recently implanted democratic framework would last." The nation "basically agreed that purging the educational system was the most important task in the process of denazification and democratization."[53] Lucius Clay, the American scholar and army officer who administered U.S.-occupied Germany for four years after the war, wrote that during the occupation "much attention was given to the writing of new textbooks free from Nazi dogma and to the reform of the educational system so that even the poorest students would have the opportunity to finish high school and to undertake university training."[54]

In both those countries, there was freer and more reasonable journalism after the war, so that better-educated citizens could find out what was happening. The governments also used reason to press forward on recovery from the war and normalization of their societies.

Also in Canada, thanks to the achievements of governmental operators such as Mildred Naismith, knowledge became essential:

> Every public official uses records. They are vital to his job, for they provide information he needs to work with, they are evidence of his performance, and they protect his interests and those of the public.....Records are the means by which public officials in a democracy are accountable to the people. They are tools of administration, the memory of an organization, the embodiment of experience, protectors of legal rights, and sources of many kinds of information. They are often taken for granted, but they merit real attention if good government is to be realized.[55]

Democracy—forgotten for centuries, remembered when history was written as a true record of the past, spreading slowly in some eras, faster in others, rejected when fantasy ruled, and salvaged when chastened peoples saw what fanatical imagination could lead to in politics—is the only form of government that has worked *for* human beings. To keep a democracy, ordinary people must know the truth and be able to talk and write freely, the elected representatives must use reason to make laws, and administrators must apply policy rationally. As history surely shows, whenever access to learning and free discussion deteriorate, democracy is likely to collapse.

BIBLIOGRAPHY

ASIMOV, ISAAC. *Words from the Myths.* New York: New American Library, 1969.

ATKINSON, BROOKS (ED.). *The Complete Essays and Other Writings of Ralph Waldo Emerson.* New York: The Modern Library, 1940.

BARBER, BENJAMIN, AND PATRICK WATSON. *The Struggle for Democracy.* Boston: Little, Brown, 1988.

BARBER, JAMES DAVID. *Citizen Politics: An Introduction to Political Behavior.* Chicago: Markham, 1969.

BARK, DENNIS L. AND DAVID R. GRESS. *From Shadow to Substance, 1945–1963.* Cambridge, Mass.: Basil Blackwell, 1989.

CLAY, LUCIUS D. *Germany and the Fight for Freedom.* Cambridge, Mass.: Harvard University Press, 1950.

CONANT, JAMES BRYANT. *Germany and Freedom: A Personal Appraisal.* Cambridge, Mass.: Harvard University Press, 1958.

CRAVEN, AVERY O. *The Coming of the Civil War.* 2nd ed. Chicago: University of Chicago Press, 1974.

CRAVEN, AVERY O. *Civil War in the Making: 1815–1860.* Baton Rouge: Louisiana State University Press, 1986.

DONALD, DAVID HERBERT. *Charles Sumner and the Coming of the Civil War.* Chicago: University of Chicago Press, 1981.

DONALD, DAVID. *Lincoln Reconsidered: Essays on the Civil War Era.* 2nd ed. New York: Vintage Books, 1961.

DOWER, J.W. *Empire and Aftermath: Yoshida Shigeru and the Japanese Experience, 1878–1954.* Cambridge, Mass.: Harvard University Press, 1988.

GIBBON, EDWARD. *The Decline and Fall of the Roman Empire.* Abridged version edited by Dero A. Saunders. London: Penguin Books, 1987.

GRANT, MICHAEL. *Gladiators.* New York: Delacorte Press, 1967.

HOFSTADTER, RICHARD. *Anti-Intellectualism in American Life.* New York: Alfred A. Knopf, 1963.

HOPKINS, KEITH. *Death and Renewal: Sociological Studies in Roman History.* Vol. 2. Cambridge, England: Cambridge University Press, 1983.

JOWETT, B. (TRANS.). *The Dialogues of Plato.* Vol. 1: "Gorgias" New York: Random House, 1937.

KIELL, NORMAN (ED.). *Psychological Studies of Famous Americans: The Civil War Era.* New York: Twayne, 1964.

MACKAY, CHARLES. *Extraordinary Popular Delusions and the Madness of Crowds.* New York: Farrar, Straus, and Giroux, 1932.

OATES, STEPHEN B., *With Malice Toward None: The Life of Abraham Lincoln.* New York: New American Library, 1977.

REISCHAUER, EDWIN O. *The United States and Japan.* 3rd ed. Cambridge, Mass.: Harvard University Press, 1981.

RILEY-SMITH, JONATHAN. *The Crusades: A Short History.* New Haven, Conn.: Yale University Press, 1987.

SCHLESINGER, ARTHUR, JR. "The Causes of the Civil War: A Note on Historical Sentimentalism." *Partisan Review.* October 1949.

STOWE, HARRIET BEECHER. *Uncle Tom's Cabin.* London: C.H. Clarke, 1852.

STOWE, HARRIET BEECHER. *A Key to Uncle Tom's Cabin.* London: Thomas Bosworth, 1853.

TUCHMAN, BARBARA W. *The March of Folly: From Troy to Vietnam.* New York: Alfred A. Knopf, 1984.

13

The Story of the Creation of the United States of America

Democracy Raised Up

A group of English people sailing west across the Atlantic Ocean got lost. They were aiming for "Virginia"—which in 1620 was a huge territory extending as far north as New York—but the ship that carried them drifted toward Cape Cod, way up in New England, some 150 miles north of where the ship was meant to land.

This was significant, because the 102 English people on board the ship had contracted with the Northern Virginia Company to get land that they would control. The main passengers in the ship were poor Puritans, a group of religious dissenters who saw England as evil and felt they had to separate from it. Years before they had gone to Holland, but there they were unhappy doing hard work for low pay. So they dreamed of settling in Virginia, but they lacked money to rent a ship to carry them across the sea. At last they appealed to London merchants to finance their passage—along with "strangers" who would work for them. The Puritans took courage—one said, "It is not with us as with other men, whom small things can discourage, or small discontents cause to wish themselves at home again"[1]—and set out for this strange place called Virginia, along with the non-Puritan "strangers" who were looking to make a better living in the new land.

As the ship approached the cold land on November 10, 1620, the "strangers" noted they had been hired by the merchants to work for the Puritans in *Virginia*. Since the ship had obviously gone far off course, they insisted "that when they came ashore they would use their own liberty, for none had power to command them, the patent they had being for Virginia."[2] To preserve their authority, the Puritans demanded that all the male passengers promise before they landed that they would join together in this strange territory and agree, "being in the presence of God, and one of another," to

> covenant & combine our selves together into a civil body politick; for our better ordering & preservation & furtherance of the ends aforesaid; and by virtue hear of to enact, constitute, and frame such just & equal laws, ordinances, Acts, constitutions, & offices, from time to time, as shall bethought most meet and convenient for the general good of the Colonie; unto which we promise all due submission and obedience.[3]

Forty-one men signed the agreement—which was all the men aboard except for eight servants and one dying Puritan Pilgrim.

Later generations of Americans were taught that this group was a clear example of *creating* self-government through reasoned discourse and *establishing* reasoned discourse as the means of self-government. In recognizing the "presence" of "one of another," the community aboard that ship started the American heritage of democratic consultation among citizens who shared their thoughts and purposes, rather than simply sharing equal devotion to a king.

Had the Puritans made it to Virginia, they might have joined the chaotic tragedy of that colony. The first Virginians had come for gold, but they failed to find it. Instead, they discovered the economic possibilities of planting, raising, picking, and selling tobacco to England. Tobacco cultivation proved so profitable that thousands of people were attracted from England to Virginia. To maintain order, the Virginia Company

> decided to give the settlers a voice in the management of the colony. The planters were allowed to elect representatives to an assembly, which, along with the governor's appointed council, would have power to make laws for the colony.[4]

But thousands died, thousands returned to England, and in one year, 1622, the Indians in Virginia killed 347 colonists. Thus the program of the Virginia Company did not save the community. Virginia fell apart. The New England agreement at least helped Puritans to help one another as they struggled to survive through the terrible winter. But they did not even know how to get food from the sea. Forty-six of the 102 died that winter. Only 19 men survived.[5] Still, the New England colony lasted, though democracy died once the Puritan ministers took charge of government.

ANNE HUTCHINSON'S COURAGE FOR REASON

In 1634, a remarkable Englishwoman arrived in New England. Anne Hutchinson was the daughter of a minister who had been silenced for 15 years because he had called for an "able clergy." But Anne Hutchinson was not silent in New England. She spoke out. She gathered worried women in her home for religious study and discussion, treated their illnesses, and taught them that they were children of

TRIAL OF ANNE HUTCHINSON.

Woodcut showing Anne Hutchinson before the General Court.

God. Married by 1648, in her mid-40s, she subsequently gave birth to a dozen children and was now a grandmother.

But then she was brought to trial by Governor John Winthrop.

The charge was that she and her friends were tangling religion and holding unauthorized meetings. At the trial, in the freezing winter, Anne Hutchinson had to stand up alone for hours before her accusers in a building with no heat. Alone she confronted 49 "inquisitors." No lawyer, or even her husband, was allowed to assist her.

The governor opened the hearing:

> Mrs. Hutchinson, you are called here as one of those that have troubled the peace of the commonwealth and the churches here; you are known to be a woman that hath had a great share in the promoting and divulging of those opinions that are causes of this trouble, and to be nearly joined not only in affinity and affections with some of those the court had taken notice of and passed censure upon, but you have spoken divers things as we have been informed very prejudicial to the honour of the churches and ministers thereof, and you have maintained a meeting and an assembly in your house that hath been condemned by the general assembly as a thing not tolerable nor comely in the sight of God nor fitting for your sex, and notwithstanding that was cried down you have continued the same.

Therefore, we have thought good to send for you to understand how things are, that if you be in an erroneous way we may reduce you so you may become a profitable member here among us; otherwise if you be obstinate in your course that then the court may take such course that you may trouble us no further.[6]

Anne Hutchinson said, "I am called here to answer before you, but I hear no things laid to my charge." The conflict was joined:

> Gov.   I have told you some already and more I can tell you.
> Mrs. H.   Name one, sir.
> Gov.   Have I not named some already?
> Mrs. H.   What have I said or done?
> Gov.   Why for your doings, this you did harbour and countenance those that are parties of this faction that you have heard of.
> Mrs. H.   That's matter of conscience, sir.[7]

The governor wanted to quiet women. He interpreted the Christian Fifth Commandment, "Honor thy father and mother," as meaning only to honor the "fathers of the commonwealth." Thus he said, "We do not mean to discourse with those of your sex...." In contrast, Ms. Hutchinson thought a "clear rule" was that "the elder women should instruct the younger, and then I must have a time wherein I must do it." She challenged Winthrop: "Do you think it not lawful for me to teach men and why do you call me to teach the court?" The governor replied, "We do not call you to teach the court but to lay open yourself."

Still, the governor allowed her to call her own witnesses, which she did—four men. The first said, "I dare say she did not say all that which they lay against her." But one of the inquisitors, Rev. Hugh Peter, responded, "How dare you look into the court to say such a word." The witness responded, "Mr. Peter takes upon him to forbid me. I shall be silent." But the other three witnesses did speak up for her. Anne Hutchinson said to the court, "You have no power over my body, neither can you do me any harm." One of her allies agreed: "Here is no law of God that she hath broken nor any law of the country that she broke and therefore deserves no censure."

The governor decided otherwise. Because of "the troublesomeness of her spirit and the danger of her course against us, which is not to be suffered," he urged the court to vote to condemn her. They did, and he pronounced "the sentence of the court" to her: "you are banished from out of our jurisdiction as being a woman not fit for our society, and are to be imprisoned till the court shall send you away." Her allies in court and the women who had visited her at home were ordered to turn in "all such guns, pistols, swords, powder, shot, and match as they are owners of." Anne Hutchinson's banishment was delayed until spring, because the court decided "the snow-filled winter season was unsuitable for banishing a woman." They also permitted her to remain at home to take care of her seven children, aged one to seventeen.[8]

Free speech and devotion to reason had not yet been firmly established in America, but at least Governor Winthrop had proceeded against Anne

Hutchinson with evidence and witnesses, in public before a range of officials. And she had had the courage to argue in court, even though the result might have been her death. There was injustice—the reason for banishing her was not her thoughts and practices, but her gender—but at least the community had focused its mind on what she had actually done and said. She was not punished without a hearing, but as a result of a thoughtful process conducted by community leaders.

In the spring, Anne Hutchinson and her family traveled to Rhode Island, to a new community led by Roger Williams, who had also been banished from New England in 1635. He and Anne Hutchinson confirmed that Rhode Island was "the one and only colony where complete religious liberty existed."[9] It was even "the first American community to call itself a democracy."[10] Anne Hutchinson did not give up working for democracy. Speaking out time and again, she set a high example for shared reason, not only for women, but *including* women. Early on, she helped to reform and develop rational politics.

In 1643, Anne Hutchinson was killed by American Indians.[11]

A MOVEMENT FOR FREE SPEECH: JOHN PETER ZENGER

Thanks to the courage of a few individuals, early American political experiences included reasoned discourse. But those efforts did not give quick birth to democracy. A century went by in which reasoned law did develop, but reasoned discourse was far from the norm.

In 1734, a newspaper editor and writer named John Peter Zenger was arrested for criticizing the government of the city of New York, then a village of about 10,000 people, 1,700 of them slaves. The articles he published were often harsh. A law issued by the commission of government in New York in 1697 was the basis for Zenger's arrest:

> For as much as great inconvenience may arise by the liberty of printing within the province of New York, you are to provide all necessary orders that no person keep any press for printing, nor that any book, pamphlet or other matter whatsoever be printed without your especial leave and consent first obtained.[12]

Zenger, who was poorly educated, wrote simply in language understandable by all. He often criticized government leaders. For example he wrote:

> A supreme Magistrate may be conceived to injure his Subjects, if in his Dealings with them, he treats them either not as Subjects, or not as Men. The Duty of a supreme Magistrate respects either the whole People, or particular Persons; and thus much he owes to the whole People, that he procures the Good and Safety of the Community, according as Laws direct and prescribe. Therefore he injures the whole People, if he evades or suffer these LAWS to be evaded to their hurt.[13]

After Zenger was arrested, he said, "I had not the Liberty of Pen, Ink, or Paper, or to see, or speak, with People." He later recalled hearing the chief justice declaring, in the full court, *"That if a Jury found Zenger Not Guilty, they would be per-jured."* A lawyer named Andrew Hamilton defended him.

The crucial issue in the case was whether Zenger's accusations could be considered libel if they were true. In other words, is a writer free to tell truth? The government's attorney argued against freedom of speech, *especially* when it was true:

> Indeed, Sir, as Mr. *Hamilton* has confessed the Printing and Publishing these Libels, I think the Jury must find a Verdict for the King; for supposing they were true, the Law says that they are not the less libelous for that; nay indeed the Law says, their being true is an Aggravation of the Crime.[14]

Hamilton disagreed: "Not so neither, Mr. Attorney....The Words themselves must be libellous, that is, *false, scandalous, and seditious,* or else we are not guilty." He criticized the government's attorney for having "omitted the Word *false.*"[15] He also challenged the attorney's argument that the truer the criticisms, the worse they were: *"That Truth is greater a Sin than Falsehood."* The chief justice intervened to argue against truth being a factor in libel. He quoted from a book to support his argument: *"It is far from being a Justification of a Libel, that the Contents thereof are true, or that the Person upon whom it is made, had a bad Reputation, since the greater Appearance there is of Truth in any malicious Invective, so much the more provoking it is."* Hamilton said he hoped that "that Practice had been dead with the court," but the chief justice answered that "you are not to be permitted to argue against the Opinion of the Court."[16]

Engraving showing the trial of Peter Zenger in New York, 1734.

To his great fortune—and that of a rational press in America—Zenger was found not guilty. The jury's decision supported "the freedom of the press."[17] As author Livingston Rutherfurd concludes:

> The trial of Zenger first established in North America the principle that in prosecution for libel the jury were the judges of both the law and the facts. The liberty of the press was secure from assault and the people became equipped with the most powerful weapon for successfully combating arbitrary power, the right of freely criticizing the conduct of public men, more than fifty years before the celebrated trial of "Junius" gave the same privilege to the people of England.[18]

In 1736, Zenger wrote a 40-page account of his trial entitled "A brief Narrative of the Case and Trial of *John Peter Zenger*." It was circulated throughout the country and even sent to London.[19]

Zenger's strong effort to publicize free reason was a signal for the future. Democracy relies—forever—upon popular discourse. The liberty of the press, not fixed for sure in Zenger's time, would eventually turn out to be an essential commitment of the United States of America.

REASON IN GOVERNMENT: BENJAMIN FRANKLIN

An equally important aspect of democracy is rational *congressional* discourse. Politics is not the main work of citizens; they are otherwise occupied. Therefore the public's part in political discourse is largely limited to setting the general purposes or directions the government is to strive for. The people's elected representatives must gather detailed factual information and through logical discussion and genuine give-and-take create laws that express those purposes, enhance progress, and enrich the community.

The early movement for rule by reason in America was advanced by Benjamin Franklin, a staunch advocate of free speech and practical democratic government.

Franklin was born on January 17, 1706, in Boston, Massachusetts, two years after America's first newspaper, the *Newsletter*, came out. As a little lad, Benjamin gained experience with politics through the give-and-take discussions in his very large family: he was the fifteenth of seventeen children, and the youngest of ten sons.[20] His mother, he said, had "an excellent Constitution" and took good care of her children. His "ingenious" father "had an excellent Constitution of Body" and was "a mechanical Genius." Despite his great number of children, Benjamin's father paid him individual attention, taking him on walks about Boston. All the Franklins' children learned to communicate well—they had to in order to persuade the others into giving them what they wanted. Growing up amid such a crowd, Ben also learned the need for cooperation.

The mature Franklin wrote about his early life, telling stories of youthful experiences that had formed him. For example, young Ben loved to swim. One day he flew a paper kite up into the air, held the string with a stick, and settled

Benjamin Franklin.

on his back floating in the pond, so "I was drawn along the surface of the water in a very agreeable manner."[21] At age eight, he started school, but attended for only two years because his father needed him to do work at home. He failed arithmetic, but learned to love reading. The grown-up Franklin reported, "From a Child I was fond of Reading, and all the little Money that came into my Hands was ever laid out in Books." And "This Bookish Inclination at length determin'd my Father to make me a Printer, tho' he had already one son [James] of that Profession."[22] So Benjamin worked at printing all day, and then "Often I sat up in my Room reading the greatest Part of the Night...." He wanted to write poetry, but "my Father discourag'd me, by ridiculing my Performances, and telling me Verse-makers were generally Beggars; so I escap'd being a Poet, most probably a very bad one." He also enjoyed debating with "another Bookish Lad in the Town." When the boy moved away, Benjamin "put my Arguments in Writing" and sent the letters to his friend, which stimulated return letters. The experience of carrying on debates through correspondence taught him "Method in the Arrangement of Thoughts."[23] Benjamin became a vegetarian at age 16 because he read a book recommending that. His brother, James, who was ten years older, ran the major newspaper in the area, the *New-England Courant*. Young Benjamin desired to have his own writings published in that newspaper.

> But being still a Boy, and suspecting that my Brother would object to printing any Thing of mine in his Paper if he knew it to be mine, I contriv'd to disguise my Hand, and writing an anonymous Paper. I put it in at Night under the Door of the

> Printing House. It was found in the Morning and communicated to his Writing Friends when they call'd in as usual. They read it, commented on it in my Hearing, and I had the exquisite Pleasure, of finding it met with their Appropriation, and that in their different Guesses at the Author none were named but Men of some Character among us for Learning and Ingenuity. [24]

He wrote many more pieces that were published, still without his brother knowing he was the author. He signed each piece "Silence Dogood," whom he described as a woman who was "A hearty Lover of the Clergy and all good Men, and a mortal Enemy to arbitrary Government and unlimited Power." [25] Under this pen name, young Benjamin wrote what he was thinking:

> Without Freedom of Thought, there can be no such Thing as Wisdom; and no such Thing as Public Liberty, without Freedom of Speech....
> This sacred Privilege is so essential to free Governments, that the Security of Property, and the Freedom of Speech always go together....Whoever would overthrow the Liberty of a Nation, must begin by subduing the Freeness of Speech; a *Thing* terrible to Public Traytors. [26]

When at last James discovered that it was his younger brother who was writing the Silence Dogood pieces, he got mad at him. But then James, the formal editor of the newspaper, was arrested for "Offence to the Assembly" and was put in jail for a month. Upon his release, he was forbidden to run the paper, so he put Benjamin in charge. But tensions between the brothers continued, and Benjamin decided to leave Boston.

At age 17, he sold a few of his books and traveled to the city of New York. Finding no printing jobs available there, he went on to Philadelphia, where he not only found a job but also got to know "the young People of the Town, that were Lovers of Reading with whom I spent my Evenings very pleasantly." [27] Young as he was, Benjamin found employment with the governor. He returned to Boston on a visit, and his parents were glad to see him, but he determined to go back to Philadelphia. He made a trip to London as a young man and put out a pamphlet titled *A Dissertation on Liberty and Necessity, Pleasure and Pain*. He worked hard, remained a vegetarian, and "I drank only Water."

Sailing home from London, Franklin made some "resolutions" for leading his life: I grew convinc'd that *Truth, Sincerity and Integrity* in Dealings between Man and Man, were of the utmost Importance to the Felicity of Life, and I form'd written Resolutions...[and decided] to practice them ever while I lived." The most important of these resolutions was that "I may live in all respects like a rational creature." Other resolutions were: "To endeavor to speak truth in every instance; to give nobody expectations that are not likely to be answered, but aim at sincerity in every word and action—the most amiable excellence in a rational being." [28]

Back in Philadelphia, Franklin took charge of a major newspaper, *The Pennsylvania Gazette*, and made a point of covering politics. His view was that

> by the Dictates of Reason there should be mutual Dependence between the *Governor* and the *Governed*, and that to make any Governour independent on his

People, would be dangerous, and destructive of their Liberties, and the ready way to establish Tyranny....[29]

He had the newspaper print letters to the editor, such as one saying, "As you sometimes take upon you to correct the Public, you ought in your Turn patiently to receive public Correction."[30] He started a discussion club called Junto, and this club created North America's first subscription library. And he created a publication called *Poor Richard* which spread throughout America, selling more than 10,000 copies a year in three editions. *Poor Richard* included such pieces of wisdom as

> Kings and Bears often worry their keepers.
> He's a Fool that makes his Doctor his Heir.
> Beware of Meat twice boil'd, and an old foe reconcil'd.
> The poor have little, beggars none, the rich too much, *enough* not one....
> Approve not of him who commends all you say....
> The Golden Age never was the present Age....
> Love your Neighbor; yet don't pull down your Hedge.
> Love your enemies, for they tell you your faults.[31]

Franklin wanted to do more in life than just make money. Once he wrote to his mother that when he died, he hoped it would say "he lived usefully, [rather] than he died rich." The most marvelously useful thing in his eyes was to gain and spread knowledge. He became fascinated by the new science of electricity. In order to have time to pursue this and other interests, he arranged to have his printing business, newspaper, and almanac run by his partner, providing him 50 percent of the profits.

In the mid-eighteenth century, electricity was a mystery. Franklin searched deeply into it and made many practical experiments that he urged others to repeat. One was: "Place an Iron shot of three or four Inches Diameter on the Mouth of a clean dry Glass Bottle. By a fine silken Thread from the Ceiling, right over the Mouth of the Bottle, suspend a small Cork Ball, about the Bigness of the Marble...." He spent *four years* of his life working mainly on electricity. He especially began to wonder how lightning could be drawn down from the sky without blowing up houses and churches. Through a series of experiments, Franklin invented the lightning rod to save people from being struck by lightning. He also explored other sciences, including meteorology, the science of weather forecasting, and demography, the study of human populations. Like so many others in his century, Franklin shifted his interest from poetry to empirical truth; he found reality more intellectually exciting than imagination.[32]

During those years, Franklin was not at all disconnected from politics. Nor was he merely an observer; later in life he recalled that "I have always set a greater value on the character of a *doer of good*."[33] Franklin initiated a remarkable series of institutions in the colony of Pennsylvania: street guards, a fire department, a university, a city hospital, and the colony's militia. He was elected to the Pennsylvania Assembly. Most importantly, in the 1750s, he developed ideas about a country called "America." In that decade, Britain was sending many of its convicts to America (Australia, which later became Britain's major dumping ground for undesirables, had not yet been settled by the British.) Franklin wrote, "I understand that the Government at home will not suffer our mistaken Assemblies to make any Law for preventing or discouraging the Importation of Convicts from Great Britain, for this kind Reason, *'That such Laws are against the Public Utility, as they tend to prevent the IMPROVEMENT and WELL PEOPLING OF THE COLONIES.'*"[34] His ironic protest was clearly supported throughout the colonies, for he was recruited from serving as postmaster of Philadelphia to become deputy postmaster general of the North American colonies.

In the 1750s, the English began to fear that the French, with whom they were often at war in Europe, were seeking to take over the western areas of their American colonies. In 1754, the governor of Virginia sent a message, carried by a young Virginia military officer named George Washington, to the French, demanding that they stop penetrating the Ohio Territory. Franklin saw the French threat as especially dangerous because of "the present disunited State of the British Colonies, and the extreme Difficulty of bringing so many different Governments and Assemblies to agree in any speedy and effectual Measures for our common Defence and Security...." He thought that "Britain and her Colonies should be considered as one Whole, and not as different States with separate Interests." Franklin repeatedly observed the ineffectiveness of royal governors appointed to rule the colonies. They were arbitrary governors who frequently lied: "False Reasons seldom appear good, their Weakness is discover'd and expos'd. The Governor persists and is despised. The people lose their Respect for him, grow Angry and rude."[35]

Threatened by the French and Indians, the British government ordered its royal governors in America to convene a colonial congress in Albany to discuss defense. Franklin, convinced that the colonies had to make common cause among themselves before they could effectively make treaties with the Indians, suggested "Short hints towards a scheme for uniting the Northern Colonies."[36] His plan supposed that a British "Governor General" would rule, but that at least there would be a "Grand Council" of representatives of the colonies. The suggestion was accepted at the Albany Conference, but rejected or ignored by the several colonial governments, which preferred to remain distinctive and independent of one another. Therefore, Franklin's specific proposal failed. But his published ideas for the development of democracy did register in many minds in America.

Franklin thought that the colonists would be loyal to a national government and would willingly furnish funds and material for its defense. Americans were better able to judge how the military should operate in America than the British Parliament in London. He saw that royal "Governors often come to the Colonies merely to make Fortunes" and "are not always Men of the Best Abilities and Integrity, have no Estates here, nor any natural Connections with us...."[37] Franklin's plan for establishing a congress of the colonies was not based on some abstract ideology, but on practical needs for defense and political and economic cooperation. He thought that a "Plan of Union" made special sense because "The Colonies so united would have been sufficiently strong to have defended themselves; there would have been no need of Troops from England...."[38]

Franklin's plan for union was ultimately rejected by the British government, which saw it as too democratic, and by the colonial assemblies, which saw it as too authoritarian. As Franklin ironically noted, "Its fate was singular: the assemblies did not adopt it, as they all thought there was too much *prerogative* in it, and in England it was judged to have too much of the *democracy*."[39] Franklin returned from Albany to Pennsylvania, where, having been appointed a general, he led some 300 volunteer troops out into the western counties. Later, he sailed to England, became sick and recovered, and subsequently spent years in London and in Paris working to advance the American cause.

When Franklin finally did come home, he resumed his participation in the movement toward American democracy. He operated as an elder counselor for such relative youths as Thomas Jefferson, with whom he worked on the Declaration of Independence, and James Madison, whom he helped establish an initial Congress in 1780, where "Madison did everything he could to support Franklin."[40] But his essential importance lies in the wide, long, and intense influence he had on the minds of Americans. As noted by the scholar Francis Graham Wilson:

> The last half of the eighteenth century was one of the creative periods in social thought when the ideas of the next hundred years were taking shape....Benjamin Franklin was not only a colonial; he was a figure that illustrates admirably the transition in political ideas from the colonial period to that of the American Revolution."[41]

Another scholar, Henry F. May, thinks that "Franklin at times can fairly be called pragmatic, and there is a lot in his early writings that can clearly be labeled utilitarian."[42] Franklin's keen mind often leapt to humor: he once remarked that "to pick legislators on the basis of heredity is just as sensible as to pick professors of mathematics in that fashion."[43] But under that plain speech and humorous manner, Franklin was "perhaps the most learned man of his time in America."[44] He learned and thought, spoke out and wrote, like the intellectual that he was. He used his exceptional reasoning skills to think creatively about politics, to contemplate what would be entailed in establishing democracy. But he also used his remarkable mind in action to help establish representative, reasoning government. Had Franklin not lived, the probability of democracy developing in America would have been much less likely.

TO MOVE TOWARD INDEPENDENCE: THOMAS JEFFERSON

Benjamin Franklin helped inspire a younger generation who loved learning and whose own thinking stimulated American thinking. Thomas Jefferson, born in Virginia in 1743, inherited a love of knowledge from his father. "My father's education had been quite neglected," Jefferson wrote, "but being of a strong mind, sound judgment and eager after information, he read much and improved himself." [45] Jefferson's family had come to America from Wales and eventually moved to Monticello, in Virginia, that high hilltop with a grand view, where Thomas learned to enjoy nature: "Where has nature spread so rich a mantle under the eye?" he asked later, and declared, "How sublime to look down into the workhouse of nature, to see her clouds, hail, snow, rain, thunder, all fabricated at our feet! And the glorious Sun, when rising as if out of distant water, just gilding the tops of the mountains, and giving life to all nature!" [46]

His father enrolled him in an English school at age five, and then a Latin school at age nine. But when Thomas was only 14, his father died. To overcome his sadness, Thomas concentrated on school. He had already learned to read Latin, Greek, and French, and he began a deep and wide course of reading. He was especially impressed by John Locke's philosophy that humans are "by nature all free, equal, and independent." [47]

Though Jefferson focused most of his energy on reading books, he also enjoyed dancing and playing the violin. (Much later, he told his daughter to "Determine never to be idle....It is wonderful how much may be done, if we are always doing.") At the small College of William and Mary in Williamsburg, Virginia, he found "my great good fortune, and what probably fixed the destinies of my life." [48] This "great good fortune" was Professor William Small of Scotland, whom Jefferson described as "a man profound in most of the useful branches of science, with a happy talent of communications, correct and gentlemanly manners, and an enlarged and liberal mind." Professor Small, "most happily for me, became soon attached to me, and made me his daily companion when not engaged in the school; and from his conversation I got my first views of the expansion of science, and of the system of things in which we are placed." [49] Thomas studied some 15 hours a day, often until 2:00 A.M., when he would go to sleep to rise again at dawn. Each day he took a break from his studies to run one mile, but even during his vacations among family and friends, he spent nearly three-fourths of his time reading books. [50] To the Latin, Greek, and French he already knew, he added Spanish and Italian; later he even learned some American Indian languages. He also read many English thinkers.

Jefferson completed college in two years and went on to law school, where he greatly enjoyed "more rational and philosophical conversations, than in all my life besides." [51] Typically he liked to focus a conversation on the subject the other person knew best, in order to learn about it and go home and write up notes on what he had learned. He also kept notes on his homeland of Virginia. For five years Jefferson studied law, then practiced it for eight years, during which time he was engaged in 948 cases. [52]

As a young lawyer, Thomas Jefferson got to know Virginia government officials and their thinking, and at age 23 he traveled to Annapolis, Philadelphia, and New York to visit their legislatures. His thinking developed. In 1768, he was elected to the House of Burgesses, colonial Virginia's legislature. Though he grew up on a Virginia plantation where slaveholding was taken for granted, Jefferson

Thomas Jefferson.

could not reconcile his Lockean ideas of human freedom with slavery: "I made one effort in that body for the permission of the emancipation of slaves, which was rejected."[53]

The House of Burgesses at this time was hardly a real legislature because the British governor personally ruled nearly everything in Virginia. In Jefferson's first session, the burgesses (i.e., members) passed unanimous resolutions demanding the governor recognize that it was their own sole right to levy taxes on the colony, affirming the right of petition, and protesting against the sending of Virginians accused of crimes to England for trial. The governor officially dissolved the House of Burgesses, but that same day the burgesses reassembled in the Raleigh Tavern to consider their "distressed Situation." They passed a series of resolutions based on a paper presented by George Washington. Though power was still firmly in the hands of the British, the burgesses had asserted Virginians' rights to some extent. That fall the governor called a new election—in which Jefferson was returned to the burgesses.

In a law case in 1770, Jefferson argued that "under the law of nature, all men are born free, every one comes into the world with a right to his own person, which includes the liberty of moving and using it at his own will."[54] In another case that year, he again stated that "we are all born free" and therefore slavery was contrary to nature. But the court threw aside that argument.[55] When the colonial legislature met again, it reasserted its right to tax and to pass laws, but

Jefferson saw "nothing of particular excitement occurring for a considerable time." He joined with other young members who thought the older, leading men in the Burgesses lacked the zeal needed for progress. Jefferson helped persuade the delegates to agree that "the most urgent of all measures was that of coming to an understanding with all the other colonies to consider the British claims as a common cause to all, and to produce an unity of action." This led to the creation of committees of correspondence throughout the colonies.[56] Now the different colonies could share news and purposes.

In 1773–74, Jefferson emerged as a leader in Virginia, to some extent because several influential men, including some of his own close friends and relatives, died. In 1793, Bostonians rebelled against the British tea tax by dressing as Indians, boarding ships full of East Indian tea, and throwing the tea into the sea. To punish them, the British closed Boston harbor. News of that event and the British government's annulment of Massachusetts' colonial charter reached Virginia. An aroused Jefferson expressed support for Massachusetts. Fearing rebellion in his own colony, Virginia's governor once again dissolved the House of Burgesses, and once again the representatives assembled in the Raleigh Tavern. They decided to boycott tea and most other items sold by the British East India Company. The crucial resolution was that "an attack, made on one of our sister colonies, to compel submission to arbitrary taxes, is an attack made on all British America." They also directed the Virginia Committee of Correspondence to organize a general congress of all the colonies "to deliberate on those general measures which the united interests of America may from time to time require."[57]

At Monticello, Jefferson prepared resolutions to put before that congress. That "The several states of British America" should make their own laws, and "no other legislature whatever may rightfully exercise authority over them," was one. Another resolution protested that the colonists' "natural and legal rights have in frequent instances been invaded by the parliament of Great Britain." At the First Continental Congress, which met in September 1774, Jefferson's work, *A Summary View of the Rights of British America,* was widely circulated.

Jefferson argued that the mere fact that England had settled America no longer justified English rule over America. He pointed out that England itself was not ruled by the nations from which England's own settlers had come. Americans had the same right to make their own laws as the English had in England. Clearly, he thought, "the British parliament has no right to exercise authority over us." The English philosopher John Locke, a century earlier, had declared that men are "by nature all free, equal, and independent," and that therefore no one could be "subjected to the political power of another, without his own consent."[58] Jefferson understood that the nation could be controlled by force, but said, "why subject it to coercion? To produce uniformity. But is uniformity desirable? No more than of face and stature. Reason and persuasion are the only practicable instruments. To make use of these, free inquiry must be indulged...."[59] Though Jefferson appealed to the king of England to revoke Parliament's rule over America, he was careful to note that the king himself was "no more than the chief officer of the people, appointed by the laws, and circumscribed with definite powers, to use, and consequently subject to their superintendence." He described English government of the colonies as "a deliberate, systematical plan of reducing us to slavery." By contrast, American grievances would be expressed "with that freedom of language and sentiment which becomes a free people, claiming their rights as derived from the laws of nature, and not as the gift of their chief magistrate." For Jefferson, the bottom line was that "the god who gave us life, gave us liberty at the same time...." [60]

Many Americans were not ready for revolution in 1774. But the new Continental Congress did affirm the colonists' rights to "life, liberty and property," and called for the repeal of all acts that in the last decade had abridged those rights in the eyes of the colonists. Organization for opposition began. Democratically elected committees were created in all the counties, cities, and towns. Jefferson spoke up repeatedly. Still, the split from Britain was not yet certain.

In May 1775, the Second Continental Congress met in Philadelphia. Serious fighting had broken out between British soldiers and colonists in Massachusetts the previous month, and Jefferson thought that "The war is now heartily entered into." [61] He drafted a "Declaration of the Causes and Necessity of taking up Arms," and the Congress directed the raising of 20,000 troops, naming George Washington the commander-in-chief of this new Continental Army.

The king of Great Britain rejected the petitions from America and declared the colonies in a state of rebellion. News came to Philadelphia that more British troops were on their way to America. Jefferson, who despite British misrule still loved England, was "sorry to find a bloody campaign is decided on." During this time, his mother unexpectedly died, and he became ill for a month. [62] But he soon returned to Philadelphia, where he read Thomas Paine's *Common Sense*, a widely circulated pamphlet demanding independence.

THE REASON FOR THE DECLARATION OF INDEPENDENCE

Never a strong speechmaker, Jefferson was a great writer and communicator of essentials. He worked up a draft constitution for Virginia after studying the Declaration of Rights written by his fellow Virginian George Mason. When the Congress appointed a committee on June 11, 1776, to draft the new nation's Declaration of Independence, Jefferson was chosen for it, along with John Adams, Benjamin Franklin, Roger Sherman, and Robert R. Livingston. Jefferson proposed that Adams draft the declaration, but Adams said Jefferson should, because "I am obnoxious, suspected, and unpopular. You are very much otherwise....You can write ten times better than I can." [63] Jefferson's draft was altered somewhat by Adams and Franklin, and then by the Congress, but all his original initiatives, except for his condemnation of slavery, stayed in. Though the Declaration is a stirring document, Jefferson's purpose was neither artistic nor inventive. As he explained, he had "turned to neither book nor pamphlet while writing it," and "did not consider it as any part of my charge to invent new ideas altogether, and to offer no sentiment which had ever been expressed before." His purpose was, rather, "to place before mankind the common sense of the subject, in terms so plain and firm as to command their assent." The Declaration "was intended to be an expression of the American mind." [64] And "the question was not whether, by a Declaration of Independence, we should make ourselves what we are not; but whether we should declare a fact which already exists...." [65]

The immediate purpose of the Declaration of Independence was to justify revolution against the British. So its long and detailed paragraphs listed what Britain's king had done to force Americans to take this drastic course. But the introduction, because of Jefferson's long and deep thinking on the subject, his discussions with his fellow committee members, and debate by the whole Congress, expressed the fundamental reasons for declaring independence. This section was the new nation's first and most significant statement of its fundamental political beliefs:

> When in the Course of human events, it becomes necessary for one people to dissolve the political bands which have connected them with another, and to assume among the powers of the earth, the separate and equal station to which the Laws of Nature and of Nature's God entitle them, a decent respect to the opinions of mankind requires that they should declare the causes which impel them to the separation.
>
> We hold these truths to be self-evident, that all men are created equal, that they are endowed by their Creator with certain unalienable Rights, that among these are Life, Liberty and the pursuit of Happiness. That to secure these rights, Governments are instituted among Men, deriving their just powers from the consent of the governed. That whenever any Form of Government becomes destructive of those ends it is the Right of the People to alter or to abolish it, and to institute new Government, laying its foundation on such principles and organizing its powers in such form, as to them shall seem most likely to effect their Safety and Happiness. Prudence, indeed, will dictate that Governments long established should not be changed for light and transient causes; and accordingly all experience hath shewn, that mankind are more disposed to suffer, while evils are sufferable, than to right themselves by abolishing the forms to which they are accustomed. But when a long train of abuses and usurpations, pursuing invariably the same Object evinces a design to reduce them under absolute Despotism, it is their right, it is their duty, to throw off such Government and to provide new Guards for their future security. Such has been the patient sufferance of these Colonies; and such is now the necessity which constrains them to alter their former Systems of Government. The history of the present King of Great Britain is a history of repeated injuries and usurpations, all having in direct object the establishment of an absolute Tyranny over these States. To prove this let Facts be submitted to a candid world. He has refused his Assent to Laws.... [66]

Then follow many accusations against the king, concluding with a final demand for independence. The Declaration was signed by 56 American leaders. It remains the most significant product of reasoned political thinking and consultation the world has ever seen.

These principles of government, largely brought forth by Thomas Jefferson, were based on life experience and solid thinking about the future of the nation. Jefferson used reason to demand a government based on reason. And such a government would have to be a democracy, run by the people through their elected representatives. Jefferson's friend Caesar Rodney wrote to him years later that the crux of the matter was reason:

> The Revolution of America, by recognizing those rights which every Man is Entitled to by the laws of God and Nature, Seems to have broken off all those devious Tramels of Ignorance, Prejudice, and Superstition which have long depressed the Human Mind. Every door is now Open to the Sons of genius and Science to enquire after Truth. Hence we may expect the darkening clouds of error will vanish fast before the light of reason; and that the period is fast arriving when the Truth will enlighten the whole world. [67]

The Declaration was fundamentally a justification for revolution against the British government. But it also expressed the main principles of democracy: human equality; guaranteed rights to life, liberty, and the pursuit of happiness; the necessity for a government responsible for ensuring those rights; and government that depended on the consent of citizens. Thus the document was published throughout the nation not only to present the case to fight against Britain, but as a basic commitment to the alternative government which that war could create. The hope of a government to make the right things happen was strengthened by the Declaration of Independence.

Jefferson was also a leader in defining what the new government should *not* do. When his wife was ill, he moved back to Virginia and took a seat in the Virginia House of Delegates, hoping that the war would be brief. He led an action to reform Virginia law. The government should not rule religion. In Virginia, the Anglican Church was still financially supported and empowered by the government, though the June 1776 Virginia Declaration of Rights had incorporated the principle of religious freedom. Jefferson noted that most citizens were religious "dissenters" but most delegates were "churchmen." [68] The problem was that the rulers "have assumed domination over the faith of others, setting up their own opinions and modes of thinking as the only true and infallible, and as endeavoring to impose them on others, hath established and maintained false religions over the greatest part of the world and through all time: that to compel a man to furnish contributions of money for the propagation of opinions which he disbelieves *and abhors,* is sinful and tyrannical...." Religious belief is meant to be independent of government: *"the opinions of men are not the object of civil government, nor under its jurisdiction."* So in 1779, Jefferson proposed a law guaranteeing religious freedom to Virginians:

> *We the General Assembly of Virginia do enact* that no man shall be compelled to frequent or support any religious worship, place, or ministry whatsoever, nor shall be enforced, restrained, molested, or burthened in his body or good, nor shall otherwise suffer, on account of his religious opinions or belief; but that all men shall be free to profess, and by argument to maintain, their opinions in matters of religion, and that the same shall in no wise diminish, enlarge, or affect their civil capacities. [69]

This Bill for Establishing Religious Freedom was not adopted by Virginia until 1786—when Jefferson was abroad. It was thanks largely to James Madison that the bill passed. Madison was glad that "this country extinguished forever the ambitious hope of making laws for the human mind." According to his biographer, Ralph Ketcham, "religious liberty stands out as the one subject upon which Madison took an extreme, absolute, undeviating position throughout his life."[70] Like Jefferson, Madison was concerned with what the government ought *not* to do.

Jefferson worked on several other issues. He tried to broaden access to land ownership by average citizens, which was opposed by aristocrats who wished to expand their estates. For several years, he tried to reform the Virginia penal code, especially by reducing the use of the death penalty, which he thought should be inflicted only for the crimes of treason and murder. State execution, he wrote, must be "the last melancholy resource."[71]

JEFFERSON'S MOVEMENT FOR EDUCATION

Perhaps Jefferson's most important move for reform was education. He had found education a great advantage in his own life. He wrote to his daughter Martha that "I expect you will write to me by every post. Inform me what books you read, what tunes you learn, and inclose me your best copy of every lesson in drawing....Take care that you never spell a word wrong....It produces good praise to a lady to spell well."[72]

Rousseau, the prophet of the French Revolution, had said, "Let us begin by laying facts aside."[74] By contrast, Jefferson was for bringing facts up front. "The whole art of government," he said, "consists in the art of being honest."[73] Real newspapers that informed people of what was going on in the political world had only been invented in the eighteenth century, and Jefferson thought that "every man should receive those papers, and be capable of reading them."[75] For that, it was necessary to have a system of public education for ordinary citizens.

Because democracy depends upon the informed opinions of citizens, education was crucial, Jefferson wrote, "to illuminate, as far as practicable, the minds of the people at large."[76] Indeed, he thought, "Reason and free inquiry are the only effectual agents against error."[77] He proposed that the government should provide for every hundred children a free school to attend, for three years, where they would learn reading, writing, arithmetic, and the histories of Greece, Rome, England, and America. He proposed that newborn children of slaves should be free and educated. His belief in education was so strong that he considered "the most important bill in our whole code is that for the diffusion of knowledge among the people. No other sure foundation can be devised for the preservation of freedom, and happiness."[78] Believing that public education is essential for democracy, Jefferson proposed a law whose general objectives were to provide an education adapted to the years, to the capacity, and the condition of every one, and directed to their freedom and happiness....But of all the views of this law none is more important, none more legitimate, than that of rendering the people safe, as they are ultimate, guardians of their own liberty. For this purpose the reading in the first stage, where *they* will receive their whole education, is proposed, as has been said, to be chiefly historical. History by apprising them of the past will enable them to judge of the future; it will avail them of the experience of other times and other nations; it will qualify them as judges of the actions and designs of men; it will enable them to know ambition under every disguise it may assume; and knowing it, to defeat its views. In every government on earth is some trace of human weakness, some germ of corruption and degeneracy, which cunning will discover, and wickedness insensible open, cultivate, and improve. Every government degenerates when trusted to the rulers of the people alone. The people themselves therefore are its own safe depositories. And to render even them safe their minds must be improved to a certain degree....The influence over government must be shared among all the people.[79]

Unfortunately, the war suspended any progress of public education. In 1778, Jefferson did succeed in getting Virginia to pass a law forbidding the further importation of slaves into the state.[80] His insights into the fundamental principles of human rights and the process of democracy strongly influenced many American political leaders from his day up to our own. He knew that the purpose of the American Revolution was not just to overthrow injustice but also to create the conditions for human justice.

DEMOCRACY IN WAR: GEORGE WASHINGTON

On June 1, 1779, in the middle of the Revolution, Thomas Jefferson was elected governor of Virginia. His chief responsibility was organizing the military and negotiating for French assistance. The American forces were led by George Washington of Virginia, who was to become the first president of the United States. Another leader might have insisted that a military dictatorship was necessary to defeat the enemy, but Washington resolved that America's war would be guided by democracy. Throughout the Revolution, he engaged in genuine rational discourse and shared decision making with the civilian government.

George Washington was born and raised in Virginia, in a family previously educated in England. They lived in a great house on a great farm named Mount Vernon. At age 16, George was a tall fellow with big hands and big feet, shy and somewhat awkward. Unlike previous generations of Washingtons, he was educated at home. Bent over the table in his room, "while the light from dripping candles flickered over the page, he slowly and carefully copied the *Rules of Civility and Decent Behavior in Company and Conversation*."[81]

As a teenager he was hired to survey a 5-million-acre tract, an outdoor job he loved, and he sailed across the sea to the West Indies, an adventure that made him seasick. In 1752, at age 20, he became the man in charge of Mount Vernon, commissioned as Major George Washington.

The governor of the Virginia Colony recruited Washington to relate to the French and the Indians. Washington took extensive notes for the governor and led troops through the forests, telling the Indians' leader "Half-King" that "we are coming in haste to support you whose interest is as dear to us as our lives."[82] In charge of military leadership, and promoted to Colonel, he was happy. However, he and other colonial officers were under the rule of all British officers, regardless of rank. Washington opposed being ruled by "any whippersnapper," and he discussed and wrote about it, but the trouble continued. While leading his 40 soldiers, Washington heard from Half-King that the Indian had found the French soldiers' camp, so Washington brought together the Indian allies and attacked the French, killing their commander and nearly half of their 50 troops. That was Washington's first war action: "I heard the bullets whistle, and, believe me, there is something charming in the sound."[83] He met with other Indians who were fighting against the English, but that was difficult. He told them the French were "always treacherous, and asserting the greatest Falsehoods whenever they think they will turn out to their Advantage," while the English had "sent an Army to Maintain your Rights; to put you again in Possession of your Lands; and to Protect your Wives and Children."[84] But, to his disgust, those Indians went off and allied with the French. To deal with the crisis, George Washington held a military council.

The British sent General Edward Braddock and a thousand trained troops to Virginia in 1755 to defend the colony from the French and Indians. The Virginia Assembly supplied money and troops: 400 Virginians were drafted into Braddock's army, and Braddock took on George Washington as an officer. When full-scale war broke out, Washington led men into battle, but found British military rule so troubling that he wanted to resign and go home to Mount Vernon. However, when Indians allied with the French burnt farmhouses and murdered settlers, he fought on, advised by his military council. He believed in military discipline—he punished soldiers for drunkenness, gaming, and immorality—yet he dealt fairly and openly with the men; as he said of himself, "My nature is open and honest, and free from guile!"[85] Despite his physical and mental aches and pains, he did his duty in the field and traveled back and forth to Mount Vernon and to meetings with the Virginia Assembly.

The French and Indian War finally ended in 1763, in an English victory so complete that England gained nearly all of France's possessions in North America. Throughout the war, Washington displayed some of the qualities that made him such a great democratic commander-in-chief during the Revolution. He knew how to take the initiative in the field, but he also regarded himself as a military leader under the authority of the civilian government—as shown by his meetings with the Assembly in the middle of the war. He also showed himself ready to discuss strategy and tactics with his military council and to take advice. He was always willing to listen to reason. As late as 1773, when he was a member of the Virginia House of Burgesses and one of the leading opponents of British policies in the colonies, he was willing to meet with the royal governor of Virginia. When, after the crisis between America and Britain boiled up in New

George Washington.

England, delegates from across the colonies convened in Philadelphia for the First Continental Congress, Washington attended, sitting quietly with them.

That colonial congress was condemned by the British and its members threatened with arrest for treason if they held another meeting. They did, in 1775. Washington also attended this Second Continental Congress, and sat quietly reading military books until he was unanimously elected to command the Continental Army. He was chosen because of his superior experience; the delegates believed he could "unite the cordial exertions of all the colonies better than any other person in the union."[86] Because he had doubts of himself, Washington refused the high pay the Congress offered of 500 dollars per month; instead he asked only to be reimbursed for his expenses. Then he marched forward as commander-in-chief of the new American Revolution against the British.

The army he commanded was hardly an army at all. Washington found it "a mixed multitude of people," soldiers "under very little discipline, order or government."[87] Many men refused to fight at all. And many of those who were willing to fight could go home when they wanted to. A number did. After fighting the British for a year, Washington urged Congress to declare war so that he could enlist soldiers for its duration. But Congress would not.

Along with the need for soldiers, Washington saw the need for reason. He told Congress that "the War in which we are engaged requires a Knowledge comprehending the Duties of the Field and Fortifications."[88] And he saw the need for unity: "The cause of America, and of liberty is the cause of every virtuous American citizen; whatever may be his religion or descent...."[89] He also held regular councils of war with his officers, and relied repeatedly upon the council's judgments, even when he disagreed with them.

When Washington urged a sudden attack on British-held Boston, the council of officers replied that it was not expedient. Washington wrote to Congress about his plan: "I cannot say that I have wholly laid it aside."[90] To his irritation and sadness, Congress much later did approve his attack on Boston, but too late for him to carry it out. Even so, when the British troops evacuated Boston and George Washington rode into the city in triumph in March 1776, the Congress praised him strongly and thanked him for his "wise and spirited conduct at the siege."[91]

Washington wrote often to Congress throughout the war, reaching not only for their support but also for their permission. For Congress was running the war, even before it had agreed to declare war and create a nation. As Washington's biographer Shelby Little notes, "everything had to be discussed and if decision on everything was postponed, that was Congress' way and Washington, for all his impatience, tried to be discreet."[92] The Virginia Convention proposed that the Congress "declare the Colonies free and independent States." New York's Richard Henry Lee and Massachusetts' John Adams backed that movement. The Declaration of Independence, drafted by Jefferson, passed, and on July 9, 1776, at six o'clock in the evening, the military brigades paraded forward to hear the Declaration read aloud to them. Throughout the colonies, artillery was fired and bonfires were set ablaze in honor of the Declaration.[93] The strength of the applause was partially because the British had just increased their army to 30,000 men. This new threat also expanded Washington's power, though he remained in continual communication with Congress.

But even the Declaration and the massing of British forces did not politically or socially unite the colonies. Southern troops fighting together with New Englanders often cursed the "damn yankees," who responded by damning the southerners. Later, John Adams wrote to his wife that "I am wearied to death with the wrangles between military officers, high and low," and "They quarrel like cats and dogs. They worry one another like mastiffs, scrambling for rank and pay like apes for nuts."[94] Washington saw these internal conflicts as a crisis, so he dictated general orders:

> It is with great concern the General understands that jealousies &c., are arisen among the troops from the different Provinces, of reflections frequently thrown out, which can only tend to irritate each other, and injure the noble cause in which we are engaged, and which we ought to support with one hand, and one heart. The General most earnestly entreats the officers and soldiers to consider the consequences; that they can no way assist our cruel enemies more effectually, than making division among ourselves.

He declared punishment:

[I]f there are any officers, or soldiers, so lost to virtue, and a love of their Country, as to continue in such practices after this order, the General assures them, and is directed by Congress, to declare to the whole Army, that such persons shall be severely punished and dismissed the service with disgrace.[95]

Still, he depended upon a various army of men who decided their own duties and naturally thought of their own futures, including the hope of getting more land. Many, many times, his strategic decisions were shared with his council and the Congress. However, he controlled his frustrations and continued to share the facts of the current situation with Congress. After debating for weeks, the Congress decided to offer 20 dollars and 100 acres of land to each man who enlisted for the whole length of the war. John Adams hated that decision, calling it "the spirit of venality" rather than patriotism, and said, "I am ashamed of the age I live in."[96]

Whenever he lost a battle, Washington was criticized, which sometimes depressed him: "I am wearied almost to death with the retrograde motion of things."[97] But he kept doing his duty, including urging Congress and obeying Congress. He congratulated Congress for getting the French to join the Americans in the war. He made his military chiefs his partners, not only giving them orders, but also sharing his hopes and ideas with them. For example, he told them, "I earnestly recommend to you to be circumspect in your choice of officers. Take none but gentlemen."[98] His communication was extensive. He not only corresponded with Congress but also by circulations to all 12 states—to urge the recruitment of soldiers.[99] (Washington's wartime correspondence was eventually collected into 25 volumes.[100]) But the conflicts among the different states were such a horror that Washington longed for the Revolution to be all over so that he could leave war and politics and return to Mount Vernon.

America won the war. Throughout the colonies, there was great rejoicing and Congress voted thanks to every person who had helped achieve the victory.

The new nation was operating under the Articles of Confederation, a weak constitutional alliance of the states that had been adopted by Congress in 1777 and at last ratified by all the states in 1781. At war's end, the popular suggestion was that the leader of the new country should be none other than George Washington—a democratic leader, not a holy emperor; as one citizen said, "I respect our great general, but let us not make a GOD of him!"[101] Though he received high honor, Washington did not want to be his nation's leader: "I can truly say that the first wish of my Soul is to return speedily into the bosom of that country, which gave me birth, and, in the sweet enjoyment of domestic happiness and the company of a few friends, to end my days in quiet, when I shall be called from this stage."[102] He thought Congress—not himself—should be the essence of the new government, but for that to happen, its powers would have to be strengthened: "I am decidedly of opinion that if the Powers of Congress are not enlarged, and made competent to all *general purposes* that the blood that has been split…will soon be broken when anarchy & confusion must ensue."[103] He worked with Congress and with the military officers to pass a resolution giving the officers five years' pay and the soldiers three months' pay.

But when, at last, the war was clearly over, the breakup of Congress and the disintegration of the united colony government was likely. Alexander Hamilton, a young leader in New York, wrote, "Our prospects are not flattering," for "every day proves the inefficiency of the present Confederation." [104] In October 1785, Washington wrote that "Illiberality, jealousy, and local policy mix too much in all our public councils for the good government of the Union. In a word, the confederation appears to me to be little more than a shadow without the substance, and Congress a nugatory body, their ordinances being little attended to." [105] The colonies were taking independent actions. New England even began threatening to secede from the Confederation, turning away from the Confederation's reasoning. [106]

George Washington saw reason as essential to preserving the Union: "From thinking proceeds speaking; thence to acting is often but a single step." [107] Because he believed that "the foundation of our empire was not laid in the gloomy age of ignorance and superstition, but at an epoch when the rights of mankind were better understood and more clearly defined than at any former period," [108] he had hope that the Union could be salvaged and strengthened. In September 1786, only five states could be induced to send delegates to a convention meeting in Annapolis, Maryland, to discuss the problem. Alexander Hamilton pointed out the weakness of the present government and the need for drastic improvements. Washington wrote to Madison that "the superstructure we have been for seven years in raising, at the expense of so much treasure and blood, must fall. We are fast verging to anarchy and confusion." [109] Plans were made to hold a constitutional conference in Philadelphia the following year.

Washington's fear of irrational breakups turned out to be accurate. Even while the Annapolis Convention was meeting, there was a revolution in Massachusetts, sparked by farmers and others who were being harshly exploited by their state government, which was forcing them to pay off debts at a time when they were suffering through an economic depression. Crowds assembled. Revolution leader Daniel Shays was asked "What shall we do?" He answered, "Close down the courts! Then they can't take our property away or throw us into jail." The rebels moved to seize guns from a federal government arsenal. Shays urged "To hell with Congress! That crowd is too weak to act." [110]

The Massachusetts revolution was defeated, but many other citizens used voting to attack their government. And resistance to pay taxes and debts spread throughout America. In Maryland in 1786, a rebellion closed down a county courthouse; in South Carolina, farmers attacked a courthouse and sent the judges scurrying home; in Virginia, a county courthouse was burned to the ground and many other courts were forced to stop action. James Madison was shocked. He wrote to Jefferson, "The nearer the crisis approaches the more I tremble for the issues." [111] Washington hoped that the national government would survive, but thought it could do so only if "the federal government, may be considered with calm and deliberate attention." He urged that "prejudices, unreasonable jealousies, and local interests, yield....Let us look to our national character, and to things beyond the present moment." [112] The disintegration of the nation was the challenge that confronted the convention gathered in Philadelphia in May 1787.

George Washington, despite his wish to retire, had been persuaded to take part. An army general urged him to work for a thorough overhaul of the government:

> Were the convention to propose only amendments and patchwork to the present defective confederation, your reputation would in a degree suffer. But, were an energetic and judicious system to be proposed with your signature, it would be a circumstance highly honorable to your fame, in the judgment of the present and future ages; and doubly entitle you to the glorious republican epithet, *The Father of your Country.* [113]

Indeed, Washington's wide public heroism had to be used to support the coalition of the colonies to form a nation. He was praised by Henry Lee as the leader *"first in war, first in peace and first in the hearts of his countrymen."* [114] As early as 1775, American babies had been christened with his name. In a 1783 sermon by Ezra Stiles at Yale University, Washington was sainted: "O Washington!...How I do love thy name! How have I often adored and blessed thy God, for creating and forming thee the great ornament of human kind!" [115]   And Thomas Jefferson once wrote admiringly of Washington's principle:

> Perhaps the strongest feature in his character was prudence, never acting until every circumstance, every consideration, was maturely weighted; refraining if he saw a doubt, but, when once decided, going through with his purpose whatever the obstacles opposed. His integrity was pure, his justice the most inflexible I have ever known, no motives of interest or consanguinity of friendship or hatred, being able to bias his decision. He was indeed, in every sense of the words, a wise, a good, and a great man. [116]

Washington agreed to go to the convention partly to encourage all the states to send their representatives—which they finally did, though some arrived nearly two weeks after the formal start of the meeting. He was selected to chair the meeting and spoke to the delegates:

> It is too probable that no plan we propose will be adopted. Perhaps another dreadful conflict is to be sustained. If, to please the people, we offer what we ourselves disapprove, how can we afterward defend our work? Let us raise a standard to which the wise and the honest can repair; the event is in the hand of God. [117]

George Washington's combination of military leadership and devotion to decision making by democratic discourse made hope for a new nation, the first democracy. Then he sat quietly in a chair as James Madison, his fellow Virginian, worked to create the democracy for which Washington had just set the standard.

WORKING FOR A CONSTITUTION: JAMES MADISON

The first essential plan for the future of the new nation was to create a constitution. That would require thought, discourse, decision, and definite application of a strongly defined and fair procedure for democracy. The new ambition was to make a universally accepted, national, ultimate document that would clearly stand as the fundamental law for political behavior. James Madison was a major leader for that cause.

Madison was born on March 16, 1751. He was his mother's first child, and was named James after his father. His father owned 13,500 acres in the wide Shenandoah Valley, where the grand Blue Ridge Mountains stood beyond the vast open lands and rolling hills that young James loved to explore. His family had lived in Virginia for a century, so he had many relatives. The Madisons went to the Anglican (Episcopal) Church, where his father was a vestryman. As a child and youth in the 1750s and 1760s, James learned the harsh lessons of the terrible French and Indian War. He also suffered the personal trauma of an attack of smallpox, which in those days was often fatal. But he survived and grew healthy.

His love of thinking and learning fed his youthful life. His family owned many books, rare possessions in those days, and he read nearly all of them. His parents came to admire him as a strong intellectual person. He boarded at the local school, where Scottish schoolmasters set him to studying Horace, Ovid,

James Madison.

Homer, and the New Testament, as well as Latin and Greek. Many years later, Madison wrote of Donald Robertson, the school's headmaster: "all that I have been in life I owe largely to that man."[118]

At age 16, James came home for two years to be further educated by the Reverend Thomas Martin, who lived with the Madisons as the "family teacher." When he was 18 and ready for college, he did not go to Virginia's College of William and Mary because it was situated in an area considered unhealthy by mountain-living Virginians. Instead, he traveled to Princeton University in New Jersey. There he felt fine: "I am perfectly pleased with my present situation."[119] He studied hard. He not only read books, but also learned to write and speak. Princeton did not bend its students' minds to some particular doctrine, but rather guaranteed "free and equal Liberty and Advantage of Education [to] any Person of any religious Denomination whatsoever," while retaining its right to "direct the conduct and studies of the youth, and to restrain them from such liberties and indulgences as would tend to corrupt their morals, or alienate their minds from a steady application."[120] Open debate was encouraged. Students were assigned such textbooks as Isaac Watts' classic *Logick: or the Right Use of Reason in the Enquiry after Truth.* At five o'clock each morning, a bell rang to wake them up; at six, they went to morning prayer; then they studied for one hour—all before breakfast. Throughout the day students had many more activities. At nine at night, they were expected to go to sleep—or keep studying. Because of his great thirst for knowledge, Madison was one of those who kept on studying; he slept only four or five hours a night.[121] There was much intellectual discussion in the Princeton Community. Group meals were a requirement; professors, and even Princeton's president, ate and chatted with the students.

In the midst of his more serious mental endeavors, James Madison wrote some awkward poetry and shared humor with his student pals, but his thinking, especially about politics, progressed. At Princeton he thought of political results. As his biographer Ralph Ketcham notes, Madison "had at the foundation of his political education a supreme emphasis on the *ends*, not the *means*, of government."[122]

After he graduated in September 1771, Madison stayed on at Princeton through the winter, writing his parents that he was too weak to journey home. His voice was weak and his health not the best, but he wanted to study Hebrew and other subjects, possibly law.

Much as Madison liked Virginia, he complained about its "Poverty… Luxury…Pride…Ignorance…Knavery…Vice and Wickedness" and longed "to breath free Air" in Philadelphia. So off he went to Benjamin Franklin's city. On May 13, 1774, a man rode into that town from New York to bring the news that the British Parliament had ruled that the port of Boston be closed because men had attacked ships carrying tea subject to British taxation. Madison was outraged against that British policy. He was probably in Philadelphia, where a meeting was held on May 20 in protest, calling itself a "Congress of deputies of all the colonies."[123] He thought that Britain's Parliament should not rule the colonies. He longed to be in the planned First Continental Congress, which he thought would "illuminate the minds of thinking people among us" and "render us more respectable at Home [in England]." [124] That Congress resolved that every county, city, and town in America should choose a "Committee of Safety" to ban trade which the new Congress had resolved, and to name violating traders in the newspapers, declaring them "universally condemned as the enemies of American Liberty."

Madison moved back to Virginia, and both he and his father were elected in December 1774 to the Orange County Committee of Safety. James Madison was made a colonel of the militia the following year, but because of his weak health, he did not serve in the Revolutionary War. He continued to work for the cause of independence, however, and in 1775 hailed the "true Eloquence" of the Second Continental Congress. During the war, he emerged as a nation-minded activist and one of the smartest of the political revolutionaries.

Madison became a strong advocate of the complete separation of church and state in Virginia. When his original proposal for religious freedom was opposed by Anglican churchmen and rejected as too radical by the Virginia legislature, Madison thought and talked with legislators and others and came up with a more acceptable proposal, which asserted that

> all men are equally entitled to enjoy the free exercise of religion, according to the dictates of conscience, unpunished and unrestrained by the magistrate, Unless the preservation of equal liberty and the existence of the State are manifestly endangered. [125]

That concept was accepted and Madison's amendment became law. One leader applauded it as "the first achievement of the wisest civilian in Virginia." [126]

Madison worked best by talking privately with representatives. He was not an accomplished public speaker—which is probably why he lost an election to Virginia's legislature in 1777. However, those who were elected to the legislature elected him by a good margin (61 to 42) to the Council of State, a small body that, under the Virginia constitution, decided what acts the governor could take. After Thomas Jefferson became governor of Virginia in 1779, he and Madison worked together for years as friends and political partners. Together they created the Library of Congress and spent hours discussing which books should be within it. In 1779 also, Madison was appointed as a member of the Continental Congress. There he learned how a government should handle money. Author Ketcham wrote that "He cast aside the enormous amount of vacuous theorizing and technical gibberish that befogged the study of money and credit in his day." [127]

Though shy and short (five feet six) the youthful Madison impressed fellow members of the Continental Congress and was making its operations successful. He did not like the formal meetings of the whole Congress, but took much pleasure in discussions with members who shared his political beliefs. Guiding the new nation through a war against one of the world's most formidable powers was a major challenge to the inexperienced Congress. They could not tell what the British would do next or whether any of the Continental powers would support the United States against Great Britain. The Continental Army was usually distant from Philadelphia and communications were difficult. Finally, members of Congress held various attitudes toward both government and the conduct of the war. Fortunately, Washington was no military dictator and pressed responsibility on the Congress, so civilian authority was firmly established. And Madison, along with Hamilton and others, worked hard—and usually successfully—to get the Congress to make the necessary policy decisions about the war, money, the western territory, and other issues. For four years, Madison served nearly every day; never once, until the war ended, did he return to Virginia.

The Articles of Confederation had created a weak national government because the majority of states and those who represented them feared a strong central government would be as tyrannical as Britain. Madison worked to gain Congress more significant powers, such as the ability to prohibit trade with Britain, to pay soldiers, to control war supplies, and to govern international relations as well as national relations. He and his allies believed that "the citizens of the United States are responsible for the greatest trust ever confided to a political society,"[128] and they wanted a Congress worthy of that trust. But Congress, under the loose union of states established by the Articles, could not exercise the kind of authority needed. In June 1783, for example, soldiers in Philadelphia were so angry that they had not received their back pay that they demonstrated against the Congress. Congress, being helpless to raise the taxes needed to pay them, responded by moving to Princeton.

Finally, in the winter of 1783–84, the war over and the peace treaty signed, Madison left Congress and took up the study of law. He did, however, stay in communication by letters with his allies, one of whom was Jefferson. In 1786, Jefferson wrote from France, where he was representing the United States, that "It is comfortable to see the standard of Reason at length erected, after so many ages during which the human mind has been held in vassalage by kings, priests and nobles, and it is honorable for us to have produced legislators who had the courage to declare that the Reason of man may be trusted with the formation of his own opinions."[129] In 1787, Jefferson wrote to Madison, wondering

> whether peace is best preserved by giving energy to the government, or information to the people. This last is the most certain and the most legitimate engine of government. Educate and inform the whole mass of the people. Enable them to see that it is their interest to preserve peace and order, and they will preserve them.[130]

From 1784 to 1787, Madison took several long journeys, though he was a delegate of the Virginia Assembly. In the Assembly, he did succeed in establishing religious freedom in the new state: "I flatter myself [we] have in this country extinguished forever the ambitious hope of making laws for the human mind."[131] But he knew much more was needed to ensure the rule by reason he treasured. Through those years that Madison was thinking about the future of America, his particular focus was the creation of a constitution to make politics work well for the citizens. He thought the government should control the flow of money, internationally and domestically, for "The value of money consists in the uses it will serve."[132] He saw the future nation as a "Union" but also as a "Federation," joining partially independent states together to govern the nation. He thought the nation should be ruled by the majority of citizens, provided they bound themselves to a common commitment to fundamental human rights and justice.

Extremely helpful to his thinking was a "cargo" of books his friend Jefferson sent him from Paris—books on history, politics, and economics. Madison read many of them and put together an extensive paper titled "Of Ancient and Modern Confederacies." He thought that "the past should enlighten us on the future."[133] For the future, he urged and supported the plan for a convention to meet in Philadelphia, in May 1787, to discuss and decide how the government should be strengthened.

THE MEETING TO CREATE THE CONSTITUTION

The outcome of the new "Federal Convention" was far from certain. Washington and Madison agreed that "no morn ever dawned more favorably than ours did; and no day was ever more clouded than the present." Rationality was the great necessity: "Wisdom and good examples are necessary at this time to rescue the political machine from the impending storm." They faced "the probable diversity of opinions and prejudices" delegates to the convention would express, but felt "the whole community is big with expectation, and there can be no doubt but that the result will in some way or other have a powerful effect on our destiny." Benjamin Franklin warned that if the convention "does not do good, it must do harm, as it will show that we have not wisdom enough among us to govern ourselves...."[134]

Madison arrived early so he could talk informally with delegates. Eventually, 55 men attended. George Washington was elected as chairman. Madison proposed 15 resolutions that came to be called the Virginia Plan. In the formal sessions, Madison sat up front and only he wrote notes of what the members said. This convention was to be a completely private meeting: "nothing spoken in the House be printed, or otherwise published, or communicated without leave."[135] The meeting was private, because, as Madison later judged, "no Constitution would ever have been adopted by the convention if the debates had been public."[136]

Summer began. The hot building was kept closed, so the men sweated for many hours each day as they argued and decided what to do. Meanwhile, off in cooler London, John Adams declared the convention "the greatest single effort of national deliberation that the world has ever seen."[137] The United States' unique Constitution developed primarily from fundamental principles, such as the standards of the Declaration of Independence, but the decisions that created that Constitution were also meant to adjust democracy to the particular circumstances of America. For example, some delegates wanted the president to be elected, not by citizens, but by the state legislatures. Others wanted the Congress to be elected by each state voting equally, even though some states had many more people than others. Opposed to that idea were those who thought that the

Congress ought to be "the grand depository of the democratic principle."[138] The differences were expressed and discussed, and a coalition formed for a national legislative system of two houses: a Senate elected by the state legislatures, with two senators from each state; and a House of Representatives elected by the people, with the number of representatives for each state to be determined by the numbers of people in the state. As James Wilson from Pennsylvania argued, "The Government ought to possess not only...the *force* but...the *mind or sense* of the people at large."[139] The legislative system was thus American, reflecting the peculiar necessities of that period, but the fundamental invention was that a Congress chosen by the people would decide law for the nation.

Should there be one top national official? The argument was that without such a president, the nation might fall apart, as there would be no single leader to stand for the country. The presence of George Washington supported that idea. But how should such a leader be chosen? Madison and others thought he should be elected by the Congress, but others thought he should be relatively independent of the legislative branch. After much discussion, it was decided that the president of the United States would be elected by an independent electoral college composed of respected people who could be counted on to choose a president for the citizens' benefit.

Much discussion followed these decisions, with votes changing time and again, but the delegates were determined to reach agreement. Madison made it clear that guessing what the people might want was not the best mode of political thought. Rather, the convention "ought to consider what was right and necessary in itself for the attainment of a proper Government." Different suggestions were proposed. Alexander Hamilton recommended, during a five- or six-hour speech, that the president, the senators, and the national judges should be allowed to serve as long as they performed well, that the president should have absolute veto power over legislation, and that the legislature itself should have "power to pass all laws whatsoever." The state governors would be appointed by the national government. Madison argued against all of those ideas. He persuaded the delegates that the government should genuinely represent contemporary people and should not be set up in such a way as to tempt leaders to use their power to enrich themselves. Madison also thought that the state governments should not decide the wages of congressmen, nor should congressmen themselves be able to increase their own salaries.

Benjamin Franklin came forth with ideas, but he made perhaps his most important contribution in reminding delegates to calm their tempers and deliberate in an amiable style.[140] Southern members agitated to veto laws regulating trade, while northern members tried to abolish slave trade. In the hot, closed-up building where the Constitutional Convention met, tempers often reached the boiling point; one member felt provoked enough to shout, "I DO NOT, GENTLEMEN, TRUST YOU."[141] George Washington was wise enough to understand that "The primary cause of all our discontents lies in the different State Governments."[142]

Through it all, Madison kept his head. He did not try to resolve crises by unworkable patched-up compromises, but strove to get the delegates to agree on the best possible decisions. On some matters, the vote was but five to four. In August, Madison was so sick that he could take only about two-thirds of the notes he wanted, and Virginia's George Mason said that he "would sooner chop off his right hand than put it to the Constitution as it now stands." [143] There were many moments of despair and anger, but the discourse went on.

At last, the Constitution was ready to be sent to the states for ratification. Despite the demanding wants of some and the threats of others to extract themselves or even their states from the process, despite the delegates' differences in ideologies and desires, the common dedication to reason at the Constitutional Convention made it possible for the U.S. Constitution to be invented. It was not a perfect product, but it was the very best that could be contrived by a majority of delegates at that convention. Madison reported how this great achievement happened:

> In all our deliberations...we kept steadily in our view...the consolidation of our Union, in which is involved our prosperity, felicity, safety, perhaps our national existence....The Constitution, which we now present, is the result of a spirit of amity, and of that mutual deference and concession which the peculiarity of our political situation rendered indispensable. [144]

Signing of the Constitution.

The essential decisions, voted by a large majority of the men who worked from May to September to create a government to save humans, were these:

> The Articles of Confederation must be discarded, not merely amended, and a new constitution substituted.
> The new government must have three departments—legislative, executive, judicial.
> The large states must have more power in the new government than the small states, thus giving to it a popular basis.
> The new Congress must have the power to legislate on all matters of national concern and all matters with which the states cannot deal competently, including the power to tax, to regulate interstate and foreign commerce, and to spend money for common defense and general welfare.
> The debts of the Confederation must be binding on the new government.
> Many restraints must be laid on the state government. [145]

In addition, the federal government was to be clearly in charge of the military.

Old Benjamin Franklin addressed the members: "On the whole, Sir, I cannot help expressing a Wish, that every Member of the Convention, who may still have Objections to it, would with me on this Occasion doubt a little of his own Infallibility, and make *manifest* our *Unanimity*, put his Name to this Instrument." [146] George Washington rose up from his elegant chair, a chair with a gilded, carved half-sun at its top. Franklin remarked, "As I have been sitting here all these weeks, I have often wondered whether yonder sun is rising or setting. But now I know that it is a rising sun." The Constitution was signed by the great majority of the delegates. George Washington signed it first. [147]

That was not the end of the process, however, for the Constitution had to be ratified by nine states before it could take effect. And out in the states it had some formidable enemies, including leading political figures and influential newspapers. For example, the Boston *Gazette* greeted the document with this screaming headline: "BRIBERY AND CORRUPTION!!!" [148] Opponents' arguments were complex, but the crux of the opposition was antifederalism: the sense that the new constitutionalized government would be too powerful, too monarchical, too much in control of the economy.

The arguments for and against the Constitution's components now rolled out of the closed-up, hot building in which the delegates had secretly debated into the public arena. Virginia's George Mason, a delegate to the convention who had refused to sign the Constitution, published a criticism titled *Objections to the Proposed Federal Constitution*. [149] Madison and Hamilton, with some help from John Jay, wrote and published a series of 85 essays, called *The Federalist*, in defense of the Constitution. In these papers, they gave the people many facts and closely reasoned arguments for supporting the Constitution. Jefferson judged *The Federalist* as the "best commentary on the principles of government which ever was written." [150] Madison pleaded that the Constitution be evaluated "on its own merits solely," and "that gentlemen in displaying their abilities on this occasion, instead of giving opinions, and making assertions, will condescend to prove and demonstrate, by a fair and regular discussion." [151] He published his arguments and facts, but he also gave as many as seven speeches in one day. While the criticisms were significant, the argument for the Constitution appeared to be moving public opinion forward, by means of thinking.

THE ORIGINS OF THE BILL OF RIGHTS

Those who were worried that they might be enslaved by the powerful national government envisioned by the Constitution began to demand that a bill of rights be added to it. That a government—even a democratic government—could gain the total confidence, because it had a fixed procedure for decision making, was thought doubtful to many. Leading Virginians had indeed urged the creation of a bill of rights during the Philadelphia meeting, but the majority of the other delegates—including Madison—had said that a specific set of protectionary rules was unnecessary because the federal government would only exercise those powers expressly granted to it in the Constitution. Fortunately for past, present, and future generations of Americans, the expanding criticism of the Constitution made it necessary to add a clear, definite, fundamental bill of rights. Madison, campaigning for a seat in the new Congress, recognized the need to reassure the public: he promised to propose and work to pass amendments guaranteeing essential rights for all citizens after the Constitution was ratified.

The year between 1788 and 1789 was crucial to the adoption of the Bill of Rights. The first national election took place during that period, even though North Carolina and Rhode Island had not yet ratified the Constitution. Madison helped to persuade a homesick George Washington to run for president, noting that "The Presidency alone unites the conjectures of the public."[152] John Adams stepped forward to run against him. Adams was no enemy of the Constitution; he had published a *Defense of the Constitution of Government of the United States*. So the two men in contention for the presidency at this crucial point were both supporters of the Constitution. Washington won, and many other men in favor of the Constitution were elected to Congress—a plus for "peaceable commencement" and to "give it a fair trial," Madison thought. In Virginia, however, there was still much opposition, though Madison, the Constitution's chief advocate in that state, was elected to the House of Representatives. There he took a leadership role, partly because President Washington typically stood apart from the Congress. At Madison's urging, Washington appointed Alexander Hamilton secretary of treasury and Thomas Jefferson secretary of state.

By the time he got to Congress, Madison had come to see the necessity for a bill of rights. Jefferson had told him that it "is what the people are entitled to against every government on earth,…and what no just government should refuse."[153] Madison himself was now convinced that it would be a great benefit "If we can make the Constitution better in the opinion of those who are opposed to it, without weakening its frame, or abridging its usefulness in the judgment of those who are attached to it."[154] In other words, he perceived that a constitution of procedures for decision making was not sufficient to guarantee fundamental human rights. The bill of rights would be amendments to the Constitution requiring the *government* to respect and safeguard certain enumerated citizens' rights.

"Equality" in the eighteenth century—The Age of Reason—did not mean that everyone was the same as everyone else, or that no one could be seen as better than anyone else. The basic right of equality was defined in relation to the government: every citizen was equal under the law. Similarly, "liberty" did not mean that anyone could do anything. Obviously the rule of law in a democracy required citizens to obey the laws their representatives made. But neither was liberty a philosophical abstraction: citizens' liberties were specified, such as the freedom of speech, and were defined in relation to the force of the government. The whole idea of a bill of rights was to restrain government from controlling the lives of human beings. Madison came to recognize that just as there had to be some restraints on citizens' behavior in a civilized society, there had to be built-in restraints on the government's behavior toward citizens. He understood that "we must not shut our eyes to the nature of man, nor to the light of experience." He knew that "If men were angels, no government would be necessary," and if men were devils, "no government can render us secure." [155] Madison was a realist, well acquainted with history.

The House of Representatives and the Senate discussed and debated numerous potential rights. In the end, they agreed upon 12 rights, but the states failed to ratify 2 of them. Finally, on December 15, 1791, the ten amendments we know as the U.S. Bill of Rights were added to the Constitution. North Carolina and Rhode Island then joined the United States.

The United States of America Bill of Rights brought forth these straight demands:

AMENDMENT I

Congress shall make no law respecting an establishment of religion, or prohibiting the free exercise thereof; or abridging the freedom of speech, or of the press; or the right of the people peaceably to assemble, and to petition the Government for a redress of grievances.

AMENDMENT II

A well regulated Militia, being necessary to the security of a free State, the right of the people to keep and bear Arms, shall not be infringed.

AMENDMENT III

No Soldier shall, in time of peace be quartered in any house, without the consent of the Owner, nor in time of war, but in a manner to be prescribed by law.

AMENDMENT IV

The right of the people to be secure in their persons, houses, papers, and effects, against unreasonable searches and seizures, shall not be violated, and no Warrants shall issue, but upon probable cause, supported by Oath or affirmation, and particularly describing the place to be searched, and the persons or things to be seized.

AMENDMENT V

No person shall be held to answer for a capital, or otherwise infamous crime, unless on a presentment or indictment of a Grand Jury, except in cases arising in the land or naval forces, or in the Militia, when in actual service in time of War or public danger; nor shall any person be subject for the same offence to be twice put in jeopardy of life or limb; nor shall be compelled in any criminal case to be a witness against himself, nor be deprived of life, liberty, or property, without due process of law; nor shall private property be taken for public use, without just compensation.

AMENDMENT VI

In any criminal prosecutions, the accused shall enjoy the right to a speedy and public trial, by an impartial jury of the State and district wherein the crime shall have been committed, which district shall have been previously ascertained by law; and to be informed of the nature and cause of the accusation; to be confronted with the witness against him; to have compulsory process for obtaining witnesses in his favor, and to have the Assistance of Counsel for his defence.

AMENDMENT VII

In Suits at common law, where the value in controversy shall exceed twenty dollars, the right of trial by jury shall be preserved, and no fact tried by a jury, shall be otherwise re-examined in any Court of the United States, than according to the rules of the common law.

AMENDMENT VIII

Excessive bail shall not be required, nor excessive fines imposed, nor cruel and unusual punishments inflicted.

AMENDMENT IX

The enumeration in the Constitution, of certain rights, shall not be construed to deny or disparage others retained by the people.

AMENDMENT X

The powers not delegated to the United States by the Constitution, not prohibited by it to the States, are reserved to the States respectively, or to the people. [156]

The failure to approve Jefferson's amendment to stop slavery left a major gap in this splendid legacy of the First Congress, and for that the nation paid with the tragedy of the Civil War. But the main effect of the Bill of Rights was to confirm fundamental confidence in the procedural democracy that the states had approved in ratifying the Constitution.

Ratification of the Constitution and Bill of Rights was essential to the future of American democracy. For the ultimate establishment of democracy, however, what is written and agreed upon has to happen. The modern Soviet Union produced a remarkably democratic constitution, but in fact the Soviet government had no intention of acting the way that document committed it to act. In the United States, the intention to act constitutionally seemed to be present in the government from the start.

THE FIRST NATIONAL GOVERNMENT OF THE NEW DEMOCRACY

Ironically, the United States of America's initial blessing was decision making by Congress. President George Washington, whose desire was to retire to Mount Vernon rather than serve in New York, became a president standing above—and mainly beyond—the Congress. The vice president was John Adams, who lost the election to Washington and thus was made vice president—a procedure that was quickly changed. Adams was reported to be "unfriendly in his sentiments to George Washington."[157] And after the election, Adams said that "If our government does well, I shall be more surprised than I ever was in my life."[158] Washington, by contrast, was worried but hopeful. From the start, he received many visitors, but because he was an awkward and obscure speechmaker, he hardly ever addressed the Congress.

What the Congress might do was very uncertain; Madison told Jefferson that "We are in a wilderness, without a single footstep to guide us."[159] Madison, as usual, considered it his duty to gather the facts. He "hunted up all the grievances and complaints of newspapers, all the articles of conventions, and the small talk of their debates."[160] Washington spent time each day looking over pieces of paper, and he did keep in touch with Madison and Hamilton. But more often he sat quietly, with a cold, stern face, up in front of the Senate—his presence inhibiting the senators from yelling against one another, despite their uneasy, restless mood. Depressed by the news that his mother had died, Washington was also bored by the Congress. In the morning, he took exercise by riding his horse or walking, sometimes with children, and on his way home, he stopped to visit with friends. Thus the first president presided over but did not attempt to rule the Congress.

By contrast, young Secretary of the Treasury Alexander Hamilton, even after his main proposal for operating national funding lost by only two votes, was enthusiastic and glad that "Our government is now happily carried into operation, although some thorny questions still remain."[161] The government soon moved to Philadelphia, where Hamilton and Secretary of State Jefferson worked to influence action, along with Madison and others. The potential Congress became an actual Congress, raising key issues, debating, deciding, and focusing on actual results. Washington did not abandon Congress; he yearned to go home, "but whilst I am in office, I shall never suffer private convenience to interfere with what I conceive to be my official duty."[162] His "official duty," as he saw it, was overseeing the representatives' reasoning rather than taking part in their arguments. Thanks to his high-minded exclusion, Congress through daily practice grew from political childhood to political adolescence, making policy not only for domestic but also for international government action.

After four years as president, Washington wanted to retire. Jefferson, who did not admire everything about Washington's presidency, nevertheless helped to persuade him to run again for president because "North and South will hang together as long as they have you to hang on."[163] Washington ran again and won. Then, after four more years in office, he insisted to retire. He did. As the first hero of the nation, Washington's name was eventually titled to 1 state, 7 mountains, 8 streams, 10 lakes, 33 counties, 9 colleges, and 121 towns and villages.[164] But even his admirable behavior during two terms as president did not ensure the future of democracy in the United States. Would future presidents operate as rationally and honorably toward Congress and the states to uphold the fundamental law of the Constitution and the Bill of Rights?

John Adams and Thomas Jefferson ran for president in 1796. Adams won and Jefferson became vice president. During the Adams presidency, the fear arose that France might take over the still-weak United States, either through war or through the manipulations of foreign agents in America. Most members of Congress increasingly agreed that the national government should hold essential, sovereign power to attack such crises. That perspective created a major crisis for democracy: the Congress, both House and Senate, passed the Alien and Sedition Acts, which sharply denied the freedoms of speech that the Bill of Rights had guaranteed. These new laws made it illegal for groups to gather "with intent to oppose any measure or measures of the government of the United States" or for anyone to write or publish "any false, scandalous, and malicious writing or writings against the United States, or the President of the United States, with intent to defame…or to bring them or either of them, into contempt or disrepute." [165] That the government was so soon ready to contradict the Bill of Rights shocked Jefferson, Madison, and others whose work to institute the Bill of Rights had been essential to the establishment of the national government.

Now that the Congress itself had violated the Constitution, what would happen? It was not yet established that the Supreme Court, at the top of law, would take responsibility for deciding about that conflict. Citizens in favor of the French began to be jailed, including even a member of Congress. [166] Jefferson and Madison worked vigorously against the Alien and Sedition Acts and convinced the Virginia and Kentucky state governments to openly oppose those acts as unconstitutional. Some Virginian legislators even thought this crisis meant that their state should secede from the United States. There was uncertainty about how to rule on this decision. In the 1800 election, Madison saw that the Acts could repress "that information and communication among the people which is indispensable to the just exercise of their electoral rights." [167] But fortunately, the Alien and Sedition Acts, passed on June 25, 1800, were set to expire on March 3, 1801—which happened.

Basic democratic rights were promised to the American people, though the Adams government nearly destroyed this. However, the controversy split the consensus among the leading politicians. For example, Alexander Hamilton privately damned Jefferson as "an *atheist* in Religion and a *fanatic* in politics" and criticized Jefferson's growing Republican party as "all tending to mischief." [168] Jefferson saw the destruction of the Bill of Rights as a "detestable thing." [169] But neither Hamilton nor Jefferson argued publicly with these harsh damnations. So discourse continued.

PRESIDENT THOMAS JEFFERSON RATIFIES DEMOCRACY

In 1800, the new election to choose a president resulted in many complications, with the House of Representatives eventually voting thirty-six times until finally deciding who won. The Republicans campaigning for Jefferson asked, "*Is it not high time for a CHANGE?*" [170] The Federalists lost, the Republicans won. Jefferson saw the Republicans' victory over the Federalists as a revolution: "The revolution of 1800 as real a revolution in the principles of our government as that of 1776 was in its form." [171] Despite that complicated public election, which had to be decided in

Congress, Thomas Jefferson finally won. At his inauguration on March 4, 1801—the first in the new capital of Washington, D.C.—previous President John Adams was absent, having quietly left town that morning. The two men remained political enemies for a long time. But President Jefferson did not speak forth to use his power to cut away his opponents. Instead, he presented himself as a president who saw general political reasoning as essential to a democratic government. He believed that

> every difference of opinion, is not a difference of principle. We have called, by different names, brethren of the same principle. We are all Republicans, we are all Federalists.
>   If there be any among us who wish to dissolve this union, or to change its republican form, let them stand undisturbed, as monuments of the safety with which error of opinion may be tolerated where reason is left free to combat it....

Earlier in the speech he said that

> the sacred principle that if the will of the Majority is in all cases to prevail that will, to be rightful, must be reasonable: that the Minority possess their equal rights, which equal laws must protect, & to violate would be oppression.
>   Let us then, fellow citizens, unite with one heart & one mind; let us restore to social intercourse that harmony & affection, without which Liberty, & even Life itself, are but dreary things....[172]

Jefferson pardoned and freed those who had been imprisoned under the Alien and Sedition Acts. Even more importantly, he did what he had said should be done: he helped the country to once again "unite with one heart & one mind," by discourse. For example, in his administration, foreign policy was decided not by him alone, or by him and the secretary of state, but by consultations with the entire cabinet.[173] Having spent his four vice presidential years presiding over the Senate, President Jefferson knew how to bring together the members of Congress for reasonable discourse. When the national government moved to the newly created town, called "Washington," most members of Congress left their families at home and lived in shared boardinghouses while Congress was in session. Social life for these lonely men was rather meager. But in the new "White House," any congressman could drop by without an appointment, and at noon Jefferson typically met with his cabinet. Three times a week he invited about 12 congressmen for dinner at 3:30 P.M. All elected members were eventually invited to dine with the president. When dining with Federalists, Jefferson typically invited one group from that party who lived together in the same boardinghouse, but when dining with Republicans, he invited them from different boardinghouses so that members of his party would get to know other members who lived elsewhere. A Jefferson dinner was a treat: good food, good wine. And the president and his guests all sat at a round table, which equalized and unified them. Waiters did not stand about them as they talked; instead, Jefferson had a "dumbwaiter" beside him, a mini-elevator that was sent up from the downstairs kitchen with food and drinks that Jefferson himself passed around. Uninhibited conversation was thus encouraged. As he told his guests, "You see we are alone and *our walls have no ears.*"[174] He wore informal clothes and slippers for shoes. As historian James Sterling Young explains, Jefferson's mode of dining brought "legislators belonging to different boardinghouse fraternities together in circumstances conducive to amicability and free from contention, and in such a way as to stimulate a sense of common party membership among them."[175]

Jefferson continued to write many letters to many people. And he was pleased that there were local Washington newspapers reporting politics, for he found that fact a confirmation of the democratic significance of journalism. As early as the 1790s, Jefferson had been a strong and effective supporter of starting newspapers, each "so that it might go through the states, and furnish a whig-vehicle of intelligence."[176] He was a genuine advocate of a free press who read opposition newspapers, not just those that supported his own ideology. As he explained, "The two papers will shew you both sides of our politics."[177] However, newspapers were never perfect. Jefferson complained in one letter that "Every word of mine which they can get hold of, however innocent, however orthodox, is twisted, tormented, perverted, and like the words of holy writ, are made to mean everything but what they were intended to mean."[178] But he never thought that freedom of the press should be curtailed, no matter how untrue and hateful some newspaper criticism of him and his government became. Such angry haters, he believed, should be "left to find their punishment in the public indignation."[179]

Jefferson held many private conversations with members of Congress to help bind together the separate parts of government. Thus he used the heritage of Philadelphia's constitution-making meetings to correct President George Washington's mistake of separating himself from Congress. President John Adams' mistake of attacking the Bill of Rights was also corrected. And the new United States government continued to exist in its fundamental democracy through the shift in leadership from the Federalist Party to the Republican Party. In 1804, Jefferson was reelected overwhelmingly.

Thomas Jefferson believed that "The general government has no powers but such as the constitution has given it."[180] Within the Constitution, President Jefferson achieved significant progress, such as a major expansion of the size of the United States with the purchase from France of the Louisiana Territory. But his essential achievement was to confirm and strengthen the American democracy that had been declared with the Declaration of Independence and then created with the Constitution. In his daily diplomacy and reasonable discourse, he focused on actuality: on facts and rational plans.

Jefferson's understanding that reason is essential to democracy inspired him to propose that the government foster reason by education. He saw that "the most legitimate engine of government" was to "Educate and inform the whole mass of the people."[181] The original purpose of general education was "to enable every man to judge for himself what will secure or endanger his freedom."[182] He thought that ignorance in the citizenry would inevitably lead to tyranny: "If a nation expects to be ignorant and free in a state of civilization, it expects what never was and never will be."[183] The education he envisioned was not a form of government propaganda, not a system enforcing uniform beliefs among citizens. He believed that "Since God had created mind free, all attempts to influence it by temporal punishments, or burthens, or by civil incapacitation, tend only to beget habits of hypocrisy and meanness, and are a departure from the plan of the holy author of our religion...." [184] Well before he became president, Jefferson wrote from Paris to his old teacher Chancellor Wythe that "by far the most important bill in our whole code, is that for the diffusion of knowledge among the people." He urged his teacher, "Preach, my dear sir, a crusade against ignorance; establish and improve the law for educating the common people." [185] Later on, when planning the gravestone to stand above his own tomb, Jefferson asked that he be honored as the author of the Declaration of Independence and of Virginia's law for religious freedom, but also as "Father of the University of Virginia." After his presidency, he returned to Virginia and, by his remarkable leadership, virtually created that university: its classic and appealing architecture as well as its education system.

Long before that achievement, Thomas Jefferson had pressed the state of Virginia to create, through legislation, a fundamental educational system for citizens. He did not see this as simply one item on a desirable agenda, but rather as the highest-priority issue for cultivating reason in the public. His *Notes on the State of Virginia*, a book written between 1781 and 1782, while he was incapacitated after being thrown by his horse, contains many empirical descriptions of the Virginia of his day, including its physical landscape, natural resources, and indigenous peoples. It also made strong empirical recommendations for the state's future course. Regarding his proposed bill for public education, Jefferson said that the key to preserving liberty is

> to diffuse knowledge more generally through the mass of the people. This bill proposes to lay off every county into small districts of five or six miles square, called hundreds, and in each of them to establish a school for teaching reading, writing and arithmetic....The ultimate result of the whole scene of education would be the teaching all the children of the state reading, writing, and common arithmetic....
>
> The general objects of this law are to provide an education adapted to the years, to the capacity, and the condition of every one, and directed to their freedom and happiness. Specific details were not proper for the law. These must be the business of the visitors intrusted with its execution....Instead...of putting the Bible and Testament into the hands of the children at an age when their judgments are not sufficiently matured for religious inquiries, their memories may here be stored with the useful facts from Grecian, Roman, European and American history. The first elements of morality, too, may be instilled into their minds; such as, when further developed as their judgments advance in strength, may teach them how to work out their own great happiness, by showing them that it does not depend on the condition of life in which chance has placed them but is always the result of a good conscience, good health, occupation and freedom in all just pursuits.

Jefferson proposed lessons for students of various ages and in various educational situations, but the following statement is the crux of his thinking about education:

> But of all the views of this law none is more important, none more legitimate, than that of rendering the people the safe, as they are the ultimate, guardians of

their own liberty. For this purpose the reading in the first stage, where they will receive their whole education, is proposed, as has been said, to be chiefly historical. History, by apprizing them of the past, will enable them to judge of the future; it will avail them of the experience of other times and other nations; it will qualify them as judges of the actions and designs of men; it will enable them to know ambition under every disguise it may assume and, knowing it, to defeat its views. In every government on earth is some trace of human weakness, some germ of corruption and degeneracy, which cunning will discover and wickedness insensibly open, cultivate, and improve. Every government degenerates when trusted to the rulers of the people alone. The people themselves, therefore, are its only safe depositories; and, to render even them safe, their minds must be improved to a certain degree. This indeed is not all that is necessary, though it be essentially necessary. An amendment of our constitution must here come in aid of the public education. The influence over government must be shared among all the people.[186]

As president, Jefferson did not succeed in establishing a national law for education, though his concern for public education did spread widely. Moreover, his establishment of the University of Virginia was a significant example for future universities. He urged the birth of the university "on a plan so broad and liberal and *modern,* as to be worth patronizing with the public support, and be a temptation to the youth of other States to come and drink of the cup of knowledge and fraternize with us."[187] In 1814, in the midst of another war with Great Britain, British forces set the Library of Congress on fire—along with the rest of Washington—a crime Jefferson called one of the "acts of barbarism which do not belong to a civilized age."[188] To rebuild the Library, he offered Congress nearly 6,500 of his own books.

Though never perfect, the democracy of the United States of America emerged as a mighty example for nations throughout the world in the first generation after the Revolution. It has stood in such superior contrast to the tyrannical and chaotic results of most other revolutions.

Even today, the United States much remember how it was created. And modern democracy must be spread throughout the world.

BIBLIOGRAPHY

ANDRIST, RALPH K. (ED.). *George Washington: A Biography in His Own Words.* Vol. 1. New York: Newsweek, 1972.

BAILYN, BERNARD. *The Ideological Origins of the American Revolution.* Cambridge, Mass.: The Belknap Press of Harvard University Press, 1967.

BARBER, BENJAMIN, AND PATRICK WATSON. *The Struggle for Democracy.* Boston: Little, Brown, 1988.

BARBER, JAMES DAVID. *The Presidential Character: Predicting Performance in the White House.* 4th ed. Englewood Cliffs, N.J.: Prentice Hall, 1992.

BARBER, JAMES DAVID. *The Pulse of Politics: Electing Presidents in the Media Age.* New Brunswick, N.J.: Transaction Publishers, 1992.

BARBER, JAMES DAVID, AND BARBER KELLERMAN, (EDS.). *Women Leaders in American Politics.* Englewood Cliffs, N.J.: Prentice Hall, 1986.

BEARD, CHARLES A., AND MARY R. BEARD. *A Basic History of the United States.* Philadelphia:

The Blakiston Company, 1994.

BLUM, JOHN M. ET AL. *The National Experience: A History of the United States.* 2nd ed. New York: Harcourt, Brace & World, Inc., 1968.

BOORSTIN, DANIEL J. (ED.). *An American Primer.* Chicago: The University of Chicago Press, 1966.

BOORSTIN, DANIEL J. *The Genius of American Politics.* Chicago: The University of Chicago Press, 1953.

BOWEN, CATHERINE DRINKER. *The Most Dangerous Man in America: Scenes from the Life of Benjamin Franklin.* Boston: Little, Brown, 1974.

BRODIE, FAWN M. *Thomas Jefferson: An Intimate History.* New York: W. W. Norton, 1974.

BURNS, JAMES MACGREGOR. *The Vineyard of Liberty.* New York: Alfred A. Knopf, 1982.

CHINARD, GILBERT. *Thomas Jefferson: The Apostle of Americanism.* 2nd ed. Ann Arbor: University of Michigan Press, 1964.

CHRISTENSON, REO M., AND ROBERT O. MCWILLIAMS. *Voice of the People: Readings in Public Opinion and Propaganda.* New York: McGraw-Hill, 1967.

CLARK, RONALD W. *Benjamin Franklin: A Biography.* New York: Random House, 1983.

COMMAGER, HENRY STEELE. *Jefferson, Nationalism, and the Enlightenment.* New York: George Braziller, 1975.

CUNNINGHAM, NOBLE E., JR. *In Pursuit of Reason: The Life of Thomas Jefferson.* Baton Rouge: Louisiana State University Press, 1987.

EDITORS OF NEWSWEEK BOOKS. *Thomas Jefferson: A Biography in His Own Words.* Vols. 1 and 2. New York: Newsweek, 1974.

FAY, BERNARD. *Franklin: The Apostle of Modern Times.* Boston: Little, Brown, 1929.

FAULKNER, HAROLD UNDERWOOD. *American Political and Social History.* 4th ed. New York: F.S. Crofts & Co., 1946.

FLEMING, THOMAS (ED.). *Benjamin Franklin: A Biography in His Own Words.* Vol. 1. New York: Newsweek, 1972.

FRIEDRICH, CARL J. *Constitutional Government and Democracy: Theory and Practice in Europe and America.* Rev. ed. Boston: Ginn, 1950.

GRADIN, HARLAN JOEL. *George Washington: The Establishment of the Presidential Office.* Social Science Course 192. Durham, N.C.: Duke University.

HALLOWELL, JOHN H. *Main Currents in Modern Political Thought.* New York: Henry Holt, 1950.

HOFSTADTER, ROBERT. *Anti-Intellectualism in American Life.* New York: Alfred A. Knopf, 1963.

JEFFERSON, THOMAS. *Autobiography of Thomas Jefferson.* New York: Capricorn Books, n.d.

KELLY, ALFRED H., AND WINFRED A. HARBISON. *The American Constitution: Its Origins and Development.* 4th ed. New York: W.W. Norton, 1970.

KETCHAM, RALPH. *James Madison: A Biography.* Charlottesville: University Press of Virginia, 1990.

KETCHUM, RICHARD M. (ED.). *The World of George Washington.* New York: American Heritage, 1974.

KOCH, ADRIENNE, AND WILLIAM PEDEN (EDS.). *The Life and Selected Writings of Thomas Jefferson.* New York: The Modern Library, 1944.

KOCH, ADRIENNE. *Jefferson and Madison: The Great Collaboration.* London: Oxford University Press, 1970.

LEWIS, R.W.B. *The American Adam: Innocence, Tragedy and Tradition in the Nineteenth Century.* Chicago: University of Chicago Press, 1955.

LIPSET, SEYMOUR MARTIN. *The First New Nation: The United States in Historical and Comparative Perspective.* New York: Basic Books, 1963.

LITTLE, SHELBY. *George Washington.* New York: Capricorn Books, 1962.

MASON, ALPHEUS THOMAS. *Free Government in the Making: Readings in American Political Thought.* New York: Oxford University Press, 1949.

MAY, HENRY F. *The Enlightenment in America.* New York: Oxford University Press, 1976.

MAYO, BERNARD (ED.). *Jefferson Himself.* Boston: Houghton Mifflin, 1942.

MORRIS, RICHARD B. *Witness at the Creation: Hamilton, Madison, Jay, and the Constitution.* New York: Holt, Rinehart and Winston, 1985.

ONUF, PETER S. (ED.). *Jeffersonian Legacies.* Charlottesville: University Press of Virginia, 1933.

ORLANDI, ENZO (ED.). *The Life and Times of Washington.* New York: Rand McNally, 1967.

PADOVER, SAUL K. (ED.). *The Complete Jefferson: Containing His Major Writings, Published and Unpublished, Except His Letters.* New York: Buell, Sloan & Pearce, 1943.

RANDALL, WILLARD STERNE. *A Little Revenge: Benjamin Franklin and His Son.* Boston: Little, Brown, 1984.

RANDOLPH, SARAH N. *The Domestic Life of Thomas Jefferson.* Charlottesville: University Press of Virginia, 1978.

RUTHERFURD, LIVINGSTON. *John Peter Zenger: His Press, His Trial and A Bibliography of Zenger Imprints.* Gloucester, Mass.: Peter Smith, 1963.

RUTLAND, ROBERT ALLEN. *The Birth of the Bill of Rights, 1776–1791.* Chapel Hill: University of North Carolina Press, 1955.

SCHATTSCHNEIDER, E.E. *Two Hundred Million Americans in Search of Government.* New York: Holt, Rinehart and Winston, 1969.

SCHWARTZ, BARRY. *George Washington: The Making of an American Symbol.* New York: Free Press, 1987.

SHAW, PETER. *The Character of John Adams.* New York: W.W. Norton, 1977.

SHENKMAN, RICHARD, AND KURT REIGER. *One-Night Stands with American History: Odd, Amusing, and Little-Known Incidents.* New York: Quill, 1982.

SMITH, BRADFORD. *Bradford of Plymouth.* Philadelphia: J.B. Lippincott Company, 1951.

STEPHENS, MITCHELL. *A History of News: From the Drum to the Satellite.* New York: Viking, 1988.

THE STAFF OF SOCIAL SCIENCES, UNIVERSITY OF CHICAGO (EDS.). *The People Shall Judge: Readings in the Formation of American Policy.* Vol. 1. Chicago: University of Chicago Press, 1949.

TUCHMAN, BARBARA W. *The March of Folly: From Troy to Vietnam.* New York: Alfred A. Knopf, 1984.

WILLS, GARRY. *Under God: Religion and American Politics.* New York: Simon & Schuster, 1990.

WILSON, FRANCIS GRAHAM. *The American Political Mind: A Textbook in Political Theory.* New York: McGraw-Hill, 1949.

WOODWARD, W.E., *George Washington: The Image and the Man.* Greenwich, Conn.: Fawcett, 1956.

YOUNG, JAMES STERLING. *The Washington Community, 1800–1828.* New York: Columbia University Press, 1966.

PART FIVE

Conclusion

14

To Make
Democracy Happen

The present worldwide movement for democracy is remarkable. According to the National Endowment for Democracy, 99 nations were democracies in 1992. The United Nations has member nations that are not democracies, but the UN has been pressing governments to refrain from using violence against people, internally and externally, and to govern more justly.

We live in an era of widespread concern for human rights. In 1993, the human rights organization Amnesty International had 1,100,000 members in 150 countries, with about 400,000 members in the United States alone. Of the 42,000 political prisoners whose cases Amnesty International took on, more than 38,000 have been released. Several other human rights organizations have been formed or expanded in recent years. In the United States, many new groups are working hard to spread democracy, especially by encouraging and monitoring elections in other countries. The Next Century Institution, a project of the 21st Century Foundation in Washington, is reaching out to organize the main national democracies to cooperate in creating new democracies in other nations.

There has never been a better time in history for the development of democracy. The Cold War is over, so the two super powers are no longer engaging other countries in their battle against each other. These nations are now freer to develop as they wish and can. But this period might not continue. Action is necessary now to make democracy the permanent norm of government throughout the world.

I have sought throughout this book to make the case for democracy as the only form of government that protects the individual's rights and truly respects human dignity. The freedoms to decide where to live, what to work at, whom to talk with, what religion (or nonreligion) to practice, what to think and say, are all much stronger under democracy than under any other form of government. Free democracy naturally allows nations to have their different cultures. Democracy is political, not totalitarian.

Within a democracy, violence against citizens is typically far less than in nondemocracies. Economically, democracies are usually better for people than the chaos and manipulation typically experienced in nondemocracies. And a democracy almost never goes to war against another democracy. Those are facts. That is why it is so important to seize this moment to make democracy the rule all over the globe.

There are many exciting democratic movements right now. Throughout Latin America, democracies have been established and are growing more secure every year. Even in the dictatorship of China, there is a large group of people arguing for the democratic transformation of their country. But I will concentrate here on two beginning democracies whose rapid progress toward democracy is confounding the gloomy predictions of just a decade ago: Russia and South Africa.

RUSSIA BEGINS DEMOCRACY

After the huge Union of Soviet Socialist Republics fell apart in the early 1990s, Russia—the heartland of that sprawling Communist empire—remained the largest country in the world. Today Russia is breaking away from Communism and moving toward democracy. The other former pieces of the USSR are clearly not trying democracy. In Belarus, for example, the leader was elected president in the middle of 1994 despite his promise to ban both private property and free enterprise. In Ukraine, about 52 million people either lack jobs or work at very poor-paying jobs; the average income is about 10% what it is in Russia. In Georgia, a leader says "It's impossible to restore the empire."[1] In Belarus, Ukraine, and Georgia, the movement for democracy has not yet begun.

In Russia, however, the foreign minister has said, "I believe we can succeed in seizing this opportunity to make Russia a democratic state."[2] At least some of the world's established democracies have tried to help Russia develop democracy. Russia's people have already voted in free elections. The present elected president of Russia, Boris Yeltsin, was very popular when he took office and, nationally and internationally, has come out strongly for democracy.

But trouble grew. As Yeltsin said in 1993, "Corruption is devouring the state from top to bottom."[3] The falsely named Liberal Democratic Party has been working against democracy and liberty. In the December 1993 parliamentary election, Yeltsin's candidates did badly. In 1994, there were 64 members of the Liberal Democratic Party sitting in the parliament. In April of that year, the LDP's 340 deputies at the party convention unanimously voted absolute power to the head of the party, Zhirinovsky. This is the man who said in 1991, "I say it quite plainly—when I come to power, there will be a dictatorship."[4] He even wanted Russia to attack Alaska!

Yeltsin, aged 63, was quite ill in March 1994, but he has remained hopeful and intends to continue as president until the next presidential election in 1996. Though the December 1993 election ratified a change in the constitution that gives the Russian president much more power, including the right to ignore certain acts of the parliament, Yeltsin seems sincerely determined not to become another Stalin. As he has noted, "The elections showed once more that the majority of voters are against the return to a communist utopia and support free enterprise and a diversified market economy."[5]

The democratic fundamentals have been put into operation in Russia: there are free elections, there is a constitution that was voted into being by the parliament, and there are human rights safeguards. But the main democratic challenges still confront Russia: how to establish full freedom and equality of citizens under the law, how to make reason and the rule of law the norm in a land that has known little of either, and, most of all, how to control violence inside Russia and on its borders.

The current Russian Federation contains 21 republics and several different ethnic groups speaking nearly 100 different languages. The country has only been independent for a few years and already some of these groups are at each other's throats. There is much resentment of the new democracy among militarists and conservatives, and even many ordinary people, because of the loss of empire and lowering of living standards that have taken place during the recent years of upheaval. Given this resentment in a country with a legacy of violence and none of democracy, some are predicting that in Russia, "civil war is more than likely."[6]

Russia has never been a democracy, though Aleksandr Kerensky almost made it one in 1917. Russians have gone through extreme violence in this century. In the civil war of 1918–20, 20 million lives were lost; then, under Stalin, more than 20 million were killed; and in World War II, about 27 million Russians died. The new Russian Federation has inherited from the old Soviet Union tens of thousands of nuclear weapons—amazingly powerful versions of the two bombs the United States dropped on Japan in 1945.[7]

Each year recently, tens of thousands of police officers have been fired and more than a thousand have been killed. In 1993, Russian military units fought in civil wars in other parts of the former USSR, though the Russian foreign minister, Andrei Kozyrev has said that the troops must be controlled by the Russian government.[8] In 1994, violent crime in Russia increased, and the threat of street violence by the right has also increased, especially from the rightist Liberal Democratic Party. Zhirinovsky said in 1994 that "I won't get votes. It's war out there, and I'm out to win." He has a significant following among military officers and members of the old Soviet secret police.[9] Kozyrev is much worried: "There is internal strife in Russia. There is a party of war, new imperialists, even fascists....The typical Soviet mentality was to take up your rifle and grab power."[10] A popular Russian writer, Aleksandr Solzhenitsyn, declared on his return to Russia from long exile that "In this country there are murderers and victims, the persecutors and the persecuted....The murderers and the persecutors must personally repent for what they have done."[11]

The first requirement for democracy is to have the parliament and president take control of the military and police. Will Yeltsin be able to do this—without becoming a dictator? In 1993, he made a serious mistake when he ordered the military to retake the building where parliamentary members were gathered, because he had demanded them to leave and they refused. The front of the building was heavily blasted. This proved to be a national and international scandal. But in 1994, Yeltsin made this pledge:

> ...I won't hide the fact that I would like Russians to remember me as the man who did his best to free his people once and for all from the legacy of the civil war. From now on, let our Russia be a homeland for all its sons and daughters, whatever political camp they may belong to. And may God help us.[12]

The second main challenge for Russia is to establish freedom and equality for its citizens. Though the old Communist totalitarian dictatorship is gone forever, a new type of totalitarianism could develop. "Totalitarianism" in Russia "has deep roots in our society," said the deputy chairman of the Moscow City Council,[13] but a Professor Lourie saw the Russian people as "clamoring for freedom."[14] With the horrors of totalitarianism still fresh in their minds, political scientist Ian Bremmer has noted, "the Russians have been stepping up demands for dual citizenship, berating the government for discriminatory language policies and discussing secessionist alternatives...."[15]

The government had not become total. Moscow correspondent Fred Coleman described that "The government and parliament differ over key issues such as the budget, but so far they have kept their differences in check—partly because neither side wants to provoke Yeltsin's anger and draw him back...."[16]

Suppose, however, that economic problems get worse instead of better, that criminal violence continues to increase. Then order may become more important to Russians than freedom and equality, and they may be willing, like the Germans in the early 1930s, to sacrifice their new liberties if they think order requires it. Suppose Yeltsin dies suddenly or loses the 1996 presidential election to Zhirinovsky—the man who has promised autocratic rule to restore the glories of old Russia and who "has vowed that his first act as President would be to throw the Jewish comic in jail."[17]

Freedom and equality were, in 1994, only potentials. It remains to be seen whether Russians will choose Zhirinovsky—or someone like him—who offers totalitarian dictatorship, or Yeltsin, who offers them freedom and equality:

> I love Russia and its people, and they feel it. I have been destined to carry out the difficult mission of leading Russia out of a totalitarian past and bringing it into the family of nations of the free world, where every person is the creator of his own happiness and can openly express his thoughts and opinions without fearing the secret police and its agents, recruited under pressure or of their own free will, and where the state serves a person rather than the other way around.[18]

The third requirement for democracy—rule by law—also seemed a very hard challenge in Russia in 1994. The Russian economy was extremely complicated and fragmented, with much business done secretly and criminally. Professor Lourie has noted that "The economy continues to disintegrate; food is used as a political weapon. The result is large-scale starvation, no stranger to Russia."[19] According to journalist Claire Sterling, "It is common knowledge that millions of ordinary citizens steal state property, trade on the black [e.g., secret] market, swindle each other and buy or sell protection."[20] Zhirinovsky has sought to take advantage of this chaos: "It's the sorry state of affairs in this country that forces me to take so tough a stand to avert something even worse....If there were a healthy economy and security for the people, I would lose all the votes I have."[21]

The murder rate in Russia was about ten times higher than that in the United States in 1994.[22] The Moscow police feel overwhelmed: "The criminals have more money, more guns, more everything." Organized crime has reached into nearly all types of activities, including drugs—Russia today has more than a million drug addicts—and "legitimate business"—approximately 150 criminal gangs control some 40,000 Russian companies.[23] Yeltsin has said that at least 1,000 *groups*—not individuals—"have contacts with international organized crime."[24] And national officials have gotten into the organized crime game, using "anti-crime crusades" to eliminate rival criminal organizations. Russian organized crime has even moved some of its operations to America and Europe.

Currency laws—very important in a nation desperate for hard currency—are widely warped. People commonly take out of Russia more than the $500 allowed under the law. In 1994, Yeltsin was trying to get "tough sanctions against those guilty of violations and holding hard currency abroad illegally." In 1993, 30 bankers were murdered.[25]

The old Communist command system of production has collapsed, but only about 31 percent of Russian businesses today are private. Transforming state enterprises into private ones has proved very hard because Russia still does not have the kind of clear commercial law needed for a free economy. Also, there is great fear that doing away with state enterprises entirely will result in massive unemployment. As Yeltsin has said, "Our road is strewn with obstacles. We have no experience of free enterprise."[26]

Government officials' attitude toward law also leaves much to be desired. The election laws have been warped, and sexism has practically been institutionalized: new government jobs are given only to men, never to women.[27]

Given Russia's long, long time of injustice, is fair law a good possibility? There are Russians who want "to create some sort of a legal framework for society to start the process of reform."[28] And Yeltsin has said, "I have fully resolved that we must keep on with the strategy of democratic reforms. At the same time, we will have to make certain corrections in our tactics."[29] But though he seems to understand that democracy requires strong, clear, just law, chaotic conditions are pushing him in the opposite direction. In June 1994, Yeltsin decreed that the police would not need warrants to search offices and homes, to investigate finances, or to arrest suspects—who can now be jailed for 30 days without challenge. These decrees violate the Russian constitution.

The fourth essential for democracy is rule by reason. Reason requires realistic perceptions, which in turn depend upon accurate information. Historically, Russia has tended toward secrecy, fantasy, and propaganda. But today there are good indications that Russians want to know the truth and that the government realizes there is a need to develop and distribute genuine factual information.

Russian government officials, especially Yeltsin, linked with the United States "to cooperate on intelligence issues when they have common interests."[30] It has also moved to develop real education for the people—not fantasies that support Russian leaders or "the dream of empire."[31] There has been a "massive educational campaign to fill the minds of disenchanted Soviets with the values and ideas that helped the nation of the civilized world to survive and prosper...the primacy of individual rights, respect for private ownership, the rule of law and ideological tolerance...."[32]

Independent professional journalists who are not afraid to report on significant issues truthfully are desperately needed if democracy is to have a real chance. The Russian news media—television, radio, and newspapers alike—have continued to convey more propaganda than real news since the breakup of the USSR—and the people know it: a poll showed that most Russians still equate "news" with "propaganda." Despite popular resentment, Russia's new "government has kept tight control over the Russian media, closing down several newspapers in the process."[33] There have been some signs that this attitude is beginning to change, however. In 1994, Russian television leaders conferred with former U.S. President Jimmy Carter's Center to learn how television news could improve.

Russia today is poised between two courses. The one leads back to the old Russia, the Russia of Ivan the Terrible and Stalin: violent, tyrannical, inward-looking, and given to fantasies. The second course leads forward to a new Russia: democratic, realistic, peaceful, and open to Western ideas about justice and freedom, rule through law and reason.

The first course is represented by Zhirinovsky. He "is one of the few leaders who speak in a language that average Russians can understand."[34] He often seems bombastic and crude almost to the point of comicality—but then, so did Hitler before he took power. In Russia, Zhirinovsky's "listeners seemed genuinely charmed by his sense of humor, his flair for dramatic gestures, his bravado."[35] He has already made it into the parliament, and he is a serious candidate for the presidency.

The second course is represented by Yeltsin. He, too, connects with the Russian people: "I am part of the people and speak to them in a language they understand."[36] And he has expressed confidence that "truth is truth and truth will overcome the left, the right, and the center."[37] Russian democracy needs him to be the kind of president Thomas Jefferson was at a crucial point in American history. Yeltsin and his democratic allies—in and out of government—need to understand how democracy has worked in other places and times so they can succeed in making it work in Russia today.

Which course Russians will choose—the Russia that was or the Russia that can be—will probably be known before the century is out. The strong need is for Russian politicians to understand how democracy has really worked, so they can work on it.

SOUTH AFRICA BEGINS DEMOCRACY

Like Russia, South Africa is at a crucial stage of transition, though it differs from Russia in one important way: it has long been a "democracy"—though only for whites. Today South Africa's fundamental challenge is to create a genuine democracy, one for *all* citizens of this large, various nation.

Throughout the continent of Africa, there has been an enormous amount of killing and torture, sickness and starvation, ethnic conflict and civil war, injustice and oppression. There have been few democracies. Most attempts to establish democracy have been defeated by military coups. Therefore the challenge to create a real democracy is tough, but South Africa's determination to meet that challenge is impressive. A majority of South Africans of all races realize the need to establish full democracy without delay. A leading South African democrat declared not long ago that "the threats to peace, stability and security for all in South Africa have never been greater." [38] In the first all-racial elections in 1994, millions of newly enfranchised citizens came out to vote. And South Africa's new president is strongly dedicated to democracy. The new Senate (90 members) and National Assembly (400 members) are working to create a permanent constitution by April 1996. [39]

The interim constitution provides for an unusual system in which the president is elected by the parliament, one deputy president is selected by the president, and another deputy president is selected by the party that came in second in the national election. The next national election is to be held in 1999. The new Bill of Rights is to be managed by a new Constitutional Court. [40]

The movement for democracy was set in motion in 1989 by Frederik Willem de Klerk, the white president elected by the minority (13 percent) white population. For decades, South African politics had been dominated by the racial segregation policy of apartheid. Essentially, whites ruled the country and kept most of its economic benefits for themselves. Some concessions were made to the mixed-race population and to Asians, but blacks—the great majority of the country's population—were either packed off to artificially created "homelands" remote from the economic center of South Africa or into segregated South African townships. They were generally allowed to work only at menial jobs for low pay. Despite years of protest, strikes, and violence, the white leaders maintained a hard line. Then, in a startling turnaround, President de Klerk started to dismantle apartheid in 1990 and to move toward creating a democracy for *all* of South Africa's people. To do away with racism, he hoped for "change of heart." In 1994, he pronounced himself convinced that "the majority of South Africans have adapted to the new situation relatively well." [41] He became one of the two deputy

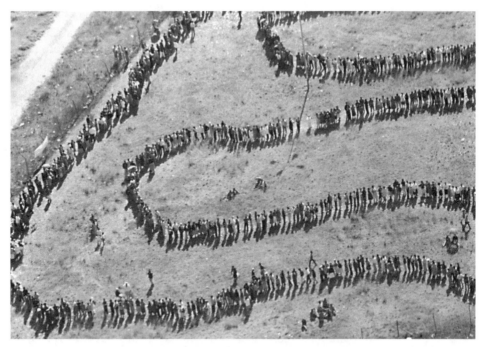

Long lines of voters wait outside the polling station in the black township of Soweto to participate in South Africa's first all-race elections.

presidents in the new government, and has worked successfully with the new president.

The new president of South Africa, a black man named Nelson Mandela, is a remarkable political leader. Back in 1964, Mandela's politics got him arrested and sent to jail—where he stayed for 27 years! Amnesty International, advocates for human rights, tried hard to have Mandela released. He was finally released in 1990, and in 1994, his party won 63 percent of the vote in the first fully democratic election.[42] Mandela was 76 years old in 1994, but he was healthy and very active. He rose at 4:30 A.M. every day to exercise and eat a healthy breakfast. His guiding principle was democracy: "What we stand for is the result of a democratic process."[43] In the past, he criticized President de Klerk, but after he became convinced de Klerk was sincerely trying to democratize the country, Mandela began to work closely with him. Democracy in South Africa was a great hope for both of them.

The largest issue in South Africa today is internal violence. One South African who spoke out for peace, and went to a meeting for peace, was shot dead within two weeks. According to police statistics, 17,467 South Africans were murdered in 1993.[44] Many more were hurt. In March 1994, the death toll was approximately 300 people—more than in any month in the past 10 years.[45] Thirteen people were killed one Friday night in April 1994.[46] There has been white violence against blacks, especially by the "neo-Nazi Afrikaner Resistance Movement," an outfit of thousands of people.[47] But there is a "war of all against all" in South Africa, and as a result, the country's murder rate is ten times more than murder in the United States.[48] Many people have grown frightened. One South African said, "I can't put my life on the line for the vote." Another noted that "because of this political problem we began to hate each other."[49] But some, like this farmer, are tired of battles and willing to give democracy a chance: "As long as they leave me to rest in peace, I'll leave them to rest in peace....I've got no more feeling for war; there's enough room for all of us in this country."[50]

President de Klerk moved to stop violence in early 1994, before the election. He assured the country that the government was "in control" and told South Africans, "There is no need for panic." He then sent 2,000 troops and police out to stop white right-wing bands from upsetting the election and brought the aspiring dictator Chief Buthelezi under control.[51] Fortunately, by the time the election took place in April, nearly all violence had stopped. So millions came out to vote—a great number of them lining up for a very long time to do so. About three-quarters of the voters—16.2 million—were blacks, who had never been permitted to vote before.[52]

Nelson Mandela said his force would stop the violence. He has acted strongly to transform South Africa from a country of harsh physical clashes—bombs against bombs—to one where differences are resolved through political discourse and debate—reason vying with reason. He taught his lieutenants to shift from fighting to arguing politics.[53] He told all South Africans, "Don't be afraid."[54] He declared that "Political persuasion and security measures must go hand in hand."[55] He suspended any members of the African National Congress who carried arms, "because one of our commitments is to ensure gun control."[56] He saw his actions as "a leap forward for peace."[57]

The new government was in no way meant to be a dictatorship, but to guarantee freedom and equality for all. Even before the new election, there were many "non-governmental organizations, trade unions, civic groups and religious associations"—institutions that promote a democratic climate.[58] But South Africa was for a long time "the most deeply and bitterly divided country in the world."[59] Not only were whites and blacks divided from each other but there were also deep divisions among blacks and among whites.

But by 1994, the blacks and whites sought connection and community. Having never voted before, 16.2 million blacks voted in 1994, about three-quarters of the voters. De Klerk said, "Apartheid has failed. The best way is negotiations."[60] He said that "We have proved we can work together."[61] Also, "I stand for a good balance of power between central governments and regional governments."[62] And his fundamental objective was citizens coming together.

President Nelson Mandela determined freedom. He has made it clear that he understands the major essential actions to create and confirm democracy. He accepts democratic decision making: "What the people decide, we accept."[63] He has declared that as president he will never "do something which is contrary to the decision of the government of national unity."[64] Fortunately, he said, "People have proved we can work together," and "This is democracy."[65] Mandela declared, "I think every one of us will agree that the people of South Africa have been victorious. They have won."[66] Now "South Africans, blacks and whites, will work together to build a new country."[67] He summed up his political creed this way: "I have fought against white domination. I have fought against black domination. I have cherished the ideal of a democratic and free society in which all people live together in harmony and with equal opportunities."[68]

In 1993, more than 8,000 people, mostly whites, left the country—about twice as many as in 1992. But 1,500 people—mostly whites and Asians—moved into South Africa in 1993.[69] There is at least a possibility that the new democracy will make good on its promise of freedom and equality.

The question of decent, clear law is still uncertain. The economy of South Africa is very fragmented, with most of the wealth concentrated among whites and most of the poverty concentrated among blacks. For example, "About 18 million black families [earned] less than $220 a month" in 1994.[70] Many not only lack jobs but homes as well. Black women are treated unfairly under the law: "The majority of black women are married under 'customary law,' the government's codification of tribal customs in the Black Administration Act, which considers black women minors whose business is to be handled by their husbands, fathers, or sons."[71] And though the election of 1994 was a great step forward, it was not up to the fairness standards of modern democracies: "Millions of ballots were inexplicably lost."[72] The new slogan, "Jobs for all," is a big challenge in a nation whose rich business people are skilled manipulators of law.[73]

South Africa does have better economic potential than most new democracies. It is rich in gold, much more of which could be sold on the world market. And it has developed modern industries. Mandela realizes that the task is to spread prosperity from the top down through the populace. "We are rolling up our sleeves to begin tackling the problems our country faces," he has said, and "This means creating jobs, building houses, providing education and bringing peace and security for all."[74] It was conceivable that Nelson Mandela would work to get the parliament to create fair laws. He declared that "We are concerned about giving confidence and security to those who are worried that by these changes they are going to be in a disadvantaged position."[75] But the establishment of just law is not only determined by the president, in a democracy, but mainly by the representatives of the citizens. What they will do is not yet certain. What will happen to law as we approach the 21st century?

Another significant challenge for South Africa is to develop the habit of reason and political realism in the population. Journalism—newspapers, magazines, radio, and television—is the chief means of conveying information to the people in a democracy. Journalism in South Africa has a mixed record. It is modern and sophisticated in many ways, but it functioned for a long time under censorship laws that prevented it from telling the truth. And some groups in the country are violently opposed to a free press. In 1993, 100 journalists were attacked and 5 of them were killed.[76] Education, another essential for rule by reason, has a long way to go. Half of black South Africans cannot read or write.[77]

About seven million of them still live in remote "homelands," isolated from the country's political and economic mainstream. "The vast majority of our people are not oriented toward participation," said one political leader, "Now we have to teach them."[78]

Mandela knows that it is crucial to improve schools throughout the nation. And he was not at all moving into silence or privacy. He intellectually linked with other members of government. For example, "I have had discussions with all the police generals who are responsible for policy."[79] And for the public, Mandela said, "I try not to be a rabble rouser." He tried to focus on reality:

> The people want things explained to them clearly and rationally. They recognize when someone is speaking to them seriously. They want to see how you handle difficult situations, whether or not you stay calm.[80]

On May 10, 1994, President Nelson Mandela gave an inaugural address containing these words:

> Your Majesties, your Highnesses, distinguished guests, comrades, and friends,
> Today, all of us do, by presence here, and by our celebrations in other parts of our country and the world, confer glory and hope to newborn liberty. Out of the experience of an extraordinary human disaster that lasted too long must be born a society of which all humanity will be proud.
> Our daily deeds as ordinary South Africans must produce an actual South African reality that will reinforce humanity's belief in justice, strengthen its confidence in the nobility of the human soul and sustain all our hopes for a glorious life for all. All this we owe both to ourselves and to the peoples of the world who are so well represented here today....
> We are both humbled and elevated by the honour and privilege that you, the people of South Africa, have bestowed on us, as the first President of a united, democratic, non-racial and non-sexist South Africa, to lead our country out of the valley of darkness.
> We understand that there is no easy road to freedom. We know well that none of us acting alone can achieve success. We must therefore act together as a united people for national reconciliation, for nation building, for the birth of a new world.
> Let there be justice for all.
> Let there be peace for all.
> Let there be work, bread, water, and salt for all.
> Let each know that for each the body, the mind, and the soul have been freed to fulfill themselves.
> Never, never and never again shall it be that this beautiful land will again experience the oppression of one by another and suffer the indignity of being the skunk of the world.
> The sun shall never set on so glorious a human achievement.
> Let freedom reign.
> God bless Africa.[81]

That remarkable statement brings hope for South Africa's democracy. Mandela knows what in the past has failed democracy and what has helped it to flourish.

Beyond hopes, actions are essential.

HOW TO CREATE DEMOCRACIES

How can we make democracy live throughout the world?

The answers lack certainty because democracy is a relatively new form of government and every country is unique. Yet we have learned from the past and can bring that knowledge to bear on contemporary situations.

Here are the actions I see as crucial:

1. *Agreement on the Essentials.* Those advocating democracy should come to agreement—not on every detail, but on the basics. This book has been driven by the requirement that there are four essentials for democracy—control of violence, liberty and equality, law, and reason—and that has been backed by historical evidence. There is one other obvious essential—elections—for whatever else a nation achieves, it is no democracy unless it is governed by elected representatives. Supporting a government lacking any one of these basic requirements is a gross mistake. All will be imperfect, but only nations clearly committed to these fundamentals can be considered democracies and worthy of support.

2. *Organization.* Both domestic and international democracy assemblies should meet regularly to strategize. The international assembly should organize as a world political party for democracy. Domestic assemblies should also organize to strategize for essential issues, so the international assembly members do not merely spend their time competing with one another. There is strength in association.

3. *Economics.* International trade has become far more potentially beneficial to societies than it used to be. The organized democracies should agree to trade among themselves—but refuse to trade in any way with a nondemocracy. Then whenever a nation *does* become a real democracy, that nation should immediately receive funding from the other democracies and be admitted into trade with the democracies. On the other hand, whenever a democracy clearly falls into the nondemocratic camp, the democracies should stop trading with it. Fine trading relationships among democracies would be free trade, but even more limited trade would be a clear benefit. Dictatorships and lawless nations would then perceive that if they became democratic, their international trade would increase and with it, their standard of living.

4. *Military.* War should be as rare as possible, and of course should only be decided on by the elected representatives of the people, not by the nation's chief executive. The organized democracies should refuse to sell or send weapons or artillery to any nondemocracy. Whenever a nondemocracy attacks or seriously threatens a democracy, the democracies should present a unified military defense. In addition, when civil war begins in a nondemocracy, the unified democracies should decide to do whatever they must do to stop the violence. This would often mean using their coordinated military forces to end the mass murder and establish peace and justice.

5. *Immigration.* Democracies should permit immigration from other democracies, but not allow immigration from nondemocracies. Today, democracies typically restrict immigration. What would change is that they would signif-

icantly increase the amount of immigration permitted from other democracies as they cut off immigration from dictatorships. This would probably motivate the people living in nondemocracies—and perhaps even their leaders—to convert to democracy so they could travel to free nations. In cases of extreme violence against citizens living in an undemocratic society, a visit to a democratic society might provide brief respite to desperate victims.

6. *Publication.* Information travels around the world mostly by radio and television, and to some extent, by newspapers and magazines. Within nondemocracies, news is usually propaganda, dishonest information churned out to support the rulers. Therefore, it is essential that the organized democracies communicate ideas and information, not only among themselves, but also to the nondemocracies. People and leaders in the nondemocracies need to be informed about the advantages of democracy—how it works, how it has developed, information about problems and failures as well as its successes. The purpose would not be to present propaganda, but truth. Truth is a great advantage for democracies, in comparison with the worse political alternatives. True publication needs to be made understandable and interesting to ordinary citizens. And the communication should include good news, not just bad news.

7. *Federalism as an Alternative.* Federalism creates serious problems for democracies, especially in representation. For example, within a nation, some states are more populated than others, yet each state is entitled to the same number of representatives in the national parliament. But federal democracy is democracy. Therefore, a nondemocracy can be encouraged to become democracy by bringing together equally the parts of the nation or perhaps even by joining with other nations. Russia as the "Russian Federation" of 21 republics is an example of the first course. Russia as part of the "Commonwealth of Independent States" (the old Soviet Union) is an example of the second course. Since it is the responsibility of the national government to ensure justice, federal democracy can improve the human situation by, for instance, stepping in to stop violence between different ethnic cultures.

FOUR STRONG POSSIBILITIES

Democracies can get better. Their basic qualities can be improved. In fact, improvement is important to their survival. History shows that when democracy is neglected, it can crumble. The power of democracy to protect and advance humans should continually improve. This objective is essential, because democracies are taken for granted too often and therefore lapse into deterioration. Organized effort works better than fragmented effort.

The essentials above are based on research. In contrast, the following ideas for improving democracies are speculative and should not be put into practice until they are researched, assessed, and debated. The four fundamentals need to be improved, even in the United States.

1. *Reason.* Reason is most important in elections. Citizens have to know how to vote and how to make a reasoned choice among candidates. The voting procedure should be simple, direct, and publicly known. Information on where and how to register to vote should be easily available to citizens, and there should be no requirements that serve to eliminate ordinary citizens. National elections should be held during the same hours throughout the nation so that voters in one area, on their way to cast their votes, will not hear news of the results of voting in another area in an earlier time zone. Election day should be a holiday, so that voting is as convenient for workers as it is for leaders and retired and unemployed people. Where to vote and how to get there should be clearly known to all citizens. Government employees who oversee the process and report the results must be carefully selected as honest champions of democracy. The local district where voters vote for their local officials should not be physically complex but simple. It should be a real community where people live relatively close together—a roughly square area rather than some odd-looking area created on a map to separate different types of humans. And election results need to be straight and simple. Voters are equal: each citizen has one vote to cast for any representative desired—not voting any more than one vote for one candidate. All citizens should be required to vote; those who fail to do that duty for democracy should be fined. Rule by reason requires that each person be well enough informed to have the capacity to vote and responsible enough to take the trouble to vote.

Political reason depends on news. For democracy to work, citizens must have political information. Prior to voting, they need to learn the facts about the candidates: their pasts, their presents, their plans. The immediate source of that information is journalism. The cost of television, radio, newspapers, and magazines should be low enough to be easily affordable by individuals; then news companies would make profits on wide sales. The news should be well researched, so that the national community would have accurate knowledge. That means news stories would be based on real investigation: reporters going out and finding out what actually happened, not simply dreaming up interesting theories and speculations. Journalism needs to cover many issues, but its most important subject is politics.

The challenge of journalism is to make reality interesting. The news should include good news: stories of successes, rather than a steady stream of horrors and failures, exciting scandals and violence. Newswriters and commentators must learn how to present the news in clear, understandable, and fascinating ways that will appeal to average citizens, including the less educated. News, of course, is what is happening now, but news stories should include history that is relevant to breaking events. Complexification and fantasy should be avoided. The political purpose of news is to help people think and act, not wonder or feel. News is essential.

Reason also depends on education. In a democracy, the ideal is public education, operated by the national government, from kindergarten through the university level. Public education should be free for all, so that rich and poor have equal access to knowledge. And the quality of schools should be equal throughout the nation. One common language should be used throughout the school system—ideally, the main language which is now the nation's most common language—because all citizens have to share communication that they understand. Education should concentrate on reading, writing, mathematics, and history, including the history of democracy. Art, music, and fiction should also be studied, but politics should be presented as reality concreted by actual truth. Throughout the educational system, teachers and professors should work together as teams, supporting one another in teaching effectively and honestly. The government should also support research to discover the most effective teaching methods and curriculum—a research subject rare in U.S. education today, even in universities. Teaching should include information on human varieties throughout the world, but the concentration should be on understanding human relations. Emphasis should be put on successful coalitions in which people have come together to strengthen the blessings of human fellowship. Education for all citizens should include the understanding of politics, taught with honesty, not ideological manipulation.

2. *Law.* A democratic government operates by rules decided on by the representatives of the people. The fundamental law is the constitution, including both governmental procedures and substantive human rights. New democracies should begin by establishing a constitution and committing themselves to obey it. Once a constitution is agreed upon, it should not be changed except by nearly complete public agreement. New democracies should study constitutions that have worked well for other democracies.

The actual procedures of democracy must be ruled by law. Laws made by the parliament should include basic procedures of the parliament itself—law ruling parliament. Members of parliament should be required to meet as a group, to discuss and then vote on the laws they pass, rather than casting votes without ever having deliberated together: the purpose of parliament is to meet in order to make common group decisions. Further, the members are equal. Everyone elected to parliament represents equal people, so every member is in an equal relationship with all other members, even with those who have been reelected many times. Law must prevent members of the parliament from being manipulated by organizations that contribute cash to their election campaigns. The laws regarding elections should be clear and fair for all, so that the voters can concentrate on comparing the candidates.

As we have seen, a major problem with the law even in established democracies is that it is manipulated often for the benefit of the powerful and rich. There is a significant need for changes in this regard. For example, law must ensure that anyone can become a member of parliament or president, not just the super-rich. Running for office should not require raising great amounts of money; rather, it should require speaking to the voters about the current, most significant government laws.

Law ruling regular citizens should be fair, so that rich and poor persons accused of crime have equal experiences with the justice system. Far too often, the poor go to jail—for a long time—even before they have been made guilty of a crime because they cannot pay the bail, while rich people accused of a crime can easily afford bail and are therefore immediately let free. That is unjust. In addition, rich people accused of crime can afford to hire strong lawyers to present the best possible case for them, while the poor who are accused of crime usually have to rely on court-assigned lawyers, who are paid far less and therefore spend little time on each case they work on. Criminal law is meant to result in justice. What should matter is the crime that has been committed, not how much money the accused is able to put up. Legal justice demands equality.

All citizens are supposed to obey the law. Therefore they need to know it. Citizens cannot become familiar with every detail of law, but they should know as much as possible. So in high school, all students should be required to take a course of law, learning the basic laws that relate to them. In the parliament of democracy, lawmaking needs to result in clarity: new laws should be clear and comprehensible to citizens. Dependency of citizens on lawyers is a necessity, but lawyers can work with law in a plain, open, honest way. The common disease of law is the tendency toward complexification: the deterioration of law into complicated specifics, rather than straightforward rules of the game of life. Democracy is based not only on the right of election, but also on clear laws applied equally throughout the nation.

3. *Liberty and Equality.* Government has the potential power to exercise absolute control over the nation. But a great discovery of democracy is that government must be limited: that is, it must be restrained by the constitution and bill of rights from exercising certain powers so that citizens' human rights are protected. For example, in a democracy, citizens should never be arrested for what they think or for any kind of political speech. "Free speech" was a remarkable invention, finally achieved after centuries of governments forcing citizens to think and say what the rulers demanded. In a democracy, the rulers do not merely seek to control the hearts of citizens. Liberty also demands, on the one hand, that the government not align itself with a particular religion, and on the other hand, that citizens have the right to practice whatever religion they want, so long as their religious practices do not infringe on the rights of other citizens (such as having people killed). No religion or political position is to be forced onto citizens by the government or by any social group. Free citizens are never required to stay in one location; they can take off and live where they want to. In short, liberty allows citizens to live mainly on their own, day by day, free from oppression by the government or other citizens.

Democracy demands liberty to relieve human torment. Killing is illegal. The death penalty is completely wrong for a democracy, a mistake that has been corrected by many modern democracies. Fortunately, nearly all religions have come out against the death penalty, and extensive evidence that the death penalty does not deter crime has been publicized by human rights groups. In addition, numerous democracies, such as Britain and Japan, concentrating on real information, have discovered that murder in society can be very effectively reduced if the government demands that all citizens give up guns—weapons that make murder far too easy. Thus research has shown how to stop killing.

Torture is also illegal in a democracy. Any nation that wants to become a democracy must immediately halt torture of prisoners. Beyond sports, a democracy does not permit citizens to use physical force against one another. Physical hurting is to be stopped, while free speech is to be encouraged. Of course, people harm others with their speech, but that, though regrettable, is not as bad as government control of speech. Let people speak out—but not hit out.

In the past, many advocates of democracy have supported socialism: government itself operating the society's businesses and farms and industries. But socialism has been unsuccessful. Clearly, Marxism, like Fascism, was a huge mistake, resulting in enormous human suffering. Democracy works better with a capitalist economy, provided the government enforces both law and liberty. A nation's economics should be seen as a sport, with the government as the referee—ruling not who wins, but how fairly the capitalists play. Competition within capitalism is complicated and sometimes harms human welfare, so law is a necessity. But ironically, it is competitive capitalism, not socialism, that instills the habit of helpfulness and kindness in people: workers in a capitalist economy generally need to act helpful, kind, and admiring toward clients and customers, not just now and then, but nearly all day every day. So people naturally get into the habit of engaging the minds of others in hopeful and admirable ways—a great advantage for the success of democracy. The *relative* liberation of capitalism is yet another lesson from history: some government rules are clearly necessary. For example, should a company be allowed to "fire" workers—sometimes by the hundreds or even thousands—who have done nothing wrong, have been laboring for the company for years, and need income to support themselves and their families? Company leaders sometimes fire people simply to improve the leaders' money-making situation. Democratic government should produce law against that kind of firing of innocent workers. When capitalism hurts human beings to that extent, change is worth considering.

The principle of equality is a fundamental of democracy. Currently, some imaginative academics are championing politics as "diverse culture"—exaggerating the differences between ethnic, racial, and other groups rather than emphasizing their human relatedness. Liberty allows cultural differences; democracy must never become totalitarian. But democracy must concern itself principally with the equality of each individual citizen—the same rights and rules for everyone. In voting, law, education, military, and other aspects of government, citizens should not be distinguished because of their race, gender, ethnic inheritance, culture, or religion; each and every individual is entitled to respect and fair treatment. The contemporary tragic spectacle of murderous conflict between citizens of different ethnic, racial, or religious groups in the old Soviet Union, Yugoslavia, South Africa, and elsewhere ought to remind politicians that the evidence strongly supports the need to emphasize equality in a democracy, not diversity.

4. *Controlling Violence.* Democratic government must be directly in charge of the nation's military in order to survive. But the modern challenges to this requirement are severe. In the past, the decision to go to war could be taken at a far more leisurely pace; there was time to gather extensive information and to debate

at length. A modern war decision often requires immediate action, especially when the nation is attacked. Modern technology has not only made the instruments of war far more powerful than they were in the days of swords or arrows, it has also made them capable of quick delivery. The modern nightmare is surprise attack by nuclear bombs and the death of millions before the government even knows it is at war. But in a democracy, even that kind of threat does not justify letting the military do whatever it wants. There is, in fact, a stronger need than ever for the government to keep control over the military and to decide definitely—in advance—how it will handle military emergencies. The representatives of the people must also decide, definitely and in advance, which military matters can be revealed to the public and which must be kept secret for the sake of security. The nation's top military leaders should meet and work together with trusted representatives chosen by the parliament on a regular basis, sharing their full information. These representatives then must relay the basics to the full body of representatives, who, in turn, inform the public of all basic decisions. Knowledge of science is essential for those government representatives who deal directly and regularly with the military so they can ask appropriate questions and understand the answers. For example: Is it possible to stop an enemy's attack immediately by fighting down weapons in the air rather than by killing the enemy's soldiers? And always it should be remembered that military technology is to serve human needs, not to be developed—at great public expense— to satisfy the grandiose desires of scientists and militarists.

Clearly democracy requires decisions about war to be made by the representatives of the people, not by the president alone. The president should not have individual authority to send soldiers off to some dangerous part of the world. Nor should the president deal privately with other nations regarding war, or delay public decision until the battle is almost underway. As I have seen, democracy is not just domestic but rules international action.

The age-old romanticization of war surely needs to be changed. People should know the actual horrors of war, which they never learn from most war movies and television stories. These depict war as jazzy and exciting, obscuring the truth of what really happens in war to both the enemy and ourselves. If journalism also fosters romantic fantasies about war, the government should take responsibility for revealing and explaining the truth.

Similarly dangerous is the romanticization of crime. The violence in homes and schools, even in churches, that has emerged in some countries in recent years is amazing. What crime actually does to people must be brought out. Research on ways to stop crime is essential. The government should enact laws to keep guns and bombs out of the hands of citizens. In addition, the national government should recruit and train and assign police where they are most needed. For police organizations to be entirely local is not effective today, when criminals have greater mobility and easily escape from one part of the country to another. Further, there is more criminal organization today: gangs that plan crimes at the regional or even national level. Therefore it makes sense to have a substantial national police force that is well trained and capable of operating effectively throughout the country.

Finally, the development of international democratic organization requires an international democratic *military* organization whose mission would be to protect and spread real democracy around the world. That requires the democracies to coordinate their armed forces so they can effectively work together internationally—even with different languages. Alliances between this international democratic military force and the armed forces of nondemocracies would be a mistake. Democracies must pull together in all things—even in war.

These thoughts are uncertain, offered in the hope of stimulating thinking and research. Before taking action to improve the workings of the four fundamentals of democracy, we need to know the details of the current situation, as well as how similar actions have worked in the past.

MAKE IT HAPPEN

What all of us should do is learn to care for our fellow human beings. We live in a time when democracy has triumphed over Communism and Fascism by showing that it is the only truly worthy form of government. People all over the world wish to be free. They wish to decide how to live their lives without being forced to serve some government ideology, without fearing the knock on the door in the middle of the night, the abrupt imprisonment, the torture and death that are the price of political opposition in too many countries. Two hundred years ago, democracy looked fragile because unjust government was the norm. Today it is injustice that is at bay.

An American clergyman named Theodore Parker said in the nineteenth century, "If powerful men will not write justice with black ink on white paper, ignorant and violent men will write it on the soil in letters of blood, and illuminate their crude legislation with burning castles, palaces and towns." [82]

That is what will happen if we let this opportunity pass.

If we put our beliefs into action instead, we can help human beings everywhere create and sustain democracy—the best hope for humanity.

References

CHAPTER 2

1. V.V. Shulgin, *Days of the Russian Revolution: Memoirs from the Right, 1905–1917,* Ed. Bruce F. Adams (Gulf Breeze, Fla.: Academic International Press, 1990), p. 112.
2. Alexander F. Kerensky, *The Crucifixion of Liberty* (New York: John Day, 1934), p. 286.
3. Adam B. Ulam, *Russia's Failed Revolutions: From the Decembrists to the Dissidents* (New York: Basic Books, 1981), p. 300.
4. Richard Abraham, *Alexander Kerensky: The First Love of the Revolution* (New York: Columbia University Press, 1987), p. 132.
5. Kerensky, *Crucifixion,* p. 286.
6. Alexander F. Kerensky, *Russia and History's Turning Point* (New York: Duell, Sloan and Pearse, 1965), p. 229.
7. Abraham *Kerensky,* p.134.
8. Ibid., pp. 134–35.
9. Ibid., p. 146.
10. Ulam, *Russia's Failed Revolutions,* p. 295.
11. Ibid., pp. 30–2.
12. Abraham, *Kerensky,* p. 142.
13. Kerensky, *Crucifixion,* p. 292.
14. Ibid., p. 285.
15. Abraham, *Kerensky,* p. 145.
16. *The New York Times,* March 19, 1917, p. 1. This and subsequent references to *The New York Times (NYT)* use U.S. dating.
17. *NYT,* March 16, 1917, p. 7.
18. *NYT,* March 17, 1917, p. 1.

19. *NYT,* March 19, 1917, p. 1.

20. *NYT,* March 16, 1917, p. 7.

21. *NYT,* March 17, 1917, p. 1.

22. *NYT,* March 16, 1917, p. 7.

23. Harold T. Parker and Marvin L. Brown, Jr., *Major Themes in Modern European History: An Invitation to Inquiry and Reflection,* Vol. II (Durham, S.C.: Moore, 1974).

24. Bertram D. Wolfe, *Three Who Made a Revolution: A Biographical Essay* (Boston: Beacon Press), 1955, p. 29.

25. Abraham, *Kerensky,* p. 38.

26. Ulam, *Russia's Failed Revolutions,* p. 253.

27. Kerensky, *Crucifixion,* p. 167.

28. Adam B. Ulam, *The Bolsheviks: The Intellectual and Political History of the Triumph of Communism in Russia,* (New York: Collier Books, 1965), p. 289.

29. Ulam, *Russia's Failed Revolutions,* p. 257.

30. Kerensky, *Russia,* p. 331.

31. Kerensky, *Crucifixion,* p. 164.

32. Ulam, *Russia's Failed Revolutions,* p. 216.

33. Ibid., p. 248.

34. Kerensky, *Crucifixion,* p. 164.

35. Alex de Jonge, *The Life and Times of Gigorii Rasputin* (New York: Dorset, 1987), p. 141.

36. Ibid., pp. 152–169.

37. Kerensky, *Crucifixion,* p.176.

38. De Jonge, *Rasputin,* p. 163.

39. Kerensky, *Crucifixion,* p. 168.

40. Ibid.

41. Ulam, *Russia's Failed Revolutions,* p. 247.

42. Louis Fischer, *The Life of Lenin* (New York: Harper and Row, 1964), p. 126. Cf. de Jonge, *Rasputin,* Chap. 21.

43. Kerensky, *Crucifixion,* p. 213.

44. Wolfe, pp. 283–286.

45. Kerensky, *Russia,* p. 48.

46. Ulam, *Russia's Failed Revolutions,* p. 163.

47. Wolfe, *Three Who Made a Revolution,* p. 286.

48. Ibid., p. 302.

49. Ibid., pp. 303–04.

50. Abraham, *Kerensky,* p. 21.

51. Ibid., p. 32.

52. Ibid., p. 39.

53. Ibid., p. 41.

54. Ulam, *Russia's Failed Revolutions,* p. 194.

55. Ibid., p. 221.

56. Abraham, *Kerensky,* pp. 54–56. See also Kerensky, *Russia,* p. 82.

57. De Jonge, *Rasputin,* p. 206.

58. Abraham, *Kerensky,* pp. 93, 129.

59. Kerensky, *Crucifixion,* p. 60.

60. Kerensky, *Russia,* p. 7.

61. Kerensky, *Crucifixion,* p. 61.

62. Kerensky, *Russia,* pp. 7–8.

63. Abraham, *Kerensky,* p. 7.

64. Kerensky, *Russia,* p. 9.

65. Abraham, *Kerensky,* pp. 8–9.

66. Kerensky, *Russia,* p. 15.

67. Kerensky, *Crucifixion,* p. 64.

68. Abraham, *Kerensky,* p. 11.

69. Kerensky, *Russia,* pp. 15–16.

70. Ibid., p. 20.

71. Abraham, *Kerensky,* p. 16.

72. Ibid., p. 14.

73. Ibid., p. 13.

74. Ibid., p. 18.

75. Ibid., p. 19.

76. Ibid., pp. 22, 25.

77. Ibid., p. 22.

78. Kerensky, *Russia,* p. 51.

79. Ibid., p. 62.

80. Abraham, *Kerensky,* p. 32.

81. Kerensky, *Russia,* pp. 66–67.

82. Ibid., p. 68.

83. Kerensky, *Crucifixion,* p. 131.

84. Kerensky, *Russia,* p. 74.

85. Abraham, *Kerensky,* pp. 58–59.

86. Ibid., p. 63.

87. Ibid., p. 73.

88. Alexander F. Kerensky, *The Catastrophe: Kerensky's Own Story of the Russian Revolution* (New York: Appleton, 1927), pp. 41–42.

89. Kerensky, *Russia,* p. 229.

90. Ibid., p. 326.

91. R.H. Bruce Lockhart, *The Two Revolutions: An Eye-witness Study of Russia 1917* (London: The Bodley Head, 1967), p. 11.

92. Robert Wallace and the Editors of Time-Life Books, *Rise of Russia* (New York: Time-Life Books, 1967), p. 11.

93. Ibid., p. 16.

94. Ibid., p. 23.

95. Ibid., p. 96.

96. Ibid., p. 77.

97. Ibid., p. 78.

98. Ibid., pp. 79, 83, 115.

99. Ibid., pp. 121–22.

100. Ibid., pp. 158–59, 164.

101. Ulam, *Russia's Failed Revolutions,* pp. 6, 23.

102. Ibid., pp. 125, 128, 47.

103. De Jonge, *Rasputin,* p. 156, recounts a sermon by the monk on the need to escape human connections in order to approach God.

104. Ibid., p. 7.

105. Kerensky, *Russia,* p. 28.

106. Ulam, *Russia's Failed Revolutions,* p. 226.

107. Fischer, *Life of Lenin,* p. 125.

108. Abraham, *Kerensky,* p. 93.

109. Ulam, *Russia's Failed Revolutions,* pp. 233–34.

110. Olivia Coolidge, *Makers of the Red Revolutions* (Eau Claire, Wis.: E.M. Hale, 1963), p. 66.

111. Fischer, *Life of Lenin*, p. 126.
112. Fischer, *Life of Lenin*, pp. 125–26.
113. Ulam, *Russia's Failed Revolutions*, p. 263.
114. Ibid., p. 267.
115. Ibid., p. 281.
116. Ibid., p. 280.
117. Otto Friedrich, "Headed for the Dustheap," *Time*, February 19, 1990, p. 36.
118. Abraham, *Kerensky*, p. 5.
119. Wolfe, *Three Who Made a Revolution*, p. 55.
120. Fischer, *Life of Lenin*, p. 7.
121. Edmund Wilson, *To the Finland Station: A Study in the Writing and Acting of History* (Garden City, N.Y.: Doubleday, 1953), pp. 354–55.
122. Fischer, *Life of Lenin*, p. 8.
123. Abraham, *Kerensky*, pp. 6–7.
124. Fischer, *Life of Lenin*, p. 12; and Wilson, *To the Finland Station*, p. 357.
125. Fischer, *Life of Lenin*, p. 10: and Wolfe, *Three Who Made a Revolution*, p. 65.
126. Fischer, *Life of Lenin*, p. 17.
127. Wolfe, *Three Who Made a Revolution*, pp. 69–70, 74.
128. Fischer, *Life of Lenin*, p. 18.
129. Wolfe, *Three Who Made a Revolution*, p. 78.
130. Ibid., pp. 83–85.
131. Wilson, *To The Finland Station*, p. 367; and Wolfe, *Three Who Made a Revolution.*, p. 86.
132. Fischer, *Life of Lenin*, p. 21.
133. Wolfe, *Three Who Made a Revolution*, p. 94.
134. Ibid., p. 150.
135. Ibid., pp. 152–53.
136. Ulam, *Russia's Failed Revolutions*, p. 143.
137. Kerensky, *Crucifixion*, pp. 104, 119.
138. Fischer, *Life of Lenin*, p. 53.
139. Wolfe, *Three Who Made a Revolution*, p. 355.
140. Ibid., p. 306.
141. Ibid., p. 318.
142. Kerensky, *Crucifixion*, p. 134.
143. Wolfe, *Three Who Made a Revolution*, p. 296.
144. Ulam, *Russia's Failed Revolutions*, pp. 225, 253, 318.
145. Fischer, *Life of Lenin*, p. 115.
146. Zbigniew Brzezinski, *The Grand Failure: The Birth and Death of Communism in the Twentieth Century* (New York: Scribner's, 1989), p. 19.
147. Wolfe, *Three Who Made a Revolution*, p. 525.
148. Fischer, *Life of Lenin*, P. 119.
149. Wolfe, *Three Who Made a Revolution*, p. 281.
150. Kerensky, *Crucifixion*, p. 298.
151. Wolfe, *Three Who Made a Revolution*, p. 119.
152. Fishcer, *Life of Lenin*, p. 119.
153. Kerensky, *Russia*, p. 304.
154. Abraham, *Kerensky*, p. 146; and Fischer, *Life of Lenin*, p. 127.
155. Abraham, *Kerensky*, pp. 148–49.
156. Fischer, *Life of Lenin*, p. 127.
157. Abraham, *Kerensky*, p. 155.
158. Ibid., p. 159.
159. Kerensky, *Crucifixion*, p. 284.

160. Ibid., p. 293.
161. Abraham, *Kerensky*, p. 168.
162. Coolidge, *Makers of the Red Revolution*, pp. 73–74.
163. Abraham, *Kerensky*, p. 179.
164. Ulam, *Russia's Failed Revolutions*, pp. 323–24.
165. Coolidge, *Makers of the Red Revolution*, pp. 74–76.
166. Ulam, *Russia's Failed Revolutions*, pp. 334, 338.
167. Fischer, *Life of Lenin*, p. 128.
168. Abraham, *Kerensky*, pp. 180–81.
169. Ulam, *Russia's Failed Revolutions*, p. 345.
170. Abraham, *Kerensky*, pp. 183–84.
171. Ulam, *Russia's Failed Revolutions*, p. 340.
172. Abraham, *Kerensky*, p. 185.
173. Ibid.
174. Ibid., p. 186.
175. Ibid., p. 190.
176. Ulam, *Russia's Failed Revolutions*, p. 348; and Abraham, *Kerensky*, p. 214.
177. Abraham, *Kerensky*, pp. 199–200.
178. Lockhart, *The Two Revolutions*, pp. 92–93.
179. Ulam, *Russia's Failed Revolutions*, p. 355.
180. Abraham, *Kerensky*, p. 213.
181. Ibid., p. 214.
182. Kerensky, *Russia*, p. 291.
183. Ibid., p. 289.
184. Abraham, *Kerensky*, p. 218.
185. Ulam, *Russia's Failed Revolutions*, p. 358.
186. Abraham, *Kerensky*, p. 219.
187. Ulam, *Russia's Failed Revolutions*, p. 361.
188. Kerensky, *Crucifixion*, p. 367.
189. Coolidge, *Makers of the Red Revolutions*, p. 80.
190. Abraham, *Kerensky*, p. 221.
191. Kerensky, *Russia*, p. 292.
192. Abraham, *Kerensky*, p. 225.
193. Ibid., p. 226.
194. Kerensky, *Russia*, p. 292.
195. Abraham, *Kerensky*, pp. 233–35.
196. Ibid., p. 238.
197. Ibid., p. 239.
198. Ibid.
199. Ibid., p. 252.
200. Ibid., p. 244.
201. Ulam, *Russia's Failed Revolutions*, pp. 363–64.
202. Abraham, *Kerensky*, p. 245.
203. Ibid., p. 251.
204. Ulam, *Russia's Failed Revolutions*, p. 366.
205. Abraham, *Kerensky*, pp. 252–55.
206. Lockhart, *The Two Revolutions*, p. 97.
207. Ulam, *Russia's Failed Revolutions*, p. 370; and Lockhart, *The Two Revolutions*, p. 98.
208. Abraham, *Kerensky*, p. 249.
209. Ulam, *Russia's Failed Revolutions*, p. 368. Cf. Robert Paul Browder and Alexander F. Kerensky

Eds., *The Russian Provisional Government, 1917: Documents* (Stanford, Cal.: Stanford University Press, 1961), Vol. II, P. 1457 fn.

210. Browder and Kerensky, *Russian Provisional Government*, III, pp. 1457–62.
211. Abraham, *Kerensky*, p. 260.
212. Browder and Kerensky, *Russian Provisional Government*, III, pp. 1457–62.
213. Ibid., p. 1510.
214. Ibid., pp. 1510–15.
215. Ulam, *Russia's Failed Revolutions*, p. 369.
216. Ibid., p. 380.
217. Coolidge, *Makers of the Red Revolution*, p. 83.
218. Kerensky, *Russia*, pp. 348–49.
219. Lockhart, *The Two Revolutions*, pp. 102–3; and Kerensky, *Russia*, p. 358.
220. Abraham, *Kerensky*, p. 275.
221. Kerensky, *Russia*, p. 351.
222. Ibid., p. 352.
223. Abraham, *Kerensky*, p. 289.
224. Kerensky, *Russia*, p. 355.
225. Abraham, *Kerensky*, p. 286.
226. Kerensky, *Russia*, p. 356.
227. David Killingray, *The Russian Revolution* (St. Paul, Minn.: Greenhaven, 1980), p. 11.
228. Ulam, *Russia's Failed Revolutions*, p. 373.
229. Lockhart, *The Two Revolutions*, pp. 103–04.
230. Abraham, *Kerensky*, p. 278.
231. Ibid., p. 280.
232. Lockhart, *The Two Revolutions*, pp. 104, 106.
233. Ulam, *Russia's Failed Revolutions*, p. 377.
234. Browder and Kerensky, *Russian Provisional Government*, III, p. 1677. Cf. Abraham, *Kerensky*, p. 293.
235. Abraham, *Kerensky*, p. 294.
236. Kerensky, *Russia*, p. 414.
237. Browder and Kerensky, *Russian Provisional Government*, III, p. 1714.
238. Ibid., p. 1724.
239. Ulam, *Russia's Failed Revolutions*, p. 378.
240. Coolidge, *Makers of the Red Revolution*, p. 84.
241. Abraham, *Kerensky*, p. 305.
242. Ulam, *Russia's Failed Revolutions*, p. 378.
243. Abraham, *Kerensky*, p. 305.
244. Ibid., p. 298.
245. Ibid., pp. 299–301.
246. Ibid., p. 313.
247. Ulam, *Russia's Failed Revolutions*, p. 383.
248. Ibid., p. 384.
249. Ibid.
250. Ibid., p. 386.
251. Coolidge, *Makers of the Red Revolution*, p. 90.
252. Ulam, *Russia's Failed Revolutions*, p. 387.
253. Ibid., p. 388.
254. Abraham, *Kerensky*, p. 321.
255. Ibid., pp. 327–28.
256. Fischer, *Life of Lenin*, p. 139.

257. Ibid., p. 137.

258. Abraham, *Kerensky*, p. 334.

259. Ibid., p. 343.

260. Ulam, *Russia's Failed Revolutions*, p. 388.

261. Friedrich, "Headed for the Dustheap," p. 37.

262. Lockhart, *The Two Revolutions*, p. 121.

263. Review of *Red Victory, The New York Times*, February 25, 1990.

264. Alfred G. Meyer, *Communism* (New York: Random House, 1960), p. 67.

265. Howard R. Swearer, *The Politics of Succession in the U.S.S.R.: Materials on Khrushchev's Rise to Leadership* (Boston: Little, Brown, 1964), p. 9.

266. Friedrich, "Headed for the Dustheap," p. 37.

267. Nikita S. Khrushchev, *The Crimes of the Stalin Era: Special Report to the 20th Congress of the Communist Party of the Soviet Union* (New York: The New Leader, 1962), p. 53.

268. Meyer, *Communism*, p. 82.

269. Raymond A. Bauer, Alex Inkeles, and Clyde Kluckhohn, *How the Soviet System Works: Cultural, Psychological, and Social Themes* (New York: Vintage Books, 1960), p. 78.

270. Brzezinski, *The Grand Failure*, p. 237.

271. Ibid., p. 236.

CHAPTER 3

1. See Joseph Campbell, *The Way of the Animal Powers* Vol. I of *Historical Atlas of World Mythology* (London: Summerfield Press, 1983).

2. See Quincy Wright, *A Study of War* (2nd ed.), abridged by Louise Leonard Wright (Chicago: University of Chicago Press, 1964), Chap. II, "The History of War"; and Robert L. O'Connell, *Of Arms and Men: A History of War, Weapons, and Aggression* (New York: Oxford University Press, 1989), Chap. 3, "Genesis."

3. Quoted in Maurice R. Davie, *The Evolution of War: A Study of Its Role in Early Societies* (New Haven, Conn.: Yale University Press, 1929), p. 9.

4. James Graham-Campbell, *The Viking World* (New Haven, Conn.: Ticknor & Fields, 1980), pp. 22 ff.

5. Doralisa Pilarte, "Nicaraguans Unhappy with Government, "AP, *Durham Morning Herald, November 19, 1990.*

6. Roberto Eisenmann, "The Struggle Against Noriega," *The Journal of Democracy*, Winter 1990.

7. Col. Jack Pryor, in *U.S. News & World Report*, December 17, 1990, p. 55.

8. Carlos H. Waisman, "The Argentine Paradox," *The Journal of Democracy*, Winter 1990, p. 95.

9. National Democratic Institute for International Affairs, "Civil-Military Relations: The Argentine Experience," NDI Report 1989, pp. 20–21.

10. Alfred Stephen, *Rethinking Military Politics: Brazil and the Southern Cone* (Princeton, N.J.: Princeton University Press, 1988), p. 89.

11. Rick Atkinson and Gary Lee, "Soviet Army Coming Apart at the Seams," *The Washington Post*, November 18, 1990, p. 1.

12. Candolezza Rice, "The Military Under Democracy," *The Journal of Democracy 3* (April 1992): pp. 30–31.

13. Benjamin Barber and Patrick Watson, *The Struggle for Democracy* (Boston: Little, Brown, 1988), pp. 63–68, 84.

14. Steve Coll, "India's Security Forces Assume New Power as Role in Ending Conflict Grows," *The Washington Post*, December 2, 1990, p. A36.

15. James David Barber, "Empire of the Sun," *The Washington Monthly*, October 1991, pp. 26, 29.

16. Samuel Eliot Morison and Henry Steele Commager, *The Growth of the American Republic* (New York: Oxford University Press, 1942), Vol. I, p. 638.

17. Avery Craven, *The Coming of the Civil War* (Chicago: University of Chicago Press, 1974), p. 436.

18. Ibid., p. 437.

19. Morrison and Commager, *American Republic,* Vol. I, p. 645.

20. Ibid., pp. 645–49.

21. Paul Fussell, *The Great War and Modern Memory* (New York: Oxford University Press, 1975), pp. 12–14.

22. Theodore Draper, "Presidential Wars," *The New York Review of Books,* September 26, 1991, pp. 66, 71.

23. See James David Barber, *The Presidential Character: Predicting Performance in the White House* (3rd ed.) (Englewood Cliffs, N.J.: Prentice Hall, 1985); Barber, "Empire of the Sun"; and Draper, "Presidential Wars," p. 64.

24. Richard J. Barnet, *The Rockets' Red Glare: When America Goes to War* (New York: Simon and Schuster, 1990), pp. 13–14.

25. Draper, "Presidential Wars," p. 73.

26. Ben Bradlee, Jr., *Guts and Glory: The Rise and Fall of Oliver North* (New York: Donald I. Fine; 1988), pp. 537, 544–47.

27. See David J. Garrow, *The FBI and Martin Luther King, Jr.: From "Solo" to Memphis* (New York: Norton, 1981).

28. Col. L Fletcher Prouty, *The Secret Team: The CIA and Its Allies in Control of the United States and the World* (Englewood Cliffs, N.J.: Prentice Hall, 1973), pp. 424–25.

29. Chapman Pincher, *Traitors: The Anatomy of Treason* (New York: St. Martin's Press, 1987), p. 193.

30. Erwin Stand, *The Roots of Evil: The Psychological and Cultural Origins of Genocide and Other Forms of Group Violence* (Cambridge, England: Cambridge University Press 1989), p. 255.

31. See Robert F. Kennedy, *Thirteen Days* (New York: Signet Books, 1969); and Chester L. Cooper, *The Lost Crusade* (New York: Dodd Mead, 1970).

32. See Irving Janis, *Victims of Groupthink.*

33. Herbert York, *Race to Oblivion: A Participant's View of the Arms Race* (New York: Simon and Schuster, 1970), p. 228.

34. Tacitus, quoted in Roland H. Bainton, *Christendom: A Short History of Christianity and Its Impact on Western Civilization,* Vol. I: *From the Birth of Christ to the Reformation* (New York: Harper Torchbooks, 1966), p. 51. Cf. Kenneth Scott Latourette, *Christianity Through the Ages* (New York: Harper Chapel Books, 1965), Chap. IV, "The Initial Five Centuries of Christianity."

35. Don Higginbotham, *War and Society in Revolutionary America: The Wider Dimensions of Conflict* (Columbia S.C.: University of South Carolina Press, 1988), pp. 179–80.

36. Quoted in Selig Adler, *The Isolationist Impulse: Its Twentieth Century Reaction* (New York: Collier Books, 1961), p. 20.

37. Ibid., p. 95.

38. Ibid., p. 234.

39. Ibid., p. 270.

40. Ibid.

41. William L. Langer and S. Everett Gleason, *The Challenge to Isolations: 1937–1940* (New York: Harper, 1952), p. 13.

42. Ibid., p. 14.

43. Sian Facer Ed., *On This Day: The History of the World in 366 Days* (New York, Crescent Books, 1992), September 6.

44. John Hope Franklin, *From Slavery to Freedom: A History of Negro Americans* (5th ed.) (New York: Alfred A. Knopf, 1980), p. 84.

45. Ibid., p. 150.

46. Ibid., p. 186.

47. Ibid., p. 198.

48. See Nick Kotz, *Wild Blue Yonder: Money, Politics, and the B-1 Bomber* (New York: Pantheon Books, 1988.)

49. Charles E. Welch, Jr. (Ed.), *Civilian Control of the Military: Theory and Cases from Developing Countries* (Albany, N.Y.: State University of New York Press, 1976), p. 8.

50. Noble E. Cunningham, Jr., *In Pursuit of Reason: The Life of Thomas Jefferson* (Baton Rouge: Louisiana State University Press, 1987), p. 62.

51. Michael B. Poliakoff, *Combat Sports in the Ancient World: Competition, Violence, and Culture* (New Haven, Conn.: Yale University Press, 1987), p. 20.

52. Ibid., p. 54.

53. Ibid., p. 92.

54. See Allen Buttman, *Sports Spectators* (New York: Columbia University Press, 1986.)

55. Welch, *Civilian Control of the Military,* p. 315.

CHAPTER 4

1. John Gunther, *Inside Australia,* completed and edited by William H. Forbes (New York: Harper & Row, 1972), p. 24.

2. Robert Hughes, *The Fatal Shore* (New York: Alfred A. Knopf, 1987), p. 41.

3. Clive Turnbull, *A Concise History of Australia* (London: Thames and Hudson, 1966), p. 15.

4. Hughes, *The Fatal Shore,* p. 9.

5. John Laffin, *ANZACS at War: The Story of Australian and New Zealand Battles* (New York: Abelard-Schuman, 1965), p. 16.

6. Turnbull, *Concise History,* p. 20.

7. Hughes, *The Fatal Shore,* p. 69.

8. Gunther, *Inside Australia,* p. 25.

9. Hughes, *The Fatal Shore,* p. 149.

10. Ibid., p. 29.

11. Ibid., p. 68.

12. Ibid., p. 99.

13. Ibid., p. 102.

14. Ibid., p. 260.

15. Ibid., p. 105.

16. Ibid., pp. 106–07.

17. Ibid., p. 109.

18. Ibid., p. 118.

19. K.S. Inglis, *The Australian Colonists: An Exploration of Social History, 1788–1870* (Carlton, Victoria, Australia: Melbourne University Press, 1974), pp. 181–84; and Hughes, *The Fatal Shore,* p. 294.

20. Hughes, *The Fatal Shore,* p. 288.

21. Ibid., pp. 293–94.

22. Ibid., p. 294.

23. Turnbull, *Concise History,* p. 33.

24. Hughes, *The Fatal Shore,* pp. 302–313.

25. Ibid., p. 325.

26. Ibid., pp. 325–326.

27. Ibid., p. 346.

28. Ibid., pp. 354 ff.

29. Ibid., p. 366.

30. Gunther, *Inside Australia,* p. 35.

31. Hughes, *The Fatal Shore,* p. 367.

32. Ibid., p. 377.

33. Ibid., p. 378.

34. Ibid., p. 409.

35. Ibid., p. 419.

36. Ibid., p. 423.
37. Ibid., p. 468.
38. Ibid., p. 480.
39. Ibid., p. 481.
40. Frederick C. Folkard, *The Remarkable Australians* (Sydney: Murray, 1965), Chap. 5.
41. Hughes, *The Fatal Shore*, p. 381.
42. Ibid., p. 395.
43. Ibid., p. 397.
44. Folkard, *The Remarkable Australians*, p. 81.
45. Hughes, *The Fatal Shore*, p. 490.
46. Ibid., p. 493.
47. Ibid., p. 499.
48. Ibid., p. 500.
49. Ibid., p. 505.
50. Ibid., p. 507.
51. Ibid., p. 509.
52. Ibid., p. 513.
53. Ibid., p. 519.
54. Ibid.
55. Ibid., p. 527.
56. Ibid., p. 544.
57. Ibid., p. 547.
58. Ibid., pp. 555–56.
59. Ibid., p. 556.
60. Ibid., p. 600.
61. Gunther, *Inside Australia*, p. 33.
62. Ibid., p. 34.
63. Hughes, *The Fatal Shore*, p. 219.
64. Roderick Cameron, *Australia: History and Horizons* (New York: Columbia University Press, 1971), p. 204.
65. Hughes, *The Fatal Shore*, p. 227.
66. J.B. Hirst, *The Strange Birth of Colonial Democracy: New South Wales, 1848–1884* (Sydney: Allen & Unwin, 1988), p. 131.
67. Cameron, *Australia*, pp. 204–05.
68. Ibid., p. 208.
69. Hirst, *Colonial Democracy*, p. 127.
70. Inglis, *The Australian Colonists*, p. 169.
71. Ibid., p. 170.
72. Ibid., pp. 218–19.
73. Ibid., pp. 219–20.
74. Ibid., p. 239.
75. Ibid., pp. 252–54.
76. A.C.V. Melbourne, *Early Constitutional Development in Australia* (St. Lucia: University of Queensland Press, 1963), p. 304.
77. Ibid., p. 382.
78. Gunther, *Inside Australia*, pp. 34–35.
79. Melbourne, *Early Constitutional Development*, p. 428.
80. Ibid., p. 444.
81. Turnbull, *Concise History*, pp. 102–04.

82. Marjorie Barnard, *A History of Australia* (Sydney: Angus & Robertson, 1963), p. 438.

83. J.A. La Nauze, *Alfred Deakin: A Biography* (London: Angus & Robertson, 1979), pp. 11–12.

84. Ibid., p. 47.

85. Ibid., p. 48.

86. Ibid., p. 69.

87. Ibid., p. 136.

88. Ibid., pp. 108, 112.

89. Ibid., p. 106.

90. Ibid., p. 113.

91. Ibid., p. 129.

92. Ibid., p. 131.

93. Ibid., p. 157.

94. Turnbull, *Concise History*, p. 112.

95. Barnard, *History of Australia*, pp. 441–45.

96. La Nauze, *Alfred Deakin*, p. 196.

97. J.A. La Nauze *The Making of the Australian Constitution* (Melbourne: Melbourne University Press, 1974), p. 287.

98. All excerpts from the constitution are from ibid., App. 7.

99. Leslie C. Jauncey, *The Story of Conscription in Australia* (South Melbourne: Macmillan of Australia, 1968), p. 3.

100. Barnard, *History of Australia*, pp. 472–73.

101. La Nauze, *Alfred Deakin*, p. 519.

102. Ibid., pp. 533, 585.

103. R. Norris, *The Emergent Commonwealth: Australian Federation—Exceptions and Fulfillment, 1889–1910* (Melbourne: Melbourne University Press, 1975), p. 158.

104. Ibid., p. 137.

105. Ibid., p. 140.

106. Jauncey, *Conscription in Australia*, p. 36.

107. Laffin, *ANZACS at War*, p. 23.

108. Ibid., p. 48; and Gunther, *Inside Australia*, p. 111.

109. Laffin, *ANZACS at War*, p. 48.

110. Barnard, *History of Australia*, pp. 511–12.

111. Jauncey, *Conscription in Australia*, p. 151.

112. Ibid., p. 163.

113. La Nauze, *Australian Constitution*, pp. 227 ff; and Melbourne, *Early Constitutional Development*, pp. 498 ff.

114. Jauncey, *Conscription in Australia*, pp. 169–74.

115. Ibid., p. 174.

116. Barnard, *History of Australia*, p. 494.

117. Jauncey, *Conscription in Australia*, pp. 176–77.

118. Turnbull, *Concise History*, p. 127.

119. Jauncey, *Conscription in Australia*, p. 215.

120. Ibid., p. 312.

121. T.B. Millar, "The Defense of Australia," *Daedalus*, Winter 1985, p. 260.

122. Barnard, *History of Australia*, pp. 516, 498.

123. Ibid., pp. 558–59.

124. Turnbull, *Concise History*, p. 159.

125. Michael Davie, "The Fraying of the Rope," *Daedalus*, Winter 1985, pp. 373–74.

126. W.J. Hudson and M.P. Sharp, *Australian Independence: Colony to Reluctant Kingdom* (Melbourne: Melbourne University Press, 1988), p. 133.

CHAPTER 5

1. Maurice de la Fuye and Emile Babeau, *The Apostle of Liberty: A Life of La Fayette* (New York: Thomas Yoseloff, 1956), p.13.
2. Ibid., p. 14.
3. Olivier Bernier, *Lafayette: Hero of Two Worlds* (New York: Dutton, 1983), pp. 7–9.
4. Fuye and Babeau, *Apostle of Liberty*, p. 15.
5. Ibid., p. 17.
6. Ibid., p. 18.
7. Bernier, *Lafayette*, p. 18.
8. Ibid., p. 21.
9. Ibid.
10. Ronald W. Clark, *Benjamin Franklin: A Biography* (New York: Random House, 1983), p. 328; and Carl Van Doren, *Benjamin Franklin* (New York: Viking, 1938), pp. 572, 578.
11. Fuye and Babeau, *Apostle of Liberty*, p. 26.
12. Ibid., p. 27.
13. Simon Schama, *Citizens: A Chronicle of the French Revolution* (New York: Alfred A. Knopf, 1989), p. 27.
14. Fuye and Babeau, *Apostle of Liberty*, p. 28.
15. Bernier, *Lafayette*, pp. 39–40.
16. Ibid., p. 44.
17. Fuye and Babeau, *Apostle of Liberty*, p. 32.
18. Ibid., p. 33.
19. Bernier, *Lafayette*, p. 48.
20. Ibid., pp. 56–57.
21. Ibid., p. 53.
22. Ibid., p. 47.
23. Schama, *Citizens*, p. 24.
24. Bernier, *Lafayette*, p. 52.
25. Fuye and Babeau, *Apostle of Liberty*, p. 43.
26. Bernier, *Lafayette*, p. 59.
27. Ibid., p. 60.
28. Ibid.
29. Ibid., p. 68.
30. Ibid., p. 77.
31. Fuye and Babeau, *Apostle of Liberty*, p. 54.
32. Ibid., pp. 61–62.
33. Gilbert Chinard (Ed.), *The Letters of Lafayette and Jefferson* (Baltimore, Md.: The Johns Hopkins Press, 1929), pp. 7, 20.
34. Ibid., p. 9.
35. Fuye and Babeau, *Apostle of Liberty*, p. 64.
36. Bernier, *Lafayette*, p. 132.
37. Ibid., p. 137.
38. Chinard, *Letters*, p. 13.
39. Ibid., p. 51.
40. Ibid., p. 55.
41. Ibid., p. 56 (from Jefferson's Autobiography, I, 96).
42. Bernier, *Lafayette*, p. 156.
43. Schama, *Citizens*, pp. 42–43.
44. Robert Sobel, *The French Revolution: A Concise History and Interpretation* (New York: Ardmore Press, 1967), p. 25.

45. Merle Severy, "The Great Revolution, " *National Geographic 176* (July 1989): 20.
46. M.J. Sydenham, *The French Revolution* (New York: Capricorn Books, 1965), p. 47.
47. Sobel, *Concise History,* p. 32.
48. Sydenham, *The French Revolution,* pp. 27–28.
49. Ibid., p. 30.
50. Ibid., p. 32.
51. Bernier, *Lafayette,* p. 156.
52. Sydenham, *The French Revolution,* p. 13.
53. Sobel, *Concise History,* p. 27.
54. Charles Breunig, *The Age of Revolution and Reaction, 1789–1850* (New York: Norton, 1970), pp. 2–3.
55. Schama, *Citizens,* Chap. 6, "Body Politics."
56. Bernier, *Lafayette,* p. 175.
57. Sydenham, *The French Revolution, p. 43.*
58. Ibid.
59. Olivier J.G. Welch, *Mirabeau: A Study of a Democratic Monarchist* (Port Washington, N.Y.: Kennikat Press, 1968), p. 193.
60. Sydenham, *The French Revolution,* p. 45.
61. Breunig, *Age of Revolution,* p. 10; and Georges Lefebvre, *The Coming of the French Revolution,* trans. R.R. Palmer (Princeton, N.J.: Princeton University Press, 1947) p. 114. The tower heights corrected by Schama, *Citizens,* p. 389.
62. Breunig, *Age of Revolution,* p. 11.
63. R.R. Palmer, *A History of the Modern World* (New York: Alfred A. Knopf, 1952), p. 351.
64. Severy, "The Great Revolution, " p. 20.
65. Sobel, *Concise History,* p. 49.
66. Ibid.
67. Sydenham, *The French Revolution,* p. 50.
68. Lefebvre, *Coming of the French Revolution,* p. 116.
69. Fuye and Babeau, *Apostle of Liberty,* p. 880.
70. Palmer, *History of the Modern World,* p. 351.
71. Breunig, *Age of Revolution,* p. 11.
72. Sobel, *Concise History,* p. 50.
73. Ibid., p. 53.
74. Bernier, *Lafayette,* p. 175.
75. Ibid., p. 183.
76. Ibid., p. 178.
77. Ibid., 199.
78. Ibid., 189.
79. Palmer, *History of the Modern World,* p. 352.
80. Lefebvre, *Coming of the French Revolution,* p. 166.
81. Chinard, *Letters,* pp. 127–28.
82. Ibid., pp. 137, 139, 140.
83. Daniel J. Boorstin (Ed.), *An American Primer* (Chicago: University of Chicago Press, 1966), p. 155.
84. Chinard, *Letters,* p. 142.
85. Lefebvre, *Coming of the French Revolution,* pp. 169–70.
86. Ibid., p. 173.
87. Ibid., pp. 173–74.
88. Bernier, *Lafayette,* p. 199.
89. Sobel, *Concise History,* pp. 54–55.
90. Adapted from ibid., p. 55.
91. Lefebvre, *Coming of the French Revolution,* p. 202.

92. Sydenham, *The French Revolution*, p. 60.

93. Sobel, *Concise History*, p. 55.

94. Ibid., p. 56.

95. Welch, *Mirabeau*, p. 150.

96. Ibid., p. 21.

97. Ibid., p. 23.

98. Ibid., p. 79.

99. Ibid., pp. 81–82.

100. Ibid., p. 149.

101. Ibid., p. 168.

102. Ibid., p. 186.

103. Ibid., p. 188.

104. Ibid., p. 197.

105. Bernier, *Lafayette*, p. 212.

106. Louis Gottschalk and Margaret Maddox, *Lafayette in the French Revolution: From the October Days Through the Federation* (Chicago: University of Chicago Press, 1973), p. 30.

107. Ibid., p. 72.

108. Ibid., p. 81.

109. Ibid., pp. 94–95.

110. Ibid., p. 104.

111. Fuye and Babeau, *Apostle of Liberty*, pp. 129–30.

112. Gottschalk and Maddox, *Lafayette in the French Revolution*, pp. 360–61.

113. Ibid., pp. 365–66.

114. Ibid., p. 511.

115. Ibid., p. 529.

116. Ibid., p. 530.

117. Ibid., p. 531.

118. Schama, *Citizens*, pp. 506–07.

119. F.W.J. Hemmings, *Culture and Society in France: 1789–1849* (Great Britain: Leicester University Press, 1987), p. 54.

120. Gottschalk and Maddox, *Lafayette in the French Revolution*, p. 538.

121. Schama, *Citizens*, p. 508.

122. Ibid., p. 509.

123. Ibid., p. 511; and Sydenham, *The French Revolution*, p. 72.

124. Gottschalk and Maddox, *Lafayette in the French Revolution*, p. 541.

125. Ibid., p. 542.

126. Ibid., p. 552.

127. Gottschalk and Maddox, *Lafayette in the French Revolution*, p. 548. Gottschalk and Maddox are the main source of the above information on the festival of July 14, 1790. Cf. Bernier, *Lafayette*, pp. 218–19; and Welch, *Mirabeau*, pp. 282–84.

128. Carol Blum, *Rousseau and the Republic of Virtue: The Language of Politics in the French Revolution* (Ithaca, N.Y.: Cornell University Press, 1986), p. 37.

129. Ibid., p. 38.

130. Ibid., p. 39.

131. Ibid., p. 49.

132. John H. Hallowell, *Main Currents in Modern Political Thought* (New York: Henry Holt, 1950), p. 175.

133. Ibid.

134. Ibid., pp. 176–80.

135. David P. Jordan, *The Revolutionary Career of Maximilien Robespierre* (Chicago: University of Chicago Press, 1985), p. 24.

136. James Michael Egan, *Maximilien Robespierre: Nationalist Dictator* (New York: Columbia University Press, 1938), p. 14.

137. Stanley Loomis, *Paris in the Terror: June 1793–July 1794* (New York: Dorset, 1989), p. 266.

138. Blum, *Rousseau,* pp. 156–57.

139. Ibid., p. 154 fn.

140. Loomis, *Paris in the Terror,* p. 273.

141. Eagan, *Maximilien Robespierre,* p. 19.

142. Ibid., p. 24.

143. Ibid., p. 34.

144. J. M. Thompson, *Robespierre and the French Revolution* (New York: Collier Books, 1967), p. 18.

145. Ibid., p. 19.

146. Eagan, *Maximilien Robespierre,* p. 38.

147. Blum, *Rousseau,* p. 160.

148. Ibid.

149. Ibid., p. 161.

150. Jordan, *Revolutionary Career of Robespierre,* p. 46.

151. Lynn Hunt, *Politics, Culture, and Class in the French Revolution* (Berkeley: University of California Press, 1984), p. 49.

152. Jordan, *Revolutionary Career of Robespierre,* p. 52.

153. Loomis, *Paris in the Terror,* p. 269.

154. Thompson, *Robespierre and the French Revolution,* p. 24; and Eagan, *Maximilien Robespierre,* pp. 52–53.

155. Eagan, *Maximilien Robespierre,* p. 64.

156. Ibid., p. 60.

157. Ibid., p. 61.

158. Ibid.

159. Ibid., p. 65.

160. Jordan, *Revolutionary Career of Robespierre,* p. 71.

161. Thompson, *Robespierre and the French Revolution,* pp. 26–27.

162. Ibid., p. 28.

163. Welch, *Mirabeau,* pp. 334 ff.

164. Loomis, *Paris in the Terror,* p. 48.

165. Sobel, *Concise History,* p. 65.

166. Bernier, *Lafayette,* p. 234.

167. Thompson, *Robespierre and the French Revolution,* p. 41.

168. Bernier, *Lafayette,* p. 236.

169. Thompson, *Robespierre and the French Revolution,* p. 41.

170. Bernier, *Lafayette,* p. 238.

171. Ibid.

172. Ibid., p. 239.

173. Thompson, *Robespierre and the French Revolution,* p. 42.

174. Bernier, *Lafayette,* p. 240.

175. Ibid.

176. Jordan, *Revolutionary Career of Robespierre,* p. 107.

177. Blum, *Rousseau,* p. 170.

178. Ibid.

179. Lafayette account primarily from Bernier, *Lafayette,* pp. 232–42.

180. Jordan, *Revolutionary Career of Robespierre,* p. 118.

181. Loomis, *Paris in the Terror,* p. 76.

182. Ibid., p. 80.

183. Ibid., p. 82.

184. Ibid., p. 83.

185. Ibid., p. 96.

186. Jordan, *Revolutionary Career of Robespierre*, p. 121.

187. Thompson, *Robespierre and the French Revolution*, p. 49.

188. Ibid., p. 57.

189. Sobel, *Concise History*, p. 91.

190. Thompson, *Robespierre and the French Revolution*, p. 60.

191. Loomis, *Paris in the Terror*, pp. 288–89.

192. Thompson, *Robespierre and the French Revolution*, p. 53.

193. Richard Cobb and Colin Jones (Eds.), *Voices of the French Revolution* (Topsfield, Mass: Salem House, 1988), p. 202.

194. Thompson, *Robespierre and the French Revolution*, p. 80.

195. Sobel, *Concise History*, p. 109.

196. Thompson, *Robespierre and the French Revolution*, p. 113.

197. Eagan, *Maximilien Robespierre*, p. 112.

198. Jordan, *Revolutionary Career of Robespierre*, p. 187.

199. Ibid., p. 227.

200. Thompson, *Robespierre and the French Revolution*, p. 114.

201. Eagan, *Maximilien Robespierre*, p. 106.

202. Blum, *Rousseau*, p. 223.

203. Ibid., p. 244.

204. Cobb and Jones, *Voices*, p. 222.

205. Thompson, *Robespierre and the French Revolution*, p. 115.

206. Cobb and Jones, *Voices*, p. 224.

207. Loomis, *Paris in the Terror*, p. 301.

208. Thompson, *Robespierre and the French Revolution*, p. 116.

209. Eagan, *Maximilien Robespierre*, pp. 176–77; and Schama, *Citizens*, p. 835.

210. Blum, *Rousseau*, p. 252.

211. Eagan, *Maximilien Robespierre*, p. 178. This book is the main source of the description of the festival.

212. Jordan, *Revolutionary Career of Robespierre*, p. 200.

213. Schama, *Citizens*, p. 831.

214. Eagan, *Maximilien Robespierre,* pp. 179–80.

215. Blum, *Rousseau*, p. 254.

216. Eagan, *Maximilien Robespierre*, p. 180.

217. Blum, *Rousseau*, p. 252.

218. Schama, *Citizens*, p. 834.

219. Ibid.

220. Ibid., p. 836.

221. Blum, *Rousseau*, p. 239.

222. Schama, *Citizens*, p. 777.

223. Ibid., p. 778.

224. Ibid., p. 779.

225. Sydenham, *The French Revolution*, p. 201.

226. Schama, *Citizens*, p. 778.

227. Loomis, *Paris in the Terror*, pp. 278–79.

228. Breunig, *Age of Revolution*, p. 45.

229. Schama, *Citizens*, p. 778.

230. Blum, *Rousseau*, p. 240.

231. Ibid., p. 242.

232. Loomis, *Paris in the Terror*, pp. 280–81.

233. Blum, *Rousseau*, p. 244.
234. Jordan, *Revolutionary Career of Robespierre*, p. 157.
235. Eagan, *Maximilien Robespierre*, p. 75.
236. Blum, *Rousseau*, p. 223.
237. Ibid., p. 194.
238. Eagan, *Maximilien Robespierre*, p. 80.
239. Ibid., pp. 76–77.
240. Ibid., p. 78.
241. Ibid., p. 77.
242. Blum, *Rousseau*, p. 191.
243. Eagan, *Maximilien Robespierre*, p. 65.
244. Sydenham, *The French Revolution*, p. 165.
245. Eagan, *Maximilien Robespierre*, p. 108.
246. Ibid., p. 98.
247. Ibid., p. 108.
248. Ibid., p. 99.
249. Ibid., pp. 100–01.
250. Ibid., p. 107. Italics added.
251. Ibid., p. 103.
252. Ibid., p. 106.
253. Ibid., p. 116.
254. Ibid.
255. Jordan, *Revolutionary Career of Robespierre*, p. 161.
256. Sydenham, *The French Revolution*, p. 207.
257. Loomis, *Paris in the Terror*, p. 294.
258. Eagan, *Maximilien Robespierre*, p. 119.
259. Blum, *Rousseau*, p. 222.
260. Thompson, *Robespierre and the French Revolution*, p. 106. Italics added.
261. Hunt, *Politics*, p. 46.
262. Loomis, *Paris in the Terror*, p. 299.
263. Eagan, *Maximilien Robespierre*, p. 152.
264. Sydenham, *The French Revolution*, pp. 190, 211.
265. Eagan, *Maximilien Robespierre*, p. 171.
266. Blum, *Rousseau*, p. 267.
267. Ibid., p. 272.
268. Thompson, *Robespierre and the French Revolution*, p. 102.
269. Ibid., pp. 108–09.
270. Schama, *Citizens*, pp. 633–34.
271. Ibid., p. 635.
272. Ibid., p. 764.
273. Ibid., p. 780.
274. Loomis, *Paris in the Terror*, p. 329.
275. Schama, *Citizens*, p. 783.
276. Ibid.
277. Ibid., p. 791.
278. Ibid., p. 792.
279. Loomis, *Paris in the Terror*, p. 330.
280. Schama, *Citizens*, p. 794.
281. Ibid., p. 796.
282. Ibid., p. 827.

283. Severy, "The Great Revolutions," p. 44. Cf. Schama, *Citizens*, p. 790.

284. Schama, *Citizens*, p. 837.

285. Loomis, *Paris in the Terror*, p. 336.

286. Jordan, *Revolutionary Career of Robespierre*, p. 216.

287. Loomis, *Paris in the Terror*, p. 386.

288. Thompson, *Robespierre and the French Revolution*, p. 129.

289. Loomis, *Paris in the Terror*, p. 387.

290. Ibid.

291. Ibid., pp. 392–93.

292. Ibid., pp. 393–94.

293. Ibid., p. 400.

294. Jordan, *Revolutionary Career of Robespierre*, p. 220.

295. Loomis, *Paris in the Terror*, p. 402.

296. Jordan, *Revolutionary Career of Robespierre*, pp. 219–20; Schama, *Citizens*, pp. 840–46; Thompson, *Robespierre and the French Revolution*, pp. 127–34; Eagan, *Maximilien Robespierre*, pp. 218–19; and Blum, *Rousseau*, pp. 274–78.

297. Bernier, *Lafayette*, p. 256.

298. Ibid., p. 258.

299. Ibid.

300. Ibid., p. 266.

301. Ibid., pp. 264–66.

302. Chinard, *Letters*, pp. 417–18.

CHAPTER 6

1. Mogens Herman Hansen, *The Athenian Democracy in the Age of Demosthenes*, trans. J.A. Crook (Oxford, England: Basil Blackwell, 1991), p. 74.

2. Gospel of St. Luke, Chapter 10, verse 27.

3. Alan Gardiner, *Egypt of the Pharaohs* (New York: Oxford University Press, 1964), p. 177.

4. Henri Frankfort, *Kingship and the Gods: A Study of Ancient Near Eastern Religion as the Integration of Society and Nature* (Chicago: The University of Chicago Press, 1978), pp. 108–09.

5. Gardiner, *Egypt*, p. 227.

6. Frankfort, *Kingship and the Gods*, p. 252.

7. T. Walter Wallbank and Alistair M. Taylor, *Civilizations Past and Present* (Chicago: Scott, Foresman, 1955), pp. 21–22.

8. Fray Diego Duran, *The Aztecs: The History of the Indies of New Spain*, trans. Doris Heyden and Fernando Horcasitas (New York: Orion, 1964), p. 120.

9. Ibid., p. 120.

10. Ibid., p. 239. See also Fray Diego Duran, *Book of the Gods and Rites and the Ancient Calendar*, trans. and ed. Fernando Horcasitas and Doris Heyden (Norman: University of Oklahoma Press, 1971), Chaps. II and III.

11. Ervin Staub, *The Roots of Evil: The Origins of Genocide and Other Group Violence* (New York: Cambridge University Press, 1989), pp. 175–76.

12. Ibid., pp. 181–82.

13. Ibid., p. 183.

14. Ibid., p. 184.

15. John Boardman, Jasper Griffin, and Osivyn Murray (Eds.), *The Roman World* (New York: Oxford University Press, 1988), p. 145.

16. Paul Johnson, *A History of Christianity* (New York: Athenaeum, 1985), p. 115

17. Ibid.

18. Ibid.
19. Ibid.
20. A.N. Sherwin-White, *The Roman Citizenship*, 2nd ed. (Oxford, England: Oxford University Press, 1973), p. 461n.
21. Johnson, *History of Christianity*, p. 116.
22. Ibid.
23. Ibid., p. 117.
24. Ibid., p. 120.
25. Donald Earl, *The Moral and Political Tradition of Rome* (Ithaca, N.Y.: Cornell University Press, 1967), p. 125.
26. Johnson, *History of Christianity*, p. 120.
27. Ibid., p. 121.
28. Regarding Augustine, See George H. Sabine, *A History of Political Theory*, 3rd ed. (New York: Holt, Rinehart, and Winston, 1961), pp. 188–92.
29. Johnson, *History of Christianity*, p. 244.
30. Ibid., p. 252.
31. Jonathan Riley-Smith, *The Crusades: A Short History* (New Haven, Conn.: Yale University Press, 1987), p. 141.
32. Johnson, *History of Christianity*, p. 254.
33. Ibid.
34. Ibid., p. 255.
35. Shlomo Avineri, *The Social and Political Thought of Karl Marx* (Cambridge, England: Cambridge University Press, 1968), p. 190.
36. Ibid., p. 189.
37. Richard Crossman (Ed.), *The God That Failed* (New York: Bantam Books, 1952), p. 44.
38. Ibid., pp. 173–74.
39. Ibid., p. 257.
40. Ibid., p. 203.
41. Ibid., p. 102.
42. G.R. Urban (Ed.), *Stalinism: Its Impact on Russia and the World* (New York: St. Martin's Press, 1982), p. 181.
43. Ibid., p. 414.
44. Maurice Latey, *Tyranny: A Study in the Abuse of Power* (London: Macmillan, 1969), p. 171.
45. Ibid., p. 170.
46. Robert C. Tucker, *Stalin in Power: The Revolution from Above, 1928–1941* (New York: Norton, 1990), p. 35.
47. Urban, *Stalinism*, p. 102.
48. Ibid., pp. 130–31.
49. Tucker, *Stalin in Power*, pp. 3ff.
50. Ibid., p. 321.
51. Ibid., p. 325.
52. Ibid., p. 332.
53. Crossman, *The God That Failed*, p. 193.
54. Urban, *Stalinism*, p. 418.
55. Ibid., p. 423.
56. Ibid., p. 106.
57. Stephen J. Lee, *The European Dictatorships, 1918–1945* (New York: Metheun, 1987), pp. 304–05.
58. Robert B. Daniels (Ed.), *A Documentary History of Communism* (New York: Random House, 1960), p. 253.
59. Ibid., p. 254.
60. Ibid., p. 255.

61. Tucker, *Stalin in Power,* p. 221.

62. Ibid., . 467.

63. Lee, *European Dictatorships,* p. 56.

64. Tucker, *Stalin in Power,* p. 311.

65. Latey, *Tyranny,* pp. 140–41.

66. Tucker, *Stalin in Power,* p. 27.

67. Ibid., pp. 27–28.

68. Ibid., p. 139.

69. Ibid., p. 181.

70. Ibid., p. 173.

71. Ibid., p. 177.

72. Ibid., p. 180.

73. Ibid., p. 191.

74. Ibid., p. 192.

75. Ibid., p. 297.

76. Ibid., p. 305.

77. Ibid., p. 316.

78. Ibid., p. 386.

79. Ibid., p. 441.

80. Ibid., p. 474.

81. Ibid., p. 497.

82. Urban, *Stalinism,* p. 106.

83. Tucker, *Stalin in Power,* p. 192.

84. Ibid., p. 415.

85. Frank N. Trager and William Henderson (Eds.), *Communist China, 1949–1969: A Twenty-Year Appraisal* (New York: New York University Press, 1970), pp. 30, 32.

86. Dennis Bloodworth, *The Messiah and the Mandarins: Mao Tse-tung and the Ironies of Power* (New York: Athenaeum, 1982), p. 81.

87. Trager and Henderson, *Communist China,* p. 28.

88. Bloodworth, *The Messiah and the Mandarins,* p. 71.

89. Ibid., p. 74.

90. Ibid., p. 87.

91. Ibid., p. 91.

92. Ibid., p. 97.

93. Ibid., p. 98.

94. Trager and Henderson, *Communist China,* p. 35.

95. Ibid., p. 37.

96. Bloodworth, *The Messiah and the Mandarins,* p. 106.

97. Ibid., p. 32.

98. Ibid., p. 88.

99. Ibid., p. 102.

100. Ibid., p. 104.

101. Ibid., pp. 106–07.

102. Aleksandr I. Solzhenitsyn, *Letter to the Soviet Leaders* (New York: Harper and Row, 1975), pp. 57–58.

103. James Bryant Conant, *Germany and Freedom: A Personal Appraisal* (Cambridge, Mass.: Harvard University Press, 1958), pp. 38, 57.

104. Edwin O. Reischauer, *The United States and Japan,* 3rd ed. (Cambridge, Mass.: Harvard University Press, 1981), pp. 255–56.

105. Daniel J. Boorstin (Ed.), *An American Primer* (Chicago: University of Chicago Press, 1966), pp. 152–53.

106. Editors of Newsweek Books, *Thomas Jefferson: A Biography in His Own Words*, Vol. I (New York: Newsweek, 1974), p. 86.
107. Lewis Perry, *Radical Abolitionism: Anarchy and the Government of God in Antislavery Thought* (Ithaca: N.Y.: Cornell University Press, 1973), pp. 240–41.
108. J.L. Talmon, *The Origins of Totalitarian Democracy* (London: Secker and Warburg, 1952), p. 254.

CHAPTER 7

1. *The New Republic,* Editorial, September 7, 1987, p. 7.
2. Stanley Wolpert, *A New History of India*, 2nd ed. (New York: Oxford University Press, 1982), p.4.
3. Ibid., p. 42.
4. Ibid, p. 58.
5. Ibid., p. 63.
6. Ibid., pp. 66–67.
7. Ibid., p. 138.
8. Ibid., p. 188.
9. Ibid., p. 203.
10. Ibid., p. 213.
11. Ibid., p. 237.
12. Ibid., pp. 240–41.
13. Ibid., pp. 258–59.
14. Percival Spear, *A History of India,* Vol. II (New York: Penguin Books, 1984), p. 223.
15. M.J. Akbar, *Nehru: The Making of India* (New York: Penguin Books, 1988), p. 70.
16. Ibid., p. 21.
17. Spear, *History of India,* pp. 194 ff.
18. Ibid., p. 183.
19. Wolpert, *New History of India,* pp. 293–94.
20. Michael Brecher, *Nehru: A Political Biography* (Boston: Beacon Press, 1959), p. 36.
21. Spear, *History of India,* p. 397.
22. Wolpert, *New History of India,* p. 300.
23. Robert L. Hardgrave, Jr., *India: Government and Politics in a Developing Nation* (New York: Harcourt, Brace, Jovanovich, 1986), p. 43.
24. Romain Rolland, quoted by Erik Erikson, *Gandhi's Truth: On the Origin of Militant Nonviolence* (New York: Norton, 1969), pp. 31–32.
25. Spear, *History of India,* pp., 197–200.
26. H.V. Hodson, *The Great Divide: Britain-India-Pakistan* (London, Hutchinson, 1970), p. 35.
27. Wolpert, *New History of India,* p. 302.
28. Donald Eugene Smith, *India as a Secular State* (Princeton, N.J.: Princeton University Press, 1963), p. 91.
29. Wolpert, *New History of India,* pp. 303–304.
30. Ibid., p. 298.
31. Ibid., p. 307.
32. Ibid., pp. 314–15.
33. Ibid., pp. 315–316.
34. Ibid., p. 319.
35. Ibid., pp. 325–27.
36. Ibid., pp. 330–31.
37. Ibid., p. 331.
38. Ibid., p. 333.
39. Ibid., p. 333 ff.

40. Wali Khan, *Facts Are Facts: The Untold Story of India's Partition* (New Delhi: Vikas, 1987), pp. 95–100.

41. Wolpert, *New History of India*, pp. 333–49.

42. Akbar, *Nehru*, p. 7.

43. Ibid., p. 22.

44. Ibid., p. 27.

45. Ibid., p. 38.

46. Brecher, *Nehru*, p. 25.

47. Akbar, *Nehru*, p. 48.

48. Ibid., p. 53.

49. Brecher, *Nehru*, p. 31.

50. Akbar, *Nehru*, p. 72.

51. Ibid., p. 74.

52. Ibid., p. 80.

53. Ibid., pp. 60–61.

54. Ibid., p. 73.

55. Ibid., p. 105.

56. Ibid., p. 107.

57. Ibid., pp. 216–217.

58. Ibid., p. 221.

59. Brecher, *Nehru*, p. 43.

60. Akbar, *Nehru*, p. 239.

61. Ibid., p. 228.

62. Ibid., p. 241.

63. Ibid., p. 267.

64. Ibid., pp. 268–69.

65. Ibid., p. 289.

66. Brecher, *Nehru*, p. 65.

67. Ibid., p. 78.

68. Ibid., p. 80.

69. Ibid., p. 81.

70. Ibid., p. 83.

71. Ibid., p. 84.

72. Ibid., p. 137.

73. Ibid., p. 128.

74. Ibid., p. 139.

75. Ibid., p. 140.

76. H.B. Hodson, *The Great Divide: Britain-India-Pakistan* (London: Hutchinson, 1970), p. 419.

77. Wolpert, *New History of India*, pp. 355–56.

78. Hodson, *The Great Divide*, pp. 434–35.

79. Ibid., p. 440.

80. Spear, *History of India*, p. 241.

81. Hodson, *The Great Divide*, p. 490.

82. Ibid., p. 494.

83. N.L. Gupta and Vinod Bhatia (Eds.), *Jawaharlal Nehru: Statesman, National Leader, and Thinker* (New Delhi: Panchsheel, 1989), pp. 170–71.

84. Smith, *India as a Secular State*, pp. 127–28.

85. Brecher, *Nehru*, p. 164.

86. Wolpert, *New History of India*, p. 356.

87. Brecher, *Nehru*, p. 165.

88. Akbar, *Nehru*, pp., 571, 507.

89. Ibid., pp. 460–63.

90. Bipan Chandra, *Communalism in Modern India* (New Delhi: Vikas, 1984), pp. 1–2.

91. Ibid., p. 320.

92. Smith, *India as a Secular State*, p. 102.

93. Ibid., p. 4–5.

94. Spear, *History of India*, p. 253.

95. Brecher, *Nehru*, p. 243.

96. Wolpert, *New History of India*, p. 356.

97. Akbar, *Nehru*, p. 456.

98. Ibid., p. 462.

99. Ibid., p. 464.

100. Ibid., pp. 507–09.

101. Wolpert, *New History of India*, p. 363.

102. Brecher, *Nehru*, p. 133.

103. Ibid., p. 235.

104. Wolpert, *New History of India*, pp. 366–67.

105. Ibid., pp. 367–70.

106. Spear, *History of India*, p. 251.

107. Jawaharlal Nehru, *The Discovery of India*, Ed. Robert I. Crane (Garden City, N.Y.: Anchor Books, 1960), pp. 406–08.

108. Wolpert, *New History of India*, p. 370.

109. Ibid.

110. "Holy War in India," *Newsweek*, December 21, 1992, p. 47.

111. *Time*, October 21, 1995, p. 50.

CHAPTER 8

1. Harold T. Parker and Marvin L. Brown, Jr., *Major Themes in Modern European History: An Invitation to Inquiry and Reflection*. Vol. II: *The Institution of Liberty* (Durham, N.C.: Moore, 1974) p. 451.

2. Ibid., p. 613.

3. Cf. T Walter Walbank and Alastair M. Taylor, *Civilization Past and Present* (Chicago: Scott, Foresman, 1956), pp. 326ff.

4. Parker and Brown, *Institution of Liberty*, pp. 455–58.

5. Ibid., p. 454.

6. Ibid.

7. Wallbank and Taylor, *Civilization*, pp. 337–38.

8. Ibid., p. 338.

9. Dorothy Thompson, *The Chartists: Popular Politics in the Industrial Revolution* (New York: Pantheon Books, 1984), p. 111.

10. Wallbank and Taylor, *Civilization*, p. 338.

11. J.T. Ward, *The Factory Movement: 1830–1855* (London: Macmillan, 1962), p. 59.

12. Ivy Pinchbeck and Margaret Hewitt, *Children in English Society. Vol. II: From the Eighteenth Century to the Children Act 1948* (London: Routledge & Kegan Paul, 1973) p. 402.

13. Thompson, *The Chartists*, p. 14.

14. Ward, *The Factory Movement*, p. 146.

15. Ibid., p. 204.

16. Ibid., pp. 56, 102.

17. Pinchbeck and Hewitt, *Children and English Society*, II, pp. 395, 398.

18. A.V. Dicey, *Lectures on the Relation Between Law and Public Opinion in England* (London: Macmillan, 1920), p. 221.

19. Ivy Pinchbeck, *Women Workers and the Industrial Revolution, 1750–1850.* London: Virago Press, 1985), p. 279.

20. Pinchbeck and Hewitt, *Children in English Society,* II, p. 396.

21. Ibid., p. 397.

22. Ibid., pp. 403, 406.

23. Pinchbeck, *Women Workers,* p. 251.

24. Pinchbeck and Hewitt, *Children in English Society,* II, p. 401.

25. Wallbank and Taylor, *Civilization,* p. 338.

26. Ward, *The Factory Movement,* p. 30.

27. Pinchbeck and Hewitt, *Children in English Society,* II, p. 408.

28. Wallbank and Taylor, *Civilization,* p. 338. CF ibid., p. 399.

29. Pinchbeck and Hewitt, *Children in English Society,* II, p. 455.

30. Ward, *The Factory Movement,* p. 2.

31. *The Trial of Feargus O'Connor, Esq., (Barrister at Law), and Fifty-eight Others at Lancaster, on a Charge of Sedition, Conspiracy, Tumult, and Riot* (London: John Cleave, 1843), pp. 248–55.

32. T.A. Jackson, *Trials of British Freedom* (New York: Burt Franklin, 1968), p. 144.

33. Julius West, *A History of the Chartist Movement* (Boston: Houghton Mifflin, 1920), p. 184.

34. Thompson, *The Chartists,* p. 250.

35. Ward, *The Factory Movement,* pp. 16–17.

36. Ibid., pp. 24, 27.

37. N.H. Brasher, *Arguments in History: Britain in the Nineteenth Century* (London: Macmillan, 1968), pp. 28–29.

38. Ibid., pp. 34, 41.

39. Ward, *The Factory Movement,* pp. 142–43.

40. Brasher, *Arguments in History,* pp. 34, 36. Cf Parker and Brown, *Institution of Liberty,* pp. 473–74; and G.D.H. Cole, *Chartist Portraits* (London: Cassell, 1989), p. 32.

41. Thompson, *The Chartists,* p. 30.

42. John Stevenson, *Popular Disturbances in England, 1700–1870* (London: Longman, 1979), pp. 245–47.

43. Donald Read, *Peel and the Victorians* (Oxford: Basil Blackwell, 1987), p. 112.

44. C. Bradlaugh, *The Real Representation of the People,* 2nd ed. [London: Freethought, 188(?)], pp. 5–6.

45. Jackson, *Trials,* p. 122.

46. F.C. Mather, "The Government and the Chartists," in Asa Briggs (Ed.), *Chartist Studies* (London: Macmillan, 1959), p. 398.

47. Parker and Brown, *Institution of Liberty,* p. 471; and Thompson, *The Chartists,* p. 13.

48. Thompson, *The Chartists,* p. 17.

49. James Epstein, *The Lion of Freedom: Feargus O'Connor and the Chartist Movement, 1832–1842* (London: Croom Helm, 1982), p. 10.

50. Cole, *Chartist Portraits,* p. 304.

51. Ibid., p. 308.

52. Epstein, *Lion of Freedom,* pp. 8–10.

53. Ibid., p. 10–11.

54. Ibid., p. 12–13.

55. Ibid., p. 14.

56. Ibid., p. 15.

57. Ibid., p. 16.

58. Ibid., p. 17.

59. Ibid., p. 18–19.

60. Ibid., p. 25.

61. Ibid., p. 30.
62. Ibid., p. 42.
63. Ibid., p. 48.
64. Ibid., p. 51.
65. Ibid., p. 60.
66. Ibid., pp. 68, 76.
67. Ibid., p. 78.
68. Ibid., p. 82.
69. Ibid., p. 96.
70. Ibid., p. 101.
71. Ibid., p. 104.
72. Norman Gash, *Aristocracy and People: Britain, 1815–1865* (Cambridge, Mass.: Harvard University Press, 1979), p. 215.
73. Epstein, *Lion of Freedom,* p. 105.
74. Thompson, *The Chartists,* p. 126.
75. Ibid., p. 124, 134.
76. Cole, *Chartist Portraits,* p. 43.
77. Ibid., pp. 42–43.
78. Epstein, *Lion of Freedom,* p. 110.
79. Ibid., p. 141.
80. Ibid., p. 114.
81. Cole, *Chartist Portraits,* pp. 50–51.
82. Jackson, *Trials,* p. 128.
83. Thompson, *The Chartists,* pp. 64–65.
84. Epstein, *Lion of Freedom,* p. 155.
85. Jackson, *Trials,* p. 129.
86. *Hansard's Parliamentary Debates,* Third Series, 2 Victoriae 1839, Vol. XLIX, 8 July–6 August, 1839, Fifth Volume of the Session, 63515, p. 254.
87. Ibid.
88. Ibid., p. 257.
89. Ibid., pp. 229–30.
90. Ibid., p. 236.
91. Ibid., p. 238.
92. Ibid., pp. 239, 267.
93. Ibid., pp. 243–49.
94. Stevenson, *Popular Disturbances,* p. 258.
95. Thompson, *The Chartists,* pp. 66–69.
96. Ibid., pp. 70–73.
97. Ibid., p. 74.
98. Cole, *Chartist Portraits,* pp. 50–55.
99. *Trial of Feargus O'Connor,* p. 12.
100. Ibid., pp. 358–59.
101. Ibid., pp. 358–64.
102. Epstein, *Lion of Freedom, p. 218.*
103. Thompson, *The Chartists,* pp. 77–82; and Jackson, *Trials,* p. 142.
104. Epstein, *Lion of Freedom,* p. 221.
105. Cole, *Chartist Portraits,* pp. 332–33.
106. Read, *Peel,* p. 139.
107. Epstein, *Lion of Freedom,* pp. 228–29.
108. Ibid., p. 235.

109. Ibid., p. 236.

110. Ibid., p. 240.

111. Ibid., p. 288.

112. Stevenson, *Popular Disturbances*, p. 264.

113. Thompson, *The Chartists*, p. 295.

114. *Hansard's Parliamentary Debates*, Third Series, 5 Victoriae 1842,. Vol. LXIII, 3 May–16 June 1842, Fourth Volume of the Session, 63529, pp. 14, 35, and 18.

115. Ibid., p. 30.

116. Ibid., pp. 46–48.

117. Ibid., p. 64.

118. Ibid., pp. 70–71.

119. Ibid., p. 78.

120. Ibid., pp. 81–82.

121. Ibid., p. 84.

122. Ibid., p. 88.

123. Thompson, *The Chartists*, p. 310.

124. *Hansard's Parliamentary Debates*, Third Series, 11 Victoriae 1847–1848, Vol. XCVIII, 7 April –26 May, 1848, Fourth Volume of the Session, 63564, p. 290.

125. Cole, *Chartist Portraits*, p. 331.

126. Thompson, *The Chartists*, pp. 312–13.

127. Ibid., pp. 316, 320.

128. Jackson, *Trials*, p. 155.

129. Thompson, *The Chartists*, p. 324.

130. Ibid., p. 325.

131. Cole, *Chartist Portraits*, p. 334.

132. Ibid., p. 353.

133. Thompson, *The Chartists*, pp. 325–29, 331.

134. Ibid., p. 335.

CHAPTER 9

1. A.S. Diamond, *The Evolution of Law and Order* (London: Watts, 1951), p. 45.

2. Ibid., pp. 204 ff.

3. Ibid., p. 209.

4. Ibid., pp. 252–53.

5. Ibid., p. 247.

6. Ibid., p. 27.

7. Ibid., pp. 73 ff.

8. Ibid., pp. 88 ff.

9. Ibid., p. 206.

10. Ibid., pp. 73–77.

11. Rev. Boniface Verheyen, *The Holy Rule of Our Most Holy Father Benedict*, 8th ed. (Atchison, Kan.: The Abbey Student Press, 1935), p. v.

12. Diamond, *Evolution of Law*, p. 151.

13. Ibid., p. 160.

14. Ibid., p. 161.

15. Ibid., p. 307.

16. Ibid., p. 146.

17. Ibid., p. 149.

18. Cf. Alma E. Guiness (Ed.), *Mysteries of the Bible: The Enduring Questions of the Scriptures.* (Pleasantville, N.Y.: Reader's Digest, 1988).

19. Frank J. Powell, *The Trial of Jesus Christ* (London: The Paternoster Press, 1949), pp. 12, 48.

20. Ibid., p. 13.

21. Ibid., p. 21.

22. John 11:50; see ibid., pp. 35, 55–56. This account of the trial is woven from three of the gospels, following Powell.

23. Powell, *Trial of Jesus Christ*, p. 58.

24. Ibid., p. 102.

25. Ibid., pp. 96–97.

26. Ibid., p. 97.

27. Ibid., p. 101.

28. Ibid., p. 106.

29. Hunter's *Roman Law*, quoted in ibid., p. 111.

30. Matthew 5:17; see Powell, *Trial of Jesus Christ*, p. 57.

31. Powell, *Trial of Jesus Christ*, p. 24.

32. Matthew 22:15, 17.

33. Powell, *Trial of Jesus Christ*, p. 44.

34. Ibid., p. 45.

35. Ibid., p. 69.

36. John 18:21, 23.

37. Matthew 26:63.

38. Matthew 26:65–66; see Powell, *Trial of Jesus Christ*, pp. 70–71.

39. Powell, *Trial of Jesus Christ*, pp. 83–85.

40. Ibid., p. 90.

41. Ibid., p. 107.

42. John 18:29.

43. John 18:31.

44. John 18:31.

45. Luke 23:2.

46. John 18:33.

47. John 18:34.

48. John 18:35.

49. John 18:36.

50. John 18:38.

51. Powell, *Trial of Jesus Christ*, p. 117.

52. Ibid., p. 52.

53. Luke 23:14–16; see ibid., p. 121.

54. John 19:6, 7; see Powell, *Trial of Jesus Christ*, pp. 124, 127.

55. John 19:9, 10, 11.

56. John 19:12, 14, 15.

57. Powell, *Trial of Jesus Christ*, p. 133.

58. Luke 23:34.

59. Quoted in John H. Hallowell, *Main Currents in Modern Political Thought* (New York: Henry Holt, 1950), p. 18.

60. Ibid., pp. 18–19.

61. Anthony Birley, *Marcus Aurelius: A Biography* (New Haven, Conn.: Yale University Press, 1987), p. 222.

62. T. Walter Wallbank and Alastair M. Taylor, *Civilization: Past and Present* (Chicago: Scott, Foresman, 1956), p. 62.

63. Edward Gibbon, *The Decline and Fall of the Roman Empire,* abridged version edited by Dero A. Saunders (London: Penguin Books, 1987), pp. 116–33.

64. James Freeman Clarke, *Anti-Slavery Days* (New York: AMS Press, 1972), pp. 11–12.

65. Fawn M. Brodie, *Thomas Jefferson: An Intimate History* (New York: Norton, 1974), p. 49.

66. Adrienne Koch and William Peden (Eds.), *The Life and Selected Writings of Thomas Jefferson* (New York: The Modern Library, 1944), p. xviii.

67. Brodie, *Jefferson*, p. 183.

68. Ibid.

69. Daniel J. Boorstin (Ed.), *An American Primer* (Chicago: University of Chicago Press, 1966), p. 68.

70. John Hope Franklin, *From Slavery to Freedom: A History of Negro Americans*, 5th ed. (New York: Alfred A. Knopf, 1980), p. 84.

71. Koch and Peden, *Life of Jefferson*, p. 29.

72. John Richard Alden, *The South in the Revolution, 1763–1789* (Louisiana: Louisiana State University Press, 1957), p. 217.

73. Franklin, *From Slavery to Freedom*, p. 89.

74. Alden, *The South in the Revolution*, p. 218.

75. Koch and Peden, *Life of Jefferson*, p. 32.

76. Ibid., p. 40.

77. Franklin, *From Slavery to Freedom*, p. 94.

78. Ibid., p. 95.

79. Ibid.

80. Ibid., p. 96.

81. Ibid., p. 104.

82. Brodie, *Jefferson*, p. 422.

83. Ibid., p. 441.

84. Franklin, *From Slavery to Freedom*, p. 134.

85. Brodie, *Jefferson*, p. 468.

86. Arthur R. Hogue, *Origins of the Common Law* (Indianapolis: Liberty Press, 1966), p. 3.

87. *Newsweek*, May 18, 1992, p. 45.

88. Ibid., p. 46.

89. Robert W. Merry, Executive Editor of *Congressional Quarterly*, quoted in *Durham Herald-Sun*, May 14, 1992, p. A9; and Donald L. Bartlett and James B. Steele, *America: What Went Wrong?* (Kansas City: Andrews and McMeel, 1992), p. xiii.

90. Merry, *Durham Herald-Sun*, p. A9.

91. *Secrets of the Temple: How the Federal Reserve Runs the Country* (New York: Simon & Schuster, 1987), p. 717.

92. Bartlett and Steele, *America*, p. x.

93. Ibid., p. 3.

94. Ibid.

95. William Greider, *The Trouble with Money* (Knoxville, Tenn.: Whittle Direct Books, 1989), p. 84.

96. Nigel Hawkes (Ed.), *Tearing Down the Curtain: The People's Revolution in Eastern Europe* (London: Hodder and Stoughton, 1990), p. 150.

97. Benjamin Barber and Patrick Watson, *The Struggle for Democracy* (Boston: Little, Brown, 1988), p. 260.

98. Peter Stein, *Legal Evolution: The Story of an Idea* (Cambridge, England: Cambridge University Press, 1980), p. 5, emphasis added.

CHAPTER 10

1. Orlando Patterson, *Freedom*, Vol. I: *Freedom in the Making of Western Culture* (New York: Basic Books, 1991), p. 369.

2. Edward S. Corwin, *The "Higher Law" Background of American Constitutional Law* (Ithaca, N.Y.: Great Seal Books, 1929), p. 42.

3. Stephen D. White, *Sir Edward Coke and "The Grievances of the Commonwealth," 1621–1628*

(Chapel Hill: University of North Carolina Press, 1979) p. 3.

4. David Lindsay Keir, *The Constitutional History of Modern Britain Since 1485* (New York: W.W. Norton, 1966), p. 198.

5. Wilfrid R. Prest, *The Rise of the Barristers: A Social History of the English Bar, 1590–1640* (Oxford: Clarendon Press, 1991), p. vii.

6. James H. Rutherford, *The Moral Foundation of United States Constitutional Democracy* (Pittsburgh: Dorrance, 1992), p. 31.

7. Catherine Drinker Bowen, *The Lion and Throne: The Life and Times of Sir Edward Coke (1552–1634)* (Boston: Little, Brown, 1957), p. 515.

8. Ibid., pp. 45–75.

9. Hastings Lyon and Herman Block, *Edward Coke: Oracle of the Law* (Boston: Houghton Mifflin, 1929), pp. 62–65.

10. Ibid., pp. 64–65.

11. Ibid., p. 67.

12. Corwin, *Higher Law*, p. 10.

13. Ibid., p. 16.

14. Ibid., p. 27.

15. Ibid., p. 33.

16. Charles Warburton James, *Chief Justice Coke: His Family and Descendants at Holkham* (London: Country Life, 1929), p. 8–9.

17. Bowen, *The Lion and the Throne*, p. 19.

18. James, *Chief Justice Coke*, pp. 22, 145.

19. Ibid., pp. 93, 142.

20. Ibid., pp. 31–32.

21. Harold T. Parker and Marvin L. Brown, Jr., *Major Themes in Modern European History: An Invitation to Inquiry and Reflection*, Vol. I: *The Institution of the State* (Durham, N.C.: Moore, 1974), p. 194.

22. Clayton Roberts and David Roberts, *A History of England*, Vol. I: *Prehistory to 1714*, 3rd ed. (Englewood Cliffs, N.J.: Prentice Hall, 1980), pp. 340–41.

23. See notes from *The Holy Bible: Containing the Old and New Testaments* (Philadelphia: A.J. Holman, 1942), Exodus, Chapters 18–40.

24. Bowen, *The Lion and the Throne*, p. 229.

25. Davis Harris Wilson, "King James I and Anglo-Scottish Unity," in *Conflict in Stuart England*, Ed. William Appleton Aiken and Basil Duke Henning (New York: New York University Press, 1960), p. 44.

26. Bowen, *The Lion and the Throne*, p. 294.

27. Winston S. Churchill, *A History of the English-Speaking Peoples*, Vol. II: *The New World* (New York: Dodd, Mead, 1983), p. 151.

28. Ibid., p. 157.

29. Bowen, *The Lion and the Throne*, p. 296.

30. Ibid., p. 178.

31. Ibid., p. 263.

32. Churchill, *History*, II, p. 148.

33. Ibid., p. 155.

34. Roberts and Roberts, *History of England*, I, p. 333.

35. Ivor Jennings, *Parliament* (Cambridge, England: Cambridge University Press, 1969), p. 473.

36. Bowen, *The Lion and the Throne*, pp. 294, 291.

37. Ibid., p. 298.

38. Ibid., pp. 304–05.

39. Corwin, *Higher Law*, p. 43.

40. Bowen, *The Lion and the Throne*, pp. 312–313.

41. Ibid., p. 315.

42. Ibid., p. 321.

43. Ibid., p. 322.

44. Ibid., p. 323.

45. James, *Chief Justice Coke*, pp. 35–36.

46. Corwin, *Higher Law*, p. 47.

47. Parker and Brown, *Institution of the State*, p. 196.

48. Bowen, *The Lion and the Throne*, pp. 450–53.

49. Parker and Brown, *Institution of the State*, p. 197.

50. Bowen, *The Lion and the Throne*, p. 466.

51. Ibid., p. 475.

52. Ibid., p. 481.

53. Ibid., p. 482–83.

54. Ibid., p. 483.

55. Ibid., p. 487.

56. Ibid., pp. 488–89.

57. Ibid., p. 490.

58. Ibid., p. 493.

59. Ibid., pp. 495–96.

60. David Harris Wilson, *A History of England* (New York: Holt, Rinehart and Winston, 1967), p. 384.

61. Bowen, *The Lion and the Throne*, p. 498.

62. Ibid., p. 499.

63. Ibid., pp. 497–503; and Lyon and Block, *Edward Coke*, p. 327.

64. Conrad Russell, *Parliaments and English Politics* (Oxford: Clarendon Press, 1979), p. 348.

65. Harold Hulme, "Charles I and the Constitution," in William Appleton Aiken and Basil Duke Henning (Eds.), *Conflict in Stuart England* (New York: New York University Press, 1960), p. 100.

66. Roberts and Roberts, *History of England*, I, p. 344.

67. Bowen, *The Lion and the Throne*, p. 521.

68. Anthony Fletcher, *The Outbreak of the English Civil War* (New York: New York University Press, 1981), p. xix.

69. Wilson, *History of England*, p. 427.

70. Parker and Brown, *Institution of the State*, p. 203.

71. J.H. Hexter (Ed.), *Parliament and Liberty: From the Reign of Elizabeth to the English Civil War* (Stanford, Cal.: Stanford University Press, 1992), p. 257.

72. Russell, *Parliaments and English Politics*, p. 350.

73. Ibid., p. 358.

74. Ibid., p. 362.

75. Rutherford, *Moral Foundations*, p. 30.

76. Bowen, *The Lion and the Throne*, pp. 505–24.

CHAPTER 11

1. Paul Fussell, *The Great War and Modern Memory* (New York: Oxford University Press, 1975), p. 115.

2. Ibid., p. 184.

3. Ibid., p. 13.

4. Willi Eichler, "Friedrich Ebert: The Exponent of the Upheaval, " in *Friedrich Ebert, 1871/1971* (Bonn–Bad Godesberg: Inter Nationes, 1971), p. 24.

5. Ibid., p. 24.

6. Ibid., p. 29.

7. Ibid., p. 32.

8. Ibid., p. 34.

9. V. Nitzschke and P. Weight, *Friedrich Ebert* (Bonn: Friedrich-Ebert-Stiftung, 1968):, p. 21. Much of the material on Ebert throughout this chapter is taken from this source.

10. Eichler, "Friedrich Ebert," p. 40.

11. Ibid., p. 42.

12. S. William Halperin, *Germany Tried Democracy: A Political History of the Reich from 1918 to 1933* (New York: Thomas Y. Crowell, 1946), p. 69.

13. Ibid., p. 72.

14. Ibid., p. 93.

15. Eichler, "Friedrich Ebert," p. 47.

16. Halperin, *Germany Tried Democracy*, p. 93.

17. Ibid., p. 120.

18. Ibid., p. 121.

19. Eichler, "Friedrich Ebert," p. 55.

20. Otto Friedrich, *Before the Deluge: A Portrait of Berlin in the 1920s* (New York: Fromm, 1986), pp. 53–54.

21. Ibid., p. 55.

22. Halperin, *Germany Tried Democracy*, p. 142.

23. Ibid., p. 157.

24. William L. Shirer, *The Rise and Fall of the Third Reich: A History of Nazi Germany* (New York: Simon & Schuster, 1960), p. 57.

25. Halperin, *Germany Tried Democracy*, p. 158.

26. Modris Eksteins, *The Limits of Reason: The German Democratic Press and the Collapse of the Weimar Democracy* (London: Oxford University Press, 1975), pp. 70, 306—7.

27. Shirer, *Third Reich*, pp. 60–61.

28. Friedrich, *Before the Deluge*, p. 124.

29. Otis C. Mitchell, *Hitler Over Germany: The Establishment of the Nazi Dictatorship (1918–1934)* (Philadelphia: Institute of the Study of Human Issues, 1983), p. 76.

30. Leonard Mosely, *The Reich Marshall: A Biography of Hermann Goering* (New York: Dell, 1974), p. 103.

31. Shirer, *Third Reich*, p. 68.

32. Ibid., pp. 68–69.

33. Ibid., p. 69.

34. Ibid.

35. Friedrich, *Before the Deluge*, p. 140.

36. Shirer, *Third Reich*, pp. 71–72.

37. Mosely, *Reich Marshall*, p. 109.

38. Halperin, *Germany Tried Democracy*, p. 277.

39. Shirer, *Third Reich*, pp. 73–75; and Mosely, *Reich Marshall*, pp. 110–13.

40. Friedrich, *Before the Deluge*, p. 141.

41. Halperin, *Germany Tried Democracy*, p. 279.

42. Ibid., p. 280.

43. Nitzschke and Weight, *Friedrich Ebert*, p. 60.

44. Adolf Hitler, *Mein Kampf*, trans. Ralph Manheim (Boston: Houghton Mifflin, 1971), pp. xi–xii.

45. Ibid., pp. 7–8.

46. Ibid., p. 9.

47. Ibid., p. 17.

48. Ibid., pp. 9–10.

49. Ibid., p. 14.

50. Ibid., pp. 14–15.

51. Walter C. Langer, *The Mind of Adolf Hitler: The Secret Wartime Report* (New York: Basic Books, 1972), p. 122.

52. Mitchell, *Hitler Over Germany,* p. 17.

53. Langer, *Mind of Hitler,* p. 126.

54. Shirer, *Third Reich,* p. 29.

55. Langer, *Mind of Hitler,* p. 130.

56. Ibid., p. 130.

57. Mitchell, *Hitler Over Germany,* p. 57.

58. Langer, *Mind of Hitler,* p. 132.

59. Ibid., p. 133.

60. Mitchell, *Hitler Over Germany,* p. 60.

61. Langer, *Mind of Hitler,* p. 206.

62. Ibid., p. 137.

63. Ibid., p. 37.

64. Ibid., p. 55.

65. Ibid.

66. Ibid.

67. Ibid., p. 56.

68. Ibid., p. 74.

69. Hitler, *Mein Kampf,* p. 35.

70. Langer, *Mind of Hitler,* p. 41.

71. Peter Viereck, *Metapolitics: The Roots of the Nazi Mind* (New York: Capricorn Books, 1961), p. 132.

72. Shirer, *Third Reich,* p. 101.

73. Viereck, *Metapolitics,* p. 143.

74. Ibid., p. 135.

75. Shirer, *Third Reich,* p. 101.

76. Horst von Maltitz, *The Evolution of Hitler's Germany: The Ideology, the Personality, the Moment* (New York: McGraw-Hill, 1973), p. 218.

77. Langer, *Mind of Hitler,* p. 144.

78. Viereck, *Metapolitics,* p. 139.

79. Ibid., p. 142.

80. Maltitz, *Hitler's Germany,* pp. 208–9, 217.

81. Friedrich, *Before the Deluge,* p. 155.

82. Ibid., p. 153.

83. Ibid., p. 147.

84. Ibid., p. 259.

85. Ibid., p. 271.

86. Ibid., p. 151.

87. Ibid., p. 146.

88. Ibid., p. 82.

89. Ibid., p. 183.

90. Ibid., p. 292.

91. Ibid., p. 91.

92. Siegfried Kracauer, *From Caligari to Hitler: A Psychological History of the German Film* (Princeton, N.J.: Princeton University Press, 1947) p. 6.

93. Bruce Murray, *Film and the German Left in the Weimar Republic: From Caligari to Kuhle Wampe* (Austin: University of Texas Press, 1990), p. 21.

94. Friedrich, *Before the Deluge,* p. 65.

95. Kracauer, *From Caligari to Hitler,* p. 46.

96. Ibid., p. 53.
97. Ibid., p. 59.
98. Ibid., p. 67.
99. Murray, *Film and the German Left*, p. 27.
100. Friedrich, *Before the Deluge*, p. 73.
101. Ibid., p. 77.
102. Ibid., p. 326.
103. Kracauer, *From Caligari to Hitler*, p. 11.
104. Carol Cohen, (Ed.), *Communism, Fascism, and Democracy: The Theoretical Foundations* (New York: Random House, 1962), p. 321; emphasis added.
105. Ibid., pp. 322, 324.
106. Ibid., p. 324.
107. Friedrich, *Before the Deluge*, p. 189.
108. Shirer, *Third Reich*, p. 26.
109. Langer, *Mind of Hitler*, p. 194.
110. Ibid., p. 197.
111. Friedrich, *Before the Deluge*, pp. 108–09.
112. Peter Peal, Preface to Alfred Rosenberg's *The Myth of the Twentieth Century: An Evaluation of the Spiritual-Intellectual Confrontations of Our Age* (Torrance, Cal.: Noontide Press, 1982), pp. xx–xxi.
113. Friedrich, *Before the Deluge*, p. 112.
114. Milton Mayer, *They Thought They Were Free: The German, 1933–1945* (Chicago: University of Chicago Press, 1955), p. 81.
115. Nitzschke and Weight, *Friedrich Ebert*, p. 114.
116. Ibid., p. 112.
117. Ibid.
118. Friedrich, *Before the Deluge*, p. 187.
119. Helmut Heiber, *Goebbels*, trans. John K. Dickinson (New York: Da Capo Press, 1972), p. 8.
120. Ibid., p. 12.
121. Ibid., p. 13.
122. Ibid., p. 27.
123. Ibid., pp. 21, 23.
124. Ibid., p. 38.
125. Shirer, *The Third Reich*, p. 127.
126. Friedrich, *Before the Deluge*, p. 198.
127. Heiber, *Goebbels*, p. 46.
128. Friedrich, *Before the Deluge*, p. 203.
129. Robert Edwin Herzstein, *The War That Hitler Won: Goebbels and the Nazi Media Campaign* (New York: Paragon House, 1987), p. 37.
130. Heiber, *Goebbels*, p. 32.
131. Ibid., p. 78.
132. Ibid., p. 76.
133. Friedrich, *Before the Deluge*, p. 206.
134. David Welch (Ed.), *Nazi Propaganda: The Power and the Limitations* (Totowa, N.J.: Barnes and Noble, 1983), pp. 44, 1.
135. Friedrich, *Before the Deluge*, p. 300.
136. Ibid., pp. 206–07.
137. Eksteins, *Limits of Reason*, pp. 273–74.
138. Heiber, *Goebbels*, p. 50.
139. Ibid., p. 95.
140. Ibid., p. 101.
141. Ibid., p. 49.

142. Ibid., p. 55.

143. Ibid., p. 80.

144. Ibid., p. 96.

145. Friedrich, *Before the Deluge*, p. 311.

146. Ibid., p. 323.

147. Ibid., p. 325.

148. Heiber, *Goebbels*, p. 93.

149. Shirer, *Third Reich*, p. 158.

150. Heiber, *Goebbels*, p. 101.

151. Friedrich, *Before the Deluge*, p. 370.

152. Ibid., p. 376.

153. Ibid., p. 382.

154. Edward Yarnall Hartshorne, Jr., *The German Universities and National Socialism* (Cambridge, Mass.: Harvard University Press, 1937), p. 14; Shirer, *Third Reich*, p. 194; and Friedrich, *Before the Deluge*, p. 383.

155. Heiber, *Goebbels*, p. 109.

156. Edward McNall Burns, *Western Civilizations: Their History and Their Culture*, 4th ed. (New York: W.W. Norton, 1954), p. 766.

157. Shirer, *Third Reich*, p. 189.

158. Welch, *Nazi Propaganda*, p. 36.

159. Ibid., p. 37.

160. Shirer, *Third Reich*, p. 190.

161. Ibid., p. 198.

162. Ibid.

163. Ibid., p. 199.

164. Ibid.

165. Ibid.

166. Ibid., p. 223.

167. Hartshorne, *German Universities*, p. 16.

168. Mayer, *They Thought They Were Free*, p. 111.

169. Maltitz, *Hitler's Germany*, pp. 215–216.

170. Friedrich, *Before the Deluge*, p. 385.

171. Shirer, *Third Reich*, p. 249.

172. Ibid.

173. George L. Mosse, *Nazi Culture: Intellectual, Cultural and Social Life in the Third Reich* (New York: Schocken Books, 1981), p. 10.

174. Shirer, *Third Reich*, p. 248.

175. Susanne Charlotte Engelmann, *German Education and Re-education* (New York: International Universities Press, 1945), p. 80.

176. Mosse, *Nazi Culture*, p. 280.

177. Ibid.

178. Shirer, *Third Reich*, p. 253.

179. Engelmann, *German Education*, p. 119.

180. Harwood L. Childs, *The Nazi Primer: Official Handbook for Schooling the Hitler Youth* (New York: Harpert Brothers, 1938), p. xxiii.

181. Shirer, *Third Reich*, p. 252.

182. Ibid., p. 249.

183. Engelmann, *German Education*, p. 82.

184. Shirer, *Third Reich*, p. 250.

185. Engelmann, *German Education*, p. 88.

186. Childs, *Nazi Primer*, p. 270.

187. Engelmann, *German Education*, pp. 87–88.

188. Mayer, *They Thought They Were Free*, p. 196.

189. Ibid., p. 193.

190. David Lehman, "Deconstructing de Man's Life," *Newsweek*, February 15, 1988.

191. David H. Hirsch, *The Deconstruction of Literature: Criticism After Auschwitz* (Hanover, N.H.: University Press of New England, 1991), p. 267.

192. Shirer, *Third Reich*, p. 256.

193. Studs Terkel, *"The Good War": An Oral History of World War Two* (New York: Ballantine Books, 1984), pp. 215–216.

194. Joseph E. Persico, *Edward R. Murrow: An American Original* (New York: McGraw-Hill, 1988), pp. 228–29.

195. Shirer, *Third Reich*, p. 981.

196. Ibid., p. 985.

197. Ibid., p. 1133.

CHAPTER 12

1. Barbara W. Tuchman, *The March of Folly: From Troy to Vietnam* (New York: Alfred A. Knopf, 1984), p. 39.

2. Ibid., p. 42.

3. Cf. ibid., Chap. 2, and Isaac Asimov, *Words from the Myths* (New York: New American Library, 1969), pp. 125–26.

4. B. Jowett (trans.) *The Dialogues of Plato*, Vol I, "Gorgias" (New York: Random House, 1937), p. 582.

5. Ibid., p. 511.

6. Ibid., p. 517.

7. Ibid., p. 522.

8. Ibid., p. 579.

9. Ibid., p. 545.

10. Ibid., p. 552.

11. Ibid., p. 564.

12. Ibid., p. 587.

13. Edward Gibbon, *The Decline and Fall of the Roman Empire*, abridged version edited by Dero A. Saunders (London: Penguin Books, 1987), p. 620.

14. Ibid., p. 626.

15. Michael Grant, *Gladiators* (New York: Delacorte, 1967), p. 7.

16. Ibid., pp. 118–19.

17. Keith Hopkins, *Death and Renewal: Sociological Studies in Roman History*, Vol. 2 (Cambridge, England: Cambridge University Press, 1983), p. 17.

18. Ibid., p. 9.

19. Jonathan Riley-Smith, *The Crusaders: A Short History* (New Haven, Conn.: Yale University Press, 1987), p. 141.

20. Ibid.

21. Charles Mackay, *Extraordinary Popular Delusions and the Madness of Crowds* (New York: Farrar, Straus, and Giroux, 1932), p. 463.

22. Ibid., p. 478.

23. Ibid., p. 528.

24. Ibid., pp. 528–29.

25. David Donald, *Lincoln Reconsidered: Essays on the Civil War Era*, 2nd ed. (New York: Vintage Books, 1961), p. 223.

26. Richard Hofstadter, *Anti-Intellectualism in American Life* (New York: Alfred A. Knopf, 1963), p. 165.

27. Brooks Atkinson (Ed.), *The Complete Essays and Other Writings of Ralph Waldo Emerson* (New York: The Modern Library, 1940), p. xxiii.
28. Donald, *Lincoln Reconsidered*, p. 226.
29. Ibid.
30. Atkinson, *Emerson*, p. 422.
31. Donald, *Lincoln Reconsidered*, p. 230.
32. Avery Craven, *The Coming of the Civil War*, 2nd ed. (Chicago: University of Chicago Press, 1974), pp. 17–18.
33. Ibid., p. 145.
34. Ibid., pp. 145–46. In addition to Stowe's *Uncle Tom's Cabin* (London: C.H. Clarke, 1852), see her *A Key to Uncle Tom's Cabin* (London: Thomas Bosworth, 1853).
35. Stephen B. Oates, *With Malice Toward None: The Life of Abraham Lincoln* (New York: New American Library, 1977), pp. 186–87.
36. Craven, *Coming of the Civil War*, p. 366.
37. Norman Kiell (Ed.), *Psychological Studies of Famous Americans: The Civil War Era* (New York: Twayne, 1964), p. 159.
38. David Herbert Donald, *Charles Sumner and the Coming of the Civil War* (Chicago: University of Chicago Press, 1981), p. 278.
39. Ibid., pp. 283–84.
40. Ibid., pp. 284–85.
41. Ibid., p. 286.
42. Ibid., pp. 287–88.
43. Craven, *Coming of the Civil War*, p. 367.
44. Donald, *Charles Sumner*, p. 288.
45. Ibid., pp. 296, 301.
46. Ibid., p. 305.
47. Arthur Schlesinger, Jr., "The Causes of the Civil War: A Note on Historical Sentimentalism," *Partisan Review*, October 1949, p. 970.
48. Benjamin Barber and Patrick Watson, *The Struggle for Democracy* (Boston: Little, Brown, 1988), pp. 191–93.
49. James David Barber, *Citizen Politics: An Introduction to Political Behavior* (Chicago: Markham, 1969), pp 38–39.
50. J.W. Dower, *Empire and Aftermath: Yoshida Shigaru and the Japanese Experience, 1878–1954* (Cambridge, Mass.: Harvard University Press, 1988), p. 7
51. Ibid., p. 349.
52. Ibid., p. 356.
53. Dennis L. Bark and David R. Gress, *From Shadow to Substance, 1945–1963* (Cambridge, Mass.: Harvard University Press, 1989), pp. 339, 165, 168.
54. Lucius D. Clay, *Germany and the Fight for Freedom* (Cambridge, Mass.: Harvard University Press, 1950), pp. 49–50.
55. Public Records Management, c. 1960s, p. 1.

CHAPTER 13

1. John M. Blum and others, *The National Experience: A History of the United States*, 2nd ed. (New York: Harcourt, Brace, and World, 1968), p. 21.
2. Daniel J. Boorstin (Ed.), *An American Primer* (Chicago: University of Chicago Press, 1966), p. 2.
3. Ibid., p. 3.
4. Blum, *The National Experience*, p. 18.
5. Bradford Smith, *Bradford of Plymouth* (Philadelphia: Lippincott, 1951), p. 18.
6. James David Barber and Barbara Kellerman (Eds.), *Women Leaders in American Politics*

(Englewood Cliffs, N.J.: Prentice Hall, 1986), p. 2–3.

7. Ibid., p. 3.

8. Ibid., pp. 4–11.

9. Harold Underwood Faulkner, *American Political and Social History* (New York: F.S. Crofts, 1946), p. 45.

10. Benjamin Barber and Patrick Watson, *The Struggle for Democracy* (Boston: Little, Brown, 1988), p. 34.

11. Garry Wills, *Under God: Religion and American Politics* (New York: Simon and Schuster, 1990), p. 345.

12. Livingston Rutherfurd, *John Peter Zenger: His Press, His Trial, and a Bibliography of Zenger of Zenger Imprints* (Gloucester, Mass.: Peter Smith, 1963), p. 29.

13. Ibid., p. 30.

14. Ibid., p. 70.

15. Ibid., p. 79.

16. Ibid., p. 88.

17. Faulkner, *American Political and Social History*, p. 63.

18. Rutherfurd, p. 131.

19. Ibid., p. 127.

20. Catherine Drinker Bowen, *The Most Dangerous Man in America: Scenes from the Life of Benjamin Franklin* (Boston: Little, Brown, 1974), p. 6.

21. Thomas Fleming (Ed.), *Benjamin Franklin: A Biography in His Own Words*, Vol. I (New York: Newsweek, 1972), p. 18.

22. Ibid., p. 20.

23. Ibid., p. 22.

24. Ibid., pp. 23–24.

25. Ibid., p. 24.

26. Bowen, *Most Dangerous Man*, pp. 23–24.

27. Fleming, *Franklin*, pp. 34–35.

28. Ibid., pp. 50–51.

29. Ibid., p. 56.

30. Ibid., p. 64.

31. Ibid., pp. 66–68; and Boorstin, *American Primer*, p. 48.

32. Fleming, *Franklin*, Chap. 4.

33. Ronald W. Clark, *Benjamin Franklin: A Biography* (New York: Random House, 1983), p. 19.

34. Fleming, *Franklin*, pp. 130–31.

35. Ibid., pp. 134–36.

36. Bowen, *Most Dangerous Man*, p. 130; and Fleming, *Franklin*, p. 136.

37. Fleming, *Franklin*, p. 139.

38. Barbara Tuchman, *The March of Folly: From Troy to Vietnam* (New York: Alfred A. Knopf, 1984), p. 157.

39. The Staff of Social Sciences, University of Chicago (Eds.), *The People Shall Judge: Readings in the Formation of American Policy*, Vol. I (Chicago: University of Chicago Press, 1949), p. 146.

40. Ralph Ketcham, *James Madison: A Biography* (Charlottesville: University Press of Virginia, 1990), p. 94.

41. Francis Graham Wilson, *The American Political Mind: A Textbook in Political Theory* (New York: McGraw-Hill, 1949), pp. 48–49.

42. Henry F. May, *The Enlightenment in America* (New York: Oxford University Press, 1976), p. 129.

43. Carl J. Friedrich, *Constitutional Government and Democracy: Theory and Practice in Europe and America* (Boston: Ginn, 1950), p. 304.

44. Alfred H. Kelly and Winfred A. Harbison, *The American Constitution: Its Origins and Development*, 4th ed. (New York: Norton, 1970) p. 33.

45. Noble E. Cunningham, Jr., *In Pursuit of Reason: The Life of Thomas Jefferson* (Baton Rouge:

Louisiana State University Press, 1987), p. 1.

46. Ibid., p. 20.

47. John H. Hallowell, *Main Currents in Modern Political Thought* (New York: Henry Holt, 1950), p. 102.

48. Cunningham, *In Pursuit of Reason*, pp. 2–5.

49. Thomas Jefferson, *Autobiography of Thomas Jefferson* (New York: Capricorn Books, n.d.), p. 20.

50. Sarah N. Randolph, *The Domestic Life of Thomas Jefferson* (Charlottesville: University Press of Virginia, 1978), p. 31.

51. Cunningham, *In Pursuit of Reason*, p. 6.

52. Randolph, *Domestic Life of Jefferson*, p. 39.

53. Jefferson, *Autobiography*, p. 21.

54. Cunningham, *In Pursuit of Reason*, pp. 15, 13.

55. Henry Steele Commager, *Jefferson, Nationalism, and the Enlightenment* (New York: George Braziller, 1975), p. 59.

56. Cunningham, *In Pursuit of Reason*, p. 23.

57. Ibid., p. 26.

58. Hallowell, *Main Currents*, p. 102.

59. Commager, *Jefferson*, p. 65.

60. Cunningham, *In Pursuit of Reason*, pp. 27–28.

61. Ibid., pp. 29–36.

62. Ibid., p. 41.

63. Ibid., p. 47.

64. Ibid., p. 48.

65. Jefferson, *Autobiography*, p. 31.

66. Boorstin, *American Primer*, pp. 68–69.

67. May, *Enlightenment*, p. 164.

68. Cunningham, *In Pursuit of Reason*, p. 55.

69. Editors of Newsweek Books, *Thomas Jefferson: A Biography in His Own Words*, Vol. I (New York: Newsweek, 1974), pp. 86–87.

70. Ketcham, *Madison*, p. 165.

71. Cunningham, *In Pursuit of Reason*, p. 58.

72. Fawn M. Brodie, *Thomas Jefferson: An Intimate History* (New York: Norton, 1974), p. 51.

73. Barber and Watson, *Struggle for Democracy*, p. 170.

74. Commager, *Jefferson*, p. 146.

75. Reo M. Christenson and Robert O. McWilliams, *Voice of the People: Readings in Public Opinion and Propaganda*, 2nd ed. (New York: McGraw-Hill, 1967), p. 119.

76. Cunningham, *In Pursuit of Reason*, p. 60.

77. *The People Shall Judge*, p. 224.

78. Editors of Newsweek Books, *Jefferson*, p. 90.

79. Ibid., pp. 89–90.

80. Adrienne Koch and William Peden (Eds.), *The Life and Writings of Thomas Jefferson* (New York: The Modern Library, 1944), p. 400.

81. Shelby Little, *George Washington* (New York: Capricorn Books, 1962), p. 4.

82. Ibid., p. 15.

83. Ibid., p. 18.

84. Ibid., p. 19.

85. Ibid., p. 45.

86. Ibid., pp. 109–16.

87. Ibid., p. 120.

88. Ibid., p. 121.

89. Ibid., p. 125.

90. Ibid., p. 126.

91. Ibid., p. 137.
92. Ibid., p. 144.
93. Ibid., p. 148.
94. Ibid., p. 190.
95. Ibid., p. 153.
96. Ibid., p. 165.
97. Ibid., p. 170.
98. Ibid., p. 180.
99. Ibid., p. 246.
100. Barry Schwartz, *George Washington: The Making of an American Symbol* (New York: The Free Press, 1987), p. 25.
101. Ibid., p. 42–43.
102. Little, *Washington*, p. 298.
103. Ibid., p. 303.
104. Ibid., p. 310.
105. Ibid., pp. 321–22.
106. Ibid., p. 324.
107. Ibid.
108. May, *Enlightenment*, p. 361.
109. Little, *Washington*, p. 328.
110. Robert B. Morris, *Witnesses at the Creation: Hamilton, Madison, Jay and the Constitution* (New York: Holt, Rinehart and Winston, 1985), pp. 172–73.
111. Ibid., pp. 176–77.
112. Boorstin, *American Primer*, p. 76.
113. Little, *Washington*, p. 330.
114. Seymour Martin Lipset, *The First New Nation: The United States in Historical Comparative Perspective* (New York: Basic Books, 1963), p. 18.
115. Ibid., p. 19.
116. Bernard Mayo (Ed.), *Jefferson Himself* (Boston: Houghton Mifflin, 1942), p. 163.
117. Little, *Washington*, p. 334.
118. Ketcham, *Madison*, p. 21.
119. Ibid., p. 28.
120. Ibid., p. 30.
121. Ibid., p. 45.
122. Ibid., p. 43.
123. Ibid., p. 60.
124. Ibid., p. 61.
125. Ibid., p. 72.
126. Ibid., p. 73.
127. Ibid., p. 87.
128. Ibid., p. 119.
129. Commager, *Jefferson*, p. xiv.
130. Alpheus Thomas Mason, *Free Government in the Making: Readings in American Political Thought* (New York: Oxford University Press, 1949), p. 249.
131. Ketcham, *Madison*, p. 165.
132. Ibid., p. 175.
133. Ibid., p. 184.
134. Ibid., p. 190.
135. Ibid., p. 196.
136. Morris, *Witnesses at the Creation*, p. 198.
137. Ibid., p. 187.

138. Ketcham, *Madison,* p. 197.

139. Ibid., p. 200.

140. Ibid., pp. 208–09.

141. Ibid., p. 210.

142. Ibid., p. 211.

143. Ibid., p. 224.

144. Ibid., p. 230.

145. Charles A. Beard and Mary R. Beard, *A Basic History of the United States* (Philadelphia: Blakiston, 1944), p. 127.

146. Boorstin, *American Primer,* p. 80.

147. Schwartz, *Washington,* p. 46.

148. Little, *Washington,* p. 344.

149. Ketcham, *Madison,* p. 234.

150. Ibid., p. 249.

151. Ibid., p. 256.

152. Ibid., p. 275.

153. Boorstin, *American Primer,* p. 153.

154. Ketcham, *Madison,* p. 290.

155. Ibid., p. 297.

156. Boorstin, *American Primer,* pp. 155–57.

157. Little, *Washington,* p. 354.

158. Ibid., p. 362.

159. Ibid., p. 364.

160. Ibid., p. 365.

161. Ibid., p. 378.

162. Ibid., p. 423.

163. Schwartz, *Washington,* p. 88.

164. Richard Shenkman and Kurt Reiger, *One-Night Stands with American History: Odd, Amusing, and Little-Known Incidents* (New York: Quill, 1982), p. 39.

165. James David Barber, *The Presidential Character: Predicting Performance in the White House,* 4th ed. (Englewood Cliffs, N.J.: Prentice Hall, 1992), pp. 10–11.

166. Robert Allen Rutland, *The Birth of the Bill of Rights, 1776–1791* (Chapel Hill: University of North Carolina Press, 1955), p. 221.

167. Ketcham, *Madison,* p. 402.

168. Rutland, *Birth of Bill of Rights,* pp. 220–21.

169. James MacGregor Burns, *The Vineyard of Liberty* (New York: Alfred A. Knopf, 1982) p. 126.

170. James David Barber, *The Pulse of Politics: Electing Presidents in the Media Age* (New Brunswick, N.J.: Transaction, 1992), p. 107.

171. Ibid., p. 107.

172. Burns, *Vineyard of Liberty,* p. 160.

173. Cunningham, *In Pursuit of Reason,* p. 243.

174. James Sterling Young, *The Washington Community, 1800–1828* (New York: Columbia University Press, 1966), p. 169.

175. Ibid., p. 172.

176. Peter S. Onuf (Ed.), *Jeffersonian Legacies* (Charlottesville: University Press of Virginia, 1993), p. 319.

177. Ibid., p. 321.

178. Gilbert Chinard, *Thomas Jefferson: The Apostle of Americanism* (Ann Arbor: University of Michigan Press, 1964), p. 391.

179. Ibid., p. 427.

180. Cunningham, *In Pursuit of Reason,* p. 265.

181. Koch and Peden, *Life and Selected Writings of Jefferson*, p. 440.

182. Ibid., p. 604.

183. Richard Hofstadter, *Anti-Intellectualism in American Life* (New York: Alfred A. Knopf, 1963), p. 300.

184. Wilson, *The American Political Mind*, p. 164.

185. Commager, *Jefferson*, p. 68.

186. *The People Shall Judge*, pp. 220–22.

187. Cunningham, *In Pursuit of Reason*, p. 336.

188. Ibid., p. 332.

CHAPTER 14

1. *Time*, July 25, 1994, pp. 41–42.

2. Ibid., July 11, 1994, p. 45.

3. *The New Republic*, April 11, 1994, p. 19.

4. *Time*, July 11, 1994, p. 43.

5. Ibid., January 24, 1994, p. 40.

6. Richard Lourie, *Predicting Russia's Future* (Washington, D.C.: Whittle Direct Books, 1991), p. 79.

7. Ibid., pp. 81, 83.

8. *The New Republic*, April 11, 1994, pp. 24–27.

9. *Time*, July 11, 1994, pp. 40, 43.

10. Ibid., p. 44.

11. *Time*, June 20, 1994, p. 46.

12. Ibid., January 24, 1994, p. 41.

13. Sergie Stankevich, in *The Unfinished Revolution* (Washington, D.C.: The National Endowment for Democracy, 1991), p. 59.

14. Lourie, *Predicting Russia's Future*, p. 79.

15. *The New Republic*, April 11, 1994, p. 26.

16. *U.S. News & World Report*, April 4, 1994, p. 10.

17. *Time*, January 10, 1994, p. 35.

18. Ibid., January 24, 1994, p. 41.

19. Lourie, *Predicting Russia's Future*, p. 82.

20. *The New Republic*, April 11, 1994, p. 19.

21. *Time*, July 11, 1994, p. 42.

22. *U.S. News & World Report*, July 18, 1994, p. 39.

23. Ibid., March 7, 1994, p. 45.

24. *The New Republic*, April 11, 1994, p. 22.

25. *U.S. News & World Report*, March 7, 1994, pp. 41, 43.

26. *Time*, January 24, 1994, p. 40.

27. *U.S. News & World Report*, March 28, 1994, p. 56.

28. *The Unfinished Revolution*, p. 65.

29. *Time*, January 24, 1994, p. 40.

30. *U.S. News & World Report*, March 7, 1994, p. 32.

31. Lourie, *Predicting Russia's Future*, p. 81.

32. Alexei Izyumov, quoted in ibid., p. 80.

33. *The New Republic*, April 11, 1994, p. 2.

34. *Time*, July 11, 1994, p. 40.

35. Ibid., p. 44.

36. Ibid., January 24, 1994, p. 41.

37. *Newsweek,* May 2, 1994, p. 49.
38. *The Unfinished Revolution,* p. 51.
39. *U.S. News & World Report,* April 24, 1994, p. 64.
40. Ibid., May, 9, 1994, p. 34.
41. Ibid., April 25, 1994, p. 59.
42. *Time,* May 16, 1994, p. 65.
43. *U.S. News & World Report,* May 9, 1994, p. 35.
44. Ibid., April 25, 1994, pp. 44, 46.
45. Ibid., April 11, 1994, p. 35.
46. *Time,* April 11, 1994, p. 48.
47. Ibid., May 9, 1994, pp 28, 34.
48. *The New Republic,* May 2, 1994, p. 20.
49. *U.S. News & World Report,* April 11, 1994, pp. 36, 38.
50. Ibid., April 26, 1994, p. 62.
51. *Time,* April 11, 1994, pp. 48, 51; March 11, 1994, p. 49.
52. Ibid., February 21, 1994, p. 36.
53. Ibid., p. 35.
54. *Newsweek,* March 28, 1994, p. 31.
55. *U.S. News & World Report,* April 11, 1994, p. 36.
56. *Time,* May 9, 1994, p. 35.
57. Ibid., May 2, 1994, p. 59.
58. National Democratic Institute, 1992, p. 11.
59. *U.S. News & World Report,* May 9, 1994, p. 31.
60. *Time,* May 16, 1994, p. 65.
61. *Newsweek,* May 16, 1994, p. 40.
62. *U.S. News & World Report,* April 25, 1994, p. 59.
63. *Time,* May 9, 1994, p. 35.
64. *U.S. News & World Report,* May 9, 1994, pp. 34–35.
65. *Newsweek,* May 16, 1994, p. 40.
66. *U.S. News & World Report,* May 9, 1994, p. 31.
67. *Time,* February 21, 1994, p. 35.
68. *U.S. News & World Report,* May 9, 1994, p. 35.
69. *Newsweek,* March 7, 1994, p. 38.
70. *Time,* May 9, 1994, p. 30.
71. *U.S. News & World Report,* March 28, 1994, p. 53.
72. Ibid., May 9, 1994, p. 31.
73. Ibid., April 25, 1994, p. 64.
74. *Newsweek,* May 16, 1994, p. 40.
75. *Time,* May 9, 1994, p. 30.
76. Ibid., May 2, 1994, p. 59.
77. Ibid., May 9, 1994, p. 30.
78. Ibid., February 21, 1994, p. 36.
79. Ibid., May 16, 1994, p. 65.
80. Ibid., May 9, 1994, p. 38.
81. *Journal of Democracy,* July 1994, pp. 133–35.
82. Avery O. Craven, *Civil War in the Making: 1815–1860* (Baton Rouge: Louisiana State University Press, 1986), p. 13.

Photo Credits

CHAPTER 2   AP/Wide World Photos, 9; Bettmann, 15; Prentice Hall Archives, 17; Bettmann, 27; Bettmann, 28; Bettmann, 32.

CHAPTER 3   AP/Wide World Photos, 67 (top and bottom); Library of Congress, 71.

CHAPTER 4   National Library of Australia, 92; Bettmann, 93; National Library of Australia, Rex Nan Kivell Collection, 98.

CHAPTER 5   National Archives, 118; Prentice Hall Archives, 125; Bettmann, 127; Bettmann, 136; Prentice Hall Archives, 143; AP/Wide World Photos, 145.

CHAPTER 6   Courtesy of St. Augustine & St. Johns County Chamber of Commerce, St. Augustine, Florida, 176; New York Public Library, 181; UPI/Bettmann, 184; UPI/Bettmann, 190.

CHAPTER 7   UPI/Bettmann, 200; United Nations, 204; AP/Wide World Photos, 206.

CHAPTER 8   Bettmann, 225; Bettmann, 227; Bettmann, 231.

CHAPTER 9   Bettmann, 251; Bettmann, 254; (no credit), 259; Bettmann, 260.

CHAPTER 10   Bettmann, 275; Library of Congress, 277; Bettmann, 280; Bettmann, 285.

CHAPTER 11   Bettmann, 295; Bettmann, 301; UPI/Bettmann, 302; UPI/Bettmann, 318; Bettmann, 320.

CHAPTER 12   New York Public Library, 337; Bettmann, 346.

CHAPTER 13   Bettmann, 356; Bettmann, 359; New York Public Library, 361; White House Collection, 367; White House Historical Association, 375; The National Geographic Society/White House Historical Association, 380; Bettmann, 386.

CHAPTER 14   AP/Wide World Photos, 407.

Index